**ANALYSIS
OF INVENTORY SYSTEMS**

PRENTICE-HALL INTERNATIONAL SERIES IN MANAGEMENT

Baumol	*Economic Theory and Operations Analysis*
Churchman	*Prediction and Optimal Decision: Philosophical Issues of a Science of Values*
Hadley and Whitin	*Analysis of Inventory Systems*
Herron, Rawdon, and Greenlaw	*Business Simulation*
Holt, Muth, Modigliani, and Simon	*Planning Production, Inventories, and the Work Force*
Massé	*Optimal Investment Decisions: Rules for Action and Criteria for Choice*
Miller and Starr	*Executive Decisions and Operations Research*
Pfiffner and Sherwood	*Administrative Organization*

PRENTICE-HALL QUANTITATIVE METHODS SERIES
Dr. W. Allen Spivey, Editor

Cyert and Davidson	*Statistical Sampling for Accounting Information*
Hadley and Whitin	*Analysis of Inventory Systems*
Kemeny, Schleifer, Snell, and Thompson	*Finite Mathematics with Business Applications*
Massé	*Optimal Investment Decisions: Rules for Action and Criteria for Choice*

PRENTICE-HALL, INC.

PRENTICE-HALL INTERNATIONAL, INC., UNITED KINGDOM AND EIRE

PRENTICE-HALL OF CANADA, LTD., CANADA

J. H. DE BUSSY, LTD., HOLLAND AND FLEMISH-SPEAKING BELGIUM

DUNOD PRESS, FRANCE

MARUZEN COMPANY, LTD., FAR EAST

C. BERTELSMANN VERLAG, WEST GERMANY AND AUSTRIA

HERRERO HERMANOS, SUCS., SPAIN AND LATIN AMERICA

ANALYSIS
OF INVENTORY SYSTEMS

G. Hadley
University of Chicago

T. M. Whitin
University of California, Berkeley

Prentice-Hall, Inc., Englewood Cliffs, N. J.   1963

PRENTICE-HALL INTERNATIONAL, INC., *London*
PRENTICE-HALL OF AUSTRALIA, PTY., LTD., *Sydney*
PRENTICE-HALL OF CANADA, LTD., *Toronto*
PRENTICE-HALL FRANCE, S.A.R.L., *Paris*
PRENTICE-HALL OF JAPAN, INC., *Tokyo*
PRENTICE-HALL DE MEXICO, S.A., *Mexico City*

Library of Congress Catalog Card No. 62-7406

Printed in the United States of America

03295-C

PREFACE

During the last fifteen years there has been a rapid growth of interest in what is often referred to as scientific inventory control. Scientific inventory control is generally understood to be the use of mathematical models to obtain rules for operating inventory systems. The subject has attracted such wide interest that today every serious student in the management science or industrial engineering areas is expected to have had some experience working with inventory models. Originally, the development of inventory models had practical application as an immediate objective. To a large extent this is still true, but as the subject becomes older, better developed, and more thoroughly explored, an increasing number of individuals are working with inventory models because they present interesting theoretical problems in mathematics. For such individuals, practical application is not a major objective, although there is the possibility that their theoretical work may be helpful in practice at some future time. Thus, today work is being done with inventory models at many different levels, ranging from a concern only for practical problems to a concern only for the abstract mathematical properties of the model.

The purpose of this text is to introduce the reader to the techniques of constructing and analyzing mathematical models of inventory systems. In doing so, it cuts across many of the levels of work being done with inventory models. Thus, by reading the entire text it should be possible for the reader to gain an understanding of the sort of work that is being done and the kinds of problems that are encountered when studying inventory models at all levels—from the purely practical to the purely theoretical.

It was recognized that in many cases readers would be only interested in one facet of the subject, such as practical applications. An effort has been made to write the text in such a way that it can be read by a broad group of readers with widely varying mathematical backgrounds. To accomplish this, the material presented first in each chapter is of practical interest, and involves the most elementary mathematics. The more detailed and exact developments, which are also more advanced mathematically, come later. Topics of theoretical interest are treated in the discussion of these more advanced models. An exception to this rule is Chapter 8, which is devoted almost exclusively to topics that are more advanced mathematically. Thus someone who was mainly interested in practical applications could read Chapter 1, the first few sections of Chapters 2 through 7, none of Chapter 8, and all of Chapter 9.

Because of its flexibility this text could be used for a variety of courses including a full semester course in inventory theory, part of a course in production, or part of a course in operations research. Both of the authors have used essentially all of the material in this text in an inventory control course. This course was one quarter in length at the University of Chicago (requiring about fifteen hours per week of work) and one semester in length at the University of California (requiring about nine hours per week of work). One of the authors (G.H.) has also used the material for slightly less than one half of a one quarter course in the production area. This course covered all of Chapter 1, Chapter 2 through Sec. 2-9, Chapter 4 through Sec. 4-4, Chapter 5 through Sec. 5-2, Chapter 6 through Sec. 6-4, and all of Chapter 9.

The material treated in this book is concerned almost exclusively with the determination of optimal operating doctrines for systems consisting of a single stocking point and a single source of supply. The reasons for doing this are: 1) Many practical problems fall into this category. 2) Many interesting mathematical problems arise even when attention is restricted to these relatively simple systems. 3) It is extremely difficult to determine optimal operating doctrines for more complex systems. Indeed, little has been done in this area. Frequently, when one desires to examine a complex multi-echelon system as a whole, he is, for a variety of reasons, far more interested in the dynamic response and the stability of the system than in determining an operating doctrine which will minimize some cost expression for a specified stochastic input. The analysis of the dynamic response and stability of a system by analytical methods and simulation techniques will be treated in a separate volume, and hence these topics are not considered in the present text either.

An effort has been made to provide a large number of original and interesting problems. The authors consider the problems to be very important, and any serious reader should at least look them over and attempt to work out a fair number.

The Graduate School of Business, University of Chicago, very generously provided the secretarial services for having the manuscript typed. Jackson E. Morris once again did an excellent job of providing the quotations which appear at the beginning of the chapters. The authors are indebted to Paul Teicholz and B. Lundh of Stanford University, who used their digital computer programs to compute one of the examples for Chapter 4 and one for Chapter 5. Also the authors are indebted to a number of their students who pointed up errors and misprints in the manuscript. Finally, the authors express their appreciation to the editor of *Operations Research* for permission to reprint a number of the Poisson properties which they first published there.

G.H.
T.M.W.

CONTENTS

1

THE NATURE

OF INVENTORY SYSTEMS

"How can it be that mathematics, being after all a product of human thought independent of experience, is so admirably adapted to the objects of reality?"

Albert Einstein

1-1 Inventory Problems

The control and maintenance of inventories of physical goods is a problem common to all enterprises in any sector of a given economy. For example, inventories must be maintained in agriculture, industry, retail establishments, and the military. In the United States the total dollar investment in inventories at any one time is immense. The sum runs to more than 50 billion dollars for defense projects alone and more than 95 billion for private enterprise sectors of the economy. There are many reasons why organizations should maintain inventories of goods. The fundamental reason for doing so is that it is either physically impossible or economically unsound to have goods arrive in a given system precisely when demands for them occur. Without inventories customers would have to wait until their orders were filled from a source or were manufactured. In general, however, customers will not or cannot be allowed to wait for long periods of time. For this reason alone the carrying of inventories is necessary to almost all organizations that supply physical goods to "customers". There are, nonetheless, other reasons for holding inventories. For example, the price of some raw material used by a manufacturer may exhibit considerable seasonal fluctuation. When the price is low, it is profitable for him to procure a sufficient quantity of it to last through the high priced season and to keep it in inventory to be used as needed in production. Another reason for maintaining inventories, a reason particularly important to retail establishments, is that sales and profits can be increased if one has an inventory of goods to display to customers.

Two fundamental questions that must be answered in controlling the inventory of any physical good are when to replenish the inventory and how much to order for replenishment. In this book we shall attempt to show how these questions can be answered under a variety of circumstances. Essentially every decision which is made in controlling inventories in any organization, regardless of how complicated the inventory supply system may be, is in one way or another associated with the questions of when to order and how much to order. There are certain types of inventory problems, such as those concerned with the storage of water within dams, in which one has no control over the replenishment of the inventory. (Is

1

other words, the resupply of the inventory of water within the dam depends on the rainfall, and the organization operating the dam has no control over this.) We shall not consider this type of problem here. The only problems with which we shall concern ourselves are those in which the organization controlling the inventory has some freedom in determining when, and in what quantity, the inventory should be replaced. On the other hand, we shall assume that, in general, the inventory system has no control over the demands which occur for the item, or items, which it stocks. Again, this is just the opposite of what one encounters in dealing with inventory problems such as storage of water within dams, since the efflux of water through the dam is completely within the control of the organization operating the dam. In short, we are going to consider the type of inventory problem encountered in business, industry, and the military.

We shall concentrate on showing how mathematical analysis can be used to help develop operating rules for controlling inventory systems. When mathematics is applied to the solution of inventory problems, it is necessary to describe mathematically the system to be studied. Such a description is often referred to as a mathematical model. The procedure is to construct a mathematical model of the system of interest and then to study the properties of the model. Because it is never possible to represent the real world with complete accuracy, certain approximations and simplifications must be made when constructing a mathematical model. There are many reasons for this. One is that it is essentially impossible to find out what the real world is really like. Another is that a very accurate model of the real world can become impossibly difficult to work with mathematically. A final reason is that accurate models often cannot be justified on economic grounds. Simple approximate ones will yield results which are good enough so that the additional improvement obtained from a better model is not sufficient to justify its additional cost.

In this book we shall study a variety of mathematical models of inventory systems. Many of these are intended for practical application. Others, however, have no immediate practical application because of the restrictive nature of the assumptions. They are interesting and relevant, however, because they exhibit some theoretical properties which are important in understanding the nature of inventory systems.

1-2 Brief Historical Sketch

Although inventory problems are as old as history itself, it has only been since the turn of the century that any attempts have been made to employ analytical techniques in studying these problems. The initial impetus for the use of mathematical methods in inventory analysis seems to have been supplied by the simultaneous growth of the manufacturing industries and the various branches of engineering—especially industrial engineering. The real need for analysis was first recognized in industries that had a combination of production scheduling problems and inventory problems, i.e., in situations in which items were produced in lots—the cost of set up being fairly high—and then stored at a factory warehouse.

The earliest derivation of what is often called the *simple lot size formula* was obtained by Ford Harris of the Westinghouse Corporation in 1915 [5]. This same formula has been developed, apparently independently, by many individuals since then; it is often referred to as the *Wilson formula* since it was also derived by R. H. Wilson as an integral part of the inventory control scheme which he sold to many organizations. The first full length book to deal with inventory problems was that of F. E. Raymond [6], written while he was at M.I.T. It contains no theory or derivations, and only attempts to explain how various extensions of the simple lot size model can be used in practice.

It was not until after World War II, when the management sciences and operations research emerged, that detailed attention was focussed on the stochastic nature of inventory problems. Prior to that the systems had been treated as if they were deterministic, except for a few isolated cases, such as the work of Wilson, where some attempts were made to include probabilistic considerations. During the war, a useful stochastic model was developed which we shall refer to in Chapter 6 as the Christmas tree model. Shortly thereafter, a stochastic version of the simple lot size model was developed by Whitin, whose book [8], published in 1953, was the first book in English which dealt in any detail with stochastic inventory models.

As has been noted above, the original interest in using analytical techniques to solve inventory problems arose in industry where engineers were seeking solutions to practical problems. It is interesting to observe that economists were not the first to take an active interest in inventory problems even though inventories play a crucial role in the study of dynamic economic behavior. The reason for this lack of interest probably lies in the fact that economists were concentrating their attention mainly on static equilibrium models. Recently, however, some economists and mathematicians have taken an interest in inventory models. They have not been especially concerned with immediate practical applications; instead, they have been interested in the models because of their mathematical properties and economic interpretations. The paper by the economists Arrow, Harris, and Marschak [1] was one of the first to provide a rigorous mathematical analysis of a simple type of inventory model. It was followed by the often quoted and rather abstract papers by the mathematicians Dvoretzky, Kiefer, and Wolfowitz [3, 4]. Since then a number of papers by mathematicians have appeared. A recent full length book devoted to the mathematical properties of inventory systems is that of Arrow, Karlin, and Scarf [2]. At the present time, work on inventory problems is being carried on at many different levels. At one extreme a considerable amount of work is concerned strictly with practical applications, while, at the other extreme, work is being done on the abstract mathematical properties of inventory models without regard to possible practical applications. The material presented in this text will, in similar fashion, cover a fairly broad area. Some material will be directly concerned with practical applications while other material will be concerned with the mathematical structure of inventory systems. In this way, the reader will be introduced to the methods of analysis used and the problems involved in carrying out investigations of inventory systems at these various levels.

1-3 Inventory Systems

There are great differences between existing inventory systems. They differ in size and complexity, in the types of items they carry, in the costs associated with operating the system, in the nature of the stochastic processes associated with the system, and in the nature of the information available to decision makers at any given point in time. All these differences can be considered to reflect variations in the structure of the inventory system. These variations can have an important bearing on the type of operating doctrine that should be used in controlling the system. By an operating doctrine we simply mean the rule which tells us when to order and how much to order.

It is desirable to spell out in somewhat more detail the differences which can exist in inventory systems—either real world systems or mathematical models. In the following sections we shall make explicit some of these differences.

1-4 The Echelon Structure of Inventory Systems

An item may be stocked in an inventory system at only a single physical location, or it may be stocked at many locations. For example, if the organization under consideration is the U.S. Air Force supply system, a spare part for a certain type of aircraft may be stocked at over 100 bases and repair facilities all over the world. If the organization under study is a single privately owned lumber yard, the entire stocks of the organization will be held at this lumber yard.

When there is more than a single stocking point, there exists the possibility for many forms of interaction between the stocking points. One of the simplest forms of interaction involves one stocking point which serves as a warehouse for one or more other stocking points. This leads to what is referred to as a multiechelon inventory system. One possible type of multiechelon system is illustrated in Fig. 1-1. The arrows indicate the normal pattern for the flow of goods through the system. This might be referred to as a four echelon system since there are four levels. Each level is called an echelon. In the system shown, customer demands occur only at the stocking points in level 1. These stocking points have their stocks

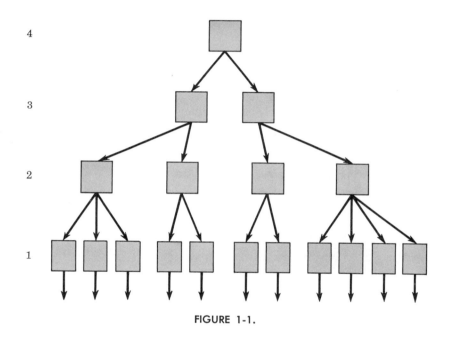

FIGURE 1-1.

replenished by shipments from warehouses at level 2, which in turn receive replenishments for their stock from level 3, etc. Figure 1-1 represents only one type of multiechelon system. In other cases, customer demands might occur at all levels, or stocking points at any level might not only receive shipments from the next highest level but might also get replenishments from any higher level or from the source. Also, it might be allowable, on occasion, to permit redistribution of stocks among various stocking points at a given level.

Most inventory systems encountered in the real world are multiechelon in nature. However, it is often true that one need not or cannot consider the multiechelon system in its entirety. The reason for this is that different organizations operate different parts of the system. For example, Fig. 1-1 might refer to a production distribution system in which the source is a plant where the item is manufactured, level 4 is a factory warehouse, level 3 represents regional warehouses, level 2 represents warehouses in various cities, and level 1 represents the retail establishments which sell the item to the public. In such a system the manufacturer might control only the plant and the factory warehouse, while different organizations operate the regional warehouses and still different organizations operate the city warehouses and the retail establishments. Note that even at a given level many different organizations may be involved. For example, each of the warehouses in different cities may be under different ownership. In such a system, each organization has the freedom to choose the operating doctrine for controlling the inventories under its jurisdiction. One could not, in general, attempt to analyze the system as a whole and dictate what operating doctrine should be used by each stocking point at each level. Instead, one might be concerned with the best way for one of the warehouses at level 2 to control its inventories. In making the analysis, the customers would be the retailers at level 1 and the source from which replenishments are obtained would be the appropriate warehouse at level 3.

Frequently, there will be just a single source from which an inventory system replenishes its stocks when it is desirable to do so. This source may be the plant where the item is made, a factory warehouse, or simply a warehouse at a higher echelon. Sometimes, however, the system has two or more alternative sources of supply available. For example, one of the retailers in Fig. 1-1 might be able to order from several different warehouses at level 2. A special case which can occur is that where the system under study also controls the source of its supplies, i.e., the plant where the item or items are made. In this case the problem is not strictly an inventory control problem but also involves production scheduling. In this book we shall not consider the general problem of combined production scheduling and inventory control except in some cases where production is carried out in lots rather than being continuous.

The basic inventory system that will be studied in this text will be much simpler than the general sort of multiechelon system shown in Fig. 1-1. It will consist of just one stocking point with a single source for resupply. Customer demands arrive at the single stocking point, and at appropriate times orders are placed with the source for replenishing the inventory. The operation of this system is illustrated schematically in Fig. 1-2.

There are good reasons for restricting our attention to the structure illustrated in Fig. 1-2. Perhaps the most important reason is that it is very difficult to study analytically multiechelon systems of the type shown in Fig. 1-1. In fact, very little work has been done in this area. It will be seen

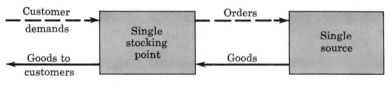

FIGURE 1-2.

that even the relatively simple structure that will be studied can become very complex to analyze. The other reason is that for practical applications the simple structure of Fig. 1-2 is often (although by no means always) adequate. This is true because, as was noted above, even though real world systems are usually of the multiechelon variety, it is often necessary to consider the various stocking points individually because different organizations control them. Even when a single organization controls a number of stocking points, however, the interactions between them are frequently sufficiently small to allow each to be studied independently of the others.

1-5 The Nature of the Items

A large military supply system stocks over 500,000 different items, while a typical department store may carry as many as 150,000 items. Other inventory systems stock only one or two items. The items stocked can differ from each other in many ways. They differ in cost, and in their physical properties, such as weight and volume. Some items are perishable and cannot be stored for long periods of time; others can be stored indefinitely without deterioration; others are subject to rapid obsolescence. Often, items can be stored only under specially controlled conditions of temperature, humidity, etc., and require special types of packaging for storage. When more than a single item is stocked there can be interactions between the items. For example, the items may be substitutes for each other so that if the system is out of stock on one item a customer will accept another. On the other hand, they may be complements so that usually one will not be sold without the other. Frequently, the interactions will take the form of having items compete for limited warehouse floor space or for investment dollars, which are also limited.

Another different form of interaction can exist between the items carried by an inventory system. This type of interaction is represented in what might be called a multistage inventory system associated with a production process. A typical block diagram for such a system is illustrated in Fig. 1-3.

A characteristic of such a system is that the product or products being manufactured can be inventoried at various stages of completion. (For example, as raw materials, rough castings, finished castings, partially assembled units, etc.). The problem is to determine what inventories, if any, should be maintained at the various stages, and what the operating doctrine should be for controlling the stocks at all the stages. Very little work has been done on problems of this sort, and they will not be considered in this text, except for a few very simple situations which are treated in the problems.

In this book the main characteristic of an item that will be of interest to us is its cost. For some of the models developed, we shall assume that the item can be stored indefinitely; in others, the item is assumed to become

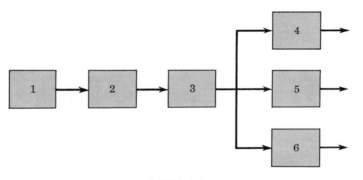

FIGURE 1-3.

obsolete ultimately. Only one of the models will deal specifically with perishable items that can be stored only for short periods of time. We shall never need to concern ourselves directly with any of the special, controlled conditions required for storage. Only a limited amount can be done in treating interactions between items. Simple cases, where items are competing for warehouse floor space or investment dollars, can be examined. In a case where there is competition for floor space we shall also make use of the unit volume of the items.

1-6 The Stochastic Processes Associated with the Inventory System

Generally speaking, it is almost never true that enough is known about the process which generates demands for items carried by an inventory system to be able to predict with certainty the time pattern of demands. In general, the best that can be done is to describe the demand in probabilistic terms. We shall study ways in which this can be done. The process for describing the demand pattern in probabilistic terms will be part of the mathematical model of the system. When the demand pattern is described probabilistically we shall say that a stochastic process generates the demand pattern. In certain cases, the demand pattern will show enough regularity so that, for an adequate approximation, it can be treated as deterministic. When this is possible, the task of analyzing the model mathematically is considerably simplified. Generally, however, it will not be possible to make such an approximation.

In the real world, the stochastic process associated with the demand pattern will always be changing with time. However, in some cases, the change with time may be so slow that in the mathematical model one can assume that it does not change with time. In other cases, the change is sufficiently rapid that a meaningful model must explicitly account for it. We shall consider both types of models—those in which the stochastic process remains constant over time and those in which it changes with time.

In general, if the inventory system under consideration has a number of stocking points at which demands can occur, it may or may not be true that the demands at the various stocking points are independent of each other. If they are not independent the analysis becomes extremely complex. Since we are limiting our study to systems having just a single stocking point, we are implicitly assuming that if the actual system contains more than a single stocking point, then the demands at the different locations are independent. Otherwise, it would not be possible to study each stocking point by itself independently of the others.

It is seldom economically sound for a system to carry enough inventory so that there will always be stock on hand when a demand occurs. Because of the stochastic nature of the demand pattern, there can be times when demands occur and the system is out of stock. An important characteristic of the process generating demands is what happens when a demand occurs and the system is out of stock. Basically, there are two possibilities. Either the demand is lost (as it might be in a department store when the customer goes to another store), or it is backordered and the customer waits until the inventory system obtains sufficient stock to meet his demand.

In the text, we shall examine the two cases where (a) all requisitions occurring when the system is out of stock are backordered, and (b) all requisitions occurring when the system is out of stock are lost. These will be referred to as the backorders case and the lost sales case, respectively. In the backorders case, all orders are ultimately filled. We shall see that it is much easier to treat the backorders case than it is the lost sales case. In fact, results for the lost sales case can be obtained only under very restrictive assumptions. The backorders case and lost sales case represent fundamentally different stochastic processes.

For any particular inventory system it can happen that some demands occurring when the system is out of stock are backordered while others are lost. If it is possible to develop models of the system for the backorders and the lost sales cases respectively, it is not difficult to develop a single model in which some sales are lost and some are backordered.

We shall define the procurement lead time (or simply the lead time) for an inventory system as the interval between the time when the stocking point decides that an order for a replenishment should be made and the time that the order arrives and is on the shelves, available to customers. Often the procurement lead time will not be constant, since the time to fill the order at the source, the shipping time, and the time required to carry out the paper work, etc., can vary from one order to another. It is seldom possible to predict in advance precisely what the lead time will be. Sometimes the variations in the lead time will be small enough so that in the mathematical model the lead time can be assumed to be absolutely constant. In other situations, however, it will exhibit sufficient unpredictable variability that it is necessary to assume that a stochastic process generates the lead times. We shall consider both models in which the lead times are constant and models in which lead times are stochastic variables.

1-7 The Relevant Costs

The costs incurred in operating an inventory system play a major role in determining what the operating doctrine should be. The costs which influence the operating doctrine are clearly only those costs which vary as the operating doctrine is changed. Costs that are independent of the operating doctrine used need not be included in any analysis where costs are used as an aid in determining an operating doctrine. Fundamentally, there are five types of costs which may be important in determining what the operating doctrine should be. These are: 1) The costs associated with procuring the units stocked, 2) The costs of carrying the items in inventory, 3) The costs of filling customers' orders, 4) The costs associated with demands occurring when the system is out of stock, 5) The cost of operating the data gathering and control procedures for the inventory system.

In the following sections, we shall examine in more detail each of these five types of costs. When doing so, it will quickly become apparent that it is quite difficult to represent mathematically all the cost components with complete accuracy. Consequently, for reasons outlined earlier, it is desirable to make some approximations when representing these costs in the mathematical models to be developed. The nature of these approximations will also be considered when discussing the costs.

1-8 Procurement Costs

We shall begin by examining the procurement costs. At the outset these costs can be divided into two parts. First there is the amount which must be paid to the source from which the procurement is made. The sum paid to this source simply represents the cost of the units procured. Then there are the costs incurred by the inventory system itself in making a procurement. These costs can arise from many different factors and they can differ considerably in nature from one inventory system to another. For example, there are the costs of processing an order through the purchasing and accounting departments. These include paper and postage costs, labor costs, perhaps the cost of a telephone call to the source, or the cost of computer time needed to make any necessary computations or to update accounting records. Sometimes the cost of transporting the order from the source of supply to the stocking point will be paid by the source and hence will be included in the cost of the units. In other cases the inventory system will pay the transportation costs. These transportation costs will, of course, depend on the mode of transportation used. Also, there are usually receiving costs incurred when the stock arrives at the warehouse. It may be necessary to uncrate the goods, perform an inspection of them, or perhaps even carry out detailed testing. Furthermore, additional accounting and control records must be prepared.

The costs incurred by the inventory system itself in placing an order, which were outlined above, can be divided into two classes—those which depend on the quantity ordered and those which are independent of the quantity ordered. Transportation costs, part of the receiving costs, and part of the inspection costs will depend on the quantity procured. We shall find it convenient to include these costs in with the cost of the units themselves. If Q units are procured, we shall denote those costs of the procurement such as the cost of the units, transportation costs, etc., which depend on Q by $C(Q)$. The average unit cost when Q units are procured will be $C(Q)/Q$. A case that will be of particular interest is that where the unit cost is a constant C, independent of the quantity ordered. Then the cost of the Q units will be simply CQ. It need not be true, of course, that this simple linear dependence on Q will always be valid even though frequently it is a satisfactory approximation. For example, it will not be correct if quantity discounts are available either on the cost of the units themselves or on transportation costs.

Consider next the costs which are independent of the quantity ordered. These costs include paper, postage, telephone charges etc., as well as the labor costs incurred in processing the order. They also include those parts of receiving and inspection costs which are independent of the order size. If the inventory system controls the plant where the item under consideration is made, then assuming that the item is made in lots, the set up costs for a production run will fall into this category. These costs which do not depend on the quantity ordered are incurred each time an order is placed. They will be referred to as the "fixed" costs of placing an order. We shall usually denote the fixed cost of placing an order by A. The total cost of placing an order for Q units will then be $A + C(Q)$.

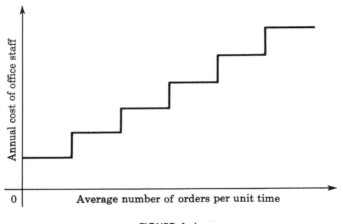

FIGURE 1-4.

It is important to note that the fixed ordering costs have the property that, usually, to a good approximation, the total fixed costs incurred on placing N orders is simply AN. In other words, the total fixed costs incurred are proportional to the number of orders placed. This proportionality of total fixed costs to the number of orders placed need not be exactly true because of phenomena like the following: The number of people in the office staff, and hence the annual cost of the office staff as a function of the average number of orders placed per unit time might look something like that shown in Fig. 1-4. As more and more orders are placed, the size of the office staff must be increased. Each step in Fig. 1-4 might indicate an increase in the office staff by one person. However, for a given size of office staff, there is a range of ordering rates which requires this size of staff and hence a range over which the annual cost of the office staff does not change.

This is indicated by the flat portion of Fig. 1-4. Often, though, in the range of interest, the curve shown in Fig. 1-4 can be approximated well enough by a straight line through the origin so that a linear dependence of annual cost on the average ordering rate is obtained.

We shall assume in the mathematical models developed in this book that the fixed cost of placing N orders is AN, where A is the fixed cost of placing a single order, so that the total fixed costs incurred are directly proportional to the number of orders placed. As seen above, this will not in general be precisely true in any real world situation. Usually, it is a quite satisfactory approximation. However, more importantly, models which make this assumption can be used to handle situations in which there exist step functions in the costs such as those shown in Fig. 1-4 which must be explicitly accounted for. The technique for doing this will be presented in Chapter 9.

1-9 Inventory Carrying Costs

Let us now examine the costs of holding inventory. Included in these costs are the real out of pocket costs such as costs of insurance, taxes, breakage and pilferage at the storage site, warehouse rental if the warehouse is not owned by the inventory system, and the costs of operating the warehouse such as light, heat, night watchmen, etc. A cost which is frequently the most important cost is not a direct out of pocket cost but rather an opportunity cost which would never appear on an accounting statement. This is the cost incurred by having capital tied up in inventory rather than having it invested elsewhere, and it is equal to the largest rate of return which the system could obtain from alternative investments. By having funds invested in inventory, one forgoes this rate of return, and hence it represents a cost of carrying inventory.

The rate at which opportunity costs are incurred will, at any instant of time, be proportional to the total investment in inventory. Similarly, the rate at which breakage and pilferage costs are incurred will normally be roughly proportional to the total investment in inventory at any point in time. The rate at which insurance costs are incurred will not usually be strictly proportional to the investment in inventory. Instead, a certain amount of insurance will be carried and so long as the policy is in effect the amount of insurance will be constant, independent of fluctuations in the inventory level. However, the policy will be revised periodically and hence insurance costs can be made to vary to a certain extent with changes in the inventory level. The precise way in which insurance costs will change with the inventory level can vary greatly from one system to another.

The nature of tax assessments is not entirely uniform, although often they are levied on the on hand inventory in the warehouse on a specified day in the year. In such cases, taxes are not incurred continuously through the year but instead are incurred at a discrete point in time. If the inventory is low on the critical day the year's taxes will also be relatively low, and conversely, if inventory is high the year's taxes will be relatively high.

When warehouse space is rented, it will normally be contracted for, and the contract will be in force for a specified length of time. The amount of space rented will then be based on the maximum amount needed for the period of the contract. Thus the rate of incurring warehouse rental charges will not fluctuate day to day with changes in the inventory level, although the rental rates can be varied from month to month or year to year when a new contract is negotiated. The costs of operating the warehouse may be essentially independent of the inventory level, or part of these costs will be independent of the inventory level, while the remainder will fluctuate more or less proportionately with the inventory level.

The above discussion shows that not all the costs of carrying inventory vary with the inventory level in the same way. Indeed, it is very difficult to represent all of these costs with great accuracy in any mathematical model. It is usually necessary to introduce some simplifying approximations. In this text we shall assume that the instantaneous rate at which inventory carrying costs are incurred are proportional to the investment in inventory at that point in time. We shall use the symbol I to denote the constant of proportionality; I will be called the carrying charge, and the physical dimensions of I are cost per unit time per monetary unit invested in inventory. The particular dimensions that we shall use in measuring I are dollars per year per dollar of inventory investment, and in these dimensions, it is usually true that $0 < I < 1$. The instantaneous rate of incurring carrying charges in the units of dollars per year can then be written ICx where C is the unit cost of the item in dollars (or sometimes the average unit cost if the unit cost is not constant) and x is the on hand inventory level.

From the above it is clear that we are assuming that the cost of carrying a unit in inventory is directly proportional to the length of time for which the unit remains in inventory. Suppose that the inventory level of the system behaved as shown in Fig. 1-5 for a period of one year. Then the carrying costs for the year are

$$IC \int_0^1 x(t) \, dt$$

Note that the integral is the area under the curve between $t = 0$ and $t = 1$ year. Since the interval of integration is unity it is also true that the integral is simply the average inventory (averaged over the period of one year). Thus it follows that our definition of the way carrying costs are incurred implies that the annual cost of carrying inventory is proportional to the average inventory computed for that year. With this interpretation the inventory carrying charge I is the fraction of the average investment in inventory for a year which is incurred as carrying charges for the year.

The method chosen to compute the inventory carrying costs does not represent with absolute accuracy any of the costs discussed above. It was chosen because it does represent quite well the opportunity cost of carrying inventory, which is normally the most important of all the costs. The reason it does not exactly represent the opportunity cost is because the largest rate of return which can be obtained from other investments depends on the length of time for which the investment is made. Other lesser problems

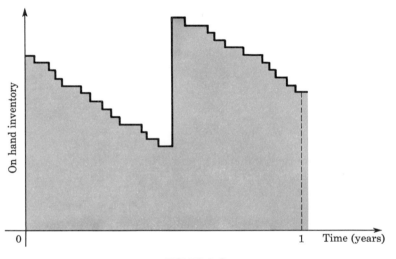

FIGURE 1-5.

concern the fact that the maximum rate of return will also depend on the sum that is available for investment and the general state of business. Thus the opportunity cost represented in I can represent only an average rate of return.

As has been noted previously, the rate of incurring breakage and pilferage costs is roughly proportional to the investment in inventory, and hence unless one has information to suggest otherwise, the method of costing we are using seems reasonable for representing these costs. On the other hand, our previous discussion has shown that the instantaneous rate of incurring insurance costs will not in general fluctuate with movements in the inventory level. However, we have shown above that making the instantaneous rate of incurring inventory carrying charges proportional to the inventory level yields an annual carrying cost which is proportional to the average inventory. Now in many situations, especially those in which the average demand rate remains relatively constant, it will be true that the annual insurance costs will be essentially proportional to the average inventory, since the insurance policy will be drawn up using the expected average inventory as a basis for the value of the policy. Hence, in such cases, the method to be used for incurring inventory carrying charges can be made to represent the insurance costs quite accurately. In other situations, however, such as those where the average rate of demand is continually changing significantly with time, it no longer follows that annual insurance costs can be made proportional to the average inventory (since it will be exceptionally difficult to predict ahead of time what the average inventory will be). For these cases, the procedure to be used for computing carrying costs will only approximately represent the way in which insurance costs are incurred.

The representation of tax costs by the method of computing carrying charges which we are going to use is even more crude than the representation of insurance costs, since if taxes depend only on the inventory in the warehouse on a particular day in the year, they need have no relation whatever to the average inventory for the year. On the other hand, the method of computing carrying costs to be used here does often represent the way in which the system sets aside funds for taxes. A tax fund will be set up, and each unit contributes to the tax fund an amount proportional to the length of time for which it remains in inventory. If the inventory system uses this sort of procedure for accumulating money for payment of taxes, then the costing procedure to be used here is the appropriate one to use. In other situations where this is not done, the attempt to include taxes in the carrying charge I can be considered to be only a rough approximation. In general, it seems realistic to attempt to include a provision for taxes in the carrying charge only when they are of such a magnitude that no special effort is made to reduce inventories to a low level on the day when the tax assessment is incurred. If special efforts are made to reduce inventories to a low level at the date when taxes are incurred, then it is appropriate to use a mathematical model which accounts for the fact that taxes are incurred at a given point in time and not to try to include a provision for them in the carrying charge. We shall later present models which could be used for this purpose.

There is one other cost not mentioned above, for which an attempt is often made to include it in the carrying charge. This is the cost of obsolescence. The cost for each unit which must be disposed of at a loss because it becomes obsolete is, at the time of obsolescence, the difference between the original cost of the unit (plus any return which could have been earned from the purchase date to the obsolescence date if the funds devoted to the procurement of the item had been invested elsewhere) and its salvage value. Obsolescence costs are always incurred at a fixed point in time, and this obsolescence date often cannot be predicted with certainty in advance. It is much more unrealistic to attempt to include obsolescence costs in the carrying charge than it is to try to make a provision for taxes in the carrying charge. The usual argument given is that by making a charge against each item in proportion to the length of time it has remained in inventory, one is setting up a fund to insure against obsolescence. However, such a procedure can seriously distort the situation and lead one to using an operating doctrine which may be far from being a good one. When obsolescence is an important consideration, one should use a mathematical model that explicitly takes into account the fact that obsolescence costs are incurred only at a single point in time. We shall consider such models in Chapter 7.

The inventory carrying charge I can then be thought of as the sum of several terms and can be written

$$I = I_1 + I_2 + I_3 + \ldots \tag{1-1}$$

where I_1 might be the carrying charge arising from opportunity costs, I_2 the carrying charge arising from pilferage and breakage, I_3 the carrying charge due to insurance costs, I_4 the carrying charge due to taxes (if taxes are included in carrying charge), etc. Thus I is obtained by evaluating each of the components I_j of the carrying charge and then summing the results. Some of the details of making such computations are illustrated in Chapter 9. It should be emphasized that in any particular application, it is not necessarily true that all the cost components referred to above will be relevant. On the other hand, there may be some costs that were not referred to above.

Certain costs, such as floor space rental, will be essentially proportional to the maximum inventory level. Although we do not in the text include any inventory carrying charge terms which are proportional to the maximum inventory level, it is very easy to include such terms in the mathematical models and some of the problems ask the reader to show how this can be done.

1-10 Costs of Filling Customers' Orders

In order to fill each customer's order, a requisition must frequently be processed through some sort of accounting operations where, among other things, a shipping invoice is prepared and sent to the warehouse. In the warehouse, someone must go to the proper bin and obtain the unit or units. Next, it may be necessary to package the order for shipment. Finally, the order is shipped to the customer. After the order has been shipped, a record of this transaction is usually sent from the warehouse to accounting where appropriate additional records are made. If a customer's order arrives when the system is out of stock, it will usually be necessary to go through special procedures to inform the customer of the existing situation.

The costs of the accounting operations referred to above, the salaries of those in the warehouse who are concerned with filling orders, the costs of packing, and the shipping costs, if paid by the inventory system, are all part of the normal costs of filling customers' orders. The important thing to note about all these costs is that, while they will vary with the demand rate, they will in general not depend on the operating doctrine used to control the inventory system. Hence they need not be considered when studying costs that vary as the operating doctrine is changed. On the other hand, the costs arising from the special action required if a customer's demand arrives when the system is out of stock will depend on the operating doctrine, since the fraction of the time that the system is out of stock will depend on the operating doctrine. We shall find it convenient to include these latter costs as a part of the stockout costs. With this convention, we shall not need to consider in the future the costs of filling customers' orders.

1-11 Stockout Costs

Let us now turn our attention to the costs incurred by having demands occur when the system is out of stock. In doing so, we must distinguish between the backorders and lost sales cases. Consider first the case where all demands occurring when the system is out of stock are backordered. In any practical situation, it is very difficult to determine accurately the nature of the backorder costs. Backorder costs are inherently extremely difficult to measure since they can include such factors as loss of customers' goodwill (i.e., in the future, he may take his business elsewhere), or in military supply systems, the cost of having part of some first line weapon system inoperative because of lack of parts. Other parts of the backorder cost can be somewhat easier to measure; however, these are usually a small part of the total backorder cost. Such costs include the cost of notifying a customer that an item is not in stock and will be backordered plus the cost of attempting to find out when the customer's order can be filled and giving him this information. If the system itself uses the part, the backorder cost may simply be the cost of keeping a machine idle for lack of parts. In such a case one can obtain a relatively good measure of the backorder cost.

When units are demanded one at a time, then there will in general be a backorder cost associated with each unit backordered. When more than a single unit can be demanded when a demand occurs, the backorder cost could depend in a complicated way on the size of the demand. However, we shall in this text assume that there is a backorder cost associated with each unit backordered, even when units need not be demanded one at a time. This cost will in general depend on the length of time for which the unit remains backordered. It will be assumed here that this cost depends only on the length of time for which the backorder exists. In principle, the cost of each unit backordered as a function of the time t for which the backorder remained on the books might be described by a nondecreasing function $\pi(t)$, and this function might change from system to system. In the real world it is essentially impossible to determine the precise shape of $\pi(t)$. About the most general function that can be used in practice is $\pi(t) = \pi + \hat{\pi}t$. In other words, there is a fixed cost for each unit backordered plus a variable cost which is linear in the length of time for which the backorder remains on the books. In the mathematical models developed in this text, when it is necessary to specify a backorder cost, the most general function used will be $\pi + \hat{\pi}t$. When $\pi(t)$ involves t in a more complicated way than $\pi + \hat{\pi}t$, it becomes considerably more difficult to work with the mathematical models. Since these more complicated possibilities are not useful in practice we shall not treat them in detail. However, some of the problems ask the reader to formulate models involving more complicated functions for $\pi(t)$.

If n units are backordered in a one year period, then the cost incurred in that year attributable to the fixed cost π per unit backordered will be πn. If the number of backorders $b(t)$ on the books as a function of time in the year under consideration looks like that shown in Fig. 1-6, then the cost incurred in that year attributable to the variable cost $\hat{\pi}t$ per unit backordered will be

$$\hat{\pi}[t_1 + t_2 + t_3 + \ldots + t_7] = \hat{\pi} \int_0^1 b(t)\, dt \qquad (1\text{-}2)$$

since the height of each rectangle is unity. Now note that if t is measured in years, then

$$\int_0^1 b(t)\, dt$$

will have the dimensions of units times years, i.e., unit years. Then if we want the cost for the year to come out in dollars, $\hat{\pi}$ must have the dimensions of dollars per unit year of shortage. Note that since the interval of integration is unity,

$$\int_0^1 b(t)\, dt$$

is simply the average number of backorders which existed for the year, i.e.,

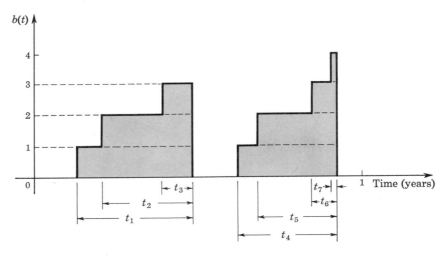

FIGURE 1-6.

the number of unit years of shortage incurred for the year under consideration is numerically equal to the average number of backorders which existed for the year.

Let us next consider the lost sales case. Since demands are lost if they occur when the system is out of stock, the cost of a lost sale cannot depend on time, for a lost sale is lost and there is nothing which corresponds to the length of time for which a unit remains backordered. Thus when units are demanded one at a time the cost of each lost sale will simply be a constant. If units need not be demanded one at a time, then the cost of a lost sale could depend in a complicated way on the size of the demand. In the text we shall assume that when there are costs incurred from lost sales, then there is a fixed cost associated with each unit demanded which cannot be met from inventory, even if units need not be demanded one at a time.

The cost of a lost sale includes a number of different factors. As in the backorders case, most of these are not direct out of pocket costs that would ever appear on a balance sheet. Perhaps the most important component of the cost of a lost sale is the somewhat intangible goodwill loss. This can include lost profits on sales of other items or on future sales of the given item due to the fact that the customer temporarily or permanently takes his business elsewhere or because he discourages other potential customers by telling them that he received unsatisfactory service. The cost of a lost sale also includes the costs of any special procedures used to inform the customer that his demand cannot be supplied, and the profit lost in not making the sale. We shall denote by π_0 the cost, exclusive of the lost profit on the unit, of a unit having been demanded when the system is out of stock. Then π will be used to denote the cost, including the lost profit on the unit, of having a unit demanded when the system is out of stock. Thus π is the sum of π_0 and the unit profit on the item.

Sometimes we shall refer to the cost of having a unit backordered as the cost of a backorder. Similarly, the cost of having a sale lost because a unit is demanded when the system is out of stock will be referred to as the cost of a lost sale. When we don't care to differentiate between the costs of backorders or of lost sales, we shall simply refer to stockout costs.

1-12 Costs of Operating the Information Processing System

In order to use any given operating doctrine, an inventory system must gather the information required for its use. The cost of obtaining the necessary information for decision making will clearly depend on the type of operating doctrine used. These costs may include such things as the cost associated with having a computer continuously update the inventory records, or the cost of making an actual inventory count, or the cost of making demand predictions. The relevance of such costs to the mathematical models to be developed will be treated in the discussion of the models.

1-13 Selection of an Operating Doctrine

The purpose in constructing a mathematical model of an inventory system is to use it as an aid in developing a suitable operating doctrine for the system. Usually one attempts to arrive at an operating doctrine that will make profits as large as possible or costs as small as possible. In other words, the criterion for selecting the operating doctrine is that of profit maximization or cost minimization. In some cases the task of determining the optimal operating doctrine is so difficult that it is either impossible or uneconomical to determine the optimal doctrine, and instead, one optimizes with respect to some subset of operating doctrines. In still other cases, the mathematical model may be so complicated that it is extremely difficult to do anything analytically. In such situations, one can use a computer and simulation to study various operating doctrines. In general, it is not possible to determine an optimal operating doctrine by use of simulation, and it can be exceptionally difficult to find the optimum with respect to some subclass of operating doctrines. About the best that can be done using simulation is to study a small number of operating doctrines and to select the one which seems to be the best. In this text we shall only be concerned with analytical techniques for working with mathematical models, and hence we shall not deal with simulation as a tool for determining operating doctrines.

In the above, we loosely referred to determining operating doctrines by maximizing profits or minimizing costs. We have not yet specified precisely what profits or costs we are referring to. We must indicate the various cost components to be included, the time period over which they are computed, and the technique to be used for handling the stochastic elements in the problem. Of course, the profit will always be the revenue minus the costs. However, the profit or cost need not be the same as that which would be obtained if we were computing the strict accounting profit or cost, since for purposes of computing optimal operating doctrines it is only necessary to include those costs which vary with the operating doctrine (the variable costs). Costs which are independent of the operating doctrine need not be included. The costs which must be included are those listed in Sec. 1-7, which are the procurement, carrying, and stockout costs, and the cost of operating the information processing system (recall that the cost of processing customers' orders need not be included since the part of this cost that depends on the operating doctrine is included in the stockout costs). There is another reason why the profit or cost will differ from what would be computed from accounting records. This is because the stockout and carrying costs include components which are not out of pocket costs, but instead represent goodwill costs or opportunity costs. In many of the models that we shall study, the revenues received will not depend on the operating doctrine, and in this case the maximization of profits will be equivalent to the minimization of the variable costs. In such cases we shall formulate the problem as a cost minimization problem.

Consider now the question of the time period over which the profit or cost is to be computed. For models which assume that an item will be carried in the inventory system for only a limited time (perhaps because it will become obsolete or is perishable), the profit that is to be maximized or the cost to be minimized is the profit or cost for the entire length of time for which the item is carried by the inventory system. However, in determining the profit or cost one must, if the time period is long enough, take account of the time value of money, so that what should be used in such situations is the present worth of the profit or cost (i.e., the discounted profit or cost). The maximization of profits or minimization of costs over a time period of finite length will also cover those models in which the mean rate of demand is allowed to change with time, since in such situations only a finite time period (planning horizon) can be treated.

For models in which the nature of the processes generating the demand pattern and lead times does not change with time (this implies, in particular, that the mean rate of demand is constant over time) and for which it can be assumed that the item can be inventoried indefinitely, it is usually convenient to imagine that the inventory system will continue to operate for all future time. One logical procedure then is to maximize the discounted profits or minimize the discounted costs over all future time. Note that discounting must be used here if the profit or cost is to be finite. Now, however, an alternative criterion suggests itself. This alternative criterion is to determine the operating doctrine by maximizing the average annual profit or minimizing the average annual cost. By definition, the average annual profit $\mathcal{P}$ and the average annual cost $\mathcal{K}$ are the long run average annual profit and cost, respectively, and are defined as follows. Let $\hat{\mathcal{W}}(\zeta)$, $\hat{\mathfrak{Z}}(\zeta)$ be the total profits received and costs incurred (not discounted), respectively, for a time period of length ζ years. Then

$$\mathcal{P} = \lim_{\zeta \to \infty} \frac{\hat{\mathcal{W}}(\zeta)}{\zeta}; \quad \mathcal{K} = \lim_{\zeta \to \infty} \frac{\hat{\mathfrak{Z}}(\zeta)}{\zeta} \tag{1-3}$$

For models of the type under discussion we shall in general find it more convenient to maximize the average annual profit or minimize the average annual cost, rather than maximizing the present worth of all future profits or minimizing the present worth of all future costs.

It would be very disconcerting if the optimization of the average annual rates of incurring profits or costs led to an operating doctrine which was quite different from that obtained by optimizing the present worth of all future profits or costs. Fortunately, this is not the case. For the range of interest rates and average times between the placement of orders which are of practical interest, both methods will give either identical results or almost identical results. It is easy to see, in fact, that if the annual profit or cost was the same each year, so that $\mathcal{P}$, $\mathcal{K}$ would also represent the profit and cost, respectively, for each and every year, then the two procedures would give identical results for any value of the interest rate. For example, let $\mathfrak{Z}$ be the present worth of all future costs, and $\mathcal{K}$ the annual (and also average annual) cost. Then if i is the interest rate and $a = (1 + i)^{-1}$, it follows that if we discount on a year by year basis

$$\mathfrak{Z} = a\mathcal{K} + a^2\mathcal{K} + a^3\mathcal{K} + \ldots = a\mathcal{K}(1 + a + a^2 + \ldots)$$

$$= \frac{a}{1 - a} \mathcal{K} = \frac{\mathcal{K}}{i} \tag{1-4}$$

Thus $\mathfrak{Z}$ and $\mathcal{K}$ differ only by the constant factor $1/i$, and hence minimizing either one also minimizes the other.

Usually, however, the actual profit or cost will fluctuate from one year to the next, sometimes being above or below the average annual values as defined above. Because of this it is possible, by making the interest rate sufficiently high, to obtain different results by minimizing the average annual cost and minimizing the present worth of all future costs, or maximizing the average annual profit and maximizing the present worth of all future profits. As has been noted above, however, the differences will be negligible in almost all cases of practical value when the interest rate remains within the limits appropriate to the real world. It might be noted, however, that the effect of the interest rate becomes more important as the average time between the placement of orders is increased. In any case where the interest rate was large enough to make a difference, then the present worth would be the function to be optimized.

There remains the question of how any stochastic elements in the problem are to be handled. For models in which the mean rate of demand is imagined to remain constant over all future times, we shall again maximize the average annual profit or minimize the average annual cost. When stochastic elements are present, however, it will be necessary to introduce probabilities and compute expected values in order to determine the average annual profit or cost. These expected values will arise in a natural way as time averages.

For situations where the mean rate of demand changes in some fashion with time, we shall use the criterion of maximizing expected profits or minimizing expected costs over some relevant time interval. It is not completely evident in such cases that expected values are what should be used. It would be quite reasonable to use expected values if it was true that the system would repeatedly encounter the same sorts of conditions and that the expected profit or cost could be interpreted as the average profit or cost averaged over all times that the system faced a particular set of circumstances. However, it will frequently be true that the system will encounter a particular set of conditions only once, and they will never be repeated again. The rationale for using expected values in such cases lies in the modern theory of utility introduced by von Neumann and Morgenstern [7]. We shall not attempt to examine this theory in detail, but instead shall merely point out that it roughly implies the following: If it is possible for an individual to express consistent preferences between various situations whose outcomes must be described probabilistically, then there exists a function having a numerical value associated with every possible outcome such that if he selects among the alternatives in such a way that the expected value of this function is maximized, then he will be acting in a way that is truly representative of his preferences. The numerical function referred to above is often called a utility function. We shall assume in this text that the system under consideration does have a utility function defined over the possible outcomes in any inventory problem. Thus the system should always behave in a way that maximizes its expected utility. We shall further assume that the utility can be measured in monetary units and is, in fact, with the proper definition of the relevant components, simply the expected profit over some appropriate time period. It is in this way that we justify the use of the expected profit even in situations where the given set of conditions can never be expected to be encountered again. We shall also see that in a number of cases the maximization of expected profit is equivalent to the minimization of expected cost. In these cases then, one can equally well minimize the expected cost over some relevant time interval.

We have noted previously that it is often very difficult in practice to determine the stockout cost functions. To avoid this problem, an alternative procedure might be to maximize the profit or minimize the cost, each exclusive of the stockout cost, subject to a constraint that the average fraction of the time for which the system is out of stock is not greater than a specified value. Here, instead of specifying the nature of the stockout cost, one instead specifies an upper limit to the average fraction of the time for which the system is out of stock. We shall also examine criteria of this sort for the determination of operating doctrines and shall also investigate their relation to the cases where a stockout cost function is specified.

Before closing this introductory chapter, we might say something about the physical dimensions that will be employed in formulating the profit or cost expressions in the remainder of the text. The equations will hold for any consistent set of physical dimensions. However, we shall always imagine that the monetary unit is the dollar and the time unit is a year. Of course, physical quantities of any good will be measured simply in units, where the unit need not be defined more precisely. A unit may, for example, be a case of screwdrivers, a dozen screwdrivers, or a single screwdriver, depending on the application. The only important thing to remember is that no matter how the unit is defined, the definition must be used consistently throughout.

As a final remark it is worth observing that while we shall be concerned with optimizing the mathematical models to be studied, it does not follow that the real world system represented by the mathematical model will also be optimized. Since a number of simplifying assumptions and approximations must be made to obtain the mathematical model, the most we can expect is that by using the optimal solution for the model in the real world we shall have a "good" operating doctrine or one that is an improvement over an existing operating doctrine. Indeed, in the real world situations, there are usually such a large number of complications that it is exceptionally difficult to define what an optimal operating doctrine means.

REFERENCES

1. Arrow, K. J., T. Harris, and J. Marschak, "Optimal Inventory Policy," *Econometrica*, **XIX** (1951), pp. 250–272.

2. Arrow, K. J., S. Karlin, and H. Scarf, *Studies in the Mathematical Theory of Inventory and Production.* Stanford, Calif.: Stanford University Press, 1958.

3. Dvoretzky, A., J. Kiefer, and J. Wolfowitz, "The Inventory Problem: **I**, Case of Known Distributions of Demand; **II**, Case of Unknown Distributions of Demand," *Econometrica,* **XX** (1952), pp. 187–222 and 450–466.

4. Dvoretzky, A., J. Kiefer, and J. Wolfowitz, "On the Optimal Character of the (*s*, *S*) Policy in Inventory Theory," *Econometrica,* **XXI** (1953), pp. 586–596.

5. Harris, F., *Operations and Cost.* (Factory Management Series.) Chicago: A. W. Shaw Co., 1915, pp. 48–52.

6. Raymond, F. E., *Quantity and Economy in Manufacture.* New York: McGraw-Hill Book Co., 1931.

7. Von Neumann, J., and O. Morgenstern, *Theory of Games and Economic Behavior.* Princeton, N.J.: Princeton University Press, 1953.

8. Whitin, T. M., *The Theory of Inventory Management.* Princeton, N.J.: Princeton University Press, 1953.

DETERMINISTIC LOT SIZE MODELS AND THEIR EXTENSIONS

Order is a lovely thing;

On disarray it lays its wing,

Teaching simplicity to sing.

Anna Hamsted Branch, The Monk in the Kitchen

2-1 Introduction

To begin our discussion of inventory systems, an especially simple collection of models will be studied for which the rate of demand for units stocked by the system will be assumed to be known with certainty and to be constant over time. This chapter will be devoted to a study of such models. As we mentioned before, in the real world demands can almost never be predicted with certainty; instead they must be described in probabilistic terms. However, the deterministic models to be discussed are still of interest because they provide a simple framework for introducing the methods of analysis that will be used in more complicated systems and because, sometimes, they are useful in examining certain aspects of real world problems. Furthermore, the results obtained from these models yield, qualitatively, the proper sort of behavior—even when the deterministic demand assumption is removed.

2-2 The Simplest Lot Size Model—No Stockouts

Let us consider the problem of controlling the inventory of a given item at a single location (a retail store, for example) when the assumption is made that the rate of demand for the item is deterministic and is a constant λ units per year independent of time. The fundamental problem for this system, and indeed for any inventory system, as was pointed out in Chapter 1, is to determine when an order should be placed and how much should be ordered. We shall suppose that the procurement lead time τ is a constant independent of λ and the quantity ordered. Furthermore, it will be assumed that the entire quantity ordered is delivered as a single package, i.e., it never happens that an order is split so that part of it arrives at one time and part at another time. We shall imagine that the item can be inventoried indefinitely, and that it will never become obsolete. Then, as suggested in Chapter 1, it is convenient to imagine that the system will continue to operate for all future time. Since λ and τ are constant and deterministic, it is immediately clear that when the system is operated optimally, the same quantity will be ordered each time an order is placed, and the on hand inventory at the point in time when an order arrives will always have the same value.*

In this section we wish to study a case where the system is never out of stock when a demand occurs. This limitation can legitimately be imposed since the demand is deterministic and the procurement lead time is a constant. Initially it will be convenient to imagine that the quantity demanded in a time t is a continuous function of t, and to ignore the fact that an integral number of units must be demanded. Later, account will be taken of the integrality of demand. Since the system is never out of stock when a demand occurs, and since λ is a constant, the annual revenues received from the sale of the item are a constant, independent of the operating doctrine, and hence, the minimization of costs will yield the same operating doctrine as the maximization of profits. Following the suggestion of Chapter 1, we shall determine the optimal operating doctrine by minimizing the average annual cost. Recall that only those costs that depend on the operating doctrine need be included. These costs have been discussed in Chapter 1. The costs appropriate to this model are the cost of the units purchased, the fixed cost of placing an order (the ordering cost), and the inventory carrying costs. It will be assumed that the costs of operating the information processing activity are independent of the order size and the reorder rule, and therefore do not need to be included in the cost expression.

To compute the average annual cost, we must compute the total cost for an arbitrary time period of length ζ, then divide by ζ to obtain the average annual cost for the period of length ζ, and finally allow ζ to approach infinity, giving the desired average annual cost. The actual cost of operating the system can vary from one year to another because the number of orders actually placed can vary. Only when a year is an integral multiple of the time between placing orders can the actual system cost be the same each year. The differences between average yearly cost and the actual system cost for a given year will be illustrated later by a concrete example. The procedure we are about to use to determine the average annual cost may, at first reading, seem unnecessarily complicated for the simple model being studied. It is introduced now because it provides a rigorous way of obtaining the average annual cost and because it allows us to introduce, in the context of a very simple model, a technique which will later prove quite useful in dealing with more complex models involving uncertainty. Further, the technique used to derive the average annual cost is of course the definition of the average annual cost, i.e., it is by definition the limit as ζ approaches infinity of the average cost for a time period of length ζ.

---

* A rigorous proof that the optimal operating doctrine has this form can be given using the methods to be introduced later in Chapter 8.

If a quantity Q is ordered each time the system orders replenishment stock, then after every Q demands an order for Q units is placed. Thus the time T between the placement of orders is $T = Q/\lambda$. Similarly, the time between the arrival of successive procurements is T. We shall say that the system goes through one cycle of operation in the time between the placement of two successive orders or the receipt of two successive procurements, or, more generally, between any two points in time separated by an interval of length T. During each cycle, the system repeats exactly its behavior during the previous cycle. The length of a cycle is T.

Let v be the largest integer less than or equal to ζ/T. Then in time ζ there are v complete cycles, and perhaps a fraction of another cycle. This is independent of where we select the time origin. Since precisely one order is placed per cycle, the number of orders placed in time ζ will be v or $v + 1$; it can be $v + 1$ if the included fraction of a cycle is long enough. The number of orders placed can be written $(\zeta/T) + \epsilon$, where $|\epsilon| < 1$ ($|\epsilon|$ is the absolute value of ϵ), or $(\lambda\zeta/Q) + \epsilon$. If A is the cost of placing an order, then the ordering costs incurred in the time ζ are $[(\zeta/T) + \epsilon]A$. The cost of the units ordered in the time ζ will be $[(\lambda\zeta/Q) + \epsilon]QC$ if C is the unit cost of the item when ordered in lots of Q units.

Let s be the on hand inventory in the system at the time of arrival of a procurement. The on hand inventory immediately after the procurement arrives will be $s + Q$. Consequently, the inventory carrying costs per cycle are

$$IC \int_0^T (Q + s - \lambda t)\, dt = IC \left[(Q + s)T - \frac{\lambda T^2}{2} \right] = ICT \left[\frac{Q}{2} + s \right] \quad (2\text{-}1)$$

This follows since at any time t from the beginning of the cycle (which is taken for convenience to be the time of arrival of an order), the on hand inventory is $Q + s - \lambda t$, and the cost incurred between t and $t + dt$ is $IC(Q + s - \lambda t)\, dt$. Summation over the length of the cycle gives (2-1) when the relation $T = Q/\lambda$ is used.

In the time ζ there are

$$v = (\zeta/T) - \xi, \quad 0 \le \xi < 1$$

full cycles. The inventory carrying costs for the time period of length ζ are

$$ICT \left[\frac{\zeta}{T} - \xi \right] \left[\frac{Q}{2} + s \right] + \eta$$

where η is the inventory carrying cost for the fractional cycle of length $\zeta - vT$; note that η is less than the inventory carrying cost for a single cycle. The total variable cost for the time period of length ζ is then

$$\left[\frac{\lambda}{Q}\zeta + \epsilon \right] QC + \left[\frac{\lambda}{Q}\zeta + \epsilon \right] A + ICT \left[\frac{\zeta}{T} - \xi \right] \left[\frac{Q}{2} + s \right] + \eta \quad (2\text{-}2)$$

The average annual cost for the time period of length ζ, $\mathcal{K}_\zeta$, is obtained by dividing the total cost by ζ. This yields

$$\mathcal{K}_\zeta = \lambda C + \frac{\epsilon Q C}{\zeta} + \frac{\lambda}{Q} A + \frac{\epsilon A}{\zeta} + IC \left[\frac{Q}{2} + s \right] - \frac{\xi}{\zeta} ICT \left[\frac{Q}{2} + s \right] + \frac{\eta}{\zeta}$$

To obtain the average annual cost of the system, we allow ζ to go to infinity. Therefore the average annual variable cost is

$$\mathcal{K} = \lambda C + \frac{\lambda}{Q} A + IC \left[\frac{Q}{2} + s \right] \tag{2-3}$$

The formula for $\mathcal{K}$ can also be derived using the following simple argument: Since there are λ demands per year and since all demands are met, then on the average λ units per year must be procured at a cost of λC. Similarly, if the order quantity is Q, then the number of orders placed per year must average to λ/Q, and the fixed procurement costs per year average to $\lambda A/Q$. Furthermore, by assumption, the inventory carrying cost per unit is proportional to the length of time it remains in inventory. Consequently, the inventory carrying cost per year must then be IC times the average inventory. The average inventory is one half the sum of the maximum inventory $Q + s$ and the minimum inventory s, i.e., $(Q/2) + s$. Summation of these three terms gives (2-3).

For the moment (indeed, in all discussions through Sec. 2-10), we shall restrict our attention to situations for which the unit cost of the item is independent of the quantity ordered. Then λC is independent of Q and the reordering rule and need not be included in the variable cost. Hence the relevant average annual variable cost in this case, which is the sum of ordering and inventory carrying costs, is

$$\mathcal{K} = \frac{\lambda}{Q} A + IC \left[\frac{Q}{2} + s \right] \tag{2-4}$$

We use the same symbol $\mathcal{K}$ in (2-4) as in (2-3) since by convention we shall use $\mathcal{K}$ to represent the average annual variable costs; $\mathcal{K}$ will be assumed to include all variable costs and no costs which are not a function of the system variables Q, s.

Examination of (2-4) shows that the only term which depends on the reorder rule is ICs. This term is minimized by having $s = 0$, so that the system just runs out of stock as the new procurement arrives. The requirement that $s = 0$ in order to minimize (2-4) allows us to determine immediately the optimal reordering rule for any given Q value. Let m be the largest integer less than or equal to τ/T, where τ is the procurement lead time. Then, if we place an order when the on hand inventory reaches the level

$$r_h = \lambda(\tau - mT) = \lambda\tau - mQ = \mu - mQ \tag{2-5}$$

where $\mu = \lambda\tau$ is the lead time demand (i.e., the number of units demanded from the time an order is placed until it arrives), the on hand inventory will be zero at the time the order arrives. The number r_h is called the reorder point; each time the on hand inventory in the system reaches r_h an order for Q units is placed. This is illustrated graphically in Fig. 2-1.

It remains to determine the optimal value of Q. We have seen that the optimal value of s is zero for any Q. Thus the average annual cost really depends only on the single variable Q; it can be written

$$K = \frac{\lambda}{Q} A + IC \frac{Q}{2} \qquad (2\text{-}6)$$

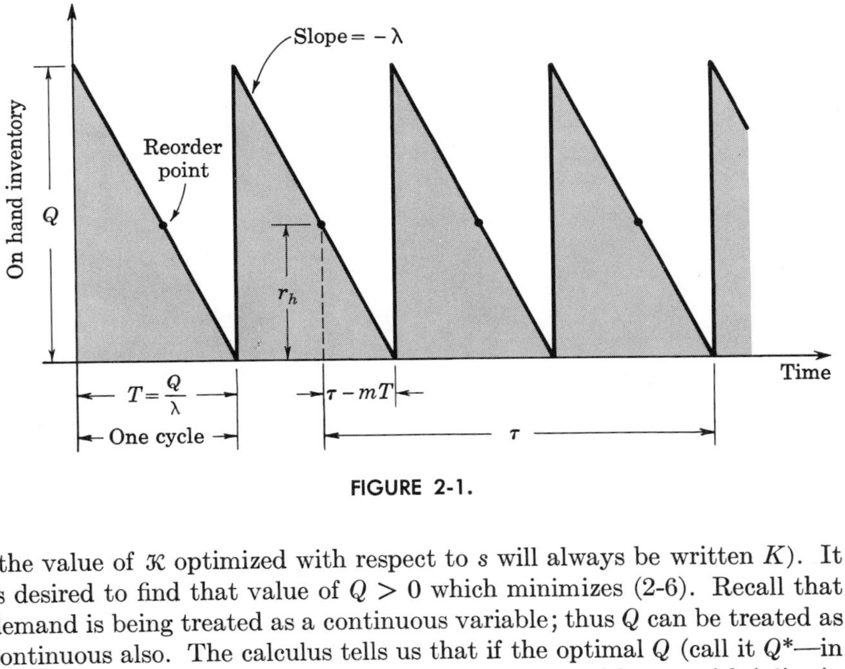

FIGURE 2-1.

(the value of $\mathcal{K}$ optimized with respect to s will always be written K). It is desired to find that value of $Q > 0$ which minimizes (2-6). Recall that demand is being treated as a continuous variable; thus Q can be treated as continuous also. The calculus tells us that if the optimal Q (call it Q^*—in fact, all optimal quantities will hereafter be indicated by asterisks) lies in the interval $0 < Q < \infty$, then it is necessary that Q^* satisfy the equation

$$\frac{dK}{dQ} = 0 = -\frac{\lambda}{Q^2} A + \frac{IC}{2} \qquad (2\text{-}7)$$

or

$$Q^* = Q_w = \sqrt{\frac{2\lambda A}{IC}} \qquad (2\text{-}8)$$

It will be noted that $K = \infty$ when $Q = 0$ or ∞ and that K is finite for any other $Q > 0$. Furthermore K is differentiable for all $Q > 0$. Thus the optimal Q must satisfy (2-7) and hence (2-8). However, (2-7) has only one solution for $Q > 0$. Consequently, (2-8) gives the value of Q which yields the unique absolute minimum of K for $Q > 0$.

The fact that (2-8) gives the Q which yields the absolute minimum of K can be seen in another way. Recall that the calculus tells us that if Q^* satisfies $dK/dQ = 0$ and if $d^2K/dQ^2 > 0$ when evaluated at Q^*, then Q^* yields a relative minimum of K. If, however, $d^2K/dQ^2 > 0$ for all Q in the region of interest, not simply at Q^*, then Q^* yields the unique absolute minimum of K in the region of interest. Now

$$\frac{d^2K}{dQ^2} = \frac{2\lambda A}{Q^3} > 0 \qquad (2\text{-}9)$$

for all $Q > 0$ and hence the Q determined from (2-7) yields the absolute minimum value of K.

The equation (2-8) is referred to in the literature under a variety of names. It is sometimes called the lot size formula, the economic order quantity, the square root formula, or the Wilson formula. We shall occasionally use several of the above names. Equation (2-8) might also be called the Harris formula since, as indicated in Chapter 1, Harris seems to have been the first to have derived it. Because the square root expression in (2-8) appears frequently in later work, we use a special symbol Q_w to identify it; whenever Q_w appears, it will always be defined by (2-8).

The problem of determining how to operate the system has now been solved. The reorder point, given by (2-5) (with Q^* replacing Q), tells us when an order should be placed. The quantity to be ordered is given by (2-8). Specification of the reorder point and the order quantity determines all other quantities of interest.

2-3 Additional Properties of the Model; An Example

It is instructive to examine in somewhat greater detail the nature of the model described in the previous section and the optimal operating doctrine for it. If the inventory carrying costs, ordering costs, and K are plotted as a function of Q on the same graph, one obtains curves something like those shown in Fig. 2-2. The figure shows clearly that the Q which yields the minimum is unique and that $d^2K/dQ^2 > 0$ for all $Q > 0$. It might also be noted that the optimal Q occurs at the point where the slope of the ordering cost curve is the negative of the slope of the inventory carrying cost curve. It will be left to Problem 2-2 to demonstrate that, in this special case, the two curves intersect at this point.

When an optimal policy is used, the average amount of inventory in the system will be

$$\frac{Q^*}{2} = \sqrt{\frac{\lambda A}{2IC}} \tag{2-10}$$

The on hand inventory fluctuates between Q^* and 0 and averages to $Q^*/2$. Equation (2-10) points out the interesting result that the average inventory (and the maximum inventory, and Q^*) should increase as the square root

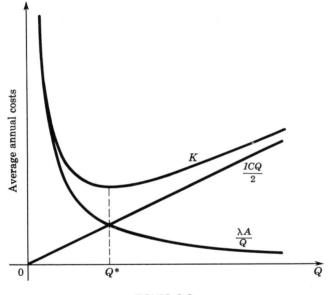

FIGURE 2-2.

of the sales rate and not proportionally with the sales rate. Similarly, the average inventory varies inversely as the square root of the cost so that the average inventory for high cost items should be lower than for low cost items, all other things being equal. The above observations merely serve to point out that in formulating an inventory policy, items with different characteristics should be treated differently. This implies, for example, that if a system was stock.ng a number of items with widely different rates of demand and costs, it would not be optimal to require that the average inventory for each item should be k weeks of stock where the same k was used for all items.

The average annual cost of procurement and holding inventory K^* under the optimal procurement policy will be

$$K^* = \lambda A \left(\frac{IC}{2\lambda A}\right)^{1/2} + \frac{IC}{2}\left(\frac{2\lambda A}{IC}\right)^{1/2} = \left(\frac{1}{2}\lambda AIC\right)^{1/2} + \left(\frac{1}{2}\lambda AIC\right)^{1/2}$$
$$= \sqrt{2\lambda AIC} = K_w \qquad (2\text{-}11)$$

The value of K^* is also proportional to $\lambda^{1/2}$. The square root expression appearing in (2-11) will appear frequently in later work and a special symbol K_w will be used to represent it; whenever K_w appears it will be defined by (2-11).

It is of interest to compare K^* with the cost K of operating the system when a Q different from Q^* is used. To make this comparison, we shall compute K/K^* as a function of Q/Q^*. Now

$$\frac{K}{K^*} = \frac{\lambda}{Q} A(2\lambda AIC)^{-1/2} + IC\frac{Q}{2}(2\lambda AIC)^{-1/2} = \frac{1}{2}\left[\frac{Q^*}{Q} + \frac{Q}{Q^*}\right] \qquad (2\text{-}12)$$

Note that this equation is completely independent of the system parameters. A plot of Eq. (2-12) yields the universal curve shown in Fig. 2-3. The interesting thing about this curve is that it is rather flat in the neigh-

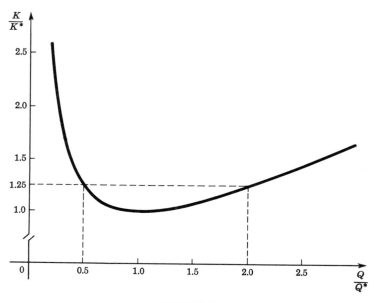

FIGURE 2-3.

borhood of the optimal Q. If the actual Q is off from the optimal Q in either direction by a factor of two, costs are increased by only 25%. The same sort of analysis can be used to study how the actual cost will vary from the optimum cost if one of the parameters such as λ or A is not measured correctly. Examinations of sensitivity analyses of this sort are left to the problems.

In the event that the procurement lead time is less than one cycle, there will never be more than a single order outstanding. Furthermore, there will be no orders outstanding at the time immediately prior to placing an order (i.e., just as the reorder point is reached). On the other hand, if the procurement lead time is longer than one cycle, there will always be at least one order outstanding. As an aid in visualizing the situation where the

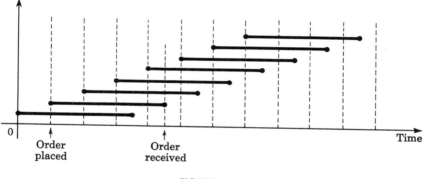

Order placed   Order received

FIGURE 2-4.

procurement lead time is longer than one cycle, it is helpful to draw a chart such as that shown in Fig. 2-4 which illustrates a case where the procurement lead time is $3\frac{1}{2}$ times the length of a cycle. It will be observed that (after period 4 in Fig. 2-4) there are always either 3 or 4 orders outstanding. For half the period three orders are outstanding and for half the period four orders are outstanding. The average number of orders outstanding is therefore $3\frac{1}{2}$. Hence the average amount on order is $3\frac{1}{2} Q$ which is precisely the lead time demand μ. We have thus shown in this special case that the average amount on order is equal to the lead time demand. Problem 2-10 asks the reader to prove that the average amount on order is equal to the lead time demand for any arbitrary lead time τ. In Fig. 2-4 the quantity on order just prior to reaching the reorder point is $3Q$ and immediately after hitting the reorder point is $4Q$. In general, the amount on order just prior to reaching the reorder point is mQ where

m is the largest integer less than τ/T, and $(m + 1)\,Q$ immediately after hitting the reorder point (or, in the razor's edge case where τ/T is an integer m, there are always precisely m orders outstanding).

It is often useful to consider the quantity on hand plus on order. At the reorder point the on hand inventory is $\mu - mQ$, and the quantity on hand plus on order increases by Q units when the order is placed. Thus the quantity on hand plus on order fluctuates between μ and $\mu + Q$. The relationship between the on hand inventory and the on hand plus on order inventory is shown in Fig. 2-5. The on hand inventory reaches its minimum value 0 just prior to receipt of a procurement, and its maximum value

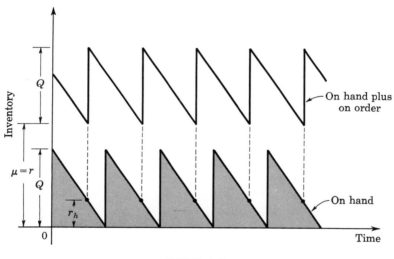

FIGURE 2-5.

Q immediately after receipt of a procurement. The on hand plus on order inventory reaches its minimum μ just prior to reordering and its maximum $\mu + Q$ immediately after placing an order.

For the system under consideration, specification of the on hand inventory uniquely determines the quantity on hand plus on order, and conversely, the specification of the quantity on hand plus on order uniquely determines the amount on hand.* One can therefore specify a reorder point

---

* Exceptional points are the reorder point when the quantity on hand plus on order jumps discontinuously, and the points in time corresponding to arrivals of procurements when the on hand inventory jumps discontinuously.

in terms of the on hand plus on order inventory. This reorder point will be denoted by r, and $r = \mu$ (μ being the lead time demand); thus when the on hand plus on order inventory reaches a level μ an order is placed. Later, when uncertainty in the demand is introduced, we shall see that the reorder point cannot always be legitimately determined in terms of an on hand inventory. Instead, it must be specified in terms of the on hand plus on order inventory (or on a more general level defined to be the quantity on hand plus on order minus backorders). It is only for certain special cases that the reorder point can be specified in terms of an on hand level.

EXAMPLE Consider a system of the type described above which inventories an item whose parameters have the following values:

$$\lambda = 600 \text{ units/yr.}, \quad I = 0.20$$

$$A = \$8.00, \quad \tau = 1 \text{ year}$$

$$C = \$0.30$$

To be more specific, it can be imagined that this is a low cost item carried by a department store. The high fixed cost of ordering arises because the item is procured in Europe. This also accounts for the long lead time.

The optimal order quantity is

$$Q^* = \sqrt{\frac{2\lambda A}{IC}} = \sqrt{\frac{2(600)(8)}{0.20(0.30)}} = 400$$

The time between placement of orders (the length of a cycle) is

$$T^* = \frac{Q^*}{\lambda} = \frac{400}{600} = \frac{2}{3} \text{ yr.}$$

The lead time demand is

$$\mu = \lambda\tau = 600 \text{ units.}$$

The reorder point based on the on hand plus on order inventory level is then $r^* = 600$. To compute the reorder point based on the on hand inventory level, we first note that $\tau/T = \frac{3}{2}$. The largest integer less than τ/T is 1. Thus

$$r_h^* = \mu - Q^* = 200 \text{ units.}$$

The minimum average yearly cost of ordering and holding inventory is

$$K^* = \sqrt{2\lambda AIC} = \sqrt{2(600)(8)(0.06)} = \sqrt{576} = \$24$$

The yearly cost of the units themselves is

$$\lambda C = \$180$$

Thus the ordering and holding costs are a small part of the total cost which includes the cost of the units.

The actual yearly procurement and holding costs vary from one year to another. This can be seen from Fig. 2-6. Assume that we start measuring time immediately after the placing of an order. Then in the first year shown, one order is placed, while in the second year two orders are placed. After the second year a repetition of the above is obtained. For the first year shown in Fig. 2-6, the actual system costs are $8 for ordering and $10 for holding, or a total of $18. In the second year, the actual costs are $16

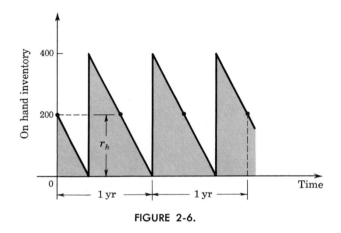

FIGURE 2-6.

for ordering and $14 for holding or a total of $30. The average of these two values gives $24, which is that obtained above for K^*.

2-4 Accounting for Integrality of Demand

In the previous sections demand has been treated as a continuous variable. For most practical applications of the simple model studied, Q^* is sufficiently large that it is quite satisfactory to treat the demand as continuous and to round off the value of Q^* to the nearest integer, since an integral number of units must be ordered. In reality, of course, each demand must be for an integral number of units, and in addition Q^* must be an integer. It is instructive to examine a case where the integrality of demand is accounted for, and the Q values are restricted to being positive integers. To be specific, it will be assumed that units are demanded one at a time and the time between demands t_s is known with certainty. Then $\lambda = 1/t_s$.

As in the continuous case, the number of units s on hand when an order arrives should be zero. Now, however, this requirement does not uniquely specify the time when an order should be placed since there is a time interval of length t_s between demands. It should be noted, however, that there is no need to have the order arrive until precisely the moment when a demand occurs for otherwise costs will be increased. Thus the order should arrive at a time t_s after the demand which reduces the on hand inventory to zero, i.e., the system will have a zero on hand stock level for a time t_s each cycle. Immediately after the procurement arrives one unit is demanded. Hence, the maximum inventory level is $Q-1$ and the minimum is zero.

The inventory carrying costs per cycle are then*

$$ICt_s[Q - 1 + Q - 2 + \ldots + 1 + 0] = IC\frac{Q}{\lambda}\left(\frac{Q-1}{2}\right) \quad (2\text{-}13)$$

The average number of cycles per year remains λ/Q so that the average inventory carrying costs per year are $\frac{1}{2}IC(Q-1)$. The average yearly procurement costs remain unchanged at $\lambda A/Q$. Thus the average annual cost of holding and procuring inventory is for a given $Q \geqslant 1$

$$K(Q) = \frac{\lambda}{Q}A + \frac{1}{2}IC(Q - 1) \quad (2\text{-}14)$$

If Q^* is the *smallest* Q value which minimizes $K(Q)$, Q^* being an integer, then if $Q^* \geqslant 2$, it is necessary that

$$K(Q^*) - K(Q^* - 1) < 0; \quad K(Q^* + 1) - K(Q^*) \geq 0 \quad (2\text{-}15)$$

The optimal Q is then the largest Q for which

$$\Delta K(Q) = K(Q) - K(Q - 1) < 0$$

or

$$Q^* = 1$$

However, for $Q > 1$

$$\Delta K(Q) = \lambda A\left[\frac{1}{Q} - \frac{1}{Q-1}\right] + \frac{1}{2}IC = -\frac{\lambda A}{Q(Q-1)} + \frac{1}{2}IC$$

$$= \frac{1}{2Q(Q-1)}[-2\lambda A + ICQ(Q-1)] < 0$$

---

*The reader should recall that

$$\sum_{=1}^{n} j = 1 + 2 + \ldots + n = \frac{n(n+1)}{2}$$

Thus Q^* is the largest positive integer Q for which

$$Q(Q - 1) < \frac{2\lambda A}{IC} \tag{2-16}$$

When unity is negligible with respect to Q and it is assumed that Q can vary continuously, then one obtains (2-8). In the discrete case just studied, Q^* need not be unique. If the strict equality holds in the second condition of (2-15), then either Q^* or $Q^* + 1$ is optimal.

The determination of the reordering rule is a little more complicated than in the continuous case. If T is the length of a cycle, τ is the procurement lead time, and if m is the largest integer less than or equal to τ/T, then $\hat{t} = \tau - mT$ gives the time before the next order arrives when an order should be placed. If $\hat{m}$ is the largest integer less than or equal to $\hat{t}/t_s$, then a reorder should be placed at a time $(1 + \hat{m})t_s - \hat{t}$ after a demand reduces the on hand inventory to $\hat{m}$ (illustrate this graphically). A similar analysis shows that in terms of the on hand plus on order inventory level an order is placed at a time $(\bar{m} + 1)t_s - \tau$ after the demand which reduces the on hand plus on order inventory to $\bar{m}$, where $\bar{m}$ is the largest integer less than or equal to τ/t_s.

2-5 Case Where Backorders Are Permitted

The model presented in Sec. 2-2 required that all demands could be met from stock, i.e., the system was never out of stock when a demand occurred. We shall now study the more general case in which all demands must be met ultimately, but it is permissible for the system to be out of stock when a demand occurs. In such a case the demands occurring when the system is out of stock are backordered until a procurement arrives. When a procurement does arrive it is assumed that all backorders are met before the procurement can be used to meet any other demands.

Clearly, if there were no costs associated with incurring backorders, then it would be optimal never to have any inventory on hand. On the other hand, if backorders are sufficiently expensive, then one should never incur any. However, for an intermediate range of backorder costs, it will be optimal to incur some backorders towards the end of a cycle. In accordance with the discussion of Chapter 1, we shall assume that the cost of a backorder has the form $\pi + \hat{\pi}t$ where t is the length of time for which the backorder exists. The cost of a backorder thus includes a fixed cost π and a cost $\hat{\pi}t$ which is proportional to the length of time for which the backorder exists.

Let s be the number of backorders on the books when a procurement of

Q units arrives (s is a non-negative number). Then, after satisfying the backorders, Q-s units will be on hand, since s units were used to fill the backorders. The time required for the Q-s units to be demanded will be $T_1 = (Q - s)/\lambda$. The length of time during one cycle over which backorders will be incurred will then be $T_2 = T - T_1$. The behavior of the system is illustrated graphically in Fig. 2-7.*

The inventory carrying costs per cycle are†

$$IC \int_0^{T_1} (Q - s - \lambda t) \, dt = \frac{IC}{2\lambda} (Q - s)^2$$

This result is also immediately evident from Fig. 2-7, since $(Q - s)^2/2\lambda$

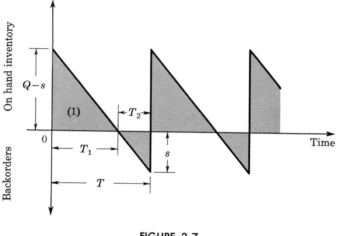

FIGURE 2-7.

is the area of triangle (1). As before, there are on the average λ/Q cycles per year, so that the average yearly cost of carrying inventory is $IC(Q - s)^2/2Q$.

The backorder cost per cycle is

$$\pi s + \hat{\pi} \int_0^{T_2} \lambda t \, dt = \pi s + \frac{1}{2} \hat{\pi} \lambda T_2^2 = \pi s + \frac{\hat{\pi} s^2}{2\lambda}$$

---

* Note that the minimum value of $Q - s$ is zero. Costs could never be reduced by having backorders on the books immediately after the arrival of a procurement. Thus, for a given Q, s must be in the interval $0 \leq s \leq Q$.

† Here and in the remainder of the chapter, we revert to treating the demand and Q and s as continuous variables.

since

$$T_2 = s/\lambda$$

The average annual cost of backorders is then

$$\frac{1}{Q}\left[\pi\lambda s + \frac{1}{2}\hat{\pi}s^2\right]$$

The average annual variable cost $\mathcal{K}$, which includes the cost of ordering, holding inventory, and backorders then becomes

$$\mathcal{K} = \frac{\lambda}{Q}A + \frac{1}{2Q}IC(Q-s)^2 + \frac{1}{Q}\left[\pi\lambda s + \frac{1}{2}\hat{\pi}s^2\right] \qquad (2\text{-}17)$$

Here, $\mathcal{K}$ is a function of Q, s. We wish to find the absolute minimum of $\mathcal{K}$ in the region $0 < Q < \infty, 0 \le s$. It is clear that for any finite s, $\mathcal{K}$ is infinite when $Q = 0$ or ∞. Thus the optimal Q, i.e., Q^*, must indeed satisfy $0 < Q^* < \infty$. If the optimal s, i.e., s^*, satisfies $0 < s^* < \infty$, then the differential calculus requires that since $\mathcal{K}$ is differentiable everywhere in the region of interest, Q^*, s^* must satisfy the equations

$$\frac{\partial \mathcal{K}}{\partial Q} = \frac{\partial \mathcal{K}}{\partial s} = 0 \qquad (2\text{-}18)$$

As we shall see, the optimal solution need not always satisfy (2-18). In certain cases, the optimal s may be on the boundaries.

Consider now the problem of finding the solution to (2-18). From (2-17) we see that

$$\frac{\partial \mathcal{K}}{\partial Q} = -\frac{1}{Q^2}\left[\lambda A + \frac{1}{2}IC(Q-s)^2 + \pi\lambda s + \frac{1}{2}\hat{\pi}s^2\right]$$

$$+ \frac{IC}{Q}(Q-s) = 0 \qquad (2\text{-}19)$$

or

$$-\frac{1}{2}(Q-s)^2 + Q(Q-s) = \frac{1}{IC}\left[\lambda A + \pi\lambda s + \frac{1}{2}\hat{\pi}s^2\right] \qquad (2\text{-}20)$$

so

$$\frac{1}{2}Q^2 = \frac{1}{IC}\left[\lambda A + \pi\lambda s + \frac{1}{2}\hat{\pi}s^2\right] + \frac{1}{2}s^2 \qquad (2\text{-}21)$$

Next observe that

$$\frac{\partial \mathcal{K}}{\partial s} = -\frac{IC}{Q}(Q-s) + \frac{1}{Q}\pi\lambda + \frac{1}{Q}\hat{\pi}s = 0 \qquad (2\text{-}22)$$

or

$$Q = \frac{\pi\lambda}{IC} + \left(1 + \frac{\hat{\pi}}{IC}\right)s \qquad (2\text{-}23)$$

To solve explicitly for Q and s in terms of the system parameters, first substitute (2-23) for Q in (2-21). This yields after regrouping the terms

$$[\hat{\pi}^2 + \hat{\pi}IC]s^2 + 2\pi\hat{\pi}\lambda s + (\pi\lambda)^2 - 2\lambda AIC = 0 \qquad (2\text{-}24)$$

We note immediately that if $\hat{\pi} = 0$, (2-24) reduces to $(\pi\lambda)^2 = 2\lambda AIC$, which is not true in general. This simply means that, in general, when $\hat{\pi} = 0$, there is no solution s such that $0 < s < \infty$. In other words, the solution is on the boundaries so that $s = 0$ or $s = \infty$. In the event that $(\pi\lambda)^2 = 2\lambda AIC$, any s value in the interval satisfies (2-24).

When $\hat{\pi} = 0$, it is easy to determine whether $s = 0$ or $s = \infty$ is optimal. It is only necessary to compare the corresponding costs optimized over Q. When $s^* = 0$, we see that (2-17) reduces to (2-6) so that the optimal Q is Q_w given by (2-8) and the minimum cost is K_w. When $s^* = \infty$, an order is never placed and the minimum yearly cost is $\pi\lambda$. This means that in reality the inventory system should not be operated at all; it is better simply to incur the backorder costs year after year. We see that if

$$\pi > \sqrt{\frac{2AIC}{\lambda}} = \delta \quad \text{or} \quad \pi\lambda > K_w \qquad (2\text{-}25)$$

then the optimal solution has $s^* = 0$, so that Q^* is given by (2-8); if $\pi < \delta$, there should not be any inventory system. When $\pi = \delta$, any value of s, $0 \le s \le \infty$ is optimal (of course, the optimal Q value depends on the s chosen). In the case where $\pi = \delta$, we have shown that the costs are the same when $s = 0$, and $s = \infty$. We leave it for Problem 2-18 to show that the same cost is obtained for any other value of s.

Next consider the case where $\hat{\pi} \neq 0$. Then solution of the quadratic equation (2-24) yields the result

$$s^* = [\hat{\pi} + IC]^{-1}\left\{-\pi\lambda + \left[(2\lambda AIC)\left(1 + \frac{IC}{\hat{\pi}}\right) - \frac{IC}{\hat{\pi}}(\pi\lambda)^2\right]^{1/2}\right\},$$

$$\hat{\pi} \neq 0 \quad (2\text{-}26)$$

To determine Q explicitly, (2-23) is used to eliminate s in (2-21). This yields

$$Q^2 = \frac{2}{IC}\left[\lambda A + \frac{\pi\lambda IC}{\hat{\pi} + IC}Q - \frac{(\pi\lambda)^2}{\hat{\pi} + IC}\right]$$

$$+ \left(\frac{\hat{\pi}}{IC} + 1\right)\left[\frac{IC}{\hat{\pi} + IC}Q - \frac{\pi\lambda}{\hat{\pi} + IC}\right]^2$$

Thus Q^*, the optimal value of Q, is

$$Q^* = \left[\frac{\hat{\pi} + IC}{\hat{\pi}}\right]^{1/2}\left[\frac{2\lambda A}{IC} - \frac{(\pi\lambda)^2}{IC(\hat{\pi} + IC)}\right]^{1/2}, \quad \hat{\pi} \neq 0 \qquad (2\text{-}27)$$

In the event that the s value computed from (2-26) is negative, then the optimal s lies on the boundary, i.e., $s^* = 0$. We leave it for the reader to demonstrate in Problem 2-62 that if $\pi\lambda \geq K_w$, $s^* = 0$. When $\hat{\pi} \neq 0$, s^* cannot be infinite (why?). Equation (2-27) holds only when the s computed from (2-26) is positive; otherwise, $Q^* = Q_w$. Furthermore, if the s computed from (2-26) is positive, it is the optimal s, i.e., s^* does not lie on the boundary $s = 0$. To prove this recall that when $s = 0, Q^* = Q_w$; however, $\partial\mathcal{K}/\partial s < 0$ at $s = 0$, when $Q = Q_w$ and $K_w > \pi\lambda$, so that $s = 0$ cannot be optimal if $K_w > \pi\lambda$.

When $\pi = 0$, (2-26), (2-27) become respectively

$$s^* = \left[\frac{2\lambda A IC}{\hat{\pi}(\hat{\pi} + IC)}\right]^{1/2} = K_w[\hat{\pi}(\hat{\pi} + IC)]^{-1/2} \tag{2-28}$$

and

$$Q^* = \left[\frac{\hat{\pi} + IC}{\hat{\pi}}\right]^{1/2}\sqrt{\frac{2\lambda A}{IC}} = Q_w\left[\frac{\hat{\pi} + IC}{\hat{\pi}}\right]^{1/2} \tag{2-29}$$

It will be noted from (2-28) that when $\pi = 0$, then $s^* > 0$ unless $\hat{\pi} = \infty$, i.e., under optimal operating conditions, some backorders will always be incurred. Give an intuitive explanation for this result.

The computation of the reorder point for this model is, in principle, the same as that presented in Sec. 2-3. Now, however, the inventory levels used must be redefined. The on hand inventory is no longer appropriate since there may be no inventory on hand, but instead there may be backorders at the time when an order should be placed. The appropriate level to replace the on hand inventory is the amount on hand minus the backorders, which will often be referred to as the net inventory.* If there is inventory on hand, there will be no backorders and this level will be positive. If there are backorders, there will be no inventory on hand and this level will be negative. In terms of the net inventory level, the reorder point is then $r_h^* = \mu - mQ^* - s^*$, where, as before, m is the largest integer less than or equal to τ/T. It is possible for r_h^* to be negative. This means that an order is placed when the backorders reach a level $|r_h^*|$. The level to replace the on hand plus on order inventory of Sec. 2-3 is the amount on hand plus on order minus backorders. This will often be referred to as the inventory position of the system. The reorder point in terms of the inventory position is $r^* = \mu - s^*$; r^* can also be negative.

---

* Some authors allow the on hand inventory to be negative, a negative value indicating that backorders exist. With this convention it is unnecessary to introduce the net inventory level. However, we prefer to follow the convention always used in industry and the military of having the on hand inventory be a non-negative variable.

EXAMPLE Consider an item with the following characteristics:

$\lambda = 200$ units/year; $C = \$25$

$I = 0.20$; $A = \$5.00$

$\pi = \$0.20$ per unit; $\hat{\pi} = \$10$ per unit per year

$\tau = 9$ months

From (2-26)

$$s^* = [10 + 5]^{-1}\{-40 + [2(200)(25)(1 + \tfrac{5}{10}) - \tfrac{5}{10}(1600)]^{1/2}\} = 5.27 \approx 5$$

Then, from (2-27)

$$Q^* = \left(1 + \frac{1}{2}\right)^{1/2}\left[\left(\frac{2(200)(5)}{5}\right) - \frac{1600}{5(15)}\right]^{1/2} = 23.8 \approx 24$$

The time between procurements is

$$T^* = \frac{24}{200} = 0.12 \text{ yr.}$$

The lead time demand is $\mu = 0.75\,(200) = 150$ units. Thus the reorder point based on the inventory position of the system is

$$r^* = \mu - s^* = 150 - 5 = 145$$

To determine the reorder point r_h based on the net inventory level, we note that m, the largest integer less than τ/T is 6. Thus

$$r_h^* = \mu - mQ^* - s^* = 150 - 144 - 5 = 1$$

2-6 The Lost Sales Case

In the previous section it was assumed that all demands incurred when the system was out of stock were backordered. We shall now examine the lost sales case, i.e., the case where a demand which occurs when the system is out of stock is lost forever. If demands occurring when the system is out of stock are lost, it is no longer true that the annual revenues received will be independent of the operating doctrine. They will depend on the length of time for which the system is out of stock, and hence on the operating doctrine. Thus we cannot immediately conclude that maximization of the average annual profit will yield the same operating doctrine as the minimization of the average annual cost. We shall now show, however, that with the proper definition of the stockout cost, the minimization of the average annual cost will yield the same result as the maximization of the average annual profit. Let S be the unit selling price of the item, $\mathcal{P}$ be the average annual profit, π_0 the cost of a lost sale exclusive of the lost profit, and C the unit cost of the item. Then if f_0 is the fraction of time during which the system is out of stock, the average annual profit is

$$\mathcal{P} = \lambda(S - C)(1 - f_0) - \pi_0 \lambda f_0 - \text{(ordering and carrying costs)}$$

$$= \lambda(S - C) - (\pi_0 + S - C)\lambda f_0 - \text{(ordering and carrying costs)}$$

It is clear that $\lambda(S - C)$ is the annual profit that would be obtained if the system was never out of stock and is independent of the operating doctrine. Thus if we write $\pi = \pi_0 + S - C$, so that π is the cost of a lost sale including the lost profit, and if in defining the average annual cost, π is taken to be the cost of a lost sale, then the minimization of the average annual cost will yield the same operating doctrine as the maximization of the average annual profit, since the two expressions differ only by $\lambda(S - C)$ which is independent of the operating doctrine. This is what we shall do, and therefore we can again proceed to determine the optimal values of Q and r by minimizing the average annual cost, which is the sum of the ordering, carrying, and stockout costs.

Let $\hat{T}$ be the length of time per cycle during which sales are lost. For any procurement quantity Q, the length of a cycle is $T = (Q/\lambda) + \hat{T}$. Thus the average annual cost is

$$\mathcal{K} = \frac{\lambda}{Q + \lambda \hat{T}} A + \frac{IC}{2} \frac{Q^2}{Q + \lambda \hat{T}} + \frac{\pi\lambda}{Q + \lambda \hat{T}} \lambda \hat{T} \qquad (2\text{-}30)$$

since on the average there are $\lambda/(Q + \lambda\hat{T})$ cycles per year, the inventory carrying cost per cycle is $ICQ^2/2\lambda$, and the cost of lost sales per cycle is $\pi\lambda\hat{T}$. Geometrically, the behavior of the system can be represented as in Fig. 2-8.

A necessary condition that $\hat{T}^*$, Q^* be optimal is that they satisfy

$$\frac{\partial \mathcal{K}}{\partial \hat{T}} = 0 = -(Q + \lambda\hat{T})^{-2}\left[\lambda^2 A + \frac{\lambda IC}{2} Q^2 + \pi\lambda^3 \hat{T}\right] + (Q + \lambda\hat{T})^{-1}\pi\lambda^2 = 0$$

or

$$\lambda\pi = \frac{\lambda A}{Q} + \frac{IC}{2} Q \qquad (2\text{-}31)$$

and

$$\frac{\partial \mathcal{K}}{\partial Q} = 0 = -[Q + \lambda\hat{T}]^{-2}\left[\lambda A + \frac{IC}{2} Q^2 + \pi\lambda^2 \hat{T}\right] + ICQ[Q + \lambda\hat{T}]^{-1}$$

or

$$-\lambda A + \frac{IC}{2} Q^2 - \pi\lambda^2 \hat{T} + ICQ\lambda\hat{T} = 0 \qquad (2\text{-}32)$$

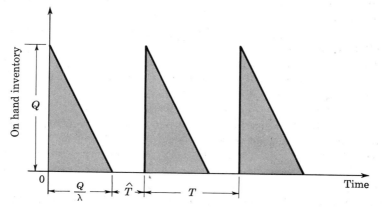

FIGURE 2-8.

provided that

$$0 < \hat{T}^* < \infty, \quad 0 < Q^* < \infty$$

Solving (2-31) for Q, we obtain

$$Q = \frac{\pi\lambda}{IC} \pm \left[\left(\frac{\pi\lambda}{IC} \right)^2 - \frac{2\lambda A}{IC} \right]^{1/2} \tag{2-33}$$

If $(\pi\lambda)^2 < 2\lambda AIC$, there is no real value of Q which satisfies (2-31). If $(\pi\lambda)^2 = 2\lambda AIC$ there is a unique positive Q value which satisfies (2-31). When $(\pi\lambda)^2 > 2\lambda AIC$ there are two *positive* values of Q which satisfy (2-31) since in this case

$$\frac{\pi\lambda}{IC} > \left[\left(\frac{\pi\lambda}{IC} \right)^2 - \frac{2\lambda A}{IC} \right]^{1/2} \tag{2-34}$$

In the event that there is no real Q satisfying (2-31), there is no $\hat{T}$, $0 < \hat{T} < \infty$, which will yield a minimum of $\mathcal{K}$; hence the optimal value of $\hat{T}$ must be zero or ∞. The optimal value is ∞ since the condition $(\pi\lambda)^2 < 2\lambda AIC$ implies that incurring the cost of lost sales all the time is cheaper than operating a system where lost sales are never incurred. Thus in this case there should not be any inventory system.

Consider now the case where either one or two positive Q values satisfy (2-31). Substitution of (2-33) into (2-32) yields after a little manipulation

$$\lambda\hat{T} = -\frac{\pi\lambda}{IC} \mp \left[\left(\frac{\pi\lambda}{IC} \right)^2 - \frac{2\lambda A}{IC} \right]^{1/2} \tag{2-35}$$

However, because of (2-34), it follows that $\hat{T} < 0$ for both signs. Hence, the optimal $\hat{T}$ again does not lie in the interval $0 < \hat{T} < \infty$. In this case the optimal value is $\hat{T} = 0$, since $(\pi\lambda)^2 \geq 2\lambda AIC$, i.e., the cost of running the system with no lost sales is at least as cheap as that of running it with any positive quantity of lost sales. In the special case where $(\pi\lambda)^2 = 2\lambda AIC$, any value of $\hat{T}$ is optimal.

What we have shown above is that if the inventory system should be operated at all, then it is never optimal to incur any stockouts. Even if lost sales are allowed, it follows that when $(\pi\lambda)^2 > 2\lambda AIC$, the optimal solution is precisely the same as the optimal solution to the model studied in Sec. 2-2. The results of this section can be seen intuitively as follows. We rearrange the time sequence of events in Fig. 2-8 so that there are no lost sales for a long time (i.e., in this region we have a situation like Fig. 2-1) and for a long time there is nothing but lost sales. This does not change the average yearly cost. However, if $(\pi\lambda)^2 > 2\lambda AIC$, and the Q in Fig. 2-8 is that given by (2-8), then costs can be reduced by stocking during the period of lost sales and ordering in lots of size Q_w.

2-7 The Case of a Finite Production Rate

In the previous sections it has been assumed that an order for Q units will arrive in the inventory system as a lot of size Q units, i.e., all Q units are received at the same time. We shall now consider a situation in which the inventory system is the factory warehouse. It will be imagined that the item is produced in lots at the factory, and goes directly from the factory to the factory warehouse. Once the factory is set up to produce a lot it will be imagined that the production rate is ψ units per year (independent of the size of the lot). It will be supposed that demands are deterministic and are incurred at the factory warehouse at a rate λ units per year. Both the number demanded and produced will be treated as continuous variables. Clearly, the system cannot operate unless $\psi > \lambda$.

Let us compute the average annual variable costs when Q is the size of the lot produced. It will be imagined that there is a fixed setup cost A for each lot produced. It will also be assumed that there is an inventory carrying cost of IC dollars per unit year where C is the unit cost of the item. The unit cost of the item will be assumed to be independent of the lot size. First the case will be studied where the requirement is made that all demands must be met from inventory, i.e., no backorders or lost sales are permitted.

During the periods when the item is being produced in the factory, there will be a net rate of inflow $\psi - \lambda$ of units into the warehouse. During the periods when the factory is not producing the item there is a net rate of outflow λ of units from the factory warehouse. If s is the quantity on hand in the factory warehouse when the factory starts to turn out units, it is

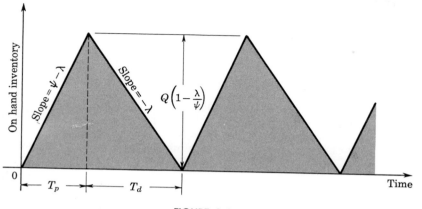

FIGURE 2-9.

clear from the analysis of Sec. 2-2 that the optimal value of s is zero. It remains to determine Q, the lot size, in such a way that the costs are minimized.

The situation is illustrated geometrically in Fig. 2-9. The length of time required to produce a lot is $T_p = Q/\psi$. The on hand inventory in the factory warehouse reaches its maximum value just as production is cut off at the factory. The maximum on hand inventory is

$$T_p(\psi - \lambda) = Q\left(1 - \frac{\lambda}{\psi}\right) \tag{2-36}$$

The time required to deplete the on hand inventory at the warehouse is

$$T_d = \frac{Q}{\lambda}\left(1 - \frac{\lambda}{\psi}\right) \tag{2-37}$$

The length of a cycle is then $T = T_d + T_p = Q/\lambda$.

The average annual costs of setup and holding inventory are

$$K = \frac{\lambda}{Q}A + IC\frac{Q}{2}\left(1 - \frac{\lambda}{\psi}\right) \tag{2-38}$$

since the inventory carrying costs per cycle are

$$IC\left\{\int_0^{T_p}(\psi - \lambda)t\,dt + \int_0^{T_d}\left[Q\left(1 - \frac{\lambda}{\psi}\right) - \lambda t\right]dt\right\}$$

$$= IC\left[\frac{Q^2}{2\psi}\left(1 - \frac{\lambda}{\psi}\right) + \frac{Q^2}{2\lambda}\left(1 - \frac{\lambda}{\psi}\right)^2\right] \tag{2-39}$$

$$= IC\frac{Q^2}{2\lambda}\left(1 - \frac{\lambda}{\psi}\right)$$

If Q^*, $0 < Q^* < \infty$, minimizes the K of (2-38), then it is necessary that Q^* satisfy

$$\frac{\partial K}{\partial Q} = 0 = -\frac{\lambda}{Q^2} A + \frac{IC}{2}\left(1 - \frac{\lambda}{\psi}\right) \tag{2-40}$$

which has the unique positive solution

$$Q^* = \left[\frac{2\lambda A}{IC} \frac{\psi}{\psi - \lambda}\right]^{1/2} = Q_w\left[\frac{\psi}{\psi - \lambda}\right]^{1/2} \tag{2-41}$$

The Q^* of (2-41) does yield the absolute minimum value of K for Q in the range $0 < Q < \infty$. If a time τ is required from the time the warehouse submits an order to the factory until the first unit comes off the production line, then to compute the reorder point r_h based on the on hand inventory level, let m be the greatest integer less than or equal to τ/T. If $\tau - mT < T_d$, the reorder point is $r_h = \mu - mQ$. However, if $\tau - mT > T_d$, the reorder point is

$$r_h = \mu - \eta + (m + 1)\left(\frac{\psi}{\lambda} - 1\right)Q \tag{2-42}$$

where $\eta = \psi\tau$. We leave for Problems 2-30, 2-31, the task of sketching the behavior of the on hand plus on order inventory and the determination of the reorder point in terms of the on hand plus on order inventory level.

It might be pointed out that it is sometimes difficult to decide what cost C to use in computing inventory carrying charges at the factory warehouse. The cost should be the variable production cost and should not include any fixed production costs.

Consider now the case where backorders are allowed. The cost of a backorder will be assumed to have the form $\pi + \hat{\pi}t$ where t is the length of time for which the backorder exists. Let Q^* be the optimal lot size and s^* be the optimal value of the maximum number of backorders incurred per cycle. Then it can be shown that if $\hat{\pi} = 0$, $s^* = 0$ or ∞ and if $s^* = 0$, Q^* is given by (2-41). When $\hat{\pi} \neq 0$

$$s^* = \left(1 - \frac{\lambda}{\psi}\right)(\hat{\pi} + IC)^{-1}\left\{-\pi\lambda\right.$$

$$\left. + \left[\frac{\psi}{\psi - \lambda}(2\lambda AIC)\left(1 + \frac{IC}{\hat{\pi}}\right) - \frac{IC}{\hat{\pi}}(\pi\lambda)^2\right]^{1/2}\right\} \tag{2-43}$$

and

$$Q^* = \left(\frac{\hat{\pi} + IC}{\hat{\pi}}\right)^{1/2}\left[\frac{\psi}{\psi - \lambda}\left(\frac{2\lambda A}{IC}\right) - \frac{(\pi\lambda)^2}{IC(\hat{\pi} + IC)}\right]^{1/2} \tag{2-44}$$

We leave to Problem 2-28 the detailed derivation of the equations which have been written down above for the backorders case, as well as a more detailed discussion of when the optimal s lies on the boundaries of the region. We also leave for Problem 2-29 the proof of the fact that if demands occurring when the system is out of stock are lost instead of backordered, then provided that the system should be operated at all, it is never optimal to incur any lost sales.

EXAMPLE   A certain company makes a complete line of valves. These valves are supplied directly to customers from the factory warehouse. The valves are made in lots and the same production facilities are used to make all the valves. One particular valve has the following properties: The demand rate can be assumed to be known with certainty and to be constant at 2500 units per year. The fixed cost of setup for each production run is $50, and the unit variable cost of production is $3. The inventory carrying charge $I = 0.20$. The production rate is 10,000 units per year. A period of 2 months is required from the time that a production requisition is received at the factory until finished units begin to come off the production line. It is desired to determine the optimal lot size and the warehouse reorder point based on the assumption that stockouts are not permitted.

From (2-41), the optimal lot size is

$$Q^* = \left[\frac{2(2500)(50)}{(0.20)(3)}\frac{(10,000)}{(10,000\text{-}2500)}\right]^{1/2} = \left[\frac{25 \times 10^4}{0.60}(1.333)\right]^{1/2}$$

$$= \sqrt{55.6} \times 10^2 = 745 \tag{2-45}$$

This lot size is 15.5% greater than the lot size that would have been obtained assuming the production rate to be infinite, i.e., by use of (2-8). The reader should answer for himself why the Q^* for the finite production rate is always greater than that for infinite production rates. Note that this approach has ignored any holding costs on units in production. These costs are independent of Q and hence do not appear in the variable cost provided that the amount of time that each unit spends in production is independent of Q.

According to the above, the time between orders $Q^*/\lambda = 0.298$ years. The on hand inventory in the warehouse reaches a maximum value of

$$Q^*\left(1 - \frac{\lambda}{\psi}\right) = 745\left(1 - \frac{2500}{10,000}\right) = 559 \tag{2-46}$$

in a time

$$T_p = \frac{745}{10,000} = 0.0745 \text{ years} = 27.2 \text{ days} \tag{2-47}$$

after the first unit comes off the production line. Since the lead time is

$\tau = 2/12 = 0.167$ years, it follows that the reorder point based on the on hand inventory is

$$r_h^* = \lambda\tau = 2500\ (0.167) = 417 \tag{2-48}$$

2-8 Constraints

Most real world inventory systems stock many items, not merely a single item. It is permissible to study each item individually only as long as there are no interactions among the items. There can be many sorts of inter-actions between items. For example, the items may be partial substitutes for each other; warehouse capacity may be limited and the items are competing for floor space; there may be an upper limit to the number of orders and the items are competing for these; or there may be an upper limit on the maximum investment in inventory and the items are competing for in-vestment dollars. Here we shall consider cases where there are constraints on the floor space, and/or on the number of orders per year which may be placed, and/or on the maximum dollar investment in inventory.

Consider first the case where there is an upper limit f to the square feet of warehouse floor space. Suppose that n items are being stocked and that one unit of item j takes up f_j square feet of floor space. We shall study the case where all demands must be met from inventory so that no backorders or lost sales are allowed. If Q_j is the order quantity for item j, then if the floor space constraint is not to be violated at any time, it must be true that

$$\sum_{j=1}^{n} f_j Q_j = f_1 Q_1 + \ldots + f_n Q_n \leq f \tag{2-49}$$

Here we shall not attempt to account for the possibility that orders can be phased in the certainty case so that it will never be necessary to have the maximum quantity of each item on hand at the same time.

Let λ_j be the yearly demand rate (assumed to be deterministic), A_j be the fixed ordering cost, C_j the unit cost (assumed to be independent of Q_j), and I_j the carrying charge for item j. Then the average annual variable cost for all the items is

$$K = \sum_{j=1}^{n} \left[\frac{\lambda_j}{Q_j} A_j + I_j C_j \frac{Q_j}{2} \right] \tag{2-50}$$

It is desired to find the absolute minimum of K in the region $0 < Q_j < \infty$, $j = 1, \ldots, n$, subject to the constraint (2-49).

In Appendix 1, we review the mathematical background needed to solve the above problem. The procedure is as follows: First we solve the problem ignoring the constraint (2-49), i.e., we minimize over each Q_j separately. This yields

$$Q_j = \sqrt{\frac{2\lambda_j A_j}{I_j C_j}}, \quad j = 1, \ldots, n \tag{2-51}$$

If the Q_j of (2-51) satisfy (2-49), then these Q_j are optimal. In such a case the constraint is not active, i.e., sufficient floor space is available so that average yearly costs could not be reduced by increasing the amount of floor space available.

On the other hand, if the Q_j of (2-51) do not satisfy (2-49), then the constraint is active and the Q_j of (2-51) are not optimal. To find the optimal Q_j, the Lagrange multiplier technique is used. We form the function

$$J = \sum_{j=1}^{n} \left[\frac{\lambda_j}{Q_j} A_j + I_j C_j \frac{Q_j}{2} \right] + \theta \left(\sum_{j=1}^{n} f_j Q_j - f \right) \tag{2-52}$$

where the parameter θ is a Lagrange multiplier. Then the set of Q_j, $j = 1$, $\ldots$, n, which yield the absolute minimum of K subject to (2-49) are solutions to the set of equations

$$\frac{\partial J}{\partial Q_j} = 0 = -\frac{\lambda_j}{Q_j^2} A_j + \frac{I_j C_j}{2} + \theta f_j, \quad j = 1, \ldots, n \tag{2-53}$$

$$\frac{\partial J}{\partial \theta} = 0 = \sum_{j=1}^{n} f_j Q_j - f \tag{2-54}$$

These have the unique and hence optimal solution

$$Q_j^* = \sqrt{\frac{2\lambda_j A_j}{I_j C_j + 2\theta^* f_j}}, \quad j = 1, \ldots, n \tag{2-55}$$

where θ^* is the value of θ such that the Q^* of (2-55) satisfy (2-54). The function

$$\sum_{j=1}^{n} f_j [2\lambda_j A_j (I_j C_j + 2\theta f_j)^{-1}]^{1/2} - f$$

is a monotone decreasing function of θ; consequently, there is a unique $\theta^* > 0$ such that (2-54) is satisfied.

As is shown in Appendix 1, $\theta^* = -\partial K^*/\partial f$, where K^* is the minimum value of K when optimized with respect to the Q_j for a given f. Thus, in an intuitive sense, θ^* gives the decrease in the minimum cost if the floor space were increased by one square foot. The Lagrange multiplier is often called an imputed cost or shadow price of floor space. Looked at another way, if there were no constraint on the floor space available, but if floor space cost

θ^* dollars per square foot per year, then the average annual variable cost would be

$$K = \sum_{j=1}^{n} \left[\frac{\lambda_j}{Q_j} A_j + I_j C_j \frac{Q_j}{2} \right] + \theta^* \sum_{j=1}^{n} f_j Q_j \tag{2-56}$$

The set of Q_j which minimize this cost expression are precisely the same as those which minimize (2-50) subject to (2-49). The problem described by (2-56) which assigns a cost but no upper limit to the amount of floor space is called a dual of the problem described by (2-50) and (2-49), which does not charge for floor space but has an upper limit on the amount of floor space available.

Consider next the case where there is a constraint on the total number of orders which can be placed. Assume that no more than h orders can be placed per year. This requires that

$$\sum_{j=1}^{n} \frac{\lambda_j}{Q_j} \leq h \tag{2-57}$$

Here we ignore the fact that in any given year the number of orders placed must be an integer and can differ from the average value λ_j/Q_j by as much as unity. It is assumed that this influence is small. We assume now that there is no fixed cost per order. (In Problem 2-35, the reader is asked to generalize the theory to be developed to the case where there is also a fixed cost associated with each order.) The only costs are then the inventory carrying charges. Thus the average annual variable cost is

$$K = \sum_{j=1}^{n} I_j C_j \frac{Q_j}{2} \tag{2-58}$$

It is desired to find the absolute minimum of (2-58) subject to (2-57). Inasmuch as only carrying costs appear in (2-58), it is immediately clear that the constraint (2-57) must always be active, i.e., as many orders will be processed as possible, since inventory carrying costs can be reduced in this way.

To determine the optimal Q_j we form the function

$$J = \sum_{j=1}^{n} I_j C_j \frac{Q_j}{2} + \eta \left(\sum_{j=1}^{n} \frac{\lambda_j}{Q_j} - h \right) \tag{2-59}$$

where η is the Lagrange multiplier. Then the optimal Q_j must satisfy the set of equations

$$\frac{\partial J}{\partial Q_j} = 0 = \frac{I_j C_j}{2} - \frac{\eta \lambda_j}{Q_j^2}, \quad j = 1, \ldots, n \tag{2-60}$$

$$\frac{\partial J}{\partial \eta} = 0 = \sum_{j=1}^{n} \frac{\lambda_j}{Q_j} - h \qquad (2\text{-}61)$$

The unique optimal solution is

$$Q_j{}^* = \sqrt{\frac{2\eta^*\lambda_j}{I_j C_j}}, \quad j = 1, \ldots, n \qquad (2\text{-}62)$$

where on substitution of (2-62) into (2-61)

$$\eta^* = \left[\frac{1}{\sqrt{2}\,h} \sum_{j=1}^{n} \sqrt{\lambda_j I_j C_j} \right]^2 \qquad (2\text{-}63)$$

In this case it is easy to solve explicitly for the optimal value of the Lagrange multiplier. The value η^* can be interpreted as the imputed cost of placing an order.

Finally consider the case where there is an upper limit D to the dollar investment in inventory at any one time. This constraint requires that

$$\sum_{j=1}^{n} C_j Q_j \leq D \qquad (2\text{-}64)$$

(here again we omit consideration of the possibility of time phasing orders in such a way that every level would not reach its maximum value simultaneously). It is desired to minimize (2-50), subject to (2-64). The constraint (2-64) is formally equivalent to the floor space constraint (2-49). Hence it is unnecessary to repeat the analysis; it is only necessary to substitute C_j for f_j and D for f. There are a number of minor variations on the above three types of constraints. Some of these are pointed out in the problems.

It is also possible to have two or more of the constraints imposed simultaneously. Suppose, for example, that there is a constraint on the number of orders placed per year and a constraint on the maximum dollar investment in inventory at any time. Thus we wish to minimize (2-58) subject to (2-57) and (2-64).* We know that the constraint (2-57) will be active. However, (2-64) may or may not be active. Thus we first solve the problem ignoring (2-64). If the optimal solution satisfies (2-64) we are finished. If (2-64) is not satisfied, we introduce two Lagrange multipliers θ, ϕ and form the function

$$J = \sum_{j=1}^{n} I_j C_j \frac{Q_j}{2} + \theta \left(\sum_{j=1}^{n} \frac{\lambda_j}{Q_j} - h \right) + \phi \left(\sum_{j=1}^{n} C_j Q_j - D \right) \qquad (2\text{-}65)$$

---

* It is conceivable that the constraints (2-57), (2-64) are inconsistent so that there is no solution. Here we assume that they are consistent.

Then the optimal Q_j must be solutions to

$$\frac{\partial J}{\partial Q_j} = 0 = \frac{I_j C_j}{2} - \frac{\theta \lambda_j}{Q_j^2} + \phi C_j, \quad j = 1, \ldots, n \qquad (2\text{-}66)$$

$$\frac{\partial J}{\partial \theta} = 0 = \sum_{j=1}^{n} \frac{\lambda_j}{Q_j} - h \qquad (2\text{-}67)$$

$$\frac{\partial J}{\partial \phi} = 0 = \sum_{j=1}^{n} C_j Q_j - D \qquad (2\text{-}68)$$

From (2-66)

$$Q_j^* = \sqrt{\frac{2\theta^* \lambda_j}{C_j(I_j + 2\phi^*)}}, \quad j = 1, \ldots, n \qquad (2\text{-}69)$$

Then substitution of (2-69) into (2-67) yields

$$\theta^* = \left[\frac{1}{\sqrt{2}\,h} \sum_{j=1}^{n} \sqrt{\lambda_j C_j(I_j + 2\phi^*)} \right]^2 \qquad (2\text{-}70)$$

Finally, substitution of (2-70) into (2-69) and (2-69) into (2-68) yields

$$\left\{ \sum_{j=1}^{n} \left[\frac{\lambda_j C_j}{I_j + 2\phi^*} \right]^{1/2} \right\} \left\{ \frac{1}{h} \sum_{j=1}^{n} [\lambda_j C_j(I_j + 2\phi^*)]^{1/2} \right\} = D \qquad (2\text{-}71)$$

The numerical procedure is as follows: 1) Determine ϕ^* from (2-71). 2) Then determine θ^* from (2-70). 3) Finally determine the Q_j^* from (2-69). The numerical value of ϕ^* can be determined from (2-71) using a trial and error technique. However, a more efficient procedure is to use Newton's method discussed in Appendix 2.

The difficulties in numerically evaluating the Q_j^* increase considerably with each additional constraint which is imposed on the system. In the event that the two constraints imposed on the system were a constraint on the floor space and a constraint on the maximum investment in inventory, then the problem is more complicated since either or both of the constraints can be inactive. The computational procedure is as follows: First determine the Q_j from (2-8) ignoring both constraints. If these Q_j satisfy the constraints they are optimal. When this is not the case include one of the constraints, say the investment constraint, in the analysis, but not the other. If the Q_j so obtained satisfy the square feet constraint they are optimal. When they do not, solve the problem including the floor space constraint but ignoring the investment constraint. If the Q_j satisfy the investment constraint they are optimal. If they do not, we are then sure that both constraints are active. Thus we introduce two multipliers and solve the problem treating both constraints as being active. It is important to note that it is necessary to examine the cases where one or both Lagrange multipliers are zero, i.e., where one or both constraints hold as strict inequalities.

2-9 Constraints—An Example

Consider a shop which produces and stocks three items. The management desires never to have an investment in inventory of more than $14,000. The items are produced in lots. The demand rate for each item is constant and can be assumed to be deterministic. No backorders are to be allowed. The pertinent data for the items are given in Table 2-1. The carrying charge on each item is $I = 0.20$. Determine the optimal lot size for each item.

TABLE 2-1

Data for Example

Item	1	2	3
Demand rate (units per year) λ_j	1000	500	2000
Variable cost (dollars per unit) C_j	20	100	50
Set up cost per lot (dollars) A_j	50	75	100

The optimal lot sizes in the absence of the constraint are:

$$Q_1 = \sqrt{\frac{2(1000)(50)}{4}} = 158; \quad Q_2 = \sqrt{\frac{2(500)(75)}{20}} = 61;$$

$$Q_3 = \sqrt{\frac{2(2000)(100)}{10}} = 200$$

If these Q_j's were used, the maximum investment in inventory would be

$$D = 20(158) + 100(61) + 200(50) = 3160 + 6100 + 10,000 = \$19,260$$

This is greater than the maximum allowable investment in inventory. Hence the constraint is active, and on introduction of a Lagrange multiplier ρ, we see by analogy with (2-55) that the optimal Q_j's are given by

$$Q_j^* = \sqrt{\frac{2\lambda_j A_j}{C_j(I + 2\rho^*)}}, \quad j = 1, 2, 3$$

where ρ^* is the solution of the equation

$$\sum_{j=1}^{3} \sqrt{\frac{2\lambda_j C_j A_j}{I + 2\rho^*}} = D = 14{,}000 = \sqrt{\frac{1 \times 10^6}{0.10 + \rho^*}}$$

$$+ \sqrt{\frac{3.75 \times 10^6}{0.10 + \rho^*}} + \sqrt{\frac{10 \times 10^6}{0.10 + \rho^*}}$$

Thus

$$\sqrt{0.10 + \rho^*} = \frac{1}{14} \left[1 + 1.935 + 3.16\right] = \frac{6.10}{14} = 0.436$$

or

$$\rho^* = 0.091$$

Consequently, the optimal Q_j are

$$Q_1^* = \sqrt{\frac{2(1000)(50)}{20(0.382)}} = 114; \quad Q_2^* = \sqrt{\frac{2(500)(75)}{100(0.382)}} = 44;$$

$$Q_3^* = \sqrt{\frac{2(2000)(100)}{50(0.382)}} = 145$$

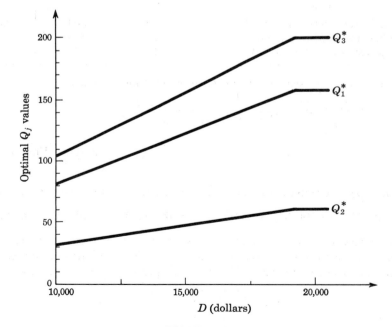

FIGURE 2-10.

Substitution of these Q_j^* values into the constraint shows that it does indeed hold as a strict equality (to the accuracy with which the calculations can be made when the Q_j^* are rounded to be integers).

The minimum cost of setups and holding inventory for the three items in the absence of any constraint on investment in inventory is

$$K = \sum_{j=1}^{3} \sqrt{2\lambda_j A_j IC_j} = 632 + 1225 + 2000 = \$3857/\mathrm{yr}.$$

The corresponding minimum cost in the presence of the constraint is

$$K^* = \sum_{j=1}^{3} \left[\frac{\lambda_j}{Q_j^*} A_j + IC_j \frac{Q_j^*}{2} \right] = 667 + 1292 + 2105 = \$4064/\mathrm{yr}.$$

The cost in the presence of the constraint on inventory investment is thus $207 per year higher than in the absence of such a constraint.

It is of interest to observe the way in which the optimal Q_j and the minimum average yearly variable cost change with D, the maximum allowable investment in inventory. This is shown in Figs. 2-10, 2-11. When $D \geq \$19,260$, the optimal Q_j's are simply those obtained in the absence of any constraint. Similarly, when $D \geq \$19,260$, $K^* = \$3857$ per year.

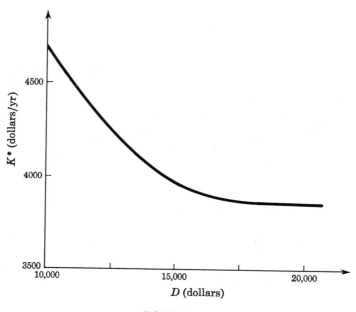

FIGURE 2-11.

2-10 Periodic Review Formulation

Consider an inventory system in which an order is placed every T units of time. It is desired to determine the optimal value of T by minimizing the average annual variable cost, this cost being the sum of the ordering and inventory carrying costs. It will be required that all demands be met from inventory so that there are never any backorders or lost sales. We assume as before that the demand rate λ is known with certainty and does not change with time. It is immediately clear that if the on hand inventory is not to continually increase or decrease with each period, then the quantity ordered each time will be $Q = \lambda T$. Furthermore, in order to minimize carrying charges, the on hand inventory when a procurement arrives should be zero. If A is the fixed cost of placing an order, C the cost of one unit, and I the inventory carrying charge, then the average annual variable cost is

$$K = \frac{A}{T} + IC\frac{\lambda T}{2} \tag{2-72}$$

and the optimal value of T is

$$T^* = \sqrt{\frac{2A}{IC\lambda}} \tag{2-73}$$

If (2-73) is multiplied by λ we obtain the quantity ordered each period, i.e.,

$$Q^* = \lambda T^* = \sqrt{\frac{2\lambda A}{IC}} = Q_w$$

which is precisely (2-8).

What we have shown is that for models in which the demand is deterministic, there is no difference between models which order a quantity Q each time the inventory reaches the reorder point (these will be referred to as $\langle Q, r \rangle$ or lot size-reorder point models) and periodic review models in which an order is placed only at times separated by an interval T. When uncertainty is introduced into the demand we shall later see that periodic review models and $\langle Q, r \rangle$ models have a somewhat different structure.

2-11 Quantity Discounts—"All Units" Discounts

In the real world, it is not always true that the unit cost of an item is independent of the quantity procured. Often, discounts are offered for the purchase of large quantities. These discounts sometimes take the form of price breaks of the following type: There are given quantities $q_0 = 0$, q_1, $q_2, \ldots, q_m$, $q_j < q_{j+1}$, $j = 1, \ldots, m$ and $q_{m+1} = \infty$, such that if a quantity Q is purchased, $q_j \leq Q < q_{j+1}$, then the unit cost of each of the Q units is

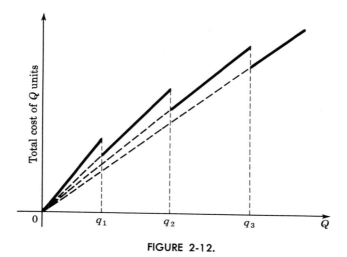

FIGURE 2-12.

C_j, i.e., the cost of Q units is C_jQ, and $C_{j+1} < C_j$. The total cost of purchasing Q units then has the form shown in Fig. 2-12. We shall refer to quantity discounts of this sort as "all units" quantity discounts since the discount applies to every unit purchased.

The introduction of "all units" quantity discounts increases the difficulty of determining the optimal order quantity for an item. Let us now examine how it is done. Let us consider the case where backorders are allowed, and $\pi = 0$, $\hat\pi \neq 0$. For any Q value, the optimal s is given by (2-23). Hence, if C_j is the unit cost of the item, the average annual variable cost optimized with respect to s is

$$K_j(Q) = \lambda C_jQ + \frac{\lambda}{Q} A + \hat\pi \left(\frac{IC_j}{\hat\pi + IC_j}\right) \frac{Q}{2}, \qquad j = 0, 1, \ldots, m \qquad (2\text{-}74)$$

For $q_j \leq Q < q_{j+1}$, K_j is the average annual variable cost. Note that it is now necessary to include the cost of the units themselves in the variable cost since the unit cost of the item depends on the quantity procured.

We can think of (2-74) as defining a cost curve for all Q, not simply for Q in the interval $q_j \leq Q < q_{j+1}$. In this way one can obtain $m + 1$ cost curves, one for each C_j. The important thing to notice is that these cost curves do not intersect and that $K_{j+1}(Q) < K_j(Q)$ for all Q (proof?). A typical set of these curves is shown in Fig. 2-13. The actual cost curve for the system is represented by the solid portions of the curves shown in Fig. 2-13. The dashed portions are not physically realizable.

The problem is to determine the lowest point on the solid (broken) curve. This can be done as follows: First we compute the Q value, call it $Q^{(m)}$,

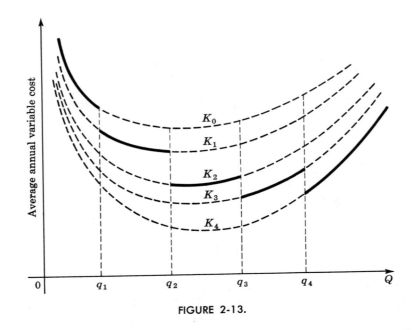

FIGURE 2-13.

which yields the minimum cost on the K_m curve. If $Q^{(m)}$ satisfies $q_m \leq Q^{(m)}$, then $Q^{(m)}$ is optimal since it yields the minimum cost on the K_m curve and no cost on any of the other K_j curves, $j < m$, can be lower than this cost. If $Q^{(m)} < q_m$, then $Q^{(m)}$ is not physically realizable. In this case compute $K_m(q_m)$ which is the cost on the K_m curve at the mth price break; $K_m(q_m)$ is to be used in the next stage.

To begin the second stage of the computation (if it is needed), determine $Q^{(m-1)}$ which is the point of minimum cost on the K_{m-1} curve. If $q_{m-1} \leq Q^{(m-1)} < q_m$, compute $K_{m-1}(Q^{(m-1)})$ and compare it with $K_m(q_m)$. If $K_{m-1}(Q^{(m-1)}) < K_m(q_m)$, then $Q^{(m-1)}$ is optimal since no cost on the curves $K_j, j < m - 1$ can be lower and no realizable cost on the K_m curve is lower. When $K_m(q_m) < K_{m-1}(Q^{(m-1)})$ then q_m is optimal (if $K_m(q_m) = K_{m-1}(Q^{(m-1)})$ then either q_m or $Q^{(m-1)}$ is optimal). In the event that $Q^{(m-1)}$ lies outside the interval $q_{m-1} \leq Q^{(m-1)} < q_m$, compute $K_{m-1}(q_{m-1})$ and $\hat{K}_{m-1} = \min [K_m(q_m), K_{m-1}(q_{m-1})]$. Let $\hat{q}_{m-1}$ be the q_j appropriate to $\hat{K}_{m-1}$, i.e., in this case either q_m or q_{m-1}.

If the optimal Q was not determined during the second stage, the third stage is begun by computing $Q^{(m-2)}$, the Q value at which K_{m-2} takes on its minimum cost. If $Q^{(m-2)}$ lies in the interval $q_{m-2} \leq Q^{(m-2)} < q_{m-1}$ compute $K_{m-2}(Q^{(m-2)})$ and compare it with $\hat{K}_{m-1}$. If $K_{m-2}(Q^{(m-2)}) < \hat{K}_{m-1}$ then $Q^{(m-2)}$ is optimal. If $\hat{K}_{m-1} > K_{m-2}(Q^{(m-2)})$ then $\hat{q}_{m-1}$ is optimal (if $\hat{K}_{m-1}$

$= K_{m-2}(Q^{(m-2)})$ either is optimal). When $Q^{(m-2)}$ is not in the physically allowable region compute $\hat{K}_{m-2} = \min \, [K_{m-2}(q_{m-2}), \, \hat{K}_{m-1}]$ and record $\hat{q}_{m-2}$. The remaining stages are merely a repetition of the above type of computations. Unless one has some prior knowledge as to where the optimal Q lies, it is probably best to begin the computational procedure as discussed above. Clearly, if there were a large number of price breaks, it could be quite time consuming to compute the optimal Q.

EXAMPLES   1.   Consider again the example presented on p. 37. Recall that $\lambda = 600$ units per yr., $A = \$8.00$, $I = 0.20$. Let us now assume that quantity discounts of the type discussed above are available. It will be imagined that there are two price breaks at $q_1 = 500$ and $q_2 = 1000$; furthermore $C_0 = \$0.30$, $C_1 = \$0.29$, $C_2 = \$0.28$.

To determine the optimal Q we first compute $Q^{(m)} = Q^{(2)}$, where $K_m = K_2$ takes on its minimum value. Thus

$$Q^{(2)} = \sqrt{\frac{2\lambda A}{IC_2}} = \sqrt{\frac{2(600)8}{0.20(0.28)}} = 414$$

We observe that $Q^{(2)}$ does not satisfy $Q^{(2)} \geq 1000$; hence $Q^{(2)}$ is not physically realizable. Thus we next compute

$$K_2(q_2) = \lambda C_2 + \frac{\lambda}{q_2} A + IC_2 \frac{q_2}{2} = \$200.80$$

The second stage is begun by computing

$$Q^{(1)} = \sqrt{\frac{2\lambda A}{IC_1}} = 406$$

However, $Q^{(1)}$ does not satisfy $500 \leq Q^{(1)} < 1000$ and $Q^{(1)}$ is not realizable. Hence we next find

$$K_1(q_1) = \lambda C_1 + \frac{\lambda}{q_1} A + IC_1 \frac{q_1}{2} = \$198.10$$

Then $\hat{K}_1 = \min \, [K_1(q_1), K_2(q_2)] = K_1(q_1) = \$198.10$ and $\hat{q}_1 = 500$. For stage three

$$Q^{(0)} = \sqrt{\frac{2\lambda A}{IC_0}} = 400$$

and $Q^{(0)}$ is allowable since $0 < Q^{(0)} < 500$. Then

$$K_0(Q_0) = \lambda C_0 + \sqrt{2\lambda A I C_0} = \$204$$

However, $\hat{K}_1 < K_0(Q_0)$. Thus $Q^* = \hat{q}_1 = 500$ is optimal and the optimal Q value occurs at a price break.

2. By slightly modifying the nature of the discounts in the above example, it is possible to illustrate a case where one of the $Q^{(j)}$ is optimal. Assume that $q_1 = 300$, $q_2 = 400$ with C_0, C_1, C_2, λ, A, and I being defined as in the previous example. Now $Q^{(2)} = 414$ satisfies $q_2 \leq Q^{(2)}$, and hence $Q^{(2)}$ is optimal. The minimum average annual cost is

$$K_2 = \lambda C_2 + \sqrt{2\lambda A I C_2} = \$191.19$$

2-12 Incremental Quantity Discounts

Another type of quantity discount, which we shall call the incremental type discount, charges C_0 per unit for units $1, \ldots, q_1$, C_1 per unit on units $q_1 + 1, \ldots, q_2$, etc. Geometrically, the total cost of Q units can then be represented graphically as in Fig. 2-14. The total cost of Q units, $C(Q)$, when $q_j < Q \leq q_{j+1}$ can be written

$$C(Q) = R_j + C_j(Q - q_j), \quad j = 0, 1, \ldots, m$$

where $R_j = C(q_j)$, $R_0 = 0$, $q_0 = 0$, and $q_{m+1} = \infty$. The average cost per unit is

$$\frac{C(Q)}{Q} = \frac{R_j}{Q} + C_j - C_j \frac{q_j}{Q}, \quad j = 0, 1, \ldots, m \tag{2-75}$$

Thus when no stockouts are allowed, the average annual variable cost if $q_j < Q \leq q_{j+1}$ is

$$K_j = \lambda C_j + \frac{\lambda}{Q}(A + R_j - C_j q_j) + \frac{IR_j}{2} + IC_j \frac{Q}{2} - IC_j \frac{q_j}{2} \tag{2-76}$$

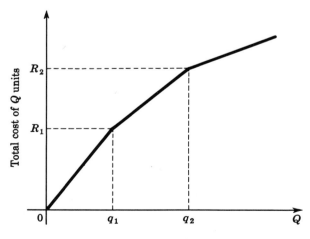

FIGURE 2-14.

(The corresponding cost equation for the case where backorders are allowed becomes somewhat complicated to write down. We leave the analysis of this case to Problem 2-66. The general results described here hold, however, when backorders are allowed.) We can imagine K_j in (2-76) to be defined for all positive Q, even though K_j is physically realizable only if $q_j < Q \le q_{j+1}$. If there are m price breaks we then obtain $m + 1$ curves as shown in Fig. 2-15. The actual total cost curve is the solid portion of these curves.

The computation of the optimal Q for incremental discounts is somewhat

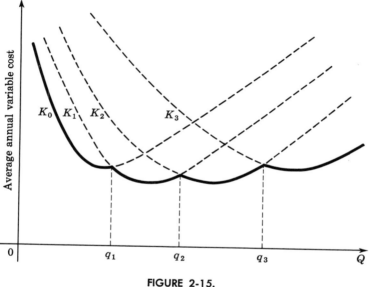

FIGURE 2-15.

different than for "all units" discounts. The important thing to notice in the present case is that the minimum of the average annual variable cost cannot occur at one of the price breaks. To see this note first of all that the total cost curve is continuous, i.e., $K_{j-1}(q_j) = K_j(q_j)$, $j = 1, \ldots, m$. Also, the slope of K_j at q_j is less than the slope of K_{j-1} at q_j (we ask the reader to prove this in Problem 2-45). Thus the average annual cost does not have a relative minimum at q_j, and therefore the absolute minimum cannot occur at q_j. The computational procedure to determine the optimal Q is then as follows: Compute $Q^{(j)}$, the value of Q which minimizes K_j for $j = 0$, $1, \ldots, m$. From (2-76) we see that

$$Q^{(j)} = \left[\frac{2\lambda(A + R_j - C_j q_j)}{IC_j}\right]^{1/2} \tag{2-77}$$

For those $Q^{(j)}$ which are physically realizable, i.e., $q_j < Q^{(j)} \leq q_{j+1}$, determine $K_j(Q^{(j)})$. The $Q^{(j)}$ corresponding to the smallest of these costs is the optimal Q. Note that for this case it does not follow that if $Q^{(m)}$ is physically realizable, then $Q^{(m)}$ is optimal (the following example illustrates a case where $Q^{(m)}$ is allowable, but not optimal).

EXAMPLE   Consider an item on which incremental quantity discounts are available. The first 100 units cost \$100 each, and additional units cost \$98 each. For this item: $\lambda = 500$ units per yr., $I = 0.20$, $A = \$50$. To determine the optimal Q value we first compute

$$Q^{(0)} = \sqrt{\frac{2\lambda A}{IC_0}} = 50$$

Since $Q^{(0)}$ is in the allowable range, we determine

$$K_0(Q^{(0)}) = \lambda C_0 + \sqrt{2\lambda A I C_0} = \$51{,}000$$

Next we compute $Q^{(1)}$ the point where K_1 takes on its minimum value.

$$Q^{(1)} = \left[\frac{2\lambda(A + R_1 - C_1 q_1)}{IC_1}\right]^{1/2} = 113$$

$Q^{(1)}$ is also in the allowable range and

$$K_1(Q^{(1)}) = \lambda C_1 + \frac{\lambda}{Q^{(1)}}(A + R_1 - C_1 q_1) + \frac{1}{2}IR_1 + \frac{1}{2}IC_1 Q^{(1)}$$

$$-\frac{1}{2}IC_1 q_1 = \$51{,}234$$

Hence the optimal Q is $Q^* = Q^{(0)} = 50$. It is unnecessary to check the price break points since they can never be optimal.

REFERENCES

1. Bowman, E. H., and R. B. Fetter, *Analysis for Production Management, Revised Ed.* Homewood, Illinois: Richard D. Irwin, Inc., 1961.

2. Churchman, C. W., R. L. Ackoff, and E. L. Arnoff, *Introduction to Operations Research.* New York: John Wiley and Sons, Inc., 1957.

Chapters 8, 9, 10 are devoted to inventory management. Chapter 8 considers the simplest lot size model with no stockouts and the case where backorders are allowed under the assumption that $\pi = 0$. Some simple probabilistic models are also treated in this chapter. Chapter 9 gives a very detailed discussion of "all units" quantity discounts and suggests essentially the same sort of computational procedure which we have used. Chapter 10 gives an elementary treatment of constraints and the Lagrange multiplier technique.

3. Fetter, R. B., and W. C. Dalleck, *Decision Models for Inventory Management.* Homewood, Illinois: Richard D. Irwin, Inc., 1961.

In Chapters 1, 2 the authors present the simplest lot size formula with no stockouts and the finite production rate case with no stockouts. Some probabilistic models are also treated. All units quantity discounts are discussed; however, the computational procedure suggested for determining the optimal Q seems to be incorrect.

4. Magee, J. F., *Production Planning and Inventory Control.* New York: McGraw-Hill Book Co., Inc., 1958.

5. Morris, W. T., *Engineering Economy.* Homewood, Illinois: Richard D. Irwin, Inc., 1960.

6. Raymond, F. E., *Quantity and Economy in Manufacture.* New York: McGraw-Hill Book Co., Inc., 1931.

7. Sasieni, M., A. Yaspan, and L. Friedman, *Operations Research, Methods and Problems.* New York: John Wiley and Sons, Inc., 1959.

Chapter 4 discusses inventory models. The simplest lot size model with no stockouts is treated as well as the backorders case for $\pi = 0$. The finite production rate model with no stockouts is also developed. Over half of the chapter is devoted to simple probabilistic models.

8. Welsh, W. E., *Scientific Inventory Control.* Greenwich, Conn.: Management Publishing Corp., 1956.

A very elementary treatment intended for those in industry with no background in mathematics who are trying to apply the subject.

9. Whitin, T. M., *The Theory of Inventory Management, Revised Ed.* Princeton, N.J.: Princeton University Press, 1957.

PROBLEMS

2-1. The soft goods department of a large department store sells 500 units per month of a certain large bath towel. The unit cost of a towel to the store is \$0.50 and the cost of placing an order has been estimated to be \$2.00. The store uses an inventory carrying charge of $I = 0.17$. Assuming that the demand is deterministic and continuous, and that no stockouts are allowed, determine the optimal order quantity. What is the time between the placing of orders? The procurement lead time for the towels is one month. What is the reorder point based on the on hand inventory level?

2-2. Prove that for the lot size model discussed in Sec. 2-2 it is true that the average annual inventory carrying charges are equal to the average annual fixed procurement costs when $Q = Q^*$, i.e., show that in Fig. 2-2 the $ICQ/2$ and the $\lambda A/Q$ curves cross at $Q = Q^*$.

2-3. A soap manufacturer makes several different detergents using the same equipment for all of them. It costs $1000 to clean the equipment and to prepare it for a run of a given detergent. A particular detergent has a demand rate of 100 tons per month. This can be considered to be deterministic. The variable production cost of one ton is $200. The firm uses an inventory carrying charge of $I = 0.17$. What is the optimal quantity to produce per run if no stockouts are to be allowed? What is the time between runs?

2-4. Derive an economic lot size formula which expresses the optimal order quantity in terms of its dollar value. Assume that no stockouts are allowed. What practical advantages might there be in using this type of lot size formula?

2-5. Derive a formula for the ratio $(K - K^*)/K^*$ in terms of γ when lots of size γQ^*, $\gamma > 0$, are ordered rather than Q^*. Assume that no stockouts are allowed. Show that if γQ^* is replaced by $1/\gamma Q^*$ the same relation is obtained.

2-6. A function $f(x)$ is said to be convex in some interval $a \le x \le b$ if for any two different values x_1, x_2 in the interval, and all α, $0 \le \alpha \le 1$

$$f[\alpha x_1 + (1 - \alpha)x_2] \le \alpha f(x_1) + (1 - \alpha)f(x_2)$$

The function is called strictly convex if the strict inequality holds for $0 < \alpha < 1$. Geometrically, a function is convex if the line joining two points on the curve $y = f(x)$ lies on or above the curve. Illustrate a convex function graphically. Show that the sum of convex functions is also convex. Prove that a strictly convex function can only have a single relative minimum in any interval, and that this is also the absolute minimum in the interval.

2-7. Show that $f_1(Q) = \lambda A/Q$ is a strictly convex function, and that $f_2(Q) = ICQ/2$ is convex, for $0 < Q < \infty$. Thus show that the function K defined by Eq. (2-6) is strictly convex. By use of the results of Problem 2-6 show that $dK/dQ = 0$ can have only one solution in the interval $0 < Q < \infty$, and that the solution will yield the absolute minimum value of K in this interval. *Hint:* Note that the proof requires that one show that K cannot have a relative maximum.

2-8. In the real world it is often difficult to estimate precisely the values of such parameters as A or I. Consider a case where λ, C, I have been estimated correctly, but A has not. Let A_a be the true value of the ordering cost and A our estimate of it. Let Q be our estimate of Q^*, Q being obtained from Eq. (2-8) using A instead of A_a. Then denote by K the average annual cost that would be incurred by using Q as the order quantity in the actual system. Determine an equation relating K/K^* to A/A_a, where K^* is the minimum average annual cost. What useful information does this curve provide? Is it better to have an estimate of A_a which is too high or too low? Also determine the relation between Q/Q^* and A/A_a. Derive a similar set of results for incorrect estimates of the carrying charge.

2-9. Determine the first and second derivatives of Eq. (2-6). How does the shape of the K curve depend on the values of A, I, C, λ? For fixed λ, I, C sketch the nature of a family of K curves with A as a parameter.

2-10. Prove in general for the case of deterministic demand and constant lead times that the average amount on order is equal to the lead time demand.

2-11. At a large automobile repair shop a certain part has a very low demand. The demand is 8 units per year. This can be assumed to be deterministic and constant over time. The cost of placing an order for this part is $1.00. The unit cost of the part is $30, and the shop uses an inventory carrying charge of $I = 0.20$. Use the theory developed in Sec. 2-4 to take account of the integrality of demand and determine the optimal order quantity. What is the time between placing of orders? What Q value would be obtained using Eq. (2-8)?

2-12. For the example solved on p. 37, what would be the optimal Q value if the approach of Sec. 2-4 was used?

2-13. From the theory of the backorders case discussed in Sec. 2-5, show that the average on hand inventory can be written $\frac{1}{2}Q - s + B(Q, s)$ where $B(Q, s)$ is the average number of backorders (this average is to be taken over all time not merely for the time over which backorders exist).

2-14. From the theory of the backorders case discussed in Sec. 2-5, show that the average annual cost of backorders arising from the $\hat{\pi}t$ term is simply $\hat{\pi}$ times the average unit years of shortage incurred per year.

Furthermore, show that the average unit years of shortage per year is numerically equal to the average number of backorders.

2-15. Introduce the reorder point r explicitly into the model of Sec. 2-5 and eliminate the variable s.

2-16. For the material presented in Sec. 2-5 show that the optimal values of Q and s will be independent of whether one bases the inventory carrying costs on the quantity on hand or the quantity on hand plus on order.

2-17. Carry out in detail the derivation of Eqs. (2-26) and (2-27).

2-18. Show that if the inequality sign is replaced by an equality in Eq. (2-25) then any $s \geq 0$ is optimal, i.e., show that the same cost will be obtained for any s provided that one optimizes over Q.

2-19. Consider the case studied in Sec. 2-5 where backorders are allowed. Instead of taking the cost of a backorder to be $\pi + \hat{\pi}t$, assume instead that the cost of a backorder has the form ae^{bt}, $a, b > 0$, where t is the length of time for which the backorder exists. Derive the equations which yield the optimal values of Q, s.

2-20. For the model discussed in Sec. 2-5 determine the fraction of the time that the system is out of stock when the optimal values of Q and s are used. Assume that $\pi = 0$, $\hat{\pi} \neq 0$.

2-21. A chemical company produces a certain organic chemical in batches. The annual demand rate for this chemical is 100,000 pounds. The demand can be considered to be known with certainty and the rate does not change with time. The fixed cost of producing a batch is $500. The variable cost of production is $2.00 per pound. There is a backorder cost of $5.00 per pound per year, and no fixed cost of a backorder, i.e., $\pi = 0$. Determine the optimal batch size and the optimal number of backorders to incur.

2-22. Show that if Eqs. (2-28), (2-29) for the case of $\pi = 0$, $\hat{\pi} \neq 0$, are substituted into Eq. (2-17), the minimum cost is

$$\mathcal{K}^* = K_w \left\{ \left[1 + \frac{IC}{\hat{\pi}} \right]^{1/2} - IC[\hat{\pi}(\hat{\pi} + IC)]^{-1/2} \right\}$$

2-23. The management policy of a certain company is to never run out of stock. The sales department carried out an analysis of a particular item to evaluate this policy. The demand is deterministic and constant over time at 625 units per year. The unit cost of the item is $50 independent of the quantity ordered. The cost of placing an order is $5.00 and the inventory carrying charge is $I = 0.20$. Units can be backordered at a cost of $0.20 per unit per week. Calculate the optimal operating doctrine under the assumption that no stockouts are allowed, and under the assumption that units can be backordered at the cost indicated above. What is the dollar loss per year caused by the no stockout policy if the sales department has correctly estimated the pertinent parameters?

2-24. For the situation described in the previous problem, the company president insisted that an additional backorder cost of $0.50 per unit be included in the cost expression. What effect does this have on Q^* and on $\mathcal{K}^*$?

2-25. Consider an item with the characteristics listed below. Solve for the optimal values of Q and s. Compute the average annual variable cost using Eq. (2-17) and also the equation of Problem 2-22.

$$\lambda = 900 \text{ units/yr.,} \quad I = 0.20, \quad C = \$90$$

$$A = \$2.00, \quad \pi = 0, \quad \hat{\pi} = \$16 \text{ per unit per year}$$

2-26. Solve the preceding problem for the case where $\hat{\pi} = \infty$. Compute the average annual variable cost and compare with the results of the previous problem.

2-27. The inventory turnover rate is a variable frequently referred to, especially in retailing. The turnover rate is defined to be the annual demand divided by the average inventory. Give an intuitive interpretation of the turnover rate. Compute the optimal turnover rate for the case where no stockouts are allowed and the case where backorders are permitted. *Hint*: What is the average inventory in the backorders case?

2-28. Derive in detail Eqs. (2-43) and (2-44). When will $s^* = 0$ if $\hat{\pi} \neq 0$?

2-29. Examine the situation in which the production rate is finite and lost sales are allowed. Show that, as in the case where the production rate is infinite, it is never optimal to have any lost sales.

2-30. Let τ be the production lead time for the finite production rate case. Obtain the reorder points, both for the no stockout case and the backorders case, in terms of the various inventory levels of interest.

2-31. Sketch on the same graph for the case of a finite production rate and no stockouts the behavior of the on hand inventory and the quantity on hand plus on order.

2-32. Re-solve Problem 2-3 assuming that the production rate of detergent is 400 tons per month.

2-33. The J electronics company produces a certain type of magnetic core in lots. These cores can be produced at a rate of 1600 cores per day. The daily demand for cores of this type is 250 per day. The cost of setting up for a production run is $700. The inventory carrying charge is $I = 0.30$ and the unit variable cost of a core is $0.10. Under the assumption that no stockouts are allowed, calculate the optimal size of a production run. How long will a production run take? What will be the time between runs?

2-34. In the preceding problem, assume that cores can be backordered and that $\pi = \$0.01$ and $\hat{\pi} = \$0.04$ per unit year. Now determine the optimal values of Q and s.

2-35. An inventory system stocks n items. The cost of placing an order for items of type j is A_j. The carrying charge I is the same for all items. There is also a constraint on the number of orders which can be processed, the maximum allowable number of orders per year being h. Derive formulas for the optimal order quantity for each item such that the average annual variable cost of procurement and holding inventories is minimized subject to the limitation on the number of orders which can be processed.

2-36. Show how one can treat a constraint on the number of man years per year that are available for making setups in some shop which makes a number of different items in lots. Derive formulas for the optimal lot size for each item. Assume that there is also a setup cost associated with each setup.

2-37. Derive in detail the equations which determine the optimal order quantities for a number of different items when the items are coupled together through a constraint on the available floor space and a constraint on the maximum investment in inventory. Assume that no stockouts are allowed.

2-38. Derive in detail the equations which determine the optimal order quantities for a number of items when the items are coupled together through a constraint on the number of orders, a constraint on the available floor space, and a constraint on the maximum investment in inventory. Assume that no stockouts are allowed.

2-39. Show what modifications are needed in the theory developed in the chapter to handle a constraint on the maximum investment in inventory if the constraint is on the average investment in inventory.

2-40. A small shop produces three machined parts 1, 2, 3 in lots. The shop has only 700 sq. ft. of storage space. The appropriate data for the three items are presented in the following table.

item	①	②	③
λ (units/yr.)	5000	2000	10,000
A (dollars)	100	200	75
C (dollars)	10	15	5
f_i (sq. ft./unit)	0.70	0.80	0.40

The shop uses an inventory carrying charge of $I = 0.20$. If no stock-outs are allowed, determine the optimal lot size for each item.

2-41. For models of the type discussed in this chapter, is it possible to place a constraint on the total dollars spent on purchasing items for inventory? Discuss the circumstances under which this type of constraint can be implemented.

2-42. The E. E. Automotive Parts Co. produces crankshafts in lots. The company has decided to use an economical lot size formula to minimize the sum of setup costs and inventory carrying charges. Eight thousand crankshafts are demanded every year. It is estimated that each setup costs $245 (based on standard hours). Inventory carrying charges are $2.00 per unit per year. Assume that requirements for setups on other parts have limited the number of setups per year on crankshafts to four. What is the optimal lot quantity to produce? If the setup crew has time available for ten setups, what is the optimal lot size?

2-43. The A. C. Trash Co. stocks containers, each of which occupies four square feet of rack space. The available rack space is limited to 600 square feet. The appropriate data on these containers are as follows: $\lambda = 2000$ units per year, $A = \$5.00$, $C = \$2.00$, $I = 0.25$. How much would the first additional foot of storage space be worth? How much would 100 additional square feet of rack space be worth?

2-44. A purchasing agent is concerned with the procurement of three types

item	①	②	③
annual demand $\left(\dfrac{\text{units}}{\text{yr.}}\right)$	1000	3000	2000
ordering cost (dollars)	10	10	10
unit cost (dollars)	30	10	20
space requirement $\left(\dfrac{\text{sq. ft}}{\text{unit}}\right)$	5	10	8

of items. The comptroller of the company has placed a $2400 constraint on the value of average inventory, and there is a 2500 square foot limitation on storage space. The data for the items are given in the preceding table. The inventory carrying charge is $I = 0.25$. Determine the optimal purchase quantity for each of the items.

2-45. Prove that when incremental quantity discounts are given, the optimal Q value can never occur at one of the price breaks. Do this by evaluating the derivative of K_j and K_{j+1} at q_{j+1} and showing that the derivative of K_{j+1} is less than the derivative of K_j.

2-46. The purchasing agent for the G. W. Dog Food Company can buy horsemeat from one source for $0.06 per pound for the first 1000 pounds and $0.058 per pound for each additional pound. The company requires 50,000 pounds per year. The cost of placing an order is $1.00. The inventory carrying charge is $I = 0.25$. Compute the optimal purchase quantity.

2-47. Derive in detail Eq. (2-74).

2-48. A supplier of made to order metal fixtures quotes the cost of Q units as $400 + 25Q$ dollars. The purchaser of these fixtures requires 2000 units per year. He uses them at a uniform rate. His direct costs for making out purchase orders, receiving, inspection, and other costs that are incurred on each shipment amount to $20 per order. The carrying charge is $I = 0.20$. The time elapsing between the placing of an order and the delivery of the units to the stockroom is three months. Calculate the economic purchase quantity and the reorder point (based on the on hand inventory level).

2-49. The XYZ Corporation has a special petty cash fund it uses for a known steady state flow of contributions to charity. The corporation periodically replenishes this fund by withdrawing cash from its savings bank account (which pays 4 percent interest on deposits). The fund is never allowed to run out. A bank messenger is paid $5.00 per delivery of cash from the bank. If the optimal withdrawal schedule involves nine withdrawals per year, what is the dollar volume of annual contributions to charity?

2-50. The fee which a particular brokerage firm charges its clients is $20 + 0.01\,v$ dollars, where v is the market value of the stocks purchased or sold on any given day. A client of the firm spends $10,000 annually over and above the 8 percent interest he receives from his investments. Assuming that the client accumulates the funds for investment at a uniform rate, how much should he accumulate before investing, i.e., what is the optimal value of v?

2-51. A firm is committed to a capital expansion program that requires a rate of borrowing of $300,000 per year. On any given quantity borrowed at a single time, the interest rate is 4 percent for the first $100,000 and 5 percent for any additional amounts. The costs of negotiating each loan are $500. The loans will not be repaid until the end of the long expansion program. What is the optimal quantity to be borrowed at each time?

2-52. Solve the previous problem when the bank charges 4 percent for the first $50,000 and 5 percent for additional amounts borrowed at the same time.

2-53. Suppose that in the last problem, the interest charged on amounts over $50,000 is $6\frac{1}{2}$ percent. Solve the revised problem.

2-54. A firm uses the policy of ordering two particular items at the same time. The characteristics of the items are: item (1); $\lambda = 5408$ units per year, $C = \$10$, $A = \$3.00$, $I = 0.30$: item (2); $\lambda = 845$ units per year, $C = \$1.00$, $A = \$3.00$, $I = 0.30$. Management's policy is to allow no stockouts. Orders can be placed only at the start of a week. Calculate the best policy for ordering the two items if both must be ordered at the same time. What are the average annual costs of this policy? Calculate what additional savings can be obtained by establishing a different ordering policy for each of the items.

2-55. A purchasing agent for consumable aircraft spare parts is to decide between three sources. Source A will sell a particular component for $10 each regardless of the quantity ordered. Source B will not accept an order for less than 600 units, but sells them for $9.50 each if an order for 600 or more units is placed. Source C will not accept an order for less than 800 units, but charges $9.00 each if an order for 800 or more units is placed. Annual demand for the component is 2500 units and $I = 0.25$. A fixed cost of $300 is incurred each time that an order is placed. Which source should the purchasing agent select? What quantity should he purchase? What annual costs will be incurred in ordering, carrying inventory, and purchasing the components?

2-56. Suppose in the preceding problem that source B requires a purchase of at least 3000 units and source C requires a purchase of at least 5500 units. Also change the ordering cost to $100 per order. Re-solve the problem.

2-57. An item in inventory is sold at a unit price of p, the rate of sales being λ units per year. If a quantity Q is ordered the unit cost is $b + (a/Q)$. The cost of placing an order is A and the inventory carrying charge is I. What procurement quantity will maximize the average annual profits if it is assumed that no stockouts are allowed?

2-58. Consider an item with an annual demand of λ units per year. If a quantity $Q \leq q_1$ of the item is ordered, the unit cost is $q_0 e^{-aQ}$ and if a quantity $Q > q_1$ is ordered, the unit cost is $b = q_0 e^{-aq_1}$. The fixed cost of placing an order is A and the inventory carrying charge is I. For the case where no stockouts are allowed, show how to determine the optimal order quantity Q.

2-59. Consider the curves defined by Eq. (2-74). Imagine that λ, A, I are fixed, but that C_j is a variable parameter. For a given C_j let Q^* be the value of Q which minimizes K. Let the minimum of K be K^*. Determine the curve which gives the locus of the points (Q^*, K^*) as C_j varies from zero to infinity.

2-60. Derive formulas which yield the optimal values of Q and s in the case where backorders are allowed when account is taken of the integrality of demand of Q and of s. Assume that $\pi = 0$ and $\hat{\pi} \neq 0$. Follow the same sort of procedure that is used in Sec. 2-4.

2-61. Give an intuitive explanation as to why in the backorders case when $\hat{\pi} = 0$, $\pi \neq 0$, it must always be true that $s^* = 0$ or ∞. *Hint*: Use a modification of the type of argument introduced in Sec. 2-6.

2-62. In Eq. (2-26) show that if $s^* = 0$ then $\pi\lambda = K_w$. Also show that in Eq. (2-27), if we set $\pi\lambda = K_w$, then $Q^* = Q_w$.

2-63. Show that

$$\frac{dQ}{Q^*} = \frac{1}{2}\frac{dA}{A}, \quad \frac{dK}{K^*} = \frac{1}{2}\frac{dA}{A}$$

for Eqs. (2-8), (2-11) respectively. What does it say about the percent change in Q^* for small percentage changes in A. For the example on p. 37 determine the approximate change in Q^* if A increases to \$8.50. What is the approximate change in K^*? What are the exact changes in Q^* and K^*? Derive formulas similar to the above for changes in λ, C, and I.

2-64. An inventory system stocks n items. It has been found necessary to review and place orders for all items at the same time. Let T be the time between reviews, A the cost of review and of placing orders for all n items, I the inventory carrying charge, λ_j the annual rate of demand for item j and C_j its unit cost. Determine a formula for the optimal value of T by minimizing the average annual variable costs of review and holding inventory for all n items under the assumption that no stockouts are allowed. Find the optimal T for a system which carries items for which the appropriate parameters are: $A = \$75$,

$I = 0.20$, $\lambda_1 = 500$, $\lambda_2 = 300$, $\lambda_3 = 1000$, $C_1 = \$2.00$, $C_2 = \$25.00$, $C_3 = \$10.00$. Compute the average annual cost and the order quantity for each item. Suppose that it was possible to use a $\langle Q, r \rangle$ model on each item separately with the ordering costs being $A_1 = \$15$, $A_2 = \$40$, $A_3 = \$20$. Determine the optimal Q values and the average annual variable cost for the three items. How much can be saved by using a $\langle Q, r \rangle$ system for each item?

2-65. Except for Sec. 2-7 it has always been assumed in this chapter that orders were never split, i.e., the entire Q units ordered arrived in a single batch. Now suppose that each order is always delivered in two parts, a fraction f_1 being delivered at a time τ_1 after the order is placed and a fraction $1 - f_1$ being delivered at a time τ_2 after the order is placed. Derive formulas for the optimal Q, and reorder point for this case under the assumption that backorders are not allowed. How does one make sure that stockouts do not occur?

2-66. Study the problem of determining the optimal Q in the presence of incremental quantity discounts when backorders are allowed. Show that the results of Sec. 2-12 hold in this more general case.

2-67. From Eq. 2-11, what can we deduce about economies of scale in the cost of operating an inventory system, i.e., all other things being equal, would there be an advantage to having a large system with a relatively high rate of demand rather than a smaller system with a relatively low rate of demand?

2-68. Consider a firm which has several different warehouses, and let the demand rate at warehouse i be λ_i. It is possible to operate this collection of warehouses on a decentralized basis, by having each warehouse order for its own needs using its own order quantity and reorder point, or the system can operate on a centralized basis, with a system reorder point and an order quantity for the entire system which is allocated in the appropriate amounts. Prove that when the unit cost of the item is constant, the carrying charge is the same at each warehouse, the ordering cost and lead time are independent of whether the system is operated on centralized or decentralized basis, and when transportation costs from the source to the warehouses do not depend on the mode of operation, then the centralized mode of operation never leads to higher costs than the decentralized mode of operation. Would the conclusion be altered if quantity discounts were offered? Assume in the analysis that stockouts are not permitted.

2-69. Consider the simplest deterministic $\langle Q, r \rangle$ model treated in this chapter, i.e., the one in which no stockouts are allowed and the unit cost is a constant independent of the quantity ordered. Suppose that instead of determining Q^* and r^* by minimizing the average annual cost, we attempt to determine these quantities by minimizing the discounted cost over all future time. Different answers for the discounted cost can be obtained depending on what point in a cycle one selects as the time origin. For simplicity, select the time origin as a point just prior to the arrival of an order so that nothing is on hand at the time origin. Imagine now that continuous discounting is used (the reader not familiar with this will find it described on p. 377) so that if i is the annual interest rate, the present worth of a cost H incurred at time t in the future is He^{-it}. Consider now any cycle, the beginning of the cycle being taken as the point when an order arrives. The cost of placing an order and of the Q units ordered, discounted to the beginning of the cycle is $(A + CQ)e^{-it_r}$ where t_r is the time from the arrival of an order until the reorder point is reached. In computing the discounted cost one must include the cost of the units even though C is constant. Why? The carrying cost discounted to the beginning of the cycle is

$$I_0 C \int_0^T (Q - \lambda t)e^{-it} \, dt$$

When introducing discounting, then, in general, the rate of return need not be included in the carrying cost since it is expressed in i. We have denoted by I_0 the carrying charge exclusive of the rate of return. (The reader should study this point in detail to see why the rate of return should not be included.) Let H be the total cost per cycle discounted to the beginning of the cycle, i.e., discounted to the time when an order arrives. Then the discounted costs over all future time are

$$\mathfrak{z} = H \sum_{n=0}^{\infty} e^{-inT}$$

Determine the value of Q which minimizes $\mathfrak{z}$. Expand the equation which determines Q^* in powers of i and show that to a first approximation

$$Q^* = \sqrt{\frac{2\lambda A}{(I_0 + i)C}} = Q_w$$

How does the frequency with which orders are placed affect the goodness of the above approximation? As a specific example consider the case where $A = \$15.00$, $C = \$20.00$, $I_0 = 0.10$, $i = 0.10$, $\lambda = 1000$ units per year. Determine the exact value of Q which minimizes $\mathfrak{z}$ and the value Q_w. Pick another point other than the point when an order arrives as the initial point of the cycle, and compute $\mathfrak{z}$ in this case. Are the results equivalent for small i? Suppose now that instead of using continuous discounting, the yearly interest rate is i and it is compounded once per cycle, i.e., the present worth at the beginning of a cycle of costs H incurred during the cycle will be taken to be $H/(1 + Qi/\lambda)$. Compute $\mathfrak{z}$ in this case. How does it differ from the $\mathfrak{z}$ obtained using continuous discounting? What is Q^* now? Use the same sort of expansion as in the continuous discounting case to find an approximate form for Q^*. Is it Q_w? Show also that different results can be obtained depending on whether the cost of units is discounted from the time of placing an order or from the time of receipt of an order. Which was used in the above? *Hint*: It can be difficult to solve explicitly the equation $d\mathfrak{z}/dQ = 0$ for Q^*. In obtaining the limiting form, determine the coefficients of A, C, $I_0 C$ and expand each of these as a power series in i retaining only the lowest nonvanishing power of i. It may be helpful initially to assume that $t_r = 0$ and $I_0 = 0$.

3

PROBABILITY THEORY

AND STOCHASTIC PROCESSES

"Lest men suspect your tale untrue,

Keep probability in view."

John Gay

3-1 Introduction

We have noted previously that the demands for units stocked by an inventory system can seldom be predicted with certainty. Instead, they must be described in probabilistic terms. Realistic inventory models must account for this uncertainty in demand. Often, it is also true that procurement lead times must be described probabilistically. It is the purpose of this chapter to present the background material from the theory of probability and stochastic processes that will be needed in the future chapters. It will be assumed, however, that the reader has previously had at least a brief introduction to the theory of probability.

3-2 Basic Laws of Probabilities

It will be recalled that the foundations of probability can be developed from several points of view, such as: (1) the a priori method, (2) the frequency approach, (3) the degree of rational belief, (4) the axiomatic approach. In practical application one will frequently use several definitions of probability—for example, the a priori and frequency definitions—simultaneously in the solution of some problem. Here we shall not attempt to develop the theory from any one of the above points of view. Instead we shall simply set down the basic laws for operating with probabilities, which should be familiar to the reader, and explain their operational meaning.

Consider an experiment whose outcome can lead to one or more of the following finite number of events, which will be denoted symbolically by $A_1, \ldots, A_n$. Imagine that the outcome of the experiment is not deterministic, but can only be described probabilistically. Let $p(A_j)$ be the probability that A_j occurs. We shall use the notation $A_i \cap A_j$, $i \neq j$, to mean that both A_i and A_j occur, the notation $A_i \cup A_j$, $i \neq j$, to mean that A_i or A_j or both occurs, and the symbol $\hat{A}_i$ to mean that A_i does not occur. Then the three basic laws of probability are:

(1) $0 \leq p(A_j) \leq 1$

$$(3-1)$$

(2) $p(A_i \cup A_j) = p(A_i) + p(A_j) - p(A_i \cap A_j), \quad i \neq j$ \hfill (3-2)

(3) $p(A_i \cap A_j) = p(A_i|A_j)p(A_j) = p(A_j|A_i)p(A_i), \quad i \neq j,$

$$p(A_j), \quad p(A_i) \neq 0$$

$$p(A_i \cap A_j) = 0 \quad \text{if} \quad p(A_j) = 0 \quad \text{or} \quad p(A_i) = 0 \tag{3-3}$$

Equation (3-1) simply indicates that $p(A_j)$ is a non-negative number which is not greater than unity. If A_j does not occur, then $p(A_j) = 0$, and if A_j always occurs, then $p(A_j) = 1$. The second law states that the probability of A_i or A_j occurring is equal to the probability that A_i occurs plus the probability that A_j occurs, minus the probability that A_i and A_j occur. Two events, A_i, A_j, $i \neq j$, are called mutually exclusive if they cannot occur together, i.e., A_i and A_j cannot occur; then $p(A_i \cap A_j) = 0$. For mutually exclusive events (3-2) reduces to the simple addition rule

$$p(A_i \cup A_j) = p(A_i) + p(A_j), \quad i \neq j \tag{3-4}$$

By the definition of $\hat{A}_j$ it follows that A_j and $\hat{A}_j$ are mutually exclusive. Furthermore, either A_j or $\hat{A}_j$ must occur. Hence

$$p(A_j \cup \hat{A}_j) = 1 = p(A_j) + p(\hat{A}_j)$$

More generally, suppose that the finite set of events $A_1, \ldots, A_r$ are mutually exclusive. This means that no combinations of two or more of these events can occur simultaneously. Then

$$p(A_1 \cup A_2 \cup \ldots \cup A_r) = p(A_1) + p(A_2) + \ldots + p(A_r) \tag{3-5}$$

To prove this we introduce the new event $A_2{}^* = A_2 \cup A_3 \cup \ldots \cup A_r$ and note that $p(A_1 \cap A_2{}^*) = 0$ since A_1 cannot occur simultaneously with any one of the events $A_2, \ldots, A_r$, i.e., with $A_2{}^*$. Thus

$$p(A_1 \cup A_2 \cup \ldots \cup A_r) = p(A_1 \cup A_2{}^*) = p(A_1) + p(A_2{}^*)$$

The same argument is now repeated with $p(A_2{}^*)$, etc. until (3-5) is obtained.

The third law (3-3) serves to define the conditional probabilities $p(A_i|A_j)$ and $p(A_j|A_i)$. These conditional probabilities have the following intuitive meaning: The quantity $p(A_i|A_j)$ is the probability that A_i has occurred (or will occur) if we know that event A_j has occurred. In practical applications, this intuitive explanation of the meaning of $p(A_i|A_j)$ often allows us to compute this probability directly without the use of (3-3). In the event that

$$p(A_i|A_j) = p(A_i)$$

so that the conditional probability is independent of A_j, then the events A_i, A_j are said to be independent and (3-3) reduces to

$$p(A_i \cap A_j) = p(A_i)p(A_j), \quad i \neq j \tag{3-6}$$

Intuitively, A_i, A_j are independent if the occurrence of A_i has no influence on whether A_j will occur or not, and vice versa.

EXAMPLE   If the foundations of probability are developed from the a priori approach, then it is possible to derive the laws (3-1) through (3-3). The a priori approach assumes that the results of the experiment under consideration can be described by a finite number n of equally likely and mutually exclusive outcomes. If n_i of these outcomes have the property A_i, then the probability of the event A_i is defined to be

$$p(A_i) = \frac{n_i}{n}$$

Since $n > 0$, $n_i \geq 0$ and $n_i \leq n$, (3-1) follows immediately from this definition. If n_{ij} outcomes have the properties A_i and A_j, then the number of outcomes which have the property A_i or A_j is $n_i + n_j - n_{ij}$ and hence

$$p(A_i \cup A_j) = \frac{n_i}{n} + \frac{n_j}{n} - \frac{n_{ij}}{n} = p(A_i) + p(A_j) - p(A_i \cap A_j)$$

which is (3-2). Finally, note

$$p(A_i \cap A_j) = \frac{n_{ij}}{n} = \frac{n_{ij}}{n_j}\frac{n_j}{n} = p(A_i|A_j)p(A_j), \quad n_j \neq 0$$

where n_{ij}/n_j is the probability of A_i given that A_j has occurred, i.e.,

$$n_{ij}/n_j = p(A_i|A_j)$$

This is (3-3). Thus the three basic laws have been derived in this case.

Often it is convenient to imagine that the n outcomes can be represented symbolically by points in a space. The resulting space is called the sample space. If we think of the outcomes as being represented by points in a plane, then it is possible to draw diagrams such as Fig. 3-1. The sample space will be assumed to consist of the points (represented by crosses) inside the rectangle. The set of outcomes with property A_i is the set of all points inside the crosshatched area marked A_i. Similarly, the set of outcomes with property A_j is the set of all points inside the crosshatched region marked A_j. The set of points with the properties A_i and A_j are those in the doubly ruled area, i.e., these points represent the set of points with the property $A_i \cap A_j$. The set of points with the property $A_i \cup A_j$ is the set of all points in the shaded areas. Fig. 3-1 makes it especially easy to derive the formula (3-2). If A_i, A_j are mutually exclusive, then in Fig. 3-1, the areas representing A_i and A_j do not intersect.

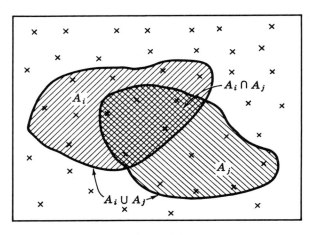

FIGURE 3-1.

3-3 Discrete Random Variables

Many of the events which will be of interest to us in this book will be capable of being represented by non-negative integers. For example, the event might be the number of units demanded in one month. This event can be represented by a non-negative integer x which gives the number of units demanded. Consider an experiment the totality of whose mutually exclusive outcomes can be described by the $n + 1$ non-negative integers $0, 1, 2, \ldots, n$. Let $p(x)$ be the probability that the outcome of the experiment can be described by the non-negative integer x. Then since one of the integers $0, 1, \ldots, n$ must describe the outcome, and since no more than one can describe the outcome (because the events are mutually exclusive), we must have

$$p(0 \cup 1 \cup 2 \cup \ldots \cup n) = 1 = p(0) + p(1) + \ldots + p(n)$$

$$= \sum_{x=0}^{n} p(x) \tag{3-7}$$

If the experiment is performed many times, then the fraction of the time that the outcome can be described by the integer x will approach $p(x)$.

The outcome of the experiment can then be thought of as being described by the variable x, and $p(x)$ can be looked upon as a function of x which gives the probability of x. The variable x which can only take on the non-negative integral values $0, 1, \ldots, n$ is called a random variable since it describes the outcome of an experiment, the outcome of which is determined by the laws of chance. The function $p(x)$ is called the probability density function for the random variable x; $p(x)$ must satisfy (3-7) and $0 \leq p(x) \leq 1$. Note that in the above $p(x)$ must be defined for every possible outcome x, and the outcomes must be defined so that they are mutually exclusive.

Consider now the probability $p(0 \cup 1 \cup \ldots \cup r)$, $r \leq n$. This is the probability that x takes on the value 0 or 1 or $\ldots$ or r, i.e., the probability that x takes on a value less than or equal to r. We shall denote this probability by $\hat{P}(r)$ and

$$\hat{P}(r) = p(0 \cup 1 \cup \ldots \cup r) = p(0) + p(1) + \ldots + p(r) \quad (3\text{-}8)$$

Note that r can take on the values $0, 1, \ldots, n$, the same values which x can assume. Thus we can define a new function $\hat{P}(x)$, which will be called the cumulative probability of x or the cumulative function for x; it is the probability that the outcome of the experiment yields a value less than or equal to x. Another function which will frequently be of use to us is sometimes called the complementary cumulative function. It is defined by

$$P(x) = 1 - \hat{P}(x - 1) = p(x) + p(x + 1) + \ldots + p(n) \quad (3\text{-}9)$$

$P(x)$ is the probability that the outcome of the experiment will yield a value greater than or equal to x. We shall find it convenient to use the complementary cumulative function much more frequently than the cumulative function.

The random variable introduced above, which could only assume one of $n + 1$ integral values, will be called a *discrete random variable*. More generally, any random variable that can only take on integral values will be called discrete. The probability law that describes a discrete random variable is uniquely defined by specifying either the density function, or the cumulative function, or the complementary cumulative function. The probability law is also referred to as the distribution of the random variable. The distribution of a discrete random variable is called a *discrete distribution*.

An important special case of the type of probability density function which we have been discussing above is called the binomial density. One way this distribution arises is in the study of repeated independent "trials" which can have only two possible outcomes. These two outcomes can without loss of generality be referred to as success or failure. Let ρ be the probability that a trial will be a success and $1 - \rho$ the probability that it will be a failure. Let us imagine that we perform n trials in sequence and we desire to determine the probability that the first x trials, $0 \leq x \leq n$, are successes and the last $n - x$ are failures. Since the trials are independent, the desired probability is simply the product of the probabilities for each event, i.e., $\rho^x(1 - \rho)^{n-x}$. This same probability is obtained if we ask for the probability of x successes and $n - x$ failures in any specified order.

Next, let us ask what is the probability of having x successes in n trials without regard to the order in which the successes are obtained. Note that events corresponding to obtaining x successes in different orders are mutually exclusive. Hence, the probability of having x successes without regard to the order in which they are obtained is simply the sum of the probabilities for each possible order. The probability for x successes in any given order is $\rho^x(1 - \rho)^{n-x}$. Thus, all that remains is to compute the number of possible orders in which x successes can occur. This is simply the number of ways in which n objects (the trials) can be separated into two groups (without regard to order within a group) such that x objects are in one group and $n - x$ in the other. Of course, this is the number of combinations of n things taken x at a time, i.e., $n!/x!(n - x)!$. Sometimes we shall use the simplified notation $\binom{n}{x}$ to represent $n!/x!(n - x)!$. We conclude, therefore, that the probability of x successes in n trials, without regard to order, is

$$p(x) = b(x; n, \rho) = \frac{n!}{x!(n - x)!} \rho^x(1 - \rho)^{n-x}, \quad 0 < \rho < 1 \quad (3\text{-}10)$$

We can think of x, the number of successes, as being a random variable which can take on the values $0, 1, \ldots, n$ and $b(x; n, \rho)$ as being the density function for this random variable. We note that $b(x; n, \rho)$ is a legitimate density function since $b(x; n, \rho) \geq 0$ and

$$\sum_{x=0}^{n} \binom{n}{x} \rho^x(1 - \rho)^{n-x} = [\rho + (1 - \rho)]^n = 1 \quad (3\text{-}11)$$

by the binomial expansion. Note that $b(x; n, \rho)$ is the xth term in the binomial expansion of $[\rho + (1 - \rho)]^n$. We shall always use the notation $b(x; n, \rho)$ for the binomial density function. If the random variable x has the density function $b(x; n, \rho)$, then x is said to have a binomial distribution. *Note:* We shall use frequently the binomial expansion and hence it might be helpful to review briefly its derivation. The binomial expansion of $(x + b)^n$ for any real number n is a special case of the Maclaurin expansion

$$f(x) = \sum_{j=0}^{\infty} \frac{1}{j!} f^{(j)}(0)x^j$$

when $f(x) \equiv (x + b)^n$. In the above expansion $f^{(j)}(0)$ is the jth derivative of f evaluated at $x = 0$. When $f(x) \equiv (x + b)^n$

$$f^{(j)}(0) = n(n - 1) \ldots (n - j + 1)b^{n-j}, \quad j \geq 1; \quad f^{(0)}(0) = f(0) = b^n$$

and hence

$$f(x) = b^n + \sum_{j=1}^{\infty} \frac{n(n-1)\ldots(n-j+1)}{j!} x^j b^{n-i}$$

when the series converges. By the ratio test, the series converges if $|x/b| < 1$. In the event that n is a positive integer, $f^{(j)}(0) = 0, j > n$ and the infinite series becomes a finite sum of $n + 1$ terms which can be written

$$(x+b)^n = \sum_{j=0}^{n} \binom{n}{j} x^j b^{n-i}, \quad n \text{ a positive integer.}$$

When n is a negative integer, we can write

$$n(n-1)\ldots(n-j+1) = (-1)^i(|n|+j-1)(|n|+j-2)\ldots|n|$$

$$= (-1)^i \frac{(|n|+j-1)!}{(|n|-1)!}$$

and so

$$(x+b)^{-n} = \sum_{j=0}^{\infty} (-1)^i \binom{n+j-1}{n-1} x^j b^{-n-i},$$

$$n \text{ a positive integer, and } |x/b| < 1.$$

EXAMPLES 1. A given base has n missiles. These missiles are inspected once per month and ρ is the probability that any single missile will not fail during the month. If all n missiles are operating at the beginning of a given month, then (3-10) gives the probability that x missiles will still be operating at the end of the month.

2. A coin is tossed n times. The probability of a head is ρ. Then the probability of obtaining x heads is given by (3-10). To check (3-10) in a very simple case, imagine that a coin is tossed three times and we wish to compute the probability of obtaining two heads. Denoting a head by H and a tail by T, then two heads can be obtained in the following ways HHT, HTH, THH, i.e., three ways. The probability of each of these orders is $\rho^2(1-\rho)$, so that the probability of two heads is $3\rho^2(1-\rho)$. Now

$$\frac{3!}{2!1!} = 3$$

so that (3-10) also gives $3\rho^2(1-\rho)$.

In the above paragraphs we have discussed random variables which are defined over a finite set of non-negative integers. We shall also have use for random variables which are defined over all the non-negative integers, so that a $p(x)$ can be defined for every non-negative integer x. As before, we assume that the outcome of the experiment will yield one and only one non-negative integer x. Thus the various x values are mutually exclusive and we must have

$$\sum_{x=0}^{\infty} p(x) = 1, \quad p(x) \geq 0 \tag{3-12}$$

Although for the case of finite n we could prove (3-7) from the fundamental laws, we cannot prove (3-12) directly. Instead we take (3-12) as a postulate.

A particularly interesting density function which is defined for all non-negative x is called the Poisson density. It is defined by

$$p(x) = p(x; \mu) = \frac{\mu^x}{x!} e^{-\mu}, \quad x = 0, 1, 2, \ldots \tag{3-13}$$

where μ is a constant whose physical interpretation will be made clear later. We shall make frequent use of the Poisson density or distribution in future chapters. The Poisson density will always be denoted by $p(x; \mu)$. The random variable x whose probabilities are given by (3-13) is said to be Poisson distributed. The cumulative and complementary cumulative Poisson functions will be denoted by $\hat{P}(x; \mu)$ and $P(x; \mu)$ respectively, where

$$\hat{P}(x; \mu) = \sum_{j=0}^{x} \frac{\mu^j}{j!} e^{-\mu}; \quad P(x; \mu) = \sum_{j=x}^{\infty} \frac{\mu^j}{j!} e^{-\mu} \tag{3-14}$$

Observe that

$$\sum_{x=0}^{\infty} p(x; \mu) = e^{-\mu} \sum_{x=0}^{\infty} \frac{\mu^x}{x!} = e^{-\mu} e^{\mu} = 1$$

since

$$e^{\mu} = \sum_{j=0}^{\infty} \frac{\mu^j}{j!}$$

Another distribution of a random variable defined over all the non-negative integers, which we shall use occasionally, is called the negative binomial distribution.

The density function for the negative binomial distribution of order n is

$$p(x) = b_N(x; n, \rho) = \binom{x + n - 1}{n - 1} \rho^n (1 - \rho)^x,$$

$$0 < \rho < 1, \quad x = 0, 1, 2, \ldots \tag{3-15}$$

where n is a positive integer and ρ is a constant. We shall always use

$b_N(x; n, \rho)$ to represent the negative binomial density. From the binomial expansion of $[1 - (1 - \rho)]^{-n} = \rho^{-n}$ we obtain

$$\rho^{-n} = \sum_{x=0}^{\infty} \binom{x + n - 1}{n - 1} (1 - \rho)^x$$

Multiplication by ρ^n shows that the sum of $b_N(x; n, \rho)$ from $x = 0$ to ∞ is unity as desired.

A random variable having a negative binomial density can arise in a variety of ways. One simple probability problem which gives rise to such a distribution is as follows: Suppose that we toss a coin which has a probability ρ of getting a head until we obtain n heads. We then ask: "What is the probability that exactly $x + n$ tosses are required to obtain n heads?" This means that $n - 1$ heads are obtained in the first $x + n - 1$ tosses and a head is obtained on the $(x + n)$th toss. The probability of $n - 1$ heads in $x + n - 1$ tosses is $b(n - 1; x + n - 1, \rho)$ and the probability of a head on the last toss is ρ. Hence, the desired probability is $\rho b(n - 1; x + n - 1, \rho)$, which is (3-15), and the random variable x (not n) has a negative binomial distribution.

When $n = 1$ in (3-15) we obtain

$$p(x) = b_N(x; 1, \rho) = \rho(1 - \rho)^x, \quad x = 0, 1, 2, \ldots \tag{3-16}$$

This density function is assigned a special name—it is called the geometric density function, and if the probability of x is given by (3-16), x is said to have a geometric distribution.

We have noted previously that the probability of an impossible event is zero. Conversely, if x is a random variable defined over a finite set of non-negative integers, or over all the non-negative integers, the expression $p(x) = 0$ for a particular x is usually interpreted in practice to mean that the integer x will never occur. Sometimes, however, since it is often necessary to estimate probabilities from historical or experimental data, the expression $p(x) = 0$ may be interpreted to mean that x can occur, but only very rarely.

3-4 Continuous Random Variables

In the previous section we discussed random variables which were defined only for a finite number of non-negative integers or for all non-negative integers. Now we would like to consider variables which can take on any value between 0 and ∞ or $-\infty$ and ∞, and which cannot be predicted with certainty, but instead can only be described in probabilistic terms. Such variables will be called continuous random or stochastic variables. It is necessary to change slightly the probabilistic description of random variables when one moves from the discrete to the continuous case. The change required is similar to that needed in mechanics in moving from the study of point masses to the study of continuous mass distributions. From the intuitive point of view, if every x value (or even every x value in some interval $a \le x \le b$) had a positive probability it would not be possible to have the sum over all x values equal to unity. Therefore, the probability of any specific value of x must be zero. The notion of a continuous random variable is really a mathematical abstraction of reality, since nothing is continuous in the real world, i.e., there are certain discrete building blocks which are not infinitely divisible. Even time, as we measure it, is not infinitely divisible. Thus in dealing with continuous random variables, what we are actually interested in is the probability that x will lie in some interval $a \le x \le b$. We shall never be concerned with the probability that x takes on a given value but rather with the probability that x lies in some interval.

To describe the probability that a continuous random variable x lies in some interval we introduce a function $f(x) \ge 0$, called the density function for x, with the property that the probability that x lies in the interval $a \le x \le b$, i.e., $p(a \le x \le b)$ is given by

$$p(a \le x \le b) = \int_a^b f(x)\, dx \qquad (3\text{-}17)$$

It is important to note that $f(x)$ is not the probability of x. Instead we can say that the probability that x lies in the infinitesimal interval x to $x + dx$ is $f(x)\, dx$. We can imagine $f(x)$ describes a curve in the plane, and the probability that x lies in the interval $a \le x \le b$ is the area between the curve and the x axis from $x = a$ to $x = b$. This is illustrated in Fig. 3-2.

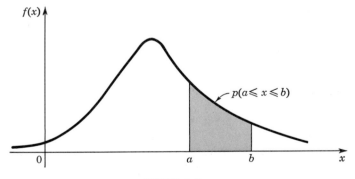

FIGURE 3-2.

Inasmuch as x must lie in the interval $-\infty$ to ∞ in any experiment, we must have

$$\int_{-\infty}^{\infty} f(x)\, dx = 1 \qquad (3\text{-}18)$$

The probabilistic description of a continuous random variable just introduced does require that the probability of a specific value of x be zero, since $p(x = a)$ is found by setting $b = a$ in (3-17), which yields a value of 0. For continuous random variables, the fact that $p(x) = 0$ does not imply that the number x cannot occur, since whenever an event involving x occurs, a specific value of x will be observed.

We shall be dealing with continuous random variables which are restricted to non-negative values, and with those which can take on any real values. In discussing the theory, we shall usually treat the random variables as if they can assume any real values, as we did in (3-18) and (3-19). There is no loss of generality in doing this, for a continuous random variable x which is restricted to be non-negative can be allowed to take on any real values if its density function is defined to be zero for all $x < 0$, since this definition will insure that the probability that x lies in an interval $x_1 \le x \le x_2$, $x_1, x_2 < 0$ will be zero as desired. To convert integrals that involve random variables which can take on any real values to a form suitable for random variables that must be non-negative, the lower limit of $-\infty$ is replaced by 0. Any function $f(x) \ge 0$, such that (3-18) holds, can be considered to be a legitimate probability density function. The function

$$\hat{F}(x) = \int_{-\infty}^{x} f(\xi)\, d\xi \qquad (3\text{-}19)$$

is called the cumulative probability function or the cumulative function of x. It gives the probability that the random variable takes on a value less than or equal to x. The complementary cumulative function $F(x)$, defined by $F(x) = 1 - \hat{F}(x)$ is the probability that the random variable takes on a value greater than or equal to x. Note that

$$\frac{d\hat{F}(x)}{dx} = f(x), \quad \frac{dF(x)}{dx} = -f(x)$$

The probability law for a continuous random variable is uniquely defined by specifying either the density function, the cumulative function or the complementary cumulative function. The probability law is also referred to as the distribution of the random variable. The distribution of a continuous random variable is called a continuous distribution.

In dealing with continuous random variables, it is often of interest to study some function $\theta(x)$ of the random variable x. Then $v = \theta(x)$ is also a random variable. Let us study how to determine the density function for v from the known density function for x. We shall assume that $v = \theta(x)$ is invertible, and that the inverse has a continuous derivative so that we can write $x = \psi(v)$, (possibly with different ψ functions needed for different ranges of x), and $dx = \psi'(v)\, dv$ where $\psi' = d\psi/dv$. Then

$$\int_{-\infty}^{\infty} f(x)\, dx = \int_{\theta(-\infty)}^{\theta(\infty)} f[\psi(v)]\psi'(v)\, dv = 1 \qquad (3\text{-}20)$$

where the limits on the second integral are those corresponding to $x = -\infty$ and $x = \infty$ respectively. The range of values for the variable v may not be from $-\infty$ to ∞. Suppose that the range is from $v_{\min}$ to $v_{\max}$. Then after we have converted the second integral in (3-20) to the form

$$\int_{v_{\min}}^{v_{\max}} h(v)\, dv = 1, \quad h(v) = 0 \quad \text{for} \quad v > v_{\max}, v < v_{\min} \qquad (3\text{-}21)$$

$h(v) \geq 0$, $h(v)$ will be the density function for the random variable v.

In the event that the transformation from x to v is one to one, and $\psi' \geq 0$, so that $v_{\min} = \theta(-\infty)$ and $v_{\max} = \theta(\infty)$, then $h(v) = f[\psi(v)]\psi'(v)$. If the transformation is one to one and $\psi' \leq 0$ so that $v_{\min} = \theta(\infty)$ and $v_{\max} = \theta(-\infty)$, then in going from (3-20) to (3-21) the limits of integration must be interchanged so that $h(v) = -f[\psi(v)]\psi'(v)$. In general, if the transformation from v to x is one to one, $h(v) = f[\psi(v)]|\psi'(v)|$.

When $\psi(v)$ is not unique so that different ψ functions are needed for different ranges of x values, then the right-hand side of (3-20) must be interpreted as the sum of two or more integrals, one for each ψ, integrated over the appropriate range of v values. An example involving a non-unique ψ function will be presented below.

We shall make use of several continuous distributions in our later work. The one to be used most frequently will be the well-known normal distribution for which the density function is

$$n(x; \mu, \sigma) = \frac{1}{\sqrt{2\pi}\,\sigma}\, e^{-(1/2\sigma^2)(x-\mu)^2} \qquad (3\text{-}22)$$

where μ, σ are specified constants whose physical interpretation will be given later. The coefficient $1/\sqrt{2\pi}\,\sigma$ appears in order that (3-18) hold. To prove that (3-18) holds when $n(x; \mu, \sigma)$ is given by (3-22), we wish to show that

$$\frac{1}{\sqrt{2\pi}\,\sigma} \int_{-\infty}^{\infty} e^{-(1/2\sigma^2)(x-\mu)^2}\, dx = 1 \qquad (3\text{-}23)$$

To do this it is convenient to introduce the new random variable

$$w = \frac{x - \mu}{\sigma}$$

so that $dx = \sigma \, dw$, i.e., $\psi' = \sigma$. Furthermore when $x = -\infty$, $w = -\infty$ and when $x = \infty$, $w = \infty$. Hence the density function for w, which we shall designate by $\phi(w)$, is a normal density with $\mu = 0$, $\sigma = 1$, i.e.,

$$\phi(w) = \frac{1}{\sqrt{2\pi}} e^{-w^2/2} = n[\psi(w); \mu, \sigma] \psi'(w) \tag{3-24}$$

so that to prove that (3-23) holds is equivalent to showing that

$$\delta = \frac{1}{\sqrt{2\pi}} \int_{-\infty}^{\infty} e^{-w^2/2} dw = 1$$

To do this note that

$$\delta^2 = \frac{1}{2\pi} \left[\int_{-\infty}^{\infty} e^{-w^2/2} \, dw \right] \left[\int_{-\infty}^{\infty} e^{-u^2/2} \, du \right]$$

$$= \frac{1}{2\pi} \int_{-\infty}^{\infty} \int_{-\infty}^{\infty} e^{-(1/2)[w^2+u^2]} \, dw \, du$$

and the product of two single integrals has been converted into a double integral. Then write $w^2 + u^2 = r^2$, $w = r \cos \theta$, $u = r \sin \theta$, so that on changing to polar coordinates

$$\delta^2 = \frac{1}{2\pi} \int_0^{\infty} \int_0^{2\pi} re^{-r^2/2} \, dr \, d\theta = \int_0^{\infty} re^{-r^2/2} \, dr = \int_0^{\infty} e^{-\xi} \, d\xi = 1$$

This proves that (3-23) is correct.

Another continuous distribution which we shall use occasionally is called the gamma distribution. The gamma density function is defined by

$$\gamma(x; \alpha, \beta) = \begin{cases} \dfrac{\beta(\beta x)^{\alpha}}{\alpha!} e^{-\beta x}, & x \geq 0 \\ 0 & , \quad x < 0 \end{cases} \tag{3-25}$$

where α is a non-negative integer and β is any positive number. Note that in this case the random variable is restricted to being a non-negative number—it can never take on negative values. The function $\gamma(x; \alpha, \beta)$ is called a gamma density of order $\alpha + 1$.

To show (3-18) holds we observe that

$$\int_{-\infty}^{\infty} \gamma(x; \alpha, \beta) \, dx = \frac{1}{\alpha!} \int_0^{\infty} \beta(\beta x)^{\alpha} e^{-\beta x} \, dx = \frac{1}{\alpha!} \int_0^{\infty} u^{\alpha} e^{-u} \, du$$

where $u = \beta x$. However, if we integrate by parts

$$\int_{-\infty}^{\infty} \gamma(x; \alpha, \beta) \, dx = \frac{1}{\alpha!} \left[-u^\alpha e^{-u} \right]_0^\infty + \frac{1}{(\alpha-1)!} \int_0^\infty u^{\alpha-1} e^{-u} \, du$$

$$= \frac{1}{(\alpha-1)!} \int_0^\infty u^{\alpha-1} e^{-u} \, du$$

We repeat the integration by parts on the right-hand side of the above equation. After α steps we are reduced to

$$\int_{-\infty}^{\infty} \gamma(x; \alpha, \beta) \, dx = \int_0^\infty e^{-u} \, du = -e^{-u} \big|_0^\infty = 1$$

which is what we desired to show.

It is possible to prove, although we shall not do so, that the integral

$$\Gamma(\alpha + 1) = \int_0^\infty \beta(\beta x)^\alpha e^{-\beta x} \, dx \tag{3-26}$$

converges to a finite positive value for any real value of $\alpha > -1$. The value of the integral depends only on α and is denoted by $\Gamma(\alpha + 1)$. The integral is called the gamma function of $\alpha + 1$. Thus it is possible to generalize the gamma density (3-25) to any real $\alpha > -1$ if $\alpha!$ is replaced by $\Gamma(\alpha + 1)$. When α is a non-negative integer, then $\Gamma(\alpha + 1) = \alpha!$.

EXAMPLES   1. If in (3-25), $\alpha = 0$, we are reduced to the density function

$$\begin{cases} \beta e^{-\beta x}, & x \geq 0 \\ 0, & x < 0 \end{cases}$$

This special case of the gamma density, i.e., a gamma density of order one, is called the exponential density and x is said to have an exponential distribution. We shall denote the exponential density by $e(x; \beta)$. The cumulative function for $e(x; \beta)$ is

$$\hat{E}(x) = \beta \int_0^x e^{-\beta \xi} \, d\xi = 1 - e^{-\beta x}$$

The complementary cumulative is

$$E(x) = 1 - \hat{E}(x) = e^{-\beta x}$$

The functions $e(x; \beta)$, $E(x)$, $\hat{E}(x)$ are plotted in Fig. 3-3 for the case of $\beta = 2$.

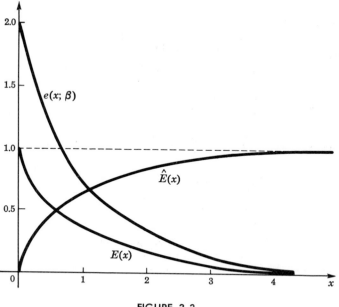

FIGURE 3-3.

2. Consider the change of variables $v = w^2/2$ or $w = \pm(2v)^{1/2}$ in the normal distribution with $\mu = 0$ and $\sigma = 1$, i.e., in (3-24). When $w = \infty$, $v = \infty$; $w = 0$, $v = 0$; $w = -\infty$, $v = \infty$. Here we have a case where ψ is double valued, and the range of v is from 0 to ∞. We can write (3-20) as

$$\frac{1}{\sqrt{2\pi}} \int_{-\infty}^{0} e^{-w^2/2} \, dw + \frac{1}{\sqrt{2\pi}} \int_{0}^{\infty} e^{-w^2/2} \, dw$$

Note that when w ranges from $-\infty$ to ∞, v moves over the interval 0 to ∞ twice. On changing to the variable v this becomes

$$-\frac{1}{2\sqrt{\pi}} \int_{\infty}^{0} v^{-(1/2)} e^{-v} \, dv + \frac{1}{2\sqrt{\pi}} \int_{0}^{\infty} v^{-(1/2)} e^{-v} \, dv = \frac{1}{\sqrt{\pi}} \int_{0}^{\infty} v^{-(1/2)} e^{-v} \, dv$$

Hence the density function for the random variable v is

$$\frac{1}{\sqrt{\pi}} v^{-(1/2)} e^{-v}, \quad v \geq 0, \text{ and } 0 \text{ for } v < 0$$

This is simply a gamma density function with $\beta = 1$, $\alpha = -\frac{1}{2}$. We leave it for Problem 3-4 to show that $\Gamma(\frac{1}{2}) = \sqrt{\pi}$.

3-5 Expected Values

In Chapter 1 it was suggested that the minimization of average annual costs was a useful criterion for the determination of operating doctrines for inventory systems. In Chapter 2 we saw how to average over time for deterministic systems to determine average annual costs. When certain inputs to an inventory system are not deterministic but instead are random variables, then in order to determine average annual costs, we shall see later that it also becomes necessary to average over the possible values which the random variables can take on.

Consider an experiment whose outcome can be described by a random variable x which can assume only the non-negative integral values 0, 1, . . . , n. Let $p(x)$ be the probability of x. Let us imagine this experiment is performed a very large number of times. We add up the x values obtained on each experiment and then divide by the number of experiments to obtain the average value of x which we shall denote by $\bar{x}$. We now ask: "To what limit will $\bar{x}$ tend as the number of times the experiment is repeated is increased to infinity?" The definition of $p(x)$ implies that as the number of times the experiment is repeated approaches infinity, then the fraction of the time when we obtain x approaches $p(x)$. Thus $\bar{x}$ should approach the value

$$\mu = \sum_{x=0}^{n} xp(x) \tag{3-27}$$

The number μ defined by (3-27) will be called the mean or expected value of x. It is also called the mean of the probability distribution of x.

Let us now consider some function of the random variable x, say $\theta(x)$ (for any inventory model x might be the demand in a given year and $\theta(x)$ the cost of operating the system). Note that $\theta(x)$ is also a random variable. Then if we find the average value of $\theta(x)$ by repeating the experiment a large number of times, as the number of times which the experiment is repeated approaches infinity, we expect the average value of $\theta(x)$ to tend to the number

$$\sum_{x=0}^{n} \theta(x)p(x) \tag{3-28}$$

which will be called the expected value of $\theta(x)$. Note that in general, the expected value of $\theta(x)$ will not be $\theta(\mu)$, μ being the expected value of x.

In the event that the random variable x can take on any non-negative integral value, it is only necessary to replace the upper limit n on the summation signs in (3-27) and (3-28) by ∞ to obtain the appropriate expected values for this case. If the expected value is to have any meaning when x

is allowed to range over all non-negative integers, the sums (3-27), (3-28) must converge. In all cases of interest to us they will.

When $\theta(x) = (x - \mu)^2$, μ being the mean of x, then (3-28) is called the variance of x and is denoted by σ^2. The variance of x is a rough measure of the sort of spread in x values about the mean that can be expected. If σ^2 is large we can expect a greater spread in the x values than if σ^2 is small. The number $\sigma = \sqrt{\sigma^2}$ is often called the standard deviation of x. The number σ^2 is also called the variance of the distribution of x.

By its definition

$$\sigma^2 = \sum_{x=0}^{n} (x - \mu)^2 p(x)$$

This can be written

$$\sigma^2 = \sum_{x=0}^{n} (x^2 - 2\mu x + \mu^2) p(x) = \sum_{x=0}^{n} x^2 p(x) - 2\mu \sum_{x=0}^{n} x p(x) + \mu^2 \sum_{x=0}^{n} p(x)$$

$$= \sum_{x=0}^{n} x^2 p(x) - 2\mu^2 + \mu^2 = \sum_{x=0}^{n} x^2 p(x) - \mu^2 \tag{3-29}$$

and we have obtained a useful result which will be of assistance below in computing the variances of specific distributions. Equation (3-29) also holds if x is defined for all non-negative integers, provided that the sums converge.

Let us now evaluate the means and variances of the discrete distributions introduced in Sec. 3-3. For the binomial distribution, we see from (3-27) and (3-10) that

$$\mu = \sum_{x=0}^{n} x \frac{n!}{x! (n - x)!} \rho^x (1 - \rho)^{n-x}$$

$$= n\rho \sum_{x=1}^{n} \frac{(n - 1)!}{(x - 1)! (n - x)!} \rho^{x-1} (1 - \rho)^{n-x} \tag{3-30}$$

$$= n\rho \sum_{u=0}^{n-1} \binom{n - 1}{u} \rho^u (1 - \rho)^{n-1-u} = n\rho[\rho + (1 - \rho)]^{n-1} = n\rho$$

In the first step we cancelled the x in $x!$ to yield $(x - 1)!$ and factored out $n\rho$. In the second step we made the substitution $u = x - 1$. The resulting summation is simply the binomial expansion of $[\rho + (1 - \rho)]^{n-1}$. Hence the mean of the binomial distribution is $n\rho$. This is to be expected intuitively, since if ρ is the probability of a success on a single trial, one would expect the average number of successes in n trials to be $n\rho$.

To compute σ^2, we use (3-29). Thus

$$\sigma^2 = \sum_{x=0}^{n} x^2 \frac{n!}{x!\,(n-x)!}\,\rho^x(1-\rho)^{n-x} - (n\rho)^2$$

$$= \sum_{x=2}^{n} x(x-1)\frac{n!}{x!\,(n-x)!}\,\rho^x(1-\rho)^{n-x}$$

$$+ \sum_{x=0}^{n} x\frac{n!}{x!\,(n-x)!}\,\rho^x(1-\rho)^{n-x} - (n\rho)^2 \qquad (3\text{-}31)$$

$$= n(n-1)\rho^2 \sum_{u=0}^{n-2} \frac{(n-2)!}{u!\,(n-2-u)!}\,\rho^u(1-\rho)^{n-2-u} + n\rho - (n\rho)^2$$

$$= n(n-1)\rho^2 + n\rho - (n\rho)^2 = n\rho(1-\rho)$$

Note that the mean and variance of the binomial distribution depend on both n and ρ.

Consider next the Poisson distribution. We first note that the mean is

$$\sum_{x=0}^{\infty} x\frac{\mu^x}{x!}e^{-\mu} = \mu\sum_{x=1}^{\infty}\frac{\mu^{x-1}}{(x-1)!}e^{-\mu} = \mu\sum_{y=0}^{\infty}\frac{\mu^y}{y!}e^{-\mu} = \mu \qquad (3\text{-}32)$$

Thus the parameter μ appearing in the definition (3-13) of the Poisson distribution is simply the mean of the distribution. The variance is, by (3-29)

$$\sigma^2 = \sum_{x=0}^{\infty} x^2\frac{\mu^x}{x!}e^{-\mu} - \mu^2 = \sum_{x=2}^{\infty} x(x-1)\frac{\mu^x}{x!}e^{-\mu} + \mu - \mu^2$$

$$\qquad (3\text{-}33)$$

$$= \mu^2\sum_{y=0}^{\infty}\frac{\mu^y}{y!}e^{-\mu} + \mu - \mu^2 = \mu$$

Thus $\sigma^2 = \mu$ and the variance of the Poisson distribution is numerically equal to its mean.

For the negative binomial distribution

$$\mu = \sum_{x=0}^{\infty} x\frac{(x+n-1)!}{(n-1)!\,x!}\,\rho^n(1-\rho)^x$$

$$= \frac{n}{\rho}(1-\rho)\sum_{x=1}^{\infty}\frac{(x+n-1)!}{n!\,(x-1)!}\,\rho^{n+1}(1-\rho)^{x-1}$$

$$\qquad (3\text{-}34)$$

$$= \frac{n(1-\rho)}{\rho}\sum_{u=0}^{\infty}\binom{u+n}{n}\rho^{n+1}(1-\rho)^u$$

$$= \frac{n(1-\rho)}{\rho}\sum_{u=0}^{\infty} b_N(u;n+1,\rho) = \frac{n(1-\rho)}{\rho}$$

Furthermore

$$\sigma^2 = \sum_{x=0}^{\infty} x^2 b_N(x; n, \rho) - \mu^2$$

$$= \sum_{x=2}^{\infty} x(x-1)b_N(x; n, \rho) + \mu - \mu^2$$

$$= \frac{n(n+1)(1-\rho)^2}{\rho^2} \sum_{u=0}^{\infty} b_N(u; n+2, \rho) + \mu - \mu^2 \qquad (3\text{-}35)$$

$$= \frac{n(n+1)(1-\rho)^2}{\rho^2} + \mu - \mu^2 = \frac{n(1-\rho)}{\rho^2}$$

The geometric distribution is a special case of the negative binomial for which $n = 1$. Thus for the geometric distribution, as defined by (3-16)

$$\mu = \frac{1-\rho}{\rho}; \quad \sigma^2 = \frac{1-\rho}{\rho^2} \qquad (3\text{-}36)$$

Consider now the computation of expected values for continuous random variables. If $f(x)$ is the density function for the random variable x, then the fraction of the time that x lies in the interval x to $x + dx$ should approach $f(x)\,dx$ as the number of times the experiment is repeated approaches infinity. Hence if $\theta(x)$ is any function of x, the average value of $\theta(x)$ in the limit as the number of experiments over which $\theta(x)$ is averaged approaches infinity will tend to

$$\int_{-\infty}^{\infty} \theta(x)f(x)\,dx \qquad (3\text{-}37)$$

provided that the integral converges. The number computed according to (3-37) is called the expected value of $\theta(x)$. The mean μ (when $\theta(x) = x$) and variance σ^2 [when $\theta(x) = (x - \mu)^2$] of x and of the distribution of x are then defined to be

$$\mu = \int_{-\infty}^{\infty} xf(x)\,dx; \quad \sigma^2 = \int_{-\infty}^{\infty} (x-\mu)^2 f(x)\,dx \qquad (3\text{-}38)$$

Let us now compute the mean and variance for the normal and gamma distributions defined in Sec. 3-4. For the normal distribution given by (3-22) the mean is

$$\frac{1}{\sqrt{2\pi}\,\sigma} \int_{-\infty}^{\infty} xe^{-(1/2\sigma^2)(x-\mu)^2}\,dx = \frac{1}{\sqrt{2\pi}} \int_{-\infty}^{\infty} \frac{(x-\mu)}{\sigma} e^{-(1/2\sigma^2)(x-\mu)^2}\,dx + \mu$$

$$= \frac{\sigma}{\sqrt{2\pi}} \int_0^{\infty} e^{-v}\,dv + \frac{\sigma}{\sqrt{2\pi}} \int_{\infty}^0 e^{-v}\,dv + \mu = \mu \qquad (3\text{-}39)$$

where

$$v = \frac{1}{2}\left(\frac{x - \mu}{\sigma}\right)^2$$

Thus the parameter μ in the definition (3-22) of the normal distribution is its mean.

The variance of the normal distribution is

$$\frac{1}{\sqrt{2\pi}\,\sigma}\int_{-\infty}^{\infty}(x - \mu)^2 e^{-(1/2\sigma^2)(x-\mu)^2}\,dx = \frac{\sigma^2}{\sqrt{2\pi}}\int_{-\infty}^{\infty}w^2 e^{-(w^2/2)}\,dw$$

Now integrate by parts writing $u = w$, $dv = we^{-w^2/2}\,dw$ so that $v = -e^{-w^2/2}$. This yields

$$\frac{\sigma^2}{\sqrt{2\pi}}\int_{-\infty}^{\infty}w^2 e^{-w^2/2}\,dw$$

$$= \frac{\sigma^2}{\sqrt{2\pi}}\left\{-we^{-w^2/2}\Big|_{-\infty}^{\infty} + \int_{-\infty}^{\infty}e^{-w^2/2}\,dw\right\} = \sigma^2 \qquad (3\text{-}40)$$

Thus the parameter σ appearing in the definition (3-22) of the normal distribution is its standard deviation.

A plot of the normal density function looks something like that shown in Fig. 3-4. It is symmetric about $x = \mu$, and the inflection points occur at one standard deviation on either side of the mean.

Let us finally examine the gamma distribution. Before turning to the computation of the mean and variance, we shall first show that for any real $\alpha > 0$, $\Gamma(\alpha + 1) = \alpha\Gamma(\alpha)$. To prove this, recall that from (3-26)

$$\Gamma(\alpha + 1) = \int_{0}^{\infty}\beta(\beta x)^\alpha e^{-\beta x}\,dx = \int_{0}^{\infty}w^\alpha e^{-w}\,dw$$

Integration by parts yields

$$\Gamma(\alpha + 1) = -w^\alpha e^{-w}\Big|_{0}^{\infty} + \alpha\int_{0}^{\infty}w^{\alpha-1}e^{-w}\,dw = \alpha\Gamma(\alpha), \quad \alpha > 0 \qquad (3\text{-}41)$$

We shall now compute the mean and variance for the gamma distribution in the case where α can be any real number greater than -1 and β is any real positive number. From the generalization of (3-25) with $\Gamma(\alpha + 1)$ replacing $\alpha!$, we see that the mean is

$$\mu = \int_{0}^{\infty}\frac{\beta x(\beta x)^\alpha}{\Gamma(\alpha + 1)}e^{-\beta x}\,dx$$

$$= \frac{\Gamma(\alpha + 2)}{\Gamma(\alpha + 1)}\frac{1}{\beta}\int_{0}^{\infty}\frac{\beta(\beta x)^{\alpha+1}}{\Gamma(\alpha + 2)}e^{-\beta x}\,dx = \frac{\alpha + 1}{\beta}$$

$$(3\text{-}42)$$

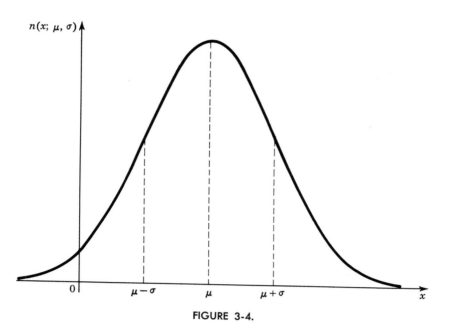

FIGURE 3-4.

by (3-41). Similarly, the variance is given by (we leave for Problem 3-22 the proof that the equivalent of (3-29) holds for continuous random variables)

$$\sigma^2 = \int_0^\infty \frac{\beta x^2 (\beta x)^\alpha}{\Gamma(\alpha + 1)} e^{-\beta x} \, dx - \left(\frac{\alpha + 1}{\beta}\right)^2 = \frac{\Gamma(\alpha + 3)}{\Gamma(\alpha + 1)} \frac{1}{\beta^2} - \left(\frac{\alpha + 1}{\beta}\right)^2$$

$$= \frac{(\alpha + 2)(\alpha + 1)}{\beta^2} - \left(\frac{\alpha + 1}{\beta}\right)^2 = \frac{\alpha + 1}{\beta^2} \tag{3-43}$$

To express α, β in terms of μ, σ note that on using (3-42) in (3-43)

$$\beta = \frac{\mu}{\sigma^2} \tag{3-44}$$

so

$$\alpha = \left(\frac{\mu}{\sigma}\right)^2 - 1 \tag{3-45}$$

A qualitative plot of the gamma densities for several integral values of α and a fixed β is shown in Fig. 3-5.

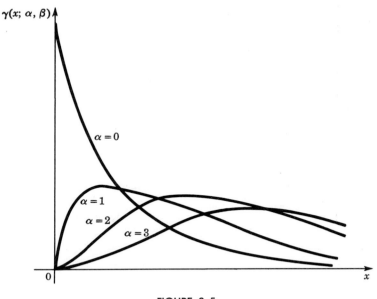

FIGURE 3-5.

3-6 Time Averages and Ensemble Averages

In the previous section we have given the mathematical definition of the expected (or mean) value of a random variable and have indicated how the expected value can be computed once the probability density function for the random variable is known. In dealing with inventory models we shall have frequent use for expected values. Physically, the expected value of a random variable will be interpretable as a *time average* of the random variable, an *ensemble average*, or both. We shall now introduce the notions of the time average and ensemble average of a random variable, and show their relation to the expected value of the random variable.

The notion of a time average is quite straightforward. We imagine that we have a system and we continue to allow it to operate for all future time, with demands and lead times being generated by the appropriate stochastic processes for the system. Then the time average of any random variable x associated with the system will be either

$$\lim_{t \to \infty} \frac{1}{t} \int_0^t x(t)dt$$

if x is defined at each point in time (such as the on hand inventory or the number of backorders) or

$$\lim_{n \to \infty} \frac{1}{n} \sum_{j=1}^{n} x(j)$$

if x is defined only with respect to a time period (such as the number of orders placed per year). Then n is the number of time periods used in computing the sum. The above definitions hold for either discrete or continuous random variables. To be specific, it will be assumed in the following discussion that x is discrete, although precisely the same results hold true if x is continuous.

In general, time averages will be of interest only when the stochastic processes associated with the system are not changing with time. The notion of a time average will be of most importance in computing the average annual cost introduced in Chapter 1. One cannot usually compute analytically the average values of a random variable in the time average sense using only the above definitions, since the average will depend on the nature of the stochastic processes involved. To relate a random variable to these stochastic processes, one determines a probability density function $p(x)$ which has the property that, as the length of the time interval taken for consideration becomes sufficiently long, the fraction of the time that the random variable has a given value x approaches $p(x)$. Then the expected value of x can be computed as described in the previous section, and because of the way $p(x)$ is defined it will be the average value in the time average sense.

The other and more important type of average is called an ensemble average. The notion of ensemble averages has been used a great deal by physicists in the study of statistical mechanics, and the same notion is quite helpful in studying inventory systems. Suppose that we are studying an inventory system for which the stochastic process generating demands is changing with time. We then ask the question, "What do we mean by saying that the probability that x units will be demanded in the next week is $p(x)$?" Clearly we cannot mean that if we observed the system for a long time the fraction of the time that x units were demanded will approach $p(x)$. The reason is that the mean rate of demand may be changing with time and hence a time average would be meaningless.

A clear physical interpretation can be given to $p(x)$ in the following way: Instead of considering just a single system, suppose that instead, we consider a large number N of identical systems. Imagine that we start them all off at the beginning of the week in identical states and allow the demands for each system to be generated by the appropriate stochastic process in such a way that the demand for each system is generated independently of the others. Since the systems are identical, the same stochastic process will be associated with each system. However, the week's demand will vary from one system to another, since we assumed that they operate independently, i.e., the stochastic processes for the various systems operate independently of each other. With this picture in mind, the fraction of the systems which have demands of precisely x will approach $p(x)$ as $N \rightarrow \infty$. Thus if one computes the expected demand in accordance with the rules given in the previous section, this expected demand will be the ensemble average demand, i.e., the average over the ensemble of systems of the week's demand.

Let us now imagine that the stochastic processes associated with a system do not change with time. Again we can imagine that we have an ensemble of N of these (identical) systems operating. After the ensemble of systems has been operating for a long time, it will reach a condition of statistical equilibrium. This means that the ensemble average of any relevant variable will become independent of time. When statistical equilibrium is reached, then, for any random variable, an ensemble average over the ensemble of systems will be precisely the same as a time average over all time for a single system,* so that $p(x)$ can be interpreted as the fraction of the time that a single system will have the value x, or the fraction of the systems in the ensemble that will have the value x at any given point in time.

The notion of an ensemble average is sufficiently general so that every expected value used in this book can be thought of as an ensemble average, and every probability as the limit as the number of systems in the ensemble approaches infinity, of the fraction of the systems in the ensemble which yield the given value of the random variable under the conditions specified. When the stochastic process under consideration does not change with time, an expected value can be interpreted both as a time average and an ensemble average. Furthermore, in this case, the expected value will be the same regardless of which way it is computed. Similarly, when the stochastic process does not change with time, a probability statement can be interpreted as referring to the long run fraction of the time that the random variables will have a specific value, or the fraction of the systems in the ensemble that will have the value.

3-7 Probabilistic Description of Demands

In this section, we would like to investigate the way in which the probabilistic nature of the demands received by an inventory system can be described in the case where the nature of the process generating the de-

---

* The equivalence of time averages and ensemble averages in this case is, roughly speaking, a statement of the celebrated ergodic theorem of statistical mechanics. No mathematically satisfactory proofs of the ergodic theorem were available until 1931 when proofs were provided by G. D. Birkhoff and John von Neumann.

mands does not change with time. Let us begin by noting that the number of units demanded in any time period will depend on the time between demands and on the number of units demanded when a demand occurs. In the real world, both the time elapsed between demands and the quantity demanded can be random variables. The time t between demands will be a continuous random variable and the number of units demanded when a demand occurs will be a discrete random variable.

Consider first the random variable t representing the time between the occurrence of demands. Let $G(t)$ be the probability that a time greater than or equal to t elapses from the time of a given demand until the time of

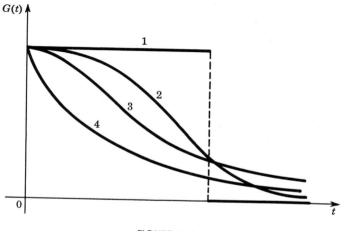

FIGURE 3-6.

the next demand. In general $G(t)$ could be a function of the times of occurrence of all previous demands, of the quantities demanded at each of the previous demands, of calendar time, and perhaps many other things. We shall here restrict ourselves to the case where $G(t)$ depends only on the time since the last demand, and not on the times of any other demands, quantities demanded, or calendar time.

If we were to plot $G(t)$ as a function of t, it might have one of the shapes shown in Fig. 3-6. Then $G(t)$ must be unity at $t = 0$, since the probability is unity that the demand under consideration will occur *after* the previous demand. Furthermore, we assume that it is certain that another demand will occur at some future time, so that $G(t)$ must approach 0 as t approaches ∞. In the event that $G(t)$ can be represented by curve 1 in Fig. 3-6, then the time between demands is deterministic, i.e., the time between demands is always t_0. Curves such as those shown in Fig. 3-6 can often be represented quite well by the complementary cumulative function of one of the gamma densities for an appropriate choice of α, β. The distribution of the time between successive demands is often referred to as the interarrival distribution.

A form of $G(t)$ which will be of greatest interest to us will be that where $G(t)$ is the complementary cumulative function for the exponential distribution (see example on p. 94), i.e.,

$$G(t) = e^{-\lambda t} \tag{3-46}$$

When $G(t)$ has the form (3-46), we say that the times between demands are exponentially distributed. The density function for t is

$$-\frac{dG}{dt} = \lambda e^{-\lambda t} = e(t; \lambda) \tag{3-47}$$

and the probability that the next demand arrives between t and $t + dt$ after the present demand is $e(t; \lambda)\, dt$. The average time $\bar{t}$ between demands is

$$\bar{t} = \int_0^\infty \lambda t e^{-\lambda t}\, dt = \frac{1}{\lambda} \tag{3-48}$$

so that the average number of demands per unit time is λ.

If $G(t)$ is given by (3-46), it is not difficult to compute the probability $V_n(t)$ that precisely n demands occur in a time period of length t immediately following the occurrence of a demand. This is most easily done by obtaining a recursive relation for the $V_n(t)$. Note first of all that

$$V_0(t) = G(t) = e^{-\lambda t} \tag{3-49}$$

When $n \geq 1$, let us imagine that the first demand occurring in the time interval of length t occurs between τ and $\tau + d\tau$ after the demand which serves as the time origin for the interval under consideration. If precisely n demands occur in the interval of length t, and if the first one occurs between τ and $\tau + d\tau$, then precisely $n - 1$ demands must occur in the interval of length $t - \tau$. The probability that $n - 1$ demands occur in an interval of length $t - \tau$ following a demand is simply $V_{n-1}(t - \tau)$. Thus the joint probability that the first demand occurs between τ and $\tau + d\tau$ and that $n - 1$ demands occur in the interval of length $t - \tau$ following this is

$$\lambda e^{-\lambda \tau} V_{n-1}(t - \tau) d\tau \tag{3-50}$$

Now events corresponding to different times of occurrence of the first demand are mutually exclusive. Hence, the probability $V_n(t)$ that there are precisely n demands in a time interval of length t is found by summing (3-50) over all τ, $0 < \tau < t$, i.e.,

$$V_n(t) = \lambda \int_0^t e^{-\lambda\tau} V_{n-1}(t - \tau)d\tau, \quad n \geq 1 \qquad (3\text{-}51)$$

By use of (3-51), we can obtain an explicit expression for $V_n(t)$. First let us note that from (3-49)

$$V_1(t) = \lambda \int_0^t e^{-\lambda\tau} V_0(t - \tau)d\tau = \lambda \int_0^t e^{-\lambda\tau} e^{-\lambda(t-\tau)} \, d\tau = \lambda e^{-\lambda t} \int_0^t d\tau = \lambda t e^{-\lambda t}$$

Then

$$V_2(t) = \lambda^2 \int_0^t (t - \tau)e^{-\lambda t} \, d\tau = \frac{(\lambda t)^2}{2} e^{-\lambda t}$$

Similarly

$$V_3(t) = \frac{(\lambda t)^3}{3(2)} e^{-\lambda t}; \quad V_4(t) = \frac{(\lambda t)^4}{4(3)(2)} e^{-\lambda t}$$

These results suggest that in general

$$V_n(t) = \frac{(\lambda t)^n}{n!} e^{-\lambda t}, \quad n = 0, 1, 2, 3, \ldots \qquad (3\text{-}52)$$

This is true and can easily be proved by induction. We have already shown that (3-52) is true for $n = 0$ and $n = 1$. It remains to show that if it is true for $n = m - 1$, it is also true for $n = m$. This follows, since if we use (3-52) evaluated for $n = m - 1$ in (3-51), we obtain

$$V_m(t) = \lambda \int_0^t e^{-\lambda\tau} \frac{[\lambda(t - \tau)]^{m-1}}{(m - 1)!} e^{-\lambda(t-\tau)} \, d\tau$$

$$= \frac{\lambda^m e^{-\lambda t}}{(m - 1)!} \int_0^t (t - \tau)^{m-1} \, d\tau = \frac{(\lambda t)^m}{m!} e^{-\lambda t}$$

and hence, by induction, (3-52) holds for all non-negative integers n.

We have obtained the interesting result that the number of demands m occurring in a time interval of length t following a demand is Poisson distributed, with the mean of the Poisson distribution being λt, i.e., $V_m(t) = p(m; \lambda t)$. Note that since λ is the mean rate of demand, λt is the mean number of demands which will occur in the time interval of length t. Thus the mean of the Poisson distribution is the average number of demands that will occur in the interval.

In the preceding derivation, the time interval was not allowed to begin at an arbitrary point in time. Instead, it was required that the time interval begin at a point in time immediately following a demand. It is also of interest to compute the probability that precisely m demands will occur in a time interval of length t when observation of the system is begun at a random point in time rather than immediately following a demand. In order to do this we must first establish another interesting property which follows from having the times between demands exponentially distributed.

Let us compute the conditional probability that the next demand after a specified demand occurs between t and $t + dt$ after the specified demand, given that it must occur after time t. If A is the event that no demand occurs up to time t, and B is the event that the demand occurs between t and $t + dt$, then $p(A) = e^{-\lambda t}$ and $p(B) = \lambda e^{-\lambda t} dt$. We wish to compute $p(B|A)$. From (3-3)

$$p(B|A) = \frac{p(A|B)p(B)}{p(A)}$$

However, $p(A|B) = 1$, since if the demand occurs between t and $t + dt$ it cannot have occurred before t. Thus

$$p(B|A) = \frac{p(B)}{p(A)} = \frac{\lambda e^{-\lambda t} dt}{e^{-\lambda t}} = \lambda \, dt \tag{3-53}$$

The important thing to note is that $p(A|B)$ is independent of t. This implies that if we start observing the system at a random point in time and ask what is the probability that a demand will occur in the next infinitesimal time interval of length dt, the probability is $\lambda \, dt$, independently of when we begin our observation, since this probability does not depend on how much time has elapsed since the last demand.

By use of (3-53) we can now compute the probability $U_0(t)$ that no demand occurs in a time period of length t from the time when we begin observing the system, if we start observation at a random point of time. To compute $U_0(t)$, observe that $U_0(t + dt)$ is simply the probability that no demands occurred up to time t multiplied by the conditional probability that no demand occurs between t and $t + dt$ given that none occurred up to t. This latter probability is $1 - \lambda \, dt$. Thus

$$U_0(t + dt) = (1 - \lambda \, dt) U_0(t)$$

or

$$\frac{dU_0}{U_0} = -\lambda \, dt$$

Hence

$$U_0 = ce^{-\lambda t}$$

where c is a constant of integration. Now at $t = 0$, $U_0 = 1$ since we begin observation at $t = 0$. Hence we obtain the unique solution

$$U_0(t) = e^{-\lambda t} \tag{3-54}$$

Recall that we began our discussion by assuming that the probability that the time from one demand to the next is greater than or equal to t is

$G(t) = e^{-\lambda t}$. We have now proved the interesting result that, if we begin observation of the system at a random point in time rather than at the time a demand occurs, the probability that the time until the next demand will be greater than or equal to t is again $e^{-\lambda t}$. In other words, the probability that the next demand will not occur for a time t or longer is independent of how long it has been since the last demand occurred.

Having computed $U_0(t)$, we can easily determine the probability $U_n(t)$ that exactly $n(n \geq 1)$ demands occur in a time period of length t when observation of the system is begun at a random point in time. If the first demand occurs between τ and $\tau + d\tau$ $(0 < \tau < t)$ after observation is begun (time 0), then to have n demands occur by time t, it must be true that precisely $n - 1$ demands occur in the period from τ to t. The probability that the first demand occurs between τ and $\tau + d\tau$ and that $n - 1$ demands occur from τ to t is

$$- \frac{dU_0(\tau)}{d\tau} V_{n-1}(t - \tau) \, d\tau = \lambda e^{-\lambda \tau} V_{n-1}(t - \tau) \, d\tau$$

Note that V_{n-1} rather than U_{n-1} appears, since the time interval beginning at time τ and extending to time t begins immediately after the occurrence of a demand. Thus on averaging over τ

$$U_n(t) = \lambda \int_0^t e^{-\lambda \tau} V_{n-1}(t - \tau) \, d\tau, \quad n \geq 1 \tag{3-55}$$

Hence, from (3-52) we see that

$$U_n(t) = V_n(t) = p(n; \lambda t) = \frac{(\lambda t)^n}{n!} e^{-\lambda t}, \quad n = 0, 1, 2, \ldots \tag{3-56}$$

and $U_n(t)$ also has a Poisson distribution with mean λt. We have proved then that the probability of having n units demanded in a time interval of length t is $p(n; \lambda t)$, and this is independent of whether we begin observation immediately after the occurrence of a demand or at a random point in time. The equality of the U_n and V_n is a peculiar feature of the exponential inter-arrival distribution and does not hold for an arbitrary interarrival distribution. When the interarrival distribution is exponential, we sometimes say that the demands are generated by a Poisson process. An important characteristic of the Poisson process is that it has no memory, i.e., the probability that a demand occurs in a time period of length dt is $\lambda \, dt$ independently of when any previous demands occurred.

Let us suppose that a Poisson process is generating demands and that units are always demanded one at a time, so that the quantity demanded is always unity. Then $U_n(t)$ is also the probability that n units are demanded in a time period of length t. Thus, in this case, the probability of having precisely n units demanded in a time period of length t is the Poisson probability $p(n; \lambda t)$. Now λ is the average rate at which units are demanded, and λt is the expected number of units demanded in the time period. In later chapters we shall use the terminology the mean or average rate of demand (or demand rate) to mean the average rate at which units are demanded. Note that when units are not demanded one at a time this will be different from the mean rate at which demands occur.

The Poisson distribution is especially easy to work with analytically. Furthermore it turns out that, in practice, it is frequently true that the process generating demands can be approximated fairly well by a Poisson process. Almost all of the future work in this book which treats demands discretely will assume that they are generated by a Poisson process.

In the event that the time between demands has a gamma distribution (3-25) with α an integer, then we say that an Erlang process of order $\alpha + 1$ is generating the demands. An Erlang process of order one is a Poisson process. We leave the task of working out the probabilities $V_n(t)$ for an Erlang process of order $\alpha + 1$ to the problems. These probabilities are quite complicated when $\alpha \geq 1$ and are rarely used in the analysis of inventory systems.

By the use of what we have learned above, let us compute for a Poisson process the probability that the Qth demand occurs between time t and $t + dt$ after we begin observing the system. This probability can be thought of as the probability of A and B where A is the event that $Q - 1$ demands occur between 0 and t and B is the event that a demand occurs between t and $t + dt$. Note that for a Poisson process B is independent of A, and hence $p(A \cap B) = p(A)p(B)$ where

$$p(A) = p(Q - 1; \lambda t), \quad p(B) = \lambda \, dt$$

Thus the desired probability is

$$\frac{\lambda(\lambda t)^{Q-1}}{(Q - 1)!} e^{-\lambda t} \, dt$$

Hence the density function for the time until the Qth demand is a gamma density with $\alpha = Q - 1$, i.e., a gamma density of order Q. We have just shown that if for some inventory system a Poisson process generates demands, and if units are demanded one at a time, then if an order is placed each time Q units are demanded, the density function for the time between the placing of orders is a gamma density of order Q.

In the event that the number of units requested when a demand occurs, i.e., the quantity demanded, can vary randomly from demand to demand, the task of determining the probability that any given number of units will be demanded in a time period of length t becomes much more complicated. We shall illustrate this by studying one of the simplest possible cases in which the number of units demanded can be a random variable. We shall assume that a Poisson process generates the demands, and that the number of units demanded when a demand occurs has a geometric distribution, i.e., the probability that when a demand occurs x units will be demanded is

$$b_N(x - 1; 1, 1 - v) = (1 - v)v^{x-1}, \quad x = 1, 2, \ldots \tag{3-57}$$

In the original definition of the geometric distribution (3-16), x could take on the value zero. Here we always want at least one unit demanded when a demand occurs—hence the change from x to $x - 1$ in going from (3-16) to (3-57).* It is also convenient to write $v = 1 - \rho$. Note that we assume that the number of units demanded per demand is independent of how long it has been since the last demand. The process formed by having a Poisson process generate demands and the quantity demanded being distributed according to a geometric distribution is sometimes referred to as a "stuttering Poisson" process.

For a stuttering Poisson process, let us now compute the probability that precisely n units will be demanded in a time period of length t. Since a Poisson process generates the demands, we know that the results are independent of the time origin. If n units are demanded, then no more than n demands could have occurred. However, it is possible to have n units demanded if there are 1, 2, . . . , or n demands. Events representing different numbers of demands in the period are mutually exclusive. The probability of precisely j demands is $p(j; \beta t)$ if $1/\beta$ is the mean time between demands. Thus if $U_n(t)$ is the probability that n units are demanded

$$U_n(t) = \sum_{j=1}^{n} p(n|j)p(j; \beta t), \quad n = 1, 2, \ldots \tag{3-58}$$

where $p(n|j)$ is the probability that precisely n units are demanded when j demands occur. Equation (3-58) does not hold for $n = 0$. The probability that no units are demanded is the probability that no demands occur. Thus

$$U_0(t) = p(0; \beta t) = e^{-\beta t} \tag{3-59}$$

It remains to compute $p(n|j)$. Let x_i be the random variable representing the number of units demanded when demand i occurs. Then $p(n|j)$ is the distribution of the random variable $n = x_1 + x_2 + \ldots + x_j$. We know the distribution of each x_i (it is geometric). Later, when we discuss convolutions, we shall show how to obtain the distribution of the sum of independent random variables. We shall state and use here the fact that if each x_i has the geometric distribution (3-57), then $n - j$, the demand in

---

* Stated differently, if y is the demand in excess of one unit, then y has the geometric distribution (3-16).

excess of one unit per demand, has a negative binomial distribution $b_N(n - j; j, 1 - \nu)$. Hence

$$p(n|j) = b_N(n - j; j, 1 - \nu) = \binom{n-1}{j-1}(1 - \nu)^j \nu^{n-j} \qquad (3\text{-}60)$$

Thus

$$U_n(t) = \nu^n e^{-\beta t} \sum_{j=1}^{n} \frac{1}{j!} \binom{n-1}{j-1}\left[\left(\frac{1-\nu}{\nu}\right)\beta t\right]^j, \quad n = 1, 2, \ldots \qquad (3\text{-}61)$$

The $U_n(t)$ given by (3-59), (3-61) are referred to as the stuttering Poisson distribution. It is rather difficult to work with this distribution, which is one of the simplest representing situations in which more than a single unit can be demanded at a time. Fortunately, as we shall see shortly, there is a simple approximation to all these distributions in terms of a continuous random variable which lends itself quite easily to analytical work and which often provides a sufficiently good approximation in practical applications.

3-8 Joint Distributions

Often in working with inventory systems it is necessary to deal with two or more variables simultaneously. For example, the random variables may refer to demands in different time periods, or one or more random variables may refer to demand while one or more different random variables may refer to the procurement lead time. We wish to study briefly here density functions involving two random variables.

Consider two discrete random variables x, y, both defined over the non-negative integers, which always occur together. We can then introduce a function $p(x, y)$ defined for each set of values x, y which gives the probability of the event $x \cap y$, i.e., the event that x and y occur. The function $p(x, y)$ is called the joint density function (or joint distribution) for the random variables x, y. It is typical to use the usual functional notation for a function of two variables, $p(x, y)$, rather than the symbol $p(x \cap y)$. Since one set of values x, y must occur, and since we as usual assume that two different values of either random variable are mutually exclusive, we must have

$$\sum_{x=0}^{\infty} \sum_{y=0}^{\infty} p(x, y) = 1 \qquad (3\text{-}62)$$

Let us now ask the question, "What is the probability of x without regard to what value y takes on?" We shall denote this probability by $p(x)$; $p(x)$ must simply be the summation of $p(x, y)$ over all possible values of y, i.e.,

$$p(x) = \sum_{y=0}^{\infty} p(x, y) \tag{3-63}$$

Similarly, $p(y)$, the probability of y without regard to the value of x is given by

$$p(y) = \sum_{x=0}^{\infty} p(x, y) \tag{3-64}$$

The functions $p(x)$, $p(y)$ are called the marginal densities for the random variables x and y respectively. Note that they are legitimate densities since $p(x) \geq 0$, $p(y) \geq 0$ and from (3-62)

$$\sum_{x=0}^{\infty} p(x) = 1, \quad \sum_{y=0}^{\infty} p(y) = 1$$

If either or both of the above random variables are defined only over a finite number of integral values, the summations are taken only over the allowed values of the variable. When $p(x) \neq 0$ and $p(y) \neq 0$, the conditional probabilities $p(x|y)$ and $p(y|x)$ are defined by

$$p(x, y) = p(x|y)p(y) = p(y|x)p(x)$$

In terms of the conditional probabilities we can write

$$p(x) = \sum_{y=0}^{\infty} p(x|y)p(y); \quad p(y) = \sum_{x=0}^{\infty} p(y|x)p(x) \tag{3-65}$$

We say that x and y are independent if $p(x, y) = p(x)p(y)$.

EXAMPLE An important application of marginal distributions in the analysis of inventory systems can be stated in an especially simple form as follows: Let the demands on the system be generated by a Poisson process and imagine that units are demanded one at a time, so that the probability that x units are demanded in a time t is $p(x; \lambda t)$, where λ is the mean demand rate. Assume also that the procurement lead time is a random variable which can only take on one of the following finite number of values $t_1, \ldots, t_k$, the probability of t_i being $l(t_i)$. We now ask what is the probability that x units will be demanded in a lead time. In other words, we want the marginal distribution of lead time demand. Note that the number of units demanded in the lead time is not independent of the lead time t_i. However, from (3-65) we see that the probability $p(x)$ that x units are demanded in a lead time is

$$p(x) = \sum_{i=1}^{k} p(x; \lambda t_i)l(t_i) \tag{3-66}$$

Consider next the case where x is a discrete random variable defined over the non-negative integers and y is a continuous random variable defined for all real y. We then take $f(x, y)$ to be the joint density function for x and y; $f(x, y)\ dy$ is the probability that the discrete random variable has the value x and that the continuous random variable lies between y and $y + dy$. Then, since some pair of values must occur, we have

$$\sum_{x=0}^{\infty} \int_{-\infty}^{\infty} f(x, y)\ dy = 1 \tag{3-67}$$

The marginal densities $p(x)$, $v(y)$ of x, y respectively are defined by

$$p(x) = \int_{-\infty}^{\infty} f(x, y)\ dy; \quad v(y) = \sum_{x=0}^{\infty} f(x, y) \tag{3-68}$$

Then $p(x)$ is the probability that the discrete random variable has the value x, and $v(y)\ dy$ is the probability that the continuous random variable lies between y and $y + dy$.

Next when $v(y) \neq 0$, $p(x) \neq 0$, we define conditional density functions $g(y|x)$ and $h(x|y)$ such that

$$f(x, y)\ dy = h(x|y)v(y)\ dy = [g(y|x)\ dy]p(x) \tag{3-69}$$

Then $h(x|y)$ is the conditional probability that the discrete variable has the value x given that the continuous variable has the value y, and $g(y|x)\ dy$ is the conditional probability that the continuous random variable lies between y and $y + dy$ given that the discrete random variable has the value x. Then (3-68) can be written

$$p(x) = \int_{-\infty}^{\infty} h(x|y)v(y)\ dy; \quad v(y) = \sum_{x=0}^{\infty} g(y|x)p(x) \tag{3-70}$$

We say that x, y are independent random variables if

$$f(x, y) = p(x)v(y) \tag{3-71}$$

If, for an inventory system, the procurement lead time is treated as a continuous random variable, and the number of units demanded in any given time period as a discrete random variable, then we have an example of the situation just discussed. For the case where the procurement lead time has a gamma distribution, and a Poisson process generates demands, with units being demanded one at a time, let us compute the marginal distribution $p(x)$ of lead time demand. This result will be of use to us later. By assumption, the probability density for the lead time t is $\gamma(t; \alpha, \beta)$ where $\gamma(t; \alpha, \beta)$ is given by (3-25), and the density function for the number of units demanded in a time t is $p(x; \lambda t)$ where λ is the mean rate of demand. Thus

$$\gamma(t; \alpha, \beta) = \frac{\beta(\beta t)^\alpha}{\Gamma(\alpha + 1)} e^{-\beta t}; \quad p(x; \lambda t) = \frac{(\lambda t)^x}{x!} e^{-\lambda t} \tag{3-72}$$

where for added generality we have replaced $\alpha!$ in (3-25) by $\Gamma(\alpha + 1)$. Note that $p(x; \lambda t)$ corresponds to $h(x|y)$ above. Then using (3-70)

$$p(x) = \int_0^\infty \frac{\beta(\lambda t)^x}{x!} \frac{(\beta t)^\alpha}{\Gamma(\alpha + 1)} e^{-(\beta+\lambda)t} \, dt = \frac{\beta^{\alpha+1}\lambda^x}{x!\Gamma(\alpha + 1)} \int_0^\infty t^{x+\alpha} e^{-(\beta+\lambda)t} \, dt$$

$$= \frac{\beta^{\alpha+1}\lambda^x}{x!\Gamma(\alpha + 1)} \frac{\Gamma(\alpha + x + 1)}{(\beta + \lambda)^{\alpha+x+1}} \int_0^\infty \frac{(\beta + \lambda)^{\alpha+x+1} t^{x+\alpha}}{\Gamma(\alpha + x + 1)} e^{-(\beta+\lambda)t} \, dt$$

$$= \frac{\Gamma(\alpha + x + 1)}{x!\Gamma(\alpha + 1)} \left(\frac{\beta}{\beta + \lambda}\right)^{\alpha+1} \left(\frac{\lambda}{\beta + \lambda}\right)^x, \quad \alpha > -1, \beta, \lambda > 0 \tag{3-73}$$

by (3-26). Thus if α is a positive integer, the marginal distribution of lead time demand $p(x)$ has the negative binomial distribution $b_N[x; \alpha + 1, \beta/(\beta + \lambda)]$. There is no reason why α must be an integer in the definition of the negative binomial distribution. We can consider (3-73) to be a generalized definition of the negative binomial distribution which includes cases where α is not an integer. We have shown, therefore, that if the lead time is gamma distributed, and demands are generated by a Poisson process, units being demanded one at a time, then the marginal distribution of lead time demand is a negative binomial distribution.

It remains to consider the case where the two random variables x, y are continuous. Now we define a density function $f(x, y)$ such that $f(x, y) \, dx \, dy$ is the probability that x lies in the interval x to $x + dx$, and y lies in the interval y to $y + dy$. Then it must be true that

$$\int_{-\infty}^\infty \int_{-\infty}^\infty f(x, y) \, dx \, dy = 1 \tag{3-74}$$

The marginal densities are given by

$$u(x) = \int_{-\infty}^\infty f(x, y) \, dy; \quad v(y) = \int_{-\infty}^\infty f(x, y) \, dx \tag{3-75}$$

where $u(x) \, dx$ is the probability that x lies in the interval x to $x + dx$ and $v(y) \, dy$ is the probability that y lies in the interval y to $y + dy$.

Conditional density functions $h(x|y)$ and $g(y|x)$ are defined by

$$f(x, y) = h(x|y)v(y) = g(y|x)u(x), \quad v(y) \neq 0, u(x) \neq 0 \tag{3-76}$$

where $h(x|y) \, dx$ is the probability that x lies in the interval x to $x + dx$ given that the other random variable has the value y, and $g(y|x) \, dy$ is the probability that y lies in the interval y to $y + dy$ given that the other random variable has the value x. Then

$$u(x) = \int_{-\infty}^{\infty} h(x|y)v(y)\,dy; \quad v(y) = \int_{-\infty}^{\infty} g(y|x)u(x)\,dx \qquad (3\text{-}77)$$

If we can write $f(x, y) = u(x)v(y)$, the random variables x, y are said to be independent.

Consider now two discrete random variables x_1, x_2 defined over the non-negative integers and let $p(x_1, x_2)$ be their density function. If $\theta(x_1, x_2)$ is any function of x_1, x_2, then the expected value of $\theta(x_1, x_2)$ is

$$\sum_{x_1=0}^{\infty} \sum_{x_2=0}^{\infty} \theta(x_1, x_2)p(x_1, x_2) \qquad (3\text{-}78)$$

As a special case, imagine that $\theta(x_1, x_2)$ depends only on x_1, i.e., $\theta(x_1, x_2) = \psi(x_1)$. Then from (3-78) the expected value of $\psi(x_1)$ is

$$\sum_{x_1=0}^{\infty} \sum_{x_2=0}^{\infty} \psi(x_1)p(x_1, x_2) = \sum_{x_1=0}^{\infty} \psi(x_1) \sum_{x_2=0}^{\infty} p(x_1, x_2) = \sum_{x_1=0}^{\infty} \psi(x_1)p(x_1) \qquad (3\text{-}79)$$

where $p(x_1)$ is the marginal density for x_1. As another special case imagine that $\theta(x_1, x_2) = x_1 \pm x_2$. Then the expected value of $x_1 \pm x_2$ is

$$\sum_{x_1=0}^{\infty} \sum_{x_2=0}^{\infty} (x_1 \pm x_2)p(x_1, x_2) = \sum_{x_1=0}^{\infty} x_1 p(x_1) \pm \sum_{x_2=0}^{\infty} x_2 p(x_2) = \mu_1 \pm \mu_2 \qquad (3\text{-}80)$$

where μ_1, μ_2 are the expected values of x_1, x_2 respectively. More generally, the expected value of a finite sum of random variables $x_1 + \ldots + x_n$ is the sum of the expected values, i.e., $\mu_1 + \ldots + \mu_n$. This is proved by letting the event $x_2^* = x_2 + \ldots + x_n$ and applying (3-80) to $x_1 + x_2^*$. Then the argument is repeated on x_2^*. Relations like (3-78), (3-79), (3-80) also hold if one random variable is discrete and the other continuous, or if both are continuous, provided that the appropriate summation signs are replaced by integrals. Similarly, the expected value of

$$x_1 \pm x_2 \pm \ldots \pm x_n \quad \text{is} \quad \mu_1 \pm \mu_2 \pm \ldots \pm \mu_n$$

3-9 Convolutions

Consider the discrete random variable x, defined over the set of non-negative integers, whose density function is $p(x)$. Then the *generating function or z-transform of x*, written $\mathcal{P}(s)$ or $z\{p(x)\}$ is defined as

$$\mathcal{P}(s) = z\{p(x)\} = p(0) + p(1)s + p(2)s^2 + \ldots = \sum_{x=0}^{\infty} p(x)s^x \qquad (3\text{-}81)$$

for those s for which the series converges. Because the $p(x)$ must sum to unity, we have $\mathcal{P}(1) = 1$. Consequently, the series (3-81) will always converge for s in the interval $-1 \leq s \leq 1$. Note that a knowledge of $\mathcal{P}(s)$ is as good as a knowledge of $p(x)$ since if $\mathcal{P}(s)$ is expanded in a power series as in (3-81) the $p(x)$ values can be found, i.e.,

$$p(x) = \frac{1}{x!}\left[\frac{d^x\mathcal{P}(s)}{ds^x}\right]_{s=0} \tag{3-82}$$

and, since the expansion of a function in a power series is unique, $p(x)$ is uniquely determined by $\mathcal{P}(s)$. Generating functions are useful in many ways. They will be of use to us in this section in finding distributions of sums of random variables.

EXAMPLES 1. The generating function for the Poisson distribution will always be denoted by $\mathcal{P}(s; \mu)$. It is

$$\mathcal{P}(s; \mu) = \sum_{x=0}^{\infty} p(x; \mu)s^x = \sum_{x=0}^{\infty} \frac{(\mu s)^x}{x!}e^{-\mu} = e^{-\mu(1-s)}\sum_{x=0}^{\infty} \frac{(\mu s)^x}{x!}e^{-\mu s}$$

$$= e^{-\mu(1-s)} \tag{3-83}$$

2. The generating function for the negative binomial distribution will be written $\mathcal{P}_N(s; n, \rho)$. It is, for integral valued n,

$$\mathcal{P}_N(s; n, \rho) = \sum_{x=0}^{\infty} \binom{x+n-1}{n-1} \rho^n(1-\rho)^x s^x$$

$$= \rho^n \sum_{x=0}^{\infty} \binom{x+n-1}{n-1}[(1-\rho)s]^x = \left[\frac{\rho}{1-(1-\rho)s}\right]^n \tag{3-84}$$

The same result is obtained for any positive n, even if it is not an integer, if (3-73) is used. The proof is left for Problem 3-23.

3. The generating function for the geometric distribution will be denoted by $\mathcal{P}_g(s; \rho)$. It is found by setting $n = 1$ in (3-84). Thus

$$\mathcal{P}_g(s; \rho) = \frac{\rho}{1-(1-\rho)s} \tag{3-85}$$

Consider two *independent*, discrete random variables x_1, x_2 defined over the non-negative integers, and let their density functions be $p_1(x_1)$ and $p_2(x_2)$. Often in applied work one is faced with the problem of finding the probability distribution for the random variable $y = x_1 + x_2$, i.e., of finding the distribution of the sum of the random variables x_1, x_2. Let us study how this can be done. The probability $p(y)$ that the random variable $x_1 + x_2$ has the value y is the sum of the probabilities of the $y + 1$ mutually exclusive events $(x_1 = j) \cap (x_2 = y - j), j = 0, 1, \ldots, y$. However, since the random variables x_1, x_2 are independent

$$p(x_1 = j \cap x_2 = y - j) = p_1(j)p_2(y - j) \tag{3-86}$$

Hence

$$p(y) = \sum_{j=0}^{y} p_1(j)p_2(y - j) \tag{3-87}$$

The density function $p(y)$ is called the convolution of the density functions $p_1(x_1)$ and $p_2(x_2)$.

Now denote by $\mathcal{P}_1(s)$ and $\mathcal{P}_2(s)$ the generating functions for $p_1(x_1)$ and $p_2(x_2)$ respectively. Then by definition

$$\mathcal{P}_1(s) = \sum_{j=0}^{\infty} p_1(j)s^j; \quad \mathcal{P}_2(s) = \sum_{j=0}^{\infty} p_2(j)s^i \tag{3-88}$$

However, a theorem on the multiplication of power series says that

$$\mathcal{P}_1(s)\mathcal{P}_2(s) = \sum_{j=0}^{\infty} \left[\sum_{k=0}^{j} p_1(k)p_2(j - k) \right] s^j \tag{3-89}$$

Note: A heuristic derivation of (3-89) can be given as follows:

$\mathcal{P}_1(s)\mathcal{P}_2(s) =$

$\quad [p_1(0) + p_1(1)s + p_1(2)s^2 + \ldots][p_2(0) + p_2(1)s + p_2(2)s^2 + \ldots]$

$= p_1(0)p_2(0) + p_1(0)p_2(1)s + p_1(0)p_2(2)s^2 + p_1(0)p_2(3)s^3$

$\qquad + p_1(1)p_2(0)s + p_1(1)p_2(1)s^2 + p_1(1)p_2(2)s^3$

$\qquad\qquad + p_1(2)p_2(0)s^2 + p_1(2)p_2(1)s^3$

$\qquad\qquad\qquad p_1(3)p_2(0)s^3 + \ldots$

$= p_1(0)p_2(0) + [p_1(0)p_2(1) + p_1(1)p_2(0)]s + [p_1(0)p_2(2) + p_1(1)p_2(1)$

$+ p_1(2)p_2(0)]s^2 + [p_1(0)p_2(3) + p_1(1)p_2(2)$

$\qquad\qquad + p_1(2)p_2(1) + p_1(3)p_2(0)]s^3 + \ldots$

$= \sum_{j=0}^{\infty} \left[\sum_{k=0}^{j} p_1(k)p_2(j - k) \right] s^j$

This immediately demonstrates the important result that the generating function for the random variable $y = x_1 + x_2$ is the product of the generating functions for x_1 and x_2. If the random variables x_1, x_2 have the same density function, and if $\mathcal{P}(s)$ is the generating function for this distribution, then the generating function for $y = x_1 + x_2$ is $\mathcal{P}^2(s)$.

Consider the random variable $y = x_1 + x_2 + \ldots + x_n$ which is the sum of n independent random variables x_i, the generating function for the probability density of x_i being $\mathcal{P}_i(s)$. To compute the density function for y, we note that the density function for $y_1 = x_1 + x_2$ is the convolution of the density functions for x_1 and x_2. The generating function for the density function of y_1 is then $\mathcal{P}_1(s)\mathcal{P}_2(s)$. The density function for $y_2 = y_1 + x_3 = x_1 + x_2 + x_3$ is the convolution of the density functions for y_1 and x_3. The generating function of the density function for y_2 is $\mathcal{P}_1(s)\mathcal{P}_2(s)\mathcal{P}_3(s)$. Continuing this process, we see that the density function for $y = y_{n-2} + x_n$ is the convolution of the density function for y_{n-2} and x_n. The generating function for the density function of y is then $\mathcal{P}_1(s)\mathcal{P}_2(s) \ldots \mathcal{P}_n(s)$, i.e., the product of the generating functions corresponding to each of the random variables x_i. In the event that each x_i has the same density function $p(x)$, then the generating function for the probability density of y is $\mathcal{P}^n(s)$ where $\mathcal{P}(s)$ is the generating function for $p(x)$, and the probability density of y is called the n-fold convolution of $p(x)$. The density function which is the n-fold convolution of $p(x)$ we shall denote by $p^{(n)}(x)$. Note that

$$p^{(1)}(x) = p(x)$$

and

$$p^{(n)}(x) = \sum_{y=0}^{x} p^{(n-1)}(y)p(x - y), \quad n = 2, 3, \ldots$$

Let us suppose that the random variables x_i, $i = 1, \ldots, n$, are Poisson distributed with means μ_i. The generating function for the Poisson distribution is given by (3-83). Then, if the x_i are independent, the generating function for the probability density of $y = x_1 + \ldots + x_n$ is

$$\mathcal{P}(s; \mu_1)\mathcal{P}(s; \mu_2) \ldots \mathcal{P}(s; \mu_n) = e^{-(\mu_1 + \ldots + \mu_n)(1-s)} = \mathcal{P}(s; \mu_1 + \ldots + \mu_n)$$
$$(3\text{-}90)$$

which is the generating function for a Poisson distribution with mean $\mu_1 + \ldots + \mu_n$. We have thus proved that if the x_i, $i = 1, \ldots, n$, are independent random variables which are Poisson distributed with means μ_i respectively, then $y = x_1 + \ldots + x_n$ is also Poisson distributed with a mean $\mu_1 + \ldots + \mu_n$.

Next let us suppose that we have n independent random variables x_i each of which has a geometric distribution with mean $(1 - \rho)/\rho$. Then the probability density of $y = x_1 + \ldots + x_n$ is the n-fold convolution of the geometric distribution with the parameter ρ. The generating function for the geometric distribution is given by (3-85). Hence the generating function of the probability distribution for y is given by

$$\mathcal{P}_g^n(s;\rho) = \left[\frac{\rho}{1-(1-\rho)s}\right]^n = \mathcal{P}_N(s;n,\rho) \tag{3-91}$$

Thus y has a negative binomial distribution $b_N(y;n,\rho)$. We have used this result previously without proof when developing the stuttering Poisson distribution. We have now provided the proof.

In the above paragraphs, we have shown how to determine the generating function of the probability for a finite sum of independent random variables $x_1 + \ldots + x_n$, n being given and specified. Let us now study a somewhat different case where n can also be a random variable. We shall imagine that each random variable x_i has the same probability density $p_1(x)$ whose generating function will be denoted by $\mathcal{P}_1(s)$. The x_i are assumed to be independent random variables. The generating function of the probability density function for n, $p_2(n)$, will be written $\mathcal{P}_2(s)$. The probability $p^*(j)$ that $y = j$, $y = x_1 + \ldots + x_n$, where j is a specified nonnegative integer is

$$p^*(j) = p(y = j) = \sum_{n=0}^{\infty} p_2(n)p(x_1 + \ldots + x_n = j) \tag{3-92}$$

If $\mathcal{P}^*(s)$ is the generating function for $p^*(j)$, then

$$\mathcal{P}^*(s) = \sum_{j=0}^{\infty} p^*(j)s^j = \sum_{j=0}^{\infty}\left[\sum_{n=0}^{\infty} p_2(n)p(x_1 + \ldots + x_n = j)\right]s^j$$

or on rearranging the summation signs

$$\mathcal{P}^*(s) = \sum_{n=0}^{\infty} p_2(n)\left[\sum_{j=0}^{\infty} p(x_1 + \ldots + x_n = j)s^j\right] \tag{3-93}$$

However, the quantity in brackets in (3-93) is precisely the generating function for $x_1 + \ldots + x_n$ for a fixed n, i.e., $\mathcal{P}_1^n(s)$. Thus

$$\mathcal{P}^*(s) = \sum_{n=0}^{\infty} p_2(n)\mathcal{P}_1^n(s) \tag{3-94}$$

However, by definition

$$\mathcal{P}_2(s) = \sum_{n=0}^{\infty} p_2(n)s^n$$

Thus

$$\mathcal{P}^*(s) = \mathcal{P}_2[\mathcal{P}_1(s)] \tag{3-95}$$

In (3-95) $\mathcal{P}^*(s)$ is written as a function of a function, i.e., $\mathcal{P}^*(s)$ is $\mathcal{P}_2$ of $\mathcal{P}_1$ of s. The result just obtained provides a way for deriving the generating function of the stuttering Poisson distribution, and hence another way to obtain the stuttering Poisson itself. For the stuttering Poisson, $p_2(n)$ is a

Poisson distribution so that $\mathcal{P}_2(s) = \mathcal{P}(s; \beta t)$ where β is the mean rate at which demands occur (see 3-83), and $\mathcal{P}_1(s)$ is the generating function for the geometric distribution. However, the generating function (3-85) for the geometric distribution must be modified slightly since for use in the stuttering Poisson, the probabilities are stepped up by unity so that the probability that one unit is demanded is the geometric probability of zero. Thus (3-85) must be multiplied by s to obtain the correct generating function, so that (recall that it is here convenient to write $\rho = 1 - \nu$)

$$\mathcal{P}_1(s) = \frac{s(1 - \nu)}{1 - \nu s} \tag{3-96}$$

Thus the generating function for the stuttering Poisson distribution, which will be written $\mathcal{P}_{sp}(s; \nu, \beta)$, is

$$\mathcal{P}_{sp}(s; \nu, \beta) = e^{-\beta t\{1 - [s(1-\nu)/(1-\nu s)]\}} = e^{-\beta t(1-s)/(1-\nu s)} \tag{3-97}$$

Let us now turn our attention to continuous random variables. We do not expect to be able to define a generating function for the probability density $f(x)$ of some continuous random variable x such that when expanded in a power series, the coefficients of the various powers will yield the density function of x for all possible x values, since x is continuous. Instead consider the function

$$\mathfrak{F}(s) = \int_{-\infty}^{\infty} e^{-sx} f(x)\, dx = \sum_{j=0}^{\infty} (-1)^j \left[\int_{-\infty}^{\infty} x^j f(x)\, dx \right] \frac{s^j}{j!} \tag{3-98}$$

In the expansion (3-98), the coefficient of s^j is $(-1)^j \mu_j/j!$ where

$$\mu_j = \int_{-\infty}^{\infty} x^j f(x)\, dx \tag{3-99}$$

The number μ_j is called the jth moment of $f(x)$ about the origin. The function $\mathfrak{F}(s)$, if it exists, is called the moment generating function of $f(x)$ or x, and it takes the place, as we shall see, of the generating function for discrete variables.* When x is defined only for non-negative x, then $\mathfrak{F}(s)$ is also called the Laplace transform of $f(x)$. It might be noted, although we shall not prove it, that a density function is uniquely determined by its moment generating function.

Let x_1, x_2 be two continuous independent random variables with densities $f_1(x_1)$, $f_2(x_2)$ and moment generating functions $\mathfrak{F}_1(s)$ and $\mathfrak{F}_2(s)$ respectively. We shall now compute the density function $g(y)$ and moment generating function $\mathcal{G}(s)$ for the random variable $y = x_1 + x_2$. The probability that

---

* It is also possible to define moment generating functions for discrete variables. We leave an analysis of these moment generating functions for discrete random variables to the problems.

y lies between y and $y + dy$ given that x_1 lies between x_1 and $x_1 + dx_1$ is $f_1(x_1)f_2(y - x_1)\, dx_1\, dx_2$ (and $dx_2 = dy$). Here the analysis is slightly different for the case where both variables are restricted to be non-negative than it is when one or both variables can take on all real values. Hence we shall present the derivation for the case where both variables are restricted to be non-negative, since this case is the more difficult to derive. Thus if $y - x_1$ is to be non-negative, x_1 can range from 0 to y so that

$$g(y) = \int_0^y f_1(x_1)f_2(y - x_1)\, dx_1 \tag{3-100}$$

Let us next compute the moment generating function of $g(y)$ in the case where x_1, x_2 and hence y must be non-negative. By (3-98)

$$\mathcal{G}(s) = \int_0^\infty \int_0^y f_1(x_1)f_2(y - x_1)e^{-ys}\, dx_1\, dy \tag{3-101}$$

This can be considered to be a double integral, whose integrand is $f_1(x_1)f_2(y - x_1)e^{-ys}$, integrated over the shaded region of the x_1y-plane shown in Fig. 3-7. As written in (3-101), the integral is found by summing over y infinitesimal strips of area parallel to the x_1 axis such as the one shown in Fig. 3-7. The integral can equally well be evaluated by summing

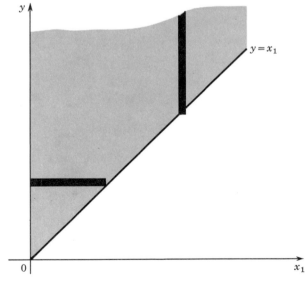

FIGURE 3-7.

over x_1, infinitesimal strips of area parallel to the y axis such as the one shown in Fig. 3-7. Thus (3-101) can be written

$$g(s) = \int_0^\infty \int_{x_1}^8 f_1(x_1)f_2(y - x_1)e^{-ys}\, dy\, dx_1$$

$$= \int_0^\infty f_1(x_1) \int_{x_1}^\infty f_2(y - x_1)e^{-ys}\, dy\, dx_1 \tag{3-102}$$

However

$$\int_{x_1}^\infty f_2(y - x_1)e^{-ys}\, dy = e^{-x_1 s} \int_0^\infty f_2(u)e^{-us}\, du = e^{-x_1 s}\mathcal{F}_2(s)$$

Thus

$$g(s) = \mathcal{F}_2(s) \int_0^\infty f_1(x_1)e^{-x_1 s}\, dx_1 = \mathcal{F}_1(s)\mathcal{F}_2(s) \tag{3-103}$$

This proves that the moment generating function for $g(y)$ is the product of the moment generating functions for $f_1(x_1)$ and $f_2(x_2)$. Precisely the same result holds if x_1, x_2 can take on any real values. The proof is left for Problem 3-24.

The above discussion shows that, given n independent random variables x_i with moment generating functions $\mathcal{F}_i(s)$, the moment generating function $g(s)$ of the random variable $y = x_1 + \ldots + x_n$ is

$$g(s) = \mathcal{F}_1(s)\mathcal{F}_2(s) \ldots \mathcal{F}_n(s) \tag{3-104}$$

In the special case where each x_i has the same density function $f(x)$ and moment generating function $\mathcal{F}(s)$, then $g(s) = \mathcal{F}^n(s)$. In this case $g(y)$ is called the n-fold convolution of $f(x)$, and when the random variables must be non-negative

$$g(y) = \int_0^y \int_0^{y_1} \ldots \int_0^{y_{n-2}} f(y - y_1)f(y_1 - y_2) \ldots f(y_{n-1} - y_{n-2})f(y_{n-2} - x)$$

$$f(x)\, dx\, dy_{n-2} \ldots dy \tag{3-105}$$

The moment generating function for the normal distribution, which will be written $\mathfrak{N}(s; \mu, \sigma)$ is

$$\mathfrak{N}(s; \mu, \sigma) = \frac{1}{\sqrt{2\pi}\,\sigma} \int_{-\infty}^\infty e^{-sx}e^{-(1/2\sigma^2)(x-\mu)^2}\, dx$$

$$= \frac{1}{\sqrt{2\pi}\,\sigma} e^{-(1/2)(\mu/\sigma)^2} \int_{-\infty}^\infty e^{-(1/2\sigma^2)[x^2 + 2(\sigma^2 s - \mu)x]}\, dx \tag{3-106}$$

$$= \frac{1}{\sqrt{2\pi}\,\sigma} e^{-(1/2)(\mu/\sigma)^2}e^{(1/2\sigma^2)(\sigma^2 s - \mu)^2} \int_{-\infty}^\infty e^{-(1/2\sigma^2)[x + (\sigma^2 s - \mu)]^2}\, dx$$

$$= e^{(1/2)(\sigma^2 s^2 - 2\mu s)}$$

If x_1, x_2 are two independent random variables which are normally distributed with means μ_1, μ_2 and standard deviations σ_1, σ_2 respectively, then the moment generating function of $y = x_1 + x_2$ is

$$e^{(1/2)(\sigma_1{}^2 s^2 - 2\mu_1 s)} e^{(1/2)(\sigma_2{}^2 s^2 - 2\mu_2 s)} = e^{(1/2)[(\sigma_1{}^2 + \sigma_2{}^2)s^2 - 2(\mu_1 + \mu_2)s]}$$

$$= \mathfrak{N}\left(s; \mu_1 + \mu_2, \sqrt{\sigma_1^2 + \sigma_2^2}\right) \qquad (3\text{-}107)$$

Therefore, since the moment generating function uniquely defines the density function, we see that y is normally distributed with mean $\mu_1 + \mu_2$ and variance $\sigma_1^2 + \sigma_2^2$.

The moment generating function or Laplace transform for the gamma distribution, which will be written $\Upsilon(s; \alpha, \beta)$ is

$$\Upsilon(s; \alpha, \beta) = \int_0^\infty \frac{\beta(\beta x)^\alpha}{\Gamma(\alpha + 1)} e^{-\beta x} e^{-sx}\, dx = \int_0^\infty \frac{u^\alpha}{\Gamma(\alpha + 1)} e^{-[1 + (s/\beta)]u}\, du$$

$$= \frac{1}{\left(1 + \dfrac{s}{\beta}\right)^{\alpha+1}} \int_0^\infty \left(1 + \frac{s}{\beta}\right) \frac{\left[\left(1 + \dfrac{s}{\beta}\right)u\right]^\alpha}{\Gamma(\alpha + 1)} e^{-[1 + (s/\beta)]u}\, du$$

$$= \frac{1}{\left(1 + \dfrac{s}{\beta}\right)^{\alpha+1}} \qquad (3\text{-}108)$$

The above result can be used to provide another way to obtain the probability density for the time required to incur Q demands when a Poisson process generates the demands. Recall that the time between demands is exponentially distributed. The moment generating function for the exponential distribution is $1/[1 + (s/\beta)]$ as is seen by setting $\alpha = 0$ in (3-108). If the Qth demand occurs at some time t after observation on the system is begun, then t can be written $t = t_1 + t_2 + \ldots + t_Q$ where the first demand occurs at the time t_1, the second demand occurs at a time t_2 after the first demand, etc. Then each t_i is exponentially distributed with the same mean. Furthermore, the t_i are independent random variables. Thus the density function for t is the Q-fold convolution of the exponential distribution, and its moment generating function is

$$\left[\frac{1}{1 + \dfrac{s}{\beta}}\right]^Q = \Upsilon(s; Q - 1, \beta) \qquad (3\text{-}109)$$

Thus the random variable t has a gamma distribution of order Q. This same result was obtained previously in a different way.

3-10 Markov Processes Discrete in Space and Time

Consider a system which is observed only at times $t_0, t_1, t_2, \ldots$ (where $t_{r+1} = t_r + \Delta t$ and $\Delta t > 0$ is a finite constant). At these times, the system will be in one of n discrete states $j, j = 1, \ldots, n$. A specific example of the general situation just outlined will be that of an inventory system whose condition is reviewed only at discrete equally spaced intervals of time. The states of the system referred to above will be the inventory position of the system. We shall assume that if the system is in state i at time t_r, then the probability that it will be in state j at time t_{r+1} is $a_{ij} \geq 0$. We shall suppose that the a_{ij} are independent of the past history of the system and independent of time, so that the a_{ij} are constants. Since the system must be in one of the states j at time t_{r+1} we must have

$$\sum_{j=1}^{n} a_{ij} = 1 \qquad (3\text{-}110)$$

The a_{ij} are called transition probabilities, and they are the conditional probabilities of finding the system in state j at time t_{r+1} if it was in state i at time t_r.

If the system is in state i at time t_r, the probability that it is in state j at time t_{r+2} is

$$a_{ij}^{(2)} = \sum_{k=1}^{n} a_{ik}a_{kj} \qquad (3\text{-}111)$$

since from t_r to t_{r+1} it can undergo a transition from i to any state k with probability a_{ik} (which may be 0) and from state k at time t_{r+1} to state j at time t_{r+2} with probability a_{kj}. The probability of transitions from i to k to j is $a_{ik}a_{kj}$, and therefore the probability of moving from i to j from time t_r to t_{r+2} is found by summing $a_{ik}a_{kj}$ over all k.

Let $p_r(i)$ be the probability that the system is in state i at time t_r. Then $p_{r+1}(j)$ is given by

$$p_{r+1}(j) = \sum_{i=1}^{n} p_r(i)a_{ij} \qquad (3\text{-}112)$$

and from (3-111)

$$p_{r+2}(j) = \sum_{i=1}^{n} p_r(i)a_{ij}^{(2)} = \sum_{i=1}^{n}\sum_{k=1}^{n} p_r(i)a_{ik}a_{kj} = \sum_{k=1}^{n} p_{r+1}(k)a_{kj} \qquad (3\text{-}113)$$

It follows thus that if we are given the probabilities $p_0(i)$ that the system is in state i at time t_0, and the transition probabilities a_{ij}, then it is possible to compute the probabilities that the system is in state j at time $t_r, r = 1, 2, \ldots$. The type of process we have been describing is called a

Markov process which is discrete in space and time (it is also referred to as a Markov chain). It is said to be discrete in space and time because the states of the system (referred to as the space variable) are discrete, i.e., can be represented by integers, and because we are interested in the states of the system only at discrete points in time. We cannot say anything about the system at times other than t_0, t_1, t_2, ... The characteristic feature of a Markov process is that the probability that the system is in a given state at time t_{r+1} depends only on the state that it was in at time t_r, and the transition probability, and is independent of the previous history of the system (i.e., how it got to the state it is in at t_r).

It might be expected that as time goes on, the probabilities $p_r(j)$ will become less and less influenced by the initial probabilities $p_0(j)$. We shall say that the system is in a steady state if the probabilities $p_r(j)$ do not change with r, i.e.,

$$p_{r+1}(j) = p_r(j) \quad \text{for all } j$$

If a steady state exists, we shall denote by $p(j)$ the probability that in steady state the system is in state j. These probabilities can be found by writing $p(j) = p_r(j) = p_{r+1}(j)$ in (3-112) to yield the following set of n homogeneous linear equations in n unknowns

$$p(j) = \sum_{i=1}^{n} p(i)a_{ij}, \quad j = 1, \ldots, n \tag{3-114}$$

This set of equations will not uniquely determine the $p(j)$. However, since the system must be in one and only one of the states, the $p(j)$ must sum to unity, i.e.,

$$\sum_{j=1}^{n} p(j) = 1 \tag{3-115}$$

With this additional constraint, the $p(j)$ will be uniquely determined for cases of interest to us (this is proved below).

We shall in our later work only have an interest in the steady state probabilities $p(j)$, and not in the transient behavior of the system starting from some initial condition. Furthermore, we shall only be interested in Markov processes for which every state can ultimately be reached from any other state. It will not necessarily be true that every state can be reached from any given state in a single time step, but if one allows a sufficient number of steps, it will be possible to reach every other state from any given state. A Markov process of this type is called an irreducible Markov process. For such a process, there exists an integer N for each pair of indices i and j such that $a_{ij}^{(N)} > 0$, where $a_{ij}^{(N)}$ is the probability that if the system is in state i at time t_r it will be in state j at time t_{r+N}.

For an irreducible Markov process with only a finite number of states, it is a well known result from the theory of Markov processes that the $p(j)$ defined by (3-114), (3-115) exist, are unique, and each $p(j) > 0$. We shall prove this without making use of the theory of Markov processes. However, the proof does require some understanding of linear algebra, which may not be familiar to the reader. An understanding of the proof is not needed in later work. It is only necessary for the reader to recall that the proof demonstrates the uniqueness of the $p(j)$. To proceed with the proof, let the matrix $\mathbf{A} = \|a_{ij}\|$ be an nth order matrix containing the transition probabilities, and $\mathbf{p} = [p(1), \ldots, p(n)]$ be a row vector containing the $p(j)$. Then (3-114) can be written $\mathbf{p}(I_n - \mathbf{A}) = 0$ where I_n is the identity matrix of order n. By (3-110), each row of $\mathbf{A}$ sums to unity and each row of $I_n - \mathbf{A}$ sums to zero. Thus the columns of $I_n - \mathbf{A}$ are linearly dependent, and $|I_n - \mathbf{A}|$, the determinant of $I_n - \mathbf{A}$, vanishes. Thus there exist $p(j)$, not all zero, which satisfy $\mathbf{p}(I_n - \mathbf{A}) = 0$.

Let us now drop the nth equation in (3-114). The resulting set of $n - 1$ equations in n variables can be written $\mathbf{p}_{n-1}(I_{n-1} - \mathbf{A}_{n-1}) = p(n)\mathbf{a}_n$, where $\mathbf{p}_{n-1}$ is a vector containing the first $n - 1$ components of $\mathbf{p}$, I_{n-1} is the identity matrix of order $n - 1$, $\mathbf{A}_{n-1}$ is the submatrix formed from $\mathbf{A}$ by crossing off the last row and column, and $\mathbf{a}_n = [a_{n1}, \ldots, a_{n,n-1}]$. Note that at least one component of $\mathbf{a}_n$ is positive, for otherwise it would be impossible to ever leave state n. Thus at least one row of $\mathbf{A}_{n-1}$ sums to a non-negative number less than unity. From the theory of Leontief matrices, we know that $(I_{n-1} - \mathbf{A}_{n-1})^{-1}$ exists and can be written as a power series. Thus

$$\mathbf{p}_{n-1} = p(n)\mathbf{a}_n[I_{n-1} + \mathbf{A}_{n-1} + \mathbf{A}_{n-1}^2 + \ldots] \tag{3-116}$$

For a given $p(n)$, the vector $\mathbf{p}_{n-1}$ is uniquely determined. If $p(n) = 0$ all $p(j)$ vanish and hence cannot sum to unity. Thus $p(n) > 0$. When $p(n) > 0$, each component of $\mathbf{p}_{n-1}$ will be positive, since for each i and j there exists an N such that element $a_{ij}^{(N)}$ in $\mathbf{A}^N$ is positive. Hence, on applying (3-115), we see that the $p(j)$ exist, are uniquely determined, and each $p(j)$ is positive. This proves what we wanted to show.

3-11 Markov Processes Discrete in Space and Continuous in Time—Queuing

In the previous section, we assumed that the state of the system was observed only at discrete points in time. We were interested in determining the steady state probabilities that, at the time of observation, the system was in one of a finite number of different discrete states. Now we wish to study situations where the system is continually under observation and the state of the system is known at each instant of time. Again we shall assume that the states are discrete and can be represented by integers;

however, we now permit an infinite number of discrete states. We wish to be able to compute the probability that the system is in any one of the states at any instant of time, and here also we shall usually be interested only in the steady state probabilities. The assumptions in this section differ from those of the previous section in that time is now a continuous variable and we allow for an infinite number of discrete states. The material to be considered will later be applicable to what will be called transactions reporting inventory systems. Again the states will refer to inventory levels in applications which will be of interest to us.

If the system is in state i at time t, we shall denote by $f(i, t; j, \tau)$ the probability that it is in state j at time $\tau > t$. As in the previous section $f(i, t; j, \tau)$ is called a transition probability. When the process is a Markov process, then the probability $p(j; \tau)$ that the system is in state j at time τ depends only on the probabilities $p(i; t)$ that the system was in state i at time t, and the transition probabilities $f(i, t; j, \tau)$; it does not in any way depend on what has happened at times previous to t except through the $p(i; t)$. Then

$$p(j; \tau) = \sum_{i=0}^{\infty} p(i; t) f(i, t; j, \tau) \qquad (3\text{-}117)$$

where in writing (3-117) we have allowed for an infinite number of discrete states. If the system is in state i at time t, it must be in some state j at time τ. Thus it must be true that

$$\sum_{j=0}^{\infty} f(i, t; j, \tau) = 1 \qquad (3\text{-}118)$$

Given the times $t < \tau_1 < \tau_2$ and the transition probabilities

$$f(i, t; j, \tau_2), \quad f(i, t; j, \tau_1), \quad f(i, \tau_1; j, \tau_2)$$

then

$$p(j; \tau_2) = \sum_{i=0}^{\infty} p(i; t) f(i, t; j, \tau_2) = \sum_{k=0}^{\infty} p(k; \tau_1) f(k, \tau_1; j, \tau_2)$$

$$= \sum_{i=0}^{\infty} p(i; t) \left[\sum_{k=0}^{\infty} f(i, t; k, \tau_1) f(k, \tau_1; j, \tau_2) \right]$$

Thus we must have for any times $t < \tau_1 < \tau_2$

$$f(i, t; j, \tau_2) = \sum_{k=0}^{\infty} f(i, t; k, \tau_1) f(k, \tau_1; j, \tau_2) \qquad (3\text{-}119)$$

For problems of physical interest, it is usually true that as τ approaches t, $f(i, t; j, \tau)$ approaches zero when $j \neq i$ and unity when $j = i$, i.e., as

$\tau \to t$ the probability of finding a change in the state of the system also approaches zero, and the probability of finding it in the same state approaches unity. Although $f(i, t; j, \tau)$ approaches zero as $\tau \to t$ when $i \neq j$, the ratio $f(i, t; j, \tau)/(\tau - t)$ can approach a finite value different from zero, which we shall denote by $a_{ij}(t)$, i.e.,

$$\lim_{\tau \to t} \frac{f(i, t; j, \tau)}{\tau - t} = a_{ij}(t), \quad i \neq j \tag{3-120}$$

When τ differs infinitesimally from t, i.e., $\tau = t + dt$, then

$$f(i, t; j, t + dt) = \frac{f(i, t; j, t + dt)}{dt} dt = a_{ij}(t) \, dt, \quad i \neq j$$

The $a_{ij}(t) \, dt$ are called the infinitesimal transition probabilities, and the $a_{ij}(t)$ are called the transition densities. Furthermore, from (3-118)

$$f(i, t; i, t + dt) = 1 - dt \sum_{\substack{j=0 \\ j \neq i}}^{\infty} a_{ij}(t) \tag{3-121}$$

By use of the infinitesimal transition probabilities, it is possible to obtain a set of differential-difference equations which determine the state probabilities $p(i; t)$. By (3-117), (3-120), (3-121)

$$p(i; t + dt) = p(i; t) \left[1 - dt \sum_{\substack{j=0 \\ j \neq i}}^{\infty} a_{ij}(t) \right] + \sum_{\substack{j=0 \\ j \neq i}}^{\infty} p(j; t) a_{ji}(t) \, dt$$

or

$$\frac{p(i; t + dt) - p(i; t)}{dt} = -p(i; t) \sum_{\substack{j=0 \\ j \neq i}}^{\infty} a_{ij}(t) + \sum_{\substack{j=0 \\ j \neq i}}^{\infty} p(j; t) a_{ji}(t)$$

However, in the limit as dt approaches zero, the quantity on the left in the above equation becomes $dp(i; t)/dt$, so that

$$\frac{dp(i; t)}{dt} = -p(i; t) \sum_{\substack{j=0 \\ j \neq i}}^{\infty} a_{ij}(t) + \sum_{\substack{j=0 \\ j \neq i}}^{\infty} p(j; t) a_{ji}(t), \quad i = 0, 1, 2, \ldots \tag{3-122}$$

Here we have an infinite set of differential-difference equations (if there are an infinite number of states). They are differential equations with respect to time and difference equations with respect to the states. If we are given the $p(j; t_0)$ at some time t_0, we expect intuitively that the equations (3-122) will determine uniquely the $p(j; t)$ at all future times.

The cases which are the easiest to solve and which are also of practical interest are those for which Poisson processes generate transitions between states. By this it is meant that Poisson processes generate certain events such as the occurrence of demands or arrivals of orders in inventory systems. To move from state i to state j will require the occurrence of one or more of these events. Thus all the probabilities $f(i, t; j, \tau)$ will be Poisson densities, or weighted sums and products of them. The important thing to note is that $f(i, t; j, t + \Delta t)/\Delta t$ will involve Δt or a higher power of Δt and hence approaches zero as $\Delta t \rightarrow 0$ in every case except that where the transition from i to j involves only the occurrence of a single Poisson event. In this case the ratio approaches a constant μ_{ij} which is the mean rate at which the Poisson event under consideration occurs. Thus all the a_{ij} will be zero except for transitions between states involving only the occurrence of a single Poisson event. We leave the detailed proof for the general case to Problem 3-25. The method of proof will be illustrated for a particular example later. Therefore, we can write

$$
a_{ij} = \begin{cases} \mu_{ij} \text{ (a constant)} & \text{if a transition from } i \text{ to } j \text{ involves the occurrence} \\ & \text{of only a single Poisson event} \\ 0 & \text{if a transition from } i \text{ to } j \text{ requires the occurrence} \\ & \text{of more than one Poisson event} \qquad \text{(3-123)} \end{cases}
$$

where $1/\mu_{ij}$ is the mean time between transitions from i to j. Note that the a_{ij} do not depend on t. For most systems discussed in subsequent chapters, it is true that for any given, fixed i, there will be only one or two values of j for which $a_{ij} \neq 0$, i.e., transitions from state i can be made only to one or two other states in an infinitesimal time interval of length dt.

The equations (3-122) tell how the state probabilities $p(i; t)$ change with time. Usually we shall be interested in cases for which the $p(i; t)$ tend toward steady state values which do not change with time. These steady state values will be denoted by $p(i)$. Since the steady state probabilities must satisfy (3-122), and since they are independent of time, i.e., $dp(i)/dt = 0$, then we see from (3-122) that the steady state probabilities must satisfy

$$
p(i) \sum_{\substack{j=0 \\ j \neq i}}^{\infty} a_{ij} = \sum_{\substack{j=0 \\ j \neq i}}^{\infty} p(j) a_{ji}, \quad i = 0, 1, 2, \ldots, j; \quad \sum_{j=0}^{\infty} p(j) = 1 \quad \text{(3-124)}
$$

When transitions are generated by Poisson processes, the a_{ij} are given by (3-123). Here we have a set of difference equations (perhaps an infinite set) to solve for the state probabilities.

The equations (3-124) can be given a simple intuitive explanation. If the probability that the system is in state i is to remain a constant, then the probability that the system leaves state i in time dt must be exactly equal to the probability that the system moves from some other state to state i.

The probability that the system leaves state i in time dt is $p(i) \sum_{j \neq i} a_{ij} \, dt$, and the probability that it changes from some other state to i is $\sum_{j \neq i} p(j) a_{ji} \, dt$. On equating these two terms and cancelling dt, we obtain (3-124) which may be called the balance equations. The left-hand side of (3-124) can be interpreted as the rate of change of $p(i)$ arising from transitions out of state i, and the right-hand side the rate of change of $p(i)$ from transitions into $p(i)$. As noted above, these two rates must be equal.

Markov processes continuous in time and discrete in space which are concerned with systems that service in some way randomly generated demands are often referred to as queuing problems. Hence, when the theory is applied to inventory systems, we often say that queuing theory is being applied to study the inventory system.

It is important to note that the theory developed above can easily be generalized to systems where the description of each state requires the specification of two or more non-negative integers rather than merely a single integer. For example, suppose that two non-negative integers are required to describe each state. Then let $p(i, j; t)$ be the probability that the system is in state (i, j) at time t, and $a_{ij;mn}(t) \, dt$ be the probability that if the system is in state (i, j) at time t, it will be in state (m, n) at time $t + dt$. With these definitions, (3-122) becomes

$$\frac{dp(i, j; t)}{dt} = -p(i, j; t) \sum_{\substack{m=0 \\ ij \neq mn}}^{\infty} \sum_{n=0}^{\infty} a_{ij;mn}(t)$$

$$+ \sum_{\substack{m=0 \\ ij \neq mn}}^{\infty} \sum_{n=0}^{\infty} p(m, n; t) a_{mn;ij}(t) \qquad (3\text{-}125)$$

EXAMPLE Perhaps the simplest example of a queuing model is that of a single service facility (perhaps a repair station) in which the time required for service is a random variable with an exponential distribution, i.e., the probability that service takes longer than t is $e^{-\mu t}$ (a Poisson process generates the service times). The arrivals of customers at the service facility are also assumed to be generated by a Poisson process, the mean arrival rate being λ. A customer arrives at the facility and goes into service immediately if the facility is not busy; otherwise the customer waits in line. Customers are serviced in order of arrival. Let the states refer to the number of customers in the system, i.e., in service or in line (note that only one customer can be in service). Thus there are an infinite number of states. We shall assume that customers arrive one at a time. If the system is in state i at time t (i.e. i customers in the system), then it can be in state $j > i$ at time τ if one of the following sets of events occurs: 1) there are $j - i$ arrivals in the time $\tau - t$ and no units are serviced, 2) there are

$j - i + 1$ arrivals and one unit completes service, 3) there are $j - i + 2$ arrivals and 2 units complete service, etc. Thus

$$f(i, t; j, \tau) = \sum_{k=0}^{\infty} p[j - i + k; \lambda(\tau - t)]p[k|j - i + k, i, \mu, \tau - t], \quad j > i$$

where

$$p[k|j - i + k, i, \mu, \tau - t]$$

is the conditional probability that k customers are serviced in time $\tau - t$ given that there were $j - i - k$ arrivals, that i were in the system originally, and that μ is the mean servicing rate. However

$$\lim_{\Delta t \to 0} \frac{p(x; \lambda \Delta t)}{\Delta t} = \begin{cases} \lambda, & x = 1 \\ 0, & x = 2, 3 \ldots \end{cases}$$

Thus, when $j > i$, $a_{ij} = 0$ unless $j = i + 1$. Furthermore

$$a_{i,i-1} = \lambda p[0|1, i, \mu, 0]$$

The conditional probability that no units are serviced in a time interval of length 0 is 1, since even if a customer is in service, the probability that a time $> t$ will be required to complete service is $e^{-\mu t}$. Consequently, we conclude that

$$a_{ij} = \begin{cases} \lambda, & j = i + 1 \\ 0, & \text{all other } j > i \end{cases}$$

Similarly, if $j < i$

$$a_{ij} = \begin{cases} \mu, & j = i - 1 \\ 0, & \text{all other } j < i \end{cases}$$

Thus we have proved for this problem that the a_{ij} are zero except for transitions to states which involve the occurrence of just a single Poisson event, i.e., an arrival or the completion of service, so that transitions in the time dt can occur only to adjacent states. The states of the system and the allowable transitions can be represented in a diagram such as Fig. 3-8.

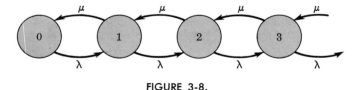

FIGURE 3-8.

We can immediately write down the balance equations (3-124) for the steady state probabilities $p(j)$ in this special case; they are

$$\mu p(1) = \lambda p(0); \quad \mu p(n+1) + \lambda p(n-1) = (\lambda + \mu)p(n), \quad n = 1, 2, \ldots$$

Then if $\rho = \lambda/\mu$ we obtain, on sequential computation beginning with $p(1) = \rho p(0)$, $p(n) = \rho^n p(0)$, $n = 1, 2, \ldots$. Now it must be true that the state probabilities sum to unity, i.e.,

$$p(0) \sum_{j=0}^{\infty} \rho^j = p(0)\left[\frac{1}{1-\rho}\right] = 1, \quad \rho < 1$$

Thus if $\rho < 1$, the steady state probabilities are distributed according to the geometric distribution, i.e.,

$$p(j) = \rho^j(1-\rho), \quad j = 0, 1, 2, \ldots$$

If $\rho \geq 1$, i.e., the mean servicing rate is not greater than the mean arrival rate, there does not exist any steady state and the expected length of the line is continually increasing.

3-12 Other Types of Markov Processes

There are two other types of Markov processes which are of interest. One is that which is discrete in time and continuous in the space (state) variable, and the other is that which is continuous in both space and time. We shall discuss very briefly Markov processes which are discrete in time and continuous in space, but shall do no more than merely mention something about the nature of those continuous in space and time.

To introduce Markov processes which are discrete in time and continuous in space, we imagine a system which is observed only at times t_r, $r = 0, 1, 2, \ldots$, where $t_r = t_{r-1} + \Delta t$, $\Delta t > 0$ being a finite constant, the state of which can be described by a continuous non-negative variable x. Let $g_r(x)\, dx$ be the probability that the state of the system lies between x and $x + dx$ at time t_r, and $f(x|y)\, dx$ be the probability that the state of the system lies between x and $x + dx$ at time $t_{r+1} > t_r$ given that the state of the system was y at time t_r. Then

$$g_{r+1}(x) = \int_0^{\infty} f(x|y)g_r(y)\, dy \tag{3-126}$$

If a steady state density $g(x)$ exists such that $g(x)\, dx$ is the steady state probability that the system lies between x and $x + dx$, then $g(x)$ is given by

$$g(x) = \int_0^{\infty} f(x|y)g(y)\, dy \tag{3-127}$$

Equation (3-127) is a homogeneous Fredholm integral equation. In general, the solution of such an equation can be quite difficult. Later, in our discussion of periodic review inventory systems, we shall have occasion to solve (3-127) in an especially simple case.

Markov processes, which are continuous in space and time, are often referred to as diffusion processes. The mathematical analysis of such systems is more complicated than those we have studied above, since the determination of the state probabilities involves the solution of partial differential equations. By use of Markov processes which are continuous in space and time, it is possible to develop a model for generating demands, in the case where demand is assumed to be a continuous random variable, along the same lines as that of the Poisson process for discrete demands. The result is a normal distribution with mean λt and variance Dt, where λ is the mean rate of demand and D is a constant which can be specified arbitrarily. We shall not go through the analysis, since the notion of a continuous demand variable will be introduced in another way.

3-13 Properties of the Poisson Distribution

We shall make use of the Poisson distribution quite frequently in later chapters. In Appendix 3 are tabulated a group of properties of the Poisson distribution which we shall have need for. This section will be devoted to showing how a number of these properties are derived. The remaining derivations will be left to the problems. Recall that the definition of the Poisson probability density is given by (3-13). Many of the relations will be expressed in terms of the complementary cumulative function

$$P(x; \mu) = \sum_{j=x}^{\infty} p(j; \mu) \tag{3-128}$$

rather than the cumulative function. This is done because the more complete tables of the Poisson distribution [2,7] tabulate the complementary cumulative function rather than the cumulative, and also because, if computations are being made with a digital computer, it is often easier to evaluate $P(x; \mu)$ rather than the cumulative function. The purpose of the derivations to follow is to express all relations involving the Poisson distribution directly in terms of $p(x; \mu)$ and $P(x; \mu)$ so that numerical computations can be made easily using the tables in [2,7]. Even when the computations are to be made on a digital computer, it will usually be desirable to make these transformations, since the resulting expressions will be easier to handle on the computer than the expressions in their original form [which may involve sums of the $P(j; \mu)$ or integrals over time of the $p(j; \mu)$ or $P(j; \mu)$]. The relations derived in the following paragraphs will hold for all non-negative integers r provided that we use the convention $p(j; \mu) = 0$ and $P(j; \mu) = 1$ when j is a negative integer. Even though r is to be non-negative, it is possible in some of the expressions to encounter negative arguments for $p(j; \mu)$ and $P(j; \mu)$ if r is small enough. The expressions will be correct in such cases if the above convention is used.

From (3-13)

$$xp(x; \mu) = \frac{x\mu^x}{x!} e^{-x} = \mu \frac{\mu^{x-1}}{(x-1)!} e^{-x}$$

$$= \mu p(x-1; \mu), \quad x = 1, 2, \ldots$$

(3-129)

This is property 1 of Appendix 3. In the future we shall refer to the properties as, for example, A3-5, which means property 5 of Appendix 3.

Sums of the following sort are often needed

$$\mu_m(r) = \sum_{j=r}^{\infty} j^m p(j; \mu), \quad m = 0, 1, 2, \ldots$$

(3-130)

An especially easy way to reduce such sums to a simple form is through the use of a recurrence relation. Note that

$$\mu_m(r) = \sum_{j=r}^{\infty} j^m p(j; \mu) = \mu \sum_{j=r}^{\infty} j^{m-1} p(j-1; \mu)$$

$$= \mu \sum_{k=r-1}^{\infty} (k+1)^{m-1} p(k; \mu) = \mu \sum_{k=r-1}^{\infty} \sum_{n=0}^{m-1} \binom{m-1}{n} k^n p(k; \mu)$$

$$= \mu \sum_{n=0}^{m-1} \binom{m-1}{n} \mu_n(r-1), \quad m = 1, 2, \ldots$$

(3-131)

This is A3-2. In particular

$$\mu_1(r) = \sum_{j=r}^{\infty} j p(j; \mu) = \mu \mu_0(r-1) = \mu P(r-1; \mu)$$

(3-132)

which is A3-3.

In determining the expected number of backorders for some of the future models to be discussed, it is necessary to evaluate numerically the expression

$$\sum_{j=r}^{\infty} (j-r) p(j; \mu)$$

This can be converted to a form which is easy to evaluate by noting that

$$\sum_{j=r}^{\infty} (j - r)p(j; \mu) = \sum_{j=r}^{\infty} jp(j; \mu) - rP(r; \mu)$$

$$= \mu P(r - 1; \mu) - rP(r; \mu) \tag{3-133}$$

by (3-132). This is A3-10.

We also have need for sums of the form

$$\Omega_m(r) = \sum_{j=r}^{\infty} j^m P(j; \mu)$$

These are also most easily reduced to computable form through the development of a recurrence relation. To obtain such a relation note that

$$\sum_{j=r}^{\infty} [(j - 1)^{m+1} - j^{m+1}]P(j; \mu)$$

$$= (r - 1)^{m+1}P(r; \mu) - r^{m+1}p(r; \mu) - (r + 1)^{m+1}p(r + 1; \mu) - \cdots$$

$$= (r - 1)^{m+1}P(r; \mu) - \mu_{m+1}(r) \tag{3-134}$$

where $\mu_{m+1}(r)$ is given by (3-130). Also, expanding by the binomial theorem, we obtain

$$\sum_{j=r}^{\infty} [(j - 1)^{m+1} - j^{m+1}]P(j; \mu)$$

$$= \sum_{j=r}^{\infty} \sum_{i=0}^{m} (-1)^{m+1-i} \binom{m + 1}{i} j^i P(j; \mu) \tag{3-135}$$

Equating (3-134), (3-135), we find that

$$\Omega_m(r) = \frac{1}{m + 1} \left[\sum_{i=0}^{m-1} (-1)^{m+1-i} \binom{m + 1}{i} \Omega_i(r) \right.$$

$$\left. + \mu_{m+1}(r) - (r - 1)^{m+1}P(r; \mu) \right], \quad m \geq 1 \tag{3-136}$$

which is A3-7.

In order to use (3-136) we must evaluate

$$\Omega_0(r) = \sum_{j=r}^{\infty} P(j; \mu) \tag{3-137}$$

This is easily done by writing $\Omega_0(r)$ as follows

$$\Omega_0(r) = p(r; \mu) + p(r + 1; \mu) + p(r + 2; \mu) + \ldots$$
$$p(r + 1; \mu) + p(r + 2; \mu) + \ldots$$
$$p(r + 2; \mu) + \ldots$$

$$= p(r; \mu) + 2p(r + 1; \mu) + 3p(r + 2; \mu) + \ldots$$

$$= \sum_{j=r}^{\infty} (j - r + 1)p(j; \mu) = \mu P(r - 1; \mu) + (1 - r)P(r; \mu) \quad (3\text{-}138)$$

from (3-133). This is A3-6.

By use of (3-138), (3-136), (3-131), and (3-132) we see that

$$\Omega_1(r) = \sum_{j=r}^{\infty} jP(j; \mu) = \frac{1}{2} [\Omega_0(r) + \mu_2(r) - (r - 1)^2 P(r; \mu)]$$

$$= \frac{\mu}{2} P(r - 1; \mu) + \frac{(1 - r)}{2} P(r; \mu) + \frac{\mu}{2} P(r - 1; \mu) + \frac{\mu^2}{2} P(r - 2; \mu)$$

$$- \frac{(r - 1)^2}{2} P(r; \mu)$$

$$= \frac{\mu^2}{2} P(r - 2; \mu) + \mu P(r - 1; \mu) - \frac{r(r - 1)}{2} P(r; \mu) \quad (3\text{-}139)$$

This is A3-8.

Several integrals over time involving the Poisson distribution will also be needed. The simplest of these is

$$\int_0^T p(r; \lambda t) \, dt = \int_0^T \frac{(\lambda t)^r}{r!} e^{-\lambda t} \, dt = \frac{1}{\lambda} \int_0^{\lambda T} \frac{x^r}{r!} e^{-x} \, dx$$

$$= \frac{1}{\lambda} \left[\frac{x^{r+1}}{(r + 1)!} e^{-x} \Big|_0^{\lambda T} + \int_0^{\lambda T} \frac{x^{r+1}}{(r + 1)!} e^{-x} \, dx \right] \quad (3\text{-}140)$$

$$= \frac{1}{\lambda} P(r + 1; \lambda T)$$

which follows from repeated integration by parts. This is A3-16. It immediately follows that

$$\int_0^T t^n p(r; \lambda t) \, dt = \int_0^T t^n \frac{(\lambda t)^r}{r!} e^{-\lambda t} \, dt = \frac{1}{\lambda^{n+1}} \frac{(n + r)!}{r!} \int_0^T \frac{x^{n+r}}{(n + r)!} e^{-x} \, dx$$

$$= \frac{1}{\lambda^{n+1}} \frac{(n + r)!}{r!} P(n + r + 1; \lambda T), \quad n = 0, 1, 2, \ldots \quad (3\text{-}141)$$

from (3-140). This is A3-17.

Finally

$$\int_0^T t^n P(r; \lambda t)\, dt$$

$$= \frac{t^{n+1}}{n+1} P(r; \lambda t)\Big|_0^T - \lambda \int_0^T \frac{t^{n+1}}{n+1} p(r-1; \lambda t)\, dt \qquad (3\text{-}142)$$

$$= \frac{T^{n+1}}{n+1} P(r; \lambda T) - \frac{1}{\lambda^{n+1}} \frac{(n+r)!}{(n+1)(r-1)!} P(n+r+1; \lambda T)$$

on integration by parts setting $du = t^n\, dt$, along with the use of A3-15 and (3-141). This is A3-19.

3-14 The Normal Distribution

The normal density function $n(x; \mu, \sigma)$ is defined by (3-22). The probability that the random variable x lies in the interval $x_1 \le x \le x_2$ is given by the integral of $n(x; \mu, \sigma)$ from x_1 to x_2. In (3-22), μ is the expected value of x and σ^2 is the variance of x. A normal distribution with $\mu = 0$ and $\sigma = 1$ is called the standardized normal distribution, and its density function given by (3-24) will always be denoted by $\phi(w)$. The complementary cumulative of $\phi(w)$ is

$$\Phi(w) = \frac{1}{\sqrt{2\pi}} \int_w^\infty e^{-y^2/2}\, dy = \int_w^\infty \phi(y)\, dy \qquad (3\text{-}143)$$

Almost all handbooks of mathematical tables [2, for example] provide tables of $\phi(w)$ and $\Phi(w)$ (or a function from which $\Phi(w)$ can be easily computed).

Given a table of $\phi(w)$, $\Phi(w)$, it is easy to make computations with the normal distribution. Note that

$$n(x; \mu, \sigma) = \frac{1}{\sigma} \phi\left(\frac{x-\mu}{\sigma}\right) = \frac{1}{\sqrt{2\pi}\,\sigma} e^{-(1/2\sigma^2)(x-\mu)^2} \qquad (3\text{-}144)$$

and

$$\int_{x_1}^{x_2} n(x; \mu, \sigma)\, dx = \int_{w_1}^{w_2} \phi(w)\, dw = \Phi\left(\frac{x_1-\mu}{\sigma}\right) - \Phi\left(\frac{x_2-\mu}{\sigma}\right) \qquad (3\text{-}145)$$

where $w = (x-\mu)/\sigma$.

It is often easier to work analytically with models of inventory systems if all variables can be treated as continuous. This allows one to eliminate the problems caused by discreteness and to take derivatives instead of dealing with differences, etc. In many cases the demand rate for an inventory system will be sufficiently high that the problems caused by discreteness can be ignored and all variables can be treated as continuous. When demand is treated as continuous, the most frequently used distribution to describe the quantity demanded in a given time is the normal distribution. There are several reasons why the normal distribution holds a central place in working with continuous random variables representing the demands on the system. One is that the normal distribution is especially easy to work with and is well tabulated. Another and more important reason is that empirical studies have shown that, quite often, the normal distribution seems to approximate very well the demand distributions over the relevant time intervals which are encountered in practice. A final theoretical reason for the importance of the normal distribution is that all the distributions studied in this chapter, the binomial, negative binomial, Poisson, gamma, and stuttering Poisson approach, as the mean of each of the distributions approaches infinity, a normal distribution whose mean and variance are the mean and variance of the appropriate distribution under consideration. We shall not prove this theorem since in itself it is not of great interest to us. The more important questions are how fast each of the distributions approaches the normal distribution and how much error can be involved if the normal distribution is used to approximate one of these distributions with a given mean and variance. These questions are in general quite difficult to answer (in fact they have not been answered completely), and we shall not attempt to present any general discussion of them.

It is important, however, to recognize that for large means, the Poisson distribution can be approximated by the normal, since tables of the Poisson distribution are available only up to $\mu = 100$. For larger μ values, the normal approximation must be used. It may be desirable to say a little more about the normal approximation to the Poisson, because at first glance it may not be clear what is meant, inasmuch as the Poisson distribution is discrete and the normal distribution is continuous.

Recall that $p(x; \mu)$ is the Poisson probability of exactly x when μ is the mean. For a given μ, a plot of $p(x; \mu)$ could be represented by a series of vertical lines as shown in Fig. 3-9. Now it is possible to represent probability as areas in Fig. 3-9 also if we draw in rectangles as shown. The length of the base of each rectangle is unity and it extends from $x - \frac{1}{2}$ to $x + \frac{1}{2}$. The probability of x is then the area of the rectangle which includes x since the length of the base of the rectangle is unity and its height is $p(x; \mu)$. Thus we can write

$$p(x; \mu) = p(x; \mu)\,\Delta x; \quad P(x; \mu) = \sum_{y=x}^{\infty} p(y; \mu)\,\Delta y$$

where $\Delta x = \Delta y = 1$ is the length of the base of the rectangle in Fig. 3-9.

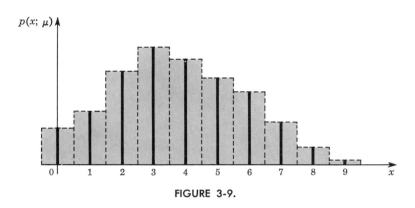

FIGURE 3-9.

Note that $p(x; \mu)$ is the area under the curve from $x - \frac{1}{2}$ to $x + \frac{1}{2}$, and $P(x; \mu)$ is the area under the curve from $x - \frac{1}{2}$ to ∞.

The theorem stated above says that as $\mu \to \infty$ for the Poisson distribution, the broken curve outlining the area of Fig. 3-9 approaches a normal curve and

$$p(x; \mu) \to n(x; \mu, \sqrt{\mu}); \quad P(x; \mu) \to \Phi\left(\frac{x - \mu}{\sqrt{\mu}}\right) \qquad (3\text{-}146)$$

Note that the mean and variance of the normal distribution are the same as the mean and variance of $p(x; \mu)$.

There is one other point related to approximating the Poisson distribution with the normal which deserves attention. Recall that $P(0; \mu) = 1$. Hence if we are approximating $P(x; \mu)$ by $\Phi(x - \mu/\sqrt{\mu})$, then we are saying that to the accuracy required in the problem, we can assume that

$$\Phi\left(\frac{-\mu}{\sqrt{\mu}}\right) = 1$$

i.e., the area under the normal curve to the left of $x = 0$ is negligible. This will of course become closer and closer to being correct as μ increases. This point will arise a number of times in later work.

When approximating $p(x; \mu)$ with the normal distribution for finite μ, increased accuracy can be obtained over using (3-146) if one notes that in Fig. 3-9, $p(x; \mu)$ is the area from $x - \frac{1}{2}$ to $x + \frac{1}{2}$ and $P(x; \mu)$ is the area from $x - \frac{1}{2}$ to infinity. Thus for finite μ, more suitable approximations are

$$\begin{aligned} p(x; \mu) &= \frac{1}{\sqrt{\mu}} \int_{x-(1/2)}^{x+(1/2)} \phi\left(\frac{y - \mu}{\sqrt{\mu}}\right) dy \\ &= \Phi\left(\frac{x - \frac{1}{2} - \mu}{\sqrt{\mu}}\right) - \Phi\left(\frac{x + \frac{1}{2} - \mu}{\sqrt{\mu}}\right) \end{aligned} \qquad (3\text{-}147)$$

$$P(x; \mu) = \Phi\left(\frac{x - \frac{1}{2} - \mu}{\sqrt{\mu}}\right) \tag{3-148}$$

Often it is suggested that the normal approximation to the Poisson will be sufficiently accurate whenever $\mu \geq 25$. One must be somewhat careful of what one means by sufficiently accurate, since the error depends on the range of x which is of interest. The approximation is best for x near the mean and becomes progressively worse as x increase towards infinity (i.e., as one moves out on the tail of the distribution). However, for practical work, one usually need not be overly concerned with precisely how well the normal distribution approximates the Poisson, since the Poisson distribution itself will only be an approximate representation of the real world demand distribution. Probably, for most practical applications, the normal approximation to the Poisson will give sufficient accuracy if $\mu \geq 25$. However, since Poisson tables [7] are available which go up to $\mu = 100$, there is no necessity for using the normal approximation until $\mu \geq 100$.

Because of (3-146) we see that as $t \to \infty$

$$p(x; \lambda t) \to \frac{1}{\sqrt{2\pi\lambda}\ t^{1/2}}\ e^{-(1/2)(x - \lambda t)^2/\lambda t} \tag{3-149}$$

In the event that the process generating demands is an Erlang of order n instead of Poisson, or if the process generating demands is Poisson but the number of units demanded per demand is a random variable, or if the lead time is a random variable and we are dealing with the marginal distribution of lead time demand, then it will still be true that the density function for the number of demands in a time t approaches a normal distribution with mean λt where λ is the mean rate at which demands occur. For this more general case, though, the variance need not be λt. It can, however, be written Dt where D is a number which may differ from λ. The proportionality of the variance to time remains unchanged. In general, then, when representing the demand in a time t by a normal distribution, we shall write the density function as

$$n(x; \lambda t, \sqrt{Dt}) = \frac{1}{\sqrt{2\pi D}\ t^{1/2}}\ e^{-(1/2)(x - \lambda t)^2/D_t} \tag{3-150}$$

and if the normal density is an approximation to the Poisson, $D = \lambda$.

3-15 Properties of the Normal Distribution

We shall need certain properties of the normal distribution, just as the corresponding properties of the Poisson distribution were needed, to convert expressions which will be obtained later to terms involving only ϕ and Φ directly so that numerical computations can be made. The properties needed are presented in Appendix 4. The derivation of several of the properties will be given here. The derivations of the others will be left for the problems. We see immediately that

$$\int_r^\infty x\phi(x)\, dx = \frac{1}{\sqrt{2\pi}} \int_r^\infty xe^{-x^2/2}\, dx = \frac{1}{\sqrt{2\pi}} \int_{r^2/2}^\infty e^{-v}\, dv$$
$$= \frac{1}{\sqrt{2\pi}} e^{-r^2/2} = \phi(r) \tag{3-151}$$

which is A4-1, and

$$\int_r^\infty x^2\phi(x)\, dx = \frac{1}{\sqrt{2\pi}} \int_r^\infty x(xe^{-x^2/2})\, dx$$
$$= \frac{1}{\sqrt{2\pi}} \left[-xe^{-x^2/2} \Big|_r^\infty + \int_r^\infty e^{-x^2/2}\, dx \right] \tag{3-152}$$
$$= \Phi(r) + r\phi(r)$$

which is A4-3.

Consider next the evaluation of

$$\int_r^\infty x^n\Phi(x)\, dx, \quad n = 0, 1, 2, \ldots$$

On integration by parts, letting $dv = x^n\, dx$, we obtain

$$\int_r^\infty x^n\Phi(x)\, dx = -\frac{1}{n+1} r^{n+1}\Phi(r)$$
$$+ \frac{1}{n+1} \int_r^\infty x^{n+1}\phi(x)\, dx, \quad n = 0, 1, 2, \ldots \tag{3-153}$$

which is A4-5. From (3-153) it immediately follows that

$$\int_r^\infty \Phi(x)\, dx = \phi(r) - r\Phi(r) \tag{3-154}$$

by (3-151). This is A4-6. Furthermore

$$\int_r^\infty x\Phi(x)\, dx = -\tfrac{1}{2}r^2\Phi(r) + \tfrac{1}{2}[\Phi(r) + r\phi(r)]$$
$$= \tfrac{1}{2}[(1 - r^2)\Phi(r) + r\phi(r)] \tag{3-155}$$

from (3-152). This is A4-7.

We shall also have need for integrals of the form

$$J_n(x, T_1, T_2) = \int_{T_1}^{T_2} \frac{t^n}{\sqrt{2\pi D}\; t^{1/2}}\, e^{-(1/2)(x-\lambda t)^2/Dt}\, dt$$

$$= \int_{T_1}^{T_2} \frac{t^n}{(Dt)^{1/2}}\, \phi\left[\frac{x-\lambda t}{(Dt)^{1/2}}\right] dt, \quad T_1, T_2 > 0 \quad (3\text{-}156)$$

where n is an integer. Consider first $J_0(x, T_1, T_2)$. This integral is some-what more difficult to evaluate than those studied above. If

$$y(t) = \frac{x-\lambda t}{(Dt)^{1/2}}; \quad dy = \left[-\frac{\lambda}{(Dt)^{1/2}} - \frac{(x-\lambda t)}{2D^{1/2}t^{3/2}}\right] dt \quad (3\text{-}157)$$

Then

$$J_0(x, T_1, T_2) = \int_{T_1}^{T_2} \frac{1}{(Dt)^{1/2}}\, \phi\left[\frac{x-\lambda t}{(Dt)^{1/2}}\right] dt$$

$$= -\frac{1}{\lambda} \int_{T_1}^{T_2} \phi\left[\frac{x-\lambda t}{(Dt)^{1/2}}\right]\left[-\frac{\lambda}{(Dt)^{1/2}} - \frac{(x-\lambda t)}{2D^{1/2}t^{3/2}}\right] dt$$

$$- \frac{1}{\lambda} \int_{T_1}^{T_2} \frac{(x-\lambda t)}{2D^{1/2}t^{3/2}}\, \phi\left[\frac{x-\lambda t}{(Dt)^{1/2}}\right] dt \qquad (3\text{-}158)$$

$$= -\frac{1}{\lambda} \int_{y(T_1)}^{y(T_2)} \phi(w)\, dw - \frac{1}{2\lambda} \int_{T_1}^{T_2} \frac{y(t)}{t}\, \phi[y(t)]\, dt$$

We now observe that

$$\frac{\partial J_0(x, T_1, T_2)}{\partial x} = -\frac{1}{D} \int_{T_1}^{T_2} \frac{y(t)}{t}\, \phi[y(t)]\, dt \qquad (3\text{-}159)$$

Substitution of (3-159) into (3-158) yields

$$J_0(x, T_1, T_2) = \frac{1}{\lambda}\, \Phi\left[\frac{x-\lambda t}{(Dt)^{1/2}}\right]\Bigg|_{T_1}^{T_2} + \frac{D}{2\lambda}\, \frac{\partial J_0(x, T_1, T_2)}{\partial x} \qquad (3\text{-}160)$$

To determine J_0 we must solve the differential equation (3-160). Multi-ply both sides of (3-160) by $e^{-(2\lambda x/D)}$. Then we see that

$$\frac{\partial}{\partial x}\left[e^{-(2\lambda x/D)} J_0\right] = -\frac{2}{D}\, e^{-(2\lambda x/D)} \Phi\left[\frac{x-\lambda t}{(Dt)^{1/2}}\right]\Bigg|_{T_1}^{T_2} \qquad (3\text{-}161)$$

On integrating both sides from x to ∞ and noting that

$$\lim_{x\to\infty} e^{-(2\lambda x/D)} J_0(x, T_1, T_2) = 0$$

we obtain

$$J_0(x, T_1, T_2) =$$

$$\frac{2}{D} e^{2\lambda x/D} \int_x^\infty e^{-(2\lambda\xi/D)} \left\{ \Phi\left[\frac{\xi - \lambda T_2}{(DT_2)^{1/2}}\right] - \Phi\left[\frac{\xi - \lambda T_1}{(DT_1)^{1/2}}\right] \right\} d\xi \quad (3\text{-}162)$$

Now

$$\int_x^\infty e^{-(2\lambda\xi/D)} \Phi\left[\frac{\xi - \lambda T}{(DT)^{1/2}}\right] d\xi = \int_x^\infty \int_{(\xi-\lambda T)/(DT)^{1/2}}^\infty e^{-(2\lambda\xi/D)} \phi(\rho)\, d\rho\, d\xi \quad (3\text{-}163)$$

can be considered to be a double integral integrated over the shaded area
of the $\rho\xi$-plane shown in Fig. 3-10. As written in (3-163), the integral is
found by summing elementary strips parallel to the ρ axis. The integral
can be evaluated by adding up elementary strips parallel to the ξ axis, like
the one shown in Fig. 3-10. The area of one of these strips is

$$\phi(\rho)\, d\rho \int_x^{(DT)^{1/2}\rho + \lambda T} e^{-(2\lambda\xi/D)}\, d\xi$$

$$= \phi(\rho)\, d\rho \left[\frac{D}{2\lambda} e^{-(2\lambda x/D)} - \frac{D}{2\lambda} e^{-(2\lambda^2 T/D)} e^{-(2\lambda T^{1/2}\rho/D^{1/2})} \right]$$

so

$$\int_x^\infty e^{-(2\lambda\xi/D)} \Phi\left[\frac{\xi - \lambda T}{(DT)^{1/2}}\right] d\xi$$

$$= \frac{D}{2\lambda} e^{-(2\lambda x/D)} \Phi\left[\frac{x - \lambda T}{(DT)^{1/2}}\right] - \frac{D}{2\lambda} e^{-(2\lambda^2 T/D)} \int_{(x-\lambda T)/(DT)^{1/2}}^\infty e^{-(2\lambda T^{1/2}\rho/D^{1/2})} \phi(\rho)\, d\rho$$

$$(3\text{-}164)$$

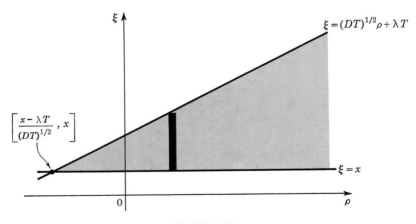

FIGURE 3-10.

But

$$\int_{(x-\lambda T)/(DT)^{1/2}}^{\infty} e^{-(2\lambda T^{1/2}\rho/D^{1/2})}\phi(\rho)\,d\rho$$

$$= \int_{(x-\lambda T)/(DT)^{1/2}}^{\infty} \frac{1}{\sqrt{2\pi}}\, e^{-(1/2)[\rho^2+(4\lambda T^{1/2}/D^{1/2})\rho+(4\lambda^2 T/D)]} e^{2\lambda^2 T/D}\,d\rho$$

$$= e^{2\lambda^2 T/D}\int_{(x-\lambda T)/(DT)^{1/2}}^{\infty} \frac{1}{\sqrt{2\pi}}\, e^{-(1/2)[\rho+(2\lambda T/(DT)^{1/2})]^2}\,d\rho$$

$$= e^{2\lambda^2 T/D}\Phi\left[\frac{x+\lambda T}{(DT)^{1/2}}\right] \tag{3-165}$$

On substitution of (3-165) into (3-164) and (3-164) into (3-162), we obtain finally

$$J_0(x, T_1, T_2) = W_0(x, T_2) - W_0(x, T_1)$$

where

$$W_0(x, T) = \frac{1}{\lambda}\,\Phi\left[\frac{x-\lambda T}{(DT)^{1/2}}\right] - \frac{1}{\lambda}e^{2\lambda x/D}\Phi\left[\frac{x+\lambda T}{(DT)^{1/2}}\right] \tag{3-166}$$

which is A4-9.

Consider next the evaluation of $J_1(x, T_1, T_2)$. As a first step, we integrate $J_0(x, T_1, T_2)$ by parts writing $dv = t^{-1/2}\,dt$. This yields

$$J_0(x, T_1, T_2) =$$

$$\frac{2t^{1/2}}{D^{1/2}}\phi\left[\frac{x-\lambda t}{(Dt)^{1/2}}\right]\Bigg|_{T_1}^{T_2} - 2\int_{T_1}^{T_2}\frac{t^{1/2}}{D^{1/2}}\left[\frac{(x-\lambda t)\lambda}{Dt} + \frac{1}{2}\frac{(x-\lambda t)^2}{Dt^2}\right]\phi\left[\frac{x-\lambda t}{(Dt)^{1/2}}\right]dt$$

$$= \frac{2t^{1/2}}{D^{1/2}}\phi\left[\frac{x-\lambda t}{(Dt)^{1/2}}\right]\Bigg|_{T_1}^{T_2} + \frac{\lambda^2}{D}\,J_1(x, T_1, T_2) - \frac{x^2}{D}\int_{T_1}^{T_2}\frac{t^{-3/2}}{D^{1/2}}\phi\left[\frac{x-\lambda t}{(Dt)^{1/2}}\right]dt \tag{3-167}$$

Next observe from (3-159) that

$$\frac{\partial J_0(x, T_1, T_2)}{\partial x} = -\frac{x}{D}\int_{T_1}^{T_2}\frac{t^{-3/2}}{D^{1/2}}\phi\left[\frac{x-\lambda t}{(Dt)^{1/2}}\right]dt + \frac{\lambda}{D}\,J_0(x, T_1, T_2) \tag{3-168}$$

After substitution of (3-168) into (3-167) and solving for $J_1(x, T_1, T_2)$, we obtain

$$J_1(x, T_1, T_2) = -\frac{2(Dt)^{1/2}}{\lambda^2}\phi\left[\frac{x-\lambda t}{(Dt)^{1/2}}\right]\Bigg|_{T_1}^{T_2}$$

$$+ \frac{D}{\lambda^2}\left[1 + \frac{\lambda x}{D}\right]J_0(x, T_1, T_2) - \frac{Dx}{\lambda^2}\frac{\partial J_0(x, T_1, T_2)}{\partial x} \tag{3-169}$$

We have now expressed $J_1(x, T_1, T_2)$ in terms of known quantities. It remains to give an explicit form for $J_1(x, T_1, T_2)$. From (3-166)

$$\frac{\partial W_0(x, T)}{\partial x} = -\frac{1}{\lambda (DT)^{1/2}} \phi \left[\frac{x - \lambda T}{(DT)^{1/2}}\right] - \frac{2}{D} e^{2\lambda x/D} \Phi \left[\frac{x + \lambda T}{(DT)^{1/2}}\right]$$

$$+ \frac{1}{\lambda (DT)^{1/2}} e^{2\lambda x/D} \phi \left[\frac{x + \lambda T}{(DT)^{1/2}}\right] \quad (3\text{-}170)$$

Substitution of (3-166) and (3-170) into (3-169) yields

$$J_1(x, T_1, T_2) = W_1(x, T_2) - W_1(x, T_1)$$

where

$$W_1(x, T) = -\frac{2(DT)^{1/2}}{\lambda^2} \phi \left[\frac{x - \lambda T}{(DT)^{1/2}}\right]$$

$$+ \frac{D}{\lambda^3} \left(1 + \frac{\lambda x}{D}\right) \left\{ \Phi \left[\frac{x - \lambda T}{(DT)^{1/2}}\right] - e^{2\lambda x/D} \Phi \left[\frac{x + \lambda T}{(DT)^{1/2}}\right] \right\}$$

$$+ \frac{D^{1/2} x}{\lambda^3 T^{1/2}} \phi \left[\frac{x - \lambda T}{(DT)^{1/2}}\right] + \frac{2x}{\lambda^2} e^{2\lambda x/D} \Phi \left[\frac{x + \lambda T}{(DT)^{1/2}}\right]$$

$$- \frac{D^{1/2} x}{\lambda^3 T^{1/2}} e^{2\lambda x/D} \phi \left[\frac{x + \lambda T}{(DT)^{1/2}}\right]$$

or

$$W_1(x, T) = \frac{D}{\lambda^3} \left(1 + \frac{\lambda x}{D}\right) \Phi \left[\frac{x - \lambda T}{(DT)^{1/2}}\right]$$

$$+ \frac{D^{1/2}}{\lambda^2} \left(\frac{x}{\lambda T^{1/2}} - 2T^{1/2}\right) \phi \left[\frac{x - \lambda T}{(DT)^{1/2}}\right] \quad (3\text{-}171)$$

$$+ e^{2\lambda x/D} \left(\frac{1}{\lambda^2}\right) \left(x - \frac{D}{\lambda}\right) \Phi \left[\frac{x + \lambda T}{(DT)^{1/2}}\right] - \frac{D^{1/2} x}{\lambda^3 T^{1/2}} e^{2\lambda x/D} \phi \left[\frac{x + \lambda T}{(DT)^{1/2}}\right]$$

which on using A4-18, is A4-10.

By use of the integration by parts trick, one can express $J_{n+1}(x, T_1, T_2)$ in terms of $J_n(x, T_1, T_2)$ and $J_{n-1}(x, T_1, T_2)$, thus obtaining a recurrence relation for the J's. Integration of $J_n(x, T_1, T_2)$ by parts with $dv = t^{n-(1/2)} dt$ yields

$$J_{n+1}(x, T_1, T_2) = -\frac{2(Dt)^{1/2} t^n}{\lambda^2} \phi \left[\frac{x - \lambda t}{(Dt)^{1/2}}\right]_{T_1}^{T_2}$$

$$+ \frac{(2n + 1)D}{\lambda^2} J_n(x, T_1, T_2) + \frac{x^2}{\lambda^2} J_{n-1}(x, T_1, T_2), \quad n = 0, 1, 2, \ldots \quad (3\text{-}172)$$

which is A4-11.

Integrals of the form

$$R_n(x, T_1, T_2) = \int_{T_1}^{T_2} t^n \Phi\left[\frac{x - \lambda t}{(Dt)^{1/2}}\right] dt, \quad n = 0, 1, 2, \ldots \quad (3\text{-}173)$$

will also be needed. On integrating (3-173) by parts with $dv = t^n \, dt$, we see that

$$R_n(x, T_1, T_2) = \frac{1}{n+1} \, t^{n+1} \Phi\left[\frac{x - \lambda t}{(Dt)^{1/2}}\right]\Big|_{T_1}^{T_2}$$

$$- \frac{\lambda}{2(n+1)} J_{n+1}(x, T_1, T_2) - \frac{x}{2(n+1)} J_n(x, T_1, T_2) \quad (3\text{-}174)$$

which is A4-14. Hence, once the J's are known, the R's can be evaluated using (3-174). For example, from A4-9, A4-10 (which were derived above)

$$R_0(x, T_1, T_2) = V_0(x, T_2) - V_0(x, T_1)$$

where

$$V_0(x, T) = T\Phi\left[\frac{x - \lambda T}{(DT)^{1/2}}\right] - \frac{D}{2\lambda^2}\left(1 + \frac{\lambda x}{D}\right)\Phi\left[\frac{x - \lambda T}{(DT)^{1/2}}\right]$$

$$+ \frac{(DT)^{1/2}}{\lambda} \phi\left[\frac{x - \lambda T}{(DT)^{1/2}}\right] - \frac{1}{2\lambda}\left(x - \frac{D}{\lambda}\right) e^{2\lambda x/D}\Phi\left[\frac{x + \lambda T}{(DT)^{1/2}}\right]$$

$$- \frac{x}{2\lambda} \Phi\left[\frac{x - \lambda T}{(DT)^{1/2}}\right] + \frac{x}{2\lambda} e^{2\lambda x/D}\Phi\left[\frac{x + \lambda T}{(DT)^{1/2}}\right]$$

or

$$V_0(x, T) = \left[T - \frac{x}{\lambda} - \frac{D}{2\lambda^2}\right]\Phi\left[\frac{x - \lambda T}{(DT)^{1/2}}\right] + \frac{(DT)^{1/2}}{\lambda} \phi\left[\frac{x - \lambda T}{(DT)^{1/2}}\right]$$

$$+ \frac{D}{2\lambda^2} e^{2\lambda x/D}\Phi\left[\frac{x + \lambda T}{(DT)^{1/2}}\right] \quad (3\text{-}175)$$

which is A4-16.

REFERENCES

1. Bharucha-Reid, A. T., *Elements of Markov Processes and Their Applications*. New York: McGraw-Hill Book Co., Inc., 1960.

2. Burrington, R. S. and D. C. May, *Handbook of Probability and Statistics with Tables*. Sandusky, Ohio: Handbook Publishers, Inc., 1953.

3. Feller, W., *An Introduction to Probability Theory and Its Applications* 2nd ed. New York: John Wiley and Sons, Inc., 1957.

This well-known work presents a good treatment of discrete random variables. However, it does not cover continuous random variables.

4. Jewell, W. S., "The Properties of Recurrent-Event Processes," *Operations Research*, Vol. 8, No. 4, 1960, pp. 446–472.

5. Kemeny, J. G., and J. L. Snell, *Finite Markov Chains*. Princeton, N. J.: D. Van Nostrand Co., Inc., 1960.

6. Kemeny, J. G., H. Mirkil, J. L. Snell, and G. L. Thompson, *Finite Mathematical Structures*. Englewood Cliffs, N. J.: Prentice-Hall, Inc., 1959.

Gives a very elementary but clear treatment of discrete and continuous random variables, including Markov processes discrete in space and time.

7. Molina, E. C., *Poisson's Exponential Binomial Limit*. Princeton, N. J.: D. Van Nostrand Co., Inc., 1942.

Gives the most complete tables of $p(x; \mu)$ and $P(x; \mu)$ generally available. However, a somewhat more complete set of tables has been computed recently by R. Pelletier of the Defense Electronics Division of the General Electric Co. (Report R 60 DSD13). These may be published in the near future.

8. Morse, P. M., *Queues, Inventories, and Maintenance*. New York: John Wiley and Sons, Inc., 1958.

Provides an introduction to queuing theory and some of its applications.

9. Takács, L., *Stochastic Processes*. London: Methuen and Co., Ltd., 1960.

Presents about one hundred problems and their solutions. The problems emphasize various physical applications of stochastic processes. A concise introduction to Markov processes is also given.

10. Wadsworth, G. P., and J. Bryan, *Introduction to Probability and Random Variables*. New York: McGraw-Hill Book Co., Inc., 1960.

Gives a fairly elementary discussion of continuous random variables as well as some discussion of discrete random variables.

PROBLEMS

3-1. Let x be a discrete random variable which can only take on the n values $j + 1, \ldots, j + n$. If $p(j + i) = 1/n, i = 1, \ldots, n$, then x is said to have a uniform or rectangular distribution. Similarly, if x is a continuous random variable, and its density function $f(x)$ is given by

$$
f(x) = \begin{cases} 0 & , \quad x < a \\ \dfrac{1}{b-a}, & a \le x \le b, b > a \\ 0 & , \quad x > b \end{cases}
$$

then x is said to have a uniform or rectangular distribution. Compute the mean and variance for the discrete and continuous uniform distributions referred to above.

3-2. Suppose that demands are being generated by an Erlang process of order n. Compute the probability that a demand occurs between t and $t + dt$, given that no demand has occurred for a time t since the previous demand.

3-3. A measure sometimes used in describing processes which generate demands is the coefficient of variation k for the process; k is defined to be $\sigma\lambda$ where $1/\lambda$ is the mean time between demands and σ^2 is the variance of the time between demands. What is k for the Poisson process and the Erlang process of order n?

3-4. Show that $\Gamma(1/2) = \sqrt{\pi}$. Also show that

$$
\Gamma\left(n + \frac{1}{2}\right) = \frac{(2n)!\sqrt{\pi}}{4n!}, \quad n = 1, 2, 3, \ldots
$$

Hint: To evaluate $\Gamma(\tfrac{1}{2})$, let $x = u^2$ in the definition of $\Gamma(\tfrac{1}{2})$.

3-5. Compare the variance of the Poisson and negative binomial distributions when they have the same mean. Express the variance of the negative binomial distribution in terms of its mean and n, the order of the negative binomial distribution. Recall that if a Poisson process is generating demands, and lead times have a gamma distribution, then the marginal distribution of lead time demand is a negative binomial distribution. What can be said then about the effects of the introduction of uncertainty on the variance of the marginal distribution of lead time demand?

3-6. Let $\mathcal{P}(s)$ be the generating function for the density function $p(x)$. Show that μ, the mean of x, is given by $\mu = \mathcal{P}'(1)$ where $\mathcal{P}'(1)$ is the derivative of $\mathcal{P}(s)$ evaluated at $s = 1$. Also show that

$$
\sigma^2 = \mathcal{P}''(1) + \mathcal{P}'(1) - [\mathcal{P}'(1)]^2
$$

where $\mathcal{P}''(1)$ is the second derivative of $\mathcal{P}(s)$ evaluated at $s = 1$. By use of these results, compute the mean and variance of the Poisson and negative binomial distributions.

3-7. Compute the generating function for the binomial distribution, and use the results of Problem 3-6 to compute the mean and variance of the binomial distribution. Let $x_1, \ldots, x_m$ be independent random variables having binomial distributions with the same value of p, but perhaps different n values. What is the distribution of $y = x_1 + \ldots + x_m$?

3-8. Consider the random variable y which is the sum of a random number of independent, identically distributed, discrete random variables x_i, i.e., $y = x_1 + \ldots + x_n$ where n is a random variable and the x_i are independent and all have the same distribution. Let μ_y, μ_x, μ_n be the expected values of y, x_i, n respectively and $\sigma_y^2, \sigma_x^2, \sigma_n^2$ the corresponding variances. By use of the results of Problem 3-6 and the generating function for y show that

$$\mu_y = \mu_x \mu_n \quad \text{and} \quad \sigma_y^2 = \mu_n \sigma_x^2 + \mu_x^2 \sigma_n^2$$

Hint: Recall that (3-95) holds and $\mathcal{P}(1) = 1$.

3-9. Derive the results of Problem 3-8 directly without the use of generating functions. *Hint:* If $p(x)$ is the density function for the x_i and $r(n)$ the density function for n, then the probability of any set $(x_1, \ldots, x_n, n)$ is

$$p(x_1)p(x_2) \ldots p(x_n)r(n)$$

and

$$\mu_y = \sum_n \sum_{\substack{x_1, \ldots, x_n \\ \text{given } n}} yp(x_1) \ldots p(x_n)r(n) = \sum_n \sum_{\substack{x_1, \ldots, x_n \\ \text{given } n}} \sum_{i=1}^{n} x_i p(x_i)r(n)$$

$$\sigma_y^2 = \sum_n \sum_{\substack{x_1, \ldots, x_n \\ \text{given } n}} (x_1 + \ldots + x_n)^2 p(x_1) \ldots p(x_n)r(n) - \mu_y^2$$

$$= \sum_n \sum_{x_1, \ldots, x_n} \left[x_1^2 + \ldots + x_n^2 + \sum_{\substack{i,j \\ i \neq j}} x_i x_j \right] p(x_1) \ldots p(x_n)r(n) - \mu_y^2$$

$$= \sum_n [n\sigma_x^2 + n\mu_x^2 + n(n-1)\mu_x^2]r(n) - \mu_y^2$$

3-10. Note that the results of Problem 3-8 allow us to compute the mean and variance of the distribution of demand in a time t when the time between demands and the number of units demanded per demand are random variables, provided that we know the means and variances of the distributions of the times between demands and the number of units demanded per demand. By use of the results of Problem 3-8 compute the mean and variance of the stuttering Poisson distribution. Note also that the results of Problem 3-8 allow us to compute the mean and variance of the marginal distribution of lead time demand in the case where the lead time is a discrete variable. Here x_i might be interpreted as the demand in day i.

3-11. Consider a situation in which demands are treated as discrete, and the procurement lead time is a continuous random variable with density function $g(t)$. Let $p(x|t)$ be the probability that x units are demanded in time t and let $\mathcal{P}(s; t)$ be the generating function for this density. Let y be the random variable representing the lead time demand, and let $\mathcal{P}^*(s)$ be its generating function. Show that

$$\mathcal{P}^*(s) = \int_0^\infty \mathcal{P}(s; t)g(t)\, dt$$

Find $\mathcal{P}^*(s)$ in the case where a Poisson process generates demands, units being demanded one at a time, and the lead time has a gamma distribution. In this way obtain another derivation of the fact that the marginal distribution of lead time demand has a negative binomial distribution.

3-12. Let $p(x|t)$ be the probability that x units are demanded in a time t. Assume that the mean of this distribution is λt where λ is the mean rate of demand and its variance is σ_{xt}^2. Let $g(t)$ be the density function for the procurement lead time with mean μ_t and variance σ_t^2. Assume that x is either discrete or continuous and that t is continuous. If y is the random variable representing the lead time demand, and μ_y, σ_y^2 are the mean and variance of y respectively, show that

$$\mu_y = \lambda \mu_t \quad \text{and} \quad \sigma_y^2 = \mu_t \sigma_x^2 + \lambda^2 \sigma_t^2$$

Hint:

$$(\lambda \mu_t)^2 + \sigma_y^2 = \int_0^\infty \int_0^\infty y^2 p(y|t)g(t)\, dy\, dt = \int_0^\infty (\sigma_{xt}^2 + \lambda^2 t^2)g(t)\, dt$$

3-13. Suppose that demands are generated by a Poisson process and that the number of units demanded per demand is described by a binomial distribution. Determine the density function for the number of units demanded in a time t. Find the generating function for this density, and the mean and variance of the density function.

3-14. Suppose that the procurement lead time is a continuous random variable with mean μ_t and variance σ_t^2. Suppose also that the process generating demands is such that the mean time between demands is μ_d and the variance of the number of demands occurring in time t is $\sigma_d^2 t$. Finally imagine that the number of units demanded per demand is a random variable with mean μ_x and variance σ_x^2. By use of the results of Problems 3-8 and 3-12 determine the mean and variance of the lead time demand in terms of the other means and variances.

3-15. Derive the mean and variance of the normal and gamma distributions using their moment generating functions.

3-16. Let x be a discrete random variable with density function $p(x)$. Then the moment generating function for x is defined to be

$$\mathfrak{M}(s) = \sum_{x=0}^{\infty} e^{-xs} p(x)$$

Given $\mathfrak{M}(s)$, how can one determine the mean and variance of x? Compute $\mathfrak{M}(s)$ for the binomial, Poisson, and negative binomial distributions.

3-17. By use of the results of Problem 3-16 compute the mean and variance of the binomial, Poisson, and negative binomial distributions.

3-18. Let x_1, x_2 be two independent discrete random variables with moment generating functions $\mathfrak{M}_1(s)$ and $\mathfrak{M}_2(s)$ respectively. Determine the moment generating function for $y = x_1 + x_2$.

3-19. Consider a process generating demands for which the density function for the time between arrivals is $g(t)$, i.e., the probability that a demand occurs between t and $t + dt$ after the last demand is $g(t)\, dt$, and this depends only on t. Suppose that we start observing a system at a time τ after the last demand and ask what is the probability $g(t|\tau)\, dt$ that the next demand will occur between t and $t + dt$ after we begin observation. Show that

$$g(t|\tau) = \frac{g(t + \tau)}{G(\tau)}; \quad G(\tau) = \int_{\tau}^{\infty} g(\xi)\, d\xi$$

Evaluate $g(t|\tau)$ for the case where a Poisson process is generating demands. Now suppose that we begin observation of the system at a random point in time. This means that when observation is begun we have no knowledge of the time when the last demand occurred. The probability that the last demand occurred between τ and $\tau + d\tau$ in the past is equal to the joint probability that the next demand after a given demand does not occur in a time τ, i.e., $G(\tau)$, and that we started observation between τ and $\tau + d\tau$. This latter probability is independent of τ if we begin at random and is proportional to $d\tau$, i.e., $\alpha d\tau$. Thus the desired probability is $\alpha G(\tau)\, d\tau$ where α is determined so that the integral over τ is equal to unity. By use of these results, show that if $u(t)\, dt$ is the probability that a demand occurs between t and $t + dt$ when observation is begun at random, then

$$u(t) = \lambda \int_0^\infty g(t + \tau) \, d\tau = \lambda G(t)$$

where λ is the mean rate at which demands occur. Compute $u(t)$ for the Poisson distribution and show that $g(t) = u(t)$.

3-20. By use of the results of Problem 3-19, show how to compute the probabilities $U_n(t)$ that n demands occur in a time t when observations are begun at random, given the probabilities $V_n(t)$ that n units are demanded in a time t when t is measured from a particular demand.

3-21. Compute $u(t)$ when an Erlang process of order m is generating demands. Attempt also to compute the $U_n(t)$ and $V_n(t)$ for this process. Note that $u(t)$ is defined in Problem 3-19 and $U_n(t)$, $V_n(t)$ in Problem 3-20.

3-22. Show that the equivalent of Eq. (3-29) holds for continuous random variables.

3-23. Show that Eq. (3-84) is the generating function for the negative binomial distribution even if n is not an integer.

3-24. Let x_1, x_2 be continuous, independent random variables which can take on any real values. Show that the moment generating function for $y = x_1 + x_2$ is the product of the moment generating functions for x_1, x_2.

3-25. Consider a Markov process discrete in space and continuous in time. Prove that if Poisson processes generate transitions between states, then the only a_{ij}, $i \neq j$, which are different from zero are those which correspond to the occurrence of a single Poisson event.

3-26. Provide a probabilistic interpretation of Eq. (3-140).

3-27. Compute the Poisson probability $p(30; 25) = p(x; \mu)$ and the normal approximation to it. Also compute $P(30; 25)$ and the normal approximation to it. Next compute $P(30; 25) - P(40; 25)$ and the normal approximation to it. Compute $p(95; 75)$, $P(95; 75)$, and $P(95; 75) - P(105; 75)$ and the corresponding normal approximations. In making the above computations, it is suggested that Molina's tables be used.

3-28. Differentiate Eq. (3-166) with respect to T and use this result to demonstrate that $W_0(x, T)$ is correct.

3-29. Determine the limiting forms of the Poisson properties derived in Sec. 3-12 obtained by replacing the Poisson terms with their normal approximations. Compare these results with the corresponding ones obtained directly, using the normal distribution.

3-30. Derive all properties in Appendix 3 not derived in the text.

3-31. Derive all properties in Appendix 4 not derived in the text.

3-32. Compute the mean and variance of the stuttering Poisson distribution from its generating function.

3-33. Consider an inventory situation in which units are demanded one at a time, and the number of units demanded in a time period of length t has a Poisson distribution, with the mean demand rate being 40 units per year. The operating doctrine is to place an order when the on hand inventory reaches a level r. If the procurement lead time is two months, determine the value of r such that the probability of running out of stock in the lead time and having one or more demands occur when the system is out of stock is less than or equal to 0.02.

4

LOT SIZE
REORDER POINT MODELS
WITH STOCHASTIC DEMANDS

"When your pills get down to four,
Order more."

     Anonymous

4-1 Introduction

Beginning with this chapter, we wish to study inventory models in which explicit account is taken of the fact that demands on the system cannot be predicted with certainty but instead must be described probabilistically. The introduction of randomness into the nature of the demand pattern brings to the fore at the outset several new considerations which did not enter into the analysis when studying the deterministic models of Chapter 2.

One of these new considerations concerns how much is known about the state of the system at any point in time. For the deterministic models of Chapter 2, it is possible to determine for all future times precisely what the state of the system will be if the state is known at a given time and if the quantity to be ordered and the reorder point are specified. However, when randomness is introduced into the demand pattern, it is no longer possible to make such predictions, since the times of occurrence of the demands (and perhaps also the number of units demanded per demand) are random variables. One cannot know the state of the system at each point in time unless each transaction (demand, placement of order, receipt of shipment, etc.) is recorded and reported as it occurs. We shall say that an inventory system is using *transactions reporting* if all transactions of interest are recorded as they occur, and the information is immediately made known to the decision maker. When transactions reporting is used, then it is possible to make decisions concerning the operation of the system, such as the decision as to whether or not to place an order each time a demand occurs. The effort required to operate a transactions reporting system can vary widely with the circumstances. In some cases, it involves nothing more than placing a card in the stock bin indicating that it is time to re-order when the stock gets down to the card. Here no actual recording or reporting is done, since in this simple situation the recording and reporting are automatic through the appearance of empty spaces in the bin. In other cases, transactions reporting may require the operation of a large scale data processing system in which all transactions are fed into a computer that automatically updates all records, prints out orders to procure when necessary, etc.

It is not always desirable to have inventory systems use transactions reporting, since it may be too expensive to do so. The other procedure commonly used in the real world will be referred to as *periodic review*. When a periodic review procedure is used, the state of the inventory system is examined only at discrete, usually equally spaced points in time. Decisions concerning the operation of the system, such as whether or not to place an order, are made only at these review times. In fact, the decision maker knows nothing about the state of the system at times other than the review times.

In this chapter we shall confine our attention to transactions reporting systems, and in the next chapter periodic review systems will be studied. We noted in Chapter 2 that there was no difference between what we have here referred to as transactions reporting systems (there they were called $\langle Q, r \rangle$ models) and periodic review systems. When randomness is introduced, however, we shall see that considerable differences exist between the two systems.

Another new consideration concerns the criterion to be used for determining the optimal operating doctrine for the system under consideration. In this chapter, as in Chapter 2, we shall only be concerned with cases in which the process generating the demands does not change with time. In particular, this implies that the mean rate of demand remains constant over time. As in Chapter 2, the criterion that will be used to determine the optimal policy is the minimization of the average annual variable cost. The average annual variable cost is still defined as the limit as ζ approaches infinity of the average annual cost for a time period of length ζ. When the demand over time is a random variable (and perhaps the procurement lead time is also a random variable), the average annual cost cannot be evaluated quite so simply as in Chapter 2. We shall show how to do this later.

A final new consideration concerns the state of the system at the time a procurement arrives. For the deterministic models of Chapter 2, it was possible to predict exactly the on hand inventory at the time of arrival of a procurement. However, when the lead time demand is a random variable, it is no longer possible to predict exactly how much inventory will be on hand when a procurement arrives. This on hand inventory level will also be a random variable. We shall define the expected value of the net inventory in the backorders case or the expected value of the on hand inventory for the lost sales case at the time a procurement arrives to be the safety stock. It will be denoted by s. The value of s can be either positive, negative, or zero for the backorders case, but must be non-negative for the lost sales case. For deterministic models, we noted in Chapter 2 that it is never optimal to have any stock on hand when an order arrives. However, when demands are described probabilistically, it will frequently be true that the optimal safety stock should be positive. The reason for this is that if the safety stock was zero, then because of the random nature of the lead time demand, the system would very frequently run out of stock before the arrival of the order, thus incurring stockout costs. When it is expensive to incur backorders or lose sales, then on the average it is cheaper to carry some additional stock to avoid these stockout costs.

In this chapter, as in Chapter 2, we shall study lot size-reorder point models for a single installation. Recall that a lot size-reorder point model is one such that a quantity Q is ordered each time the appropriate inventory level (the on hand inventory, the net inventory, the on hand plus on order inventory, or the inventory position) reaches the reorder level. The purpose of the analysis is to determine the optimal value of the order quantity Q and the reorder point.

It is important to observe that by its definition, a lot size-reorder point model assumes that an order is placed when the inventory level reaches the reorder point, i.e., there is no overshoot of the reorder point. In order for this to be true the state of the system must be examined after every demand. Thus the use of a lot size-reorder point model (a $\langle Q, r \rangle$ model) implicitly requires that a transactions reporting system be used.

The ability to place an order precisely as the reorder point is reached also implies that, when the integrality of demand is taken into account, the number of units demanded per demand cannot be a random variable. When the number of units demanded per demand is a random variable, then it is possible to overshoot (unavoidably) the reorder point. For such situations, it may no longer be appropriate to order a fixed quantity each time an order is placed. An alternative procedure is to set two levels $r, R (R > r)$ such that if the inventory level falls to $x, x \le r$ on some demand, we order up to the level R, i.e., a quantity $R - x$ is ordered. We shall refer to such an operating doctrine as an Rr doctrine, and a transactions reporting model which uses such a doctrine as an $\langle R, r \rangle$ model. The task of working with $\langle R, r \rangle$ models when the number of units demanded per demand is a random variable is much more difficult than for the models to be discussed in this chapter. We shall discuss such models in Chapter 8. It should be noted that a $\langle Q, r \rangle$ model is a special case of an $\langle R, r \rangle$ model, with $R = r + Q$, which is appropriate when units are demanded one at a time and there is never any overshoot of the reorder point.

In the real world, even if the number of units demanded per demand is a random variable, then provided that the probability of a large overshoot is very small, one will often operate the system using a $\langle Q, r \rangle$ model. To do this one might compute a Q^* and r^* using the model described in the next section, and then either order Q^* each time an order is placed, or order up to $Q^* + r^*$ each time the reorder level is crossed.

4-2 Heuristic Approximate Treatment of the Backorders Case

Before turning to the presentation of the detailed, exact formulations of $\langle Q, r \rangle$ models for some special cases, we shall present a heuristic approximate treatment of $\langle Q, r \rangle$ models. In this section, the backorders case will be examined, and in the following section the lost sales case will be studied. It is these simple approximate treatments that are almost always to be found in the texts which discuss $\langle Q, r \rangle$ models [2, 6]. Such developments require a large number of assumptions and approximations. Frequently, in the presentations given of these models, only a small fraction of the assumptions and approximations needed are explicitly stated. Indeed, it is hard to be able to appreciate all of them until the exact treatment is covered. For this reason no attempt will be made to list every approximation and assumption at this time. A number of assumptions and approximations will be listed here, however. We shall see later what additional implicit assumptions were made. In addition, we shall later examine the ways in which models to be derived here are more general than might be apparent from the discussion to follow. Even though many approximations and assumptions are made in this and the following section, the resulting models are especially useful for practical applications because of their simplicity, and because, often, the special cases for which the exact equations are available do not represent the real world situation much more accurately than the approximate models, i.e., the additional assumptions needed to reduce the exact model to the simple model are frequently warranted in practice.

We shall assume that the system under consideration consists of a single installation which uses transactions reporting. We wish to determine the optimal order quantity Q and reorder point r for a given item. If the system stocks more than a single item, it will be assumed that there are no interactions between the items. The optimal values of Q and r will be found by minimizing the average annual variable cost. At the outset, we shall make the following assumptions:

(1) The unit cost C of the item is a constant independent of Q.

(2) The backorder cost is π per unit backordered. There is no cost $\hat{\pi}t$ which depends on the length of time t for which the backorder exists, i.e., $\hat{\pi} = 0$.

(3) There is never more than a single order outstanding.*

(4) The cost of operating the information processing system is independent of Q and r.

---

* We shall prove later that the simple model developed can also be applied when an arbitrary number of orders can be outstanding.

Assumption (3) implies that at the time the reorder point is reached there are no orders outstanding, so that the inventory position (the amount on hand plus on order minus backorders) is equal to the net inventory (on hand minus backorders). Thus the order point will be the same regardless of whether it is based on the inventory position or net inventory. The additional assumption will now be made that:

(5) The reorder point r (based on the inventory position or net inventory) is positive.

This is almost always true in practice, since one will not normally wait until there are backorders on the books before placing an order. Because of (5), there will be no backorders outstanding at the reorder point. In

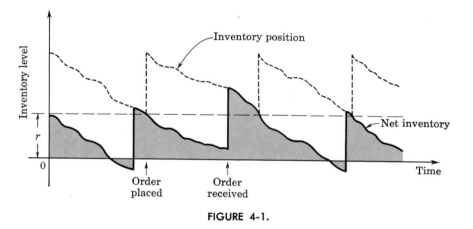

FIGURE 4-1.

fact, at the reorder point, the inventory position is equal to the on hand inventory. The behavior of the on hand inventory and the inventory position for a system of the type being described is illustrated in Fig. 4-1. For the model being examined, any one of the inventory levels, on hand, net, or inventory position can be used to define the reorder point, and the reorder point has the same value for any one of them. Note that to use the on hand level we must assume that after an order arrives, it is sufficient to meet all backorders and raise the on hand inventory level above the reorder point. If this ever failed to happen, the reorder point would never be reached again and the system would proceed to accumulate backorders. When the reorder point is thought of in terms of the inventory position of the system, then assumption (3) guarantees that the on hand inventory will always be raised above the reorder point when an order arrives, for otherwise it would not be possible to have only a single order outstanding.

As in Chapter 2, we say that the system goes through one cycle in the time between the placing of two successive orders or the receipt of two successive procurements. Unlike the case for deterministic models, it is no longer true that the system repeats itself exactly each cycle. Even the length of the cycle is now a random variable. However, the system does repeat itself in the sense that the inventory position varies between r and $r + Q$ during each cycle.

We shall now proceed to evaluate the various terms in the average annual cost. These terms include the ordering costs, the cost of carrying inventory, and the cost of backorders. Because of assumption (1), it is unnecessary to include the cost of the units. The average annual cost of units procured is independent of Q and r, since the unit cost C is independent of Q. We shall here treat all variables as continuous. It is a trivial task to modify the analysis to the case where Q, r and the demand variable are treated as discrete; this is left to Problems 4-1 through 4-3. Let $f(x; t) \, dx$ be the probability that the number of units demanded in a time t lies between x and $x + dx$, and suppose that the mean rate of demand, which is constant over time, is λ.

The cost of placing an order will be taken to be A. Since the average annual demand is λ and since an order is placed after every Q demands, the average annual cost of placing orders is $\lambda A / Q$. The inventory carrying charge will be denoted as usual by I. The average annual cost* of carrying inventory will be IC times the average number of unit years of stock held per year. Some variation of the following argument is often given to obtain the average number of unit years of stock held per year. First observe that by definition the net inventory is the on hand inventory minus the backorders, i.e., the net inventory is the difference of two random variables. Then, by the results of Sec. 3-8, the expected value of the net inventory at any time is the expected value of the on hand inventory minus the expected value of the backorders. Thus the expected on hand inventory is equal to the expected net inventory plus the expected number of backorders. Now when backorders are expensive, then if they are incurred at all during a cycle, they will be incurred only close to the time when a procurement is due in. However, to determine the average unit years of stock held per year it is necessary to integrate the expected on hand inventory over time, or equivalently integrate the expected net inventory plus the expected backorders over time. The expected backorders term will be significantly different from zero only a very small fraction of the time if the backorder

---

* In this chapter and the next, we shall employ the convention that the expected value of any random variable computed on an annual basis will be referred to as the average annual value of the variable, while expected values for all other time intervals, or at given points in time, will be referred to as expected values.

cost is high and will therefore make only a slight contribution to the integral. Thus it will be assumed that the expected number of backorders is negligible, and for computing the inventory carrying charges, the expected on hand inventory can be taken to be equal to the net inventory.

By definition, the expected net inventory at the time of arrival of a procurement is the safety stock s. The expected net inventory immediately after the arrival of a procurement is then $Q + s$. Thus, if the arrival of an order initiates a cycle, the expected net inventory at the beginning of a cycle is $Q + s$ and is s at the end of a cycle. These will also be the expected values of the on hand inventory at the corresponding times, when the expected number of backorders can be neglected. In this case, since the mean rate of demand is constant, the expected on hand inventory will decrease linearly from $Q + s$ at the beginning of the cycle to s at the end of the cycle and will average to

$$\frac{1}{2}(Q + s) + \frac{1}{2}s = \frac{Q}{2} + s \tag{4-1}$$

which is the average number of unit years of stock held per year (illustrate this graphically).

In Chapter 2 we introduced the equivalent of s directly as one of the variables. When dealing with probabilistic models, it is convenient to eliminate the variable s and replace it by r (Problem 2-15 showed that this was easy to do in the deterministic case). Since the reorder point in terms of the on hand or net inventory is r, and since nothing arrives between the time an order is placed on reaching r and the time this order arrives (i.e., assumption (3) holds), then if the order requires a time τ to arrive and if x units are demanded in this time, the net inventory $\xi(x, r)$ will be $\xi(x, r) = r - x$ at the time of arrival of the order, and the expected value of the net inventory averaged over all x for a given τ is

$$\int_0^\infty \xi(x, r)f(x; \tau) \, dx = \int_0^\infty (r - x)f(x; \tau) \, dx \tag{4-2}$$

If the procurement lead time is constant, then (4-2) is the safety stock. Suppose, however, that the procurement lead time is a random variable such that $g(\tau) \, d\tau$ is the probability that the procurement lead time lies between τ and $\tau + d\tau$. Then by (3-70), the expected value of $\xi(x, r)$ averaged over x and τ is

$$\int_0^\infty \int_0^\infty \xi(x, r)f(x; \tau)g(\tau) \, dxd\tau = \int_0^\infty (r - x)h(x) \, dx \tag{4-3}$$

where

$$h(x) = \int_0^\infty f(x; \tau)g(\tau) \, d\tau \tag{4-4}$$

is the marginal distribution of lead time demand.

We can therefore write

$$s = \int_0^\infty (r - x)h(x)\, dx = r - \mu \qquad (4\text{-}5)$$

where μ is the expected lead time demand, i.e.,

$$\mu = \int_0^\infty xh(x)\, dx \qquad (4\text{-}6)$$

and where $h(x) = f(x;\tau)$ if the lead time is a constant τ or $h(x)$ is given by (4-4) when the procurement lead time is a random variable with density $g(\tau)$. The average annual inventory carrying costs are therefore $IC[(Q/2) + r - \mu]$.

It remains to evaluate the average annual cost of backorders. The argument used to obtain this cost usually runs as follows: The average number of backorders incurred per year is simply the expected number of backorders incurred per cycle times the average number of cycles per year, i.e., λ/Q times the expected number of backorders incurred per cycle. (This argument is correct, as we shall see later.) Now the number of backorders $\eta(x, r)$ incurred in a cycle will simply be the number of backorders on the books when a procurement arrives. If the lead time demand is x, the number of backorders will be

$$\eta(x, r) = \begin{cases} 0 & \text{if } x - r < 0 \\ x - r & \text{if } x - r \geq 0 \end{cases} \qquad (4\text{-}7)$$

Thus the expected number of backorders per period $\bar{\eta}(r)$ is

$$\bar{\eta}(r) = \int_0^\infty \eta(x, r)h(x)\, dx = \int_r^\infty (x - r)h(x)\, dx$$

$$= \int_r^\infty xh(x)\, dx - rH(r) \qquad (4\text{-}8)$$

where, as above, $h(x)$ is the marginal distribution of lead time demand and $H(x)$ is the complementary cumulative of $h(x)$. The average annual cost of backorders is then

$$\frac{\pi\lambda}{Q}\left[\int_r^\infty xh(x)\, dx - rH(r)\right]$$

All the terms in the average annual variable cost $\mathcal{K}$ have now been found; $\mathcal{K}$ is

$$\mathcal{K} = \frac{\lambda}{Q}A + IC\left[\frac{Q}{2} + r - \mu\right] + \frac{\pi\lambda}{Q}\left[\int_r^\infty xh(x)\, dx - rH(r)\right] \qquad (4\text{-}9)$$

since by assumptions (1) and (4) it is unnecessary to include the cost of the units or the cost of operating the information processing system. We wish to determine the values of Q and r which minimize the $\mathcal{K}$ of (4-9). If the optimal values Q^*, r^* satisfy $0 < Q^* < \infty, 0 < r^* < \infty$, then Q^*, r^* must satisfy the equations

$$\frac{\partial \mathcal{K}}{\partial Q} = 0 = -\frac{\lambda A}{Q^2} + \frac{IC}{2} - \frac{\pi\lambda}{Q^2}\bar{\eta}(r) \qquad (4\text{-}10)$$

$$\frac{\partial \mathcal{K}}{\partial r} = 0 = IC + \frac{\pi\lambda}{Q}[-rh(r) + rh(r) - H(r)] \qquad (4\text{-}11)$$

Here we have two equations to be solved for Q and r. It is convenient to write (4-10), (4-11) as

$$Q = \sqrt{\frac{2\lambda[A + \pi\bar{\eta}(r)]}{IC}} \qquad (4\text{-}12)$$

and

$$H(r) = \frac{QIC}{\pi\lambda} \qquad (4\text{-}13)$$

Recall that $\bar{\eta}(r)$ is given by (4-8). A procedure for numerically solving for Q^* and r^* will be given in Sec. 4-4.

Often it is desirable to evaluate $\mathcal{K}$ numerically for given values of Q and r. If we assume that $h(x)$ is a normal distribution with mean μ (the expected lead time demand) and standard deviation σ, i.e., $h(x) = n(x; \mu, \sigma)$, then

$$\int_r^\infty xh(x)\, dx = \int_r^\infty xn(x; \mu, \sigma)\, dx = \int_r^\infty \frac{x}{\sigma}\phi\left(\frac{x-\mu}{\sigma}\right) dx \qquad (4\text{-}14)$$

$$= \sigma \int_{(r-\mu)/\sigma}^\infty v\phi(v)\, dv + \mu \int_{(r-\mu)/\sigma}^\infty \phi(v)\, dv \qquad (4\text{-}15)$$

$$= \sigma\phi\left(\frac{r-\mu}{\sigma}\right) + \mu\Phi\left(\frac{r-\mu}{\sigma}\right)$$

Thus

$$\mathcal{K} = \frac{\lambda}{Q}A + IC\left[\frac{Q}{2} + r - \mu\right] + \frac{\pi\lambda}{Q}\left[(\mu - r)\Phi\left(\frac{r-\mu}{\sigma}\right)\right.$$
$$\left. + \sigma\phi\left(\frac{r-\mu}{\sigma}\right)\right] \qquad (4\text{-}16)$$

In this form, $\mathcal{K}$ is easily evaluated with the aid of normal tables.

4-3 Heuristic Approximate Treatment for the Lost Sales Case

The simple approximate treatment of the lost sales case differs very little from the backorders case studied in the previous section. From our study of the lost sales case in Sec. 2-6, it is clear that the minimization of the average annual cost is equivalent to the maximization of the average annual profit if in the cost expression the cost of a lost sale includes the lost profit. It is also clear that, in general, the average number of cycles per year is no longer λ/Q but is instead $\lambda/(Q + \lambda\hat{T})$, where $\hat{T}$ is the average length of time per cycle for which the system is out of stock. In the real world $\hat{T}$ is usually a very small fraction of the total length of the cycle. Since it is very inconvenient to include $\hat{T}$ in the analysis, the following assumption is usually made in the simple treatments.

(a) The value of $\hat{T}$ is small enough to be neglected, so that the average number of cycles per year is λ/Q.

We shall suppose that assumptions (1), (3) and (4) of Sec. 4-2 also apply here. Assumption (2) of Sec. 4-2 is not needed here, since for the lost sales case the cost of a lost sale will always be π; there is never a term proportional to time, as it does not make any sense to talk about the time for which a lost sale exists. We do assume, however, that π includes the lost profit.

The only difference between the lost sales and backorders models comes in evaluating the safety stock expression. The expected on hand inventory when a procurement arrives will be s, the safety stock, and the expected on hand inventory immediately after a procurement arrives will be $Q + s$. Thus the expected on hand inventory varies between $Q + s$ and s in a cycle and averages to $(Q/2) + s$. Let $\epsilon(x, r)$ be the on hand inventory when the procurement arrives if the lead time demand is x. Then

$$\epsilon(x, r) = \begin{cases} r - x, & r - x \geq 0 \\ 0, & r - x < 0 \end{cases}$$

and the expected amount on hand when a procurement arrives is

$$s = \int_0^\infty \epsilon(x, r)h(x)\, dx = \int_0^r (r - x)h(x)\, dx \tag{4-17}$$

where $h(x)$ represents the marginal distribution of lead time demand. However

$$s = \int_0^\infty (r - x)h(x)\, dx - \int_r^\infty (r - x)h(x)\, dx$$

$$= r - \mu + \int_r^\infty xh(x)\, dx - rH(r) \tag{4-18}$$

Thus the average annual cost of carrying inventory is

$$IC\left[\frac{Q}{2} + r - \mu\right] + IC\left[\int_r^\infty xh(x)\,dx - rH(r)\right] \tag{4-19}$$

It will be noted that the expected number of lost sales per cycle is precisely the same as the expected number of backorders per cycle in Sec. 4-2, i.e., is given by (4-8). This follows, since if the lead time demand is x, the number of lost sales will be $x - r$ if $x - r > 0$ and 0 otherwise. Averaging this over x, we obtain (4-8). It follows that the average annual variable cost in the lost sales case is

$$\mathcal{K} = \frac{\lambda}{Q}A + IC\left[\frac{Q}{2} + r - \mu\right]$$
$$+ \left(IC + \frac{\pi\lambda}{Q}\right)\left[\int_r^\infty xh(x)\,dx - rH(r)\right] \tag{4-20}$$

Again we wish to determine the values of Q and r which minimize $\mathcal{K}$. If $0 < Q^* < \infty$, $0 < r^* < \infty$, then Q^*, r^* must satisfy $\partial\mathcal{K}/\partial Q = \partial\mathcal{K}/\partial r = 0$. The equivalents of (4-12), (4-13) then become

$$Q = \sqrt{\frac{2\lambda[A + \pi\bar{\eta}(r)]}{IC}} \tag{4-21}$$

$$H(r) = \frac{QIC}{\lambda\pi + QIC} \tag{4-22}$$

A numerical example illustrating the solution of these equations will be given in the next section. If $h(x)$ is a normal distribution, then the equivalent of (4-16) for the lost sales case is

$$\mathcal{K} = \frac{\lambda}{Q}A + IC\left[\frac{Q}{2} + r - \mu\right]$$
$$+ \left(IC + \frac{\pi\lambda}{Q}\right)\left[(\mu - r)\Phi\left(\frac{r - \mu}{\sigma}\right) + \sigma\phi\left(\frac{r - \mu}{\sigma}\right)\right] \tag{4-23}$$

4-4 Discussion of the Simple Models and a Numerical Example

In this section we shall discuss some interesting properties of the two models developed in the previous two sections, present a numerical technique for determining the optimal Q and r values, and give a numerical example to illustrate the use of the models.

First note from (4-12), (4-21) and (4-8) that in both the backorders and lost sales cases $Q^* \geq Q_w$, i.e., the optimal Q value is never less than the Wilson Q. In fact, for all normal cases, $Q^* > Q_w$ for any r (not simply the optimal r). The intuitive reason for this is that the expected number of backorders or lost sales per cycle depends on r but is independent of Q. However, the average annual cost of backorders or lost sales is proportional to $1/Q$. Therefore, for a fixed, specified value of r, when $\pi > 0$, it always pays to increase Q somewhat thus incurring more carrying charges per year in order to gain the benefits of correspondingly reducing the average annual cost of backorders or lost sales. The value of Q should not be increased indefinitely because after a point the incremental savings in expected stockout costs becomes less than the incremental increases in expected carrying costs.

Secondly, it will be observed that (4-13) does not make any sense if $QIC/\pi\lambda > 1$. This will never occur for cases for which this model is intended to apply, i.e., to high backorder costs. This anomaly arises because the backorders term was omitted in determining the inventory carrying costs. Note that a similar problem does not arise in the corresponding equation (4-22) for the lost sales case.

Before going on to a third observation concerning the models, it will be convenient to introduce a numerical procedure for solving the pairs of equations (4-12), (4-13) or (4-21), (4-22). This procedure is as follows: Use Q_w as the initial estimate of Q, i.e., write $Q_1 = Q_w$. Then use Q_1 in (4-13) or (4-22) to compute r_1. The r_1 so obtained is used in (4-12) or (4-21) to compute Q_2. This Q_2 is used in (4-13) or (4-22) to compute r_2, etc. This iterative procedure is continued until Q and r are obtained with sufficient accuracy. If the equations have a solution at all, then the above iterative scheme must converge to a minimum cost solution.

A proof of the convergence of the iterative scheme will be carried out using a graphical argument for the backorders case. The corresponding argument for the lost sales case can easily be made and is left for Problem 4-4. Equations (4-12) and (4-13) can be thought of as describing two curves in the Qr-plane. For the curve described by equation (4-13), we note that when $Q = 0$, $r = \infty$ and when $Q = \pi\lambda/IC$, $H(r) = 1$ or $r = 0$. Furthermore, from (4-13)

$$\frac{dQ}{dr} = -\frac{\pi\lambda}{IC} h(r) \quad \text{or} \quad \frac{dr}{dQ} = -\frac{IC}{\pi\lambda} \frac{1}{h(r)} < 0 \qquad (4\text{-}24)$$

For the curve described by (4-12) note that when $r = 0$

$$Q = \hat{Q} = \sqrt{\frac{2\lambda[A + \pi\mu]}{IC}}$$

and when $r = \infty$, $Q = Q_w$. Furthermore $dr/dQ < 0$. If one plots the two curves something like Fig. 4-2 will be obtained.

To initiate the iterative scheme, (4-13) is used to compute r when $Q = Q_w$, i.e., we start on the curve defined by (4-13) at the point where $Q = Q_w$. The r value so obtained is used in (4-12) to compute a new Q value Q_2, i.e., we move from the point (Q_w, r_1) on the curve defined by (4-13) to a point on the curve defined by (4-12) having the ordinate r_1. The Q_2 value is used in (4-13) to compute a new r, i.e., we move from the curve defined by (4-12) to the curve defined by (4-13) at constant Q. Thus a series of steps is obtained as shown in Fig. 4-2. It is clear that the iterative scheme

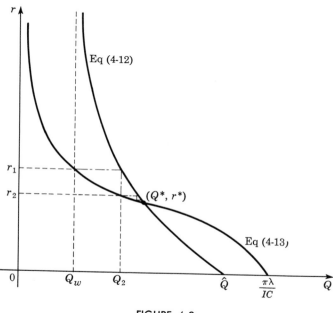

FIGURE 4-2.

must converge to Q^* and r^*. In practice, the convergence is usually quite rapid.

It turns out that the solution Q^*, r^* to (4-12), (4-13) or (4-21), (4-22) is always unique. The proof of this follows from the fact that $\mathcal{K}(Q, r)$ is convex. The details of this proof are to be developed in Problems 4-5 through 4-8. In the backorders case, it is not necessarily true that a solution will always exist. An investigation of when a solution does not exist is left to Problem 4-9. For the lost sales case, however, it is easy to show that there will always be a solution. The proof is left to Problem 4-10.

We are now able to make a third observation concerning the backorders and lost sales models. If we examine the optimal values of Q and r computed from the lost sales model and the backorders model when the same values of the parameters, i.e., the same values of λ, A, I, C, and π are used in both, it will be found Q^* for the backorders case is *larger* than Q^* for the lost sales case while r^* for the backorders case is *smaller* than r^* for the lost sales case. This can be seen immediately if one follows through the iterative computational procedure. At the first step with $Q_1 = Q_w$, a larger r_1 is obtained in the lost sales case than the backorders case. This in turn gives a smaller Q_2 in the lost sales case than the backorders case. Consequently, the ratio on the right of (4-22) will again be smaller than that of (4-13) and r_2 for the lost sales case will be larger than r_2 for the backorders case. Continuing in this way we see that the result stated above holds. In practice the difference between the Q^*, r^* values for the lost sales and backorders cases will generally be very small.

The intuitive explanation of the above behavior is roughly as follows: Note that if the same values of Q and r are used in both models, the average annual inventory carrying cost will be less for the backorders model than for the lost sales case (since in the backorders model for those cycles when backorders occur, the initial inventory in the next cycle is reduced by the backorders to being less than Q, while it is never less than Q in the lost sales case). Consequently, other things being equal, it pays to have a larger Q in the backorders case than in the lost sales case. On the other hand, an increase in r causes less of an increase in average annual inventory carrying charges for the lost sales case than for the backorders case, while yielding the same change in the expected stockout cost in both cases (provided the Q's are the same). Hence, other things being equal, it will be advantageous to have a higher r in the lost sales case than in the backorders case.

Sometimes it is of interest to compare the average annual cost of operation obtained from one of the two models discussed above with that for the corresponding deterministic model using the same values of the parameters. The average annual cost for the deterministic model will never be greater than the average annual cost for the model which treats demand as a stochastic variable. The difference in average annual costs of the probabilistic model and the deterministic model will be called the average annual cost of uncertainty. This indicates what annual savings one could obtain, on the average, if all uncertainties in the demand and lead time variables could be eliminated, the mean values remaining unchanged.

We now give an example illustrating the use of the simplified models.

EXAMPLE A large military installation stocks a special purpose vacuum tube for use in radar sets. The average annual demand for this tube is 1600 units. Each tube costs $50. The tube must be made to order, and hence each time an order is placed it is necessary to go through a process of accepting bids and negotiating a contract. It is estimated that the cost of placing an order is \$4000. The installation uses an inventory carrying charge of $I = 0.20$. It has been found that if a demand occurs when the system is out of stock, it is possible to obtain such a tube from a small stock carried at one of the manufacturers. However, the cost of sending a plane there to obtain it and the other concomitant expenses amount to \$2000 over the cost of the unit. An empirical investigation has shown that the marginal distribution of lead time demand is essentially normally distributed with mean 750 units and standard deviation 50 units. It is desired to compute the optimal order quantity, the reorder point, and the safety stock.

The description of the operation of the system presented above indicates that we here need the model for the lost sales case, since if a demand occurs when the system is out of stock it is not backordered, but is instead procured from outside the system. The cost of a lost sale π to be used in the model is \$2000, for by definition, π includes the lost profit which, in this case, since the selling price is zero, means the stockout cost net of the item's cost. The optimal values of Q and r are found using (4-21), (4-22). The iterative procedure discussed above will be used to solve the equations. We note that $\lambda = 1600$ units per year, $C = \$50$, $I = 0.20$, $A = \$4000$. The initial estimate for Q is

$$Q_1 = Q_w = \sqrt{\frac{2\lambda A}{IC}} = \sqrt{\frac{2(1600)(4000)}{0.20(50)}} = \sqrt{1,280,000} = 1130$$

Then r_1 is computed from (4-22). In this case

$$H(r) = \Phi\left(\frac{r - 750}{50}\right)$$

since the lead time demand is normally distributed with mean 750 and standard deviation 50. Thus

$$\Phi\left(\frac{r_1 - 750}{50}\right) = \frac{Q_1 IC}{\lambda\pi + Q_1 IC} = \frac{1130(10)}{1600(2000) + 1130(10)} = \frac{1.130}{321.1} = 0.00352$$

From the normal tables we find that

$$\frac{r_1 - 750}{50} = 2.695$$

or

$$r_1 = 750 + 134.7 = 884.7$$

To compute Q_2 we use (4-21). First we compute $\bar\eta(r_1)$ from

$$\bar\eta(r_1) = (\mu - r_1)\Phi\left(\frac{r_1 - \mu}{\sigma}\right) + \sigma\phi\left(\frac{r_1 - \mu}{\sigma}\right)$$

From the normal tables, $\phi(2.695) = 0.01057$, so

$$\bar{\eta}(r_1) = -134.7(0.00352) + 50(0.01057)$$

$$= -0.47414 + 0.52850 = 0.05436$$

Thus

$$Q_2 = \sqrt{\frac{2(1600)[4000 + 2000(.05436)]}{10}} = \sqrt{2(160)(4108.72)} = 1147$$

Then for r_2

$$\Phi\left(\frac{r_2 - 750}{50}\right) = \frac{1.147}{321.1} = 0.00357$$

and

$$\frac{r_2 - 750}{50} = 2.69$$

or

$$r_2 = 750 + 134.5 = 884.5 \approx 884$$

There has been essentially no change in the safety stock. Additional iterations are not needed since the changes will be negligible. The optimal values are $Q^* = 1147$, $r^* = 884$, $s^* \approx 134$. Because of the high cost of stockouts a safety stock of 134 tubes is carried. The expected time between the placing of orders is 8.60 months.

The average annual cost of ordering, carrying inventory, and stockouts is easily computed from (4-23). It is

$$\mathcal{K} = \frac{1600}{1147}(4000) + 10\left[\frac{1147}{2} + 884 - 750\right]$$

$$+ \left[10 + \frac{2000(1600)}{1147}\right][-134(0.00357) + 50(0.01071)]$$

$$= 5580 + 7075 + 160 = \$12{,}815/\text{yr}.$$

The corresponding cost for the deterministic case is

$$K_w = \sqrt{2\lambda AIC} = \sqrt{2(1600)(4000)(10)} = \sqrt{1.28} \times 10^4 = \$11{,}305/\text{yr}.$$

since it is never optimal to have lost sales in the certainty case. Thus the average annual cost of uncertainty is

$$\mathcal{K} - K_w = 12{,}815 - 11{,}305 = \$1510$$

which is \$170 more than the average annual cost of \$1340 incurred to carry the 134 units of safety stock. Of the \$170, \$160 is the average annual cost of stockouts while the remaining \$10 is incurred because Q^* differs from Q_w. Note that when using the optimal Q and r values, the average annual stockout cost is only $160. This means that on the average a lost sale will be incurred only once every 12.5 years.

Often it is desirable to know how sensitive $Q*$ and $r*$ are to changes in the parameters such as A, I, or π. In Fig. 4-3, it is shown how $Q*$ and $r*$ vary with π. It will be observed that $Q*$ is very insensitive to π while $r*$ is slightly more sensitive but not really too sensitive, since a change in π from $500 to $5000 increases $r*$ by only about 40 units, i.e., increases the safety stock by 40 units. Since the mean lead time demand is 750 units, the safety stock changes from about 109 units to 149 units or a change of less than 50 percent for a factor of 10 change in the cost of a lost sale. This

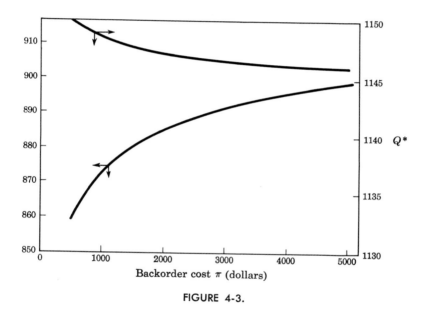

FIGURE 4-3.

points out that even if one cannot measure π too accurately, then provided it is of the right order of magnitude, the Q and r values computed will not be very far from the optimal ones that would be obtained on using the correct value of π.

4-5 The Exact Development—Introductory Discussion

After having presented the elementary approximate treatment of lot size-reorder point models in the previous three sections, we would now like to turn to a consideration of the exact formulation. Recall from the introduction to this chapter that a lot size-reorder point type of operating doctrine can be optimal only if transactions reporting is used, and if, in the discrete case, units are demanded one at a time. These assumptions will be made here.

The main emphasis will be concentrated on developing the exact average annual cost expression for the case where a Poisson process generates demands, the procurement lead time is a constant, and units demanded when the system is out of stock are backordered. We shall also consider extensions of this case to situations where the lead time is allowed to be a random variable. It will be seen, however, that it is not at all an easy matter to develop an exact treatment of this case, except under very restrictive or unrealistic assumptions. The lost sales case will be studied also. The lost sales case is much more difficult to treat than the backorders case, and, indeed it is only when the restriction is made that never more than one order is outstanding that it is possible to obtain exactly the cost expression.

Except for the material to be presented in the next section, we shall in this chapter only consider cases where a Poisson process generates demands, and units are demanded one at a time. The discussion of cases where the order size can be a random variable, or where the interarrival distribution is something other than exponential will be deferred to Chapter 8. These latter cases lead to much more complicated expressions than the cases to be considered here. We shall, however, also consider in this chapter the normal approximation to the Poisson distribution. This normal approximation is, in addition, the continuous approximation to some of the more complicated cases to be examined in Chapter 8.

The procedure used to determine the average annual cost for the simple approximate models developed in Secs. 4-2 and 4-3, was to compute the expected cost per cycle and then to multiply by the average number of cycles per year. This is a very powerful technique for developing the average annual cost expression. It can be used under a very wide variety of circumstances as we shall see in this chapter, the next chapter, and in the problems of Chapter 8. We shall use this procedure to treat the lost sales case in this chapter. To illustrate a different and interesting approach we shall treat the backorders case with constant lead times and a Poisson process generating demands as a Markov process discrete in space and continuous in time. Here, one first computes the state probabilities, and then uses them to obtain the average annual cost. While the Markov type of analysis is useful in a variety of cases, it does not seem to have nearly the general applicability of the procedure which first computes the excepted cost per cycle and then multiplies by the average number of cycles per year. The Markov form of analysis, however, does have the advantage that it yields directly the state probabilities, which are not obtained directly from the other method of generating the average annual cost.

Before going on to develop the exact annual cost expression for the backorders case with constant lead times, we shall first compute some time averages that will be needed, and also say a word about the possible interpretations of the state probabilities and their use in computing the time averages.

4-6 Computation of Time Averages

The criterion to be used in determining the optimal values of Q and r will be the minimization of the average annual cost, where the average annual cost is defined to be the limit as $\zeta \to \infty$ of the average cost for a time period of length ζ. Assume that we select arbitrary values for Q and r, and that we start out the system in operation using these values. At any arbitrary point in time after the system starts to operate we begin observing the system. Suppose that in a time ζ since observation was begun the system goes through n complete cycles and perhaps part of another one. We can use either the placement or receipt of an order as convenient events to define the beginning of a cycle. Assume that demands occurring when the system is out of stock are backordered. In this section, we shall not make any special assumptions concerning the nature of the stochastic processes generating demands and lead times except to assume that they do not change with time, and that units are demanded one at a time.

Let T_i be the length of cycle i, T'_i be the length of time during which the system has stock on hand in cycle i, T''_i be the length of time for which the system is out of stock in cycle i ($T_i = T'_i + T''_i$), Ω_i be the unit years of inventory held during cycle i, Δ_i be the unit years of shortage incurred during cycle i, and ξ_i the number of backorders incurred during cycle i.

The number of orders placed in the time period of length ζ is $n + \epsilon$ where $\epsilon = 0$ or 1, depending on whether or not an order is placed in the fraction of a cycle which may be included. The average number of orders per year placed over the time span ζ is $(n + \epsilon)/\zeta$. As $\zeta \to \infty$, it must be true that $n \to \infty$, and the average number of orders placed per year approaches*

---

* The limits of random variables studied in this section cannot rigorously be considered to be limits in the strict mathematical sense. The reason for this is that one cannot guarantee that there exists a $T_0(\epsilon)$ so large that for *all* $T > T_0(\epsilon)$, the difference between the random variable and its limiting value is less in absolute value than ϵ, for any $\epsilon > 0$, simply because of the stochastic nature of the process. The sort of statement which can be made is that the random variable approaches a given limit with probability one, i.e., the probability that the random variable differs in absolute value from its limiting value by any specified positive quantity approaches zero as $T \to \infty$. The limits employed in this section will be interpreted in this way.

$$\lim_{\zeta \to \infty} \frac{n}{\zeta} = \frac{1}{Q} \lim_{\zeta \to \infty} \frac{nQ}{\zeta} = \frac{\lambda}{Q} \tag{4-25}$$

since $\epsilon/\zeta \to 0$, nQ approaches the total demand in the period ζ, and by definition of the mean demand rate λ,

$$\lim_{\zeta \to \infty} \frac{nQ}{\zeta} = \lambda \tag{4-26}$$

Hence we have shown that in the backorders case, the average number of orders per year, i.e., the average number of cycles per year is λ/Q. This is independent of the specific nature of the demand or lead time distributions provided that an order is placed after every Q demands.

The fraction of the time that the system is out of stock which will be written P_{out}, is

$$P_{\text{out}} = \lim_{\zeta \to \infty} \frac{\sum\limits_{i=1}^{n} T_i''}{\zeta} \tag{4-27}$$

This then is, by definition, the probability that the system is out of stock if we observe the system at a random point in time. Also

$$D = \lim_{\zeta \to \infty} \frac{\sum\limits_{i=1}^{n} \Omega_i}{\zeta}, \quad B = \lim_{\zeta \to \infty} \frac{\sum\limits_{i=1}^{n} \Delta_i}{\zeta}, \quad E = \lim_{\zeta \to \infty} \frac{\sum\limits_{i=1}^{n} \xi_i}{\zeta} \tag{4-28}$$

are the average unit years of stock held per year, the average unit years of shortage incurred per year, and the average number of backorders incurred per year. If the on hand inventory were always a constant D, then the unit years of stock held per year would be D. Thus, D is the expected value of the on hand inventory at any instant of time. Similarly, B is the expected number of backorders on the books at any point of time.

It is desirable to rewrite the expression for E. Note that since the limit of a product is the product of the limits

$$E = \lim_{\zeta \to \infty} \frac{\sum\limits_{i=1}^{n} \xi_i}{\zeta} = \lim_{\zeta \to \infty} \left\{ \frac{\sum\limits_{i=1}^{n} T_i''}{\zeta} \frac{\sum\limits_{i=1}^{n} \xi_i}{\sum\limits_{i=1}^{n} T_i''} \right\}$$

$$= \lim_{\zeta \to \infty} \frac{\sum\limits_{i=1}^{n} T_i''}{\zeta} \lim_{\zeta \to \infty} \frac{\sum\limits_{i=1}^{n} \xi_i}{\sum\limits_{i=1}^{n} T_i''} = \lambda P_{\text{out}} \tag{4-29}$$

The second limit is λ, since $\sum_{i=1}^{n} \xi_i$ is the total number of units demanded in the time $\sum_{i=1}^{n} T_i''$. The ratio, in the limit as $\zeta \to \infty$, must be λ by the definition of the mean demand rate. We have just shown that the average number of backorders incurred per year is the mean rate of demand times the probability that the system has no stock on hand.

Another interesting result can be obtained using the fact that the limit of a product is the product of the limits. We note that

$$D = \lim_{\zeta \to \infty} \left\{ n \frac{\sum_{i=1}^{n} \Omega_i}{\zeta} \right\} = \lim_{\zeta \to \infty} \frac{n}{\zeta} \lim_{\zeta \to \infty} \frac{\sum_{i=1}^{n} \Omega_i}{n} = \frac{\hat{\Omega}}{Q} \lim_{\zeta \to \infty} \frac{nQ}{\zeta} = \frac{\lambda}{Q} \hat{\Omega} \qquad (4\text{-}30)$$

where by definition

$$\hat{\Omega} = \lim_{\zeta \to \infty} \frac{\sum_{i=1}^{n} \Omega_i}{n} \qquad (4\text{-}31)$$

is the average number of unit years of stock held per cycle. Furthermore, by definition of λ, $\lim_{\zeta \to \infty} nQ/\zeta = \lambda$. Thus (4-30) follows. The above shows that the average number of unit years of stock held per year is λ/Q times the average number of unit years held per cycle.

The values of D, B, E, and P_{out} will depend on the nature of the stochastic processes generating demands and lead times. They can be computed by first computing the corresponding expected value per cycle and then multiplying by λ/Q. The expected values per cycle are computed by using the information given about the demand and lead time distributions. However, if we can determine the steady state probabilities $\psi(x)$ that the net inventory has the value x, then the values of D, B, E, and P_{out} may be computed directly. Thus

$$D = \sum_{x=0}^{x_{max}} x\psi(x); \quad B = - \sum_{x=-\infty}^{-1} x\psi(x); \quad P_{out} = \sum_{x=-\infty}^{0} \psi(x) \qquad (4\text{-}32)$$

It is important to note that the steady state probability $\psi(x)$ can be given several interpretations. It is the probability that the inventory position is x if we observe the system at a random point in time (after the system is in a steady state mode of operation). It is also the long run fraction of the time that the net inventory will have the value x. Finally, it is the limit as $N \to \infty$ of the fraction of an ensemble of N systems in statistical equilibrium that will have the inventory position x at any given point in time.

The analysis for the lost sales case is precisely the same as for the backorders case examined above. If the same definitions are used as in the backorders case, it is immediately clear that the average number of lost sales per year is λP_{out}, and D, the average unit years of storage per year, is given by (4-28) and (4-32). The average number of cycles per year is different in the lost sales case than in the backorders case, however. We shall now compute the average number of cycles per year in the lost sales case. For this case, Q units are demanded in T'_i, not in time T_i as in the backorders case. The average number of cycles is, by definition

$$
\lim_{\varsigma \to \infty} \frac{n}{\varsigma} = \lim_{\varsigma \to \infty} \frac{nQ}{Q\varsigma} = \frac{1}{Q} \lim_{\varsigma \to \infty} \left[\frac{nQ}{\sum\limits_{i=1}^{n} T'_i} \right] \left[\frac{\sum\limits_{i=1}^{n} T'_i}{\varsigma} \right]
$$

(4-33)

$$
= \frac{1}{Q} \lim_{\varsigma \to \infty} \frac{nQ}{\sum\limits_{i=1}^{n} T'_i} \lim_{\varsigma \to \infty} \frac{\sum\limits_{i=1}^{n} T'_i}{\varsigma}
$$

However, nQ is the demand in time $\sum_{i=1}^{n} T'_i$ and hence the ratio of these two quantities must approach λ. Next observe that

$$
\sum_{i=1}^{n} T'_i = \sum_{i=1}^{n} T_i - \sum_{i=1}^{n} T''_i
$$

(4-34)

and hence

$$
\lim_{\varsigma \to \infty} \frac{\sum\limits_{i=1}^{n} T'_i}{\varsigma} = 1 - \lim_{\varsigma \to \infty} \frac{\sum\limits_{i=1}^{n} T''_i}{\varsigma} = 1 - P_{\text{out}}
$$

(4-35)

Thus

$$
\lim_{\varsigma \to \infty} \frac{n}{\varsigma} = \frac{\lambda}{Q} (1 - P_{\text{out}})
$$

(4-36)

and the average number of cycles per year is $(\lambda/Q)(1 - P_{\text{out}})$. It is also true that

$$
\lim_{n \to \infty} \frac{n}{\varsigma} = \lim_{n \to \infty} \frac{1}{\dfrac{1}{n}\sum\limits_{i=1}^{n} T'_i + \dfrac{1}{n}\sum\limits_{i=1}^{n} T''_i} = \lim_{n \to \infty} \frac{1}{Q\left[\dfrac{\sum\limits_{i=1}^{n} T'_i}{nQ}\right] + \dfrac{1}{n}\sum\limits_{i=1}^{n} T''_i}
$$

$$
= \frac{1}{\dfrac{Q}{\lambda} + \hat{T}} = \frac{\lambda}{Q + \lambda \hat{T}}
$$

(4-37)

where $\hat{T}$ is the average length of time per cycle for which the system is out of stock.

4-7 Exact Formulas for the Backorders Case with Poisson Demands and Constant Procurement Lead Time

We shall now determine an exact expression for the average annual cost in the case where a Poisson process generates the times between demands, units are demanded one at a time, the mean rate of demand being λ units per year, and the procurement lead time is a constant τ. In addition to treating the demand variable as being discrete, the order quantity Q, the reorder point r, and all the inventory levels will also be treated as discrete variables.

As yet, we have not discussed which inventory level (or levels) can be used to define the reorder point. We can see at once that the on hand inventory (or net inventory) cannot be used to rigorously define the reorder point, since, if there was a very heavy demand during some cycle and a huge number of backorders were incurred, then the arrival of whatever outstanding orders there were might never bring the on hand inventory back up to the reorder point again, and hence another order would never be placed. This leaves only the inventory position (the amount on hand plus on order minus backorders) as a suitable level for defining the reorder point. The inventory position does provide a suitable level, since the difficulty referred to above with the on hand level cannot occur. If during some cycle there is very heavy demand and a considerable number of backorders are incurred, it will also be true that a correspondingly large number of orders will be placed, for the reorder point in terms of the inventory position will be crossed a number of times.

If r is the reorder point in terms of the inventory position, then immediately after an order is placed the inventory position is $Q + r$. Thus the inventory position must have one of the values $r + 1, \ldots, r + Q$. It is never in a state r for a finite length of time, since as soon as a demand occurs which reduces the inventory position to state r an order is placed bringing the state to $r + Q$. Note that specification of the inventory position tells us nothing about the on hand inventory or net inventory. If the inventory position is $r + j$, there may be no orders outstanding with the net inventory being $r + j$, one order outstanding with the net inventory being $r + j - Q$, etc. For Poisson demands, where there is a positive probability for an arbitrarily large quantity being demanded in any time interval, it is theoretically possible to have any number of orders outstanding at a particular instant of time. (Of course the probability of a large number of orders outstanding will often be very small.) In a case where there was a finite upper limit to the amount that could be demanded in any time period, then there could never be more orders outstanding than total to an amount equal to the maximum lead time demand. On the other hand, specification of the net inventory does uniquely determine the number of orders outstanding and the inventory position, since if x is the net inventory and n orders are outstanding, the inventory position is $x + nQ$, and this can be written $r + j, j = 1, \ldots, Q$. This restriction determines both n and j. The value of n is the largest non-negative integer which makes $r < x + nQ \leq r + Q$.

In the simple approximate model discussed in Sec. 4-2, we assumed that there was never more than a single order outstanding, and that the reorder point could be based on the on hand inventory. We have just seen that in general such restrictions cannot be made rigorously. It may be justifiable to stipulate, however, that the probability that more than one order is outstanding is very small.

In order to compute P_{out}, the expected number of backorders on the books at any point in time, and the expected on hand inventory at any point in time we need the state probabilities for the net inventory. The straightforward way to compute these would be to attempt to write down

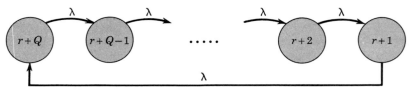

FIGURE 4-4.

the difference equations (3-124) which describe transitions between the net inventory states. Difficulties are encountered with this procedure, however, since the lead times are constant and are not generated by a Poisson process. We shall therefore use a different approach, and instead we begin by finding the state probabilities $\rho(r + j)$ that the inventory position of the system is $r + j, j = 1, \ldots, Q$. A knowledge of these permits the computation of the state probabilities for the net inventory. The advantage of doing this is that the nature of the procurement lead times does not enter into the computation of the $\rho(r + j)$.

In a time dt, the system inventory position moves from state $r + j$ to $r + j - 1, j \geq 2$, if a demand occurs. This happens when a Poisson process generates demands and units are demanded one at a time with probability $\lambda \, dt$. If the system is in state $r + 1$ and a demand occurs, it moves to state $r + Q$ since the demand triggers the placement of an order. Thus we have the diagram representing the transitions shown in Fig. 4-4.

The balance equations (3-124) then read for this particular case

$$\lambda\rho(r + j + 1) = \lambda\rho(r + j), \quad j = 1, \ldots, Q - 1$$
$$\lambda\rho(r + Q) = \lambda\rho(r + 1) \tag{4-38}$$

Thus,

$$\rho(r + Q) = \rho(r + Q - 1) = \ldots = \rho(r + 1)$$

and since $\sum_{j=1}^{Q} \rho(r + j) = 1$, it follows that the unique solution for $\rho(r + j)$ is

$$\rho(r + j) = \frac{1}{Q}, \quad j = 1, \ldots, Q \tag{4-39}$$

We have shown that, in the steady state, each of the inventory position states $r + j$ has the same probability $1/Q$ which is independent of j. We say that the states are uniformly distributed and that $\rho(r + j)$ is a uniform distribution.

To compute the state probabilities for the on hand inventory and the number of backorders, consider the system at any instant of time t. Also consider the time $t - \tau$, τ being the procurement lead time. Note that everything on order at time $t - \tau$ will have arrived in the system by time t and nothing not on order at time $t - \tau$ can have arrived in the system by time t. Thus, if the inventory position of the system was $r + j$ at time $t - \tau$, the probability that there are x units on hand at time t is the probability that $r + j - x$ units were demanded in the lead time τ if $r + j - x \geq 0$ and is zero otherwise. For Poisson demands, the probability of having this number of units demanded is $p(r + j - x; \lambda\tau)$ when $r + j - x \geq 0$. However, the probability that the inventory position is $r + j$ at time $t - \tau$ is $1/Q$. Then if $\psi_1(x)$ is the state probability that x units are on hand at any time t, to find $\psi_1(x)$ we multiply $p(r + j - x; \lambda\tau)$ by $1/Q$ and sum over the j for which $r + j - x \geq 0$. Thus

$$\psi_1(x) = \frac{1}{Q} \sum_{j=1}^{Q} p(r + j - x; \lambda\tau)$$

$$= \frac{1}{Q} \sum_{u=r+1-x}^{r+Q-x} p(u; \lambda\tau)$$

$$= \frac{1}{Q} \left[\sum_{u=r+1-x}^{\infty} p(u; \lambda\tau) - \sum_{u=r+Q+1-x}^{\infty} p(u; \lambda\tau) \right] \tag{4-40}$$

$$= \frac{1}{Q} [P(r + 1 - x; \lambda\tau) - P(r + Q + 1 - x; \lambda\tau)], \quad 0 \leq x < r + 1$$

$$\psi_1(x) = \frac{1}{Q} \sum_{j=x-r}^{Q} p(r + j - x; \lambda\tau) = \frac{1}{Q} \sum_{u=0}^{r+Q-x} p(u; \lambda\tau)$$

$$\tag{4-41}$$

$$= \frac{1}{Q} [1 - P(r + Q + 1 - x; \lambda\tau)], \quad r + 1 \leq x \leq r + Q$$

Here we have the state probabilities for the on hand inventory.

In the same way, if the system is in state $r + j$ at time $t - \tau$, the probability that there are y backorders at time t is $p(y + r + j; \lambda\tau)$, $y \geq 0$. Thus the state probability $\psi_2(y)$ that there are y backorders at time t is

$$\psi_2(y) = \frac{1}{Q} \sum_{j=1}^{Q} p(y + r + j; \lambda\tau) = \frac{1}{Q} \sum_{u=y+r+1}^{y+r+Q} p(u; \lambda\tau)$$

$$= \frac{1}{Q} [P(y + r + 1; \lambda\tau) - P(y + r + Q + 1; \lambda\tau)], \quad y \geq 0$$

(4-42)

These same state probabilities have been obtained previously in a different form in [3].

With the help of Appendix 3 we can now easily compute the expected values needed. First of all P_{out}, the probability that there is no stock on hand at time t, is

$$P_{\text{out}} = \sum_{y=0}^{\infty} \psi_2(y) = \frac{1}{Q} \left[\sum_{y=0}^{\infty} P(y + r + 1; \lambda\tau) - \sum_{y=0}^{\infty} P(y + r + Q + 1; \lambda\tau) \right]$$

$$= \frac{1}{Q} \left[\sum_{u=r+1}^{\infty} P(u; \lambda\tau) - \sum_{u=r+Q+1}^{\infty} P(u; \lambda\tau) \right]$$

(4-43)

and from A3-6

$$P_{\text{out}} = \frac{1}{Q} [\alpha(r) - \alpha(r + Q)]$$

(4-44)

where

$$\alpha(v) = \sum_{u=v+1}^{\infty} P(u; \lambda\tau) = \lambda\tau P(v; \lambda\tau) - v P(v + 1; \lambda\tau)$$

(4-45)

Thus $E(Q, r)$, the average number of backorders incurred per year, is by (4-29)

$$E(Q, r) = \lambda P_{\text{out}} = \frac{\lambda}{Q} [\alpha(r) - \alpha(r + Q)]$$

(4-46)

The expected number of backorders on the books $B(Q, r)$ at any time t is by definition

$$B(Q, r) = \sum_{y=0}^{\infty} y\psi_2(y)$$

$$= \frac{1}{Q} \sum_{y=0}^{\infty} y[P(y + r + 1; \lambda\tau) - P(y + r + Q + 1; \lambda\tau)]$$

$$= \frac{1}{Q} \left[\sum_{u=r+1}^{\infty} (u - r - 1)P(u; \lambda\tau) - \sum_{u=r+Q+1}^{\infty} (u - r - Q - 1)P(u; \lambda\tau) \right]$$

(4-47)

Now

$$\sum_{u=v+1}^{\infty} (u - v - 1)P(u; \lambda\tau)$$

$$= \sum_{u=v+1}^{\infty} uP(u; \lambda\tau) - (v + 1) \sum_{u=v+1}^{\infty} P(u; \lambda\tau) \qquad (4\text{-}48)$$

and by A3-8, A3-6

$$\sum_{u=v+1}^{\infty} uP(u; \lambda\tau) = \frac{(\lambda\tau)^2}{2} P(v - 1; \lambda\tau) + \lambda\tau P(v; \lambda\tau)$$

$$- \frac{v(v + 1)}{2} P(v + 1; \lambda\tau) \qquad (4\text{-}49)$$

$$(v + 1) \sum_{u=v+1}^{\infty} P(u; \lambda\tau) = (\lambda\tau)(v + 1)P(v; \lambda\tau)$$

$$- v(v + 1)P(v + 1; \lambda\tau) \qquad (4\text{-}50)$$

Hence if

$$\beta(v) = \sum_{u=v+1}^{\infty} (u - v - 1)P(u; \lambda\tau) = \frac{(\lambda\tau)^2}{2} P(v - 1; \lambda\tau)$$

$$- (\lambda\tau)vP(v; \lambda\tau) + \frac{v(v + 1)}{2} P(v + 1; \lambda\tau) \qquad (4\text{-}51)$$

Then

$$B(Q, r) = \frac{1}{Q} [\beta(r) - \beta(r + Q)] \qquad (4\text{-}52)$$

We have now evaluated the expected number of backorders at any point in time. As we observed in Sec. 4-6, $B(Q, r)$ is also the average unit years of shortage incurred per year.

It remains to evaluate the expected on hand inventory at any time. By definition, the expected on hand inventory $D(Q, r)$ is

$$D(Q, r) = \sum_{x=0}^{r+Q} x\psi_1(x)$$

$$= \frac{1}{Q} \left\{ \sum_{x=0}^{r} x[P(r + 1 - x; \lambda\tau) - P(r + Q + 1 - x; \lambda\tau)] \right.$$

$$+ \left. \sum_{x=r+1}^{r+Q} x[1 - P(r + Q + 1 - x; \lambda\tau)] \right\} \qquad (4\text{-}53)$$

$$= \frac{1}{Q} \left\{ \sum_{x=r+1}^{r+Q} x + \sum_{x=0}^{r} xP(r + 1 - x; \lambda\tau) \right.$$

$$- \left. \sum_{x=0}^{r+Q} xP(r + Q + 1 - x; \lambda\tau) \right\}$$

Now

$$\frac{1}{Q}\sum_{x=r+1}^{r+Q} x = \frac{1}{Q}\sum_{j=1}^{Q}(r+j) = \frac{1}{Q}\left[Qr + \frac{Q(Q+1)}{2}\right] = \frac{Q+1}{2} + r \quad (4\text{-}54)$$

Also

$$\sum_{x=0}^{v} xP(v+1-x; \lambda\tau) = \sum_{x=1}^{v} xP(v+1-x; \lambda\tau) = \sum_{u=1}^{v}(v+1-u)P(u; \lambda\tau)$$

$$= \sum_{u=1}^{\infty}(v+1-u)P(u; \lambda\tau) + \sum_{u=v+1}^{\infty}(u-v-1)P(u; \lambda\tau) \quad (4\text{-}55)$$

Thus

$$D(Q, r) = \frac{Q+1}{2} + r$$

$$+ \frac{1}{Q}\left\{\sum_{u=1}^{\infty}(r+1-u)P(u; \lambda\tau) - \sum_{u=1}^{\infty}(r+Q+1-u)P(u; \lambda\tau)\right.$$

$$\left. + \sum_{u=r+1}^{\infty}(u-r-1)P(u; \lambda\tau) - \sum_{u=r+Q+1}^{\infty}(u-r-Q-1)P(u; \lambda\tau)\right\}$$

However,

$$\sum_{u=1}^{\infty}(r+1-u)P(u; \lambda\tau) - \sum_{u=1}^{\infty}(r+Q+1-u)P(u; \lambda\tau)$$

$$= -Q\sum_{u=1}^{\infty}P(u; \lambda\tau) = -Q\mu \quad (4\text{-}56)$$

when $\mu = \lambda\tau$ is the mean lead time demand. The last step follows from A3-6. Then from (4-47), we see that

$$D(Q, r) = \frac{(Q+1)}{2} + r - \mu + B(Q, r) \quad (4\text{-}57)$$

There is another simple procedure that one can use to compute the expected value of the on hand inventory. By comparison of the result so obtained with (4-57), an interesting result can be obtained. Note that the expected value of the inventory position is the expected value of the on hand inventory plus the expected amount on order minus the expected number of backorders, since the expected value of the sum of several random variables is the sum of the expected values. Thus the expected on hand inventory is equal to the expected inventory position minus the expected amount on order plus the expected number of backorders. Now the expected value of the inventory position is

$$\sum_{j=1}^{Q} (r+j)\rho(r+j) = \frac{1}{Q}\sum_{j=1}^{Q}(r+j) = \frac{(Q+1)}{2} + r \qquad (4\text{-}58)$$

and so

$$D(Q, r) = \frac{Q+1}{2} + r - J + B(Q, r) \qquad (4\text{-}59)$$

where J is the expected amount on order. Comparison of (4-59) with (4-57) shows that

$$J = \mu \qquad (4\text{-}60)$$

i.e., the expected amount on order is equal to the mean lead time demand. This result, which we have just proved rigorously for the case under consideration, holds under much more general assumptions. The fact that the expected amount on order should be the mean lead time demand can be seen intuitively as follows. Imagine that orders flow into one end of a pipeline and that procurements flow out the other end. Since all demands are ultimately met, the mean rate of flow of units ordered into the pipeline must be λ. Since an order remains in the pipeline for a time τ, the expected number in the pipeline should be $\lambda\tau = \mu$.

All the terms in the average annual variable cost $\mathfrak{K}$ have been evaluated; $\mathfrak{K}$ consists of the expected ordering costs, holding costs, and backorders costs. It is

$$\mathfrak{K} = \frac{\lambda}{Q}A + IC\left[\frac{Q}{2} + \frac{1}{2} + r - \mu + B(Q, r)\right] + \pi E(Q, r) + \hat{\pi}B(Q, r)$$

$$= \frac{\lambda}{Q}A + IC\left[\frac{Q}{2} + \frac{1}{2} + r - \mu\right] + \pi E(Q, r) + (\hat{\pi} + IC)B(Q, r) \qquad (4\text{-}61)$$

where $E(Q, r)$ and $B(Q, r)$ are defined by (4-46) and (4-52) respectively. We are here assuming that the unit cost C of the item is constant and is independent of Q, so that the cost of the units themselves need not be included. We are also assuming that the cost of operating the information processing system is independent of Q and r and hence need not be included in $\mathfrak{K}$.

We have in the above derivations carried out the operations acting as if r was positive. In actuality, with the proper interpretations, the above formulas also hold when r is negative or zero. The proper interpretation is to take $P(v; \lambda\tau) = 1$ if $v < 0$. We ask the reader to prove these statements in Problem 4-56. For example, if v is negative

$$\alpha(v) = \lambda\tau + |v| \tag{4-62}$$

$$\beta(v) = \frac{(\lambda\tau)^2}{2} + \lambda\tau|v| + \frac{|v|}{2}(|v| - 1) \tag{4-63}$$

In general, it is not very easy to determine the optimal values of Q and r by use of the exact expression (4-61) for $\mathfrak{K}$, since E and B depend on Q and r in a rather complicated fashion. Indeed, when the $\alpha(r + Q)$ and $\beta(r + Q)$ terms are included, it does not seem easy to prove that there cannot exist local minima different from the absolute minimum. To determine Q^* and r^* in the case where the $\alpha(r + Q)$ and $\beta(r + Q)$ terms are included, it seems necessary to use a digital computer along with an appropriate search routine to find Q^* and r^*. A digital computer code to determine the Q and r values which minimize the $\mathfrak{K}$ of (4-61) has been developed by P. Teicholz and B. Lundh of Stanford University. This program determines a relative minimum but does not provide any guarantee that the minimum so obtained is the absolute minimum if there exist local minima different from the absolute minimum. In Sec. 4-10 we shall present an example, some of the calculations for which were made with this code. It is worthwhile to point out that although it seems difficult to rule out theoretically the existence of local minima, the authors have been unable to detect the existence of such in making numerical computations with specific problems.

Fortunately, it turns out that in practice it is seldom necessary to use the exact formulation developed above. In the next section, it will be pointed out that for almost all cases of practical interest, $\mathfrak{K}$ reduces to a form which makes it fairly easy to determine Q^* and r^*. About the only time that the exact formulation is required is when it costs very little to incur backorders. Such cases do not occur too frequently in the real world.

4-8 An Important Special Case

In problems of practical interest, it is usually true that the terms $\alpha(r + Q)$, $\beta(r + Q)$ in $E(Q, r)$ and $B(Q, r)$ respectively, are negligible. These terms are important only if there is a significant probability that the lead time demand will be greater than $r + Q$. If this happens, then there will still be backorders on the books after the arrival of a procurement, i.e., the procurement will not be sufficient to remove all the backorders. It will never be optimal to have a sizeable probability that so many backorders will be incurred that the arrival of an order will not be sufficient to meet all of them unless it costs very little to incur backorders. This is seldom the case for most real world problems, and hence in practice it is usually a very good approximation to neglect $\alpha(r + Q)$ and $\beta(r + Q)$. When $\alpha(r + Q)$,

$\beta(r + Q)$ are negligible, a considerable simplification of $\mathcal{K}$ occurs. It can be written

$$\mathcal{K} = \frac{\lambda}{Q} A + IC \left[\frac{Q}{2} + \frac{1}{2} + r - \mu \right] + \frac{\lambda}{Q} \pi\alpha(r) + \frac{1}{Q} (\hat{\pi} + IC)\beta(r) \qquad (4\text{-}64)$$

Then if Q^*, r^* are the smallest values of Q, r which minimize $\mathcal{K}(Q, r)$ it is necessary that

$$\left.\begin{array}{l} \Delta_Q\mathcal{K}(Q^*, r^*) = \mathcal{K}(Q^*, r^*) - \mathcal{K}(Q^* - 1, r^*) < 0 \\ \Delta_Q\mathcal{K}(Q^* + 1, r^*) = \mathcal{K}(Q^* + 1, r^*) - \mathcal{K}(Q^*, r^*) \geq 0 \end{array}\right\} \text{ or } Q^* = 1 \qquad (4\text{-}65)$$

$$\left.\begin{array}{l} \Delta_r\mathcal{K}(Q^*, r^*) = \mathcal{K}(Q^*, r^*) - \mathcal{K}(Q^*, r^* - 1) < 0 \\ \Delta_r\mathcal{K}(Q^*, r^* + 1) = \mathcal{K}(Q^*, r^* + 1) - \mathcal{K}(Q^*, r^*) \geq 0 \end{array}\right\} \qquad (4\text{-}66)$$

Thus Q^* is the largest Q for which $\Delta_Q\mathcal{K}(Q, r^*) < 0$, or $Q^* = 1$, and r^* is the largest r for which $\Delta_r\mathcal{K}(Q^*, r) < 0$.

When $\mathcal{K}$ is given by (4-64)

$$\Delta_Q\mathcal{K}(Q, r) = [\lambda A + \lambda\pi\alpha(r) + (\hat{\pi} + IC)\beta(r)]\left[\frac{1}{Q} - \frac{1}{Q - 1} \right] + \frac{IC}{2} \qquad (4\text{-}67)$$

If $\Delta_Q\mathcal{K}(Q, r) < 0$, this implies that

$$Q(Q - 1) < \frac{2\lambda}{IC}\left[A + \pi\alpha(r) + \frac{(\hat{\pi} + IC)}{\lambda} \beta(r) \right] \qquad (4\text{-}68)$$

To determine $\Delta_r\mathcal{K}(Q, r)$ note first from (4-45) that

$$\Delta_r\alpha(r) = -P(r; \lambda\tau) \qquad (4\text{-}69)$$

Also, from (4-51)

$$\Delta_r\beta(r) = -\frac{(\lambda\tau)^2}{2} p(r - 2; \lambda\tau) + r(\lambda\tau)p(r - 1; \lambda\tau) - \lambda\tau P(r - 1; \lambda\tau)$$

$$-\frac{r^2}{2} p(r; \lambda\tau) + \frac{r}{2} [P(r + 1; \lambda\tau) + P(r; \lambda\tau)]$$

$$= \frac{(\lambda\tau)^2}{2} p(r - 2; \lambda\tau) + rp(r; \lambda\tau) - \lambda\tau P(r; \lambda\tau) - \lambda\tau p(r - 1; \lambda\tau)$$

$$-\frac{r^2}{2} p(r; \lambda\tau) + rP(r; \lambda\tau) - \frac{r}{2} p(r; \lambda\tau)$$

$$= (r - \lambda\tau)P(r; \lambda\tau) - rp(r; \lambda\tau) \qquad (4\text{-}70)$$

Thus

$$\Delta_r\mathcal{K}(Q, r) = IC + \frac{1}{Q} \{[-\lambda\pi + (\hat{\pi} + IC)(r - \lambda\tau)]P(r; \lambda\tau)$$

$$- (\hat{\pi} + IC)rp(r; \lambda\tau)\} \qquad (4\text{-}71)$$

and if $\Delta_r \mathcal{K}(Q, r) < 0$ this implies that

$$\left[1 - \frac{(\hat{\pi} + IC)}{\lambda \pi} (r - \lambda \tau) \right] P(r; \lambda \tau) + \frac{(\hat{\pi} + IC)r}{\lambda \pi} p(r; \lambda \tau) > \frac{QIC}{\pi \lambda} \qquad (4\text{-}72)$$

A computational procedure for finding the optimal Q and r is to begin with Q_w in (4-72) and determine the largest r satisfying (4-72). Use this r, call it r_1, in (4-68) to determine Q_2 by finding the largest Q which satisfies (4-68). Then Q_2 is used in (4-72) to determine r_2, etc. Continue until there is no change in r and Q.

Often it is possible to treat Q as continuous even though it is desirable to treat r as discrete. For example, when Q gets to be of the order of 10 or 12, it is normally satisfactory to treat Q as continuous. However, r will not usually be treated as continuous unless μ is at least 25. For continuous Q, (4-68) becomes:

$$Q = \sqrt{\frac{2\lambda}{IC} \left[A + \pi \alpha(r) + \frac{\hat{\pi} + IC}{\lambda} \beta(r) \right]} \qquad (4\text{-}73)$$

When Q is treated as a continuous variable and r as a discrete one, then (4-73) is used with (4-72) to determine Q^* and r^*. Although the task of determining Q^* and r^* for the case being considered here is considerably more time consuming than for the simple approximate model discussed in Sec. 4-2, it can easily be carried out by hand in a short time.

EXAMPLE   The Milex Company sells reflector lenses at an average rate of 50 per year. Units are almost always demanded one at a time, and it is felt that to an adequate approximation it can be assumed that a Poisson process generates demands. Ordering and receiving costs amount to $100 for each order. The cost of each lens is $50, independent of the quantity ordered, and the company uses an inventory carrying charge of $I = 0.20$. Demands occurring when there is no stock on hand are backordered and the cost of a backorder has been estimated to be $50 per backorder plus $500 per unit year of shortage. The procurement lead time is always very close to 0.4 years. The company in the past has been using a periodic review system, but has recently changed to using transactions reporting. Therefore, the company would like to install a lot size-reorder point system for controlling the reflector inventory. Compute the optimal order quantity and reorder point.

From the data given above, we see that $\lambda = 50$ units per year, $A = \$100$, $IC = \$10$, $\pi = \$50$, $\hat{\pi} = \$500$ per unit year, $\tau = 0.4$ years. To begin the iterative procedure we compute

$$Q_w = \sqrt{\frac{2\lambda A}{IC}} = \sqrt{1000} \approx 31.6$$

It is seen that Q_w is large enough that we should be able to treat Q as continuous. However, the mean lead time demand $\mu = \lambda\tau = 20$ is small enough that r should be treated as discrete. Thus equations (4-72), (4-73) will be used in the iterative procedure.

Now observe that when $Q = Q_w = 31.6$, and $r = 31$, (4-72) becomes

$$\left[1 - \frac{500 + 10}{50(50)}\right](31 - 20)(0.013475) + \frac{(500 + 10)(31)}{50(50)}(0.005383)$$

$$= 0.152 > \frac{(31.6)(10)}{50(50)} = 0.126$$

However, if $r = 32$, the direction of the inequality is reversed. Thus the largest r satisfying (4-72) when $Q = Q_w$ is 31, i.e., $r_1 = 31$. This value of r was determined after trying out several different values.

Substituting r_1 into (4-73), we find that

$$Q_2 = \left[10\left\{100 + 50(0.0186) + \frac{510}{50}(0.0227)\right\}\right]^{1/2} = 31.8$$

On using Q_2 in (4-72) we find that $r_2 = 31$ so that r is unchanged. Hence the iteration process terminates. If we round Q to 32 units and use this in (4-72), r again turns out to be 31. Thus the optimal order quantity is 32 and the optimal reorder point based on the inventory position is 31. Since the expected lead time demand is 20 units, the safety stock is 11 units.

4-9 The Normal Approximation

For large lead time demands the Poisson probabilities appearing in the model developed in the last sections can be conveniently approximated by a normal distribution. In such cases, it is usually a good approximation to treat Q and r as continuous variables also. Here we shall develop the equations corresponding to those in the previous section for the case where the lead time demand can be considered to be normally distributed. Recall from Sec. 3-14 that as $\mu \to \infty$, $p(x; u)$ approaches a normal distribution with mean μ and with variance $\sigma^2 = \mu$. In the development here, we shall not specifically set $\sigma^2 = \mu$ in the normal distribution. The reason for this is that later we shall want to consider the case of variable lead times. It will be found that it is often desirable to represent the marginal distribution of lead time demand by a normal distribution. However, in such cases, the variance σ^2 will be greater than μ because of the influence of variable lead times. In this section, we shall imagine the lead times to be constant. However, by not specifically setting $\sigma^2 = \mu$, and instead leaving σ as an independent parameter, we shall simultaneously obtain the appropriate equations that will be useful when considering the lead times to be random variables also.

Since r and Q are now being treated as continuous the inventory position can take on any value between r and $r + Q$ rather than only the values $r + 1, \ldots, r + Q$. The probability that the inventory position lies between x and $x + dx$, $r \le x < r + Q$ is simply dx/Q, because in Sec. 4-7 we showed that $\rho(r + j)$, the probability that the system was in the state $r + j$ was $1/Q$. This follows by using the same trick of drawing in rectangles used in Sec. 3-14 to show how the Poisson distribution approached the normal. Note that if the same procedure was used as in Sec. 3-14 the inventory position would range from $r + \frac{1}{2}$ to $r + Q + \frac{1}{2}$. This gives a slightly better approximation than using the range r to $r + Q$, but since for practical purposes the difference is negligible, and since in the physical system the inventory position cannot get above $r + Q$, we prefer to use the range r to $r + Q$. Note that

$$\int_r^{r+Q} \frac{dx}{Q} = 1 \qquad (4\text{-}74)$$

as desired. In place of the Poisson density $p(x; \mu)$ for the probability that x units are demanded in a lead time, we shall now use

$$n(x; \mu, \sigma) = \frac{1}{\sigma} \phi\left(\frac{x - \mu}{\sigma}\right) \qquad (4\text{-}75)$$

as the probability density for lead time demand, where μ is the expected lead time demand. In the following, we shall make use of the fact that when it is valid to use the normal approximation, then one can assume that $\Phi(-\mu/\sigma) = 1$ (see Sec. 3-14).

Then, if $\psi_1(x)$ is the probability density for the quantity on hand at any time t, it follows that

$$\psi_1(x) = \frac{1}{Q\sigma} \int_r^{r+Q} \phi\left(\frac{v - x - \mu}{\sigma}\right) dv$$

$$= \frac{1}{Q}\left[\Phi\left(\frac{r - x - \mu}{\sigma}\right) - \Phi\left(\frac{r + Q - x - \mu}{\sigma}\right)\right], \quad 0 \le x \le r \qquad (4\text{-}76)$$

$$\psi_1(x) = \frac{1}{Q\sigma} \int_x^{r+Q} \phi\left(\frac{v - x - \mu}{\sigma}\right) dv = \frac{1}{Q}\left[1 - \Phi\left(\frac{r + Q - x - \mu}{\sigma}\right)\right],$$

$$r \le x \le r + Q \qquad (4\text{-}77)$$

Similarly, the density function $\psi_2(y)$ for the number of backorders on hand at any time t is

$$\psi_2(y) = \frac{1}{Q\sigma} \int_r^{r+Q} \phi\left(\frac{x+y-\mu}{\sigma}\right) dx$$

$$= \frac{1}{Q}\left[\Phi\left(\frac{r+y-\mu}{\sigma}\right) - \Phi\left(\frac{r+Q+y-\mu}{\sigma}\right)\right], \quad y \geq 0 \qquad (4\text{-}78)$$

Then

$$P_{\text{out}} = \int_0^\infty \psi_2(y)\, dy = \frac{1}{Q}\left[\int_0^\infty \Phi\left(\frac{r+y-\mu}{\sigma}\right) dy\right.$$

$$\left. - \int_0^\infty \Phi\left(\frac{r+Q+y-\mu}{\sigma}\right) dy\right] \qquad (4\text{-}79)$$

Now by A4-6

$$\int_0^\infty \Phi\left(\frac{v+y-\mu}{\sigma}\right) dy = \sigma \int_{(v-\mu)/\sigma}^\infty \Phi(\xi)\, d\xi$$

$$= \sigma\phi\left(\frac{v-\mu}{\sigma}\right) - (v-\mu)\,\Phi\left(\frac{v-\mu}{\sigma}\right)$$

Thus the expected number of backorders incurred per year is

$$E(Q,r) = \lambda P_{\text{out}} = \frac{\lambda}{Q}\left[\alpha(r) - \alpha(r+Q)\right] \qquad (4\text{-}80)$$

Where

$$\alpha(v) = \sigma\phi\left(\frac{v-\mu}{\sigma}\right) - (v-\mu)\,\Phi\left(\frac{v-\mu}{\sigma}\right) \qquad (4\text{-}81)$$

Next, the expected number of backorders at any time is

$$B(Q,r) = \int_0^\infty y\psi_2(y)\, dy = \frac{1}{Q}\left\{\int_0^\infty y\Phi\left(\frac{r+y-\mu}{\sigma}\right) dy\right.$$

$$\left. - \int_0^\infty y\Phi\left(\frac{r+Q+y-\mu}{\sigma}\right) dy\right\} \qquad (4\text{-}82)$$

From A4-6 and A4-7

$$\int_0^\infty y\Phi\left(\frac{v+y-\mu}{\sigma}\right) dy = \frac{1}{2}\left[\sigma^2 + (v-\mu)^2\right]\Phi\left(\frac{v-\mu}{\sigma}\right)$$

$$- \frac{\sigma}{2}(v-\mu)\phi\left(\frac{v-\mu}{\sigma}\right) \qquad (4\text{-}83)$$

Therefore

$$B(Q,r) = \frac{1}{Q}\left[\beta(r) - \beta(r+Q)\right] \qquad (4\text{-}84)$$

where

$$\beta(v) = \frac{1}{2} \left[\sigma^2 + (v - \mu)^2 \right] \Phi \left(\frac{v - \mu}{\sigma} \right) - \frac{\sigma}{2} (v - \mu) \phi \left(\frac{v - \mu}{\sigma} \right) \qquad (4\text{-}85)$$

Finally

$$D(Q, r) = \int_0^{r+Q} x \psi_1(x) \, dx = \frac{Q}{2} + r - \mu + B(Q, r) \qquad (4\text{-}86)$$

All the terms needed in the average annual cost $\mathcal{K}$ have been evaluated; $\mathcal{K}$ is

$$\mathcal{K} = \frac{\lambda}{Q} A + IC \left[\frac{Q}{2} + r - \mu \right] + \pi E(Q, r) + (\hat{\pi} + IC) B(Q, r) \qquad (4\text{-}87)$$

The values of Q and r which minimize $\mathcal{K}$ will be solutions to

$$\frac{\partial \mathcal{K}}{\partial Q} = \frac{\partial \mathcal{K}}{\partial r} = 0 \qquad (4\text{-}88)$$

Problem 4-16 asks the reader to obtain all the first and second derivatives of $\mathcal{K}$.

In the usual case where the $\alpha(r + Q)$ and $\beta(r + Q)$ terms are negligible and can be ignored, the equations of (4-88) reduce to

$$Q = \sqrt{\frac{2\lambda [A + \pi\alpha(r)] + 2(\hat{\pi} + IC)\beta(r)}{IC}} \qquad (4\text{-}89)$$

$$[\pi\lambda - (\hat{\pi} + IC)(r - \mu)] \Phi \left(\frac{r - \mu}{\sigma} \right) + (\hat{\pi} + IC)\sigma\phi \left(\frac{r - \mu}{\sigma} \right) = QIC \qquad (4\text{-}90)$$

The same sort of iterative scheme used to determine Q^* and r^* for the simple model of Sec. 4-2 can also be applied here. That is, we first set $Q = Q_w$ in (4-90) and determine r_1, the value of r which satisfies this equation. Then r_1 is used in (4-89) to yield Q_2, etc. Now, of course, it will be somewhat harder to solve (4-90) than it was to solve the corresponding equation for the simple case.

At this point we might note that when $\hat{\pi} = 0$, $\alpha(r + Q)$ is negligible, and the contribution of $B(Q, r)$ to the inventory carrying charge is negligible, (4-87), (4-89), and (4-90) reduce to (4-16), (4-12), (4-13) respectively. This shows us that the model of Sec. 4-2 is applicable, when the assumptions stated above apply, for any number of orders outstanding, and is not restricted merely to the case of never more than a single order outstanding.

It is not simple to make numerical computations using the exact form for $\mathcal{K}$ obtained in this section. When the $\alpha(r + Q)$ and $\beta(r + Q)$ terms are included, $\mathcal{K}$ is not generally convex. This nonconvexity makes it difficult to rule out the existence of local minima which differ from the absolute minimum. The nonconvexity has also caused convergence difficulties with Newton's method and the method of steepest descents in examples which the authors have attempted to work out in which the $\alpha(r + Q)$ and $\beta(r + Q)$ terms were important. When the $\alpha(r + Q)$ and $\beta(r + Q)$ terms must be included, it would seem necessary to use a computer and an appropriate search routine to determine Q^* and r^*. It is fortunate that in practice it is seldom necessary to include these terms.

4-10 An Example Involving the Use of the Exact Form of $\mathcal{K}$

Consider an item for which the demand over any time interval can be considered to be Poisson distributed with $\lambda = 400$ units per year. The procurement lead time is a constant, and $\tau = 0.25$ yr. The values of the other relevant parameters are $A = \$0.16$, $C = \$10.00$, $I = 0.20$, $\pi = \$0.10$, $\hat{\pi} = \$0.30$ per unit year. It is desired to determine Q^* and r^* when a Qr operating doctrine is used to control the system, and Q^*, r^* are determined by minimizing the exact expression for $\mathcal{K}$ given by (4-61). This problem was solved on the Burrough's 220 computer using the code referred to in Sec. 4-7. The results obtained were

$$Q^* = 19, \quad r^* = 96, \quad \mathcal{K}^* = \$31.75 \text{ per year} \tag{4-91}$$

As was noted in Sec. 4-7, the code determines a relative minimum, but does not guarantee that it is the absolute minimum, if there exists more than one relative minimum. The authors could find no indication that there exist other relative minima, and hence it seems very likely that the above values are indeed the optimal values of Q and r. One finds that in $\mathcal{K}^*$, the various cost components have the following values

$$\frac{\lambda}{Q^*} A = 3.368 \tag{4-92}$$

$$IC \left[\frac{Q^*}{2} + r^* - \mu + B(Q^*, r^*) \right] = 15.386 \tag{4-93}$$

$$\pi E(Q^*, r^*) = 12.341 \tag{4-94}$$

$$\hat{\pi} B(Q^*, r^*) = 0.658 \tag{4-95}$$

Observe that the backorder costs account for slightly over 40 percent of the average annual cost. To show that the above answer does yield a relative minimum, we present the values of $\mathcal{K}$ for neighboring (Q, r) points in the following table

TABLE 4-1

Values of $\mathcal{K}\,(Q,\,r)$

r \\ Q	18	19	20
95	31.94	31.91	31.95
96	31.90	31.75	31.91
97	31.99	32.11	32.27

Note that Q^* is much larger than Q_w which is

$$Q_w = \sqrt{\frac{2(400)(0.16)}{2}} = 8 \tag{4-96}$$

For this example, the $\alpha(r + Q)$, $\beta(r + Q)$ terms are not completely negligible, but are not really large as compared to the $\alpha(r)$, $\beta(r)$ terms, when evaluated at Q^* and r^*, i.e.,

$$\alpha(r^*) = 6.204 \qquad \alpha(r^* + Q^*) = 0.3241 \tag{4-97}$$

$$\beta(r^*) = 42.86 \qquad \beta(r^* + Q^*) = 1.18 \tag{4-98}$$

Even though the values of π and $\hat{\pi}$ are absurdly small, the values of the $\alpha(r + Q)$, $\beta(r + Q)$ terms evaluated at Q^*, r^* are not very large compared to the $\alpha(r)$, $\beta(r)$ terms. This suggests that the approximate model studied in Sec. 4-8 which neglects the $\alpha(r + Q)$, $\beta(r + Q)$ terms should converge and yield Q and r values close to Q^* and r^*. This is indeed correct. In fact, the r value obtained from the approximate model is r^*, and the Q value obtained treating Q as continuous comes within one unit of Q^*. The sequence of Q and r values obtained starting with $Q_1 = Q_w = 8$ in (4-72) and then using (4-73) to obtain the new Q is: $Q_1 = 8$, $r_1 = 105$; $Q_2 = 12.9$, $r_2 = 101$; $Q_3 = 15$, $r_3 = 99$; $Q_4 = 17.5$, $r_4 = 98$; $Q_5 = 18.4$, $r_5 = 97$; $Q_6 = 19.4$, $r_6 = 96$; $Q_7 = 20.3$, $r_7 = 96$. It should be pointed out that the manual computations with the approximate model are quite arduous and required about three hours of computation, whereas, working with the exact cost expression, Q^* and r^* were obtained in only about 15 seconds on the Burroughs computer (which is not a really high speed computer).

It is interesting that the approximate model did so well in this case where π and $\hat{\pi}$ are exceptionally small. At the outset one might have expected that it would do rather poorly. It would appear that the approximate model of Sec. 4-8 is applicable under very general circumstances. It might be noted that if we attempted to use the simple, approximate model of Sec. 4-2, which neglects the backorders term in the carrying cost and which assumes $\hat{r} = 0$, we do not obtain convergence. The sequence of iterations is: $Q_1 = Q_w = 8, r_1 = 102$; $Q_2 = 14, r_2 = 95$; $Q_3 = 18, r_3 = 87$; $Q_4 = 24$ and r_4 should be the largest integer satisfying

$$P(r;\ 100) > \frac{Q_4 IC}{\pi\lambda} = \frac{48}{40} > 1 \tag{4-99}$$

which is impossible.

4-11 The Lost Sales Case for Constant Lead Times

Interestingly enough, the exact equations for the lost sales case are much more difficult to develop than the corresponding equations for the backorders case. In fact, the exact equations have not been developed for the lost sales case when more than one order is allowed to be outstanding except for the case where $Q = 1$. In this section we wish to examine what makes the lost sales case so difficult to treat, and to derive the exact formulas for the case where only a single order can be outstanding. In Sec. 4-13 we shall consider the case where units are ordered one at a time ($Q = 1$), but any number of orders are allowed to be outstanding.

Consider a system in which demands occurring when the system is out of stock are lost. Again, as with the backorders case, we imagine that the stochastic processes generating the demands and lead times are such that the system can be described by a Markov process for which there exists a steady state. To be specific, imagine that the procurement lead time is a constant τ and that a Poisson process generates demands with units being demanded one at a time. As usual, assume that we desire to determine the optimal values of Q and r when the system is operated using a lot size-reorder point control policy.

If the inventory on hand plus on order is used to define the reorder point r, then the quantity on hand plus on order fluctuates between $Q + r$ and $r + 1$ during each cycle. The states are not necessarily, however, uniformly distributed. The reason for this is that the amount on hand plus on order will not move from $r + j$ to $r + j - 1$ when a demand occurs if the system is out of stock. When the system is out of stock the amount on hand plus on order does not change when a demand occurs. Unlike the inventory position in the backorders case, it is not possible in the lost sales case to treat the changes in the amount on hand plus on order independently of the amount on hand. This is in part what makes it so difficult to treat the lost sales case. It is necessary to take explicit account of the number of orders outstanding and the times at which they were placed. However, even if it was possible to obtain the distribution of the amount on hand plus on order, additional difficulties would be encountered. The procedure used to compute the distribution of the on hand inventory from the inventory position in the backorders case will not work here. It is still true that everything on order at time $t - \tau$ will arrive in the system by time t and nothing not on order at time $t - \tau$ can arrive by t. However, it no longer follows that if the amount on hand plus on order is $r + j$ at time $t - \tau$, the probability that $x \geq 0$ units are on hand at time t is the probability that $r + j - x$ units were demanded in the time τ. The reason is that it is possible for the system to run out of stock and have one or more demands occur while the system is out of stock in the period $t - \tau$ to t. Those demands occurring when the system is out of stock are lost, and hence x units can be on hand at time t even if more than $r + j - x$ demands occurred in the lead time.

In the backorders case there could be any number of orders outstanding when a Poisson process generated demands. Since there cannot be backorders in the lost sales case, the number of orders outstanding cannot be greater than the largest integer less than or equal to $(Q + r)/Q = 1 + (r/Q)$. The maximum number of orders which can be outstanding is therefore determined by the values of r and Q. If $r < Q$ then there can never be more than a single order outstanding. In the lost sales case then, it is possible to stipulate that there is only a single order outstanding if one requires that $r < Q$.

We shall now derive the exact equations for the lost sales case when the stipulation is made that there is never more than a single order outstanding. To obtain the average annual cost we shall here first compute the expected cost per cycle and then multiply by the average number of cycles per year, rather than attempting to find the state probabilities and compute the costs directly as was done in the backorders case. The reason for changing the approach is that it is not too easy to compute the state probabilities directly.

Let us first compute the expected length of time per cycle during which the system is out of stock. Since there is never more than one order outstanding, nothing is on order when the reorder point is reached, i.e., at the reorder point r units are on hand. If the system reaches an out of stock condition in the time interval t to $t + dt$ after the reorder point is hit, this means that in the time 0 to t, $r - 1$ units have been demanded and the rth one is demanded between t and $t + dt$. This probability is $\lambda p(r - 1; \lambda t)\, dt$. If the system does reach an out of stock position between t and $t + dt$, it will be out of stock for a length of time $\tau - t$ during the cycle. Hence the expected length of time out of stock per cycle is

$$\hat{T} = \int_0^\tau \lambda(\tau - t)\, \frac{(\lambda t)^{r-1}}{(r - 1)!}\, e^{-\lambda t}\, dt = \tau P(r; \lambda\tau) - \frac{r}{\lambda} P(r + 1; \lambda\tau) \qquad (4\text{-}100)$$

From (4-37) the average number of cycles per year is $\lambda/(Q + \lambda\hat{T})$ where $\hat{T}$ is given by (4-100).

It is very easy to compute the expected number of lost sales per cycle. If the demand in the lead time τ is $x > r$, the number of lost sales is $x - r$. Thus the expected number of lost sales is

$$\sum_{x=r+1}^{\infty} (x - r)p(x; \lambda\tau) = \lambda\tau P(r - 1; \lambda\tau) - rP(r; \lambda\tau) \qquad (4\text{-}101)$$

by A3-10. However, by A3-13 we see that the expected time out of stock (4-100) is the expected number of lost sales times the expected time between demands $1/\lambda$. This correspondence is what one would expect intuitively.

It remains to compute the expected unit years of stock held per cycle. First note that the probability that w units are on hand when the order arrives is $P(r; \lambda\tau)$, for $w = 0$, and $p(r - w; \lambda\tau)$, $1 \leq w \leq r$. These are also the probabilities that $w + Q$ units are on hand after the arrival of a procurement. Thus the probability that v units are on hand after the arrival of a procurement is

$$\psi(v) = \begin{cases} P(r; \lambda\tau), & v = Q \\ p(Q + r - v; \lambda\tau), & Q < v \leq Q + r \end{cases} \qquad (4\text{-}102)$$

The expected unit years of stock held per cycle will be computed in two parts. First, for the time period up to the time the reorder point is reached (this time is a random variable), and second for the period of fixed length τ from the time the reorder point is reached until the next order arrives. Given that v units are on hand after an order arrives, there will be v units in stock until the first demand occurs, and there will be $v - 1$ in stock from the time that the first demand occurs until the second occurs, etc., and $r + 1$ in stock from the time the $(v - r - 1)$th demand occurs until the $(v - r)$th demand occurs which reduces the on hand inventory to the reorder point. The mean time between demands is $1/\lambda$. Thus, given that the on hand inventory is v, the expected number of unit years of stock held until the reorder point is reached is

$$\frac{1}{\lambda} [v + v - 1 + \ldots + v - (v - r - 1)]$$

$$= \frac{v}{\lambda} (v - r) - \frac{1}{2\lambda} (v - r - 1)(v - r) = \frac{1}{2\lambda} [v(v + 1) - r(r + 1)]$$

Averaging over the initial inventory, i.e., over v, it is seen that the expected unit years of stock held until the reorder point is reached is

$$\frac{1}{2\lambda} \sum_{v=Q}^{Q+r} [v(v+1) - r(r+1)]\psi(v) = \frac{1}{2\lambda} [Q(Q+1) - r(r+1)]P(r; \lambda\tau)$$

$$+ \frac{1}{2\lambda} \sum_{u=0}^{r-1} [(r+Q-u)(r+Q+1-u) - r(r+1)]p(u; \lambda\tau) \quad (4\text{-}103)$$

The expected unit years of stock held from the time the reorder point is reached until the next order arrives is the integral from 0 to τ of the expected amount on hand at time t, i.e.,

$$\int_0^\tau \sum_{x=0}^{r-1} (r-x)p(x; \lambda t)\, dt \quad (4\text{-}104)$$

On expanding out (4-103) and (4-104) and summing the results, we find that the expected number of unit years of stock held per cycle is (to be worked out in Problem 4-62)

$$\frac{1}{2\lambda} Q(Q+1) + \frac{Qr}{\lambda} - \frac{Q\mu}{\lambda} + \frac{Q\mu}{\lambda} P(r-1; \lambda\tau) - \frac{Qr}{\lambda} P(r; \lambda\tau) \quad (4\text{-}105)$$

Therefore the average annual cost becomes

$$\mathcal{K} = \frac{\lambda}{Q + \lambda\hat{T}} \left\{ A + IC\left[\frac{1}{2\lambda} Q(Q+1) + \frac{Qr}{\lambda} - \frac{Q\mu}{\lambda} \right] \right.$$

$$\left. + \left(\frac{ICQ}{\lambda} + \pi \right)\left[\mu P(r-1; \lambda\tau) - \frac{r}{\lambda} P(r; \lambda\tau) \right] \right\} \quad (4\text{-}106)$$

where π is the cost of a lost sale including the lost profit and $\hat{T}$ is given by (4-100). We ask the reader to prove in detail in Problem 4-74 that minimization of the average annual cost with the cost of a lost sale being defined to include the lost profit will yield the same Q^* and r^* as the maximization of the average annual profit.

It is interesting to note that when $\hat{T}$ is negligible, (4-106) becomes simply the discrete version of the simple lost sales model studied in Sec. 4-3. In practice it is rather difficult to determine the optimal values of Q and r by use of (4-106). Fortunately, for most real world computations, it is almost always true that the simple model will suffice, and it is unnecessary to use (4-106). The reader should recall, of course, that (4-106) holds rigorously only if never more than one order is outstanding, and that the theory for more than a single order outstanding has not been worked out.

4-12 Stochastic Lead Times

In the simple approximate models we allowed the procurement lead time to be a random variable with density function $g(\tau)$. The exact formulations of the $\langle Q, r \rangle$ models presented in the last several sections have assumed that the lead time was constant. We would now like to investigate the problems involved in attempting to properly account for lead time variations in the exact models. As long as there is never more than a single order outstanding, no theoretical difficulties are encountered. If it is imagined that the procurement lead time can be described by a random variable with density function $g(\tau)$, it is only necessary to average the expected annual cost for a given τ over τ to obtain the appropriate average annual cost. Thus if $\mathcal{K}(Q, r, \tau)$ is the average annual cost for a given τ, the appropriate average annual cost averaged over τ is

$$\mathcal{K}(Q, r) = \int_0^\infty \mathcal{K}(Q, r, \tau)g(\tau)\, d\tau \qquad (4\text{-}107)$$

and $\mathcal{K}(Q, r)$ is the expression to be minimized. It is easy to see that $\mathcal{K}(Q, r)$ will be obtained directly if in computing the various expected values one uses the marginal distribution of lead time demand rather than the lead time demand for a fixed τ. The detailed proof of this for the various cases studied is left for Problem 4-58.

Unfortunately, however, for $\langle Q, r \rangle$ models in which the demand is Poisson distributed, and demands occurring when the system is out of stock are backordered, it is not possible to specify rigorously that never more than a single order is outstanding. For any time interval of length $t > 0$, there is a positive probability that an arbitrarily large number of demands will occur in this interval, and hence a positive probability that any given number of orders will be placed in the time interval. This in turn implies that there is a positive probability that any given number of orders will be outstanding at any point in time. The only sort of statement that one can legitimately make is that the probability that more than a single order is outstanding is very small.

Let us now examine the situation where more than a single order is allowed to be outstanding at any point of time. In the general derivation of the backorders case we allowed an arbitrary number of orders to be outstanding. When more than a single order can be outstanding, however, difficulties are encountered in properly representing the lead times as random variables. We would like to treat the procurement lead times as independent random variables when more than a single order is outstanding, i.e., we would like to assume that the lead time for a given order is independent of the lead times of the other orders which are outstanding. However, if this is to be rigorously correct, then we must allow orders to cross, i.e., they need not be received in the same order in which they were placed. This is illustrated geometrically in Fig. 4-5. There is a positive probability that order 2 will arrive before order 1. Order 2 can arrive before order 1 if order 1 arrives between t' and t''.

In practice, it is almost always true that orders are received in the same sequence in which they were placed, so that orders cannot cross. If this is true, then lead times cannot be considered to be independent random variables, i.e., the time of an arrival of an order placed at time t can depend on the times of arrival of the other orders on the books when the order is placed at time t. For example, if orders are backed up at the source for some reason, new orders will also have to wait in line until the previous orders have been processed. Unfortunately, there seems no easy way to handle situations where the lead times are not independent. In general, it is very difficult to describe the dependence between lead times without developing a detailed model of the source. No work has appeared in the literature as yet which deals with models having the lead times being dependent random variables.

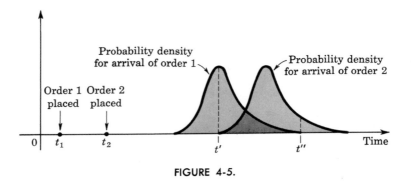

FIGURE 4-5.

We see therefore that it is very difficult to give a precise treatment of variable lead times when more than a single order can be outstanding. It might be pointed out that even if we imagined that orders could cross and that the lead times were independent variables, it is not easy to develop the exact equations in general. The reason is that it is hard to rigorously allow for orders to cross. The reader should note that the procedure used for the constant lead time case to obtain the state probabilities for the on hand inventory assumes that all orders on the books when an order is placed arrive before that order. It would not be correct, for example, if we are going to allow orders to cross, to say that for the case of Poisson demands that the equivalent of (4-40), when the lead times are independent random variables with density $g(\tau)$, is

$$\psi_1(x) = \frac{1}{Q} \int_0^\infty \sum_{j=1}^{Q} p(r + j - x; \lambda\tau)g(\tau)\,d\tau = \frac{1}{Q} \sum_{j=1}^{Q} h(r + j - x) \qquad (4\text{-}108)$$

where $h(r + j - x)$ is the marginal distribution of lead time demand. The reason is that this approach assumes that orders arrive in the sequence placed and do not cross. There is one special case which can be solved exactly when the lead times are independent random variables and orders can cross. This is when a Poisson process generates the lead times, i.e., the lead time density is

$$g(\tau) = \delta e^{-\delta \tau}$$

Then, for Poisson demands, the system can be solved by using Markov analysis for a system continuous in time and discrete in space, since Poisson processes generate all transitions. This has been carried out in [3]. The details will not be presented here since the state probabilities become fairly complicated. Furthermore the specific lead time distribution is not very realistic, usually, from a practical point of view, and in addition, since orders do not normally cross, the generalization is not particularly helpful in the real world. We shall, however, illustrate the method of analysis for a particularly simple case in the following section.

Often in the real world it is true that even although two or more orders are outstanding at any point in time, the interval between the placing of orders is usually large enough that there is essentially no interaction between orders, and to a good approximation, it can be assumed that the lead times are independent as well as assuming that orders do not cross. In this case (4-108) is correct, i.e., to develop the appropriate expected values for the cost expression it is only necessary to replace in the discrete case $p(x; \lambda \tau)$ by $h(x)$.

When treating lead times as independent while simultaneously making the assumption that orders do not cross, it is often convenient when demand is Poisson distributed to assume that the lead time density can be described by a gamma distribution. In practice, the lead time distribution, when known, can often be fitted fairly well by a gamma distribution. From Sec. 3-7 we know that if the random variable representing demand in any time period is Poisson distributed and the lead time has a gamma distribution, then the marginal distribution of lead time demand has a negative binomial distribution. Thus to compute the expected costs it is only necessary to replace $p(x; \lambda \tau)$ by $b_N[x; \alpha + 1, \beta/(\beta + \lambda)]$ in the expressions for $\psi_1(x)$ and $\psi_2(y)$. For hand computations, of course, it is much more difficult to work with the negative binomial distribution rather than the Poisson since the negative binomial is not well tabulated. Intuitively, as the variance of the procurement lead time distribution increases, the variance of the distribution of states for the net inventory increases. This in turn means that the safety stock and r must be increased. The computation of Q and r treating the lead time as a constant equal to the mean procurement lead time, when in actuality the procurement lead time is a random variable, can lead to carrying a safety stock which is much too low. The amount of the error increases as the variance of the lead time distribution increases. When the model is being used which treats Q and r as continuous and assumes the demand variable to be normally distributed, one usually assumes that the marginal distribution of demand is also normally distributed and the variance of the normal distribution is chosen to give the proper variance. In this case the formulas of Sec. 4-8 can be used for variable lead times without modification.

4-13 Models with $Q = 1$

In certain real world situations it is optimal to order units one at a time as demanded. This can be true, for example, if the demand for the item is very low or the item is very expensive. The solution to the $\langle Q, r \rangle$ model of Sec. 4-7 will indicate whether or not a $Q = 1$ is optimal. In this section we shall study models in which it is required that $Q = 1$. These simple models provide an excellent means for illustrating the effects of various ways of handling stochastic lead times.

The backorders case will be considered first. The state probabilities and cost expression can be readily obtained from the results of Sec. 4-7 by setting $Q = 1$. However, it is instructive and also very easy to derive the results directly, and hence we shall do this. Since $Q = 1$, i.e., an order is placed each time there is a demand, then the inventory position must remain constant. Denote the inventory position by R; the problem is to determine the optimal value of R. For situations where this model is of interest, it will be desirable to treat demands as discrete and R as an integer. It will be assumed then that the number of units demanded in any time interval has a Poisson distribution and that the mean rate of demand is λ.

Suppose that the procurement lead time is a constant τ. Then to compute the probability $\psi_1(x)$ that $x \geq 0$ units are on hand at time t, note that everything on order at time $t - \tau$ will have arrived in the system by time t and nothing not on order at time $t - \tau$ can have arrived in the system. The inventory position at time $t - \tau$ is R. Thus $\psi_1(x)$ is the probability that $R - x$ units were demanded in the lead time, i.e.,

$$\psi_1(x) = \begin{cases} p(R - x; \lambda\tau), & 0 < x \leq R \\ P(R; \lambda\tau), & x = 0 \end{cases} \tag{4-109}$$

Similarly $\psi_2(y)$, the probability that there are $y \geq 0$ backorders at time t is

$$\psi_2(y) = p(R + y; \lambda\tau), \quad y \geq 0 \tag{4-110}$$

Thus P_{out} and the expected number of backorders $B(R)$ are respectively

$$P_{\text{out}} = \sum_{y=0}^{\infty} \psi_2(y) = P(R; \lambda\tau) \qquad (4\text{-}111)$$

$$B(R) = \sum_{y=0}^{\infty} y\psi_2(y) = \sum_{v=R}^{\infty} (v - R)p(v; \lambda\tau)$$

$$= \lambda\tau P(R - 1; \lambda\tau) - RP(R; \lambda\tau) \qquad (4\text{-}112)$$

The expected value of the on hand inventory at time t is

$$\sum_{x=0}^{R} x\psi_1(x) = \sum_{u=0}^{R-1} (R - u)p(u; \lambda\tau) = R - \mu + B(R) \qquad (4\text{-}113)$$

The average annual cost of backorders and holding inventory is therefore

$$\mathcal{K}(R) = IC(R - \mu) + \pi\lambda P(R; \lambda\tau) + (IC + \hat{\pi})[\lambda\tau P(R - 1; \lambda\tau) - RP(R; \lambda\tau)] \qquad (4\text{-}114)$$

Note that the average annual ordering costs λA are independent of R and hence need not be included in $\mathcal{K}$.

If R^* is the smallest R which minimizes $\mathcal{K}(R)$, then it is necessary that R^* satisfy

$$\Delta\mathcal{K}(R^*) < 0; \quad \Delta\mathcal{K}(R^* + 1) \geq 0 \qquad (4\text{-}115)$$

Now

$$\Delta\mathcal{K}(R) = IC - \pi\lambda p(R - 1; \lambda\tau) - (IC + \hat{\pi})P(R; \lambda\tau)$$

Thus R^* is the largest R for which

$$P(R; \lambda\tau) + \frac{\pi\lambda}{IC + \hat{\pi}} p(R - 1; \lambda\tau) > \frac{IC}{\hat{\pi} + IC} \qquad (4\text{-}116)$$

If $\Delta\mathcal{K}(R^* + 1) = 0$, then R^* and $R^* + 1$ both minimize $\mathcal{K}$. When $\pi = 0$, (4-116) reduces to finding the largest R such that

$$P(R; \lambda\tau) > \frac{IC}{\hat{\pi} + IC} \qquad (4\text{-}117)$$

When $\hat{\pi} = 0$, (4-116) reduces to finding the largest R such that

$$\frac{IC}{\pi\lambda} P(R; \lambda\tau) + p(R - 1; \lambda\tau) > \frac{IC}{\pi\lambda} \qquad (4\text{-}118)$$

Having obtained the average annual cost and the optimality condition for the case of constant lead times, we now turn to the case where we allow the lead times to be random variables. To begin, we shall imagine that lead times are generated by a Poisson process, i.e., the lead time density is exponential, with mean $\tau = 1/\delta$, and that the lead times are independent random variables. This implies that orders can cross and need not be received in the same sequence in which they were placed. The problem can be solved in this case as a Markov process. Let the states be the net inventory (there are an infinite number of these). The probability that the system moves from state v to $v - 1$ in time dt is the probability that a demand occurs, i.e., $\lambda \, dt$. The probability that the system moves from state v to $v + 1$ in

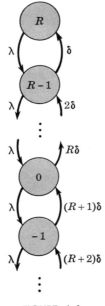

FIGURE 4-6.

time dt is the probability that an order arrives. To compute this probability note that if the system is in state v (net inventory $= v$) then $R - v$ orders are outstanding. The probability that any one of these orders arrives is $\delta \, dt$. The probability that some one of them arrives is therefore $(R - v)\delta \, dt$. Only transitions to adjacent states correspond to the occurrence of a single Poisson event, and hence only such transitions can occur in time dt. The diagram representing the transitions then looks like that in Fig. 4-6. If $\psi(v)$ is the steady state probability that the net inventory is v, the balance equations are

$$\lambda\psi(v+1) + (R-v+1)\delta\psi(v-1) = [\lambda + (R-v)\delta]\psi(v),$$
$$v = R-1, R-2, \ldots$$
$$\lambda\psi(R) = \delta\psi(R-1)$$

Then if

$$\mu = \frac{\lambda}{\delta} = \lambda\tau$$

which is the mean lead time demand, we find on successive substitution beginning with $\psi(R-1) = \mu\psi(R)$ that

$$\psi(R-k) = \frac{\mu^k}{k!}\psi(R), \quad k = 1, 2, \ldots \tag{4-119}$$

Since

$$\sum_{k=0}^{\infty} \psi(R-k) = \psi(R)\sum_{k=0}^{\infty}\frac{\mu^k}{k!} = e^\mu\psi(R) = 1$$

it follows that

$$\psi(R) = e^{-\mu} \tag{4-120}$$

and from (4-119)

$$\psi(v) = p(R-v; \lambda\tau), \quad v = R, R-1, R-2, \ldots \tag{4-121}$$

Comparison with (4-109) and (4-110) leads to the interesting result that precisely the same state probabilities are obtained as for the case of constant lead times, i.e., it makes no difference whether the lead time is a constant τ or whether the lead time is exponentially distributed with mean τ, provided that when the lead time is a random variable the lead times corresponding to different orders are independent random variables. The same optimal R will be obtained in either case. This result is peculiar to the case where $Q = 1$. If $Q > 1$ it is not true that the state probabilities for the constant lead time case are the same as where the lead times are exponentially distributed, independent random variables. This is shown in [3], referred to above, where the state probabilities are computed for arbitrary Q when the lead times are exponential, independent random variables.

An even more surprising result can be proved for the case where $Q = 1$. It says that if demand is Poisson distributed, then when $Q = 1$, and the lead times are independent random variables (i.e., orders can cross), (4-121) gives the state probabilities for any lead time density $g(\tau)$ with mean τ. In other words, the state probabilities and the optimal value of R are independent of the nature of the lead time distribution if the lead times are independent. The proof which we shall present is patterned after that of Takács [5].

Before presenting the proof we shall demonstrate an interesting property of the Poisson distribution which will be needed. Suppose that we know that $n > 0$ Poisson events have occurred in the interval 0 to t. Let us compute the conditional probability that the first occurs between t_1 and $t_1 + dt_1$, the second occurs between t_2 and $t_2 + dt_2$, etc., and the n-th occurs between t_n and $t_n + dt_n$, $t_1 < t_2 < \ldots < t_n$. The probability that n events occur in the time interval and the ith one occurs between t_i and $t_i + dt_i$, $i = 1, \ldots, n$, must be

$$[e^{-\lambda t_1}\lambda\, dt_1][e^{-\lambda(t_2-t_1)}\lambda\, dt_2] \ldots [e^{-\lambda(t_n-t_{n-1})}\lambda\, dt_n][e^{-\lambda(t-t_n)}] \quad (4\text{-}122)$$

since no event must occur for times ξ in the intervals

$$0 \le \xi < t_1, \quad t_1 < \xi < t_2, \quad \ldots, \quad t_n < \xi \le t$$

while event i does occur between t_i and $t_i + dt_i$. Equation (4-122) can be condensed to

$$\lambda^n e^{-\lambda t}\, dt_1 \ldots dt_n \quad (4\text{-}123)$$

Now the probability that n events occur in the interval 0 to t is simply $p(n; \lambda t)$. Hence the conditional probability that they occur as outlined above, given that n events occur in the interval, is obtained by dividing (4-123) by $p(n; \lambda t)$ which yields

$$\frac{n!}{t^n}\, dt_1\, dt_2 \ldots dt_n \quad (4\text{-}124)$$

We leave to Problem 4-63 the proof that $n!/t^n$ is a legitimate density function. We note from (4-124) that since the density function is independent of the t_i, the occurrences of the different events are independent random variables. Furthermore, the probability that any one occurs between t_i and $t_i + dt_i$ is simply dt_i/t. To see how the $n!$ comes about in the joint density it can be imagined that the time interval from 0 to t is divided up to yield $2n + 1$ boxes, n boxes corresponding to the time intervals t_i to $t_i + dt_i$ and the remaining $n + 1$ corresponding to the remaining $n + 1$ time intervals. The Poisson events can be imagined to be balls which are tossed into the boxes. Now suppose that the n balls are tossed into the boxes. All balls must go into one of the boxes, and for boxes corresponding to the time intervals t_i to $t_i + dt_i$ only one ball can fit into a box. The probability that one of the balls goes into the box corresponding to the interval t_1 to $t_1 + dt_1$ is then $n\, dt_1/t$. Given that one of the balls goes into the box corresponding to the interval t_1 to $t_1 + dt_1$, the probability that one of the $n - 1$ remaining balls goes into the box corresponding to the interval t_2 to $t_2 + dt_2$ is $(n - 1)\, dt_2/t$, etc. Thus the probability that one of the balls goes into each of the n boxes corresponding to the intervals t_i to $t_i + dt_i$

is (4-124). What we have shown is that if we are given that at least one Poisson event occurs in the time interval 0 to t, then the probability that any one occurs between ξ and $\xi + d\xi$ is $d\xi/t$, and this is independent of how many events have occurred in the interval or of their times of occurrence.

Let us now return to the proof that the state probabilities are independent of the lead time distribution. The probability that a unit ordered at time t_i will arrive by time $t > t_i$ is

$$S(t - t_i) = \int_0^{t-t_i} g(\tau) \, d\tau \qquad (4\text{-}125)$$

Then if we know that at least one demand has occurred in the time interval 0 to t, the probability that any one occurred between t_i and $t_i + dt_i$ and that the unit ordered arrives by time t is

$$\frac{S(t - t_i)}{t} \, dt_i$$

Consequently, the probability that any particular order placed in the interval 0 to t has arrived by time t is

$$\frac{1}{t} \int_0^t S(t - t_i) \, dt_i = \frac{1}{t} \int_0^t S(\xi) \, d\xi \qquad (4\text{-}126)$$

Suppose now that the system has been operating for a length of time t. We assume that R units were on hand initially. Let us compute the probability that the net inventory is x at time t if there have been in total n demands since the system began operation. If the net inventory is x, then $n + x - R$ of the orders have arrived and $R - x$ have not arrived. The probability of this, which will be written $q(x; n, t)$ is simply the binomial probability of $n + x - R$ successes in n trials when the probability of a success is given by (4-126), i.e.,

$$q(x; n, t) =$$
$$\binom{n}{R - x} \left[\frac{1}{t} \int_0^t S(\xi) \, d\xi \right]^{n+x-R} \left[\frac{1}{t} \int_0^t [1 - S(\xi)] \, d\xi \right]^{R-x} \qquad (4\text{-}127)$$

On weighting $q(x; n, t)$ by the probability of having n units demanded, we find that $W_x(t)$ the probability that the net inventory is x at time t is

$$W_x(t) = \sum_{n=R-x}^{\infty} p(n; \lambda t) q(x; n, t)$$
$$= \frac{\{\lambda \int_0^t [1 - S(\xi)] \, d\xi\}^{R-x}}{(R - x)!} e^{-\lambda \int_0^t [1-S(\xi)] \, d\xi} \qquad (4\text{-}128)$$

To determine $\lim_{t \to \infty} W_x(t)$ we note that

$$\lim_{t \to \infty} \int_0^t [1 - S(\xi)] \, d\xi = \int_0^\infty [1 - S(\xi)] \, d\xi = \int_0^\infty -\xi \, d[1 - S(\xi)]$$

$$= \int_0^\infty \xi \frac{dS}{d\xi} \, d\xi = \int_0^\infty \xi g(\xi) \, d\xi = \bar{\tau} \qquad (4\text{-}129)$$

Use of (4-129) in (4-128) shows that

$$\lim_{t \to \infty} W_x(t) = p(R - x; \lambda \bar{\tau}) \qquad (4\text{-}130)$$

i.e., the limiting state probabilities are Poisson and they depend only on the mean procurement lead time $\bar{\tau}$.

We have demonstrated above that when $Q = 1$, demand is Poisson distributed, and lead times are independent (and orders can cross), then the state probabilities and the optimal R are independent of the nature of the procurement lead time distribution. Let us now examine what happens if we do not allow orders to cross but instead require that they arrive in the same sequence as placed. The procedure suggested in Sec. 4-12 will be used in which it is imagined that lead times can be treated as independent and that they arrive in the same sequence in which they were placed. Then, if $g(\tau)$ is the lead time density, the average annual cost is given by (4-107). Suppose now that $g(\tau)$ is a gamma distribution, i.e., $g(\tau) = \gamma(\tau; \alpha, \beta)$. Then, from (3-73), we know that the marginal distribution of lead time demand has the negative binomial distribution $b_N[x; \alpha + 1, \beta/(\beta + \lambda)]$. Hence the average annual cost has the form

$$\mathcal{K}(R) = IC[R - \mu] + \lambda \pi \sum_{x=R}^\infty b_N[x; \alpha + 1, \beta/(\beta + \lambda)]$$

$$+ (\hat{\pi} + IC) \sum_{x=R}^\infty (x - R) b_N[x; \alpha + 1, \beta/(\beta + \lambda)] \qquad (4\text{-}131)$$

and by analogy with (4-116), R^* is the largest R for which

$$\frac{\pi \lambda}{\hat{\pi} + IC} b_N[R - 1; \alpha + 1, \beta/(\beta + \lambda)]$$

$$+ \sum_{x=R}^\infty b_N[x; \alpha + 1; \beta/(\beta + \lambda)] > \frac{IC}{\hat{\pi} + IC} \qquad (4\text{-}132)$$

The optimal R computed from (4-132) will in general be larger than the R computed from (4-116). It can be considerably larger if the variance of the marginal distribution of lead time demand is much greater than the variance of the Poisson distribution for the mean lead time. Thus, for the case of $Q = 1$, the procedure suggested in Sec. 4-12 yields a higher variance of the net inventory distribution, and will in general yield a larger R^* than would have obtained under the assumption that orders can cross.

To close this section let us examine briefly the lost sales case. Even when $Q = 1$, it is not easy to treat rigorously the case where more than a single order can be outstanding (here R would have to be one in order to specify rigorously that no more than one order could be outstanding—this case is of no interest). However, the problem can be solved if it is assumed that the procurement lead time has an exponential distribution with mean $\bar{\tau} = 1/\delta$ and that lead times are independent random variables (and orders can cross). Markov analysis can be used to solve the problem just as it

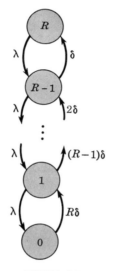

FIGURE 4-7.

could for the backorders case under similar assumptions. If x is the value of the on hand inventory at any point in time, x can only have one of the values $0, 1, 2, \ldots, R$. Fig. 4-7 shows the transition diagram from which the balance equations can immediately be written down.

If $\psi(x)$ is the steady state probability that x units are on hand at time t then

$$\lambda\psi(v + 1) + (R - v + 1)\delta\psi(v - 1) = [\lambda + (R - v)\delta]\psi(v),$$
$$v = 1, \ldots, R - 1 \quad (4\text{-}133)$$

and

$$\lambda\psi(R) = \delta\psi(R - 1), \quad \lambda\psi(1) = R\delta\psi(0)$$

Thus

$$\psi(v) = \frac{(\lambda \bar{\tau})^{R-v}}{(R - v)!} \psi(R), \quad v = 0, 1, \ldots, R \tag{4-134}$$

and since

$$\sum_{v=0}^{R} \psi(v) = 1$$

it follows that

$$\psi(R) = \left[\sum_{v=0}^{R} \frac{(\lambda \bar{\tau})^{R-v}}{(R - v)!} \right]^{-1} = \left[\sum_{v=0}^{R} \frac{(\lambda \bar{\tau})^{v}}{v!} \right]^{-1} \tag{4-135}$$

Hence

$$\psi(v) = \frac{(\lambda \bar{\tau})^{R-v}}{(R - v)! \displaystyle\sum_{v=0}^{R} \frac{(\lambda \bar{\tau})^{v}}{v!}}, \quad v = 0, 1, \ldots, R \tag{4-136}$$

Multiplication of the numerator and denominator by $e^{-\lambda \bar{\tau}}$ shows that

$$\psi(v) = \frac{p(R - v; \lambda \bar{\tau})}{1 - P(R + 1; \lambda \tau)}, \quad v = 0, 1, \ldots, R \tag{4-137}$$

It has been shown in [1] that the $\psi(j)$ are given by (4-137) if lead times are independent and orders can cross, for any lead time distribution $g(\tau)$ such that the cumulative distribution is continuous (the proof did not include the case of constant lead times, however). Conny Palm [4] has also presented a proof that the $\psi(j)$ are independent of the lead time distribution if lead times are independent and orders can cross. We shall not present either of these proofs.

When the state probabilities are given by (4-137), the average annual cost is

$$\mathcal{K} = IC \left[R - \lambda \bar{\tau} \frac{1 - P(R; \lambda \bar{\tau})}{1 - P(R + 1; \lambda \bar{\tau})} \right] + \lambda \pi \frac{p(R; \lambda \bar{\tau})}{1 - P(R + 1; \lambda \bar{\tau})} \tag{4-138}$$

provided that the unit cost of the item is constant. We leave a discussion of the determination of the optimal R to Problem 4-64.

4-14 Quantity Discounts

The preceding analysis has assumed that the unit price of the item was a constant independent of the size of the order quantity Q. In the real world quantity discounts are frequently available on the purchase of large quantities. Two types of discounts sometimes encountered are all units and incremental quantity discounts discussed in Secs. 2-11, 2-12 respectively. Precisely the same computational procedures that were valid in the deterministic case can be applied to the case of stochastic demands discussed in this chapter. The average annual cost curves optimized with respect to r will again behave like those shown in Figs. 2-13, 2-15. It then follows that the computational procedures given in Secs. 2-11, 2-12 also apply to the case of stochastic demands. The only modification in wording necessary is where it reads compute the optimal Q value, it should now read compute the optimal Q and r values, and in the all units discount case, when the cost is computed at a break point, the optimal value of r corresponding to the order quantity at the break point should be used.

For the lost sales case, it will be recalled that the cost of the unit appears in the stockout cost and hence the stockout cost will change as the unit cost is changed. Usually, however, the effect of quantity discounts on the stockout cost is negligible and can be ignored.

4-15 Constraints

The previous discussion in this chapter has assumed that the item under consideration can be treated independently of any other items carried by the system. When more than a single item is carried there will almost always be some sort of interaction between the items. These interactions may or may not have an important influence on determining the optimal Q and r values. When they are not important, the models already discussed may be used to determine Q^* and r^*. When the interactions are of consequence, things become more complicated, and some attempt must be made to account for the interactions. Typical simple interactions are of the form discussed in Sec. 2-8, i.e., competition for warehouse space, for the limited number of orders that can be placed, or for the allowable total investment in inventory. Formally, these constraints can be handled in much the same way as in Sec. 2-8. However, as we shall see, this formal generalization may not always be satisfactory. It will also become apparent that it is not a simple matter to develop a satisfactory means for treating these constraints when demand is a stochastic variable.

Assume that the system stocks n items. Consider first the case where there is a limitation on the total number of orders (or setups) which can be handled per year. Immediately a problem of interpretation arises. Because of the stochastic nature of the demands, it is theoretically possible (if the demand variable is being described by a Poisson or normal distribution) to have any arbitrarily large number of orders placed in one year. Thus one cannot guarantee that there will never be more than a given number of orders placed per year. One can, however, talk about the probability that no more than a given number of orders will be placed, or we can require that the expected number of orders placed be less than or equal to a given value.

The situation where one places a limitation on the expected number of orders placed is the easiest to handle. The expected number of orders placed per year for all n items is

$$\overline{N} = \sum_{j=1}^{n} \frac{\lambda_j}{Q_j} \tag{4-139}$$

The computational procedure is to first solve the problem ignoring the constraint, i.e., compute the Q_j and r_j values using one of the models given in the previous sections. Then if $\overline{N} \leq h$, h being the limitation on the expected number of orders placed per year, the solutions so obtained are optimal. If $\overline{N} > h$, the constraint is active. Then from the theory of Lagrange multipliers, we know that we should consider the function

$$\mathfrak{F} = \sum_{j=1}^{n} \mathcal{K}_j(Q_j, r_j) + \eta \left(\sum_{j=1}^{n} \frac{\lambda_j}{Q_j} - h \right) \tag{4-140}$$

where η is a Lagrange multiplier. Then the set of Q_j and r_j which minimize the average annual cost $\sum_{i=1}^{n} \mathcal{K}_j(Q_j, r_j)$ subject to the constraint $\overline{N} = h$ is the same set which minimize $\mathfrak{F}$ when η is adjusted so that $\overline{N} = h$. Now since Q_j, and r_j appear in $\mathfrak{F}$ only in the terms

$$\mathfrak{F}_j(Q_j, r_j) = \mathcal{K}_j(Q_j, r_j) + \eta \frac{\lambda_j}{Q_j}, \quad j = 1, \ldots, n \tag{4-141}$$

it follows that for any η, $\mathfrak{F}$ will be minimized when each of the n expressions $\mathfrak{F}_j(Q_j, r_j)$ is minimized. The computational procedure then is to minimize each $\mathfrak{F}_j(Q_j, r_j)$ for a given η and thus determine a set of Q_j and r_j, compute $\overline{N}$ and compare it with h, select a new η and repeat the process until $\overline{N} = h$. The set of Q_j, r_j so obtained will be optimal.

It must be recognized that the above procedure only sets an upper limit on the expected number of orders placed per year. In any given year the number of orders placed could be greater than h or less than h. The computation of the probability that precisely M orders will be placed is not especially easy, in general, when there are n items, although it is easy for a single item in certain cases. Let us then first consider the case of a single item when a Poisson process generates demands, units are demanded one at a time, and all demands occurring when the system is out of stock are backordered. Thus if the inventory position is $r + j$ at the beginning of the year, precisely m orders will be placed ($m \geq 1$) if the demand lies in the interval $(m - 1)Q + j$ to $mQ + j - 1$. The probability of this is

$$P[(m - 1)Q + j; \lambda] - P(mQ + j; \lambda)$$

No orders will be placed if the demand is less than j. The probability of this is

$$1 - P(j; \lambda)$$

Now the probability that the system will be in state j at the beginning of the year is $1/Q$. Hence $\Theta(m)$, the probability that precisely m orders will be placed, is

$$\Theta(m) = \frac{1}{Q} \sum_{j=1}^{Q} \{P[(m-1)Q + j; \lambda] - P(mQ + j; \lambda)\}, \quad m \geq 1$$

$$= \frac{1}{Q} \left\{ \sum_{u=(m-1)Q+1}^{\infty} P(u; \lambda) - 2 \sum_{u=mQ+1}^{\infty} P(u; \lambda) \right.$$

$$\left. + \sum_{u=(m+1)Q+1}^{\infty} P(u; \lambda) \right\} \quad (4\text{-}142)$$

and from A3-6

$$\Theta(m) = \frac{1}{Q} \{\lambda P[(m-1)Q; \lambda] - (m-1)QP[(m-1)Q + 1; \lambda]$$
$$- 2\lambda P(mQ; \lambda) + 2mQP(mQ + 1; \lambda) + \lambda P[(m+1)Q; \lambda]$$
$$- (m+1)QP[(m+1)Q + 1; \lambda]\}, \quad m \geq 1 \quad (4\text{-}143)$$

When $m = 0$, we see that

$$\Theta(m) = \frac{1}{Q} \sum_{j=1}^{Q} [1 - P(j; \lambda)]$$

$$= 1 - \frac{1}{Q} \{\lambda - \lambda P(Q; \lambda) + QP(Q + 1; \lambda)\} \quad (4\text{-}144)$$

Equations (4-143) and (4-144) thus give the probability that precisely m orders are placed in a one year period for a single item.

When there are n items it is much more complicated to find the probability that precisely M orders are placed. Let $\Theta_j(m_j)$ be the probability that precisely m_j orders are placed for item j in one year. Assuming that demands for the various items are independent, we see that the probability that m_1 orders are placed for item 1, m_2 for item 2, etc., is

$$\prod_{j=1}^{n} \Theta_j(m_j) = \Theta_1(m_1) \Theta_2(m_2) \ldots \Theta_n(m_n) \quad (4\text{-}145)$$

where Π is used to denote a product. Thus the probability $\Theta(M)$ that $\sum_{j=1}^{n} m_j = M$ is the sum of (4-145) over all integers $m_j \geq 0$ such that $\sum_{j=1}^{n} m_j = M$. Clearly, the resulting probability distribution is not especially simple in form. The easiest way to generate the probabilities is by use of generating functions. We leave a discussion of this to Problem 4-59. There does not seem to be any simple explicit form for the distribution unless n is large, in which case $\Theta(M)$ should be approximately normally distributed by the central limit theorem.

As suggested above, another approach to dealing with a restriction on the number of orders placed is to make explicit use of the probability density $\Theta(M)$ that M orders are placed. We might for example assume that there is an additional cost G for each order placed over a given number h. The expected extra ordering cost is then

$$G \sum_{M=h}^{\infty} (M - h) \Theta(M) \tag{4-146}$$

Where $\Theta(M)$ is a function of $Q_1, \ldots, Q_n$ but not of the r_j. In this case there is no constraint. The cost function to be minimized is

$$\mathfrak{K} = \sum_{j=1}^{n} \mathfrak{K}_j(Q_j, r_j) + G \sum_{M=h}^{\infty} (M - h) \Theta(M) \tag{4-147}$$

Still another procedure which makes use of $\Theta(M)$ would be to minimize $\sum_{j=1}^{n} \mathfrak{K}_j(Q_j, r_j)$ subject to the constraint that the probability that more than h orders are placed is less than or equal to α, i.e.,

$$\sum_{M=h+1}^{\infty} \Theta(M) \leq \alpha \tag{4-148}$$

This constraint, if it is active, could be handled by the Lagrange multiplier technique.

The last two procedures suggested cannot easily be used analytically even when n is large enough to assume that $\Theta(M)$ is normally distributed. The reason for this is that $\Theta(M)$ will depend on all n of the Q_j. Hence it does not become possible to solve for one set of Q_j, r_j independently of the others. They will all be coupled together and this makes the computational problem much more difficult. From a practical point of view then, about the only thing that one can do is to use the constraint on the expected number of orders placed. This is not too satisfactory unless one knows about the sort of fluctuations there can be about the average. This cannot be easily determined analytically. Thus it is difficult to handle this constraint in an entirely satisfactory way.

The same sorts of problems are encountered in handling the other types of constraints discussed in Sec. 2-8, i.e., constraints on floor space and investment in inventory. We leave a discussion of these to Problems 4-60 and 4-61. Fortunately, in practical situations, the interactions between items giving rise to the types of constraints considered here often turn out to be not too important and can be neglected. Hence each item can be studied independently of the others and the models developed in the previous sections can be applied.

4-16 Determination of Operating Doctrines without Specifying Stockout Costs

Inasmuch as it can be very difficult to assign numerical values to the stockout costs in the real world, it is interesting to examine procedures for determining operating doctrines which do not require that one assign explicit values to the stockout costs. A procedure which immediately comes to mind is that of minimizing the average annual costs of ordering and carrying inventory, subject to the constraint that the average fraction of the time out of stock is not greater than a fixed value. This criterion has been suggested in Chapter 1. It can be used either in the backorders or lost sales cases. Another criterion which is applicable to the backorders case only is to minimize the average annual costs of ordering and carrying inventory subject to the constraint that the expected number of back-orders on the books at any point in time is not greater than a specified value. We would now like to investigate in somewhat more detail these two alternative criteria for determining values of Q and r.

Consider first the case where there is a constraint on the average fraction of time that the system can be out of stock. The average fraction of time which the system is out of stock is what we previously defined as P_{out}. It is also the expected number of backorders or lost sales incurred per year divided by the average rate of demand, i.e., $E(Q, r)/\lambda$. Thus we wish to minimize (in the backorders case)

$$\frac{\lambda}{Q} A + IC \left[\frac{Q}{2} + r - \mu + B(Q, r) \right] \qquad (4\text{-}149)$$

subject to the constraint

$$\frac{E(Q, r)}{\lambda} \leq f \qquad (4\text{-}150)$$

where f is the upper limit to the average fraction of time for which the system is out of stock. Now it is clear that if the costs (4-149) are to be minimized, the average fraction of time out of stock should be as large as possible. Hence the constraint (4-150) will be active, i.e., $E(Q, r) = \lambda f$ (or when Q and r are treated as discrete, $E(Q, r)$ should be as close to λf as possible while not being greater than λf).

To minimize (4-149) subject to $E(Q, r) = \lambda f$, we know from the theory of Lagrange multipliers (see Appendix 1) that we form the function

$F(Q, r, \theta) =$

$$\frac{\lambda}{Q} A + IC \left[\frac{Q}{2} + r - \mu + B(Q, r) \right] + \theta \left[E(Q, r) - \lambda f \right] \quad (4\text{-}151)$$

where θ is a Lagrange multiplier, and Q^*, r^* and θ^* will be solutions to

$$\frac{\partial F}{\partial Q} = \frac{\partial F}{\partial r} = \frac{\partial F}{\partial \theta} = 0 \quad (4\text{-}152)$$

since we do not expect the optimal values of any of the variables to lie on the boundaries.

Note, however, that minimizing $F(Q, r, \theta)$ for a given θ will yield the same $Q^*(\theta)$ and $r^*(\theta)$ as minimizing

$$\mathcal{K} = \frac{\lambda}{Q} A + IC \left[\frac{Q}{2} + r - \mu + B(Q, r) \right] + \theta E(Q, r) \quad (4\text{-}153)$$

since $\theta \lambda f$ is independent of Q and r. Hence, to determine Q^* and r^* we can first determine the functions $Q^*(\theta)$ and $r^*(\theta)$ by minimizing (4-153) and then selecting that value of θ, i.e., θ^*, for which $E[Q^*(\theta), r^*(\theta)] = \lambda f$. The values of $Q^*(\theta)$ and $r^*(\theta)$ evaluated at θ^* are Q^* and r^* respectively.

We can now make the interesting observation that $\mathcal{K}$ is simply the average annual cost, including backorder costs if for the backorder cost $\pi = \theta$, $\hat{\pi} = 0$. Thus we can use the models developed in this chapter to handle the present case. Indeed specification of the average fraction of time out of stock is equivalent to having a backorder cost with $\hat{\pi} = 0$ and $\pi = \theta^*$. Note that the imputed value of π will be uniquely determined by f. The computational procedure to determine Q^* and r^* is, however, more complicated when f is specified than when π and $\hat{\pi}$ are given. The computational procedure is as follows. Set $\hat{\pi} = 0$ and select an initial estimate of π, say θ_0. Compute $Q^*(\theta_0)$, $r^*(\theta_0)$ using whatever model developed in this chapter may be appropriate. Also compute $E[Q^*(\theta_0), r^*(\theta_0)]/\lambda = f_0$. If $f_0 > f$ select a new value of π, say θ_1, such that $\theta_1 > \theta_0$. If $f_0 < f$ select a $\theta_1 < \theta_0$ (if $f_0 = f$, the Q and r values are optimal and no additional computations are needed). Then determine

$$Q^*(\theta_1), \; r^*(\theta_1) \quad \text{and} \quad E[Q^*(\theta_1), r^*(\theta_1)]/\lambda = f_1$$

and repeat the above procedure. As additional computations are made, it becomes possible to quickly zero in by interpolation on the value of θ such that the expected fraction of the time out of stock is the desired value. It should be clear that the procedure of assigning a value to f in reality assigns a value to the backorder cost also, so that in the end one has implicitly assigned a numerical value to the backorder cost. The method of handling the lost sales case is precisely the same as for the backorders case examined above.

Consider next the case where the constraint requires that the expected number of backorders at any point in time be less than or equal to a specified value. Again it is clear that the constraint will be active, and will have the form $B(Q, r) = \delta$. Thus we wish to minimize (4-149) subject to this constraint. From the theory of Lagrange multipliers and what has been shown above, this is equivalent to minimizing

$$\mathcal{K} = \frac{\lambda}{Q} A + IC \left[\frac{Q}{2} + r - \mu \right] + (\eta + IC) B(Q, r) \qquad (4\text{-}154)$$

with respect to Q and r for a given η, thus yielding $Q^*(\eta)$ and $r^*(\eta)$, and then determining the optimal value η^* of the Lagrange multiplier η such that $B[Q^*(\eta), r^*(\eta)] = \delta$. Then $Q^*(\eta^*)$ and $r^*(\eta^*)$ are the optimal values of Q and r. The numerical procedure for making the computations is the same as that outlined above. It follows that specification of the expected number of backorders is equivalent to setting $\pi = 0$ and uniquely determining $\hat{\pi}$. Thus by specifying δ we implicitly determine a unique value of $\hat{\pi}$ when $\pi = 0$.

A more general procedure than the two possibilities discussed above would be to specify both the average fraction of the time which the system could be out of stock and the expected number of backorders at any point in time. The theory of Lagrange multipliers immediately shows that this would impute nonzero values to both π and $\hat{\pi}$, since in this case two Lagrange multipliers would be needed.

REFERENCES

1. Arrow, K. J., S. Karlin, and H. Scarf, *Studies in The Mathematical Theory of Inventory and Production.* Stanford, California: Stanford University Press, 1958.

2. Fetter, R. B., and W. C. Dalleck, *Decision Models for Inventory Management.* Homewood, Illinois: Richard D. Irwin, Inc., 1961.

3. Galliher, H. P., P. M. Morse, and M. Simond, "Dynamics of Two Classes of Continuous Review Inventory Systems," *Operations Research,* Vol. 7, No. 3, June 1959, pp. 362–384.

4. Palm, Conny, "Analysis of the Erlang Formula for Busy-Signal Arrangements," *Ericsson Technics,* Vol. 6, 1938, p. 39.

5. Takács, L., "On the Generalization of Erlang's Formula," *Acta Mathematica, Academiae Scientiarum Hungericae,* Tomus VII, 1956, pp. 419–432.

6. Whitin, T. M., *The Theory of Inventory Management, Rev. Ed.* Princeton, New Jersey: Princeton University Press, 1957.

7. Whitin, T. M., and J. W. T. Youngs, "A Method for Calculating Optimal Inventory Levels and Delivery Times," *Naval Research Logistics Quarterly*, September 1955, pp. 157–173.

PROBLEMS

4-1. Derive the equivalent of the model presented in Sec. 4-2 when a Poisson process generates demands, units are demanded one at a time, and the procurement lead time is a constant τ. Treat Q and r as discrete variables. Show that the following numerical procedure can be used to determine Q^* and r^*. To begin, set $Q = Q_w$ in the following expression and determine the largest integer r, call it r_1 which satisfies this inequality

$$P(r; \lambda\tau) > \frac{QIC}{\pi\lambda}$$

Then substitute r_1 into

$$Q(Q - 1) < \frac{2\lambda}{IC} \{A + \pi[\lambda\tau P(r; \lambda\tau) - rP(r + 1; \lambda\tau)]\}$$

and determine the largest Q, call it Q_2, which satisfies this expression. Use Q_2 in the previous relation and determine r_2 by finding the largest r which satisfies the inequality, etc.

4-2. Derive the equivalent of the lost sales model presented in Sec. 4-3 when a Poisson process generates demands and the procurement lead time is a constant τ. Develop a numerical procedure for determining Q^* and r^*.

4-3. Modify the results of Problems 4-1, 4-2 for the case where Q can be treated as continuous, but r is to be treated as discrete.

4-4. Draw the equivalent of Fig. 4-2 for the lost sales case and prove that the iterative scheme suggested in Sec. 4-4 converges in this case.

4-5. A function of two variables $\mathcal{K}(Q, r)$ is said to be convex over some region of the Qr-plane if for any two distinct points (Q_1, r_1) (Q_2, r_2) in the region and for any α, $0 \leq \alpha \leq 1$,

$$\mathcal{K}[\alpha Q_1 + (1 - \alpha)Q_2, \alpha r_1 + (1 - \alpha)r_2]$$
$$\leq \alpha\mathcal{K}(Q_1, r_1) + (1 - \alpha)\mathcal{K}(Q_2, r_2) \quad (4\text{-}155)$$

If we think of $\mathcal{K}$ as being a surface in three dimensions, then $\mathcal{K}$ is convex if the line joining any two points on the surface lies on or above the surface. Intuitively, a convex function will then have a shape of a bowl. $\mathcal{K}$ is said to be strictly convex if the strict inequality holds in Eq. (4-155) when $0 < \alpha < 1$. The convex function $\mathcal{K}$ is said to be strictly convex with respect to one of the variables, say Q, if for any points (Q_1, r), (Q_2, r), $Q_1 \neq Q_2$ and any r, the strict inequality holds in Eq. (4-155) for $0 < \alpha < 1$. Prove that the sum of convex functions is also a convex function. Prove that the absolute minimum of a *strictly* convex function over some region in the Qr-plane is unique. Show that if $\mathcal{K}$ is convex and if the absolute minimum of $\mathcal{K}$ over some region is taken on at two distinct points (Q_1, r_1), (Q_2, r_2), then it is also taken on at any point $[\alpha Q_1 + (1 - \alpha)Q_2, \alpha r_1 + (1 - \alpha)r_2]$, $0 \leq \alpha \leq 1$. Prove that any relative minimum of a convex function is also the absolute minimum.

4-6. Prove that

$$\frac{1}{Q} \int_r^\infty (x - r) \, h(x) \, dx$$

is a convex function of Q and r for $Q > 0, r \geq 0$ when $h(x)$ is a probability density function. Prove that it is strictly convex if $h(x)$ is everywhere positive over the allowable range of x. Note that the result still holds for all non-negative $r \leq r_m$ if $h(x) = 0$, $x > r_m$ and the upper limit in the integral is replaced by r_m (i.e., in the context of an inventory problem, there is an upper limit to the lead time demand). Note that the above results depend only on the non-negativity of $h(x)$ and not on its shape.

4-7. By making use of the results of Problems 4-5, 4-6, prove that the cost functions for the backorders and lost sales models presented in Secs. 4-2, 4-3 are convex. Also show that they are strictly convex if $h(x)$ is a normal distribution, and in this instance show that Q^* and r^* are unique. Show that in any case $\mathcal{K}(Q, r)$ is a strictly convex function of Q, so that there cannot be two or more different optimal solutions with the same r^* but different Q values.

4-8. The results of Problems 4-6, 4-7 show that Q^* and r^* are unique when $h(x) > 0$ for all x in the range of interest. However, Q^* and r^* are unique even if $h(x) = 0$ over some interval. Suppose for example that $h(x)$ has the form shown in Fig. 4-8 and $h(x) = 0$ between r_0 and r_1. Sketch the shape of $H(x)$ and the shape of the curve defined by Eq. (4-13) or (4-22). What is the slope of the curve defined by Eq. (4-13) or (4-22) between r_0 and r_1? Now prove that Q^* and r^* must be unique. *Hint:* For r in the interval 0 to r_0,

$\mathcal{K}(Q, r)$ is strictly convex. Similarly $\mathcal{K}(Q, r)$ is strictly convex for r in the interval r_1 to r_m. This shows (why?) that if the minimum is not unique, two or more r values in the interval r_0 to r_1 must yield the minimum value. Show by finding the slope of the curve corresponding to Eq. (4-12) or (4-21) that this cannot happen.

4-9. Under what conditions is there no solution to Eqs. (4-12), (4-13)? How can this be interpreted on Fig. (4-2)?

4-10. Prove that there always exists a solution to Eqs. (4-21), (4-22).

4-11. Modify the derivations presented in Secs. 4-2, 4-3 for the backorders and lost sales models to show that they hold for any number of orders outstanding, provided that r is based on the inventory position in the backorders case and the quantity on hand plus on order

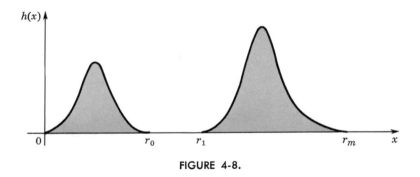

FIGURE 4-8.

in the lost sales case. Are any additional assumptions required in either case?

4-12. A warehouse which deals in hardware products services a large number of hardware stores in a given city. Solder of a certain type is sold by the warehouse to the stores in a carton containing two dozen rolls of solder. It is almost always true that a store will not place an order for more than a single carton. The warehouse will not ship less than a carton and hence it almost always ships a single carton per order. The inventory manager at the warehouse is planning to institute a lot size–reorder point system to control the inventory of this particular type of solder. An analysis of historical records shows that the procurement lead time demand for the solder is approximately normally distributed with mean of 125 cartons and standard deviation of 25. The average yearly rate of demand is 500 cartons per year. He estimates that the paper work cost in preparing an order invoice is $1.50 and the cost of receiving an order and placing it in the storage bin, along with the accompanying paper work on receipt of procurement, is $2.00 plus $0.15 times the size of the order. A carton of solder costs $12.00. The warehouse uses an inventory carrying charge of $I = 0.18$. All demands occurring when the warehouse is out of stock are backordered. It is estimated that the goodwill cost plus the cost of writing a special letter to the hardware store if a demand occurs when the system is out of stock amounts to $25.00. Compute the optimal order quantity and re-order point for the warehouse. What is the cost of uncertainty?

4-13. For the example worked out in Sec. 4-4, determine how Q^* and r^* vary with A. Allow A to vary from $500 to $50,000 and plot the results.

4-14. A large discount house is planning to install a $\langle Q, r \rangle$ system to control the inventory of a particular model of an AM-FM radio. The number of units demanded has been found to be essentially Poisson distributed with a mean of 5 radios per week (this does not include the Christmas season demand which will be handled separately). The procurement lead time is essentially constant and requires 3 weeks. Each radio costs the store $40.00. An inventory carrying charge of $I = 0.20$ is used. If a demand occurs when the model is not in stock, the customer will almost always go to another of the nearby discount stores rather than selecting a different model or waiting until a new shipment arrives. The store has decided that each such demand occurring when the model is not in stock costs the store a goodwill loss of $20.00 plus a loss in gross profits of $25.00. The total cost of placing an order is estimated to be $3.00. Determine Q^* and r^*. What is the cost of uncertainty? On the average, how many lost sales will be incurred per year?

4-15. A military supply center stocks air bearing gyros for a ballistic missile. The mean rate of demand for these gyros has been 100 per year over the past three years and the number of units demanded appears to be described quite well by a Poisson distribution. The procurement lead time is essentially constant and has the value 6 months. The gyros cost $2000 each. The cost of placing an order, incoming inspection, etc., is estimated to be $100.00. An inventory carrying charge of $I = 0.20$ is used. All units demanded when the system is out of stock are backordered. It is difficult to estimate the cost of being out of stock. Instead, the requirement has been made that the probability of being out of stock must not be greater than 0.0005. If the system is to operate using a $\langle Q, r \rangle$ model, determine Q^* and r^*. What is the imputed cost of a backorder? What is the cost of uncertainty?

4-16. Compute all the first and second derivatives of the cost function $\mathcal{K}(Q, r)$ given in Eq. (4-87).

4-17. Assume that $\mathcal{K}(Q, r)$ is approximated by the nonhomogeneous quadratic form

$$\mathcal{K}(Q, r) \approx \mathcal{K}(Q_0, r_0) + \frac{\partial \mathcal{K}}{\partial Q_0} (Q - Q_0) + \frac{\partial \mathcal{K}}{\partial r_0} (r - r_0)$$

$$+ \frac{1}{2} \frac{\partial^2 \mathcal{K}}{\partial Q_0^2} (Q - Q_0)^2 + \frac{\partial^2 \mathcal{K}}{\partial Q_0 \partial r_0} (Q - Q_0)(r - r_0) + \frac{1}{2} \frac{\partial^2 \mathcal{K}}{\partial r_0^2} (r - r_0)^2$$

where the derivatives are evaluated at Q_0, r_0. Show that the set of equations whose solution minimizes the quadratic form are precisely the same set of equations obtained using Newton's method to solve the equations $\partial \mathcal{K}/\partial Q = \partial \mathcal{K}/\partial r = 0$ when Q_0, r_0 are the initial guess at the solution.

4-18. Show that $\mathcal{K}(Q, r)$ in Eq. (4-87) is not a convex function of Q and r in general. *Hint:* Is it a convex function of r for a given Q?

4-19. Solve Problem 4-12 under the assumption that the cost of a backorder is $5.00 plus $10.00 per carton per week rather than a fixed charge of $25.00 per backorder.

4-20. Solve Problem 4-15 under the assumption that the cost of a backorder is $1000 plus $5000 per unit week of shortage.

4-21. Consider an item for which the demand can be treated as deterministic, the demand rate being 500 units per year. The item's cost is $20.00 per unit and the system which stocks the item uses an inventory carrying charge of $I = 0.20$. The cost of placing an order is $40.00. The procurement lead time is not a constant. However, it is always either 3 weeks or 6 weeks, the probability that it is 3 weeks being 0.6. All demands occurring when the system is out of stock are backordered, and the cost is $250 per backorder. The inventory is controlled using a $\langle Q, r \rangle$ system. Determine Q^* and r^*. What is the cost of uncertainty?

4-22. The housewares department of a large retail store is installing a $\langle Q, r \rangle$ system to control certain of the items it stocks. The procedur⌐ is to have the sales people count these critical items at the end of each day, and if any level has dropped to the reorder point an order is placed the next day. Occasionally, there is an overshoot of the reorder point, but it has been decided that its effect on the results will be small and can be ignored. An analysis of sales data over the past year (excluding the Christmas season) has yielded the following for weekly demand on a particular electric coffeemaker:

Number of units demanded in one week	0	1	2	3	4	5	6	7
Frequency	2	6	3	8	2	4	2	1

There were never more than 7 units demanded in one week. The unit cost of the coffee pot is $8.00 and the store uses an inventory carrying charge of $I = 0.13$. The procurement lead time is one week. The cost of placing an order is estimated to be $0.50. The store feels that because of goodwill loss, the cost of a lost sale including lost profit is $10.00. Compute Q^*, r^* under the assumption that the above data represent the true probability distribution for demand. What are the values of Q^*, r^* if one assumes that the number of units demanded per week is represented by a Poisson distribution whose mean is that obtained from the data given above?

4-23. An automotive repair shop installs new mufflers on autos. Past history indicates that the number of units demanded for a certain model of muffler is Poisson distributed with a mean of 1 per day. The procurement lead time is always either 8 or 15 days, the probability of 15 days being 0.7. A muffler costs the shop $6.00 and it uses an inventory carrying charge of $I = 0.20$. The cost of placing an order is estimated to be $1.00. Requests for muffler changes which occur when the dealer is out of stock are taken elsewhere, and the goodwill loss plus lost profits is estimated to be $25.00. If a $\langle Q, r \rangle$ system is used to control the inventory of this muffler, what are Q^*, r^*? What is the average annual cost of uncertainty? What assumption was made about the nature of the lead times? Is it valid?

4-24. Work out the equations which determine Q^* and r^* for the simple model discussed in Sec. 4-2 when

$$h(x) = \frac{1}{\delta} e^{-x/\delta}$$

i.e., $h(x)$ has an exponential distribution. Is there anything unusual about the resulting equations?

4-25. Solve the example presented in Sec. 4-4 when the marginal distribution of lead time demand has an exponential distribution rather than a normal distribution. Assume that the mean of the exponential is the same as the mean of the normal, and that all cost data given in the example apply here. Use the results of Problem 4-24 in making the computations.

4-26. Work out the equations which determine Q^* and r^* for the simple model discussed in Sec. 4-2 when the marginal distribution of lead time demand is gamma distributed with mean μ and standard deviation σ.

4-27. Solve the example presented in Sec. 4-4 when the marginal distribution of lead time demand has a gamma distribution with the same mean and standard deviation as the normal distribution in the example.

4-28. Derive the exact cost equation and the equations which determine Q^* and r^* under the assumption that the marginal distribution of lead time demand is exponential. Assume that lead times are independent and that orders do not cross.

4-29. Derive the exact cost expression and the equations which determine Q^* and r^* when the marginal distribution of lead time demand is a gamma distribution with mean μ and standard deviation σ. Assume that lead times are independent and that orders do not cross.

4-30. Solve Problem 4-12 under the assumption that the marginal distribution of lead time demand has an exponential distribution whose mean is the same as that of the normal distribution referred to in the problem.

4-31. Examine Molina's tables and note that often by adding merely a single unit of safety stock, the probability of incurring a backorder or lost sale during the lead time can be reduced from a sizable value to an exceptionally small value. Would one normally expect such an increment in protection by the addition of a single unit in the real world? Why or why not?

4-32. Is it possible when the demand variable is treated as continuous to have the demand in any time period of length t described by a gamma distribution with mean λt, instead of by a normal distribution, while still being able to describe the $\langle Q, r \rangle$ system as a Markov process continuous in space and time? Why or why not?

4-33. A low demand, expensive spare part for an aircraft is stocked at a large military depot. The average rate of demand is 3 per year. The demands behave as if they were generated by a Poisson process. Units are ordered one at a time as demanded. Each unit costs $2000 and the system uses a carrying charge of $I = 0.20$. Demands occurring when the system is out of stock are backordered. There is no fixed cost for a backorder, but the grounding of an aircraft for lack of this part costs $10,000 per week. The procurement lead time can be assumed to be a constant equal to 6 months. Determine the optimal value of the inventory position which is to be maintained at a constant value through time.

4-34. Solve Problem 4-33 under the assumption that the procurement lead time has a gamma distribution with mean equal to 6 months and standard deviation equal to 1 month. Imagine that lead times are independent random variables and that orders are received in the same sequence in which they were placed.

4-35. Solve Problem 4-33 assuming that in addition to the backorder cost of $10,000 per week, there is a fixed cost per backorder of $5000.

4-36. Solve Problem 4-34 assuming that in addition to the backorder cost of $10,000 per week, there is a fixed cost per backorder of $5000.

4-37. Plot a curve showing how in Problem 4-33 the optimal inventory position varies with the backorder cost $\hat{\pi}$.

4-38. Solve Problem 4-12 under the assumption that there is no fixed cost for incurring a backorder but that instead a backorder costs $20.00 per week out of stock.

4-39. Solve Problem 4-15 under the assumption that instead of specifying the probability of being out of stock, there is a cost of $10,000 per unit week of shortage.

4-40. A paint store orders a type of one pint cans of red paint by the carton. There are 24 pints in a carton and after each twenty-four demands, a carton is ordered. The order size is always one carton. One carton costs $12.00, and the store uses an inventory carrying charge of $I = 0.20$. Demands occurring when the store is out of stock are lost, and the owner estimates the cost of a lost sale to be $1.00. Three weeks are required from the time that an order is placed until the shipment is received. What is the optimal reorder point?

4-41. Solve the example given in Sec. 4-4 under the assumption that "all units" quantity discounts are available of the following sort: the unit cost is $50.00 if $0 < Q < 1200$; the unit cost is $49.50 if $1200 \leq Q < 2500$; and the unit cost is $49.00 if $2500 \leq Q < \infty$.

4-42. Solve the example given in Sec. 4-4 under the assumption that incremental quantity discounts are available of the following sort: for all units between 0 and 1200 the unit cost is $50.00. For additional units up to 3000 units the unit cost is $45.00. For all units above 3000, the unit cost is $40.00.

4-43. Solve Problem 4-12 under the assumption that "all units" quantity discounts of the following sort are available: the unit cost is \$12.00 if $0 < Q < 50$ and is \$11.00 if $50 \leq Q < \infty$.

4-44. Solve Problem 4-14 under the assumption that "all units" quantity discounts of the following sort are available: the unit cost of a radio is \$40.00 if $0 < Q < 39$, and is \$37.00 if $40 \leq Q < 99$ and is \$33.00 if $100 \leq Q < \infty$.

4-45. Consider the problem of developing a $\langle Q, r \rangle$ system for an item when the order quantity must be an integral multiple of a fixed package quantity. Modify the simplified models developed in Secs. 4-2, 4-3 to take account of this, and obtain the equations which determine Q^* and r^*.

4-46. The cosmetics department of a large department store has recently introduced a $\langle Q, r \rangle$ system to control many items in the department. A particular type of expensive perfume must be ordered in multiples of one dozen bottles since the standard package contains 12 bottles. The demand for this type of perfume averages 3 per week and is Poisson distributed. A standard package costs the store \$70.00. An inventory carrying charge of $I = 0.20$ is used. The cost of placing an order amounts to \$0.50. This particular perfume is not easy to obtain elsewhere, and hence demands occurring when the store is out of stock are backordered. However, only the store's most wealthy customers purchase this perfume and hence the store considers it bad policy to be out very frequently. The cost of a backorder is taken to be \$100.00. Determine Q^* and r^* if the procurement lead time is 5 weeks. How much would the average annual savings be if no restrictions were placed on the size of the order quantity?

4-47. For the model presented in Sec. 4-7 compute the probability that precisely n orders are outstanding at any point in time. Also compute the expected amount on order and show that it is equal to the expected lead time demand. *Hint:* Specification of the net inventory uniquely determines the number of orders outstanding.

4-48. For the model presented in Sec. 4-9 compute the probability that precisely n orders are outstanding at any point in time. Also compute the expected amount on order and show that it is equal to the expected lead time demand. *Hint:* Same as for Problem 4-47.

4-49. Compute the mean of the distribution $\Theta(m)$ defined by Eqs. (4-143), (4-144) and show that it is equal to λ/Q.

4-50. Consider an item with the following characteristics

$$\lambda = 700 \text{ units/yr.} \quad A = \$15.00$$
$$C = \$50.00 \qquad \qquad \pi = \$1.00$$
$$I = 0.20 \qquad \qquad \hat{\pi} = \$15.00 \text{ per unit year}$$

The lead time demand can be considered to be normally distributed with a mean of 300 and a standard deviation of 50. The lead time can be assumed to be constant. Try to determine Q^* and r^* using Eqs. (4-89) and (4-90). Are any difficulties encountered?

4-51. What changes are needed in the equations used to determine Q^* and r^* for the simple models developed in Secs. 4-2 and 4-3 if there is also an annual carrying cost which is proportional to the maximum on hand inventory which can exist. Answer the same question for the model presented in Sec. 4-9.

4-52. In the text we have always assumed that the cost of a backorder never had a more complicated form than $\pi + \hat{\pi}t$, where t is the time for which the backorder exists. In general, of course, the cost of a backorder can be an arbitrary function of the time for which the backorder exists. When the cost of a backorder depends on t in a more complicated way than $\pi + \hat{\pi}t$, then the procedures used in the text cannot be used to compute the expected annual cost of backorders. One must use a procedure which explicitly takes account of the length to time for which each backorder exists. To do this it is convenient to imagine that each unit ordered is tagged to meet a particular demand, so that no backorder costs are incurred for any given unit ordered, unless the demand it is to satisfy occurs before the order arrives. Imagine that the Q units ordered at a particular point in time are to satisfy demands $r + 1, \ldots, r + Q$ occurring after the order is placed. Show that when the lead time is a constant τ, then for the case where demand is Poisson distributed, and $\pi(t)$ is the cost of a backorder which lasts for a length of time t, the expected backorder costs associated with the order (i.e., per cycle) are

$$\sum_{j=1}^{Q} \int_0^\tau \lambda \pi(\tau - \zeta) p(r + j - 1; \lambda\zeta) \, d\zeta$$

What then are the expected annual backorder costs? For the case where $\pi(t) = \pi + \hat{\pi}t$ show that the above formula leads to the same results as those obtained in the text. Compute the average annual backorder costs when

(a) $\pi(t) = \pi_0 + \pi_1 t + \pi_2 t^2$ \qquad (b) $\pi(t) = \pi_0 e^{bt}, \quad b > 0$

What sort of modifications are needed when the lead time is a stochastic variable?

4-53. Solve Problem 4-52 under the assumption that the demand in any time period is represented by a normal distribution.

4-54. Compute the variance of the distribution of the on hand inventory for the model developed in Sec. 4-7.

4-55. Compute the variance of the distribution of the on hand inventory for the model developed in Sec. 4-9.

4-56. Derive the expression for $\mathcal{K}$ corresponding to Eq. (4-61) under the assumption that r is negative. Show that Eq. (4-61) is correct provided that $\alpha(v)$, $\beta(v)$ are given by Eqs. (4-62) and (4-63) respectively.

4-57. Derive in detail Eq. (4-83).

4-58. Show that the $\mathcal{K}(Q, r)$ defined by Eq. (4-107) will be obtained directly if the marginal distribution of lead time demand is used in computing the state probabilities rather than the distribution of lead time demand for a fixed τ.

4-59. Attempt to compute the generating function for $\Theta(m)$ defined by Eqs. (4-143) and (4-144). How would one obtain the generating function for $\Theta(M)$ where M is the total number of orders placed for all n items in one year. Attempt to obtain an explicit expression for $\Theta(M)$. Why is $\Theta(M)$ approximately normally distributed when n is large?

4-60. Discuss the use of floor space constraints in $\langle Q, r \rangle$ models with stochastic demands when there are n items. Show that the same sort of problems are encountered as those encountered in placing a limitation on the number of procurements made.

4-61. Discuss the problems involved in applying a constraint on investment in inventory for $\langle Q, r \rangle$ models with stochastic demands when there are n items. Note that in this case there is an upper limit to the inventory that can be on hand. What is it? How relevant is the upper limit to a constraint on the average investment in inventory? How difficult is it to compute the probability that the total investment in inventory will go above a specified value?

4-62. Derive in detail Eq. (4-105).

4-63. Prove that $n!/t^n$ obtained from Eq. (4-124) is a legitimate density function for the situation discussed there. *Hint:* What is the allowable range of variation for t_i?

4-64. How can R^* be determined when the average annual cost is given by Eq. (4-138)?

4-65. Obtain the $E(Q, r)$ and $B(Q, r)$ terms for the model of Sec. 4-7 by first computing the expected number of backorders or unit years of shortage incurred per cycle and then convert to an annual basis. *Hint:* Take a cycle to be the time between the arrival of two successive procurements. Note that it is necessary to take explicit account of the fact that the length of the cycle is a random variable.

4-66. Note that when units are demanded one at a time, there are precisely Q demands in every cycle. Imagine here that a cycle refers to the time between the placing of two successive orders. Then the inventory position is $r + Q$ until the first demand occurs, $r + Q - 1$ until the second demand occurs, etc., and $r + 1$ until the Qth demand occurs. Compute the expected costs (displaced by a lead time) of carrying inventory and of backorders incurred between the occurrence of the jth and the $(j + 1)$st demands. Then the corresponding costs per cycle are the sum of these costs from $j = 0$ to $Q - 1$. In this way compute the costs per cycle of carrying inventory and of backorders when a Poisson process generates demands and the lead times are constant. *Hint:* The time between demands is not constant but is exponentially distributed.

4-67. For any real world system the ultimate use of any item demanded may vary widely from one demand to the next. It is conceivable that a different backorder cost might be associated with each end use. This is especially true in military supply systems where the item may be used in a variety of ways. Suppose that there are N different end uses and for end use i, the cost of a backorder is $\pi_i + \hat{\pi}_i t$. Let f_i be the fraction of the demands that will be for end use i (or the probability that any given demand will be for end use i). Show how to account for this sort of behavior within the framework of the models developed in this chapter. Do they really implicitly include this case also?

4-68. Combine the models developed in Secs. 4-2 and 4-3 to obtain a model for the case where a fraction f of the demands occurring when the system is out of stock are backordered while the remainder are lost. Assume that the cost of a lost sale is different from the cost of a backorder.

4-69. Solve Problem 4-12 under the assumption that instead of specifying the cost of a backorder, it is required that the average fraction of the time that the system is out of stock not be greater than 0.01. What is the imputed cost of a backorder?

4-70. Solve Problem 4-14 under the assumption that instead of specifying the cost of a lost sale, it is required that the average fraction of the time that the system is out of stock not be greater than 0.05. What is the imputed cost of a lost sale?

4-71. Solve Problem 4-22 under the assumption that instead of specifying the cost of a lost sale, it is required that the average fraction of the time that the system is out of stock not be greater than 0.02. What is the imputed cost of a lost sale?

4-72. Solve Problem 4-33 under the assumption that instead of specifying the cost of a backorder, it is required that the average fraction of the time that the system is out of stock not be greater than 0.005. What is the imputed cost of a backorder?

4-73. Consider a system for which the mean rate of demand is constant over time, and the number of units demanded in any given time interval is Poisson distributed. The procurement lead time is always a constant τ, and demands occurring when the system is out of stock are backordered. Imagine that there is no fixed cost of incurring a backorder, and if there are any backorders on the books at time t, the backorder cost incurred between t and $t + dt$ is $\pi_0 \, dt$. Note that the backorder cost is independent of the number of backorders outstanding. Furthermore, assume that annual carrying costs are proportional to the maximum value of the inventory position. The cost of placing an order is A, and the unit cost of the item is C independent of the size of an order. Develop the average annual cost expression for a $\langle Q, r \rangle$ model for the above item, and obtain formulas for computing Q^* and r^*.

4-74. In the lost sales case studied in Sec. 4-11, prove that the minimization of the average annual cost with the cost of a lost sale defined so as to include the lost profit will yield the same Q^* and r^* as the maximization of the average annual profit.

4-75. In order to treat r and Q as continuous and to differentiate $\mathcal{K}$ with respect to these variables, what restrictions must be placed on $h(x)$ in the model of Sec. 4-2 if the derivatives are to exist for all $Q > 0$, $r > 0$?

PERIODIC REVIEW MODELS

WITH STOCHASTIC DEMANDS

"*A decision has to be made once each orbit. Each 90 minutes the astronaut — and Mercury control —* have to decide over the Pacific whether he is going to be brought down in the Atlantic. This is a recurring, tough decision they have to make.*"

Newspaper Report

5-1 Introduction

Although there is no difference between $\langle Q, r \rangle$ and periodic review models for deterministic systems, the nature of the two types of models becomes somewhat different for stochastic demands. This chapter will be devoted to studying different types of periodic review models. In the real world, one can find both transactions reporting and periodic review systems in operation. However, at the present time, the number of systems using periodic review appears to be much greater than the number using trans-actions reporting. The reason for this, of course, is that transactions reporting systems can be costly and difficult to operate in practice. It might be pointed out, though, that with the increased use of high speed data processing equipment, the trend is more and more in the direction of changing over to transactions reporting. This is especially true in military supply systems. There are benefits to be gained from using transactions reporting if it is not too costly because, among other things, it is possible to cut down on the average investment in inventory by doing so. This will be examined in more detail later in the chapter.

What is involved in making a "review" when a periodic review procedure is used can vary widely from one system to another. In some situations, transactions may have been recorded as they occurred but were not trans-mitted to the decision maker in a form that could be used. In this case it may only be necessary to aggregate, either by hand or on a digital com-puter, all the transactions over the past period, determine the relevant variables of interest, and send them to the decision maker. In other cases it may be necessary to make an actual physical count of the inventory before any decisions are made. This will often be done even when there is some form of transactions recording, because the recorded data may not be accurate enough for use. A typical example of this latter situation is a department store where the buyer will make a stock count, even though information from sales slips or tickets is available, simply because the information taken from sales slips or tickets will, for a variety of reasons, often be considerably in error. Of course, it should be noted that even when transactions reporting systems are used, actual inventory counts will be needed occasionally to eliminate errors arising from breakage, spoilage, pilferage, mistakes, etc.

For transactions reporting systems in which the mean rate of demand is constant, units are demanded one at a time, and the process generating lead times does not change with time, it is clear that if the operating doctrine is also to remain time invariant, then a Qr doctrine is the only one that can be thought of which makes full use of the ability to make a decision after every transaction, and hence is an optimal operating doctrine. This can be proved rigorously using the methods introduced in Chapter 8. In the case of periodic review systems, however, things are somewhat more complicated. Several possible operating policies suggest themselves.

One operating doctrine for periodic review systems which is frequently used in practice requires that an order be placed at each review time if there have been any demands at all in the past period (a periodic review system will be said to have gone through one period's operation in the time between two successive reviews). A sufficient quantity is ordered to bring the inventory position or the amount on hand plus on order up to a level R. Note that with this system, the quantity ordered can vary from one review period to the next. This operating doctrine will be called an "order up to R" doctrine.

An alternative operating doctrine is to make a procurement at a review time only if the inventory position or the amount on hand plus on order is less than or equal to r. In such a case a sufficient quantity is ordered to bring the appropriate inventory level up to $R(R > r)$. This operating doctrine will be referred to as an Rr rule. An order up to R rule is a special case of an Rr rule in which $r = R - 1$ when the inventory levels are treated as discrete variables, and $r = R$ when they are treated as continuous variables.

An intermediate type of operating doctrine is that in which, as above, a procurement is made at a review period only if the inventory position or the amount on hand plus on order at the review time is less than or equal to r. However, the quantity ordered is chosen to be an integral multiple of some fundamental quantity Q, i.e., the quantity ordered is nQ where $n = 1, 2, 3, \ldots$. The value of n is chosen to be the largest integer such that after the order is placed the appropriate inventory level is less than or equal to $R = r + Q$. Such an operating doctrine will be referred to simply as an nQ doctrine. It will be observed that when the inventory levels are treated as discrete variables, then an order up to R rule is a special case of the nQ rule for which $Q = 1$ and $R = r + 1$. When the inventory levels are treated as continuous variables, it is still true that the order up to R rule is a special case of the nQ doctrine in the limit as $Q \rightarrow 0$.

The three operating doctrines described above are essentially the only ones ever used in practice for periodic review systems. This chapter will develop and compare a set of models which use these three operating doctrines in the case where the stochastic processes generating demands and lead times are time invariant. The purpose of these models will be not only to determine the appropriate values of r, R for a given T, but also to determine the optimal value of T, the time between reviews, in cases where this time is also a variable. Models which use an order up to R policy will be referred to as $\langle R, T \rangle$ models, those which use an Rr policy as $\langle R, r, T \rangle$ models, and those which use an nQ policy as $\langle nQ, r, T \rangle$ models. Of course, any model which can be used to determine the optimal value of T as well as R, r can also be used to determine the optimal values of R, r for a given T.

In Chapter 4, the annual cost of operating the transactions reporting system was not included in the average annual cost. The reason was that it was assumed that this cost was independent of Q and r and hence did not need to be included.

In this chapter, however, in order to determine the optimal value of T, it is necessary to introduce the cost of making a review. The cost of making a review will be assumed to be independent of the model variables. The review cost will not include the cost of placing an order since, in general, an order may not be placed at each review.

As in Chapter 4 we shall begin with two simple approximate models which are also the most useful ones for practical applications.

5-2 Simple, Approximate $\langle R, T \rangle$ Models

In the real world the most widely used operating doctrine for periodic review systems is the order up to R doctrine. We shall here present the analogues of the backorders and lost sales models of Secs. 4-2 and 4-3 respectively, for periodic review systems using an order up to R policy. Again all variables will be treated as continuous.

Consider first the backorders case. The time between reviews will be denoted by T, and at each review time a sufficient quantity is ordered to bring the inventory position of the system up to a level R. The problem is to determine the optimal values of R and T. At the outset, the following assumptions will be made:

1. The cost J of making a review is independent of the variables R and T.

2. The unit cost C of the item is constant independent of the quantity ordered.

3. Backorders are incurred only in very small quantities. This will be taken to imply that when an order arrives, it is almost always sufficient to meet any outstanding backorders.

4. The cost of each backorder is π, and the cost is independent of the length of time for which the backorder exists.

5. When the procurement lead time is a random variable, it is assumed that orders are received in the same sequence in which they were placed, and furthermore, the lead times for different orders can be treated as independent random variables. It might be noted that for $\langle Q, r \rangle$ models, the dual assumptions that orders were received in the sequence placed and that lead times for different orders were independent random variables could not both hold rigorously, since there existed a positive probability that two successive orders could be separated by an arbitrarily short time interval. Here, however, orders can never be more closely spaced than by an interval of length T, and hence if T is great enough, it is possible, provided that there is a sufficiently small range of variation in the lead time, to have both assumptions hold simultaneously.

As in Chapter 4, let A be the cost of placing an order and I be the inventory carrying charge. The density function for the demand x in a time interval of length t will be written $f(x; t)$, and λ will denote the average demand rate. The variable costs which must be included in average annual cost are: (a) review, (b) ordering, (c) carrying and (d) backorder costs.

Since the time between reviews is T, the average annual review cost is J/T. Furthermore, since an order will be placed at each review (when demand is treated as continuous, the probability of no demands occurring in the period is zero), the average annual ordering cost is A/T. If we write $L = A + J$, then the average annual costs of review and ordering are L/T. In this case the ordering and review costs can be combined since an order is placed at each review time.

The average annual cost of holding inventory will be found by computing the expected holding cost per period and then multiplying by $1/T$ to obtain the average annual cost. It is convenient to use as a period the time between the arrival of two successive orders rather than between the placement of two successive orders in making this computation. Inasmuch as the inventory position of the system is R immediately after reviewing and placing an order, and since everything on order will have arrived in a procurement lead time and nothing which is not on order can arrive in this time, the expected net inventory immediately after the arrival of a procurement must be $R - \mu$, where μ is the expected lead time demand. Because the mean rate of demand remains constant over time, the expected net inventory must decrease linearly with time and have the value $R - \mu - \lambda T$ just prior to the arrival of the next order, since the expected demand per period must be the expected amount ordered, i.e., λT, so that if the expected net inventory immediately after the arrival of a procurement is $R - \mu$, it is therefore $R - \mu - \lambda T$ just prior to the arrival of a procurement. Now because of assumption 3 it must be true that the integral over time of the net inventory must very closely approximate the integral over time of the on hand inventory. Hence the expected unit years of storage incurred per period is to a good approximation

$$T \left[\frac{1}{2} (R - \mu) + \frac{1}{2} (R - \mu - \lambda T) \right] = T \left[R - \mu - \frac{\lambda T}{2} \right]$$

so that the average annual cost of carrying inventory is

$$IC \left[R - \mu - \frac{\lambda T}{2} \right] \tag{5-1}$$

It will be shown later when the precise expressions are derived that the simple argument given above is correct in the case where the expected unit years of backorders incurred per year is negligible with respect to the expected unit years of storage. Note that the above argument applies even if the procurement lead time is a random variable.

In order to compute the average annual cost of backorders, it is necessary to compute the average number of backorders incurred per year. This will be done by computing the expected number of backorders incurred per period and multiplying by $1/T$. Consider first the case where the procurement lead time is a constant τ. Then an order placed at time t will arrive in the system at time $t + \tau$, and the next procurement will arrive in the system at time $t + \tau + T$. After the order is placed at time t, the inventory position of the system is R. We wish to compute the expected number of backorders occurring between $t + \tau$ and $t + \tau + T$. A backorder will occur in this period under assumption 3 if and only if the demand in the time period $\tau + T$ exceeds R. Assumption 3 assures us that after the arrival of the order placed at time t there will be no backorders on the books, and hence they must all be incurred between times $t + \tau$ and $t + \tau + T$. Hence the expected number of backorders incurred per period is

$$\int_R^\infty (x - R) f(x; \tau + T) \, dx \tag{5-2}$$

Note that it is no longer the lead time demand but instead the lead time plus one period's demand which is relevant. Intuitively, the reason for this is that once the order is placed at time t, another order cannot be placed until time $t + T$ regardless of what happens, i.e., protection is needed for a lead time plus T. We found above that the expected value of the net inventory at the time of arrival of a procurement is $R - \mu - \lambda T$. This is by definition the safety stock, and as expected, it does depend on the expected demand in time $\tau + T$.

Suppose now that the procurement lead time τ is a random variable with density $g(\tau)$, and let $\tau_{\min}$, $\tau_{\max}$ be the lower and upper limits respectively to the possible range of lead time values. Then if τ_1, τ_2 are the lead times for the orders placed at times t and $t + T$ respectively, the expected number of backorders incurred per period must be

$$\int_{\tau_{\min}}^{\tau_{\max}} \int_{\tau_{\min}}^{\tau_{\max}} \int_{R}^{\infty} (x - R)f(x; \tau_2 + T)g(\tau_2)g(\tau_1)\, dx\, d\tau_2\, d\tau_1$$

$$= \int_{R}^{\infty} (x - R)\hat{h}(x; T)\, dx \qquad (5\text{-}3)$$

where

$$\hat{h}(x; T) = \int_{\tau_{\min}}^{\tau_{\max}} f(x; \tau_2 + T)g(\tau_2)\, d\tau_2 \qquad (5\text{-}4)$$

This follows since

$$\int_{\tau_{\min}}^{\tau_{\max}} g(\tau_1)\, d\tau_1 = 1$$

In order for (5-3) to hold rigorously, it is necessary that there be no overlap of the lead time distributions, i.e.,

$$\tau_{\max} < \tau_{\min} + T$$

However, the result will be approximately correct if the overlap is small. Note that $\hat{h}(x; T)$ is not the marginal distribution of lead time demand.

If we define $\hat{h}(x; T)$ to be $f(x; \tau + T)$ when the procurement lead time is a constant and to be (5-4) when the procurement lead time is a random variable, then in all cases, the expected number of backorders incurred per period is given by (5-3). The average number of backorders incurred per year is

$$E(R, T) = \frac{1}{T} \int_{R}^{\infty} (x - R)\hat{h}(x; T)\, dx \qquad (5\text{-}5)$$

and the average annual cost of backorders is $\pi E(R, T)$.

All the terms needed in the cost expression have now been evaluated. The average annual variable cost is

$$\mathcal{K} = \frac{L}{T} + IC\left[R - \mu - \frac{\lambda T}{2}\right] + \pi E(R, T) \qquad (5\text{-}6)$$

For a given T, the value of R which minimizes $\mathcal{K}$ must satisfy

$$\frac{\partial \mathcal{K}}{\partial R} = 0 = IC - \frac{\pi}{T}\hat{H}(R; T) \qquad (5\text{-}7)$$

where

$$\hat{H}(R; T) = \int_{R}^{\infty} \hat{h}(x; T)\, dx \qquad (5\text{-}8)$$

is the complementary cumulative of $\hat{h}(x; T)$. Thus R^*, the optimal value of R, is a solution to

$$\hat{H}(R; T) = \frac{ICT}{\pi} \tag{5-9}$$

For a given T, (5-9) will normally yield a unique R although in certain cases (to be examined in Problem 5-4) R may not be unique. There will be no solution if $ICT/\pi > 1$. This cannot happen, however, if the assumptions originally made are to be valid, since it would imply that backorders would be incurred very frequently.

To determine the optimal T value, one could attempt to solve $\partial \mathcal{K}/\partial T = 0$ simultaneously with (5-9), say by Newton's method, thus obtaining R^* and T^* at the same time. The method of steepest descents could also be used. In this case, however, it is also quite simple merely to tabulate $\mathcal{K}$ as a function of T, using the R^* for the given T in computing $\mathcal{K}$, plot the results and in this way determine T^*. The development of the details of using Newton's method or the method of steepest descents is left to Problems 5-5 and 5-7.

The equations for the lost sales case differ little from those for the backorders case. The review-ordering and stockout costs are precisely the same. A slight correction is made in the inventory carrying cost. Since for the lost sales case the safety stock is the expected value of the on hand inventory at the time of arrival of a procurement, we see using the same arguments as in Sec. 4-3 that the safety stock is

$$R - \mu - \lambda T + \int_R^\infty (x - R)\hat{h}(x; T)\, dx \tag{5-10}$$

For periodic review systems this expression is approximate even when there is never more than a single order outstanding and holds only when lost sales are incurred in very small quantities. Equation (5-10) ignores the effects of lost sales which can occur between the time an order is placed and the time it arrives. It considers only lost sales occurring between the time the order arrives and the time the next order arrives. So long as the system is out of stock on the average only a very small fraction of the time, the correction to (5-10) itself will be small, and hence (5-10) is a sufficiently good approximation. As long as the average fraction of time out of stock is very small, the model also applies to cases where more than a single order can be outstanding at any point in time. The average annual cost of holding inventory in the lost sales case is then

$$IC\left[R - \mu - \frac{\lambda T}{2} + \int_R^\infty (x - R)\hat{h}(x; T)\, dx \right] \tag{5-11}$$

The average annual variable cost for the lost sales case is thus

$$\mathcal{K} = \frac{J}{T} + IC\left[R - \mu - \frac{\lambda T}{2}\right] + \left(IC + \frac{\pi}{T}\right)\int_R^\infty (x - R)\hat{h}(x; T)\, dx \quad (5\text{-}12)$$

and the equivalent of (5-9) becomes

$$\hat{H}(R; T) = \frac{ICT}{\pi + ICT} \quad (5\text{-}13)$$

This completes the development of the simple order up to R models. With the approximations made, they can be applied when lead times are random variables and when more than a single order is outstanding.

EXAMPLE A large California warehouse follows a policy of reviewing all items quarterly. It uses an order up to R policy for every item. Consider one item it carries—say a particular type of tractor tire. The mean demand rate has been constant over time at the value of 600 per year. The warehouse orders tires directly from the manufacturer and the lead time τ is nearly constant, and has the value 6 months. The demand in the time $\tau + T$ can be represented quite well by a normal distribution with mean $600(\tau + T)$ and variance $900(\tau + T)$. The variance is not equal to the mean (as would be true if a Poisson process were generating demands), since the number of units demanded per demand is also a random variable, and this increases the variance. The cost to the warehouse of each tire is $15.00; the warehouse uses an inventory carrying charge of $I = 0.20$. All demands occurring when the warehouse is out of stock are backordered and the cost of a backorder is estimated to be $25.00. It is desired to determine the optimal value of R.

Note first of all that when T is specified, R^* can be found without a knowledge of the review or ordering costs. From the data given above $T + \tau = \frac{3}{4}$ years and the expected demand in time $T + \tau$ is $600(\frac{3}{4}) = 450$, and the variance of the demand in this time is $900(\frac{3}{4}) = 675$, or the standard deviation is 25.981. Thus from (5-9), R^* is the solution to

$$\Phi\left(\frac{R - 450}{25.981}\right) = \frac{ICT}{\pi} = \frac{0.20(15)}{25(4)} = 0.030$$

From the normal tables it follows that

$$\frac{R^* - 450}{25.981} = 1.881$$

and

$$R^* = 450 + 48.8 = 498.8 \approx 499$$

From (5-5) and A4-25 the average number of backorders incurred per year is

$$4[25.98\phi(1.881) + (450 - 499)\Phi(1.881)] = 4[25.98(0.0679) - 49(0.030)]$$
$$= 1.175$$

Thus the average fraction of time out of stock is $\frac{1.175}{600} = 0.00196$, which is small as the use of the model requires. Note that since $\tau = 6$ months and $T = 3$ months, there will always be precisely two orders outstanding.

Suppose now that the combined cost of ordering and reviewing is $25.00. Let us then determine the optimal value for T, the time between reviews. This will be done simply by tabulating $\mathcal{K}$ as a function of T, where for each T the optimal R for that T is used. The cost expression for the case under consideration is

$$\mathcal{K} = \frac{25}{T} + 3[R - 300 - 300T]$$

$$+ \frac{25}{T} \left\{ \sqrt{900(0.5 + T)} \; \phi \left[\frac{R - 600(0.5 + T)}{\sqrt{900(0.5 + T)}} \right] \right.$$

$$+ [600(0.5 + T) - R]\Phi \left[\frac{R - 600(0.5 + T)}{\sqrt{900(0.5 + T)}} \right] \right\}$$

The results are presented in Table 5-1, and $\mathcal{K}$ is plotted as a function of T in Fig. 5-1. It is seen that the optimal value of T is about 1.9 months, and the use of this T value would result in an average annual savings of about $24.00 as compared to the T value of 3 months now in use. The value of T^* could be computed more accurately. The value given is within 0.05 months of the exact value. For real world applications this accuracy is quite sufficient, especially since it would not be possible to save more than a fraction of a dollar per year by computing T^* more accurately. The values

TABLE 5-1
Data for Example

T (months)	$R^*(T)$ (units)	Safety Stock (units)	Average Annual Review and Ordering Cost	Average Annual Carrying Cost	Average Annual Backorder Cost	Average Annual Cost $\mathcal{K}$
0.5	382	57	$600	$208	$23	$831
1.0	403	53	300	234	23	557
1.5	426	51	200	265	27	492
1.7	436	51	177	281	25	483
1.8	440	50	167	285	27	479
1.9	445	50	158	292	27	477
2.0	449	49	150	297	31	478
3.0	499	49	100	372	29	501

in Table 5-1 have been rounded off to the nearest dollar value. The back-order costs jump around somewhat because R is rounded to the nearest integer.

The behavior of the safety stock in Table 5-1 deserves some comment. At first it seems rather surprising that it should decrease with increasing T. The reader can easily check that it continues to decrease even for higher T. Intuitively, the reason for this is that the more frequently that the net inventory gets down in the neighborhood of the safety stock, the greater

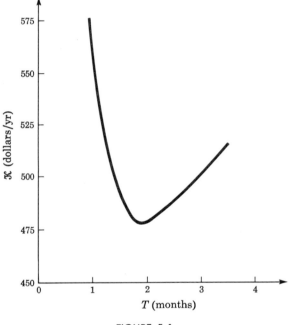

FIGURE 5-1.

will be the required safety stock to prevent unduly large backorder costs. However, in the periodic review model being studied, the net inventory gets in the neighborhood of the safety stock once each period. Hence, the smaller T, the larger the safety stock required. Another peculiar feature is that the model has the safety stock approach infinity as $T \to 0$. We know intuitively that this is not correct. The problem lies in the formulation of the model. We have assumed that there are no backorders on the books at the time an order arrives. This assumption is not valid when T is small. The exact formulation given later will rectify this problem.

An interesting comparison of the $\langle R, T \rangle$ model being studied and the simple $\langle Q, r \rangle$ model of Sec. 4-2 can be made using the present example if one assumes that the \$25.00 combined ordering and review cost is entirely an ordering cost, i.e., reviews are free. If the values of A, C, I, π are used in the $\langle Q, r \rangle$ model of Sec. 4-2 to obtain an optimal Q and r, one finds on carrying out the iteration process that $Q_w = 100$, $Q^* = 108$, and $r^* = 343$. The average time between procurements for the $\langle Q, r \rangle$ model is $T = Q/\lambda = \frac{108}{600} = 0.18$ yr. $= 2.16$ mo.

The above results show that for the periodic review model T^* is slightly less than the average time between procurements for the $\langle Q, r \rangle$ model while the safety stock of 50 is higher for the periodic review model than the value 43 for the $\langle Q, r \rangle$ model. This sort of behavior will always occur when comparing $\langle Q, r \rangle$ models and periodic review models as was done above. The reason for this behavior lies in the fact that in the periodic review system, the safety stock must offer protection for a lead time plus one period, while in the $\langle Q, r \rangle$ model protection is needed only for the lead time. This means that the safety stock will be greater for the $\langle R, T \rangle$ model. Also, it simultaneously pays to order somewhat more frequently, thus reducing the average on hand inventory to partially offset the extra carrying charges arising from the increased safety stock needed.

5-3 The Exact Formulation of the $\langle nQ, r, T \rangle$ Model for the Backorders Case with Poisson Demands and Constant Lead Times

At this point, instead of obtaining the exact form of the $\langle R, T \rangle$ models in certain cases, we shall instead move on to obtain the exact equations for the $\langle nQ, r, T \rangle$ model in the backorders case where the number of units demanded in any time period can be described by a Poisson distribution and the procurement lead time is always a constant τ. Recall that an $\langle R, T \rangle$ model is a special case of the $\langle nQ, r, T \rangle$ model with $Q = 1$ and $R = r + 1$. Thus once having obtained the exact equations for the $\langle nQ, r, T \rangle$ model we can immediately obtain the exact equations for an $\langle R, T \rangle$ model under the same assumptions which apply in deriving the $\langle nQ, r, T \rangle$ model.

We shall in the derivations treat the inventory levels as discrete variables as well as the demand variable. Recall that an nQ operating doctrine is one such that, at a review time, an order is placed if and only if the inventory position y of the system at the review time is less than or equal to r. If $y \leq r$, then a quantity nQ is ordered, $n = 1, 2, 3, \ldots$, where n is chosen so that $r < y + nQ \leq r + Q$. Thus, immediately after a review, the inventory position of the system will be in one of the Q states $r + 1, r + 2, \ldots, r + Q$.

To begin, we shall compute the steady state probability $\rho(r + j)$ that the inventory position of the system is $r + j$ immediately after a review. To do this, we note that if we concern ourselves only with the state of the system immediately after a review, the process generating transitions between states can be considered to be a Markov process discrete in space and time, provided that the demands in different periods are independent random variables. For a fixed T, these variables can be independent even if a Poisson process does not generate demands. However, if the variables representing demands in different periods are to be independent for any $T > 0$, this will be true only if a Poisson process generates demands. It need not be true, though, that units are demanded one at a time. The quantity demanded per demand can be a random variable, and demands in different periods will be independent for any $T > 0$, so long as a Poisson process generates demands and the order size does not depend on past history. Thus, for example, the stuttering Poisson distribution has the property that demands in different periods are independent for any $T > 0$.

Let us now compute the transition probabilities a_{ij}, where a_{ij} is the probability that if the inventory position is $r + i$ immediately after a given review it will be $r + j$ immediately after the next review. Denote by $p(x; T)$ the probability that x units are demanded in the time interval between reviews.

We shall first compute a_{ij} when $j \leq i$. Then the inventory position can be $r + j$ immediately after a review when it was $r + i$ immediately after the previous review if $i - j$, $i - j + Q$, $i - j + 2Q$, etc. units have been demanded in the period between reviews, since if d is the demand then d must satisfy the equation (see Fig. 5-2)

$$r + i - d + nQ = r + j, \quad n = 0, 1, 2, \ldots$$

or

$$d = i - j + nQ, \quad n = 0, 1, 2, \ldots \tag{5-14}$$

The probability that the demand is $i - j + nQ$ is $p(i - j + nQ; T)$. Since the probabilities for different n values are mutually exclusive, it follows that

$$a_{ij} = \sum_{n=0}^{\infty} p(i - j + nQ; T), \quad j \leq i \tag{5-15}$$

However, when $j > i$, the system cannot be in state j unless the demand has been at least $i - j + Q$. Thus

$$a_{ij} = \sum_{n=1}^{\infty} p(i - j + nQ; T), \quad j > i \tag{5-16}$$

From Sec. 3-10 we know that the $\rho(r + j)$ must satisfy the equations

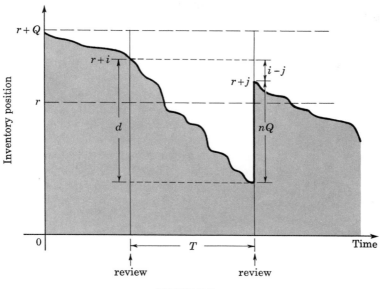

FIGURE 5-2.

$$\rho(r + j) = \sum_{i=1}^{Q} \rho(r + i) a_{ij}, \quad j = 1, \ldots, Q \qquad (5\text{-}17)$$

Now note that

$$\sum_{i=1}^{j-1} \sum_{n=1}^{\infty} p(i - j + nQ; T) + \sum_{i=j}^{Q} \sum_{n=0}^{\infty} p(i - j + nQ; T)$$

$$= \sum_{n=0}^{\infty} \left[\sum_{v=1}^{j-1} p(nQ + Q - v; T) + \sum_{v=0}^{Q-j} p(nQ + v; T) \right]$$

$$= \sum_{k=0}^{\infty} p(k; T) = 1, \quad j = 1, \ldots, Q \qquad (5\text{-}18)$$

where, when $j = 1$, any summation whose upper limit is $j - 1$ is taken to be 0. Then the sum of the a_{ij} over i is equal to unity for all j. We see immediately from (5-17) that $\rho(r + j) = $ constant satisfies (5-17). Furthermore, since $\sum_{j=1}^{Q} \rho(r + j) = 1$, it follows that

$$\rho(r + j) = \begin{cases} \dfrac{1}{Q} & j = 1, \ldots, Q \\[2mm] 0 & \text{otherwise} \end{cases} \qquad (5\text{-}19)$$

Thus in the periodic review case the distribution of the inventory position immediately after a review is uniform. Recall that for $\langle Q, r \rangle$ models, the distribution was uniform at each instant of time. Note that (5-19) holds for any distribution of demand as long as the demands in different periods are independent. Also observe that each $a_{ij} > 0$, so that from the results of Sec. 3-10 we know that (5-19) is the unique solution to (5-17).

We are now in a position to develop the average annual cost expression. At this point we shall restrict our attention to the case where units are demanded one at a time, and a Poisson process generates the demands. In principle, we could consider a case where the order size is a random variable, say the stuttering Poisson distribution, but the equations become exceptionally complex and difficult to work with. We shall here also restrict our attention to the case where the unit cost of the item is a constant independent of the quantity ordered. The cost of a backorder will be assumed to have the form $\pi + \hat{\pi}t$ where t is the length of time for which the backorder exists. The costs of review and placing an order will be denoted by J, A respectively. As usual, the inventory carrying charge will be denoted by I. The average annual cost will be computed by determining the expected cost per period and multiplying by $1/T$ to obtain the average annual cost. Problem 5-12 asks the reader to go through the same sort of analysis used in Sec. 4-6 to show that this is correct.

Since there are on the average $1/T$ reviews per year, the average annual cost of reviews is J/T. The average annual ordering cost is not A/T, since an order need not be placed at each review. Instead, the average annual cost of placing orders is Ap_{or}/T, where p_{or} is the probability that an order will be placed at any given review time. Let us now compute p_{or}. If the inventory position of the system is $r + j$ immediately after a review, the probability that it will be less than or equal to r at the time of the next review is the probability that j or more units are demanded in the time T between reviews, i.e., $P(j; \lambda T)$. The probability that the inventory position is $r + j$ immediately after a review is $1/Q$. Thus

$$p_{or} = \frac{1}{Q} \sum_{j=1}^{Q} P(j; \lambda T)$$

and from A3-6

$$p_{or} = \frac{\lambda T}{Q} [1 - P(Q; \lambda T)] + P(Q + 1; \lambda T) \tag{5-20}$$

Note that p_{or} is a function of T and Q but is independent of r.

Consider now the problem of determining the average annual cost of backorders. First the average number of backorders incurred per year will be computed by multiplying by $1/T$ the expected number of backorders per period. Suppose that a review takes place at time t. The next review takes place at time $t + T$. We shall compute the expected number of backorders incurred between time $t + \tau$ and $t + \tau + T$. The reason for doing this is that everything on order immediately after the review at time t will arrive in the system by $t + \tau$ but nothing not on order can arrive before time $t + \tau + T$. The random variable representing the number of backorders incurred between $t + \tau$ and $t + \tau + T$ can then be thought of as the difference between two random variables, the first giving the number of backorders on the books at time $t + \tau + T$ and the second being the number of backorders on the books at time $t + \tau$. If the inventory position of the system is $r + j$ immediately after the review at time t, the expected number of backorders on the books at time $t + \tau + T$ is

$$\sum_{x=r+j}^{\infty} (x - r - j) p[x; \lambda(\tau + T)]$$

and at time $t + \tau$

$$\sum_{x=r+j}^{\infty} (x - r - j) p(x; \lambda\tau)$$

Thus, if the inventory position is $r + j$ immediately after the review at time t, the expected number of backorders incurred between time $t + \tau$ and $t + \tau + T$ is

$$\sum_{x=r+j}^{\infty} (x - r - j) \{p[x; \lambda(\tau + T)] - p(x; \lambda\tau)\}$$

On averaging over the states j and dividing by T, we see that the average number of backorders incurred per year is

$$
\begin{aligned}
E(Q, r, T) &= \frac{1}{QT} \sum_{j=1}^{Q} \sum_{x=r+j}^{\infty} (x - r - j) \{p[x; \lambda(\tau + T)] - p(x; \lambda\tau)\} \\
&= \frac{1}{QT} \sum_{u=r+1}^{r+Q} \sum_{x=u}^{\infty} (x - u) \{p[x; \lambda(\tau + T)] - p(x; \lambda\tau)\} \\
&= \frac{1}{QT} \sum_{u=r+1}^{r+Q} \{\lambda(\tau + T) P[u - 1; \lambda(\tau + T)] \qquad (5\text{-}21)
\end{aligned}
$$

$$- uP[u; \lambda(\tau + T)] - \lambda\tau P(u - 1; \lambda\tau) + uP(u; \lambda\tau)\}$$

Then on using A3-6 and A3-8 we can write

$$E(Q, r, T) = \frac{1}{Q} [\Lambda(r, T) - \Lambda(r + Q, T)] \qquad (5\text{-}22)$$

where

$$\Lambda(v, T) = \frac{1}{T} [\beta(v, \tau + T) - \beta(v, \tau)] \tag{5-23}$$

and

$$\beta(v, t) = \frac{(\lambda t)^2}{2} P(v - 1; \lambda t) - (\lambda t)vP(v; \lambda t) + \frac{v(v + 1)}{2} P(v + 1; \lambda t) \tag{5-24}$$

The same sort of procedure is used to compute the average number of unit years of shortage incurred per year. The expected number of unit years of shortage incurred per period is the expected value of the integral of the backorders from time $t + \tau$ to $t + \tau + T$ with t being defined as above. However, the expected value of the integral is the integral of the expected number of backorders (since the expected value of a sum of random variables is the sum of the expected values). For any time $t + \xi$ between $t + \tau$ and $t + \tau + T$, the expected number of backorders on the books when the inventory position of the system was $r + j$ immediately after the review at time t is

$$\sum_{x=r+j}^{\infty} (x - r - j)p(x; \lambda\xi)$$

and the expected unit years of shortage incurred from $t + \tau$ to $t + \tau + T$ is

$$\int_{\tau}^{\tau+T} \sum_{x=r+j}^{\infty} (x - r - j)p(x; \lambda\xi) \, d\xi$$

Averaging over the states j and dividing by T, we find that the average number of unit years of shortage incurred per year is

$$B(Q, r, T) = \frac{1}{QT} \sum_{u=r+1}^{r+Q} \int_{\tau}^{\tau+T} \sum_{x=u}^{\infty} (x - u)p(x; \lambda\xi) \, d\xi$$

or from A3-10

$$B(Q, r, T) = \frac{1}{QT} \sum_{u=r+1}^{r+Q} \int_{\tau}^{\tau+T} [\lambda\xi P(u - 1; \lambda\xi) - uP(u; \lambda\xi)] \, d\xi \tag{5-25}$$

However,

$$\int_{\tau}^{\tau+T} [\lambda\xi P(u - 1; \lambda\xi) - uP(u; \lambda\xi)] \, d\xi = \frac{\lambda}{2} \{(\tau + T)^2 P[u - 1; \lambda(\tau + T)]$$

$$- \tau^2 P(u - 1; \lambda\tau)\} + \frac{u(u + 1)}{2\lambda} \{P[u + 1; \lambda(\tau + T)] - P(u + 1; \lambda\tau)\}$$

$$- u\{(\tau + T)P[u; \lambda(\tau + T)] - \tau P(u; \lambda\tau)\} \tag{5-26}$$

By continued application of the properties in Appendix 3, $B(Q, r, T)$ can be written

$$B(Q, r, T) = \frac{1}{Q} [\Upsilon(r, T) - \Upsilon(r + Q, T)] \qquad (5\text{-}27)$$

where

$$\Upsilon(v, T) = \Xi(v, T + \tau) - \Xi(v, \tau) \qquad (5\text{-}28)$$

and

$$\Xi(v, t) = -\frac{\lambda v t^2}{2T} P(v; \lambda t) + \frac{\lambda^2 t^3}{6T} P(v - 1; \lambda t)$$

$$+ \frac{v(v + 1)t}{2T} P(v + 1; \lambda t) - \frac{v(v + 1)(v + 2)}{6\lambda T} P(v + 2; \lambda t) \qquad (5\text{-}29)$$

The detailed derivation of (5-26) through (5-29) is left for Problem 5-13. The average annual cost of backorders is then $\pi E(Q, r, T) + \hat{\pi} B(Q, r, T)$.

It remains to evaluate the average unit years of storage incurred per year. Again the procedure used above will be applied. The expected unit years of storage incurred between $t + \tau$ and $t + \tau + T$ will be multiplied by $1/T$ to obtain the desired answer. If the inventory position of the system was $r + j$ immediately after the review at time t, the expected value of the net inventory at any time ξ between $t + \tau$ and $t + \tau + T$ is

$$\sum_{x=0}^{\infty} (r + j - x)p(x; \lambda\xi) = r + j - \lambda\xi$$

The expected value of the on hand inventory at any time is the expected net inventory plus the expected number of backorders. Thus at time ξ, the expected on hand inventory is

$$r + j - \lambda\xi + \sum_{x=r+j}^{\infty} (x - r - j)p(x; \lambda\xi)$$

Integrating from τ to $T + \tau$, averaging over the states j, and dividing by T, we find that the average number of unit years of storage incurred per year is

$$D(Q, r, T) = \frac{1}{QT} \sum_{j=1}^{Q} \int_{\tau}^{\tau+T} (r + j - \lambda\xi) \, d\xi + B(Q, r, T) \qquad (5\text{-}30)$$

$$= \frac{Q}{2} + \frac{1}{2} + r - \frac{\lambda T}{2} - \mu + B(Q, r, T) \qquad (5\text{-}31)$$

where μ is the expected lead time demand. Of course, (5-31) is also the expected value of the on hand inventory at any point in time. The procedure used to compute E, B, and D here differs from that used to compute the corresponding quantities for the $\langle Q, r \rangle$ model in Chapter 4, because here we have available the probability distribution for the inventory position only at points immediately following a review, while for the corresponding $\langle Q, r \rangle$ model, the distribution was known at each point in time.

It is possible to compute the average unit years of storage incurred per year in another way. Since the expected on hand inventory at any point in time is equal to the expected inventory position minus the expected quantity on order plus the expected number of backorders, it is clear that $D(Q, r, T)$ is equal to $1/T$ times the integral over one period of the expected inventory position as a function of time minus $1/T$ times the integral over one period of the expected quantity on order as a function of time plus $B(Q, r, T)$. To compute the integral of the expected inventory position over a period it is convenient to use the time between two reviews to define the period. If the inventory position is $r + j$ immediately after the review at time t, the expected value of the inventory position at time $t + \xi$, $0 \leq \xi \leq T$ is $r + j - \lambda \xi$. Integrating this from 0 to T and averaging over j, we have

$$\frac{1}{Q} \sum_{j=1}^{Q} \int_0^T (r + j - \lambda \xi)\, d\xi = T\left[\frac{Q}{2} + \frac{1}{2} + r - \frac{\lambda T}{2}\right] \qquad (5\text{-}32)$$

Now $1/T$ times the integral over one period of the expected quantity on order as a function of time is simply the expected amount on order at any point in time. Thus by comparison with (5-31), we have proved again in this case that the expected amount on order at any point in time is equal to the expected lead time demand.

All the terms needed in the cost expression have now been evaluated. The average annual cost is

$$\mathfrak{K} = \frac{J}{T} + \frac{A}{T} p_{or} + IC\left[\frac{Q}{2} + \frac{1}{2} - \mu - \frac{\lambda T}{2}\right] + \pi E(Q, r, T)$$
$$+ (\hat{\pi} + IC)B(Q, r, T) \qquad (5\text{-}33)$$

Just as with the exact form of the $\langle Q, r \rangle$ model of Chapter 4, it is difficult to determine Q^*, r^*, and T^* for the $\langle nQ, r, T \rangle$ model manually. Again it is the terms in $E(Q, r, T)$ and $B(Q, r, T)$ involving $r + Q$ which cause the difficulty. Here, however, unlike the situation encountered for the $\langle Q, r \rangle$ model, it is not in general a good approximation to drop these terms. It is quite possible that the optimal Q will be small even though the average quantity ordered is not; in such cases, the $r + Q$ terms will not be negligible. To determine Q^*, r^*, and T^*, a digital computer will usually be required to perform the search needed to determine the values of Q, r, and T which minimize $\mathfrak{K}$.

A code to compute $Q^*(T)$ and $r^*(T)$ for the $\langle nQ, r, T \rangle$ model discussed above has been written by P. Teicholz and B. Lundh of Stanford University for the Burroughs 220 computer. The search procedure used in this code determines a relative minimum, but does not necessarily determine the absolute minimum if there exist a number of relative minima. The results presented in the following example were computed using this code.

EXAMPLE Let us compute Q^*, r^*, and T^* when an nQ operating doctrine is used to control an item for which the number of units demanded in any time period is Poisson distributed with the mean rate of demand being 100 units per year. The lead time is a constant and has the value 0.25 yr. The values of the other relevant parameters are: $J = \$2.00$, $A = \$4.00$, $C = \$10.00$, $I = 0.20$, $\pi = \$20.00$, and $\hat{\pi} = \$1.00$. Note that the ordering cost is twice the review cost. When the ordering cost is small with respect to the review cost, then it should be optimal to order at essentially every review, so that we would expect in such a case that $Q^* = 1$ and the $\langle nQ, r, T \rangle$ model is equivalent to an $\langle R, T \rangle$ model. It is only when the ordering cost is high with respect to the review cost that one would expect Q^* to be greater than unity. This is the case to be studied here.

By use of the computer program referred to above, $Q^*(T)$ and $r^*(T)$ were computed for various values of T. The results are presented in Fig. 5-3. The results are somewhat surprising in that $Q^*(T) = 1$ until T becomes less than 0.15 years. Indeed $Q^* = 1$, $r^* = 63$, and $T^* \approx 0.25$ years. Thus in a situation where one might expect $Q^* > 1$, it turned out that $Q^* = 1$. Another interesting feature of the computation is that when $T < 0.15$, $Q^*(T)$ changes very rapidly from unity to $Q_w = 20$. The computer program referred to above also provided for the possibility of setting $Q = 1$ and optimizing over r for a given T. Thus the optimal order up to R policy and the corresponding cost could be found. As has already been noted, the optimal nQ doctrine for a given T is an order up to R doctrine down to $T = 0.15$. The divergence between the two doctrines at $T = 0.10$ is also illustrated in Fig. 5-3. The cost differences grow rapidly as T is reduced below 0.10.

The above example seems to suggest that an order up to R policy will be as good as an nQ policy under broader circumstances than one might have guessed originally. It is only when the probability of placing an order at any review is not too high that an $\langle nQ, r, T \rangle$ model can yield significantly lower costs than an $\langle R, T \rangle$ model. There do arise cases where the review interval will arbitrarily be set to a very small value so that the periodic review system becomes almost a transactions reporting system (viz., a computer will be used to process all transactions, but instead of doing it on a transactions basis, it will be done once per day or once every couple of days). In such situations Q^* may be quite large compared to the average demand in the time between reviews, and here, of course, an nQ operating doctrine would be much preferred to an order up to R doctrine. However, for these cases one could almost use the results of a $\langle Q, r \rangle$ model for the periodic review Q and r. It may not always be possible to do this, though,

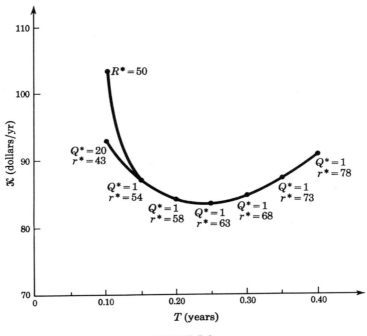

FIGURE 5-3.

and have r determined accurately enough. When Q^* is of the order of Q_w, then normally, the $r + Q$ terms in E and B can be ignored. In the next section, we shall present a simplified version of the $\langle nQ, r, T \rangle$ model obtained by dropping the $r + Q$ terms in E and B, which will hold for large Q values.

Suggestions for the use of an nQ type of operating doctrine have appeared in several places [4, for example]. The model developed in this section was first presented in [3].

5-4 Approximate Form of the $\langle nQ, r, T \rangle$ Model for Large Q

We shall here consider the case where Q is sufficiently large to justify ignoring the $r + Q$ terms in $E(Q, r, T)$ and $B(Q, r, T)$ in (5-33). Then (5-33) reduces to

$$\mathcal{K} = \frac{J}{T} + \frac{A}{T} p_{or} + IC \left[\frac{Q}{2} + \frac{1}{2} + r - \mu - \frac{\lambda T}{2} \right]$$

$$+ \frac{\pi}{Q} \Lambda(r, T) + \frac{\hat{\pi} + IC}{Q} \Upsilon(r, T) \quad (5\text{-}34)$$

If Q^*, r^* are the smallest values of Q, r which minimize $\mathcal{K}$ for a given T, it is necessary that

$$\Delta_Q \mathcal{K}(Q^*, r^*) = \mathcal{K}(Q^*, r^*) - \mathcal{K}(Q^* - 1, r^*) < 0;$$

$$\Delta_Q \mathcal{K}(Q^* + 1, r^*) \geq 0 \quad (5\text{-}35)$$

$$\Delta_r \mathcal{K}(Q^*, r^*) = \mathcal{K}(Q^*, r^*) - \mathcal{K}(Q^*, r^* - 1) < 0;$$

$$\Delta_r \mathcal{K}(Q^*, r^* + 1) \geq 0 \quad (5\text{-}36)$$

Let us now compute $\Delta_Q \mathcal{K}(Q, r)$. From (5-21) it follows that

$$\Delta_Q p_{or} = - \frac{\lambda T}{Q(Q-1)} [1 - P(Q - 1; \lambda T)] \quad (5\text{-}37)$$

Hence

$$\Delta_Q \mathcal{K}(Q, r) = - \frac{1}{Q(Q-1)} \left\{ \lambda A [1 - P(Q - 1; \lambda T)] - \frac{IC}{2} Q(Q-1) \right.$$

$$\left. + \pi \Lambda(r, T) + (\hat{\pi} + IC) \Upsilon(r, T) \right\} \quad (5\text{-}38)$$

Next consider $\Delta_r \mathcal{K}(Q, r)$. The following are needed in performing the differencing:

$$\Delta_r \{P(r - 1; \lambda t)\} = - \frac{r(r-1)}{(\lambda t)^2} p(r; \lambda t) \quad (5\text{-}39)$$

$$\Delta_r \{rP(r; \lambda t)\} = - \frac{r(r-1)}{\lambda t} p(r; \lambda t) + P(r; \lambda t) \quad (5\text{-}40)$$

$$\Delta_r \{r(r + 1)P(r + 1; \lambda t)\} = - r(r + 1)p(r; \lambda t) + 2rP(r; \lambda t) \quad (5\text{-}41)$$

$$\Delta_r \{r(r + 1)(r + 2)P(r + 2; \lambda t)\} = r(r + 1) \left\{ 3P(r; \lambda t) \right.$$

$$\left. - \left[\lambda t \left(\frac{r + 2}{r + 1} \right) + 3 \right] p(r; \lambda t) \right\} \quad (5\text{-}42)$$

In each of the above, the differences were converted to a form which involve only $p(r; \lambda t)$ and $P(r; \lambda t)$.

It follows that

$$\Delta_r \Lambda(r, T) = \frac{1}{T} [\Delta_r \beta(r, \tau + T) - \Delta_r \beta(r, \tau)] \qquad (5\text{-}43)$$

where

$$\Delta_r \beta(r, t) = (r - \lambda t)P(r; \lambda t) - rp(r; \lambda t) \qquad (5\text{-}44)$$

Similarly

$$\Delta_r \Upsilon(r, T) = \Delta_r \Xi(r, \tau + T) - \Delta_r \Xi(r, \tau) \qquad (5\text{-}45)$$

where

$$\Delta_r \Xi(r, t) = \frac{1}{2\lambda T} [(\lambda t)^2 - 2r\lambda t + r(r + 1)]P(r; \lambda t)$$

$$\qquad (5\text{-}46)$$

$$+ \frac{r}{2\lambda T} [\lambda t - (r + 1)]p(r; \lambda t)$$

Then

$$\Delta_r \mathcal{K}(Q, r) = IC + \frac{\pi}{Q} \Delta_r \Lambda(r, T) + \frac{(\hat{\pi} + IC)}{Q} \Delta_r \Upsilon(r, T) \qquad (5\text{-}47)$$

In (5-47) it is in general not a good approximation to neglect the terms involving τ in comparison to the terms involving $\tau + T$. This is especially true since we are assuming that Q is large, which will often imply that T is relatively small.

To evaluate numerically $Q^*(T)$, $r^*(T)$ one can begin with an initial guess for Q, call it Q_1. Then using Q_1 for Q in (5-47) determine r_1 by finding the largest r for which $\Delta_r \mathcal{K}(Q, r) < 0$. Use r_1 in (5-38) and determine Q_2 by finding the largest Q for which $\Delta_Q \mathcal{K}(Q, r) < 0$. Then use Q_2 in (5-47) to determine r_2, etc. The computational procedure is fairly time consuming, but not nearly so much as the one suggested in the previous section. The example of the previous section suggests that one should begin with $Q_1 = Q_w$. In fact, it may often be quite satisfactory to use Q_w as Q^*, and simply determine the optimal value of r when $Q = Q_w$ using (5-47).

5-5 The $\langle nQ, r, T \rangle$ Model for Normally Distributed Demands

We shall now work out the equations for the $\langle nQ, r, T \rangle$ model for the case where the demand density for a time interval of length t is normal with mean λt and variance Dt. The demand variable in any relevant time interval will therefore be treated as continuous. Furthermore, Q and r will also be treated as continuous variables.

To begin we shall show that if $v(x; T)$ is the density function for the demand per period (x assumed continuous), then, immediately after a review, the distribution of the inventory position will be uniform, provided that demands in different periods are independent random variables. Note that this result depends only on the fact that demands in different periods are independent, not that demands in any non-overlapping intervals are independent. It is only when we wish to allow T to vary over any positive values that this latter restriction is required. Let $\rho(r + y)\, dy$ be the steady state probability that the inventory position lies between $r + y$ and $r + y + dy$ immediately following a review. The same sort of analysis used in Sec. 5-3 shows that $\rho(r + y)$ must satisfy

$$\rho(r + y) = \int_0^Q \rho(r + \xi) q(\xi; y)\, d\xi \qquad (5\text{-}48)$$

where

$$q(\xi; y) = \sum_{n=\epsilon}^{\infty} v(\xi - y + nQ; T) \qquad (5\text{-}49)$$

and $\epsilon = 0$ if $y \le \xi$, $\epsilon = 1$, if $y > \xi$. Now it is only necessary to note that

$$\int_0^Q \sum_{n=\epsilon}^{\infty} v(\xi - y + nQ; T)\, d\xi = \int_0^{\infty} v(\xi; T)\, d\xi = 1$$

Therefore $\rho(r + y) = \text{constant } 0 \le y \le Q$, is a solution to (5-48). Since

$$\int_0^Q \rho(r + y)\, dy = 1$$

it follows that

$$\rho(r + y) = \begin{cases} \dfrac{1}{Q}, & 0 \le y \le Q \\ 0, & \text{otherwise} \end{cases} \qquad (5\text{-}50)$$

We are now ready to work out the various average annual costs for the case where demand is normally distributed. The average annual review cost is again J/T, and the average annual ordering cost is $A p_{or}/T$ where the probability of placing an order at any review time is now

$$p_{or} = \frac{1}{Q} \int_0^Q \Phi\left(\frac{y - \lambda T}{\sqrt{DT}}\right) dy = \frac{\sqrt{DT}}{Q} \int_{-\lambda T/\sqrt{DT}}^{(Q - \lambda T)/\sqrt{DT}} \Phi(\xi)\, d\xi \qquad (5\text{-}51)$$

Thus on using A4-6, and recalling that if the normal approximation is to be valid, the value of the normal density at $y = 0$ must be essentially zero and the value of the complementary cumulative essentially unity, we see that

$$p_{or} = \frac{\lambda T}{Q}\left[1 - \Phi\left(\frac{Q - \lambda T}{\sqrt{DT}}\right)\right] + \Phi\left(\frac{Q - \lambda T}{\sqrt{DT}}\right) - \frac{\sqrt{DT}}{Q}\phi\left(\frac{Q - \lambda T}{\sqrt{DT}}\right) \qquad (5\text{-}52)$$

It is easily seen that the average annual cost of carrying inventory is

$$IC\left[\frac{Q}{2} + r - \mu - \frac{\lambda T}{2} + B(Q, r, T)\right] \tag{5-53}$$

where $B(Q, r, T)$ is, of course, the average number of unit years of shortage incurred per year, i.e., the expected number of backorders at any point in time.

It remains to obtain explicit formulas for the average number of backorders incurred per year and the average number of unit years of shortage incurred per year. The same method of analysis is used as for the discrete case studied in Sec. 5-3. It is clear that the average number of backorders incurred per year is

$$E(Q, r, T) = \frac{1}{QT}\int_0^Q \int_{r+y}^{\infty} (\xi - r - y)\left\{\frac{1}{\sqrt{D(\tau+T)}}\phi\left[\frac{\xi - \lambda(\tau+T)}{\sqrt{D(\tau+T)}}\right]\right.$$

$$\left. - \frac{1}{\sqrt{D\tau}}\phi\left(\frac{\xi - \lambda\tau}{\sqrt{D\tau}}\right)\right\}d\xi\,dy$$

$$= \frac{1}{QT}\int_r^{r+Q} \int_u^{\infty} (\xi - u)\left\{\frac{1}{\sqrt{D(\tau+T)}}\phi\left[\frac{\xi - \lambda(\tau+T)}{\sqrt{D(\tau+T)}}\right]\right.$$

$$\left. - \frac{1}{\sqrt{D\tau}}\phi\left(\frac{\xi - \lambda\tau}{\sqrt{D\tau}}\right)\right\}d\xi\,du \tag{5-54}$$

However, by A4-25

$$\frac{1}{\sqrt{Dt}}\int_u^{\infty} (\xi - u)\,\phi\left(\frac{\xi - \lambda t}{\sqrt{Dt}}\right)d\xi = \sqrt{Dt}\,\phi\left(\frac{u - \lambda t}{\sqrt{Dt}}\right)$$

$$- (u - \lambda t)\,\Phi\left(\frac{u - \lambda t}{\sqrt{Dt}}\right) \tag{5-55}$$

Thus from A4-6, A4-26,

$$l(v, t) = \frac{1}{\sqrt{Dt}}\int_v^{\infty} \int_u^{\infty} (\xi - u)\,\phi\left(\frac{\xi - \lambda t}{\sqrt{Dt}}\right)d\xi\,du$$

$$= \frac{Dt}{2}\left\{\left[1 + \left(\frac{v - \lambda t}{\sqrt{Dt}}\right)^2\right]\Phi\left(\frac{v - \lambda t}{\sqrt{Dt}}\right) - \frac{v - \lambda t}{\sqrt{Dt}}\phi\left(\frac{v - \lambda t}{\sqrt{Dt}}\right)\right\} \tag{5-56}$$

and

$$E(Q, r, T) = \frac{1}{Q}\left[h(r, T) - h(r + Q, T)\right] \tag{5-57}$$

where

$$h(v, T) = \frac{1}{T}\left[l(v, T + \tau) - l(v, \tau)\right] \tag{5-58}$$

Similarly

$$B(Q, r, T) = \frac{1}{QT} \int_0^Q \int_\tau^{\tau+T} \int_{r+y}^\infty (\xi - r - y) \frac{1}{\sqrt{Dt}} \phi\left(\frac{\xi - \lambda t}{\sqrt{Dt}}\right) d\xi \, dt \, dy$$

$$= \frac{1}{QT} \int_r^{r+Q} \int_\tau^{\tau+T} \int_u^\infty (\xi - u) \frac{1}{\sqrt{Dt}} \phi\left(\frac{\xi - \lambda t}{\sqrt{Dt}}\right) d\xi \, dt \, du \tag{5-59}$$

We shall evaluate $B(Q, r, T)$ in several steps. First, by use of the properties in Appendix 4, we see that

$$U(u, \tau) = \int_0^\tau \int_u^\infty (\xi - u) \frac{1}{\sqrt{Dt}} \phi\left(\frac{\xi - \lambda t}{\sqrt{Dt}}\right) d\xi \, dt = \left[\frac{D^2 + 2\lambda^4\tau^2}{4\lambda^3}\right.$$

$$+ \frac{(D - 2\lambda^2\tau)u}{2\lambda^2} + \frac{u^2}{2\lambda}\bigg] \Phi\left(\frac{u - \lambda\tau}{\sqrt{D\tau}}\right) + \frac{1}{2}\left[D^{1/2}\tau^{3/2} - \frac{D^{3/2}\tau^{1/2}}{\lambda^2}\right.$$

$$- \frac{D^{1/2}\tau^{1/2}u}{\lambda}\bigg] \phi\left(\frac{u - \lambda\tau}{\sqrt{D\tau}}\right) - \frac{D^2}{4\lambda^3} e^{2\lambda u/D} \Phi\left(\frac{u + \lambda\tau}{\sqrt{D\tau}}\right) \tag{5-60}$$

Next

$$\Xi(r, \tau) = \int_r^\infty U(u, \tau) \, du = \left[\frac{\lambda^2\tau^3}{6} - \frac{D^2 r}{4\lambda^3} - \frac{\lambda\tau^2 r}{2} - \frac{Dr^2}{4\lambda^2} + \frac{D\tau^2}{4} + \frac{\tau r^2}{2}\right.$$

$$- \frac{r^3}{6\lambda} - \frac{D^3}{8\lambda^4}\bigg] \Phi\left(\frac{r - \lambda\tau}{\sqrt{D\tau}}\right) + \left[\frac{\lambda\tau^{5/2}D^{1/2}}{6} - \frac{D^{1/2}\tau^{3/2}r}{3} + \frac{D^{1/2}\tau^{1/2}r^2}{6\lambda}\right.$$

$$+ \frac{D^{3/2}\tau^{3/2}}{12\lambda} + \frac{D^{3/2}\tau^{1/2}r}{4\lambda^2} + \frac{D^{5/2}\tau^{1/2}}{4\lambda^3}\bigg] \phi\left(\frac{r - \lambda\tau}{\sqrt{D\tau}}\right)$$

$$+ \frac{D^3}{8\lambda^4} e^{2\lambda r/D} \Phi\left(\frac{r + \lambda\tau}{\sqrt{D\tau}}\right) \tag{5-61}$$

Then

$$B(Q, r, T) = \frac{1}{Q} \left[\Upsilon(r, T) - \Upsilon(r + Q, T)\right] \tag{5-62}$$

where

$$\Upsilon(v, T) = \frac{1}{T} \{\Xi(v, \tau + T) - \Xi(v, \tau)\}$$

and Ξ is defined by (5-61).

The average annual cost can now be written

$$\mathcal{K} = \frac{J}{T} + \frac{A}{T} p_{or} + IC\left[\frac{Q}{2} + r - \mu - \frac{\lambda T}{2}\right] + \pi E(Q, r, T)$$

$$+ (IC + \hat{\pi})B(Q, r, T) \tag{5-63}$$

Unfortunately, $\mathcal{K}$ is not in general a convex function of Q and r. This complicates the task of computing Q^* and r^*, since there is no guarantee that there won't be a number of local minima. Furthermore, it is very difficult to obtain any solution to $\partial \mathcal{K}/\partial Q = \partial \mathcal{K}/\partial r = 0$. The task of determining Q^* and r^* is quite arduous. It appears to be necessary to use a computer and to apply some appropriate search procedure just as in the discrete case.

5-6 Exact Equations for $\langle R, T \rangle$ Models

It is easy to determine the exact equations for an $\langle R, T \rangle$ model when the number of units demanded in any time period is Poisson distributed and the lead time is constant, since it is only necessary to set $Q = 1$ and $R = r + 1$ in the results of Sec. 5-3. First, from (5-20), it is clear that

$$p_{or} = \lambda T p(0; \lambda T) + P(2; \lambda T) = p(1; \lambda T) + P(2; \lambda T) = P(1; \lambda T) \quad (5\text{-}64)$$

as expected. It is easy to evaluate $E(1, R - 1, T)$, $B(1, R - 1, T)$, since in (5-21), (5-25), when $Q = 1$, it is unnecessary to sum over u from $r + 1$ to $r + Q$; it is only necessary to set $u = r + 1 = R$. Thus

$$E(1, R - 1, T) = \frac{1}{T} \{\lambda(\tau + T)P[R - 1; \lambda(\tau + T)] - RP[R; \lambda(\tau + T)]$$
$$- \lambda \tau P(R - 1; \lambda \tau) + RP(R; \lambda \tau)\} \quad (5\text{-}65)$$

and

$$B(1, R - 1, T) = \frac{1}{T} \left[\frac{\lambda}{2} \{(\tau + T)^2 P[R - 1; \lambda(\tau + T)] - \tau^2 P(R - 1; \lambda \tau)\} \right.$$
$$+ \frac{R(R + 1)}{2\lambda} \{P[R + 1; \lambda(\tau + T)] - P(R + 1; \lambda \tau)\}$$
$$\left. - R\{(\tau + T)P[R; \lambda(\tau + T)] - \tau P(R; \lambda \tau)\} \right] \quad (5\text{-}66)$$

Thus, the average annual cost is

$$\mathcal{K}(R) = \frac{J}{T} + \frac{A}{T} P(1; \lambda T) + IC \left[R - \mu - \frac{\lambda T}{2} \right] + \pi E(1, R - 1, T)$$
$$+ (IC + \hat{\pi})B(1, R - 1, T) \quad (5\text{-}67)$$

Then

$$\Delta \mathcal{K}(R) = IC - \frac{\pi}{T} \{P[R; \lambda(\tau + T) - P(R; \lambda \tau)\} + \frac{IC + \hat{\pi}}{T}$$

$$\left[-\frac{\lambda}{2} \{(\tau + T)^2 p[R - 2; \lambda(\tau + T)] - \tau^2 p(R - 2; \lambda \tau)\} \right.$$

$$+ \frac{1}{2\lambda} \{2RP[R; \lambda(\tau + T)] - 2RP(R; \lambda\tau)$$

$$- R(R + 1)p[R; \lambda(\tau + T)]$$

$$+ R(R + 1)p(R; \lambda\tau)\} - \{(\tau + T)P[R; \lambda(\tau + T)] - \tau P(R; \lambda\tau)$$

$$- (\tau + T)(R - 1)p[R - 1; \lambda(\tau + T)] + \tau(R - 1)p(R - 1; \lambda\tau)\} \Bigg]$$

$$= IC - \frac{1}{T}\left[\pi - \frac{R}{\lambda}(IC + \hat{\pi})\right]\{P[R; \lambda(\tau + T)] - P(R; \lambda\tau)\}$$

$$- \frac{(IC + \hat{\pi})}{T} \{(\tau + T)P[R; \lambda(\tau + T)] - \tau P(R; \lambda\tau)\}$$

$$- \frac{(IC + \hat{\pi})R}{\lambda T} \{p[R; \lambda(\tau + T)] - p(R; \lambda\tau)\} \quad (5\text{-}68)$$

The smallest value of R which minimizes $\mathcal{K}$ is the largest R for which $\Delta\mathcal{K}(R) < 0$. The expression for $\Delta\mathcal{K}(R)$ is fairly simple, and it is not too difficult to carry out numerical computations using it. In many instances, however, the terms involving $\lambda\tau$ are negligible with respect to those involving $\lambda(\tau + T)$, and in this case, $\Delta\mathcal{K}(R)$ reduces to the simpler form

$$\Delta\mathcal{K}(R) = IC - \frac{1}{T}\left\{\pi - \left[\frac{R}{\lambda} - (\tau + T)\right](IC + \hat{\pi})\right\} P[R; \lambda(\tau + T)]$$

$$- \frac{(IC + \hat{\pi})}{\lambda T} Rp[R; \lambda(\tau + T)] \quad (5\text{-}69)$$

Note that (5-68) holds for all T while (5-69) holds only if T is sufficiently large. To determine the optimal T it is probably simplest to tabulate $\mathcal{K}$ optimized with respect to R as a function of T.

Let us next obtain the exact equations for the $\langle R, T \rangle$ model when R is treated as continuous and the demand in any relevant time interval can be assumed to be normally distributed with mean λt and variance Dt. To obtain the desired formulas from the results of Sec. 5-5, we must set $r = R$ and take the limit as $Q \to 0$ rather than setting $r + 1 = R$, $Q = 1$ as in the discrete case. For the continuous case it is clear that p_{or} should be unity, since the probability that a positive quantity will be demanded in any time period is unity. This is indeed the result obtained from (5-52) when $Q = 0$, and the assumption is made that the normal density function is essentially zero for non-positive arguments.

To compute the average number of backorders incurred per year and the average unit years of shortage incurred per year, i.e., $E(0, R, T)$, $B(0, R, T)$, note that for any function $f(y)$ that

$$\lim_{Q \to 0} \frac{1}{Q} \int_0^Q f(y) \, dy = f(0) \tag{5-70}$$

since by definition of the derivative, if $F(y) = \int f(y) \, dy$ then

$$\lim_{Q \to 0} \frac{1}{Q} \int_0^Q f(y) \, dy = \lim_{Q \to 0} \frac{F(Q) - F(0)}{Q} = \frac{dF}{dQ}\Big|_{Q=0} = f(0) \tag{5-71}$$

It follows immediately from (5-54) that

$$E(0, R, T) = \frac{1}{T}\left\{ \sqrt{D(\tau + T)} \, \phi\left[\frac{R - \lambda(\tau + T)}{\sqrt{D(\tau + T)}}\right]\right.$$

$$- [R - \lambda(\tau + T)] \, \Phi\left[\frac{R - \lambda(\tau + T)}{\sqrt{D(\tau + T)}}\right] - \sqrt{D\tau} \, \phi\left(\frac{R - \lambda\tau}{\sqrt{D\tau}}\right)$$

$$\left. + (R - \lambda\tau) \, \Phi\left(\frac{R - \lambda\tau}{\sqrt{D\tau}}\right)\right\} \tag{5-72}$$

Similarly, from (5-59) and (5-60)

$$B(0, R, T) = \frac{1}{T}\left[U(R, \tau + T) - U(R, \tau)\right] \tag{5-73}$$

where U is defined by (5-60).

Thus the average annual cost is

$$\mathcal{K} = \frac{L}{T} + IC\left[R - \mu - \frac{\lambda T}{2}\right] + \pi E(0, R, T)$$

$$+ (IC + \hat{\pi})B(0, R, T) \tag{5-74}$$

where $L = J + A$. The optimal value of R for a given T can be found by solving the equation

$$\frac{\partial \mathcal{K}}{\partial R} = 0 = IC + \pi \frac{\partial E}{\partial R} + (IC + \hat{\pi})\frac{\partial B}{\partial R} \tag{5-75}$$

where

$$\frac{\partial E}{\partial R} = \frac{1}{T}\left\{\Phi\left(\frac{R - \lambda\tau}{\sqrt{D\tau}}\right) - \Phi\left[\frac{R - \lambda(\tau + T)}{\sqrt{D(\tau + T)}}\right]\right\} \tag{5-76}$$

and

$$\frac{\partial B}{\partial R} = \frac{1}{T}\left[\frac{\partial U(R, \tau + T)}{\partial R} - \frac{\partial U(R, \tau)}{\partial R}\right] \tag{5-77}$$

$$\frac{\partial}{\partial R} U(R, t) = \left(\frac{D}{2\lambda^2} - t + \frac{R}{\lambda}\right)\Phi\left(\frac{R - \lambda t}{\sqrt{Dt}}\right) - \frac{\sqrt{Dt}}{\lambda}\phi\left(\frac{R - \lambda t}{\sqrt{Dt}}\right)$$

$$- \frac{D}{2\lambda^2} e^{2\lambda R/D} \, \Phi\left(\frac{R + \lambda t}{\sqrt{Dt}}\right) \tag{5-78}$$

Probably the simplest way to determine T^* is to compute $\mathcal{K}(R^*)$ for a sequence of T values and to determine T^* graphically as described in Sec. 5-2.

5-7 The $\langle Q, r \rangle$ Model as the Limit as $T \rightarrow 0$ of the $\langle nQ, r, T \rangle$ Model

The total cost expression (5-33) for the $\langle nQ, r, T \rangle$ model holds for all $T > 0$. As $T \rightarrow 0$, the average annual cost approaches infinity if the review cost $J > 0$. However, if the review costs are omitted, then the average annual cost should approach a finite limit as $T \rightarrow 0$. In fact, this limit should be precisely the average annual cost for a $\langle Q, r \rangle$ model, and $Q^*(T)$, $r^*(T)$ should approach Q^*, r^* for the $\langle Q, r \rangle$ model with the same values of the parameters. We shall now prove this. Recall that in the derivation of (5-33) it was assumed that the demand over any time interval was Poisson distributed and that lead times were constant. Thus the limit as $T \rightarrow 0$ should be a $\langle Q, r \rangle$ model with demand being Poisson distributed and constant lead times, i.e., the model developed in Sec. 4-7. The result also holds true when the lead times must be considered to be random variables, provided the approximations introduced in Chapter 4 that the lead times can be simultaneously treated as independent random variables without any crossing of orders are valid. The proof in this case is left for Problem 5-18.

The continuity of transition between $\langle Q, r \rangle$ models and $\langle nQ, r, T \rangle$ models referred to above is important, because by including the review costs in the $\langle nQ, r, T \rangle$ model, and adding the average annual cost of operating the transactions reporting system to the average annual cost of the $\langle Q, r \rangle$ model, it is theoretically possible to determine whether it is better to use a transactions reporting system or a periodic review system with an nQ type of operating doctrine.

Let us now show that as $T \rightarrow 0$, $\mathcal{K}$ for the $\langle nQ, r, T \rangle$ model with demand being Poisson distributed and constant lead times approaches $\mathcal{K}$ for the $\langle Q, r \rangle$ model when the review costs are omitted. It follows from this that $Q^*(T)$, $r^*(T)$, the optimal Q, r values for a given T, approach Q^*, r^* for the $\langle Q, r \rangle$ model, since the review costs do not influence the determination of Q^* and r^*.

First observe from (5-33) and (5-20)

$$\lim_{T \rightarrow 0} \frac{p_{or}}{T} = \frac{\lambda}{Q} - \frac{\lambda}{Q} \lim_{T \rightarrow 0} P(Q; \lambda T) + \lim_{T \rightarrow 0} \frac{1}{T} P(Q + 1; \lambda T)$$

Inasmuch as $Q \geq 1$

$$\lim_{T \rightarrow 0} P(Q; \lambda T) = \lim_{T \rightarrow 0} \frac{1}{T} P(Q + 1; \lambda T) = 0$$

since $p(j; \lambda T)$ approaches zero as $T \to 0$ for all j except $j = 0$ (which is excluded in the above summations). Thus

$$\lim_{T \to 0} \frac{p_{or}}{T} = \frac{\lambda}{Q} \tag{5-79}$$

and the ordering costs approach $\lambda A / Q$, which is the correct term for the $\langle Q, r \rangle$ model.

Consider next

$$\lim_{T \to 0} E(Q, r, T) = \lim_{T \to 0} \frac{1}{QT} \sum_{u=r+1}^{r+Q} \sum_{x=u}^{\infty} (x - u) \{p[x; \lambda(\tau + T)] - p(x; \lambda\tau)\}$$

By definition of the derivative

$$\lim_{T \to 0} \frac{p[x; \lambda(\tau + T)] - p(x; \lambda\tau)}{T} = \frac{d}{dt} p(x; \lambda t)|_{t=\tau}$$

$$= \lambda[p(x - 1; \lambda\tau) - p(x; \lambda\tau)]$$

However

$$\sum_{x=u}^{\infty} (x - u)[p(x - 1; \lambda\tau) - p(x; \lambda\tau)]$$

$$= \sum_{x=u}^{\infty} (x - u)p(x - 1; \lambda\tau) - \sum_{x=u}^{\infty} (x - u)p(x; \lambda\tau)$$

$$= \sum_{y=u-1}^{\infty} (y - u)p(y; \lambda\tau) + \sum_{y=u-1}^{\infty} p(y; \lambda\tau)$$

$$- \sum_{x=u}^{\infty} (x - u)p(x; \lambda\tau) = P(u; \lambda\tau)$$

Therefore

$$\lim_{T \to 0} E(Q, r, T) = \frac{\lambda}{Q} \sum_{u=r+1}^{r+Q} P(u; \lambda\tau) \tag{5-80}$$

which from (4-45), (4-46) is $E(Q, r)$.

Finally, consider

$$\lim_{T \to 0} B(Q, r, T) = \lim_{T \to 0} \frac{1}{QT} \sum_{u=r+1}^{r+Q} \int_{\tau}^{T+\tau} \sum_{x=u}^{\infty} (x - u)p(x; \lambda\xi) \, d\xi$$

By definition of the derivative

$$\lim_{T \to 0} \frac{1}{T} \int_{\tau}^{T+\tau} \sum_{x=u}^{\infty} (x - u)p(x; \lambda\xi) \, d\xi = \sum_{x=u}^{\infty} (x - u)p(x; \lambda\tau)$$

Thus

$$\lim_{T \to 0} B(Q, r, T) = \frac{1}{Q} \sum_{u=r+1}^{r+Q} \sum_{x=u}^{\infty} (x - u)p(x; \lambda\tau) \qquad (5\text{-}81)$$

which is equivalent to (4-47). Of course, the inventory carrying cost term approaches the corresponding one for the $\langle Q, r \rangle$ model, since $\lambda T/2$ goes to zero with T.

We have shown that each term of the average annual cost for the $\langle nQ, r, T \rangle$ model approaches the corresponding term for the $\langle Q, r \rangle$ model as $T \to 0$. Hence $Q^*(T)$ and $r^*(T)$ for the $\langle nQ, r, T \rangle$ model approach Q^* and r^* for the $\langle Q, r \rangle$ model, and this demonstrates what we desired to show.

5-8 Models of the $\langle R, r, T \rangle$ Type

It will be recalled that if a periodic review system uses an Rr operating doctrine, then if at a review time the inventory position (in the backorders case) or the quantity on hand plus on order (in the lost sales case) is less than or equal to r, a quantity is ordered which is sufficient to bring the inventory position or the quantity on hand plus on order up to R. For the types of costs and stochastic demands used in this chapter it is usually true that an Rr operating doctrine is the optimal one, if all demands occurring when the system is out of stock are backordered. This will be shown in Chapter 8. The nQ and order up to R doctrines are only approximations to the optimal Rr doctrine. We shall obtain below the exact expression for the average annual cost in the backorders case when an Rr operating doctrine is used, the number of units demanded in any time period is Poisson distributed, and the lead times are constant. The derivation, however, will not be quite so simple as for the $\langle R, T \rangle$ and $\langle nQ, r, T \rangle$ models. Furthermore, it will be seen that the task of computing R^* and r^* is exceptionally arduous and would be almost impossible to carry out manually, although the computations could be made easily on a large scale digital computer.

Before restricting our attention to the case where the number of units demanded in any time period is Poisson distributed, let us begin as we did for the $\langle nQ, r, T \rangle$ model by attempting to compute the steady state probability $\rho(r + j)$ that the inventory position immediately after a review has the value $r + j$, for any distribution $p(x; T)$ of the demand in a period. The only assumption to be made will be that demands in different periods are independent random variables. If we knew the $\rho(r + j)$, then we could compute the average annual cost just as we did for the $\langle nQ, r, T \rangle$ model. Here also, transitions between these states can be considered to be a

Markov process discrete in space and time. Let us then set up the equations whose solution yields the $\rho(r+j)$. The inventory position of the system immediately after a review can only have one of the $R-r$ values $r+1, r+2, \ldots, R$. To compute the transition probabilities a_{ij}, assume that the inventory position immediately after a review is $r+i, i=1, \ldots, R-r$. We must compute the probability that it is in state $r+j$ immediately after the next review. If $j>i$ and $j<R-r$ this probability is zero, since there is no way in which such a transition can be made. If $j \leq i$, the probability is $p(i-j; T)$. When $j=R-r$ and $i<R-r$, the probability is $P(i; T)$, where $P(x; T)$ is the complementary cumulative of $p(x; T)$, since any number of demands which reduce the inventory position by the next review to or below r will result in having the inventory position immediately after the next review be R. When $i=R-r$, then $j=R-r$ if there are no demands or if there are $R-r$ or more demands, i.e., the probability of this is $p(0; T) + P(R-r; T)$. Thus

$$a_{ij} = \begin{cases} p(i-j; T), & j \leq i, \quad j \neq R-r \\ 0, & j > i, \quad j \neq R-r \end{cases} \tag{5-82}$$

$$a_{i, R-r} = P(i; T), \quad i \neq R-r \tag{5-83}$$

$$a_{R-r, R-r} = p(0; T) + P(R-r; T) \tag{5-84}$$

These transition probabilities can be conveniently represented as shown in Table 5-2.

TABLE 5-2

Transition Probabilities for Rr Doctrine
Inventory Position After Review at Time $t+T$

		R	$R-1$	$R-2$	$R-3$		$r+1$
	R	$p(0; T) +$ $P(R-r; T)$	$p(1; T)$	$p(2; T)$	$p(3; T)$	$\cdots$	$p(R-r-1; T)$
Inventory Position After Review at Time t	$R-1$	$P(R-r-1; T)$	$p(0; T)$	$p(1; T)$	$p(2; T)$	$\cdots$	$p(R-r-2; T)$
	$R-2$	$P(R-r-2; T)$	0	$p(0; T)$	$p(1; T)$	$\cdots$	$p(R-r-3; T)$
	$R-3$	$P(R-r-3; T)$	0	0	$p(0; T)$	$\cdots$	$p(R-r-4; T)$
	$\cdots$	$\cdots$	$\cdots$	$\cdots$	$\cdots$	$\cdots$	$\cdots$
	$r+1$	$P(1; T)$	0	0	0	$\cdots$	$p(0; T)$

The steady state probabilities $\rho(r+j)$ that the inventory position immediately after a review is $r+j$ will be the unique solution to the set of equations

$$\rho(r + j) = \sum_{i=1}^{R-r} \rho(r + i)a_{ij}, \quad j = 1, \ldots, R - r$$

$$\sum_{j=1}^{R-r} \rho(r + j) = 1 \tag{5-85}$$

However, it is not at all apparent from what we have studied previously how we can solve (5-85) and obtain explicit values for the $\rho(r + j)$. It is immediately obvious, though, that the states are no longer uniformly distributed, since it is intuitively clear that state R should have a higher probability than the other states. We shall make no further attempt to solve these equations directly. In the next section we shall obtain the $\rho(r + j)$. We shall not do so, however, by solving (5-85) directly. Instead, we shall derive the exact expression for the average annual cost by computing the expected cost per cycle (as usual, the system is said to go through one cycle's operation in the time between the placement of two successive orders), and then multiplying by the average number of cycles per year. The $\rho(r + j)$ will be obtained as a byproduct of this computation.

It might be pointed out that if we knew the distribution of the inventory position at the review times prior to placing any order it would be a simple matter to compute the $\rho(r + j)$. Let $\theta(x)$ be the steady state probability that the inventory position of the system has the value x at a review time prior to placing an order. Note that x can have any integral value from R to $-\infty$. Then

$$\rho(r + j) = \theta(r + j), \quad j = 1, 2, \ldots, R - r - 1 \tag{5-86}$$

$$\rho(R) = \theta(R) + \sum_{x=-\infty}^{r} \theta(x) \tag{5-87}$$

We can also characterize transitions from the inventory position at one review time (before any order is placed) to those at the next review time as a Markov process. This makes it possible to develop a set of equations from which the $\theta(x)$ can in principle be determined directly. We shall now obtain these equations and note that they cannot be easily solved explicitly either. It should be observed that a state y can be reached from states x such that $x \geq y, r + 1 \leq x$ and states x for which $x \leq r$ (since for these states an order will be placed raising the inventory position to R at the start of the period). Thus it follows that the equations relating the $\theta(y)$ are

$$\theta(y) = p(R - y; T) \sum_{x=-\infty}^{r} \theta(x) + \sum_{x=r+1}^{R} p(x - y; T)\theta(x), \quad y \leq r \tag{5-88}$$

$$\theta(y) = p(R - y; T) \sum_{x=-\infty}^{r} \theta(x) + \sum_{x=y}^{R} p(x - y; T)\theta(x),$$

$$r + 1 \leq y \leq R \quad (5\text{-}89)$$

These balance equations can be written down directly. However, the reader is asked to provide a step-by-step derivation in Problem 5-19. Equations (5-88), (5-89) represent an infinite set of equations to be solved for $\theta(y)$. Unfortunately, it is no more apparent how to solve these equations explicitly than it was (5-85). Hence we shall abandon the attempt to derive the average annual cost treating the operation of the system as a Markov process, and instead go on to use the technique of computing the expected cost per cycle and then multiply by the average number of cycles per year.

5-9 Derivation of Average Annual Cost for $\langle R, r, T \rangle$ Model

In this section we shall derive the exact average annual cost expression for an $\langle R, r, T \rangle$ model by computing the expected cost per cycle and then multiplying by the average number of cycles per year. First, we shall obtain the form of the average annual cost without specifying in detail the nature of the stochastic process generating demands. The only assumptions that will be made concerning the stochastic process generating demands is that it does not change with time and that demands in different periods are independent. We shall also assume that the lead times are constant. It will not be possible to write down explicitly all the cost terms since no special assumptions are being made about the nature of the demand distribution. However, from this cost expression, we shall be able to obtain the general solution to (5-85) for the $\rho(r + j)$, which we were unable to do in the previous section. After this we shall restrict our attention to the case where a Poisson process generates demands and units are demanded one at a time. In this case we shall obtain explicitly the average annual cost as a function of R, r, and T.

When an Rr operating doctrine is used, an order need not be placed at each review. The time between the placing of two successive orders (i.e., the length of a cycle) will always be an integral multiple of the time T between reviews; however, the number of periods included in a cycle will be a random variable. Hence the length of a cycle is also a random variable which can only assume the values nT, $n = 1, 2, 3, \ldots$.

Let $p(x; T)$ be the probability that x units will be demanded in one period. Then, since the demands in different periods are assumed to be independent $p^{(n)}(x; T)$ is the probability that precisely x units are demanded in n periods, where $p^{(n)}(x; T)$ is the n-fold convolution of $p(x; T)$.

If t is a review time, let the inventory position after the decision as to whether or not to order has been made be $r + j$, and $H(r + j, T)$ be the expected cost of carrying inventory and of backorders incurred from $t + \tau$ to $t + \tau + T$, where τ is the procurement lead time.

Suppose now that an order is placed at time t_0. Next imagine that at review time $t_0 + nT$, the inventory position of the system is $r + j$ and that no order has been placed since t_0. This means that precisely $R - r - j$ units have been demanded in the time period of length nT since t_0. The probability of this is $p^{(n)}(R - r - j; T)$. The expected cost of carrying inventory and of backorders incurred from $t_0 + nT + \tau$ to $t_0 + (n + 1)T + \tau$ will be $H(r + j, T)$. Now the time from t_0 until the next order will be placed may require more than one or more than two or more than three, etc., periods. If more than n periods are required, then there will be a contribution to the cost in period $n + 1$. The contribution to the expected cost in period $n + 1$ will depend on the inventory position at the beginning of period $n + 1$, and will be $H(r + j, T)$ if the inventory position is $r + j$ at the beginning of the period. The probability that more than n periods will be included in the cycle and that the inventory position is $r + j$ at the beginning of period $n + 1$ is simply $p^{(n)}(R - r - j; T)$. Thus the contribution to the expected cost per cycle of carrying inventory and backorders from period $n + 1(n \geq 1)$ is

$$\sum_{j=1}^{R-r} p^{(n)}(R - r - j; T)H(r + j, T)$$

There will always be at least one period per cycle and the contribution to the expected cost from the first period is simply $H(R, T)$, since immediately after placing an order the inventory position is R. The expected cost per cycle of carrying inventory and of backorders is then found by summing the expected contributions for period n over all $n \geq 1$. Thus the expected cost per cycle is

$$H(R, T) + \sum_{n=1}^{\infty} \sum_{j=1}^{R-r} p^{(n)}(R - r - j; T)H(r + j, T)$$

which can be written

$$\sum_{n=0}^{\infty} \sum_{j=1}^{R-r} p^{(n)}(R - r - j; T)H(r + j, T) \tag{5-90}$$

if we use the definitions

$$p^{(0)}(0; T) = 1, \quad p^{(0)}(x; T) = 0 \quad \text{for } x \neq 0$$

Having found the expected cost per cycle of carrying inventory and of backorders, we must next compute the average number of cycles per year. This is simply the reciprocal of the expected length of a cycle. Since the length of a period is T, the expected length of a cycle is T times the expected number of periods per cycle. Let us then compute the expected number of periods per cycle. A cycle will be precisely one period if the demand in the first period is greater than $R - r$. The probability of this is $P(R - r; T)$, where $P(x; T)$ is the complementary cumulative of $p(x; T)$. Consider now the probability that a cycle will contain precisely $n(n \geq 2)$ periods. If $R - r - j$ units have been demanded in the first $n - 1$ periods after the previous order was placed, then the cycle will contain precisely n periods if the demand in period n is for j or more units. Thus the probability that a cycle contains precisely n periods is

$$\sum_{j=1}^{R-r} p^{(n-1)}(R - r - j; T)P(j; T)$$

Hence the expected number of periods in a cycle is

$$P(R - r; T) + \sum_{n=2}^{\infty} \sum_{j=1}^{R-r} np^{(n-1)}(R - r - j; T)P(j; T)$$

which can be written

$$\sum_{n=1}^{\infty} \sum_{j=1}^{R-r} np^{(n-1)}(R - r - j; T)P(j; T) \tag{5-91}$$

if we use the convention described above with respect to $p^{(0)}(x; T)$.

We are now able to write down the average annual cost. If, as usual, J is the cost of a review and A is the cost of placing an order, then

$$\mathcal{K}(R, r, T) = \frac{J}{T} + \frac{A + \displaystyle\sum_{n=0}^{\infty} \sum_{j=1}^{R-r} p^{(n)}(R - r - j; T)H(r + j, T)}{T \displaystyle\sum_{n=1}^{\infty} \sum_{j=1}^{R-r} np^{(n-1)}(R - r - j; T)P(j; T)} \tag{5-92}$$

When the distribution of demand is specified, it then becomes possible to evaluate $p^{(n)}(x; T)$ and $H(r + j, T)$ explicitly. Before doing this for the case where a Poisson process generates demands and units are demanded one at a time, we shall obtain from (5-92) the steady state probabilities $\rho(r + j)$ that the inventory position immediately after a review is $r + j$, and hence we shall obtain the solution to the equations (5-85).

Note that the average annual cost of carrying inventory and of back-orders is $1/T$ times

$$\sum_{j=1}^{R-r} \left[\frac{\displaystyle\sum_{n=0}^{\infty} p^{(n)}(R - r - j; T)}{\displaystyle\sum_{n=1}^{\infty} \sum_{j=1}^{R-r} np^{(n-1)}(R - r - j; T)P(j; T)} \right] H(r + j, T) \tag{5-93}$$

so that (5-93) is the corresponding expected cost per period. However, from the definition of the $\rho(r + j)$ and $H(r + j, T)$ the expected cost per period is $\sum_{j=1}^{R-r} \rho(r + j)H(r + j, T)$. This suggests that

$$\rho(r + j) = \frac{\sum_{n=0}^{\infty} p^{(n)}(R - r - j; T)}{\sum_{n=1}^{\infty} \sum_{j=1}^{R-r} np^{(n-1)}(R - r - j; T)P(j; T)},$$

$$j = 1, \ldots, R - r \quad (5\text{-}94)$$

We shall now show that this is indeed true. All that is required is to show that the $\rho(r + j)$ of (5-94) satisfy (5-85). When the a_{ij} given in Table 5-2 are substituted into the equations $\rho(r + j) = \sum_{i=1}^{R-r} \rho(r + i)a_{ij}$, they become

$$\rho(R) = \sum_{i=1}^{R-r-1} \rho(r + i)P(i; T) + \rho(R)[p(0; T) + P(R - r; T)] \quad (5\text{-}95)$$

$$\rho(r + j) = \sum_{i=j}^{R-r} \rho(r + i)p(i - j; T), \quad j = 1, \ldots, R - r - 1 \quad (5\text{-}96)$$

Let us next show that

$$\rho(r + j) = \delta \sum_{n=0}^{\infty} p^{(n)}(R - r - j; T), \quad j = 1, \ldots, R - r \quad (5\text{-}97)$$

satisfy (5-95), (5-96) for any value of δ. Consider first the equations (5-96). When $\rho(r + j)$ is given by (5-97)

$$\sum_{i=j}^{R-r} \rho(r + i)p(i - j; T) = \delta \sum_{n=0}^{\infty} \sum_{i=j}^{R-r} p^{(n)}(R - r - i; T)p(i - j; T)$$

$$= \delta \sum_{n=1}^{\infty} \sum_{u=0}^{R-r-j} p^{(n-1)}(R - r - j - u; T)p(u; T) = \delta \sum_{n=1}^{\infty} p^{(n)}(R - r - j; T)$$

The last step follows from the definition of $p^{(n)}(R - r - j; T)$ in terms of $p^{(n-1)}$ and p (see p. 119). However, when $j = 1, \ldots, R - r - 1$, according to the definition used above $p^{(0)}(R - r - j; T) = 0$ so that

$$\sum_{n=0}^{\infty} p^{(n)}(R - r - j; T) = \sum_{n=1}^{\infty} p^{(n)}(R - r - j; T)$$

Thus the $\rho(r + j)$ given by (5-97) do indeed satisfy (5-96).

We shall now prove that the $\rho(r + j)$ of (5-97) also satisfy (5-95). This requires that we demonstrate that

$$1 + \sum_{n=1}^{\infty} p^{(n)}(0; T) = \sum_{n=1}^{\infty} \sum_{i=1}^{R-r-1} p^{(n)}(R - r - i; T)P(i; T)$$

$$+ \left[1 + \sum_{n=1}^{\infty} p^{(n)}(0; T)\right][p(0; T) + P(R - r; T)] \quad (5\text{-}98)$$

since $p^{(0)}(0; T) = 1$ and $p^{(0)}(x; T) = 0$, $x \neq 0$. Now because $p(0; T) = p^{(1)}(0; T)$, it follows that

$$p(0; T) + p(0; T) \sum_{n=1}^{\infty} p^{(n)}(0; T) = p^{(1)}(0; T) + \sum_{n=2}^{\infty} p(0; T)p^{(n-1)}(0; T)$$

$$= \sum_{n=1}^{\infty} p^{(n)}(0; T)$$

Thus the right hand side of (5-98) can be written

$$\sum_{n=0}^{\infty} \sum_{i=1}^{R-r} p^{(n)}(R - r - i; T)P(i; T) + \sum_{n=1}^{\infty} p^{(n)}(0; T)$$

Consequently, to show that (5-98) holds is equivalent to showing that

$$\sum_{n=0}^{\infty} \sum_{i=1}^{R-r} p^{(n)}(R - r - i; T)P(i; T) = 1 \quad (5\text{-}99)$$

Clearly (5-99) does sum to unity since it is merely the probability that one or more periods are required to have $R - r$ units demanded. The analytic proof can be obtained as follows

$$\sum_{n=0}^{\infty} \sum_{i=1}^{R-r} p^{(n)}(R - r - i; T)P(i; T)$$

$$= \sum_{n=0}^{\infty} \sum_{i=1}^{R-r} p^{(n)}(R - r - i; T) - \sum_{n=0}^{\infty} \sum_{i=1}^{R-r} \sum_{u=0}^{i-1} p^{(n)}(R - r - i; T)p(u; T)$$

$$= 1 + \sum_{n=1}^{\infty} \sum_{i=1}^{R-r} p^{(n)}(R - r - i; T) - \sum_{n=0}^{\infty} \sum_{v=0}^{R-r-1} \sum_{u=0}^{R-r-v-1} p^{(n)}(v; T)p(u; T)$$

Thus the proof of (5-98) reduces to showing that

$$\sum_{n=1}^{\infty} \sum_{i=1}^{R-r} p^{(n)}(R - r - i; T) = \sum_{n=0}^{\infty} \sum_{v=0}^{R-r-1} \sum_{u=0}^{R-r-v-1} p^{(n)}(v; T)p(u; T)$$

However

$$\sum_{n=0}^{\infty} \sum_{v=0}^{R-r-1} \sum_{u=0}^{R-r-v-1} p^{(n)}(v; T)p(u; T) = \sum_{n=0}^{\infty} \sum_{i=0}^{R-r-1} \sum_{u=0}^{i} p^{(n)}(i - u; T)p(u; T)$$

$$= \sum_{i=1}^{R-r-1} p(i; T) + \sum_{n=2}^{\infty} \sum_{i=0}^{R-r-1} \sum_{u=0}^{i} p^{(n-1)}(i - u; T)p(u; T)$$

$$= \sum_{n=1}^{\infty} \sum_{i=0}^{R-r-1} p^{(n)}(i; T) = \sum_{n=1}^{\infty} \sum_{i=1}^{R-r} p^{(n)}(R - r - i; T)$$

which is what we desired to show. Thus the $\rho(r + j)$ of (5-97) do satisfy (5-95) and (5-96).

It remains to show that when

$$\delta^{-1} = \sum_{n=1}^{\infty} \sum_{j=1}^{R-r} np^{(n-1)}(R - r - j; T) \, P(j; T)$$

that $\sum_{j=1}^{R-r} \rho(r + j) = 1$. This is equivalent to showing that

$$\sum_{n=0}^{\infty} \sum_{j=1}^{R-r} p^{(n)}(R - r - j; T)$$

$$= \sum_{n=1}^{\infty} \sum_{j=1}^{R-r} np^{(n-1)}(R - r - j; T) \, P(j; T) \quad (5\text{-}100)$$

To show that (5-100) is valid, note that

$$\sum_{n=1}^{\infty} \sum_{j=1}^{R-r} np^{(n-1)}(R - r - j; T) \, P(j; T)$$

$$= \sum_{n=0}^{\infty} \sum_{j=1}^{R-r} (n + 1) \, p^{(n)}(R - r - j; T) \, P(j; T)$$

$$= \sum_{n=0}^{\infty} \sum_{j=1}^{R-r} p^{(n)}(R - r - j; T) \, P(j; T)$$

$$+ \sum_{n=0}^{\infty} \sum_{j=1}^{R-r} np^{(n)}(R - r - j; T) \, P(j; T)$$

However, by (5-99), we are reduced to showing that

$$\sum_{n=1}^{\infty} \sum_{j=1}^{R-r} p^{(n)}(R - r - j; T) = \sum_{n=1}^{\infty} \sum_{j=1}^{R-r} np^{(n)}(R - r - j; T) \, P(j; T)$$

Now

$$\sum_{n=1}^{\infty} \sum_{j=1}^{R-r} n p^{(n)}(R - r - j; T)\, P(j; T) = \sum_{n=1}^{\infty} \sum_{j=1}^{R-r} n p^{(n)}(R - r - j; T)$$

$$- \sum_{n=1}^{\infty} \sum_{j=1}^{R-r} \sum_{u=0}^{j-1} n p^{(n)}(R - r - j; T)\, p(u; T)$$

$$= \sum_{n=1}^{\infty} \sum_{j=1}^{R-r} p^{(n)}(R - r - j; T) + \sum_{n=2}^{\infty} \sum_{j=1}^{R-r} (n - 1)\, p^{(n)}(R - r - j; T)$$

$$- \sum_{n=1}^{\infty} \sum_{i=0}^{R-r-1} \sum_{u=0}^{R-r-i-1} n p^{(n)}(i; T)\, p(u; T)$$

$$= \sum_{n=1}^{\infty} \sum_{j=1}^{R-r} p^{(n)}(R - r - j; T) + \sum_{n=1}^{\infty} \sum_{j=1}^{R-r} n p^{(n+1)}(R - r - j; T)$$

$$- \sum_{n=1}^{\infty} \sum_{j=1}^{R-r} n p^{(n+1)}(R - r - j; T) = \sum_{n=1}^{\infty} \sum_{j=1}^{R-r} p^{(n)}(R - r - j; T)$$

which is what we needed to demonstrate. We have thus shown that the probability $\rho(r + j)$ that the inventory position of the system immediately after a review is $r + j$ is given by (5-94). This holds for any distribution of demand, the only assumption required being that demands in different periods are independent. Furthermore, the result is independent of the nature of the stochastic process which generates the lead times.

Let us now concentrate our attention on the case where the number of units demanded in any time period is Poisson distributed. Then $p(x; T) = p(x; \lambda T)$ and $p^{(n)}(x; T) = p(x; n\lambda T)$. We can next evaluate $H(r + j, T)$ explicitly. We have already done this in developing $\langle nQ, r, T \rangle$ model. The expected number of backorders incurred from $t + \tau$ to $t + \tau + T$ if the inventory position is $r + j$ at time t is

$$\epsilon(r + j, T) = \sum_{x=r+j}^{\infty} (x - r - j)\, \{p[x; \lambda(\tau + T)] - p(x; \lambda\tau)\}$$

$$= \lambda(\tau + T)\, P[r + j - 1; \lambda(\tau + T)] - (r + j)\, P[r + j; \lambda(\tau + T)]$$

$$- \lambda\tau\, P(r + j - 1; \lambda\tau) + (r + j)\, P(r + j; \lambda\tau) \tag{5-101}$$

Similarly, the expected number of unit years of shortage incurred from $t + \tau$ to $t + \tau + T$ is

$$b(r+j, T) = \int_\tau^{\tau+T} \sum_{x=r+j}^\infty (x - r - j)\, p(x; \lambda\xi)\, d\xi$$

$$= \frac{\lambda}{2} \{(\tau + T)^2\, P[r + j - 1; \lambda(\tau + T)] - \tau^2\, P(r + j - 1; \lambda\tau)\}$$

$$+ \frac{(r+j)(r+j+1)}{2\lambda} \{P[r + j + 1; \lambda(\tau + T)] - P(r + j + 1; \lambda\tau)\}$$

$$- (r + j) \{(\tau + T)\, P[r + j; \lambda(\tau + T)] - \tau P(r + j; \lambda\tau)\} \qquad (5\text{-}102)$$

by (5-26). Finally, the expected unit years of storage incurred from $t + \tau$ to $t + \tau + T$ is

$$d(r+j, T) = \int_\tau^{\tau+T} (r + j - \lambda\xi)\, d\xi + b(r+j, T)$$

$$= T\left(r + j - \mu - \frac{\lambda T}{2}\right) + b(r+j, T) \qquad (5\text{-}103)$$

Then $H(r + j, T)$ is simply

$$H(r+j, T) = T\left(r + j - \mu - \frac{\lambda T}{2}\right) + \pi\epsilon(r + j, T)$$

$$+ (\hat{\pi} + IC)\, b(r + j, T) \quad (5\text{-}104)$$

The average annual cost is then

$$\mathfrak{K}(R, r, T) = \frac{J}{T} + \frac{A + \sum_{n=0}^\infty \sum_{j=1}^{R-r} p(R - r - j; n\lambda T)\, H(r + j, T)}{T \sum_{n=1}^\infty \sum_{j=1}^{R-r} np[R - r - j; (n - 1)\lambda T]\, P(j; \lambda T)} \qquad (5\text{-}105)$$

It does not seem easy to reduce the summations appearing in (5-105) to a more simple form. Clearly, it would be an impossibly laborious task to try to determine R^*, r^*, and T^* manually using (5-105). However, the computation could be carried out quite easily on a large computer such as the IBM 7090 and should not take over one minute on this computer.

5-10 The $\langle R, r, T \rangle$ Model When Demand is Treated as a Continuous Variable

In this section we shall develop the analog of the $\langle R, r, T \rangle$ model studied in the previous section for the case where R, r, and the demand variable are treated as continuous.

Let $v(x; T)$ be the density function for the demand in a period. Demands in different periods will be assumed to be independent random variables. Again we shall assume that the lead time τ is a constant. If the inventory position immediately after a review occurring at time t is $r + x$, let $H(r + x, T)$ be the expected costs of carrying inventory and of backorders incurred from $t + \tau$ to $t + \tau + T$. Suppose that an order is placed at time t_0. The probability that at time $t_0 + nT$, $n \geq 1$, the inventory position of the system lies between x and $x + dx$ given that no order has been placed since time t_0 is $v^{(n)}(R - r - x; T)dx$, where $v^{(n)}(x; T)$ is the n-fold convolution of $v(x; T)$. Thus the expected cost per cycle is

$$\sum_{n=1}^{\infty} \int_0^{R-r} v^{(n)}(R - r - x; T)H(r + x, T) \, dx + H(R, T) \quad (5\text{-}106)$$

The second term comes about because at t_0 the inventory position is R; here it is not convenient to try to include this term in the first term by summing from $n = 0$ rather than from $n = 1$, as was done in the discrete case.

The expected length of a cycle is

$$T\left[\sum_{n=2}^{\infty} \int_0^{R-r} nv^{(n-1)}(R - r - x; T)V(x; T) \, dx + V(R - r; T)\right] \quad (5\text{-}107)$$

where $V(x; T)$ is the complementary cumulative of $v(x; T)$. The average annual cost then becomes

$$\mathcal{K}(R, r, T) =$$

$$\frac{J}{T} + \frac{A + \sum_{n=1}^{\infty} \int_0^{R-r} v^{(n)}(R - r - x; T)H(r + x, T) \, dx + H(R, T)}{T\left[\sum_{n=2}^{\infty} \int_0^{R-r} nv^{(n-1)}(R - r - x; T)V(x; T) \, dx + V(R - r; T)\right]}$$

$$(5\text{-}108)$$

We ask the reader in Problem 5-22 to work out $H(r + x, T)$ and $v^{(n)}(R - r - x; T)$ explicitly for the case where $v(x; T)$ is a normal distribution.

It is interesting to examine the behavior of the inventory position immediately after a review. The behavior of the inventory position immediately after a review is peculiar in the sense that there is a positive probability that the inventory position will be R, while for other values of the inventory position, the probability of a specific value is zero (as is true with continuous random variables), while there is a probability $\rho(r + y) \, dy$ that the inventory position lies between $r + y$ and $r + y + dy$.

Let $p(R)$ be the probability that the inventory position is R immediately after a review. Then it is clear that the equations which $p(R)$ and $\rho(r + y)$ must satisfy are

$$p(R) = p(R)V(R - r; T) + \int_0^{R-r} \rho(r + y)V(y; T)\, dy \quad (5\text{-}109)$$

and

$$\rho(r + y) = \int_y^{R-r} \rho(r + x)\, v(x - y; T)\, dx \quad (5\text{-}110)$$

From the average annual cost it is clear that

$$p(R) = \cfrac{1}{T\left[\displaystyle\sum_{n=2}^{\infty} \int_0^{R-r} nv^{(n-1)}(R - r - x; T)V(x; T)\, dx + V(R - r; T)\right]} \quad (5\text{-}111)$$

$$\rho(r + y) = \cfrac{\displaystyle\sum_{n=1}^{\infty} v^{(n)}(R - r - y; T)}{T\left[\displaystyle\sum_{n=2}^{\infty} \int_0^{R-r} nv^{(n-1)}(R - r - x; T)V(x; T)\, dx + V(R - r; T)\right]},$$

$$0 \le y < R - r \quad (5\text{-}112)$$

We shall leave the proof that (5-111) and (5-112) are indeed the solutions to (5-109) and (5-110) to Problem 5-23. For any given distribution $v(x; T)$, it is generally very difficult by use of (5-111) and (5-112) to obtain $p(R)$ and $\rho(r + y)$ in a simple form not involving a sum over n.

When one deals with the inventory position at a review time prior to the placing of any order the peculiar behavior at $r + x = R$ is not encountered. If $\theta(x)$ is the density function for the inventory position at a review time prior to placing any order, then it is clear, on considering the possible transitions from one review time to the next, that $\theta(x)$ must satisfy the equations.

$$\theta(x) = v(R - x; T) \int_{-\infty}^r \theta(y)\, dy + \int_r^R \theta(y)\, v(y - x; T)\, dy,$$

$$x \le r \quad (5\text{-}113)$$

$$\theta(x) = v(R - x; T) \int_{-\infty}^r \theta(y)\, dy + \int_x^R \theta(y)\, v(y - x; T)\, dy,$$

$$r \le x \le R \quad (5\text{-}114)$$

In general, it is very difficult to attempt to solve (5-113), (5-114) for $\theta(x)$. Note that if $\theta(x)$ is known, then

$$\rho(x) = \theta(x), \quad r \le x < R, \quad p(R) = \int_{-\infty}^{r} \theta(x)\, dx \qquad (5\text{-}115)$$

There is one special form of $v(x; T)$ for which it is possible to solve (5-113), (5-114) explicitly for $\theta(x)$, and for which it is also possible to carry out the summation over n in (5-111), (5-112). This is the case where $v(x; T)$ is a gamma distribution. The difficulty of carrying out the solution increases very quickly with the order of the gamma distribution. We shall illustrate the procedure only for the first order case, i.e., that where $v(x; T)$ is an exponential distribution. We shall assume that

$$v(x; T) = \beta e^{-\beta x}$$

Note that we do not implicitly indicate the time dependence here. We imagine that T is fixed.

We shall first show how (5-113), (5-114) can be solve explicitly for $\theta(x)$. Note that

$$\frac{dv}{dx} = -\beta^2\, e^{-\beta x} = -\beta v \qquad (5\text{-}116)$$

To solve (5-113), (5-114) we shall convert them to differential equations with the aid of (5-116). Differentiating (5-113), (5-114) with respect to x, we obtain

$$\theta'(x) = -v'(R - x; T) \int_{-\infty}^{r} \theta(y)\, dy - \int_{r}^{R} \theta(y)\, v'(y - x; T)\, dy,$$

$$x \le r \quad (5\text{-}117)$$

$$\theta'(x) = -v'(R - x; T) \int_{-\infty}^{r} \theta(y)\, dy - \theta(x)\, v(0; T) - \int_{x}^{R} \theta(y)\, v'(y - x; T)\, dy,$$

$$r \le x \le R \quad (5\text{-}118)$$

Substitution of (5-116) into (5-117), (5-118) along with $v(0; T) = \beta$ yields

$$\theta'(x) = \beta\theta(x), \quad x \le r; \quad \theta'(x) = 0, \quad r \le x \le R \qquad (5\text{-}119)$$

Integration of (5-119) yields

$$\theta(x) = k_1 e^{\beta x}, \quad x \le r; \quad \theta(x) = k_2, \quad r \le x \le R \qquad (5\text{-}120)$$

where k_1, k_2 are constants yet to be determined. From (5-113), (5-114) we see that $\theta(x)$ must be continuous at $x = r$. This requires that

$$k_2 = k_1 e^{\beta r}$$

In order that $\theta(x)$ be a legitimate density function, it is necessary that

$$\int_{-\infty}^{R} \theta(x)\, dx = 1 = k_1 e^{\beta r}(R - r) + k_1 \int_{-\infty}^{r} e^{\beta x}\, dx = k_1 e^{\beta r}\left[R - r + \frac{1}{\beta}\right]$$

so

$$k_1 = \frac{e^{-\beta r}}{R - r + \dfrac{1}{\beta}}$$

and hence

$$\theta(x) = \begin{cases} \dfrac{1}{R - r + \dfrac{1}{\beta}}, & r \le x \le R \\[3ex] \dfrac{e^{\beta(x-r)}}{R - r + \dfrac{1}{\beta}}, & x \le r \end{cases} \qquad (5\text{-}121)$$

Therefore from (5-115)

$$p(R) = \int_{-\infty}^{r} \theta(x) \, dx = \frac{1}{\beta\left(R - r + \dfrac{1}{\beta}\right)}$$

$$p(r + y) = \frac{1}{R - r + \dfrac{1}{\beta}}, \qquad 0 \le y < R - r \qquad (5\text{-}122)$$

Let us now compute $\rho(r + y)$ and $p(R)$ from (5-111), (5-112) to show that the same result is obtained. From (3-108), it follows that if $v(x; T) = \beta e^{-\beta x}$, then $v^{(n)}(x; T)$ is a gamma distribution of order n, i.e.,

$$v^{(n)}(x; T) = \frac{\beta(\beta x)^{n-1}}{(n-1)!} e^{-\beta x} = \beta p(n - 1; \beta x) \qquad (5\text{-}123)$$

Also

$$V(x; T) = e^{-\beta x}$$

and

$$\int_{0}^{R-r} v^{(n-1)}(R - r - x; T) V(x; T) \, dx = \frac{1}{\beta} v^{(n)}(R - r; T) \qquad (5\text{-}124)$$

$$= p[n - 1; \beta(R - r)]$$

Hence

$$\sum_{n=2}^{\infty} \int_{0}^{R-r} n v^{(n-1)}(R - r - x; T) V(x; T) \, dx + V(R - r; T)$$

$$= \sum_{n=1}^{\infty} np[n - 1; \beta(R - r)] = \sum_{n=0}^{\infty} (n + 1)p[n; \beta(R - r)]$$

$$= \sum_{n=0}^{\infty} np[n; \beta(R - r)] + \sum_{n=0}^{\infty} p[n; \beta(R - r)] = \beta(R - r) + 1$$

Finally

$$\sum_{n=1}^{\infty} v^{(n)}(R - r - x; T) = \beta \sum_{n=1}^{\infty} p[n - 1; \beta(R - r - x)]$$

$$= \beta \sum_{n=0}^{\infty} p[n; \beta(R - r - x)] = \beta$$

Hence

$$p(R) = \frac{1}{\beta(R - r) + 1}; \quad \rho(r + y) = \frac{1}{R - r + \dfrac{1}{\beta}}, \quad 0 \le y < R - r$$

which is precisely (5-122). Thus, we have obtained the same result in two different ways. To solve (5-113), (5-114) explicitly for $\theta(x)$ is considerably more difficult when $v(x; T)$ is a gamma density of order two. We leave this case to be worked out in Problem 5-32. The procedure for solving (5-113), (5-114) when $v(x; T)$ is gamma distributed by reducing them to differential equations has been presented by Karlin in Chapter 14 of [1].

To have obtained simple expressions for $\rho(r + y)$ and $p(R)$ when the distribution of demand for a period is exponential is not especially valuable from a practical point of view for several reasons. First, the exponential distribution is seldom a realistic representation of the density for the demand in a period. Secondly, in order to compute $H(x, T)$ it would be necessary to use some other distribution such as the normal since $H(x, T)$ involves the demand from τ to $\tau + T$, and the exponential distribution does not provide for introducing time explicitly. Finally, the average annual cost even in this case does not reduce to an expression which can be easily handled manually. While the result just obtained does not seem to be of great practical value, it is of interest from a theoretical point of view to show how $p(R)$, and $\rho(r + y)$ may be computed in two entirely different ways.

5-11 Comparison of the Periodic Review Operating Doctrines

In this chapter, three different operating doctrines have been considered for use with periodic review systems. They are: (a) order up to R, (b) nQ policy, (c) Rr doctrines. We have already noted that the order up to R doctrine is a special case of both the nQ and Rr doctrines. The nQ doctrine is also really a special type of Rr doctrine for which $R - r = Q$ and the order size must be a multiple of Q. Thus the doctrines are all related to a certain extent. We have seen, however, that it is not equally easy to make numerical computations for each type of operating doctrine. It is relatively easy to make numerical computations manually for $\langle R, T \rangle$

models, but for $\langle nQ, r, T \rangle$ or $\langle R, r, T \rangle$ models a computer will normally be required. Because of the differences in computational effort required, it is of interest to inquire under what circumstances will the order up to R policy be essentially optimal, i.e., under what circumstances will the average annual cost using an order up to R policy differ so little from the average annual cost of an nQ or Rr policy that it is not worthwhile to make the computations for the nQ or Rr cases.

The answer to the question just posed depends, of course, on the relative magnitudes of the review and ordering costs. In the event that review costs are high relative to ordering costs, then normally, it will be undesirable to have a review without placing an order since otherwise, the review is essentially wasted. This means that an $\langle R, r, T \rangle$ model optimized with respect to T should have the property that an order will be placed at almost every review. However, this in turn means that the use of an $\langle R, T \rangle$ model will yield essentially all the benefits of the $\langle R, r, T \rangle$ model, i.e., will yield almost as low an average annual cost. Therefore, when review costs are high relative to ordering costs, an order up to R doctrine should be essentially optimal. In the real world, it seems to be frequently true that the review costs are considerably higher than the cost of placing an order, and hence one would expect to find that in many practical situations one could use an order up to R policy without great deviations from optimality.

It is only when ordering costs are high with respect to review costs that an Rr doctrine could be considerably better than an order up to R doctrine. In such cases the question arises as to whether it would not be better to change over to a transactions reporting system rather than using periodic review. If this is not the case, then it may be advantageous to use either an nQ or Rr operating doctrine. Although the $\langle R, r, T \rangle$ model will in general yield a lower average annual cost than an $\langle nQ, r, T \rangle$ model, it would be expected that the differences would be rather small, and in any real world situation, one could probably use either one if an order up to R doctrine was not satisfactory.

5-12 Comparison of Periodic Review and Transactions Reporting Systems

When review costs are ignored, a transactions reporting system always has lower average annual costs, all other things being equal, than a periodic review system. The principal reason for this is that in the periodic review system, sufficient safety stock must be held to offer protection for a length of time $\tau + T$, while for a transactions reporting system τ is the relevant length of time. Thus the periodic review system will require higher safety stocks and have higher costs. The thing that really determines which system is to be preferred is the cost of operating a transactions reporting system, as compared with that of operating a periodic review system. These costs can vary widely with the type of inventory system under consideration, and in any particular case, either transactions reporting or periodic review may be favored. No general statement can be made as to whether one is to be preferred or the other. As has been already noted, in industry and the military, periodic review systems have in the past been used much more extensively than transactions reporting, but with the advent of automatic data processing equipment, there has been an increasing trend both in industry and the military towards using transactions reporting. It does not follow that, when a system that carries many items changes from periodic review to transactions reporting, it will do so for all items. In many cases it will be profitable to use transactions reporting for some items but not on others. Of course, there exist some relatively rare situations in which one must use a periodic review system, perhaps, for example, because orders can be placed only at certain specified times, and in these cases a comparison with the costs of operating a transactions recording system is irrelevant.

5-13 The Lost Sales Case

Except for the simple, approximate model of Sec. 5-2, all the models in this chapter have concentrated on the backorders case. We noted in Chapter 4 that it was not possible to treat rigorously the lost sales case when more than a single order was outstanding. For periodic review systems, things are even more difficult, and trouble is encountered even in treating the case where only a single order is outstanding.

To illustrate the difficulties, consider the simplest case, i.e., that where the number of units demanded in any time period is Poisson distributed, the procurement lead time is a constant τ, and an order up to R policy is used. The additional stipulation will be imposed that there is never more than a single order outstanding. This will be rigorously true if $\tau < T$. In order to compute the average annual carrying costs and stockout costs, it is necessary to determine the distribution of the on hand inventory, either at a review time or immediately after an order arrives.

Let $\theta(x)$ be the probability that x units are on hand at a review time. If x units are on hand, then $R - x$ units are ordered, so that the quantity on hand plus on order immediately after the order is placed is R. To set up the equations which determine $\theta(x)$, it is convenient to divide the time between two successive reviews into two sub-periods, the first extending over a time period of length τ from the time that the order is placed until it arrives, and the other extending over a time period of length $T - \tau$ from the time that the order arrives until the next order is placed. It should be noted that it is possible to incur lost sales in both of these sub-periods.

Let $\psi(z)$ be the probability that z units are on hand immediately after an order arrives. The time after an order arrives until the next review is $T - \tau$. The probability that x units are on hand at the next review, if z units are on hand immediately after an order arrives, is

$$
\begin{cases}
p[z - x; \lambda(T - \tau)], & 0 < x \leq z \\
P[z; \lambda(T - \tau)], & x = 0 \\
0, & x > z
\end{cases}
\tag{5-125}
$$

Thus

$$\theta(x) = \sum_{z=x}^{R} \psi(z) p[z - x; \lambda(T - \tau)], \quad x > 0 \tag{5-126}$$

$$\theta(0) = \sum_{z=0}^{R} \psi(z) P[z; \lambda(T - \tau)] \tag{5-127}$$

Next, by considering the time period extending from 0 to τ, we shall express $\psi(z)$ explicitly in terms of $\theta(x)$. This can then be substituted into the above equations to yield a set of equations involving $\theta(x)$ only (or involving $\psi(z)$ only). If z units are on hand after an order arrives at time τ, the quantity on hand x at the time the order was placed could not have been less than $R - z$, since the size of the order is $R - x$. If the quantity on hand at the review time satisfies $x > R - z$, then in order to have z units on hand after the order arrives, it is necessary that the lead time demand be $R - z$. If $x = R - z$, then for any lead time demand $\geq R - z$, the quantity on hand after the arrival of the order must be z. Thus we have

$$\psi(z) = p(R - z; \lambda\tau) \sum_{x=R-z+1}^{R} \theta(x) + P(R - z; \lambda\tau)\theta(R - z),$$

$$z > 0 \tag{5-128}$$

$$\psi(0) = P(R; \lambda\tau)\theta(R) \tag{5-129}$$

Substitution of (5-128), (5-129) into (5-126), (5-127) yields

$$\theta(x) = \sum_{z=x}^{R} \left\{ p(R - z; \lambda\tau) p[z - x; \lambda(T - \tau)] \sum_{y=R-z+1}^{R} \theta(y) \right\}$$

$$+ \sum_{z=x}^{R} \left\{ P(R - z; \lambda\tau) p[z - x; \lambda(T - \tau)]\theta(R - z) \right\}, \quad x > 0 \tag{5-130}$$

$$\theta(0) = \sum_{z=1}^{R} \left\{ p(R - z; \lambda\tau)P[z; \lambda(T - \tau)] \sum_{y=R-z+1}^{R} \theta(y) \right\}$$

$$+ \sum_{z=0}^{R} \left\{ P(R - z; \lambda\tau)P[z; \lambda(T - \tau)]\theta(R - z) \right\} \tag{5-131}$$

These equations can be rearranged to read

$$\theta(x) = \sum_{y=0}^{R} \alpha(x, y)\theta(R - y), \quad x = 0, 1, \ldots, R \tag{5-132}$$

where

$$\alpha(x, y) = \sum_{z=x}^{R} p(R - z; \lambda\tau)p[z - x; \lambda(T - \tau)],$$
$$y = 0, 1, \ldots, x - 1; x > 0 \tag{5-133}$$

$$\alpha(x, y) = \sum_{z=y+1}^{R} p(R - z; \lambda\tau)p[z - x; \lambda(T - \tau)] \tag{5-134}$$

$$+ P(R - y; \lambda\tau)p[y - x; \lambda(T - \tau)], \quad y = x, \ldots, R - 1; x > 0$$

$$\alpha(x, R) = P(0; \lambda\tau)p[R - x; \lambda(T - \tau)], \quad x > 0 \tag{5-135}$$

$$\alpha(0, y) = \sum_{z=y+1}^{R} p(R - z; \lambda\tau)P[z; \lambda(T - \tau)]$$

$$+ P(R - y; \lambda\tau)P[y; \lambda(T - \tau)], \quad y = 0, 1, \ldots, R - 1 \tag{5-136}$$

$$\alpha(0, R) = P(0; \lambda\tau)P[R; \lambda(T - \tau)] \tag{5-137}$$

If the values of $\theta(x)$ from (5-126), (5-127) are substituted into (5-128), (5-129) we obtain the set of equations which involve $\psi(z)$ only. They are

$$\psi(z) = p(R - z; \lambda\tau) \sum_{x=R-z+1}^{R} \sum_{y=x}^{R} \psi(y)p[y - x; \lambda(T - \tau)]$$

$$+ P(R - z; \lambda\tau) \sum_{y=R-z}^{R} \psi(y)p[y - R + z; \lambda(T - \tau)],$$
$$z = 1, \ldots, R - 1 \tag{5-138}$$

$$\psi(R) = p(0; \lambda\tau) \sum_{x=1}^{R} \sum_{y=x}^{R} \psi(y)p[y - x; \lambda(T - \tau)]$$

$$+ P(0; \lambda\tau) \sum_{y=0}^{R} \psi(y)P[y; \lambda(T - \tau)] \tag{5-139}$$

$$\psi(0) = P(R; \lambda\tau)p[0; \lambda(T - \tau)]\psi(R) \tag{5-140}$$

These equations can also be rearranged to read

$$\psi(z) = \sum_{y=0}^{R} \beta(z, y)\psi(R - y) \tag{5-141}$$

We leave for Problem 5-25 the computation of the $\beta(z, y)$.

Unfortunately, it does not seem possible to solve the set of equations (5-132) or (5-141) explicitly. For any given value of R, it is straightforward to determine numerically either the $\theta(x)$ or $\psi(z)$, but this is not what is needed.

If one could compute the $\theta(x)$ or $\psi(z)$ it would be somewhat more convenient to have the $\psi(z)$, because then it would be unnecessary to divide the period up into two sub-periods. The average number of lost sales incurred per year would be

$$E(R, T) = \frac{1}{T} \sum_{z=0}^{R} \psi(z) \sum_{u=z}^{\infty} (u - z)p(u; \lambda T) \tag{5-142}$$

and the average unit years of storage incurred per year would be

$$D(R, T) = \frac{1}{T} \sum_{z=0}^{R} \psi(z) \int_{0}^{T} \sum_{x=0}^{z} (z - x)p(x; \lambda t) \, dt \tag{5-143}$$

The average annual cost when the unit cost of the item is constant is then

$$\mathcal{K} = \frac{J}{T} + \frac{A}{T} P(1; \lambda T) + ICD(R, T) + \pi E(R, T) \tag{5-144}$$

We have now seen how to formulate the model if the distribution $\psi(z)$ was available. Unfortunately, as we have noted, it does not seem possible to solve for the $\psi(z)$ explicitly, and thus the terms $D(R, T)$ and $E(R, T)$ cannot be evaluated explicitly. Hence, for periodic review systems, it is not possible to formulate exact models for the lost sales case even when the requirement is made that never more than a single order is outstanding. About the best one can do is to use the simple approximate treatment of lost sales given in Sec. 5-2. Fortunately, for many practical applications, this is adequate.

5-14 Stochastic Lead Times

It has already been noted in Sec. 5-2 that for periodic review models, unlike $\langle Q, r \rangle$ models, it is possible to treat rigorously stochastic lead times when more than a single order can be outstanding at any point in time provided that the range of lead time values is less than T. In this case, there can be no overlap of the lead time densities, and one can rigorously require that lead times be independent random variables and also that orders be received in the same sequence in which they were placed. The reason that stochastic lead times can be treated rigorously in certain cases for periodic review systems, while this is not possible with $\langle Q, r \rangle$ models, lies in the fact that for periodic review systems, the time between the placement of orders must be at least T, while for $\langle Q, r \rangle$ models there is a positive probability that two orders will be placed in an arbitrarily small time interval.

Let us show how to incorporate stochastic lead times into the $\langle nQ, r, T \rangle$ model of Sec. 5-3. The notation and terminology of that section will be employed here. We shall assume that the lead times are independent random variables and that orders are received in the same sequence in which they were placed. This can be done rigorously if the range of possible lead time values is less than T; otherwise, the treatment is only approximate.

If a review takes place at time t and an order is placed, and if an order is also placed at time $t + T$, then let τ_1, τ_2 be the random variables representing the lead times of the orders placed at t and $t + T$ respectively. The lead time density function will be written $g(\tau)$. Thus the expected number of backorders incurred in the period between the arrival of the two orders under consideration is

$$\frac{1}{Q} \int_0^\infty \int_0^\infty \sum_{u=r+1}^{r+Q} \sum_{x=u}^\infty (x - u) \left\{ p[x; \lambda(\tau_2 + T)] - p(x; \lambda\tau_1) \right\} g(\tau_2) g(\tau_1) \, d\tau_2 \, d\tau_1$$

$$= \frac{1}{Q} \sum_{u=r+1}^{r+Q} \sum_{x=u}^\infty (x - u) \left\{ \hat{h}(x; T) - h(x) \right\} \qquad (5\text{-}145)$$

where

$$h(x) = \int_0^\infty p(x; \lambda\tau) g(\tau) \, d\tau \qquad (5\text{-}146)$$

is the marginal distribution of lead time demand and

$$\hat{h}(x; T) = \int_0^\infty p[x; \lambda(\tau + T)] g(\tau) \, d\tau \qquad (5\text{-}147)$$

The limits on the integrals have been taken to be 0 to ∞. Of course, $g(\tau)$ may be 0 over most of this range so that the limits could be replaced by $\tau_{\min}$ and $\tau_{\max}$. Clearly, the assumption that lead times are independent and arrive in the order placed could not hold rigorously if $g(\tau) > 0$ for all τ between 0 and ∞. In particular, the assumption could not hold rigorously if $g(\tau)$ was represented by a gamma distribution. In this case, the treatment would at best be approximate.

The expected value of the unit years of shortage incurred between the arrival of the two orders is

$$\frac{1}{Q} \int_0^\infty \int_0^\infty \int_{\tau_1}^{\tau_2+T} \sum_{u=r+1}^{r+Q} \sum_{x=u}^\infty (x - u)p(x; \lambda\xi)g(\tau_1)g(\tau_2) \, d\xi \, d\tau_1 \, d\tau_2 \quad (5\text{-}148)$$

It is not necessarily true that an order will be placed at each review. In such cases it is necessary to apportion the expected number of backorders and unit years of shortage incurred between the arrival of two successive orders to as many periods as are involved in the time between the placement of two successive orders. This can be done in any way we choose provided that all backorders and unit years of shortage are counted somewhere. A convenient way to do this is to proceed as if an order was placed at each review, the number of units ordered being zero when an order is not in actuality placed.* The lead time density for a zero order quantity is the same as for a positive order quantity. With this convention, the expected number of backorders and unit years of shortage incurred per period are in every case given by (5-145), (5-148) respectively. Then the expected number of backorders and unit years of shortage incurred per year are

$$E(Q, r, T) = \frac{1}{QT} \sum_{u=r+1}^{r+Q} \sum_{x=u}^\infty (x - u)[\hat{h}(x; T) - h(x)] \quad (5\text{-}149)$$

$$B(Q, r, T) = \frac{1}{QT} \int_0^\infty \int_0^\infty \int_{\tau_1}^{\tau_2+T} \sum_{u=r+1}^{r+Q} \sum_{x=u}^\infty$$

$$(x - u)p(x; \lambda\xi)g(\tau_1)g(\tau_2) \, d\xi \, d\tau_1 \, d\tau_2 \quad (5\text{-}150)$$

These changes allow the inclusion of stochastic lead times in the model developed previously.

It is only for very special forms for $g(\tau)$ that it is at all simple to work out explicitly $E(Q, r, T)$ and $B(Q, r, T)$. This can be done quite easily if τ is gamma distributed. Problem 5-27 asks the reader to do this. Of course, for a gamma distribution, it will never be rigorously true that the range of lead time values will be less than T. When the demand variable is treated as continuous and normally distributed, the usual procedure used to take account of stochastic lead times is simply to change the variance of the normal distribution, i.e., the value of D. In this case, the value of D for the τ terms need not be the same as the value of D in the $\tau + T$ terms.

Stochastic lead times can be handled in $\langle R, r, T \rangle$ models in precisely the same way as for the $\langle nQ, r, T \rangle$ model illustrated above. The details are left for Problem 5-28.

---

* The reader should be careful to note that the use of this artifice in no way changes the fact that an ordering cost is incurred only if a positive quantity is ordered.

5-15 Quantity Discounts

When quantity discounts are offered which depend on the order size, an Rr or order up to R policy need not be optimal. To operate the system optimally, a function $Q(\xi)$ would have to be computed, using the techniques of dynamic programming discussed in Chapters 7 and 8, which gives the quantity Q to order as a function of the inventory position ξ at the review time. In the real world, one will often use an order up to R, Rr or nQ policy even when quantity discounts which depend on the order size are available, since it is too complicated to attempt to compute and use the $Q(\xi)$ function. The quantity discounts may, however, influence the optimal values of R^*, r^* and T^*. The main effect of quantity discounts on a periodic review system, if any, is to increase T^*. We shall illustrate how to account for quantity discounts in an $\langle R, T \rangle$ model.

Let us study the backorders case under the assumption that the number of units demanded in any time period is Poisson distributed. Let $C(x)$ be the cost of the units when x are procured. The probability that x units are procured at any given review is the probability that x units were demanded in the past period, i.e., $p(x; \lambda T)$. Thus the expected cost of the units procured at any given review is

$$\sum_{x=0}^{\infty} C(x)p(x; \lambda T)$$

and the average annual cost is

$$M = \frac{1}{T} \sum_{x=0}^{\infty} C(x)p(x; \lambda T) \tag{5-151}$$

Let us now evaluate this expression explicitly for the case of all units quantity discounts. Assume that there are m price breaks $q_1, \ldots, q_m (q_0 = 0, q_{m+1} = \infty)$, and that the unit cost is C_i if the quantity ordered x satisfies $q_i \leq x < q_{i+1}$. Then, the average annual cost of the units procured is

$$M(T) = \frac{1}{T} \sum_{i=1}^{m} \sum_{x=q_{i-1}}^{q_i-1} C_{i-1}xp(x; \lambda T) + \frac{C_m}{T} \sum_{x=q_m}^{\infty} xp(x; \lambda T)$$

$$= \lambda \sum_{i=1}^{m} C_{i-1} \sum_{x=q_{i-1}}^{q_i-1} p(x-1; \lambda T) + \lambda C_m \sum_{x=q_m}^{\infty} p(x-1; \lambda T) \tag{5-152}$$

$$= \lambda \sum_{i=1}^{m} C_{i-1}[P(q_{i-1}-1; \lambda T) - P(q_i-1; \lambda T)] + \lambda C_m P(q_m-1; \lambda T)$$

The expected unit cost $\overline{C}$ of the item is simply the average annual cost divided by the mean rate of demand, i.e.,

$$\overline{C} = \sum_{i=1}^{m} C_{i-1}[P(q_{i-1} - 1; \lambda T) - P(q_i - 1; \lambda T)] + C_m P(q_m - 1; \lambda T)$$

It is this expected unit cost that must be used in the inventory carrying cost term. Note that R^* for a given T can be found without including the $M(T)$ term in the cost expression. However, the expected unit cost $\overline{C}$ will now be a function of T. To determine T^* it is necessary to include the $M(T)$ term in the cost expression.

The computational procedure in the lost sales case is precisely the same as in the backorders case, provided that the influence of quantity discounts on the cost of a lost sale can be ignored. This is usually a valid approximation in practice.

We shall leave for Problem 5-29 the development of the average annual cost of units procured when incremental quantity discounts are available. The same general computational procedure applies in this case. However, (5-152) must be replaced by an equation of somewhat different form.

It is straightforward but tedious to compute M and $\overline{C}$ for nQ and Rr operating doctrines also. We ask the reader to attempt this in Problem 5-30.

REFERENCES

1. Arrow, K. J., T. Harris, and J. Marschak, "Optimal Inventory Policy," *Econometrica*, **XIX** (1951), pp. 250–272.

2. Arrow, K. J., S. Karlin, and H. Scarf, *Studies in the Mathematical Theory of Inventory and Production.* Stanford, Calif.: Stanford University Press, 1958.

3. Hadley, G., and T. M. Whitin, "A Family of Inventory Models," *Management Science*, Vol. 7, No. 4, July 1961, pp. 351–371.

4. Morse, P. M., "Solutions of a Class of Discrete Time Inventory Problems," *Operations Research*, Vol. 7, No. 1, Jan.–Feb. 1959, pp. 67–78.

PROBLEMS

5-1 A warehouse has a policy of reviewing each item in its inventories once every six months. It uses an order up to R policy. One particular item costs \$25 per unit independently of the quantity ordered. The cost of placing an order is \$2.00 and the cost of the review apportioned to this item is \$15. Demands occurring when the system is out of stock are backordered and the cost of a backorder is taken to be \$100. The system uses an inventory carrying charge of $I = 0.20$. The number of units demanded in any time period is normally distributed with mean $240t$ and variance $500t$, where t is the length of the period in years. The lead time is constant at 2.5 months. What is the optimal value of R for the presently used review period? What is the optimal review interval and $R^*(T^*)$? What average annual savings could be obtained by using T^* as the time between reviews?

5-2 Derive the discrete analogue of the model developed in Sec. 5-2 for the case where demand is Poisson distributed. Consider both the case of constant and stochastic lead times. What is the inequality which is used to determine $R^*(T)$. Consider both the backorders and lost sales cases.

5-3 A certain item carried in a large military supply system is reviewed every three months. An order up to R policy is used. The number of units demanded in any time period can be considered to be Poisson distributed with the average annual demand being 15. The procurement lead time is essentially constant with the value five months. The unit cost of the item is \$500, the cost of a backorder is taken to be \$5000, and the cost of placing an order is \$30. The system uses an inventory carrying charge of $I = 0.20$. Determine the optimal value of R for the specified time between reviews. What is the safety stock? What is the cost of uncertainty?

5-4 Under what conditions will the solution to Eq. (5-9) not be unique? *Hint:* The solution is unique if $h(x; T) > 0$ for all $x > 0$.

5-5 For the model developed in Sec. 5-2 develop the derivatives needed for Newton's method to solve for R^* and T^* simultaneously.

5-6 Apply the results of Problem 5-5 to the example given in Sec. 5-2 and determine R^* and T^* simultaneously.

5-7 Discuss how the method of steepest descents could be used to determine R^* and T^* for the model developed in Sec. 5-2.

5-8 Use the method of steepest descents to determine R^* and T^* for the example presented in Sec. 5-2.

5-9 Prove that the cost function of Eq. (5-6) is a convex function of R for a given T. Under what conditions is it strictly convex? Is $\mathcal{K}$ a convex function of R and T?

5-10 Discuss the behavior of the safety stock for the model developed in Sec. 5-2 as $T \to 0$. How do you explain this?

5-11 A department store reviews the stock of a particular white shirt each week. An order up to R policy is used. The number of units demanded in any time period for a particular size of the shirt can be considered to be Poisson distributed with a mean of 25 per week. Each shirt costs the store $3.00 and the selling price is $5.95. An inventory carrying charge of $I = 0.17$ is used. Demands occurring when the store is out of stock are lost, and the cost of a lost sale aside from lost profit is $10.00. The procurement lead time can be assumed to be constant at 10 days. Determine the optimal value of R.

5-12 Go through the same sort of analysis employed in Sec. 4-6 for the $\langle Q, r \rangle$ model to obtain the various time averages for the $\langle nQ, r, T \rangle$ and $\langle R, r, T \rangle$ models, and show their relation to expected values. In particular, show that the average annual cost of carrying inventory, stockouts, etc. is the expected cost per period times $1/T$. Also show that the average annual cost is the expected cost per cycle times the average number of cycles per year.

5-13 Derive Eqs. (5-27) through (5-29).

5-14 For the $\langle nQ, r, T \rangle$ model compute the steady state probability $\psi(x)$ that the inventory position at a review time is x (before the placement of any order). Do this by making use of the $\rho(r + j)$. Also develop the set of equations from which the $\psi(x)$ can be computed directly by considering the related Markov process for generating transitions between the inventory position states at the beginning of a review. Can you solve these equations directly?

5-15 Compute the mean and variance of the density $\psi(x)$ defined in Problem 5-14.

5-16 For the continuous version of the $\langle R, T \rangle$ model presented in Sec. 5-6 determine the derivatives that would be needed if Newton's method were to be used to determine R^* and T^* simultaneously.

5-17 Is the cost expression (5-74) a convex function of R for a given T? Is it a convex function of R and T then. What are the implications of this result for the determination of and consequences of R^* and T^*?

5-18 Carry through the limiting processes of Sec. 5-7 for the case of stochastic lead times. What approximations and/or assumptions are needed?

5-19 Provide a step-by-step derivation of Eqs. (5-88), (5-89).

5-20 For a given value of r and R, develop a numerical procedure for solving the set of equations (5-88), (5-89).

5-21 For a periodic review system determine an explicit form for the average annual cost expression in the backorders case when an Rr policy is used and the demand in the time between reviews has an exponential distribution. Assume that the lead time is precisely one period in length, $\hat{\tau} = 0$, and that the inventory carrying cost for a period depends only on the on hand inventory at the end of the period. Determine R^* and r^*.

5-22 In Eq. (5-108) work out explicitly $H(x, T)$ and $v^{(n)}(x; T)$ when $v(x; T)$ is a normal distribution.

5-23 Show that Eqs. (5-111), (5-112) are solutions to Eqs. (5-109), (5-110). Also show that with the proper interpretation, $p(R)$ and $\rho(r + y)$ represent a legitimate density function.

5-24 Derive in detail Eqs. (5-113), (5-114).

5-25 Evaluate explicitly the $\beta(z, y)$ in Eq. (5-141).

5-26 Develop a numerical procedure for solving the set of equations (5-132) and (5-141) for a given value of R.

5-27 Work out the explicit form for Eqs. (5-149), (5-150) when the lead time is gamma distributed.

5-28 Discuss the introduction of stochastic lead times into $\langle R, r, T \rangle$ models.

5-29 Develop the equations needed to handle incremental quantity discounts in order up to R models when demand is Poisson distributed.

5-30 Study the problem of handling quantity discounts in $\langle nQ, r, T \rangle$ and $\langle R, r, T \rangle$ models under the assumption that an nQ or Rr policy is to be used.

5-31 Show that the equations for quantity discounts developed in Sec. 5-15 reduce to the correct values when the unit cost of the item is a constant independent of the quantity ordered.

5-32 Obtain $\theta(x)$ and $\rho(r + y)$, $p(R)$ by solving Eqs. (5-113), (5-114), in the case where $v(x; T)$ is a gamma distribution of order two. Also obtain $\rho(r + y)$ and $p(R)$ from (5-111) and (5-112). *Hint:* Use the properties of $v(x; T)$ to obtain second order differential equations for $\theta(x)$. These equations are

$$\theta'' - 2\beta\theta' + \beta^2\theta = 0, \quad x \le r; \quad \theta'' - 2\beta\theta' = 0, \quad r \le x \le R$$

Determine the four constants of integration by noting that $\theta(R) = 0$; $\theta(x)$, $\theta'(x)$ are continuous at $x = r$; and $\theta(x)$ must be a legitimate density function. The resulting expression for $\rho(r + y)$ and $p(R)$ are

$$\rho(r + y) = 2\beta\Delta[1 - e^{2\beta(r+y-R)}], \quad 0 \le y < R - r$$

$$p(R) = 4\Delta, \quad \Delta = [3 + 2\beta(R - r) + e^{-2\beta(R-r)}]^{-1}$$

5-33 Suppose that instead of specifying a stockout cost, it is desired to minimize the costs of review, ordering, and carrying inventory subject to the constraint that the average fraction of time out of stock is not greater than f. For each type of operating doctrine discussed in this chapter, show how such a criterion can be used to determine the optimal values of the parameters for the specific operating doctrine under consideration. Show that this really imputes a value of 0 to $\hat{\pi}$ and a unique value to π. Also discuss the case where it is desired that an upper limit to the expected number of backorders at any point in time be specified.

5-34 Solve Problem 5-1 under the assumption that in addition to the fixed cost of $100 per backorder, there is also a variable backorder cost of $2000 per unit per year.

5-35 Solve Problem 5-3 under the assumption that in addition to the fixed cost of $5000 per backorder, there is a variable cost of $50,000 per unit per year.

5-36 Determine T^* for Problem 5-1 if all units quantity discounts are available of the following type: the unit cost is $25 if the quantity ordered Q lies in the range $0 < Q < 100$, and is $20 if $Q \geq 100$.

5-37 Determine T^* for Problem 5-3 if all units quantity discounts are available of the following sort: the unit cost is $500 if the quantity ordered is less than 10 and is $300 if the quantity ordered is greater than 10. Assume that the cost of making a review is $50.

5-38 Discuss how to compute the state probability $\psi(x)$ that the inventory position of a periodic review system is x at any randomly chosen instant of time t. Carry out the computation to determine $\psi(x)$ when an order up to R policy is used and demand is Poisson distributed. *Hint:* Show how to compute the probability that the inventory position is x at a time ξ after a review. Then average ξ over the period. Can you use these state probabilities to obtain the same E and B terms obtained in the text?

5-39 Consider a low demand, high cost item carried in a military supply system which has the following characteristics. The number of units demanded in any time period can be considered to be Poisson distributed with a mean rate of demand of 4 per year. The unit cost of the item is $1000 independently of the quantity ordered. All demands occurring when the system is out of stock are backordered and the cost of a backorder is taken to be $30,000 independently of the length of time for which the backorder exists. The procurement lead time shows quite a bit of variability. Its mean is 6 months and it has a standard deviation of 3 months. It is felt that the distribution of lead time demand can be represented with sufficient accuracy by a gamma distribution. The system uses an inventory carrying charge of $I = 0.20$. All items in inventory are reviewed every six months and an order up to R policy is used. Determine the optimal value of R for the part under consideration.

5-40 Solve Problem 5-39 under the assumption that it was not possible for the military to specify a backorder cost, but they did feel that the average fraction of time out of stock should not be greater than 0.001. What is the imputed backorder cost?

5-41 Solve Problem 5-1 under the assumption that instead of specifying the cost of a backorder, it is specified that the average fraction of time out of stock should be 0.01.

5-42 Solve Problem 5-3 under the assumption that instead of specifying the cost of a backorder, it is specified that the average fraction of time out of stock should be 0.001.

5-43 Solve Problem 5-11 under the assumption that instead of specifying the cost of a lost sale, it is specified that the average fraction of time out of stock should be 0.05.

5-44 Discuss the problems involved in handling non-linear stockout costs in periodic review systems. Consider a system which uses an order up to R policy. Let $\pi(t)$ be the cost of a backorder, if it lasts for a time t. If demand is Poisson distributed, can you develop the expression for the average annual cost of backorders?

5-45 Use the notion of an ensemble average to justify the fact that the integral of the expected on hand inventory or backorders is the expected value of the integral.

5-46 In a military supply system, a policy is followed of reviewing a certain critical item weekly. An nQ ordering policy is to be used. The demand for the item can be imagined to be Poisson, with the average annual rate being 50 units. The procurement lead time is essentially constant at 2 months. The unit cost of the item is $500 independently of the quantity ordered, and the system uses an inventory carrying charge of $I = 0.20$. The cost of placing an order is estimated to be $200. Any demands occurring when the system is out of stock are backordered, and the cost of a backorder is placed at $10,000. Determine Q^* and r^*.

5-47 For the simple model discussed in Sec. 5-2, show how to include an inventory carrying cost which is based on the maximum inventory level. How does this term change the equation which determines R^*?

5-48 Assume that an inventory system stocks n items. Imagine that an order up to R policy is used for each item. Also imagine that the time between reviews must be the same for each item. Show how to determine T^*.

5-49 Show what sorts of problems are encountered in introducing floor space constraints, or constraints on investment in inventory when n items are carried by a system and a periodic review policy is used for each of them.

5-50 Derive the average annual cost for an $\langle nQ, r, T \rangle$ model by first computing the expected cost per cycle and then multiplying by the average number of cycles per year.

5-51 Determine the limiting form of the $\langle R, r, T \rangle$ model with Poisson demands and constant lead times as $T \to 0$. Is the limiting form the familiar $\langle Q, r \rangle$ model?

SINGLE

PERIOD MODELS

"Deliberate often; decide once."

Publilius Syrus

6-1 Introduction

The models to be discussed in this chapter are perhaps the simplest of all inventory models in which demand is treated as a stochastic variable. The essential characteristic of these models is that only a single time period, usually of finite length, is relevant and only a single procurement is made. A rather wide variety of real world inventory problems including the stocking of spare parts, perishable items, style goods, and special season items offer practical examples of the sort of situations to be studied here. Since only a single time period is to be considered, there is no steady state associated with the models analyzed in this chapter. These models then provide a transition between the steady state models of Chapters 2, 4, 5 and the dynamic models to be presented in the next chapter.

6-2 The General Single Period Model with Time Independent Costs

The type of problem to be studied in this section is often referred to as the Christmas tree problem or newsboy problem, since it can be phrased as a problem of deciding how many trees a dealer in Christmas trees should purchase for the season, or how many newspapers a boy should buy on a given day for his corner newsstand.

Let us illustrate by formulating the Christmas tree problem. Assume that a Christmas tree vendor must order his trees a month before the season begins, and that he has no opportunity to reorder later in the season if he needs more trees. Thus in a given season he has only one opportunity to place an order. The cost of a tree is C and the selling price is S. Any trees not sold at the end of the season are a total loss. Let $p(x)$ be the probability that x trees will be demanded during the season.* Then his expected profit $\mathcal{G}$ for the season if he procures h trees is

---

* We here ignore the fact that in reality he will stock trees of different sizes and costs, and that the demand variables for trees of different sizes will not be independent, since if he is out of one size a customer will often accept a different size.

$$g(h) = S \sum_{x=0}^{h} xp(x) + Sh \sum_{x=h+1}^{\infty} p(x) - Ch \qquad (6\text{-}1)$$

since the revenue received is Sx if $x \leq h$, and is Sh if $x > h$. The problem is to determine the value of h which maximizes his expected profit.

The Christmas tree problem is a special case of a more general model which can be formulated as follows: An item can be procured only at the beginning of a period. The unit cost of the item is C, independent of the number of units procured. The selling price per unit is S. Let $p(x)$ be the probability that x units are demanded during the period. If a demand occurs when the system is out of stock, a goodwill cost π_0 is incurred in addition to the lost profit. Any units remaining at the end of the period can be sold at a price of L dollars per unit ($L < C$). It is desired to determine the optimal number of units to have on hand at the start of the period in order to maximize the expected profit for the period.

If h units are procured, the expected profit is

$$g(h) = S \sum_{x=0}^{h} xp(x) + Sh \sum_{x=h+1}^{\infty} p(x)$$

$$+ L \sum_{x=0}^{h-1} (h - x) \, p(x) - Ch - \pi_0 \sum_{x=h}^{\infty} (x - h) \, p(x)$$

$$= (S - L)\mu - (C - L)h - (S + \pi_0 - L) \sum_{x=h}^{\infty} (x - h) \, p(x) \qquad (6\text{-}2)$$

where μ is the expected demand for the period. The smallest h which maximizes the expected profit is the largest h for which $\Delta g(h) > 0$. However

$$\Delta g(h) = (S + \pi_0 - L) \, P(h) + L - C \qquad (6\text{-}3)$$

where $P(x)$ is the complementary cumulative of $p(x)$. Thus the largest h such that

$$P(h) > \frac{C - L}{S + \pi_0 - L} = \frac{C - L}{(S - C) + \pi_0 + (C - L)} \qquad (6\text{-}4)$$

is optimal, i.e., is h^*. Note that $C - L$ is the loss per unit on any units remaining at the end of the period, $S - C$ is the unit profit, and $(S - C) + \pi_0$ is the cost incurred if a demand occurs when the system is out of stock. Note also that no restrictions whatever are placed on the demand distribution for the period $p(x)$. For example, units need not be demanded one at a time, and demand in non-overlapping time intervals need not be independent. If $\Delta g(h^* + 1) = 0$, both h^* and $h^* + 1$ are optimal.

Often it is convenient to treat h and the demand variable as continuous.

Then if $f(x)$ is the density function for demand in the period and $F(x)$ is its complementary cumulative, the expected profit for the period when h units are procured is

$$\mathcal{G}(h) = S \int_0^h x f(x)\, dx + Sh \int_h^\infty f(x)\, dx$$

$$+ L \int_0^h (h - x) f(x)\, dx - Ch - \pi_0 \int_h^\infty (x - h) f(x)\, dx$$

$$= (S - L)\mu - (C - L)h - (S + \pi_0 - L) \int_h^\infty (x - h) f(x)\, dx \quad (6\text{-}5)$$

The optimal h is then a solution to $d\mathcal{G}/dh = 0$, i.e., h^* satisfies the equation

$$F(h) = \frac{C - L}{S + \pi_0 - L} \quad (6\text{-}6)$$

In Problem 6-4 we ask the reader to show that (6-5) is a concave function of h. Furthermore, $\mathcal{G}(h)$ is usually strictly concave. These results imply that any relative maximum of $\mathcal{G}$ is the absolute maximum. When $\mathcal{G}$ is strictly concave, then the absolute maximum is unique. Problem 6-5 asks for a discussion of the conditions under which the solution to (6-6) is not unique.

6-3 Examples

Several examples will now be given to illustrate the wide variety of problems to which the simple model developed in the previous section is applicable.

1. A large supermarket must decide how much bread to purchase each day. For shopping days Monday through Thursday, past history has shown that the daily demand can be considered to be normally distributed with mean 300 and standard deviation 50. A loaf of bread sells for $0.25 and costs the store $0.19. Any bread not sold by the end of the day is, on the following day, placed on a counter where it is sold for $0.15 per loaf. All bread on this counter can be sold at this price. It is desired to determine the optimal number of loaves to purchase to maximize the expected daily profit.

In the notation of the previous section, $S = \$0.25$, $C = \$0.19$, $L = \$0.15$, $\pi_0 = 0$. Then h^* is the solution to

$$\Phi\left(\frac{h - 300}{50}\right) = \frac{0.04}{0.10} = 0.40$$

Hence from the normal tables

$$\frac{h - 300}{50} = 0.253 \quad \text{or} \quad h = 300 + 12.65 \approx 313$$

Thus 313 loaves should be purchased.

The expected number of loaves per day of bread to be placed on the stale bread counter when h loaves are stocked is

$$\frac{1}{\sigma} \int_0^h (h - x) \, \phi\left(\frac{x - \mu}{\sigma}\right) dx = h - \mu + (\mu - h) \, \Phi\left(\frac{h - \mu}{\sigma}\right) + \sigma\phi\left(\frac{h - \mu}{\sigma}\right)$$

Then since $h^* = 313$ and $\mu = 300$, the expected number of loaves to be placed on the stale bread counter each day is

$$13 - 13(0.40) + 50(0.3863) = 13 + 14.1 = 27.1$$

It is of interest to compare the expected daily profit when h^* loaves are stocked with that in the case where the number of loaves ordered is equal to μ, the expected demand. When $f(x)$ is a normal distribution, (6-5) can be written

$$g(h) = (S - L)\, \mu - (C - L)\, h + (S - L + \pi_0)\, (h - \mu) \, \Phi\left(\frac{h - \mu}{\sigma}\right)$$

$$- \sigma(S - L + \pi_0) \, \phi\left(\frac{h - \mu}{\sigma}\right)$$

Then for the case at hand where $\pi_0 = 0$

$$g(h^*) = 30.00 - 12.52 + 0.52 - 1.93 = \$16.07$$

and

$$g(\mu) = 30.00 - 12.00 + 0 - 1.99 = \$16.01$$

Thus the increase in expected profit by using h^* rather than $h = \mu$ is only \$0.06 per day, i.e., about a $\frac{1}{2}$ percent increase in expected profit.

2. Let us now solve the above problem in the case where the super-market also attaches a goodwill loss of $\pi_0 = \$0.50$ to every loaf of bread demanded when the store is out of stock. In this case the optimal h is the solution to

$$\Phi\left(\frac{h - 300}{50}\right) = \frac{0.04}{0.10 + 0.50} = \frac{0.04}{0.60} = 0.06667$$

Hence

$$\frac{h - 300}{50} = 1.500 \quad \text{or} \quad h = 300 + 75 = 375$$

Now the expected number of loaves which will be placed on the stale bread counter is 76.48. The expected daily profits using h^* and μ are respectively

$$g(h^*) = 30.00 - 15.00 + 3.00 - 3.88 = \$14.12$$

$$g(\mu) = 30.00 - 12.00 + 0 - 11.97 = \$6.03$$

In this case there is a very large difference between the expected profit when h^* is used and the expected profit when μ is used. It should be observed that in this example, the expected daily profit is not what would be obtained by averaging the profit obtained from the accounting records over a long time, since it includes the influence of the goodwill loss which would not appear in the accounting records. Indeed, on the basis of what would be taken from the accounting records, the expected profit would be lower using $h^* = 375$ than using $h = 313$ or $h = \mu$. The reader should check this by computing the expected profit with $\pi_0 = 0$ when $h^* = 375$.

3. A fashionable candy store does not make its own chocolates, but instead buys from a large producer which caters to a number of different stores. The store under consideration must decide how many large chocolate rabbits to order for the Easter season. They must be ordered two months in advance and there is no possibility of placing a reorder. Each rabbit costs the store \$2.50 and sells for \$7.00. Any rabbits not sold at the end of the season are a total loss. The store feels sure that it can sell at least 100 of these rabbits and not more than 500. Any number between 100 and 500 is felt to be equally likely, i.e., the store feels that the distribution of demand is uniform over the interval 100 to 500. If the demand variable is treated as continuous, this means that the density function $f(x)$ is

$$f(x) = \frac{1}{400}, \quad 100 \leq x \leq 500; \quad f(x) = 0, \quad \text{otherwise}$$

The complementary cumulative function $F(x)$ of $f(x)$ is

$$F(x) = \begin{cases} 1, & 0 \leq x \leq 100 \\ 1 - \frac{1}{400}(x - 100), & 100 \leq x \leq 500 \\ 0, & x \geq 500 \end{cases}$$

From the data given above, $S = \$7.00$, $C = \$2.50$, $L = 0$, $\pi_0 = 0$. Thus (6-6) becomes

$$F(h) = 1 - \frac{1}{400}(h - 100) = \frac{2.50}{7.00} = 0.3571$$

or

$$h^* = 357.2 \approx 357$$

The expected number of rabbits remaining at the end of the season when h ($100 \leq h \leq 500$) rabbits are stocked is

$$\int_0^h (h - x) f(x) \, dx = h - \mu + \int_h^\infty x f(x) \, dx - hF(h)$$

$$= h - \mu + \frac{1}{800} [h^2 - 1000 \, h + 25 \times 10^4]$$

Then, since $h^* = 357$ and $\mu = 300$, the expected number of rabbits remaining when h^* are stocked is

$$57 + \frac{1}{800} [12.75 \times 10^4 - 35.7 \times 10^4 + 25 \times 10^4] = 82.6$$

The expected profit on the rabbits if h ($100 \leq h \leq 500$) units are stocked is

$$\mathcal{G}(h) = (S - L) \mu - (C - L) h$$

$$- \frac{1}{800} (S - L + \pi_0) [h^2 - 1000 \, h + 25 \times 10^4]$$

Then

$$\mathcal{G}(h^*) = 2100.00 - 892.50 - 178.93 = \$1028.57$$

and

$$\mathcal{G}(\mu) = 1350.00 - 350.00 = \$1000.00$$

Thus by carrying 57 rabbits above the mean demand, the expected profit is increased by \$28.57.

4. Certain spare parts for aircraft are made at the same time the aircraft is produced. Once production on the aircraft has ceased, it is extremely difficult to obtain these spare parts. Production is about to cease on a certain military aircraft. It is desired to determine how many spares of a certain low demand item should be available at the time production stops. For the number of planes in the force, past data indicate that the demand for the part will be Poisson distributed with the mean rate of demand being 0.75 per year. It is uncertain precisely what the operational life of the aircraft will be. However, it has been decided that the probability density for the time until obsolescence can be described by a gamma distribution with a mean of 6 years and a standard deviation of 1.5 years. The parts cost \$2000 each and their scrap value, if any remain unused at the end of the plane's operational life, is \$100 each. If a demand should occur when no spares are available, the cost of obtaining one is estimated to be \$13,000.

In order to determine the optimal number of spares which should be on hand, it is first necessary to determine the marginal distribution of demand over the operational life of the aircraft. We know from (3-73) that this distribution is the negative binomial $b_N[x; \alpha + 1, \beta/(\beta + \lambda)]$, since demands are Poisson distributed and the operational life has a gamma distribution. To determine α, β we use (3-44), (3-45) which relate the mean and standard deviation of the gamma distribution to α, β. Thus

$$\beta = \frac{6}{2.25} = 2.67; \quad \alpha = \left(\frac{6}{1.5}\right)^2 - 1 = 15$$

Then, $\lambda = 0.75$, $\beta/(\beta + \lambda) = 0.781$, $\alpha + 1 = 16$, and

$$b_N[x; \alpha + 1; \beta/(\beta + \lambda)] = \frac{(15 + x)!}{x! \, 15!} (0.781)^{16} (0.219)^x$$

From the above data we see that $C = \$2000$, $L = \$100$, $\pi_0 = \$13,000$ and $S = 0$. Now maximization of profits with $S = 0$ is equivalent to minimization of expected costs. Hence (6-4) applies in this case also. If h is the quantity on hand when production ceases, the optimal value of h is the largest h for which

$$\sum_{x=h}^{\infty} b_N(x; 16, 0.781) > \frac{1900}{12,900} = 0.1475$$

It is not too difficult to compute the optimal h, since once $b_N(x; 16, 0.781)$ has been calculated for a given x, it is easy to compute successively values for other x values using

$$b_N(x + 1; 16, 0.781) = \frac{16 + x}{x + 1} (0.219) \, b_N(x; 16, 0.781)$$

Denoting the complementary cumulative by $B_N(x)$, the cumulative function by $\hat{B}_N(x)$, and noting that $B_N(x) = 1 - \hat{B}_N(x - 1)$, we find that $B_N(6) = 0.3061$, $B_N(7) = 0.1906$, $B_N(8) = 0.1111$, and $B_N(9) = 0.0609$. Thus it is clear that $h^* = 7$.

If h units are on hand when production ceases, the expected number still on hand when the aircraft becomes obsolete is

$$\sum_{x=0}^{h} (h - x) \, b_N[x; \alpha + 1, \beta/(\beta + \lambda)]$$

$$= h - \mu + \sum_{x=h}^{\infty} (x - h) \, b_N[x; \alpha + 1, \beta/(\beta + \lambda)]$$

Since the expected demand until obsolescence is $\mu = 6(0.75) = 4.5$, the expected number to be scrapped if $h^* = 7$ units are on hand when production ceases is

$$2.5 + 0.0502 + 2(0.0275) + 3(0.01421) + 4(0.00702) + \ldots \approx 2.7$$

6-4 Constrained Multiple Item Problems

Another class of single period inventory problems which frequently arise in practice is concerned with the stocking of n different items when the items are not completely independent but are related by some constraint such as a budget or floor space constraint. The only interaction between the items is assumed to be through the constraint. In particular, this implies that the variables representing the demand for different items are independent random variables. We shall discuss one typical problem which is often referred to as a flyaway-kit problem [3]. A practical example of such a problem is as follows: It is desired to stock a nuclear submarine about to go on patrol with spare parts for the submarine itself and for the missiles which it carries. The probability distributions for the demands for the spare parts over the length of time of the patrol mission are assumed to be known. It will be imagined that for each demand for part i which occurs when no spares are available a cost π_i is incurred. The volume available in the submarine for stocking spares is severely limited. The problem then reduces to that of determining the quantity of each spare to stock so as to minimize the expected stockout costs while not exceeding the available space.

Suppose that there are n spare parts of interest. Let v_i be the volume of one unit of spare part i and V the total volume available for storage. The probability that x units of spare part i will be demanded will be written $p_i(x)$. Then, if h_i units of part i are stocked, it is desired to determine non-negative integers h_i which minimize the expected cost

$$\mathcal{K} = \pi_1 \sum_{x=h_1}^{\infty} (x - h_1)\, p_1(x) + \ldots + \pi_n \sum_{x=h_n}^{\infty} (x - h_n)\, p_n(x) \qquad (6\text{-}7)$$

subject to the constraint that the total volume of the spares does not exceed V, i.e.,

$$\sum_{i=1}^{n} v_i h_i = v_1 h_1 + \ldots + v_n h_n \leq V \qquad (6\text{-}8)$$

Let us now consider how the h_i^* may be determined. First, imagine that each h_i^* will be large enough that the h_i can be treated as continuous. Assume that $p_i(x)$ can be approximated by the continuous density $f_i(x)$, whose complementary cumulative function is $F_i(x)$. It is clear that when we treat the h_i as continuous, then the h_i^* will satisfy (6-8) as a strict equality. To solve the problem we can use the Lagrange multiplier approach. We introduce a Lagrange multiplier θ and form the function

$$\mathcal{W} = \sum_{i=1}^{n} \pi_i \int_{h_i}^{\infty} (x - h_i)\, f_i(x)\, dx + \theta \left[\sum_{i=1}^{n} v_i h_i - V \right] \qquad (6\text{-}9)$$

Then if each $h_i^* > 0$, the h_i^* must be solutions to the set of equations

$$\frac{\partial \mathcal{W}}{\partial h_i} = 0 = -\pi_i F_i(h_i) + \theta v_i, \quad i = 1, \ldots, n \tag{6-10}$$

or

$$\frac{\pi_i}{v_i} F_i(h_i) = \theta, \quad i = 1, \ldots, n \tag{6-11}$$

A computational procedure is to select a θ and compute the h_i from (6-11). Then compute $\hat{V} = \sum_{i=1}^{n} v_i h_i$. If $\hat{V} > V$, select a larger value of θ and repeat the process. If $\hat{V} < V$, select a smaller value of θ and repeat. If $\hat{V} = V$ the solution is optimal. One can make the computation quite readily by hand if there are not too many items. The h_i values so obtained will have to be rounded to integral values. This should not lead to serious deviations from optimality when the h_i are sufficiently large that the continuous approximation is valid.

In many practical situations, however, the h_i will tend to be very small (i.e., 0, 1, or 2), and any attempt to use the above procedure and round the results could lead to considerable deviations from optimality. An approximate procedure for handling this case is to proceed as follows: Note first of all that if we change the number of units of item i stocked from $h_i - 1$ to h_i, the expected reduction in cost is $\pi_i P_i(h_i)$, where $P_i(x)$ is the complementary cumulative of $p_i(x)$. The additional volume used in adding this unit is v_i. Thus the expected cost reduction per unit increase in volume is $\pi_i P_i(h_i)/v_i$. The procedure is then to progressively assign units to the item which yields the greatest reduction in expected cost per unit increase in volume. The first step is to compute

$$\max_i \left\{ \frac{\pi_i}{v_i} P_i(1) \right\}$$

If the maximum is taken on for $i = j$ set $h_j = 1$, and then compute

$$\max \left\{ \max_{i \neq j} \left[\frac{\pi_i}{v_i} P_i(1) \right], \frac{\pi_j}{v_j} P_j(2) \right\}$$

The next unit is assigned to the index where the maximum is taken on, etc. This is continued until adding an additional unit would exceed the volume restriction. We ask the reader to explain in Problem 6-28 why this procedure should often yield a satisfactory computational procedure and under what conditions it might not be expected to work too well. The problem of finding non-negative integers which maximize (6-7) subject to (6-8) can be solved exactly by the technique of dynamic programming to be introduced in the next chapter. We shall illustrate the procedure there. It might be pointed out that even dynamic programming cannot give the exact solution to the actual physical problem. The reason for this is that specification of the unit volumes v_i and V is not sufficient. It is also necessary to consider the actual shape of the units and of the space available for storage. In other words it does not follow that simply because (6-8) tells us that an additional 2 cubic feet of storage space are available that an item having a volume of 1.75 cubic feet can be fitted into this space. It depends on the shape of the available space and of the item.

In some cases there may be two constraints on the problem such as a volume and weight constraint. The addition of one more constraint makes the problem much more difficult to solve, but again the dynamic programming technique can be used.

Single period models involving a number of items connected by one or more constraints can take a variety of forms. The following example presents a situation which is slightly different from that given above, but the method of analysis is just the same.

EXAMPLE The buyer for the housewares department of a Midwest retail store is making his annual trip to Europe. In the real world he might be purchasing as many as 100 or more different items. For the purpose of this example, imagine that only three items are to be purchased. These are: (1) copper skillets, (2) handcarved salt and pepper sets, and (3) coffee makers. The copper skillets cost $6.50 each and retail for $15.00. The buyer believes that the demand in the coming year for these skillets will be normally distributed with a mean of 50 and a standard deviation of 10. Any skillets unsold at the end of the year will be disposed of at 10 percent below cost. The salt and pepper sets cost $8.00 each and retail for $25.00. The buyer feels that he will not sell less than 50 of these sets or more than 200. Any number between these two values seems equally likely. Sets not sold by the end of the year will be disposed of at 20 percent below cost. The coffee makers cost $3.50 each and retail for $9.00. The buyer believes the demand for this item is normally distributed with a mean of 100 and a standard deviation of 15. Any units unsold at the end of the year can be disposed of at cost. The buyer has an open to buy of $1600 (i.e., he can spend up to $1600 on these three items). How many units of each item should he procure?

If the buyer purchases h_i units of item i his expected profit $\mathcal{G}_i(h_i)$ will have the form (6-5). He desires to maximize $\sum \mathcal{G}_i(h_i)$ subject to $\sum C_i h_i \leq 1600$, where C_i is the unit cost of item i. Introducing a Lagrange multiplier θ, we form the function

$$\mathcal{W} = \sum_{i=1}^{3} \mathcal{G}_i(h_i) + \theta \left[\sum_{i=1}^{3} C_i h_i - 1600 \right]$$

and the necessary conditions which the h_i^* must satisfy (if they are all positive) are

$$\frac{\partial \mathcal{W}}{\partial h_i} = 0 = \frac{\partial \mathcal{G}_i(h_i)}{\partial h_i} + \theta C_i$$

or in the notation of Sec. 6-2

$$F_i(h_i) = \frac{C_i - L_i - \theta C_i}{S_i - L_i}, \quad i = 1, 2, 3$$

Using the appropriate values for the individual items, we see that the necessary conditions become

Skillets: $\quad \Phi\left(\dfrac{h_1 - 50}{10}\right) = \dfrac{0.65 - 6.50\theta}{9.15}$

Salt and
Pepper Sets: $\quad \dfrac{1}{150}(200 - h_2) = \dfrac{1.60 - 8.00\theta}{18.60}$

Coffee
Makers: $\quad \Phi\left(\dfrac{h_3 - 100}{15}\right) = \dfrac{-3.50\theta}{5.50}$

In this problem, it does not follow that it will be optimal to use the entire budget. However, one sees immediately from the coffee maker equation that if there was no budget restriction (i.e., $\theta = 0$) an infinite number of coffee makers would be purchased (why?). Thus θ must be different from 0. In particular, it is clear that θ must be negative. Table 6-1 presents the results of the numerical computations. To the accuracy with which rounding to integral values permits the computation to be made, one might select either $\theta = -0.99$ with $h_1 = 42$, $h_2 = 123$, $h_3 = 95$ or $\theta = -0.98$ with $h_1 = 43$, $h_2 = 124$, $h_3 = 95$. There would be no practical value in attempting to be more precise.

TABLE 6-1

Computational Results for Example

$-\theta$	h_1	h_2	h_3	Cost of units (dollars)
0.1	61	181	123	2275
0.2	58	174	117	2178
1.0	42	123	95	1590
0.99	42	123	95	1590
0.98	43	124	95	1604

6-5 Single Period Models with Time Dependent Costs

The single period model introduced in Sec. 6-2 did not involve any costs that were time dependent. We would now like to generalize that model to include carrying costs which are proportional to the length of time that a unit remains in inventory, and a stockout cost which is proportional to the length of time from the point when the demand occurs until the end of the period. As usual, the cost per unit year of keeping the item in stock will be written IC, where C is the unit cost of the item. Furthermore, as usual, $\hat{\pi}$ will be the cost per unit year of a stockout. When including these costs, one is forced to be somewhat less general than in Sec. 6-2, since it is necessary to introduce a distribution for the demand from the beginning of the period to any time t in the period. The only case that can be worked out easily when the variables are treated as discrete is that where demand is Poisson distributed over any time period. This is the case we shall examine.

Consider first the case where the mean rate of demand λ is constant over time, and the length of the period is fixed and is not a random variable. Then if h units are on hand at the beginning of the period, the expected on hand inventory at time t is from A3-11

$$\sum_{x=0}^{h} (h - x)p(x; \lambda t) = h - \lambda t + \lambda t P(h; \lambda t) - hP(h + 1; \lambda t) \quad (6\text{-}12)$$

and the expected inventory carrying charges for the period are

$$
\begin{aligned}
ICD(h) &= IC \int_0^T [h - \lambda t + \lambda t P(h; \lambda t) - hP(h + 1; \lambda t)]\, dt \\
&= IC \left\{ hT - \frac{\lambda T^2}{2} + \frac{\lambda T^2}{2} P(h; \lambda T) - \frac{h(h + 1)}{2\lambda} P(h + 2; \lambda T) \right. \\
&\qquad\qquad \left. - hTP(h + 1; \lambda T) + \frac{h(h + 1)}{\lambda} P(h + 2; \lambda T) \right\} \\
&= ICT \left\{ h - \frac{\lambda T}{2} + \frac{\lambda T}{2} P(h; \lambda T) - hP(h + 1; \lambda T) \right. \\
&\qquad\qquad\qquad \left. + \frac{h(h + 1)}{2\lambda T} P(h + 2; \lambda T) \right\} \quad (6\text{-}13)
\end{aligned}
$$

by A3-18, A3-19.

If at time t the demand has exceeded h by y, then between t and $t + dt$ the variable stockout cost incurred is $\hat{\pi}y\, dt$. The expected value of y at time t is by A3-10, A3-13

$$\sum_{x=h}^{\infty} (x - h)p(x; \lambda t) = \lambda t P(h; \lambda t) - hP(h + 1; \lambda t)$$

and the expected time dependent stockout cost for the period is $\hat{\pi}B(h)$ where

$$B(h) = \int_0^T [\lambda t P(h; \lambda t) - h P(h + 1; \lambda t)]\, dt$$

$$= \frac{\lambda T^2}{2} P(h; \lambda T) - hTP(h + 1; \lambda T) + \frac{h(h + 1)}{2\lambda} P(h + 2; \lambda T) \quad (6\text{-}14)$$

Thus the cost terms which must be added to (6-2) are

$$ICT\left[h - \frac{\lambda T}{2}\right] + (IC + \hat{\pi})B(h) \quad (6\text{-}15)$$

Written out explicitly the expected profit becomes

$$\mathcal{G}(h) = (S - L)\mu - (C - L - ICT)h - \frac{1}{2} IC\lambda T^2 - \mu\left[S - L + \pi_0\right.$$

$$\left. - \frac{T}{2}(\hat{\pi} + IC)\right] P(h; \lambda T) + h[S - L + \pi_0 \quad (6\text{-}16)$$

$$- T(\hat{\pi} + IC)]P(h + 1; \lambda T) + \frac{IC + \hat{\pi}}{2\lambda} h(h + 1)P(h + 2; \lambda T)$$

where $\mu = \lambda T$. Then

$$\Delta\mathcal{G}(h) = -(C - L - ICT) + \left[S - L + \pi_0\right.$$

$$\left. + \left(\frac{h}{\lambda} - T\right)(\hat{\pi} + IC)\right] P(h; \lambda T) - \frac{h}{\lambda}(\hat{\pi} + IC)p(h; \lambda T) \quad (6\text{-}17)$$

The largest h for which $\Delta\mathcal{G}(h)$ is positive will be optimal. It is not so simple to determine the optimal h using (6-17) as it is to use (6-4). However, it only involves a straightforward tabulation and can usually be carried out quite quickly.

The reader should be careful not to misinterpret the stockout cost $\hat{\pi}B(h)$. It is not normally a backorder cost incurred while waiting for the arrival of the next procurement, since, usually, demands occurring when the system is out of stock are not backordered, or if they are, the backorder cost will not be time dependent. This cost usually arises in a different way. For example, the item may be a spare part for a machine which is used to turn out some product. Then $\hat{\pi}$ will be the rate at which revenue is lost if a machine must halt operation for lack of the spare part.

Often in situations where the type of model under discussion would be useful, the date of obsolescence is not known with certainty. It must be described by a probability distribution. For example, one might assume that the time to obsolescence has a gamma distribution. Then in place of the Poisson terms in (6-16) the negative binomial distribution will appear. We leave for Problem 6-13 the derivation of the equivalent of (6-17) when the length of the period is gamma distributed. Frequently, it is difficult to estimate reliably what the nature of a continuous density function for the length of the period should look like. About the best that can be done is to select n times T_j at which the period may end, and assign probabilities ω_j that the period will end at times T_j. Then if $\mathcal{G}(h, T_j)$ is the expected profit when h units are on hand at the beginning of the period and the length of the period is T_j, the expected cost (averaged over the possible period lengths) is

$$\mathcal{G}(h) = \sum_{j=1}^{n} \omega_j \mathcal{G}(h, T_j) \tag{6-18}$$

It is desired to determine the h which maximizes $\mathcal{G}(h)$. This h is the largest h for which

$$\Delta \mathcal{G}(h) = \sum_{j=1}^{n} \omega_j \Delta \mathcal{G}(h, T_j) \tag{6-19}$$

is positive. Each $\Delta \mathcal{G}(h, T_j)$ has the form (6-17) (with T replaced by T_j). Of course, the determination of h^* is now more complicated than in the determination of h^* using (6-17).

One final generalization of the model is often needed. The mean rate of demand will now be allowed to vary with time. Imagine a curve is available giving the cumulative mean demand $D(t)$ from the beginning of the period until time t. It will be assumed that the cumulative demand up to time t is Poisson distributed with mean $D(t)$. Then write $D(t) = t\lambda(t)$. If the rate of demand remained constant at the value $\lambda(t)$ from the beginning of the period until time t, then there would be the same probability of having x units demanded by time t as in the case when the mean rate of demand changes with time and the expected mean demand up to time t is $D(t)$.

Let us first consider the case where the mean rate of demand can vary with time, but the length of the period is fixed at the value T. To compute the optimal quantity to have on hand at the beginning of the period, it is convenient to subdivide the period into m subperiods, subperiod i extending from time t_{i-1} to t_i ($t_0 = 0$, $t_m = T$). Within each subperiod i the mean rate of demand will be assumed constant at the value $\lambda_i = \lambda(t_i)$. By choosing $t_i - t_{i-1}$ sufficiently small, the approximation made by taking the rate of demand to be constant within each subperiod, will come arbitrarily close to representing the actual time pattern of demands.

Then the expected cost of holding inventory, and the expected time variable stockout costs in subperiod i are respectively

$$IC \int_{t_{i-1}}^{t_i} [h - \lambda_i t + \lambda_i t P(h; \lambda_i t) - h P(h+1; \lambda_i t)] \, dt = IC t_i \left[h - \frac{\lambda_i t_i}{2} \right]$$

$$- IC t_{i-1} \left[h - \frac{\lambda_i t_{i-1}}{2} \right] + IC[\mathcal{C}(h, t_i, \lambda_i) - \mathcal{C}(h, t_{i-1}, \lambda_i)] \quad (6\text{-}20)$$

and

$$\hat{\pi}[\mathcal{C}(h, t_i, \lambda_i) - \mathcal{C}(h, t_{i-1}, \lambda_i)] \quad (6\text{-}21)$$

where

$$\mathcal{C}(h, t, \lambda) = \frac{\lambda t^2}{2} P(h; \lambda t) - ht P(h+1; \lambda t) + \frac{h(h+1)}{2\lambda} P(h+2; \lambda t) \quad (6\text{-}22)$$

These results follow from (6-13) and (6-14) on breaking the integral from t_{i-1} to t_i into the integral from 0 to t_i minus the integral from 0 to t_{i-1}.

The expected profit for the period is then

$$\mathcal{G}(h) = (S - L)\mu - (C - L - ICT)h - \frac{1}{2} IC \sum_{i=1}^{m} \lambda_i (t_i^2 - t_{i-1}^2)$$

$$- \mu(S - L + \pi_0)P(h; \lambda T) + h(S - L + \pi_0)P(h+1; \lambda T) \quad (6\text{-}23)$$

$$+ (\hat{\pi} + IC) \sum_{i=1}^{m} [\mathcal{C}(h, t_i, \lambda_i) - \mathcal{C}(h, t_{i-1}, \lambda_i)]$$

The optimal h is then the largest h which yields a positive value for the following expression for $\Delta \mathcal{G}(h)$.

$$\Delta \mathcal{G}(h) = -(C - L - ICT) + (S - L + \pi_0)P(h; \lambda T)$$

$$+ (\hat{\pi} + IC)h \sum_{i=1}^{m} \frac{1}{\lambda_i} [P(h; \lambda_i t_i) - P(h; \lambda_i t_{i-1})]$$

$$\qquad\qquad (6\text{-}24)$$

$$- (\hat{\pi} + IC) \sum_{i=1}^{m} [t_i P(h; \lambda_i t_i) - t_{i-1} P(h; \lambda_i t_{i-1})]$$

$$- (\hat{\pi} + IC)h \sum_{i=1}^{m} \frac{1}{\lambda_i} [p(h; \lambda_i t_i) - p(h; \lambda_i t_{i-1})]$$

Again the optimal h can be found by tabulation, although the task could be quite arduous to carry out by hand. Several of the expressions in (6-24) such as $P(h; \lambda_i t_i) - P(h; \lambda_i t_{i-1})$ involve the difference of two terms which are almost equal. In Problem 6-14 we ask the reader to show how Taylor's expansion can be used to simplify such terms and thus yield a considerably simpler expression for $\Delta \mathcal{G}(h)$.

A variable mean rate of demand can be combined with a situation in which the length of the period is a discrete random variable having n

possible values T_j, with the probability of T_j being ω_j. For each T_j there will in general be a different function describing the mean rate of demand over time. We can then obtain expressions like (6-23), (6-24) for each possible T_j. Let $\mathcal{G}(h, T_j)$ be the expected profit if the length of the period is T_j. To obtain $\mathcal{G}(h, T_j)$ from (6-23), T is replaced by T_j, λ_i by λ_{ij}, and m by m_j (for each j we may wish to use a different number of subperiods). Then

$$\mathcal{G}(h) = \sum_{j=1}^{n} \omega_j \mathcal{G}(h, T_j) \tag{6-25}$$

and

$$\Delta\mathcal{G}(h) = \sum_{j=1}^{n} \omega_j \Delta\mathcal{G}(h, T_j) \tag{6-26}$$

The task of determining the optimal h from (6-26) will usually involve too much work to be done manually. However, it can be done quite easily on a digital computer. It is not easy to allow the mean rate of demand to be time dependent if the length of the period is described by a continuous density function. We ask the reader in Problem 6-15 to explain why this is so. Models of the type presented in this section have been discussed in [4, 5].

6-6 Marginal Analysis

In Sec. 6-2 we determined $\Delta\mathcal{G}(h)$ by first computing $\mathcal{G}(h)$ and then finding the difference $\mathcal{G}(h) - \mathcal{G}(h - 1)$. In economic terms $\Delta\mathcal{G}(h)$ is the change in expected profits if we change the number of units on hand at the beginning of the period from $h - 1$ to h. It will be profitable to add the extra unit so long as $\Delta\mathcal{G}(h) > 0$. We now wish to point out that it is easy to compute $\Delta\mathcal{G}(h)$ directly without first computing the expected cost. Note that $\Delta\mathcal{G}(h)$ is the expected change in revenue from sales minus the expected change in cost plus the expected change in income from liquidation sale minus the expected change in stockout costs.

Now the expected change in revenue from sales is S if the additional unit is sold and 0 otherwise. The probability that the unit will be sold is the probability that the demand will be $\geq h$, i.e., $P(h)$. Thus the expected increase in revenue is $SP(h)$. The change in cost is simply C, the cost of the unit. The increase in revenue on liquidation will be L if the additional unit is not sold, and 0 otherwise. The probability that the unit will not be sold is $[1 - P(h)]$ and the expected gain of liquidation revenue is $L[1 - P(h)]$. Finally, note that on adding an additional unit, expected stockout costs must be reduced or left unchanged so that the change in expected stockout cost must be non-positive. The change will be $-\pi_0$ if the additional unit is demanded (i.e., the stockout cost is avoided on this unit) and 0 otherwise. Hence the expected change in stockout cost is $-\pi_0 P(h)$. Therefore

$$\Delta \mathcal{G}(h) = SP(h) - C + L[1 - P(h)] - (-\pi_0)P(h)$$

$$= (S + \pi_0 - L)P(h) - (C - L) \qquad (6\text{-}27)$$

which is precisely (6-3). We have thus obtained $\Delta \mathcal{G}(h)$ without ever having written down the expected cost.

What we have introduced above is, of course, nothing but the marginal analysis so familiar to economists. Marginal analysis is a very useful tool for deriving optimizing conditions, and is applicable to a very wide variety of problems. In particular, marginal analysis can be used to obtain the optimizing conditions for most of the models discussed in the previous sections. The essential feature of marginal analysis is that one examines what happens when a unit change is made in the variable under consideration. As another simple example, consider the order up to R model for the backorders case discussed in Sec. 5-2. Observe that $\Delta \mathcal{K}(R)$ is equal to the expected change in carrying costs plus the expected change in backorder costs on changing from $R - 1$ to R. Now when the time over which backorders exist is negligible, then adding an additional unit implies that it will be carried in inventory essentially all the time, and the expected change in annual carrying costs will be IC. The change per period in the backorder cost is $-\pi$ if the additional unit is demanded in the period and 0 otherwise. Thus, per period, the change in expected backorder cost is $-\pi \hat{H}(R; T)$, and per year is $-\pi \hat{H}(R; T)/T$. Therefore

$$\Delta \mathcal{K}(R) = IC - \frac{\pi}{T} \hat{H}(R; T) \qquad (6\text{-}28)$$

which is the same as (5-7).

Unfortunately, it is not always so easy to carry out the marginal analysis as it was in the above two simple examples. The analysis is usually fairly straightforward as long as there are no time dependent costs. It may become more complicated, however, when time dependent costs must be included. The inventory carrying cost in the above example was a time dependent cost. The analysis was made simple because of the assumption that the unit remained in stock essentially all the time.

The simple deterministic model of Sec. 2-4 is also easy to analyze by marginal analysis. It illustrates, however, a case where it is difficult to proceed without having first evaluated the cost terms. Note that $\Delta \mathcal{K}(Q)$ is the sum of the change in ordering costs and the change in carrying costs on going from $Q - 1$ to Q. The average annual change in the carrying cost is simply

$$\lambda A \left[\frac{1}{Q} - \frac{1}{Q-1} \right] = \frac{-\lambda A}{Q(Q-1)}$$

and, since the average inventory is $(Q-1)/2$, the average annual change in carrying costs is $IC/2$. Summation of these two terms yields the proper expression for $\Delta \mathcal{K}(Q)$. In this case, however, marginal analysis did little to simplify the analysis, since one essentially had to have the cost terms to difference them. In essence, one could not analyze the effects of adding one unit without considering its effects on the costs associated with the other $Q-1$ units.

The computation of $\Delta_r B(Q, r)$ for the model of Sec. 4-7 by marginal analysis provides an illustration of a case where it is easy to handle a time dependent cost. Consider $\Delta_r B(Q, r)$. If the inventory position of the system is j units above the reorder point at time $t - \tau$, then in going from $r - 1$ to r, the expected number of backorders at time t will be reduced by one if the extra unit is demanded and will be unchanged otherwise. The probability that the extra unit is demanded is $P(r + j; \lambda \tau)$. Thus

$$\Delta_r B(Q, r) = \frac{1}{Q} \sum_{j=1}^{Q} P(r + j; \lambda \tau) \qquad (6\text{-}29)$$

This expression can be simplified using the Poisson properties. The direct computation of $\Delta_Q B(Q, r)$ by marginal analysis is more tricky and the reader is asked to try it in Problem 6-16.

Marginal analysis is often a helpful way to look at a problem. In some cases it can simplify considerably the amount of work required to obtain the optimization conditions. In other cases the analysis is so complicated that no great savings in time results. In principle, however, marginal analysis could be used to obtain the optimization equations for all the models developed thus far in this book. Of course, often it is desired to have an explicit expression for the profit or cost, and in this case, the potential savings in labor by use of marginal analysis to avoid computing the profit or cost expression are not realized. In such cases, however, marginal analysis can be helpful in checking the result obtained by directly differencing the cost or profit expression. Infinitesimal marginal analysis can be used when the variables are treated as continuous. Here one considers the change on going from say x to $x + dx$. Some examples of infinitesimal marginal analysis are considered in the problems.

REFERENCES

1. Bowman, E. H., and R. B. Fetter, *Analysis for Production Management*, Rev. Ed., Homewood, Illinois: Richard D. Irwin, Inc., 1961.

Chapter 10 is devoted to incremental analysis. The procedure given is not rigorous when the variables are discrete, since the authors assume that the optimizing condition has the marginal profit equal to zero, whereas it is not necessarily true that it can be zero when the variables are discrete. This point is not of great importance for the types of problems which they consider, however.

2. Fetter, R. B., and W. C. Dalleck, *Decision Models for Inventory Management.* Homewood, Illinois: Richard D. Irwin, Inc., 1961.

3. Geisler, M. A., and H. W. Karr, "A Fruitful Application of Static Marginal Analysis," *Management Science,* Vol. 2, No. 4, July, 1956, pp. 313–326.

4. Hadley, G., and T. M. Whitin, "An Optimal Final Inventory Model," *Management Science,* Vol. 7, No. 2, January, 1961, pp. 179–183.

5. Hadley, G., "Generalizations of the Optimal Final Inventory Model," *Management Science,* Vol. 8, No. 4, July, 1962, pp. 454–457.

PROBLEMS

6-1. A dealer in Christmas trees is attempting to determine how many to stock. Past experience indicates that demand will be normally distributed with a mean of 200 and a variance of 300. The dealer sells a tree for $7.50 and it costs him $4.00. Any trees not sold are a complete loss. How many trees should he procure to maximize his expected profit? What is his expected profit if he purchased a number of trees equal to the expected demand? What is the expected number of trees that will remain unsold if he procures the optimal number of trees?

6-2. Solve Problem 6-1 under the assumption that the distribution of demand is uniform with the same mean and variance given in Problem 6-1.

6-3. Consider a low demand item which is to be produced only once. This item is to be used in a system which will be obsolete in a number of years. The date of obsolescence is not known with certainty, but there have been assigned probabilities 0.5, 0.3, 0.2 that it will become obsolete at the end of the fifth, sixth, and seventh years respectively. The number of units demanded in any time period is expected to be Poisson distributed with a mean rate of 1 per year. The item costs $50.00 and has no scrap value. All items not used when the system becomes obsolete will be scrapped. The cost of each stockout is

$3000. How many items should be stocked to minimize the expected costs? What is the expected number of items that will be scrapped?

6-4. Show that Eq. (6-5) is a concave function of x. A function $f(x)$ is said to be concave if $f[\alpha x_1 + (1 - \alpha)x_2] \geq \alpha f(x_1) + (1 - \alpha)f(x_2)$ for all α, $0 \leq \alpha \leq 1$, and all x_1, x_2 in the relevant interval of interest. Note that if $f(x)$ is concave, $-f(x)$ is convex (see Problems 2-6, 2-7). We say that $f(x)$ is strictly concave if $-f(x)$ is strictly convex. Under what circumstances is $\mathcal{G}(h)$ strictly concave? Prove that any relative minimum of $\mathcal{G}(h)$ is also the absolute minimum. Also prove when $\mathcal{G}(h)$ is strictly concave, then the absolute minimum is unique.

6-5. Under what circumstances is the solution to Eq. (6-6) not unique? Illustrate this geometrically.

6-6. An international oil company is buying a large tanker for moving crude from the Middle East to the United States. Spare parts such as rudders must be made when the ship is built. They are very expensive to obtain later. Consider one particular part of the steering gear. This part costs $5000 each when procured at the time the ship is constructed and $25,000 each if procured later. Past experience on other ships has indicated that the number of units demanded in any time period will be Poisson distributed with a mean of 0.2 per year. The useful life of the ship cannot be determined precisely ahead of time, but it is expected to be gamma distributed with a mean of 20 years and a standard deviation of 10 years. From the available information, how many spares of the item under consideration should be purchased when the ship is built?

6-7. Show how to incorporate "all units" quantity discounts in the model of Sec. 6-2. Assume that the selling price remains constant. Devise a procedure for computing the optimal order quantity. Sketch curves equivalent to those of Fig. 2-13 for the case at hand.

6-8. Show how to incorporate incremental quantity discounts in the model of Sec. 6-2. Devise a procedure for computing the optimal order quantity. Assume that the selling price remains constant. Sketch curves equivalent to those of Fig. 2-15 for the case at hand.

6-9. Solve Problem 6-1 under the assumption that "all units" quantity discounts are available. If a quantity h is purchased, the unit cost is $4.00 if $0 < h < 225$, $3.00 if $225 \leq h < \infty$.

6-10. Solve Problem 6-1 under the assumption that incremental quantity discounts are available. The first 225 trees cost $4.00 each and additional trees cost $3.00 each.

6-11. Consider Problem 6-1. Assume that "all units" quantity discounts are available. If a quantity h is purchased, the unit cost is \$4.00 if $0 < h < q$, and \$3.50 if $q \leq h < \infty$. Determine the value of q such that the optimal order quantity occurs at the price break. For what range of q values will \$4.00 be the optimal unit cost. For what range of q values will \$3.50 be the optimal unit cost.

6-12. The buyer of a large West Coast department store must decide what quantity of a high priced women's leather handbag to procure in Italy for the coming Christmas season. The unit cost of the handbag to the store is \$17.50 and it will retail for \$50.00. The buyer is confident that all handbags not sold by the end of the season can be disposed of at cost. However, for every dollar invested in a handbag not sold at the end of the season, the buyer feels that he is really losing \$0.30 since the dollar invested in something else could have yielded this gross profit. The buyer believes that he will sell more than 50 of the handbags but not more than 250. Sales of any number within these limits seem equally likely. How many handbags should the buyer procure? Suppose now that, after discussions with other buyers, he can sharpen his sales estimate to a point where he believes sales will be normally distributed with mean 175 and a standard deviation of 20. Now what is the optimal quantity to procure? How much was it worth to the buyer to gain the additional information?

6-13. Consider the model described in Sec. 6-5 whose expected profit is given by (6-16). Suppose now that the length of the period is gamma distributed. Determine the expected profit $\mathcal{G}(h)$ and $\Delta\mathcal{G}(h)$.

6-14. Recall that for a first order approximation in $\Delta t = t_1 - t_0$, Taylor's theorem reads $f(t_1) - f(t_0) = f'(t_0)\Delta t$, where $f'(t_0)$ is the derivative of f with respect to t evaluated at t_0. Use this result to simplify $P(h; \lambda_i t_i) - P(h; \lambda_i t_{i-1})$, $t_i P(h; \lambda_i t_i) - t_{i-1}P(h; \lambda_i t_{i-1})$, $p(h; \lambda_i t_i) - p(h; \lambda_i t_{i-1})$ and $t_i p(h; \lambda_i t_i) - t_{i-1}p(h; \lambda_i t_{i-1})$. What does Eq. (6-24) reduce to in this case? Why is it now much easier to evaluate numerically?

6-15. Point out the problems involved in attempting to allow the length of the period to be a continuous random variable when the mean rate of demand is also allowed to change with time.

6-16. Attempt to compute $\Delta_Q B(Q, r)$ by marginal analysis, $B(Q, r)$ being the backorders term for the model of Sec. 4-7.

6-17. Derive Eq. (6-6) by computing directly the change in expected profits when the quantity procured is changed from h to $h + dh$.

6-18. The demand for a spare engine part is expected to behave in accordance with a Poisson distribution with mean rate 0.01 units per day. After 600 days elapse, it is known that the part will be obsolete and will be scrapped for $200 less than its original cost. The costs of carrying the unit in inventory amount to $0.10 per unit per day. If parts are not available when engines break down, the daily costs of idle time are $900 per part needed and not in stock. What number of spare parts should be acquired in advance for the 600 day period of usage if all parts must be purchased at this time?

6-19. A farmer has to decide on which crops to take into the city on his weekly trip. He has more than enough ripe crops to fill his truck which can carry only 8000 lbs. of vegetables. Cabbage, cauliflower, and tomato crops are the farmer's leading candidates. The demands for these three crops (in pounds) are normally distributed with means 1000, 3000, and 2000 respectively. The corresponding standard deviations are 200, 300, and 400. If the crops are not sold they are worthless, while the profits per pound are 4 cents for cabbage, 6 cents for cauliflower, and 7 cents for tomatoes. How should the farmer load his truck to maximize expected profits?

6-20. A dressmaker is interested in buying a special type of imported fabric for manufacture for the coming one week fiesta season. The fabric must be ordered well in advance of the fiesta. The dressmaker knows that one-third of the customers are willing to wait for the cloth to be made into dresses while the remaining two-thirds would take their business elsewhere. The number of customers is equally likely to be any number from 101 to 200. The cost of making the fabric into dresses is $20 per dress made in advance of the season and $30 per dress made during the season. The dresses sell for $100 each. Any fabric remaining in stock at the end of the season can be returned at $15 per dress unit, while finished dresses can be sold after the season for $50. What is the optimum number of (dress) units of fabric to purchase? What number of dresses should be completed before the season? What is the expected value of the dressmaker's profits?

6-21. Suppose the dressmaker in Problem 6-20 must make all the dresses in advance of the season (either because a negligible fraction of customers will wait or because too much time or incremental expense is involved in making them during the season). What is the optimal number of dresses to make. What profits are expected?

6-22. Given that demand for a spare part is Poisson distributed with mean 0.1 units per day and two alternative modes of delivery, namely two days and eight days at costs of $18.00 and $10.00 per unit respectively.

The incremental costs incurred when a unit is demanded but not in stock are $5.00 per unit per day and the inventory carrying charges per unit per day are $1.00. Parts demanded but not in stock are backordered. Design an inventory control system which minimizes the sum of stockout costs, inventory carrying charges, and transportation costs, assuming that only one of the two modes of transportation can be used. What does such a system cost per average day of operation? For what transportation cost for the two-day model would the average cost per day be equal?

6-23. Assume in a one-period model that a cost of A_i is incurred for each of N warehouses ($i = 1, 2, \ldots, N$) in which the quantity demanded exceeds stock on hand. Obtain a rule for allocating x units to the N warehouses in order to minimize the expected value of the cost, when the demand at each warehouse is a stochastic variable. Suppose that the cost of stockouts was B_i per unit demanded but not in stock. How should the x units be allocated in order to minimize the stockout costs? (Assume continuous probability density functions).

6-24. A hula hoop manufacturer can store finished hoops, or plastic which can be made into hoops in a week. Only one-third of his customers are willing to wait for the hoops to be manufactured. Assume that there is one discrete time period under consideration and that the probability density function is uniform from 100 to 200 (0 elsewhere). Finished hoops have no liquidation value. The plastic for one hoop costs $0.50 and can be sold as surplus for $0.20. Manufacturing costs are $0.10 per hoop. The hoops are sold for $1.20 each. What is the optimal number of hoops to stock? What amount of plastic should be stored in unfinished form?

6-25. The probability density function for sales volume during a given period is $f(v) = \frac{3}{2500} v^2(10 - v)$, $0 < v < 10$, and the units are in hundreds of pieces. The cost of raw material is $3.00 per item with an added cost of $2.00 per item for manufacturing cost. The raw material is made up only as orders are received and raw material not used up will be sold for scrap at $1.00 per piece. Find an expression for the number of items of raw material that should be ordered at the beginning of the period as a function of the mark-up price M per item when expected profits are maximized. The raw material must be on hand at the beginning of the period.

6-26. In Example 2 of Sec. 6-3, calculate the differences between $\mathcal{G}(h^*)$ and $\mathcal{G}(\mu)$ associated with differences in expected profits on units sold, expected losses on units not sold, and expected losses of goodwill on units demanded but not in stock.

6-27. Assume in Example 3 of Sec. 6-3 that a goodwill loss of $1.00 per rabbit demanded but not in stock is incurred. What is the increase in optimal stock? What is the change in expected profits?

6-28. Consider the computational procedure discussed in Sec. 6-4 for handling constrained problems when the variables are treated as discrete. Under what circumstances is the procedure exact? When it is not exact, under what circumstances should it yield a good approximation?

6-29. Discuss the relationship between Eq. (6-4) and Eq. (4-116) with $\pi = 0$ for steady state models with $Q = 1$. Why should they be of the same form?

6-30. Show for the general single period model discussed in Sec. 6-2 that h^* is the solution to

$$F(h) = \frac{c_1}{c_1 + c_2}$$

where h is treated as continuous, where c_1, c_2 are the cost of overage and underage respectively. Derive this equation by incremental analysis by balancing the expected cost of overage against the expected cost of underage. What is the corresponding result in the discrete case? What are c_1, c_2 in terms of π_0, C, L, S?

DYNAMIC

INVENTORY MODELS

"When we mean to build,

We first survey the plot, then draw the model;

And when we see the figure of the house,

Which if we find outweighs ability,

What do we then but draw anew the model

in fewer offices?"

Shakespeare, Henry IV, Part II.

7-1 Introduction

In a strict sense, steady state conditions are a fiction in the real world. The essential characteristic of all economic systems is that they are continually changing with time. For inventory systems, the processes generating demands and lead times change with time, as do the various costs of interest, and even the items carried by the system. In many cases, however, the changes occur slowly enough so that for considerable lengths of time the system can be treated as if it were in a steady state mode of operation. In other instances, however, the changes occur with such rapidity that they must be explicitly accounted for. Usually it is the changes in the process generating demands which are most important. It is the purpose of this chapter to study multi-period models in which the mean rate of demand changes with time.

As might be expected, the difficulty of formulating and obtaining numerical solutions to realistic dynamic inventory models is considerably greater than for the case where it was permissible to assume that the system was in steady state. In fact, when demand is treated as a stochastic variable whose mean is time dependent, only the most trivial problems can be solved manually. Usually a large digital computer is needed to obtain numerical results. The natural formalism for setting up dynamic models in a form for numerical computations is dynamic programming.

Before turning to dynamic inventory models themselves, we shall first introduce dynamic programming and cover the topics in this subject that will be needed here.

7-2 Dynamic Programming

Consider the problem of determining non-negative integers x_j which minimize the function $g(x_1, \ldots, x_n)$ defined by

$$g(x_1, \ldots, x_n) = \sum_{j=1}^{n} f_j(x_j) = f_1(x_1) + f_2(x_2) + \ldots + f_n(x_n) \qquad (7\text{-}1)$$

323

subject to the constraint

$$\sum_{j=1}^{n} v_j x_j \leq V \tag{7-2}$$

where the v_j, V are specified constants, and $f_j(x_j)$ is a function of x_j only. We shall assume that the v_j, V are integers. There is no real loss in generality in doing so, since by proper choice of the physical dimensions (i.e., perhaps using cubic centimeters instead of cubic feet), it is always possible to obtain an arbitrary degree of accuracy with the v_j, V being integers. The single period, multi-item problems subject to a constraint, such as the flyaway-kit problem discussed in Chapter 6, are special cases of the general problem just formulated.

We shall introduce dynamic programming by studying how one might attempt to solve numerically a problem such as that formulated above. The important thing to notice is that we can minimize over the variables in any way we choose, provided that the procedure we select does permit the examination of all possible combinations of values for all the variables, if necessary. Suppose then that we proceed as follows: We select a value of x_n and we minimize g over $x_1, \ldots, x_{n-1}$ for this given value of x_n. By (7-2), we see that the variables $x_1, \ldots, x_{n-1}$ must satisfy

$$\sum_{j=1}^{n-1} v_j x_j \leq V - v_n x_n \tag{7-3}$$

so that the allowable range of variation for $x_1, \ldots, x_{n-1}$ will depend on the value of x_n selected. Note that the value selected for x_n can only have the integral values $0, 1, 2, \ldots, [V/v_n]$, where $[V/v_n]$ denotes the largest integer less than or equal to V/v_n.

Now*

$$\min_{x_1, \ldots, x_{n-1}} g = f(x_n) + \min_{x_1, \ldots, x_{n-1}} \sum_{j=1}^{n-1} f_j(x_j) \tag{7-4}$$

and in computing

$$\min_{x_1, \ldots, x_{n-1}} \sum_{j=1}^{n-1} f_j(x_j) \tag{7-5}$$

$x_1, \ldots, x_{n-1}$ must satisfy (7-3). We can observe that the minimum value expressed by (7-5) will depend on $V - v_n x_n$ because of (7-3). Denote (7-5) by $Z_{n-1}(V - v_n x_n)$. Then $Z_{n-1}(V - v_n x_n)$ is the minimum of $\sum_{j=1}^{n-1} f_j(x_j)$

---

* The notation $\min_{x_1, \ldots, x_{n-1}} g$ will be taken to mean the absolute minimum of $g(x_1, \ldots, x_n)$ over $x_1, \ldots, x_{n-1}$ for a fixed value of x_n.

for non-negative integers which satisfy (7-3). Equation (7-4) can therefore be written

$$\min_{x_1, \ldots, x_{n-1}} g = f(x_n) + Z_{n-1}(V - v_n x_n) \tag{7-6}$$

If g^* is the optimal value of g, we see that

$$g^* = \min_{x_n} \left[f_n(x_n) + Z_{n-1}(V - v_n x_n) \right] \tag{7-7}$$

Hence, if we knew the function $Z_{n-1}(\xi)$ for all integral arguments ξ from 0 to V, we could determine g^* simply by computing $f_n(0) + Z_{n-1}(V)$, $f_n(1) + Z_{n-1}(V - v_n)$, $f_n(2) + Z_{n-1}(V - 2v_n)$, etc., up to $x_n = [V/v_n]$, and picking the smallest of these. We would simultaneously determine x_n^*, the optimal value of x_n, in doing so.

The question then arises as to how we determine $Z_{n-1}(\xi)$ for any argument ξ. By definition

$$Z_{n-1}(\xi) = \min_{x_1, \ldots, x_{n-1}} \sum_{j=1}^{n-1} f_j(x_j) \tag{7-8}$$

for non-negative integers x_j, $j = 1, \ldots, n-1$, satisfying

$$\sum_{j=1}^{n-1} v_j x_j \leq \xi$$

We can now resort to the same trick as above. Suppose that we pick a value of x_{n-1}, and minimize $\sum_{j=1}^{n-1} f_j(x_j)$ over $x_1, \ldots, x_{n-2}$ for non-negative integers x_j, $j = 1, \ldots, n-2$, satisfying

$$\sum_{j=1}^{n-2} v_j x_j \leq \xi - v_{n-1} x_{n-1}$$

For any argument ξ, let us now define the function $Z_{n-2}(\xi)$ by

$$Z_{n-2}(\xi) = \min_{x_1, \ldots, x_{n-2}} \sum_{j=1}^{n-2} f_j(x_j) \tag{7-9}$$

for non-negative integers x_j, $j = 1, \ldots, n-2$, satisfying

$$\sum_{j=1}^{n-2} v_j x_j \leq \xi \tag{7-10}$$

Then

$$Z_{n-1}(\xi) = \min_{x_{n-1}} \left[f_{n-1}(x_{n-1}) + Z_{n-2}(\xi - v_{n-1} x_{n-1}) \right] \tag{7-11}$$

We can continue working down in this way until we are reduced to evaluating

$$Z_1(\xi) = \min_{x_1} f_1(x_1) \tag{7-12}$$

for non-negative integers x_1 satisfying $x_1 \leq [\xi/v_1]$. It is a straightforward task to evaluate $Z_1(\xi)$ for any given ξ. We need the value of $Z_1(\xi)$ in general for all integers ξ between 0 and V (if this is not clear to the reader now it will be later). Once we have a table giving $Z_1(\xi)$ as a function we can then compute a table giving $Z_2(\xi)$ by use of

$$Z_2(\xi) = \min_{x_2} [f_2(x_2) + Z_1(\xi - v_2 x_2)]$$

Then we can compute a table giving $Z_3(\xi)$, etc., until finally from the table for $Z_{n-1}(\xi)$ we obtain g^* using (7-7).

Let us now repeat the computational procedure for determining g^*, and at the same time indicate how $x_1^*, \ldots, x_n^*$ are determined. We define the sequence of functions

$$Z_k(\xi) = \min_{x_1, \ldots, x_k} \sum_{j=1}^{k} f_j(x_j), \quad k = 1, \ldots, n \qquad (7\text{-}13)$$

for non-negative integers $x_j, j = 1, \ldots, k$, satisfying

$$\sum_{j=1}^{k} v_j x_j \leq \xi \qquad (7\text{-}14)$$

Then

$$g^* = Z_n(V) \qquad (7\text{-}15)$$

and the $Z_k(\xi)$ can be computed recursively using the recurrence relation

$$Z_k(\xi) = \min_{0 \leq x_k \leq \left[\frac{\xi}{v_k}\right]} [f_k(x_k) + Z_{k-1}(\xi - v_k x_k)], \quad k = 2, \ldots, n \qquad (7\text{-}16)$$

where in the minimization x_k can take on only integral values in the range shown. In order to compute $Z_k(\xi)$ for a given ξ, we will quite possibly need to know $Z_{k-1}(\eta)$ for all $\eta = 0, 1, \ldots, \xi$. But then in order to compute $Z_{k+1}(\zeta)$, we will quite possibly need $Z_k(\xi)$ for all $\xi = 0, 1, \ldots, \zeta$. Finally, since $g^* = Z_n(V)$, it follows that each $Z_k(\xi)$ may need to be known for all $\xi = 0, 1, 2, \ldots, V$.

The computational procedure can be thought of as an n stage process. At the first stage we compute a table of $Z_1(\xi)$ for $\xi = 0, 1, \ldots, V$, and at stage 2 a table of $Z_2(\xi)$, and finally at stage n the single value $Z_n(V)$. Note that once the table $Z_k(\xi)$ had been obtained the tables for $Z_i(\xi)$, $i < k$, are no longer needed.

In computing $Z_k(\xi)$ from (7-16) or $Z_1(\xi)$ from (7-12) we also obtain for each ξ the value of x_k which yields the minimum. Denote by $\hat{x}_k(\xi)$ the value of x_k which yields $Z_k(\xi)$ in (7-16) or (7-12). Suppose now that as we record the table of $Z_k(\xi)$ we also record a table of $\hat{x}_k(\xi)$. At the last step, when $Z_n(V)$ is computed, we automatically determine x_n^* and no table is recorded. However, we will have $n - 1$ tables giving the $\hat{x}_k(\xi)$ for $k = 1, \ldots, n - 1$. The question now is how do we determine $x_1^*, \ldots, x_{n-1}^*$ from these tables. This is done by working backwards from x_n^*. To find x_{n-1}^*, we only need to determine $\hat{x}_k(\xi)$ for $\xi = V - v_n x_n^*$, i.e., $x_{n-1}^* = \hat{x}_{n-1}(V - v_n x_n^*)$. Having determined x_{n-1}^* we are now able to compute x_{n-2}^* since $x_{n-2}^* = \hat{x}_{n-2}(V - v_n x_n^* - v_{n-1} x_{n-1}^*)$. We continue this procedure until finally we find that

$$x_1^* = \hat{x}_1 \left(V - \sum_{j=2}^{n} v_j x_j^* \right)$$

Thus in general

$$x_k^* = \hat{x}_k \left(V - \sum_{j=k+1}^{n} v_j x_j^* \right), \quad k = 1, \ldots, n - 1 \tag{7-17}$$

It is by no means true that the optimal solution must be unique, i.e., the $\hat{x}_k(\xi)$ functions need not be single valued. In numerical computations, if one finds at stage k that more than one value of x_k yields $Z_k(\xi)$, one can tabulate each x_k which yields the minimum, thus making it possible at the end to find all alternative optimal solutions, or simply tabulate one of these x_k, thus yielding finally only one of the alternative optimal solutions.

We have now presented a numerical procedure for solving exactly the problem formulated at the beginning of the section. The procedure can be considered to be an n stage process where at stage k we construct tables of $Z_k(\xi)$ and $\hat{x}_k(\xi)$ for each integer $\xi = 0, 1, 2, \ldots, V$. To obtain each entry in these tables, it is necessary to carry out a minimization over a single variable. If there are a large number of stages and if V is also a reasonably large integer, it is clear that the computational procedure would be beyond what could be done manually. The computational procedure suggested can usually be carried out quite easily and quickly using a digital computer. We might note, incidentally, that depending on the v_j values, it may not be necessary to evaluate $Z_k(\xi)$ for each integer ξ between 0 and V. However, the task of determining precisely what ξ are needed can be so complicated (it is necessary to work back from the last stage) that it is often simpler merely to tabulate $Z_k(\xi)$ for each integer in the range of interest. This is especially true if the problem is being solved on a computer.

An interesting and helpful physical interpretation can be given to the $Z_k(\xi)$. $Z_k(\xi)$ is the minimum cost if only stages $1, 2, \ldots, k$ existed, and the quantity of the limiting resource which could be devoted to these stages was ξ. The physical interpretation of (7-16) is that an optimal policy for k stages must have the property that whatever the choice of the decision variable for the kth stage, the policy must be optimal for the remaining $k - 1$ stages for this choice of x_k. Bellman [1] refers to this as the principle of optimality.

The amount of numerical work required using the dynamic programming formalism will in general be much less than if we simply attempted to determine the minimum by examining every possible combination of values which the variables could assume. We shall now illustrate the computational technique described above by a very simple example.

EXAMPLE Consider a grossly simplified flyaway-kit problem involving only three items. The volume available for storage is 9 cubic feet. Item 1 has a unit volume v_1 of 1 cubic foot, item 2 a unit volume v_2 of 2 cubic feet, and item 3 also has a unit volume v_3 of 2 cubic feet. The demand for each item is Poisson distributed with the mean for the period being 4 for item 1, 2 for item 2, and 1 for item 3. The stockout costs π_i are \$900, \$700, \$1400 for items 1, 2 and 3 respectively. It is desired to determine how many units of each item to stock in order to minimize expected stockout costs while not exceeding the available volume.

If x_i units of item i are stocked, we desire to minimize

$$\mathcal{K} = \sum_{i=1}^{3} \pi_i \left[\sum_{y=x_i}^{\infty} (y - x_i)\, p(y; \mu_i) \right]$$

$$= \sum_{i=1}^{3} \pi_i [\mu_i P(x_i - 1; \mu_i) - x_i P(x_i; \mu_i)]$$

for non-negative integers x_i which satisfy

$$x_1 + 2x_2 + 2x_3 \leq 9$$

We then define the functions

$$Z_k(\xi) = \min_{x_1, \ldots, x_k} \sum_{i=1}^{k} \pi_i [\mu_i P(x_i - 1; \mu_i) - x_i P(x_i; \mu_i)], \quad k = 1, 2, 3$$

for non-negative integers x_i satisfying

$$\sum_{i=1}^{k} v_i x_i \leq \xi$$

Then, if $\mathcal{K}^*$ is the optimal value of $\mathcal{K}$, $\mathcal{K}^* = Z_3(9)$. For $k \geq 2$, the $Z_k(\xi)$ can be computed sequentially from

$$Z_k(\xi) = \min_{0 \leq x_k \leq \left[\frac{\xi}{v_k} \right]} \{ \pi_k [\mu_k P(x_k - 1; \mu_k) - x_k P(x_k; \mu_k)] + Z_{k-1}(\xi - v_k x_k) \}$$

$Z_1(\xi)$ is given by

$$Z_1(\xi) = \min_{0 \leq x_1 \leq \xi} \{ 900 [4P(x_1 - 1; 4) - x_1 P(x_1; 4)] \}$$

since $v_1 = 1$. It is clear that the minimum in the above expression will be taken on when $x_1 = \xi$, since the expression in braces is the expected stock-out cost for item 1 when x_1 units are stocked. Hence

$$Z_1(\xi) = 900\ [4\ P(\xi - 1; 4) - \xi P(\xi; 4)]$$

and if $\hat{x}_1(\xi)$ is the value of x_1 which yields $Z_1(\xi)$, then $\hat{x}_1(\xi) = \xi$.

In the text it was suggested that the $Z_k(\xi)$ would in general be determined for each $\xi = 0, 1, \ldots, V$. For this simple example, however, it is easy to work backwards to determine which arguments ξ will be needed. It saves some work here to do this at the outset. To compute $Z_3(9)$ we need $Z_2(9 - 2x_3)$ where x_3 can take on every integral value from 0 to $[9/2] = 4$. Thus $Z_2(\xi)$ is needed for $\xi = 9, 7, 5, 3, 1$. To compute $Z_2(\xi)$ for any one of these arguments we need $Z_1(\xi - 2x_2)$ for all integral values of x_2 from 0 to $[\xi/2]$. Thus $Z_1(\xi)$ will be needed only for the arguments 9, 7, 5, 3, 1. The values of $Z_1(\xi)$ and $\hat{x}_1(\xi)$ and $\hat{x}_2(\xi)$ are given in Table 7-1 for the ξ values needed. For example

$$Z_1(5) = 900\ [4(0.56653) - 5(0.37116)] = 369.3$$

To compute $Z_2(\xi)$ we use

$$Z_2(\xi) = \min_{0 \le x_2 \le \left[\frac{\xi}{2}\right]} \{700[2P(x_2 - 1; 2) - x_2\ P(x_2; 2)] + Z_1(\xi - 2x_2)\} \tag{7-18}$$

For $\xi = 1$, it must be true that $x_2 = 0$, and hence

$$Z_2(1) = 1400 + Z_1(1) = 1400 + 2716 = 4116$$

For $\xi = 3$, x_2 can be 0 or 1. To determine which x_2 value is optimal, we compute the quantity in braces in (7-18) for $x_2 = 0$ and $x_2 = 1$, and pick the smallest value, to yield $Z_2(\xi)$. When $x_2 = 0$ the quantity in braces is 2613. When $x_2 = 1$, we need $Z_1(1) = 2716$ which is itself greater than the entire quantity in braces when $x_2 = 0$. Hence $Z_2(3) = 2613$ and $\hat{x}_2(3) = 0$. When $\xi = 5$, x_2 can be 0, 1, 2. For $x_2 = 0$, the quantity in braces in (7-18) is 1769, and is 2008 if $x_2 = 1$, and is greater than 2716 if

TABLE 7-1

Data for Example

ξ	$Z_1(\xi)$	$\hat{x}_1(\xi)$	$Z_2(\xi)$	$\hat{x}_2(\xi)$
1	2716	1	4116	0
3	1213	3	2613	0
5	369.3	5	1769.3	0
7	76.29	7	1164	1
9	11.04	9	748.2	2

$x_2 = 2$. Thus $\hat{x}_2(5) = 0$ and $Z_2(5) = 1769$. The same computational procedure is repeated for $\xi = 7, 9$ and the results are shown in Table 7-1.

We are now ready to make the final step and compute $\mathcal{K}^* = Z_3(9)$. To do this we use

$$Z_3(9) = \min_{0 \le x_3 \le 4} \{1400[P(x_3 - 1; 1) - x_3 P(x_3; 1)] + Z_2(9 - 2x_3)\} \quad (7\text{-}19)$$

Computing the quantity in braces in (7-19) for $x_3 = 0$, we obtain 2148; and for $x_3 = 1$, 1679; and for $x_3 = 2$, the value is greater than 1769. For $x_3 = 3, 4$ the value is still greater. Hence $\hat{x}_3(9) = x_3^* = 1$, and $\mathcal{K}^* = Z_3(9)$ = 1679. It only remains to determine x_2^*, x_1^*. We know from (7-17) that $x_2^* = \hat{x}_2(9 - 2x_3^*) = \hat{x}_2(7) = 1$. We find $\hat{x}_2(7)$ in Table 7-1 for $\xi = 7$. Finally $x_1^* = \hat{x}_1(9 - 2x_3^* - 2x_2^*) = \hat{x}_1(5) = 5$. Thus 5 units of item 1 and 1 unit of items 2 and 3 should be stocked. The expected stockout cost is $1679.

7-3 Dynamic Programming Formulation of Other Problems

Let us generalize the problem studied in the previous section to the case where two constraints are present, i.e., we now wish to minimize

$$g(x_1, \ldots, x_n) = \sum_{j=1}^{n} f_j(x_j) \quad (7\text{-}20)$$

for non-negative integers $x_j, j = 1, \ldots, n$, which satisfy the two constraints

$$\sum_{j=1}^{n} v_j x_j \le V; \quad \sum_{j=1}^{n} w_j x_j \le W \quad (7\text{-}21)$$

where the v_j, w_j, V, W are integers. Precisely the same procedure can be used as before except that now $Z_k(\xi)$ must be replaced by a function of two arguments $Z_k(\xi, \eta)$. Let us define the set of functions

$$Z_k(\xi, \eta) = \min_{x_1, \ldots, x_k} \sum_{j=1}^{k} f_j(x_j), \quad k = 1, \ldots, n \quad (7\text{-}22)$$

for non-negative integers x_j satisfying

$$\sum_{j=1}^{n} v_j x_j \le \xi; \quad \sum_{j=1}^{n} w_j x_j \le \eta \quad (7\text{-}23)$$

Then $g^* = Z_n(V, W)$. Since the minimization can be carried out in any way that we desire provided that all possible combinations of the values of the variables are considered if necessary, it follows that for $k \ge 2$

$$Z_k(\xi, \eta) = \min_{x_k} \left[f_k(x_k) + \min_{x_1, \ldots, x_{k-1}} \sum_{j=1}^{k-1} f_j(x_j) \right]$$

and in computing

$$\min_{x_1, \ldots, x_{k-1}} \sum_{j=1}^{k-1} f_j(x_j)$$

the variables must satisfy

$$\sum_{j=1}^{k-1} v_j x_j \leq \xi - v_k x_k; \quad \sum_{j=1}^{k-1} w_j x_j \leq \eta - w_k x_k$$

However, by definition, this minimum is simply $Z_{k-1}(\xi - v_k x_k, \eta - w_k x_k)$. Thus the $Z_k(\xi, \eta)$ can be computed using the recurrence relation

$$Z_k(\xi, \eta) = \min_{x_k} [f_k(x_k) + Z_{k-1}(\xi - v_k x_k, \eta - w_k x_k)], \quad k \geq 2 \quad (7\text{-}24)$$

and x_k can assume every integral value between 0 and

$$\min \left\{ \left[\frac{\xi}{v_k} \right], \left[\frac{\eta}{w_k} \right] \right\}$$

Finally

$$Z_1(\xi, \eta) = \min_{x_1} f_1(x_1) \quad (7\text{-}25)$$

The task of numerically solving this problem involving two constraints is much more difficult than the problem involving only a single constraint. The reason for this is that the Z_k now involve two arguments, and hence tables of two arguments must be constructed. Thus if for the case of one constraint ξ could take on 100 values, then for the case of two constraints, if both ξ and η can take on 100 values each, a table of 10,000 values will be needed, since Z_k must in general be computed for every combination of ξ and η values. It can easily require a computer one hundred times as long to solve a problem with two constraints as it would a problem with only a single constraint. Furthermore, a great deal more memory capacity is needed for the larger tables. The formulation of this problem points out one of the serious limitations of the dynamic programming technique. Only problems which can be formulated in a way such that the Z_k functions depend on a very small number of parameters are feasible computationally. In fact, any problem with Z_k involving more than three parameters is outside the range of feasibility, even with the largest computer available, and problems with three parameters require a tremendous amount of computer time to solve.

Let us now turn our attention to a slightly different type of problem that will be of interest to us, which can also be cast into the dynamic programming framework. Suppose that we wish to determine non-negative integers x_j, $j = 1, \ldots, n$, which minimize

$$g(x_1, \ldots, x_n) = \sum_{j=1}^{n} f_j(y_j, x_j) \tag{7-26}$$

where y_1 is specified and

$$y_{j+1} = y_j + x_j - d_j, \quad j = 1, \ldots, n - 1 \tag{7-27}$$

Intuitively, the interpretation of the above problem that will be of interest to us is that where g is the cost of operating a deterministic inventory system for n periods, and $f_j(y_j, x_j)$ is the cost associated with period j when x_j is the quantity ordered at the beginning of period j and y_j is the inventory position at the beginning of period j before an order is placed. Equation (7-27) is the material balance equation which relates the inventory position at the beginning of period $j + 1$ to that at the beginning of period j, the quantity ordered x_j at the beginning of period j, and the demand d_j in period j.

We shall now show how to cast this problem into the dynamic programming framework. The important thing to note is that g^* will depend on y_1, and as the problem is stated, y_1 is the only parameter which can be varied. This suggests that y_1 should play the same role as V in the problem of the previous section. In other words, the inventory position at the beginning of period k will be the parameter appearing in Z_k. Here again we can imagine the problem to be an n stage process. Now, however, in making the computations we must start with the last stage and work backwards (physically this will usually mean working backwards in time), since y_1 is specified at the beginning of the first stage. In the example of the previous section, it did not matter which stage was considered to be the first, but here it does.

Let us define the sequence of functions

$$Z_k(\xi) = \min_{x_k, \ldots, x_n} \sum_{j=k}^{n} f_j(y_j, x_j) \tag{7-28}$$

for non-negative integers x_j, $j = k, \ldots, n$, where the parameters y_j must satisfy

$$y_{j+1} = y_j + x_j - d_j, \quad j = k, \ldots, n - 1 \tag{7-29}$$

and

$$y_k = \xi \tag{7-30}$$

Then $g^* = Z_1(y_1)$. Furthermore, for $k < n$

$$Z_k(\xi) = \min_{x_k} \left[f_k(\xi, x_k) + \min_{x_{k+1}, \ldots, x_n} \sum_{j=k+1}^{n} f_j(y_j, x_j) \right]$$

where

$$y_{k+1} = \xi + x_k - d_k$$

and $y_{k+2}, \ldots, y_n$ must satisfy (7-29). Thus

$$Z_k(\xi) = \min_{x_k} \left[f_k(\xi, x_k) + Z_{k+1}(\xi + x_k - d_k) \right] \qquad (7\text{-}31)$$

and

$$Z_n(\xi) = \min_{x_n} f_n(\xi, x_n) \qquad (7\text{-}32)$$

In carrying out the minimization in (7-31), (7-32), x_k can take on any non-negative integral values.

The computational procedure is precisely the same as in the previous section. First, one computes $Z_n(\xi)$ for all integers ξ from the minimum possible value to the maximum possible value. Simultaneously $\hat{x}_n(\xi)$, the value of x_n which yields $Z_n(\xi)$, is tabulated. Then (7-31) is used to compute recursively the other $Z_k(\xi)$. As these are computed, $\hat{x}_k(\xi)$ is also tabulated. At the last stage it is only necessary to compute $Z_1(y_1)$. A table of $Z_1(\xi)$ is not needed. The value of x_1^* is found at this point also. Then

$$x_2^* = \hat{x}_2(y_1 + x_1^* - d_1); \quad x_3^* = \hat{x}_3(y_2^* + x_2^* - d_2), \text{ etc.} \qquad (7\text{-}33)$$

The method of solution just presented is sometimes referred to as the backward solution since it works back from the last stage (i.e., usually backwards in time). The $Z_k(\xi)$ can be interpreted physically as the minimum cost for periods k through n if the inventory position at the beginning of period k is ξ.

Suppose now it is also required that

$$y_{n+1} = y_n + x_n - d_n \qquad (7\text{-}34)$$

where y_{n+1} is a specified constant. This places restrictions on y_n and x_n. Physically the new constraint specifies the inventory position at the end of the last period. In this case the problem can be formulated using a forward solution as well as a backward solution. To obtain the forward solution formulation define the set of functions

$$Z_k(\xi) = \min_{x_1, \ldots, x_k} \sum_{j=1}^{k} f_j(y_j, x_j) \qquad (7\text{-}35)$$

where

$$y_k + x_k - d_k = \xi$$

and $y_2, \ldots, y_k$ satisfy (7-29). Then the recurrence relations take the form

$$Z_k(\xi) = \min_{x_k} \left[f_k(\xi + d_k - x_k, x_k) + Z_{k-1}(\xi + d_k - x_k) \right], \quad k > 1 \qquad (7\text{-}36)$$

and

$$Z_1(\xi) = \min_{x_1} f_1(\xi + d_1 - x_1, x_1) \qquad (7\text{-}37)$$

so that $g^* = Z_n(y_{n+1})$. The computational procedure is precisely the same as above. Here the $Z_k(\xi)$ can be interpreted physically as the minimum cost for periods 1 through k if the inventory position at the end of period k is ξ.

Let us now turn our attention to the case where the d_j are discrete, independent random variables with distributions $p_j(d_j)$. Physically we might think of this as a problem in which demand is a stochastic variable. The functions $f_j(y_j, x_j)$ can now be interpreted as the expected cost for period j if the inventory position immediately after the review is $y_j + x_j$. The function we now wish to minimize is the expected cost, i.e.,

$$g = \sum_{\text{all } d_j \geq 0} \left[\prod_{j=1}^{n} p_j(d_j) \right] \left[\sum_{j=1}^{n} f_j(y_j, x_j) \right] \qquad (7\text{-}38)$$

where $\sum_{j=1}^{n} f_j(y_j, x_j)$ is evaluated for a given set of y_j (the y_j being related to the d_j by (7-29)) and

$$\prod_{j=1}^{n} p_j(d_j) = p_1(d_1)p_2(d_2) \ldots p_n(d_n) \qquad (7\text{-}39)$$

is the probability of the given set of d_j, since the d_j are independent random variables.

As before, we assume that y_1 is specified. For a stochastic process it is not possible in general to specify the state of the system at the end of the last period, and hence a backward solution will always be needed in this case. By analogy with the deterministic case we define the set of functions

$$Z_k(\xi) = \min_{x_k, \ldots, x_n} \left\{ \sum_{\substack{\text{all } d_j \geq 0 \\ j=k, \ldots, n}} \left[\prod_{j=k}^{n} p_j(d_j) \right] \left[\sum_{j=k}^{n} f_j(y_j, x_j) \right] \right\},$$
$$k = 1, \ldots, n \qquad (7\text{-}40)$$

where $y_k = \xi$. Then $g^* = Z_1(y_1)$ as before.

Let us now consider the derivation of the recurrence relations. Note that in Z_k, the function $f_k(y_k, x_k) = f_k(\xi, x_k)$ is independent of the d_j. Also

$$\sum_{\substack{\text{all } d_j \geq 0 \\ j=k, \ldots, n}} \left[\prod_{j=k}^{n} p_j(d_j) \right] = \prod_{j=k}^{n} \left[\sum_{d_j=0}^{\infty} p_j(d_j) \right] = 1$$

Hence

$$Z_k(\xi) = \min_{x_k} \left\{ f_k(\xi, x_k) + \min_{x_{k+1}, \ldots, x_n} \sum_{\substack{\text{all } d_j \geq 0 \\ j=k, \ldots, n}} \left[\prod_{j=k}^{n} p_j(d_j) \right] \left[\sum_{j=k+1}^{n} f_j(y_j, x_j) \right] \right\}$$

$$= \min_{x_k} \left\{ f_k(\xi, x_k) \right.$$

$$+ \sum_{d_k=0}^{\infty} p_k(d_k) \left[\min_{x_{k+1}, \ldots, x_n} \sum_{\substack{\text{all } d_j \geq 0 \\ j = k+1, \ldots, n}} \left\{ \prod_{j=k+1}^{n} p_j(d_j) \right\} \left\{ \sum_{j=k+1}^{n} f_j(y_j, x_j) \right\} \right] \right\}$$

$$= \min_{x_k} \left\{ f_k(\xi, x_k) + \sum_{d_k=0}^{\infty} p_k(d_k) Z_{k+1}(\xi + x_k - d_k) \right\}$$

Thus the recurrence relations are

$$Z_k(\xi) = \min_{x_k} \left\{ f_k(\xi, x_k) + \sum_{d_k=0}^{\infty} p_k(d_k) Z_{k+1}(\xi + x_k - d_k) \right\}, \quad k < n \qquad (7\text{-}41)$$

and

$$Z_n(\xi) = \min_{x_k} f_n(\xi, x_n)$$

The computational procedure is precisely the same as for the deterministic case. It is somewhat more difficult here, however, because in (7-41) it is necessary to sum Z_{k+1} over the possible values of d_k. In any practical problem, some upper limit to the demand would be used rather than ∞ as shown on the summation sign in (7-41). A subtle difference enters into the determination of the x_j^*. The formulas are precisely the same as in the deterministic case. However, a numerical value can be obtained only for x_1. To obtain numerical values for $x_2, \ldots, x_n$ the d_j must be known. This is very plausible intuitively since, for example, one would not want to make a decision as to how much to order in period 2 until the quantity demanded in the first period was known. As in the deterministic case, $Z_k(\xi)$ can be thought of physically as the minimum expected cost for periods k through n if the inventory position at the beginning of period k is ξ.

Dynamic programming can also be used for problems in which all variables are treated as continuous. For continuous variables, however, one must develop some sort of search procedure to carry out the minimization over x_k in the recurrence relations. The procedure of examining each of the possible values suggested in the text can no longer be applied because of the continuum of values allowed. One straightforward way to find the minimum is to begin by using a relatively coarse grid to divide up the interval over which x_k can vary, and to determine the relative minimum (or minima) for these points. Then progressively finer grids are used in the neighborhood of the minimum (or minima) until sufficient accuracy is obtained. There exist a great variety of specialized search procedures which can be applied if the functions f_j have certain special properties (such as being concave). (Indeed, even when the x_k are treated as discrete it may be advantageous in some cases to use a specialized search procedure.)

When x_k is continuous, ξ will usually be continuous also. In this case, $Z_k(\xi)$ will be tabulated for some gridwork of points, and interpolation will be used to determine $Z_k(\xi)$ for ξ values other than those for which Z_k is tabulated. Such a procedure is legitimate, since $Z_k(\xi)$ will normally be a continuous function of ξ. It is clear that the case of continuous variables is more difficult to treat using dynamic programming than that where the variables are discrete. This is just the opposite of what was true for the computational procedures used in the previous chapters.

7-4 Dynamic-Deterministic Lot Size Model

We would here like to consider a dynamic generalization of the simple lot size model of Sec. 2-2. In dealing with dynamic models it is difficult to use an infinite planning horizon (i.e., consider all future times) since numerical calculations using dynamic programming can be made for only a finite number of periods. This is no serious restriction in practice, because the distant future has essentially no effect on decisions to be made at the present, and because for many situations in which a dynamic model will be applied, the item becomes obsolete after a certain length of time, and a planning horizon longer than the time until obsolescence would have no meaning.

For the model to be developed it will be assumed that the demand rate is deterministic. No backorders or lost sales are to be allowed, i.e., the system can never be out of stock when a demand occurs. The unit cost C of the item is assumed to be a constant which is independent of the quantity ordered. We shall imagine that there are n times $\zeta_1, \ldots, \zeta_n$ at which orders can be placed. The procurement lead time associated with any order placed at time ζ_j will be τ_j, here assumed to be constant. Note that the value of the procurement lead time is allowed to vary with j. However, it is assumed that the τ_j are such that orders cannot cross. The possible times at which orders can arrive are then $t_j = \zeta_j + \tau_j$. The cost of placing an order at time ζ_j will be written A_j. Observe that an order need not be placed at time ζ_j. One can be placed at this time if it is desirable to do so.

The quantities $Q_j (Q_j \geq 0)$ to order at times ζ_j will be determined by minimizing the sum of the ordering and carrying costs over the planning horizon, which will be assumed to end at time $\zeta (\zeta > \zeta_n + \tau_n)$. We suppose that the desired on hand inventory at time ζ is specified; it will be denoted by y_{n+1}. It will be noted that we have no influence whatever over the carrying costs incurred from the time ζ_1 when the first order can be placed until the time $\zeta_1 + \tau_1 = t_1$ when the first order arrives. In addition, these costs are independent of the Q_j, and hence need not be included in the cost expression. The only holding costs that are relevant are those incurred between t_1 and ζ.

By period j we shall mean the time from t_j to t_{j+1} $(t_{n+1} = \zeta)$. Write $T_j = t_{j+1} - t_j$. Let y_1 be the on hand inventory at time t_1. The demand rate as a function of time will be written $\lambda(t)$. Then the demand d_j in period j is

$$d_j = \int_{t_j}^{t_{j+1}} \lambda(t)\, dt$$

We are now ready to develop the total variable cost expression. All variables will be treated as continuous. Let $I_j C$ be the cost of carrying one unit in inventory for period j. Note that this is not an annual cost but the cost for period j. If y_j is the on hand inventory at the beginning of period j before any order placed at time ζ_j has arrived, then the inventory carrying charges for period j are

$$\frac{I_j C}{T_j} \int_{t_j}^{t_{j+1}} \left[y_j + Q_j - \int_{t_j}^{t} \lambda(u)\, du \right] dt = I_j C [y_j + Q_j] - \frac{I_j C}{T_j} \int_{t_j}^{t_{j+1}} \int_{t_j}^{t} \lambda(u)\, du\, dt$$

It is convenient, for reasons which will soon become apparent, to express this in terms of the on hand inventory at the end of the period rather than that at the beginning of the period. This can easily be done using the material balance equation

$$y_{j+1} = y_j + Q_j - d_j, \quad j = 1, \ldots, n \tag{7-42}$$

Here y_{j+1} is the on hand inventory at the end of period j (and the beginning of period $j + 1$ before any order arrives). Thus the carrying costs for period j can be written

$$I_j C y_{j+1} + I_j C \left[d_j - \frac{1}{T_j} \int_{t_j}^{t_{j+1}} \int_{t_j}^{t} \lambda(u)\, du\, dt \right] \tag{7-43}$$

Now note that $I_j C y_{j+1}$ is the inventory carrying cost in period j for those units carried into period $j + 1$. The other term in (7-43) is the cost in period j of carrying the d_j units which are demanded in period j. This latter cost is independent of the Q_j and is unavoidable, since the d_j units demanded in period j must be on hand at the beginning of period j. Hence the carrying cost in period j for these d_j units need not be included in the variable cost expression.

Thus the variable costs of ordering and holding inventory which are incurred over the planning horizon are

$$\mathcal{K} = \sum_{j=1}^{n} [A_j \delta_j + I_j C y_{j+1}] \tag{7-44}$$

where

$$\delta_j = \begin{cases} 0 \text{ if } Q_j = 0 \\ 1 \text{ if } Q_j > 0 \end{cases}$$

and the y_j are related by (7-42). As formulated above, $\mathcal{K}$ is the variable cost over the planning horizon and not the present worth of the variable cost. It can equally well, though, be interpreted as the discounted cost if it is imagined that the discounting factors are included in the A_j and I_j. However, when discounting is used, it is necessary to include in (7-44) the discounted cost of the units themselves. Problem 7-5 asks the reader to work out a means for solving the problem when discounting is introduced.

The dynamic programming formalism introduced in the previous section can be usefully employed to yield a computational procedure which can easily be carried out by hand to determine the Q_j^*. Since the ending inventory is specified as well as the beginning inventory, it is possible to use either a forward or backward solution. The forward solution turns out to be the most interesting, for reasons which will become clear below. The forward solution formulation will now be developed.

Let us define the sequence of functions

$$Z_k(\xi) = \min_{Q_1, \ldots, Q_k} \sum_{j=1}^{k} \{A_j \delta_j + I_j C y_{j+1}\}, \quad k = 1, \ldots, n \qquad (7\text{-}45)$$

where $y_{k+1} = \xi$ and (7-42) holds for the other y_j. Then from (7-36), (7-37), the recurrence relations are

$$Z_k(\xi) = I_k C \xi + \min_{Q_k} \{A_k \delta_k + Z_{k-1}(\xi + d_k - Q_k)\} \qquad (7\text{-}46)$$

Also

$$Z_1(\xi) = I_1 C \xi + \begin{cases} A_1 & \text{if } Q_1 > 0 \\ 0 & \text{if } Q_1 = 0 \end{cases} \qquad (7\text{-}47)$$

where

$$Q_1 = \begin{cases} \xi + d_1 - y_1 & \text{if } \xi > y_1 - d_1 \\ 0 & \text{otherwise} \end{cases} \qquad (7\text{-}48)$$

We shall now restrict our attention to the case where $y_1 = 0$, i.e., the time ζ_1 is chosen so that everything on hand at time ζ_1 will be used up just as the first order arrives. There is normally no reason to have a procurement arrive before everything on hand is used up, and hence the case of $y_1 = 0$ is the one that is usually of interest. If $y_1 = 0$, it is possible to make several observations that will considerably reduce the computational effort below that required if the problem was solved directly using the above recurrence relations. Let us note first of all that if $Q_k^* > 0$ then $y_k^* = 0$, i.e., the on hand inventory at the time of arrival of an order should be zero. The reason for this is that if $y_k > 0$, a saving in inventory carrying costs could be effected by increasing the quantity procured at time ζ_k from Q_k^* to $Q_k^* + y_k$. There would be no increase in ordering costs on doing this, and hence a net reduction in costs would result. The argument above is based on the assumption that the unit cost of the item is a constant.

Given that $y_k^* = 0$ if $Q_k^* > 0$, it follows that Q_k^* must be equal to an integral number of periods demand, i.e., if $Q_k^* > 0$ then

$$Q_k^* = d_k \quad \text{or} \quad d_k + d_{k+1} \quad \text{or} \ldots \text{or} \quad d_k + \ldots + d_n \qquad (7\text{-}49)$$

This observation considerably reduces the number of Q_k values which need to be examined in determining the minimum in (7-46). It will be noted that if the demand in period $j > k$ is satisfied by Q_k^*, then the demands in all periods $k + 1, \ldots, j - 1$ will also be satisfied by Q_k^*. If this was not so, i.e., if $Q_v^* > 0$, $k < v < j$, and Q_v^* satisfies the demand in period v and perhaps one or more of periods $v + 1, \ldots, j - 1$, then $Q_v^* y_v > 0$, since some of Q_k^* must be kept to satisfy the demand in period j. This contradicts what we have obtained above.

Next, let us show that if for $Z_k(0)$ it is optimal to have $Q_k^* > 0$ (and hence $y_k^* = 0$), it is also optimal to have $Q_k^* > 0$ for $Z_k(\xi)$, $\xi > 0$. This can be proved by considering (7-46). Note first of all that

$$Z_k(0) = \min_{Q_k} \{A_k \delta_k + Z_{k-1}(d_k - Q_k)\}$$
$$= \min \begin{cases} A_k + Z_{k-1}(0) \\ Z_{k-1}(d_k) \end{cases} \qquad (7\text{-}50)$$

Since we have assumed that $Q_k^* > 0$, i.e., $Q_k^* = d_k$ when $\xi = 0$ in $Z_k(\xi)$, it follows that $A_k + Z_{k-1}(0) \leq Z_{k-1}(d_k)$. Furthermore, it must be true that $Z_{k-1}(\xi) > Z_{k-1}(d_k)$ if $\xi > d_k$, for if we end period $k - 1$ with more units, it was at least necessary to store these units for period $k - 1$, and hence the cost will be greater for the first $k - 1$ periods. Now

$$Z_k(\xi) = \min_{Q_k} \{A_k \delta_k + Z_{k-1}(\xi + d_k - Q_k)\} \qquad (7\text{-}51)$$

However, we have noted above that

$$A_k + Z_{k-1}(0) \leq Z_{k-1}(d_k) < Z_{k-1}(\xi) \quad \text{when } \xi > d_k.$$

Thus

$$Q_k^* = d_k + \xi > 0$$

and we have proved what we set out to show.

The result we have just proved has the following physical interpretation. If it is optimal to have an order arrive at the beginning of period k when there are only k periods and the on hand inventory is to be zero at the end of period k, then it will be optimal to have an order arrive at the beginning of period k regardless of how many additional periods there are.

One final computational simplification will be introduced. Note that an optimal policy for k periods, when nothing is on hand at the end of period k must have the form that an order arrives at the beginning of period w which satisfies the demands in periods w through k, and an optimal policy is followed in periods 1 through $w - 1$ given that nothing is on hand at the end of period $w - 1$. Thus

$$Z_k(0) = \min_{w} \left\{ A_w + C \sum_{j=w}^{k-1} \left[I_j \sum_{i=j+1}^{k} d_i \right] + Z_{w-1}(0) \right\}, \quad w = 1, 2, \ldots, k$$

where $Z_0(0) = 0$, or if

$$Y_k(w) = A_w + C \sum_{j=w}^{k-1} \left[I_j \sum_{i=j+1}^{k} d_i \right] + Z_{w-1}(0) \tag{7-52}$$

then

$$Z_k(0) = \min_{w} Y_k(w), \quad w = 1, 2, \ldots, k \tag{7-53}$$

Note that $Y_k(w)$ is the cost for periods 1 through k under the assumptions that the on hand inventory at the end of period k is zero, an optimal policy is followed for periods 1 through $w - 1$ given that the ending inventory for period $w - 1$ is zero, and an order arrives at the beginning of period w which satisfies the demand for periods w through k.

We can now show that if for $Z_{k-1}(0)$, the order which satisfies the demand in period $k - 1$ arrives at the beginning of period v, then in computing $Z_k(0)$, the order which satisfies the demand in period k will arrive at the beginning of period v or a later period, i.e., in computing $Z_k(0)$ it is unnecessary to consider the possibility that the order which satisfies the demand in period k arrives before period v. Then in (7-53), it is only necessary to allow w to range from v to k. We shall prove this by contradiction. Assume that

$$Z_k(0) = Y_k(u) = A_u + C \sum_{j=u}^{k-1} \left[I_j \sum_{i=j+1}^{k} d_i \right] + Z_{u-1}(0) < Y_k(v)$$

where

$$Z_{k-1}(0) = Y_{k-1}(v) = A_v + C \sum_{j=v}^{k-2} \left[I_j \sum_{i=j+1}^{k-1} d_i \right] + Z_{v-1}(0)$$

and $v > u$. However, on factoring out in $Z_k(0)$ the carrying costs for the items carried from period u through k to satisfy the demand in period k, we have

$$Z_k(0) = Cd_k \sum_{j=u}^{k-1} I_j + Y_{k-1}(u) = Y_k(u)$$

But

$$Y_k(v) = Cd_k \sum_{j=v}^{k-1} I_j + Y_{k-1}(v)$$

On subtracting $Y_k(v)$ from $Z_k(0)$, we obtain

$$Z_k(0) - Y_k(v) = Cd_k \sum_{j=u}^{v-1} I_j + Y_{k-1}(u) - Y_{k-1}(v) \geq 0$$

since by assumption

$$Y_{k-1}(u) \geq Y_{k-1}(v) = Z_{k-1}(0) \quad \text{and} \quad Cd_k \sum_{j=u}^{k-1} I_j \geq 0$$

Hence $Z_k(0) \geq Y_k(v)$, which is a contradiction.

Thus we see that the computational procedure has been reduced to a very simple form. At stage k, we compute $Z_k(0)$ from (7-53) using (7-52) for $Y_k(w)$, and we allow w to range over the values v to k, where in $Z_{k-1}(0)$, the order satisfying the demand for period $k - 1$ arrived at the beginning of period v. The optimal policy will normally be obtained on computing $Z_n(0)$. If it is desired to have ξ units on hand at the end, then at the last step we compute instead

$$Z_n(\xi) = \min_w \left\{ A_w + C \sum_{j=w}^{n-1} \left[I_j \left(\sum_{i=j+1}^{n} d_i + \xi \right) \right] + Z_{w-1}(0) \right\}$$

and again w only needs to run from v to n, where in $Z_{n-1}(0)$ the order which satisfied the demand of period $n - 1$ arrived at the beginning of period v. The reason that the same computational procedure holds for $Z_n(\xi)$ as for $Z_n(0)$ is that having ξ units remaining at the end is equivalent, insofar as the previous periods are concerned, to increasing the demand in period n by ξ.

A convenient tabular format for making the computations is given in Table 7-2. In the last line, the optimal Q_j values are indicated by enclosing in parentheses all periods whose demands are met by the order arriving at the beginning of the period whose number appears first in the parentheses. Thus (3, 4, 5) would mean that it is optimal to meet the demands in periods 3, 4, and 5 with the order arriving at the beginning of period 3. Table 7-2 indicates the results which might be obtained in a typical case. The asterisks on the $Y_k(w)$ indicate the minima over w, i.e., $Z_k(0)$.

In the above model the times at which orders could be placed were specified. A more general problem would be to determine both the times at which orders should be placed and the quantities to be ordered. The problem of determining the precise times at which orders should be placed when the demand rate varies with time turns out to be quite difficult even in the simplest cases. Problem 7-6 will ask the reader to derive the equa-

TABLE 7-2
Computational Format for the Dynamic Lot Size Model

				Period			
	1	2	3	4	$\cdots$	$n-1$	n
$Y_k(w)$	$Y_1^*(1)$	$Y_2^*(1)$	$Y_3(1)$		$\cdots$		
		$Y_2(2)$	$Y_3(2)$		$\cdots$		
			$Y_3^*(3)$	$Y_4^*(3)$	$\cdots$		
				$Y_4(4)$	$\cdots$		
					$\cdots$	$Y_{n-1}(v)$	
					$\cdots$	$\cdot \ \cdot \ \cdot$	
					$\cdots$	$Y_{n-1}^*(n-1)$	$Y_n^*(n-1)$
					$\cdots$		$Y_n(n)$
$Z_k(0)$	$Z_1(0) = Y_1(1)$	$Z_2(0) = Y_2(1)$	$Z_3(0) = Y_3(3)$	$Z_4(0) = Y_4(3)$	$\cdots$	$Z_{n-1}(0) = Y_{n-1}(n-1)$	$Z_n(0) = Y_n(n-1)$
Q_k^*	(1)	$(1,2)$	$(1,2)(3)$	$(1,2)(3,4)$	$\cdots$	$(1,2)(3,4,\ldots)\cdots(n-1)$	$(1,2)(3,4,\ldots)\cdots(n-1,n)$

tions which determine these times for the case where there are no fixed ordering costs, and to examine the difficulties involved in solving them. It will be noted, however, that by allowing the times at which orders can be placed to be sufficiently close together in the model developed in this section, it is possible to come arbitrarily close to the solution where the optimal times at which orders are to be placed are to be determined.

7-5 Example of the Dynamic Lot Size Model

A sub-contractor to a major missile manufacturer has a contract to deliver at the beginning of each month for the coming year specified numbers of a particular die cast part. The number of units to be delivered varies from month to month, and the specific monthly values are given in Table 7-3. This particular item is produced in lots. The setup cost for a production run is $300. The variable production costs on the item amount to $120 per unit. The sub-contractor uses an inventory carrying charge of $I = 0.20$. It is desired to determine how many production runs should be made and when they should be made. Production decisions are made only at the beginning of each month, and for the item under consideration, if a run is scheduled at the beginning of a month it will be completed by the end of the month, and any units not shipped immediately to the missile manufacturer at the end of the month will be sent to the sub-contractor's warehouse. The sub-contractor does not want to have any units in stock at the end of the year when the contract terminates.

In the notation of the previous section $A_j = A = \$300$ independently of when the setup is made, and $I_jC = IC/12 = \$2.00$ per unit per month. Here a period is one month, and it is convenient to imagine that the number of units which must be delivered to the missile manufacturer at the beginning of month $k + 1$ represents the sub-contractor's demand in period k. Then

$$Z_1(0) = A = 300 = Y_1(1)$$

$$Z_2(0) = \min \begin{cases} 2A = 600 = Y_2(2) \\ 2(100) + 300 = 500 = Y_2(1) \end{cases} = 500 = Y_2(1)$$

This shows that it is not optimal to have another setup at the beginning of the second period, if the on hand inventory at the end of the second period is to be 0. Next

$$Z_3(0) = \min \begin{cases} A + Z_2(0) = 800 = Y_3(3) \\ 2(125) + 2A = 850 = Y_3(2) \\ 2(125) + 2(225) + A = 1000 = Y_3(1) \end{cases}$$

$$= 800 = Y_3(3)$$

TABLE 7-3
Computations for Example

Month

	1	2	3	4	5	6	7	8	9	10	11	12
Demand	80	100	125	100	50	50	100	125	125	100	50	100
$Y_k(w)$	300*	500* 600	1000 850 800*	1000* 1100	1200 1200* 1300	1400 1400* 1500	1800 1700 1700*	1950* 2000	2450 2250 2250*	2450* 2550	2650 2650* 2750	3050 2950 2950*
$Z_k(0)$	300	500	800	1000	1200	1400	1700	1950	2250	2450	2650	2950
Q_k^*	(1)	(1, 2)	(1, 2)(3)	(1, 2)(3, 4)	(1, 2, 3) (4, 5)	(1, 2)(3, 4) (5, 6)	(1, 2)(3, 4) (5, 6)(7)	(1, 2)(3, 4) (5, 6)(7, 8)	(1, 2) (3, 4)(5, 6) (7, 8)(9)	(1, 2) (3, 4)(5, 6) (7, 8)(9, 10)	(1, 2)(3, 4) (5, 6)(7, 8) (9)(10, 11)	(1, 2) (3, 4)(5, 6) (7, 8)(9) (10, 11)(12)

In the three period case it is optimal to set up at the beginning of period 3 to satisfy the demand for period 3, and in period 1 for the demand of the first two periods. In computing $Z_4(0)$ we know that there will be a setup in period 3. Hence it is unnecessary to consider the possibility of producing for period 4 in any period prior to period 3.

$$Z_4(0) = \min \begin{Bmatrix} A + Z_3(0) = 1100 = Y_4(4) \\ 2(100) + A + Z_2(0) = 1000 = Y_4(3) \end{Bmatrix}$$

$$= 1000 = Y_4(3)$$

It is optimal to set up in period 3 to satisfy period 4 demand. The remainder of the computations are presented in Table 7-3. It is seen that an optimal solution is

$$Q_1^* = 180, \ Q_2^* = 0, \ Q_3^* = 225, \ Q_4^* = 0, \ Q_5^* = 100, \ Q_6^* = 0, \ Q_7^* = 225,$$
$$Q_8^* = 0, \ Q_9^* = 125, \ Q_{10}^* = 150, \ Q_{11}^* = 0, \ Q_{12}^* = 100$$

where Q_j^* is the quantity to be produced in month j. It should be noted that the optimal solution is not unique. In periods 5, 6, 7, 9, 11, and 12 other choices are possible. The cost of setups and carrying inventory is $2950.

7-6 Dynamic Models with Stochastic Demands and a Fixed Horizon

We shall now turn our attention to dynamic models in which demand is a stochastic variable. As in the previous section, it will be imagined that orders can be placed only at times $\zeta_1 = 0, \zeta_2, \ldots, \zeta_n$. The planning horizon is assumed to be of a fixed length ζ. As usual, we shall examine the case where all demands occurring when the system is out of stock are backordered. The procurement lead time τ_j for any order placed at time ζ_j will be assumed to be constant (the lead time can vary with j, however, subject to the restriction that orders cannot cross). The times at which orders can arrive will be denoted by $t_1, \ldots, t_n$, where $t_j = \zeta_j + \tau_j$. It is assumed that $\zeta > t_n$. The time between t_j and t_{j+1} ($t_{n+1} = \zeta$) will be referred to as period j. The inventory position y_1 at time ζ_1 when the first order can be placed is assumed to be specified. Because of the stochastic nature of the process, it is not possible to specify the ending inventory at time ζ.

It will be imagined that the cumulative expected demand from time $\zeta_1 = 0$ to time $t(t \leq \zeta)$ can be represented by the continuous function $D(t)$. Furthermore, it will be supposed that the demand in any time interval, say from t' to t'' ($0 \leq t' < \zeta, t' < t'' \leq \zeta$) is Poisson distributed with mean $D(t'') - D(t')$. Let

$$T_j = \zeta_{j+1} - \zeta_j, \quad j = 1, \ldots, n \tag{7-54}$$

Then it will be convenient to define λ_j, σ_j such that

$$\lambda_j(T_j + \tau_{j+1}) = D(t_{j+1}) - D(\zeta_j), \quad \sigma_j T_j = D(\zeta_{j+1}) - D(\zeta_j) \quad (7\text{-}55)$$

Thus λ_j is the mean rate of demand which if maintained constant during the time from ζ_j to t_{j+1} would lead to the same probability distribution for the demand over this interval as that appropriate to the actual time varying rate. A similar interpretation can be given to σ_j.

The cost of placing an order at time ζ_j will be written A_j, and the quantity ordered will be denoted by Q_j ($Q_j \geq 0$). The cost of the Q_j units ordered at ζ_j will be taken to be $C_j(Q_j)$, and we allow this cost to be nonlinear in the quantity procured. The cost of holding a unit in stock for period j will be written $I_j \hat{C}_j$, where $\hat{C}_j$ is an average unit cost, which can be defined in any way desired. The fixed cost of a backorder incurred in period j will be written π_j and the cost of a unit year of shortage will be written $\hat{\pi}_j$. In a number of instances in which the present model is of interest, all items remaining on hand at time ζ will be sold. Let L be the unit selling price at time ζ.

As was the case for the deterministic model of the previous section, the costs incurred from the time ζ_1 to t_1 are independent of the Q_j and need not be included in the analysis.

Let us now compute the expected carrying and backorder costs incurred in period j if y_j is the inventory position of the system at time ζ_j prior to placing an order. The inventory position after any order is placed will be $y_j + Q_j$. We shall imagine that the ζ_j are chosen to be sufficiently close together that for any t value lying between t_j and t_{j+1} we can write to a sufficiently good approximation

$$\lambda_j(t - \zeta_j) = D(t) - D(\zeta_j)$$

i.e., λ_j can be assumed to be constant from t_j to t_{j+1}.

The expected costs of carrying inventory in period j are then

$$\frac{I_j \hat{C}_j}{T_j + \tau_{j+1} - \tau_j} \int_{t_i}^{t_{i+1}} \sum_{x=0}^{y_i+Q_i} (y_j + Q_j - x) p[x; \lambda_j(t - \zeta_j)]\, dt$$

$$= \frac{I_j \hat{C}_j}{T_j + \tau_{j+1} - \tau_j} \int_{\tau_i}^{T_i + \tau_{i+1}} \left\{ y_j + Q_j - \lambda_j \tau \right.$$

$$\left. + \sum_{x=y_i+Q_i}^{\infty} (x - y_j - Q_j) p(x; \lambda_j \tau) \right\} d\tau \quad (7\text{-}56)$$

$$= I_j \hat{C}_j \left[y_j + Q_j - \frac{\lambda_j}{2}(T_j + \tau_{j+1} + \tau_j) + B(y_j + Q_j, T_j + \tau_{j+1}, \tau_j) \right]$$

where

$$(T_j + \tau_{j+1} - \tau_j) B(y_j + Q_j, T_j + \tau_{j+1}, \tau_j)$$

is the expected unit years of shortage incurred in period j. Note, however, that this expression has been evaluated in Sec. 5-3 and is given by (5-26), if there instead of $\tau + T$ we use $T_j + \tau_{j+1}$ and instead of τ we use τ_j.

The expected number of backorders incurred during period j is simply

$$E(y_j + Q_j, T_j + \tau_{j+1}, \tau_j)$$

$$= \sum_{x = y_i + Q_i}^{\infty} (x - y_j - Q_j)\{p[x; \lambda_j(T_j + \tau_{j+1})] - p(x; \lambda_j \tau_j)\} \quad (7\text{-}57)$$

$E(y_j + Q_j, T_j + \tau_{j+1}, \tau_j)$ can be written down explicitly by use of A3-10. The expected gain from sale of units remaining at time ζ is

$$G(y_n + Q_n) = L \sum_{x=0}^{y_n + Q_n} (x - y_n - Q_n)p[x; \lambda_n(\zeta - \zeta_n)] \quad (7\text{-}58)$$

All the terms needed in the cost expression have now been evaluated. The y_j are related by the material balance equation

$$y_{j+1} = y_j + Q_j - d_j \quad (7\text{-}59)$$

where d_j is the demand from ζ_j to ζ_{j+1}. The probability of d_j is $p(d_j; \sigma_j T_j)$. It follows that the expected variable cost over the planning horizon of procurement, carrying, and backorders, net of the expected gain from sales at time ζ, is

$$\mathcal{K} = \sum_{\text{all } d_k \geq 0} \left[\prod_{j=1}^{n} p(d_j; \sigma_j T_j) \right] \left[\sum_{j=1}^{n} \left\{ A_j \delta_j + C_j(Q_j) \right. \right.$$

$$+ I_j \hat{C}_j \left[y_j + Q_j - \frac{\lambda_j}{2}(T_j + \tau_{j+1} + \tau_j) \right] + \pi_j E(y_j + Q_j, T_j + \tau_{j+1}, \tau_j)$$

$$+ \left. [(T_j + \tau_{j+1} - \tau_j)\hat{\pi}_j + I_j \hat{C}_j] B(y_j + Q_j, T_j + \tau_{j+1}, \tau_j) \right\} - G(y_n + Q_n) \right] \quad (7\text{-}60)$$

$\mathcal{K}$ can also be interpreted as the discounted cost if it is imagined that the discount factors are included in the A_j, $C_j(Q_j)$, I_j, π_j, $\hat{\pi}_j$ and L.

Dynamic programming provides a natural way to determine numerically the functions $Q_j^*(y_j)$. Because of the stochastic nature of the process a backward solution is needed. Let us define the set of functions

$$Z_k(\xi) = \min_{Q_k, \ldots, Q_n} \left\{ \sum_{\substack{\text{all } d_i \geq 0 \\ j = k, \ldots, n}} \left[\prod_{j=k}^{n} p(d_j; \sigma_j T_j) \right] \left[\sum_{j=k}^{n} A_j \delta_j + C_j(Q_j) \right. \right.$$

$$+ I_j \hat{C}_j \left[y_j + Q_j - \frac{\lambda_j}{2}(T_j + \tau_{j+1} + \tau_j) \right] + \pi_j E(y_j + Q_j, T_j + \tau_{j+1}, \tau_j)$$

$$+ [(T_j + \tau_{j+1} - \tau_j)\hat{\pi}_j + I_j\hat{C}_j)]B(y_j + Q_j, T_j + \tau_{j+1}, \tau_j)$$

$$- G(y_n + Q_n) \Big] \Big\}, \quad k = 1, \ldots, n \tag{7-61}$$

Then from (7-41), the recurrence relations are

$$Z_k(\xi) = \min_{Q_k} \Big\{ A_k\delta_k + C_k(Q_k) + I_k\hat{C}_k \Big[\xi + Q_k - \frac{\lambda_k}{2}(T_k + \tau_{k+1} + \tau_k) \Big]$$

$$+ \pi_k E(\xi + Q_k, T_k + \tau_{k+1}, \tau_k)$$

$$+ [(T_k + \tau_{k+1} - \tau_k)\hat{\pi}_k + I_k\hat{C}_k]B(\xi + Q_k, T_k + \tau_{k+1}, \tau_k)$$

$$+ \sum_{d_k=0}^{\infty} p(d_k; \sigma_k T_k)Z_{k+1}(\xi + Q_k - d_k) \Big\}, \quad k = 1, \ldots, n-1 \tag{7-62}$$

$$Z_n(\xi) = \min_{Q_n} \Big\{ A_n\delta_n + C_n(Q_n) + I_n\hat{C}_n \Big[\xi + Q_n - \frac{\lambda_n}{2}(\zeta - \zeta_n + \tau_n) \Big]$$

$$+ \pi_n E(\xi + Q_n, \zeta - \zeta_n, \tau_n) \tag{7-63}$$

$$+ [(\zeta - \zeta_n - \tau_n)\hat{\pi}_n + I_n\hat{C}_n]B(\xi + Q_n, \zeta - \zeta_n, \tau_n) - G(\xi + Q_n) \Big\}$$

It should be recalled that a numerical value can be obtained only for Q_1. For the other Q_j's, we obtain a function $Q_j^*(y_j)$, and it is not possible to determine Q_j^* until y_j is known, i.e., until the time is reached when Q_j is to be selected. In practice one will often only be interested in Q_1^*, and will not be interested in the $Q_j^*(y_j)$, $j > 1$. The reason for this is that the problem will often be solved each time a procurement is to be considered, using additional information obtained since the last time the computation was made.

The procedure for numerically solving the problem has been outlined in Sec. 7-3. In most cases the task is much too burdensome to carry out by hand. It can be solved fairly readily on a large scale computer, however. Even on a large scale computer, though, it is sometimes desirable to introduce shortcuts to save time. For example, if it is possible for Q_k^* to be quite large, say over 100, the task of minimizing over Q_k when Q_k is changed by only one unit at a time may be excessively time consuming. To reduce the time required to make these computations, one might, for example, vary Q_k one unit at a time between 1 and 25, five units at a time between 25 and 100, and ten units at a time over 100. In other words, Q_k cannot take on any integral value when $Q_k > 25$, but instead can only take on the values 30, 35, 40, etc., to 100 and then 110, 120, etc. The upper limit on ξ will simply be the maximum level that it is ever expected that the inventory position will reach. Again, to save computational time, it is advisable to keep it as small as feasible. If the expected lead time demands are sufficiently large, it will be desirable to replace the Poisson terms by their normal approximations.

It is also possible to give a formulation of the above model in the case where the lead times are random variables. Problem 7-9 asks the reader to do this. The lost sales case is, as usual, very difficult to handle. All the problems encountered in the steady state period review systems are also present here. In the event that more than a single order can be outstanding, it is no longer possible to have the Z_k be a function of a single argument only. This means, essentially, that at the present time, it is impossible to solve such problems numerically. We ask the reader to examine the lost sales case in Problem 7-10.

7-7 Dynamic Models with Stochastic Demands and a Variable Horizon

On occasions one encounters situations in which it is desirable to use a dynamic model of the type discussed in the previous section. However, it is now no longer true that the planning horizon is fixed. Instead, the planning horizon must be considered to be a random variable. A practical example of such a situation arises in stocking spare parts for a military aircraft which will become obsolete at some date in the future that is not known with certainty, but which can be described probabilistically. Here the planning horizon is the time until obsolescence. We would now like to generalize the model presented in the previous section to the case where ζ, the time at which any units still on hand are disposed of, is a random variable.

It is very difficult to treat the case where ζ is allowed to be a continuous random variable. Furthermore, in any real world situation it is usually very difficult to attempt to decide on a continuous density function for ζ. About the best that can be done is to select a finite number of times $\zeta(i)$, $i = 1, \ldots, m$, and the probability ρ_i that the date of obsolescence will occur at time $\zeta(i)$. For example, the $\zeta(i)$ may be years 5, 6, and 7 and the ρ_i give the probability that the plane will become obsolete at the end of years 5, 6, and 7 respectively. We shall follow this same procedure in the development of the model.

In general, we would expect the cumulative mean demand to depend on the date of obsolescence. Hence, in place of the function $D(t)$ defined in the previous section we now have m functions $D_i(t)$, where $D_i(t)$ is the expected cumulative mean demand if $\zeta(i)$ is the date of obsolescence. Similarly, the times at which orders can be placed may depend on the date of obsolescence. In particular, for the larger values of $\zeta(i)$ it was desirable to have more times at which procurements can be made than for the smaller $\zeta(i)$. In general, we shall suppose that if $\zeta(i)$ is the time of obsolescence, there are $n(i)$ times at which procurements will be considered, and these times will be denoted $\zeta_j(i), j = 2, \ldots, n(i); \zeta_1 = 0$, which is the time that the first procurement is to be considered will, of course, be the same for all i, since at and prior to ζ_1, it is not known which value of $\zeta(i)$ will actually occur. Corresponding to the $\lambda_j, \sigma_j, T_j, \tau_j$ defined in the previous section, we now have a corresponding set of these for each i, i.e., $\lambda_j(i), \sigma_j(i), T_j(i), \tau_j(i)$. Also $A_j(i), I_j(i), \hat{C}_j(i), \pi_j(i), \hat{\pi}_j(i), L(i)$ replace $A_j, I_j, \hat{C}_j, \pi_j, \hat{\pi}_j, L$ respectively.

As before, y_1 will be taken to be the inventory position of the system at time ζ_1. Let $W_i(y_1 + Q_1)$ be the expected cost if Q_1 units are ordered at time ζ_1, $\zeta(i)$ is the date of obsolescence, and an optimal policy is followed after time ζ_1. Then

$$W_i(y_1 + Q_1) = A_1(i)\delta_1 + C_1(Q_1) + I_1\hat{C}_1\left\{y_1 + Q_1\right.$$

$$\left. - \frac{\lambda_1}{2}\left[T_1(i) + \tau_2(i) + \tau_1\right]\right\} + \pi_1 E\left[y_1 + Q_1, T_1(i) + \tau_2(i), \tau_1\right]$$

$$+ \left\{[T_1(i) + \tau_2(i) - \tau_1]\hat{\pi}_1 + I_1\hat{C}_1\right\}B[y_1 + Q_1, T_1(i) + \tau_2(i), \tau_1]$$

$$+ \sum_{d_1=0}^{\infty} p[d_1; \sigma_1(i)T_1(i)]Z_2^{(i)}(y_1 + Q_1 - d_1) \qquad (7\text{-}64)$$

$Z_2^{(i)}$ and the other $Z_k^{(i)}$ are defined by (7-62), (7-63), except that all relevant parameters must now involve i.

The expected cost for any choice of Q_1 is then

$$\sum_{i=1}^{m} \rho_i W_i(y_1 + Q_1) \qquad (7\text{-}65)$$

and the optimal Q_1 is that value which minimizes (7-65). To solve this problem, we must essentially solve m problems of the type discussed in the previous section, since we need the m functions $Z_2^{(i)}(\xi)$. Then at the last step these are joined together by (7-65) and Q_1^* is determined. At each time a procurement is to be considered the problem will be solved and any additional information on the date of obsolescence obtained since the previous solution will be incorporated.

7-8 The Prediction Problem

In Secs. 7-6, 7-7 we assumed that the distribution of demand over any time period was Poisson and that the mean rate of demand was known as a function of time. In the real world, of course, it will be necessary to use some sort of prediction method to estimate the mean rate of demand at future times. The mean rate of demand as a function of time will not be known with certainty, but will be subject to errors inherent in the prediction technique used. The type of prediction technique which might be used can vary widely. In some instances it will be based only on past demand data for the item. In other cases there will be no historical data available and the predictions will be based only on planned requirements. In still other cases, the predictions will be based on a detailed economic forecast.

The accuracy with which the mean demand can be predicted will decrease the farther into the future the prediction is carried. The increasing uncertainty in the mean demand rate as one moves into the future should be reflected in the demand distributions used in the model, i.e., the variance should increase as one moves into the future. What we would like to use is the distribution of forecast errors, i.e., the distribution of the difference between the actual demand and the forecast demand. Usually, however, it is exceedingly difficult to obtain the distribution of forecast errors. Furthermore, this distribution may depend on calendar time, i.e., changes as the nature of the process generating demands changes. The problem of attempting to account for forecast errors is another difficult problem encountered when dealing with dynamic models, which is usually hard to handle easily for lack of sufficient data. It should be recognized that if one knows very little about the future it will not be easy to make accurate computations, regardless of how much mathematical manipulation is performed.

REFERENCES

1. Bellman, R., *Dynamic Programming*. Princeton, N. J.: Princeton University Press, 1957.

2. Bellman, R., and S. Dreyfus, "On the Computational Solution of Dynamic-Programming Processes—X: The Flyaway-Kit Problem," RM-1889, The RAND Corp., April 5, 1957.

3. Bellman, R., and S. Dreyfus, "On the Computational Solution of Dynamic-Programming Processes—IX: A Multistage Logistic-Procurement Model," RM-1901, The RAND Corp., November 5, 1956.

4. Bellman, R., and S. Dreyfus, "On the Computational Solution of Dynamic-Programming Processes—II: On A Cargo-Loading Problem," RM-1746, The RAND Corp., November 5, 1956.

5. Bellman, R., "Combinatorial Processes and Dynamic Programming," P-1284, The RAND Corp., February 24, 1958.

6. Dreyfus, S., "Dynamic Programming Solution of Allocation Problems," P-1083, The RAND Corp., May 9, 1957.

7. Hadley, G., and T. M. Whitin, "A Family of Dynamic Inventory Models," *Management Science*, Vol. 8, No. 4, July, 1962, pp. 458–469.

8. Wagner, H. M., and T. M. Whitin, "Dynamic Version of the Economic Lot Size Model," *Management Science*, Vol. 5, No. 1, Oct. 1958, pp. 89–96.

PROBLEMS

7-1. An isolated air base is supplied with spare parts only once every month when a plane from the main depot arrives to replenish the inventory. There are n parts which are stocked at the air base. Just prior to the time the base is to be replenished, it radios to the main depot the on hand inventory of each of the n spare parts. Let y_i be the number on hand of item i just prior to replenishment. The plane which brings the spares can carry a volume V and the unit volume of item i is v_i. A cost π_i is incurred each time a demand occurs when the base is out of stock. Monthly demand for each of the items is essentially Poisson distributed with mean μ_i. Set up as a dynamic programming problem the problem of determining the quantity x_i of each item i which should be loaded on the plane, so as to minimize the expected stockout costs for the coming month.

7-2. Consider a simplified version of Problem 7-1 which involves only three items. Assume that: $V = 15$ cu. ft.; $v_1 = 5$ cu. ft.; $v_2 = 3$ cu. ft.; $v_3 = 4$ cu. ft.; $y_1 = 1$; $y_2 = 0$; $y_3 = 2$; $\pi_1 = \$5000$, $\pi_2 = \$2000$, $\pi_3 = \$10,000$; $\mu_1 = 1$, $\mu_2 = 5$, $\mu_3 = 3$. Determine the optimal values of x_1, x_2, and x_3.

7-3. A newsboy can carry only N papers with him in the evening. There are two papers which he sells. The first is an out-of-town paper which costs him c_1 cents each and sells for p_1 cents. Any papers not sold can be returned for a credit of d_1 cents. The other is a local paper which costs him c_2 cents each and sells for p_2 cents. Any papers not sold can be returned for a credit of d_2 cents. Assume that if y_1, y_2 are the demands for the out-of-town and local papers respectively then y_1, y_2 are independent random variables with densities $p_1(y_1)$, $p_2(y_2)$. Formulate the problem of determining the quantities x_1, x_2 of each of the papers to procure as a dynamic programming problem. Solve the problem in the particular case where $c_1 = 7$, $p_1 = 10$, $d_1 = 4$, $c_2 = 5$, $p_2 = 7$, $d_2 = 3$. The demand for each is Poisson distributed, the mean being 7 for the out-of-town paper and 8 for the local paper. He can carry no more than 15 papers.

7-4. Consider a flyaway kit problem in which there are only three items to be considered. The total volume available is 11 cu. ft. The unit volume of item 1 is 2 cu. ft., of item 2 is 3 cu. ft., and of item 3 is 4 cu. ft. The cost of stockout for item 1 is $500, for item 2 is $1000, and for item 3 is $2000. The demand for each item is Poisson distributed with mean 3 for item 1, 2 for item 2, and 1 for item 3. How many of each item should be loaded in order to minimize the expected stockout costs?

7-5. Consider the cost equation given by Eq. (7-44). Assume that a rate of interest i is being used. Determine the discount factors which should appear in the A_j, I_j if it is desired to have $\mathcal{K}$ be the discounted cost. Include the discounted cost of the units, and work out a means for solving the problem in this case.

7-6. Consider a situation in which the demand for an item can be taken to be deterministic, with the cumulative demand as a function of time being $D(t)$. Assume that from $t = 0$ to $t = T$, n procurements will be allowed. There is no fixed cost of making a procurement. Derive the equations which determine the times t_i at which procurements should be scheduled to arrive, so as to minimize carrying costs over the interval 0 to T. Show that the t_i are solutions to

$$\frac{d}{dt_j} D(t_j) = \frac{D(t_{j+1}) - D(t_j)}{t_j - t_{j-1}}, \quad j = 2, 3, \ldots, n-1$$

$$\frac{d}{dt_n} D(t_n) = D(T) - D(t_n) + y_T$$

where y_T is the inventory at time T. Discuss the problems involved in solving these equations. Give a geometric interpretation. *Hint*: The solution to these equations need not be unique. Can you illustrate a case where this is so?

7-7. A television manufacturer produces its own capacitors in lots. The setup cost to produce a lot of capacitors is $200. The particular capacitor under consideration costs $1.00 to produce. An inventory carrying charge of $I = 0.20$ is used. The production schedule for television sets over the next year calls for the following quantities of capacitors to be used each month: 10,000, 20,000, 20,000, 15,000, 10,000, 5000, 5000, 10,000, 10,000, 20,000, 25,000, 10,000. The time required to produce the capacitors can be ignored. Compute the optimal times at which lots should be produced and the size of the lots, if 5000 capacitors are now on hand and it is desired to have 5000 on hand at the end of the year.

7-8. A manufacturer of actuators for rocket motors is under contract to deliver the following quantities to a producer of rocket motors on the first of each month for the coming year: 25, 50, 100, 175, 200, 200, 175, 150, 100, 75, 200, 150. The actuators are produced in lots and the setup cost is $800. Each actuator costs $300 to produce. The manufacturer uses an inventory carrying charge of $I = 0.20$. Determine when setups should be made and the optimal lot sizes. Ignore the time required to produce a lot.

7-9. Generalize the model developed in Sec. 7-6 to the case where the procurement lead times are random variables. What assumptions must be made?

7-10. Investigate the problems in treating the lost sales version of the model developed in Sec. 7-6. Show that in the Z_k, one must include parameters for the size of each of the orders outstanding. Formulate the model in the case where there is never more than a single order outstanding.

7-11. What simplifications occur in the model developed in Sec. 7-6 if $\hat{\pi} = 0$, the terms involving τ can be neglected in comparison to those involving $T + \tau$, and the backorders term in the inventory carrying charge can be neglected?

7-12. Demands for the three weeks of a season are deterministic and have the values 1, 2, 2 units respectively. The total costs of the product delivered at the beginning of each period are given by the following table.

Weeks	1	2	3
No. Units			
0	0	0	0
1	1.00	0.75	2.00
2	2.00	1.50	3.50
3	1.50	2.00	5.00
4	4.00	5.00	6.50
5	6.00	8.00	8.00

Inventory carrying charges are estimated at $1.00 per unit per period, and are applied to the ending inventory each period. Calculate the optimal purchasing program or programs. Assume that stockouts are not allowed.

7-13. Parts A, B, and C may be put in a container which can hold a maximum of 4 cubic feet of contents. The maximum cost allowable for the inputs of the container is $4.00. Use dynamic programming to maximize the profits from selling one container. The profits, cost, and weight data are given below.

	Cubic Feet	Cost ($)	Profit/unit ($)
Part A	1	3.00	5.00
Part B	1	1.00	2.00
Part C	1	0	1.50

7-14. A retailer sells an item with the following characteristics. The item costs $5.00, has a selling price of $9.00, and a liquidation value of $2.00. The supplier arrives with his merchandise at the start of each week of the three week season. The initial inventory is 0 and inventory carrying charges are negligible. Demand in the three weeks is given by the following table of probabilities, the entry in each cell being the probability that demand is exactly equal to the number of units indicated in the left hand column. Determine the optimal

Week	1	2	3
No. Units			
0	$\frac{3}{4}$	0	$\frac{1}{3}$
1	$\frac{1}{4}$	$\frac{1}{2}$	$\frac{1}{3}$
2	0	$\frac{1}{2}$	$\frac{1}{3}$

number of units to order the first week and an optimal policy for the remaining two weeks.

7-15. A manufacturer is able to increase production in any month at a cost of $4.00 per unit increase in the production rate (when measured in the dimensions of units per period). Reductions in the production rate cost $3.00 per unit decrease. It is known that demands in the next three periods are 2, 4, and 1 units respectively. Production costs per unit are $6.00, $10.00, and $8.00 in periods 1, 2, and 3 respectively. Inventory carrying charges are applied to ending inventory and amount to $2 per unit. Assuming that demands must be met as they occur and that initial and final inventories are zero, determine the least cost levels of production in the three periods.

7-16. A camera store sells its Developo Camera at $120 per unit. Its supplier appears each Monday morning and will sell additional sets to the firm at a specified price S or buy sets back at price B. There are no cameras in stock at the start of a two-week period and the Develop will be obsolete at the end of the second week but have a liquidation value of $50 per set. Given the following data, solve for the optimal inventory policy for the two-week period. Assume that carrying costs are negligible.

	Period 1	Period 2
$S(\$)$	80	90
$B(\$)$	70	70

Probability Distribution of Demand

	Period 1	Period 2
No. Units 2	$\frac{1}{3}$	0
3	$\frac{1}{3}$	$\frac{1}{4}$
4	$\frac{1}{3}$	$\frac{1}{4}$
5	0	$\frac{1}{4}$
6	0	$\frac{1}{4}$

7-17. A manufacturer produces a highly stylized item which will be worthless at the end of the second of two periods. The purchase price for the item in question is $9.50 the first period and $8.00 the second period. Initial inventory is zero at the start of the first period. The set up cost for the first period is $1.00 and increases to $4.00 the second period. The selling price for the first period is $10.00 and the first period's demand is equally likely to be 0, 1, or 2 units. In the second period the manufacturer can charge either $10.00 or $12.00 per unit for the product. At the $10.00 price there is a probability of 0.1 that demand will be 2 units, and 0.9 that demand will be for 3 units. At the $12.00 price, the probability that one unit is demanded is 3/8, and that 2 units are demanded is 5/8. What is the optimal production level in the first period? What is the optimal price and production policy for the second period? What is the level of expected profits under optimal policy for the two periods?

7-18. Two items, A and B, have certainly known demands with the annual demands being 1000 and 3125 units respectively. The total volume occupied by the two items must never exceed 210 cubic feet. Item A requires 1 cubic foot of volume, while item B requires 3 cubic feet. Ordering costs amount to $10 per order placed for either item and inventory carrying charges are 20 percent of average inventory value. Item A costs $10 per unit. Item B costs $20 per unit. No stockouts are allowed to occur. Find the ordering policy which minimizes annual costs of the two items by means of dynamic programming. Compare with the Lagrange multiplier solution which can be obtained by the methods of Chapter 2.

7-19. Indicate how Problem 2-44 could be solved by dynamic programming.

7-20. Suppose that demand for an item is deterministic with the cumulative demand as a function of time being $D(t) = t^2$. Three procurements are allowed between time 0 and 10. If initial inventory is 4 units and final inventory (at $t = 10$) is 0, calculate the minimum cost policy by means of the equations in Problem 7-6. Does this solution provide an absolute minimum?

7-21. Solve Problem 7-20 as a dynamic programming problem with the length of the period being one unit of time. Compare the solution to that obtained in Problem 7-20.

7-22. Change the example in Sec. 7-5 to allow production runs to be scheduled at the middle of each month as well as at the beginning. How much can management save because of the increased number of possible production opportunities?

7-23. The value of various numbers of parts A, B, and C is indicated in the table below, as well as the cost schedule for these parts. The total cost cannot exceed $4.00. The total weight cannot exceed 5 pounds. Item A weighs 3 pounds per unit. Items B and C weigh one pound each. Maximize the value of the parts subject to the constraints on total cost and weight. No more than three units of any item can be acquired.

Value ($)

No.	A	B	C
1	6	4	5
2	8	6	7
3	10	7	9

Cost ($)

No.	A	B	C
1	1	1	2
2	3	2	3
3	5	4	4

7-24. A business has the average cost and revenue schedules described below, where x_1, x_2, x_3 represent the quantities produced in periods one, two, and three respectively, and y_1, y_2, y_3 represent the quantities demanded in periods one, two, and three.

Average Cost and Revenue Schedules

	Period 1	Period 2	Period 3
Average Cost	$2 + 0.5x_1$	$1 + 0.3x_2$	$3 + 0.6x_3$
Average Revenue	$12 - 1.5y_1$	$6 - 0.6y_2$	$10 - y_3$

An inventory carrying charge of \$1.00 per unit will be applied to the ending inventory of each period. Each set up costs \$3.00. It is assumed that production in each period can be carried out in time to meet the sales, and that total production up to and including any period must be at least as great as total sales. Calculate the optimal price, production, and inventory policy for the three periods. Assume that initial inventory before the first period is zero and that inventory on hand after the three periods is without value.

7-25. The type of dynamic model presented in Sec. 7-7 can, in a simplified form, be useful in treating other sorts of situations. Suppose, for example, that it is not possible to predict over the planning horizon the mean demand in each time period, and then to treat the demands in different periods as independent random variables. Instead, the best that can be done is to say that the mean demand will follow one of n different curves with the probability of curve i being ρ_i. This is essentially the problem treated in Sec. 7-7, except for the fact that now obsolescence may not be a factor at all. Often in practice it is desirable to introduce a simplification of the model introduced in Sec. 7-7 and eliminate the stochastic elements in the demand. The only stochastic element is that which determines which demand curve will be the one actually observed. Thus the determination of the W_i in Eq. (7-64) involves the solution of a deterministic dynamic programming problem, so far as the demand is concerned. Equation (7-65) will remain unchanged. Formulate in detail this simplified version of the problem in the case where the lead time is allowed to be a random variable.

8 USES OF DYNAMIC PROGRAMMING

IN THE ANALYSIS

OF STEADY STATE MODELS

We do not what we ought;

What we ought not, we do;

And lean upon the thought

That chance will bring us through.

Matthew Arnold, Empedocles on Etna

8-1 Introduction

Dynamic programming was introduced in the previous chapter as a technique for obtaining numerical answers to dynamic inventory problems with a finite number of periods. The dynamic programming formalism has also been found useful in studying certain theoretical aspects of steady state models. In fact, it is in this way that, under suitable assumptions, the optimality of Rr policies can be demonstrated. Furthermore, the dynamic programming approach provides another means for obtaining the average annual cost, both for transactions reporting and periodic review systems. Indeed, we shall derive in this way the average annual cost expressions for the models developed in Chapters 4 and 5. Also, expressions for the average annual cost for transactions reporting systems when units are not demanded one at a time can be obtained by means of dynamic programming.

In applying the dynamic programming approach to steady state models we imagine that there are an infinite number of periods rather than a finite number, i.e., the system is imagined to continue to operate for all future time. For an infinite number of stages, the recurrence relations of dynamic programming become what is called a functional equation. It is through the analysis of these functional equations that the various results of interest can be derived.

8-2 The Basic Functional Equation for Periodic Review Systems

In the previous chapter where we allowed the mean rate of demand to change with time, it was possible to include only a finite number of periods in the formulation. Now we wish to discuss the steady state behavior of periodic review systems, where the mean rate of demand does not change with time. Here it will be possible and desirable to consider an infinite number of periods, and to imagine that the system will continue operating in steady state for all future time.

Let us consider a periodic review system in which all demands occurring when the system is out of stock are backordered. As usual J will denote the review cost, A the cost of placing an order, C the unit cost of the item (assumed to be a constant independent of the quantity ordered), I the inventory carrying charge, $\pi + \hat{\pi}t$ the cost of a backorder, T the time between reviews, and τ the procurement lead time (here assumed to be constant). Demands in different periods will be assumed to be independent, and $p(x; T)$ will denote the probability that x units are demanded in a period of length T.

Suppose that time ζ is a review time for the system. Nothing can be done about the carrying and backorder costs incurred between time ζ and the time $\zeta + \tau$ when any order placed at time ζ arrives. Hence, as in the previous chapter, we shall associate with the review time ζ the expected carrying costs and backorder costs incurred from time $\zeta + \tau$ to $\zeta + \tau + T$. Denote by $f(\xi + Q; T)$ the sum of the expected carrying and backorder costs incurred in the period from $\zeta + \tau$ to $\zeta + \tau + T$, discounted to time ζ, when ξ is the inventory position at time ζ prior to the placing of any order, and $Q \geq 0$ is the quantity ordered. Then

$$f(\xi + Q; T) = ICD_T(\xi + Q; T) + \pi E_T(\xi + Q; T) + \hat{\pi}B_T(\xi + Q; T) \quad (8\text{-}1)$$

where ICD_T and $\pi E_T + \hat{\pi}B_T$ are the expected carrying and backorder costs respectively incurred from $\zeta + \tau$ to $\zeta + \tau + T$ (and discounted to time ζ). Let $a(T)$, $0 < a < 1$, be the discount factor which discounts any costs known at $\zeta + T$ to their present worth at time ζ.

We shall define $Z_\zeta(\xi; T)$ to be the present worth (discounted cost) at time ζ of all future costs (with the convention that no carrying or backorder costs incurred from ζ to $\zeta + \tau$ are included) if an optimal quantity is ordered at time ζ and at all future review times, ξ is the inventory position of the system at time ζ *before any order is placed*, and T is the time between reviews. In order that $Z_\zeta(\xi; T)$ will be finite, it is necessary to introduce discounting and to assume that the interest rate is positive. Similarly, $Z_{\zeta+T}(\xi; T)$ will be defined to be the present worth at time $\zeta + T$ of all future costs if an optimal quantity is ordered at time $\zeta + T$ and all future times, and ξ is the inventory position of the system at time $\zeta + T$ before any order is placed. By convention $Z_{\zeta+T}(\xi; T)$ will not include the carrying or holding costs incurred between $\zeta + T$ and $\zeta + \tau + T$. Then we see from the methods introduced in the previous chapter that

$$Z_\zeta(\xi; T) = \min_Q \{ J + A\delta + CQ + f(\xi + Q; T)$$

$$+ a(T) \sum_{x=0}^{\infty} p(x; T)Z_{\zeta+T}(\xi + Q - x; T)\} \quad (8\text{-}2)$$

where

$$\delta = \begin{cases} 0 & \text{if } Q = 0 \\ 1 & \text{if } Q > 0. \end{cases}$$

An important observation can now be made. It is

$$Z_\xi(\xi; T) = Z_{\xi+T}(\xi; T) = Z_{\xi+nT}(\xi; T), \quad n = 2, 3, \ldots \quad (8\text{-}3)$$

In other words, the present worth of all future costs at a review time, when the inventory position is ξ prior to placing an order and an optimal policy is followed at that review time and all future reviews, is the same at any review time. The reason is of course that we are considering the discounted cost over an infinite planning horizon.

Therefore, if we define $Z(\xi; T)$ to be the present worth at a review time of all future costs (with the convention that no carrying or backorder costs are included until a lead time has elapsed) when an optimal policy is followed at the review time and at all future review times, the inventory position of the system is ξ at the review time prior to placing any order, and the time between reviews is T, then (8-2) reduces to

$$Z(\xi; T) = \min_Q \left[J + A\delta + CQ + f(\xi + Q; T) \right.$$

$$\left. + a \sum_{x=0}^{\infty} p(x; T)Z(\xi + Q - x; T) \right] \quad (8\text{-}4)$$

Equation (8-4) is an equation involving the function $Z(\xi; T)$. It is called a functional equation since it involves an unknown function rather than simply a variable. The solution to this functional equation yields $Z(\xi; T)$ and also $Q^*(\xi; T)$, the optimal quantity to order as a function of ξ. In general, it is very difficult to solve this equation to determine $Z(\xi; T)$ and $Q^*(\xi; T)$. Later we shall show how a modified form of the functional equation can be solved explicitly for $Z(\xi; T)$. Now we shall only be interested in saying something about the optimal ordering policy $Q^*(\xi; T)$.

Usually, for the analysis to follow, it will be simplest to treat Q, ξ, and the demand variable as continuous. Thus, instead of $p(x; T)$ we shall introduce $v(x; T)$, the demand density for a period of length T. Then to modify (8-4) to take account of continuous variables it is only necessary to replace $p(x; T)$ by $v(x; T)$ and the summation by an integral sign. This yields

$$Z(\xi; T) = \min_Q \left[J + A\delta + CQ + f(\xi + Q; T) \right.$$

$$\left. + a \int_0^{\infty} v(x; T)Z(\xi + Q - x; T) \, dx \right] \quad (8\text{-}5)$$

Equation (8-5) will be the basic functional equation to be used in the analysis of the next section.

8-3 Optimality of R_r Policies for Periodic Review Systems— Qualitative Discussion

The functional equation approach was first employed in the study of periodic review inventory systems in the paper by Arrow, Harris, and Marschak [1], although the use of functional equations had appeared earlier, for example, in the work of Massé [8]. The paper by Arrow, Harris, and Marschak stimulated interest in the nature of optimal operating doctrines for periodic review systems, and since its publication, a number of papers have appeared which discuss optimal operating doctrines for periodic review systems [2, 5, 6, 7, 9]. Perhaps the best known of these are the two papers by Dvoretzky, Kiefer, and Wolfowitz [6, 7]. Most of the authors made exceptionally restrictive assumptions in their analyses, such as assuming zero lead times. Also, it was frequently assumed that the cost of placing an order was zero. Even with these simplifying assumptions, the mathematical analysis employed often became rather involved. The most interesting paper from a practical point of view is the recent paper by Scarf [9]. It allows assumptions of sufficient generality to include a number of cases of practical importance. Interestingly enough, it is also the simplest mathematically. In this section we would like to show how the functional equation approach can be used to obtain information concerning the optimal operating doctrine for steady state periodic review systems. In the next section we shall present the results derived by Scarf [9].

Let $F(y; T)$ be defined by

$$F(y; T) = Cy + f(y; T) + a \int_0^\infty v(x; T)Z(y - x; T) \, dx \qquad (8\text{-}6)$$

For a fixed value of T, F depends only on y. Then from (8-5)

$$Z(\xi; T) = J - C\xi + \min \begin{cases} A + \min\limits_Q F(\xi + Q; T) \\ F(\xi; T) \end{cases} \qquad (8\text{-}7)$$

Note that we added and subtracted $C\xi$ so that F could be made a function of $\xi + Q$ only.

Let us now consider $F(y; T)$. Clearly, when given A, the optimal operating doctrine will depend on the shape of $F(y; T)$ and only on the shape of $F(y; T)$. First of all imagine that for a fixed T, $F(y; T)$ has the shape shown in Fig. 8-1. Let $F(R^*; T)$ be the absolute minimum of $F(y; T)$ with respect to y, and $R^*(T)$ the unique point where this minimum is taken on (R^* will be a function of T). Also let r^* be the value of $y (y < R^*)$ for which $F(y; T) = A + F(R^*; T)$, i.e.,

$$F(r^*; T) = A + F(R^*; T) \tag{8-8}$$

This is illustrated in Fig. 8-1.

It is clear that if ξ lies between r^* and R^*, say ξ_1, then $Q^* = 0$, i.e., it is optimal not to order anything. The reason is that by placing an order $F(y; T)$ cannot be reduced below $F(R^*; T)$. However, $F(R^*; T) + A > F(\xi; T)$ when ξ lies between r^* and R^*, i.e., the expected cost would only

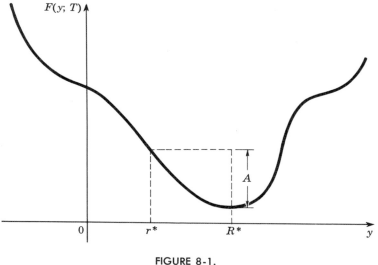

FIGURE 8-1.

be increased if an order was placed. On the other hand if $\xi < r^*$, say ξ_2, then it will be optimal to place an order, and the quantity ordered should be sufficient to make $F(y;T)$ as small as possible, i.e., $R^* - \xi_2$ should be ordered. Then the costs of placing an order and future discounted costs come to $A + F(R^*; T) < F(\xi_2; T)$. Furthermore, for Q different from $Q^* = R^* - \xi_2$, the expected discounted costs would be greater than $A + F(R^*; T)$. It is also clear that if $\xi > R^*$, an order should not be placed. However, if the system is operated optimally, ξ will never be greater than R^*. What we have shown then is that an Rr operating doctrine is the optimal one to use in this case. It is interesting to note that the same sort of analysis shows that if $A = 0$, then an order up to R policy is optimal.

This is obvious intuitively, since if it does not cost anything to place an order, and if the unit cost of the item is constant, then it will be optimal to place an order every time, and each time to bring the inventory position to the same level R. We might note in passing that if $F(y; T)$ is a convex function of y, its shape will be such that an Rr operating doctrine will be optimal.

If $F(y; T)$ had the shape shown in Fig. 8-2, an Rr policy would not be optimal. Instead, the optimal policy would have the form: If $\xi < r_1^*$ order a quantity $R^* - \xi$; if $r_1^* \leq \xi \leq r_2^*$, do not order; if $r_2^* < \xi < r_3^*$, order a

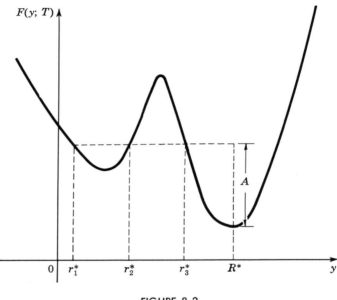

FIGURE 8-2.

quantity $R^* - \xi$, if $\xi \geq r_3^*$ do not order. We suspect that the curve of $F(y; T)$ shown in Fig. 8-2 is not a type that will be encountered in practice. This is usually correct. However, it is easy to provide practical examples where an Rr policy is not optimal. We shall do this below. First, however, we would like to study in a little more detail the circumstances under which we expect an Rr policy to be optimal.

Let us note that except for the yC term, $F(y; T)$ is simply the discounted expected cost for all future times when we begin the period under consideration with an inventory position of y (after placing any order) and follow an optimal policy for all future periods. We expect that if the inventory position y is relatively low, the expected costs will be relatively high because of high backorder costs in the present period. As y is increased the expected costs should decrease until y is large enough so that the increase in carrying charges outweighs the decrease in backorder costs. Then the expected costs will begin to rise and continue rising as y is increased: Addition of the linear yC term will not change the basic shape of the curve. Hence we expect $F(y; T)$ to yield a curve of the shape shown in Fig. 8-1 and not that shown in Fig. 8-2. Thus, we expect in general that, when the unit cost is constant, an *Rr* policy should be optimal.

In the event that the unit cost of the item is not a constant, it is no longer true that an *Rr* policy must be optimal. Now we can no longer introduce a function $F(\xi + Q; T)$ which depends on $\xi + Q$ alone. Instead, the functional equation has the form

$$Z(\xi; T) = J + \min \begin{cases} A + \min\limits_{Q} F(\xi, Q; T) \\ F(\xi, 0; T) \end{cases}$$

where

$$F(\xi, Q; T) = C(Q) + \hat{F}(\xi + Q; T)$$

and

$$\hat{F}(\xi + Q; T) = f(\xi + Q; T) + a \int_0^\infty v(x; T)Z(\xi + Q - x; T)\, dx$$

with $C(Q)$ being the cost of Q units.

Imagine that all units quantity discounts are available so that $C(Q)$ is of the form shown in Fig. 2-12. In Fig. 8-3, we have shown what $F(\xi, Q; T)$ might look like for two different values of ξ. An *Rr* policy is not optimal in this case, since the level up to which one orders depends on ξ. In both cases it is optimal to order just enough to take advantage of a price break, but it is a different price break in each case, and the level up to which one orders is different.

8-4 Proof that an *Rr* Policy is Optimal When $f(y; T)$ is Convex and the Unit Cost is Constant

While the above intuitive argument suggests that normally we expect an *Rr* doctrine to be optimal when the unit cost is constant, it is surprisingly difficult to prove this under very general conditions. However, there is one important practical case where the proof can be carried out. This is the case where $f(y; T)$ is a convex function of y (review Problem 2-6 for the definition of a convex function). It is this case that was studied by Scarf.

To carry out the proof, we do not use (8-5) directly. Instead, we make use of the observation that the steady state case with an infinite number of periods can be thought of as the limit as n approaches infinity of an n period system. Let $Z_n(\xi; T)$ be the discounted expected cost for an n period system when ξ is the inventory position at the beginning of period n before any order is placed (period n, however, comes first in time) and

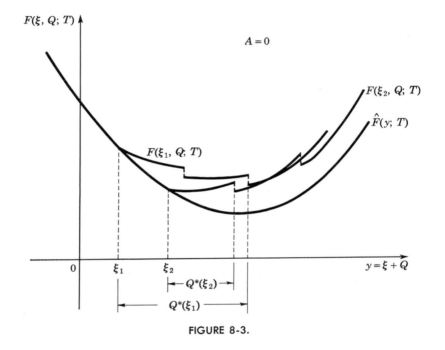

FIGURE 8-3.

an optimal policy is used for each decision. Note that the periods are being numbered in an order opposite to their time sequence. Then

$$Z(\xi; T) = \lim_{n \to \infty} Z_n(\xi; T) \tag{8-9}$$

and

$$Z_n(\xi; T) = \min_{Q_n} \left[J + A\delta + CQ_n + f(\xi + Q_n; T) \right.$$

$$\left. + a \int_0^\infty v(x; T) Z_{n-1}(\xi + Q_n - x; T)\, dx \right] \tag{8-10}$$

$$= J - C\xi + \min_{Q_n} \left[A\delta + F_n(\xi + Q_n; T) \right]$$

where

$$F_n(\xi + Q_n; T) = (\xi + Q_n)C + f(\xi + Q_n; T)$$

$$+ a \int_0^\infty v(x; T) Z_{n-1}(\xi + Q_n - x; T)\, dx, \qquad (8\text{-}11)$$

$$n = 2, 3, \ldots$$

Also

$$Z_1(\xi; T) = \min_{Q_1} [J + A\delta + CQ_1 + f(\xi + Q_1; T)] \qquad (8\text{-}12)$$

The proof would be very simple if it followed that the $F_n(\xi; T)$ were convex if $f(y; T)$ was convex. This is not in general true, however. The sort of phenomenon that arises which prevents the $F_n(\xi; T)$ from being convex can be seen by studying just a simple two period case. Now from (8-12)

$$Z_1(\xi; T) = J - C\xi + \min_{Q_1} [A\delta + F_1(\xi + Q_1; T)]$$

where

$$F_1(y; T) = Cy + f(y; T)$$

and $F_1(y; T)$ is a convex function of y, since $f(y; T)$ and Cy are. Thus from the discussion of the previous section, we know that an Rr policy will be optimal for the one period case and hence

$$Z_1(\xi; T) = \begin{cases} J + F_1(\xi; T) - C\xi = J + f(\xi; T), \xi \geq r^* \\ J + A + F_1(R^*; T) - C\xi, \xi < r^* \end{cases} \qquad (8\text{-}13)$$

$Z_1(\xi; T)$ is plotted in Fig. 8-4 for the case where $f(y; T)$ is differentiable everywhere with respect to y. Note that $Z_1(\xi; T)$ is not a convex function of ξ. $Z_1(\xi; T)$ is continuous, however, although there is a discontinuity in the derivative at $\xi = r^*$. Hence, we see from (8-11) that since $F_2(y; T)$ involves $Z_1(\xi; T)$, $F_2(y; T)$ cannot be expected to be convex, in general. By continuing the argument, it can be seen that the $F_n(y; T)$, $n > 1$ will not necessarily be convex.

It is the fixed ordering cost A which causes $Z_1(\xi; T)$, or more generally $Z_n(\xi; T)$ and $F_n(y; T)$, not to be convex even though $f(y; T)$ is convex. In fact, one can prove that when $A = 0$, the $F_n(y; T)$ and $F(y; T)$ are convex functions of y if $f(y; T)$ is. This result will follow from what is demonstrated below. It can be obtained directly, however, and we ask the reader to do this in Problem 8-2.

The above shows that since we do not expect $F(y; T)$ to be convex, the proof cannot be based on demonstrating the convexity of $F(y; T)$. Indeed, F may have a number of relative maxima and minima. As before, denote by R^* the point at which F takes on its absolute minimum. If this point is not unique, R^* will denote the smallest value of y for which F takes on its absolute minimum. Also, let $\hat{R}$ denote any point at which F takes on a relative minimum (R^* will be one such point). Suppose now that the following conditions are satisfied. For each $\hat{R}$, it is true that there are no points $y < \hat{R}$ with $F(y; T) > A + F(\hat{R}; T)$ at which F takes on a relative maximum. This means that the curve $z = F(y; T)$ can *cross* the horizontal line $z = A + F(\hat{R}; T)$ only once for $y < \hat{R}$. Thus if $r^* < \hat{R}$ is the point where the curve $z = F(y; T)$ crosses the horizontal line $z = A + F(R^*; T)$, $Q^* = 0$ if $\xi \geq r^*$ and $Q^* = R^* - \xi$ if $\xi < r^*$, so that an Rr policy is optimal. When the above conditions are satisfied, cases like that shown in

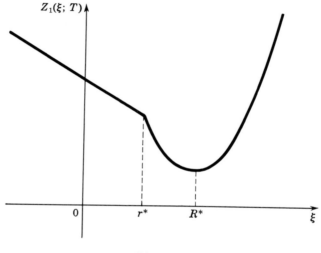

FIGURE 8-4.

Fig. 8-2, and cases where there exist relative minima with $\hat{R} > R^*$ such that for certain ranges of $\xi > R^*$ it is optimal to order up to $\hat{R}$ (illustrate this graphically), are ruled out.

We shall prove below that if $f(y; T)$ is convex and differentiable everywhere with respect to y, then $F(y; T)$ is continuous and differentiable everywhere with respect to y (even though $Z(\xi; T)$ need not be differentiable everywhere with respect to ξ), and that for any $\alpha \geq 0$

$$A + F(\alpha + y; T) - F(y; T) - \alpha F'(y; T) \geq 0 \qquad (8\text{-}14)$$

where a prime indicates the derivative with respect to y. However, the condition (8-14) does indeed assure us that $F(y; T)$ cannot have a relative maximum at a point $y < \hat{R}$ if $F(y; T) > A + F(\hat{R}; T)$. To see this, assume that $F(y; T)$ has a relative maximum at $y_1 < \hat{R}$ with $F(y_1; T) > A + F(\hat{R}; T)$. A contradiction is obtained on using (8-14), if we set $\hat{R} = \alpha + y_1$, since at y_1, $F'(y_1; T) = 0$, and (8-14) becomes $A + F(\hat{R}; T) - F(y_1; T) \geq 0$. Hence, the truth of (8-14) assures us that an Rr policy will be optimal.

It remains, then, to prove that (8-14) holds if $f(y; T)$ is convex and differentiable everywhere. For carrying costs and backorder costs of the type we use in this book $f(y; T)$ is always differentiable everywhere with respect to y when all variables are treated as continuous. We have previously defined a function $f(y)$ as convex if for any values y_1, y_2 and any α, $0 \leq \alpha \leq 1$, then

$$f[\alpha y_1 + (1 - \alpha)y_2] \leq \alpha f(y_1) + (1 - \alpha)f(y_2)$$

When $f(y)$ is differentiable everywhere, an equivalent definition of convexity is that for any $\alpha \geq 0$

$$f(\alpha + y) - f(y) - \alpha f'(y) \geq 0 \tag{8-15}$$

where $f'(y) = df/dy$. We ask the reader to show this equivalence and to give a geometric interpretation in Problem 8-3.

Scarf defines a modified form of convexity called A-convexity, which is a useful concept in carrying out the proof. For any number $A \geq 0$, the differentiable function $f(y)$ is said to be A-convex if for all y and any $\alpha \geq 0$

$$A + f(\alpha + y) - f(y) - \alpha f'(y) \geq 0 \tag{8-16}$$

From (8-15) we see that a 0-convex function is convex. The following properties of A-convex functions will be needed. These properties may be easily proved and the details are left for Problem 8-4.

(a) If $f(y)$ is A-convex, then $f(y + x)$ is A-convex for any fixed x.

(b) If $f_1(y)$ is A_1-convex and $f_2(y)$ is A_2-convex, then $\theta_1 f_1(y) + \theta_2 f_2(y)$ is $(\theta_1 A_1 + \theta_2 A_2)$-convex when θ_1, $\theta_2 > 0$.

(c) If $f(y)$ is A-convex, then

$$a \int_0^\infty v(x)f(y - x) \, dx, \quad 0 < a \leq 1$$

is A-convex when $v(x)$ is a probability density function.

(d) If $f(y)$ is A_1-convex, it is also A_2-convex for $A_2 > A_1$.

We shall now give the proof of (8-14). We shall first show that the functions $F_n(y; T)$ defined by (8-11) for the n stage approximation are A-convex. This is done sequentially (i.e., by induction). We observe that $F_1(y; T) = Cy + f(y; T)$ is A-convex, since y and $f(y; T)$ are 0-convex, and by property (b) above $F_1(y; T)$ is 0-convex, and hence is A-convex by property (d) above.

Now assume that $F_1(y; T), \ldots, F_{n-1}(y; T)$ are A-convex for any positive integer $n > 1$. We shall then show that $F_n(y; T)$ is A-convex. By induction it thus follows that $F_j(y; T)$ is A-convex for all positive integers j. From (8-11), we see that $F_n(y; T)$ will be A-convex if

$$a \int_0^\infty v(x) Z_{n-1}(y - x; T)\, dx$$

is. However, from property (c) above, this will be true when $Z_{n-1}(y; T)$ is A-convex. To prove that $Z_{n-1}(y; T)$ is A-convex, we observe first that, since by assumption $F_{n-1}(y; T)$ is A-convex, the optimal ordering policy at stage $n - 1$ will be of an Rr type, i.e., there exist numbers r_{n-1}^* and R_{n-1}^* such that if $\xi < r_{n-1}^*$, $Q_{n-1}^* = R_{n-1}^* - \xi$ and if $\xi \geq r_{n-1}^*$, $Q_{n-1}^* = 0$. Thus

$$Z_{n-1}(\xi; T) = \begin{cases} J + A - C\xi + F_{n-1}(R_{n-1}^*; T), & \xi < r_{n-1}^* \\ J - C\xi + F_{n-1}(\xi; T), & \xi \geq r_{n-1}^* \end{cases} \quad (8\text{-}17)$$

We ask the reader to show in Problem 8-5 that if $F_{n-1}(y; T)$ is everywhere a continuous and differentiable function of y, then $Z_{n-1}(\xi; T)$ is a continuous function of ξ everywhere, and $F_n(y; T)$ is a continuous and differentiable function of y everywhere. It is also true that $F_1(y; T)$ is a continuous and differentiable function of y everywhere if $f(y; T)$ is. Hence, all the $F_j(y; T)$ are continuous and differentiable functions of y everywhere.

Let us now use (8-17) to show that $Z_{n-1}(\xi; T)$ is A-convex. This requires that we show that (8-16) holds for all ξ and any $\alpha \geq 0$. Three cases must be considered depending on the values of $\xi, \xi + \alpha$ relative to r_{n-1}^*.

Case 1: $\xi + \alpha, \xi \geq r_{n-1}^*$.

From (8-17) we see that in this region $Z_{n-1}(\xi; T)$ is the sum of a 0-convex and A-convex function and hence is A-convex.

Case 2: $\xi < r_{n-1}^* \leq \xi + \alpha$.

Here we need to determine the sign of

$$A + Z_{n-1}(\xi + \alpha; T) - Z_{n-1}(\xi; T) - \alpha Z_{n-1}'(\xi; T) \quad (8\text{-}18)$$

where the prime indicates differentiation with respect to ξ. To do this observe that from (8-17)

$$Z_{n-1}'(\xi; T) = -C \quad (8\text{-}19)$$

since $\xi < r_{n-1}^*$. Also for $\xi < r_{n-1}^*$

$$Z_{n-1}(\xi; T) = \min_{Q_{n-1}} \{J + A + CQ_{n-1} + f(\xi + Q_{n-1}; T)$$

$$+ a \int_0^\infty v(x; T) Z_{n-2}(\xi + Q_{n-1} - x; T)\, dx\} \le J + A + Ca$$

$$+ f(\xi + \alpha; T) + a \int_0^\infty v(x; T) Z_{n-2}(\xi + \alpha - x; T)\, dx \qquad (8\text{-}20)$$

since the optimal Q_{n-1} will yield a value less than or equal to that for $Q_{n-1} = \alpha$. However, when $\xi + \alpha \ge r_{n-1}^*$

$$Z_{n-1}(\xi + \alpha; T) = J + f(\xi + \alpha; T)$$

$$+ a \int_0^\infty v(x; T) Z_{n-2}(\xi + \alpha - x; T)\, dx \quad (8\text{-}21)$$

since it is optimal not to order in this case. Therefore, on combining (8-21) with (8-20)

$$Z_{n-1}(\xi; T) \le A + C\alpha + Z_{n-1}(\xi + \alpha; T)$$

or because of (8-19)

$$A + Z_{n-1}(\xi + \alpha; T) - Z_{n-1}(\xi; T) - \alpha Z'_{n-1}(\xi; T) \ge 0$$

as desired.

Case 3: $\xi, \xi + \alpha < r_{n-1}^*$.

From (8-17), $Z_{n-1}(\xi; T)$ is linear and hence A-convex in this region.

This then completes the proof that $Z_{n-1}(\xi; T)$ is A-convex if $F_{n-1}(\xi; T)$ is. Hence $F_n(y; T)$ is A-convex if $F_1(y; T), \ldots, F_{n-1}(y; T)$ are A-convex. Thus by induction the $F_j(y; T)$ are A-convex for all positive integers j.

To prove that $F(y; T)$ is A-convex, we must pass to the limit as $n \to \infty$. It is clear that $Z_n(\xi; T)$ approaches $Z(\xi; T)$ as $n \to \infty$, and hence $F_n(y; T)$ approaches a unique limit $F(y; T)$ (proof?). Furthermore, for fixed values of y, α, T the sequence

$$G_n(y, \alpha; T) = A + F_n(y + \alpha; T) - F_n(y; T) - \alpha F'_n(y; T) \ge 0$$

so that 0 is a lower bound on the sequence and hence (how do we know that F' exists?)

$$G(y, \alpha; T) = \lim_{n \to \infty} G_n(y, \alpha; T)$$

$$= A + F(y + \alpha; T) - F(y; T) - \alpha F'(y; T) \ge 0$$

for any y and any $\alpha \ge 0$. Thus $F(y; T)$ is A-convex, and an *Rr* policy is optimal for the steady state periodic review system if $f(y; T)$ is a convex function of y and the unit cost is constant.

Geometrically, the fact that $F(y; T)$ is A-convex rules out cases such as those shown in Fig. 8-2 where an Rr policy is not optimal. It does not, however, rule out behavior such as that shown in Fig. 8-5 where an Rr policy is optimal.

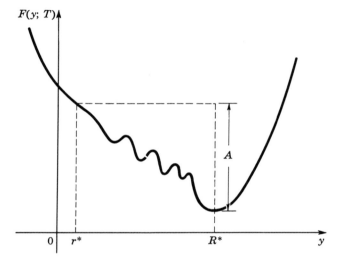

FIGURE 8-5.

8-5 Use of Dynamic Programming to Compute Optimal Values of R and r

The solution to the functional equation (8-5) will yield $Z(\xi; T)$ and $Q^*(\xi; T)$. If an Rr policy is optimal, $Q^*(\xi; T)$ will yield the values of R^* and r^*, since $Q^* = 0$, $\xi \geq r^*$, and $Q^* = R^* - \xi$ for $\xi < r^*$. Hence Q^* will have the form of the curve shown in Fig. 8-6. Thus r^* is the point where Q^* changes discontinuously from 0 to $R^* - r^*$ and the magnitude of the jump then determines R^*.

A possible procedure for computing numerically R^* and r^* for a given T is to approximate the infinite period system using n periods, as was done in the previous section in proving the optimality of Rr policies. The appropriate recurrence relations for the n period case are given by (8-10) and (8-12). Then $Q_n^*(\xi; T)$ is used as an approximation to $Q^*(\xi; T)$, and R^* and r^* can be determined from $Q_n(\xi; T)$ as indicated above. The n period system can be solved numerically using a digital computer. The value of n used might be something like 100. It is fairly easy to decide whether or not $Q_n^*(\xi; T)$ is a close enough approximation to $Q^*(\xi; T)$. If there has been only a negligible change in $Q_n^*(\xi; T)$ for a number of periods, then it should be satisfactory to use $Q_n^*(\xi; T)$ for $Q^*(\xi; T)$. In making the numerical computations, one would, of course, treat all variables as discrete rather than continuous.

In order to make the computations, it is necessary to specify a value of the interest rate, that is, it is necessary to specify a. For sufficiently

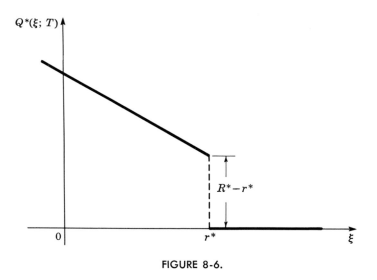

FIGURE 8-6.

small values of the interest rate the results will be independent of the interest rate. However, when the interest rate becomes large, the computed results may depend on the value of the interest rate selected. It will be shown later that the results computed using the n stage approximation will most closely approximate the R^* and r^* that would be obtained using the average annual cost expression of Sec. 5-9 if the interest rate is taken to be zero.

To determine T^*, the computations would have to be made for different T values. In order to select the optimal T it is necessary to have some costs to compare. Now if the n used in making the computation is sufficiently large, then the minimum expected cost $Z_n(\xi; T)$ will be essentially the same for any ξ lying between R and r since any one of these values are allowable at a review time when the steady state system is operated. Thus T^* can be determined by finding the T which minimizes $Z_n[R^*(T); T]$. If the reader does not see why any $Z_n(\xi; T)$ for between r and R can be used, a more rigorous justification will be presented later.

It would, of course, be an impossibly laborious task to compute manually R^*, r^*, and T^* by the method outlined above. However, it is quite feasible to make the computation using a large scale digital computer. The method outlined above will, in general, require more computer time than the computational procedure suggested in Sec. 5-9. It does, though, provide an alternative procedure for computing R^* and r^*.

8-6 The Functional Equation for Transactions Reporting Systems

The functional equation approach can be used to study transactions reporting systems as well as periodic review systems. In fact, the functional equation approach provides a way to study cases where the number of units demanded per demand is a random variable, and cases where the density function describing the time between demands is not exponential. Not nearly as much has appeared in the literature discussing the functional equations for transactions reporting systems as for periodic review systems. In fact, the papers by Beckmann [4] and Beckmann and Muth [3] are the only ones which discuss the subject.

Let us then consider a transactions reporting system with constant procurement lead times, in which demands occurring when the system is out of stock are backordered. Define $Z(\xi)$ to be the discounted expected cost over all future time when an optimal policy is followed at all future times, the time origin is immediately after a demand occurs, and ξ is the inventory position at the time origin *after* taking whatever action is appropriate (i.e., after the placing of an order if it is desirable to do so). As above, we do not include in $Z(\xi)$ any backorder or carrying costs incurred before time τ (τ being the lead time). To obtain the functional equation, we write $Z(\xi)$ as the sum of the expected discounted costs occurring until the next demand and those occurring after the next demand.

We shall assume that the unit cost of the item is constant; A, I, C, π, $\hat{\pi}$ will have their usual meanings. In formulating the functional equation for $Z(\xi)$, we shall allow the number of units demanded per demand to be a random variable, and also allow the probability that a demand occurs in the time interval t to $t + dt$ following a demand to be a function of t. A variety of probability distributions introduced in Chapter 3 will be used here. Let $g(t) dt$ be the probability that the time between two successive demands lies between t and $t + dt$, $d(j|t)$ the probability that j units are demanded when a demand occurs if a time t has elapsed since the previous demand (note that we can allow the number of units to depend on the time since the last demand), and $V_n(t)$ the probability that precisely n units are demanded in a time interval of length t following a demand.

Suppose that a demand occurs at time 0, and after taking whatever action is appropriate, the inventory position of the system is ξ. It will be supposed that it is never optimal to have $\xi < 0$. Assume also that the next demand occurs between t and $t + dt$. The probability of this is $g(t)\, dt$. We would like to compute the expected cost (discounted to time 0) of carrying inventory and of backorders in the time interval τ to $\tau + t$. Imagine that the demand at time t is for j units. The probability of this is $d(j|t)$. We shall perform the computation in two parts, depending on whether $\tau > t$ or $\tau \leq t$.

In making the computations, we must, as in the periodic review case, introduce a discount factor in order that the cost will be finite. Here there is no natural period, and hence it is convenient to use continuous discounting. By this we mean that if we have a sum $S(t)$ at time t, and if the interest rate is i, then at time $t + \Delta t$, the sum $S(t + \Delta t)$ which we have will be given by

$$S(t + \Delta t) = (1 + i\Delta t)S(t)$$

for small Δt, or taking the limit as $\Delta t \to 0$ and solving the resulting differential equation, we obtain

$$S(t) = S(0)e^{it} \quad \text{or} \quad S(0) = S(t)e^{-it} \tag{8-22}$$

Thus the present worth $S(0)$ at time 0 of a sum $S(t)$ at time t is $S(t)e^{-it}$ so that the discount factor is e^{-it}.

Consider first the case where $\tau > t$. The probability that x demands have occurred between time 0 and ζ, $\tau \leq \zeta \leq \tau + t$, is

$$\sum_{j=1}^{x} d(j|t) V_{x-j}(\zeta - t) \tag{8-23}$$

The discounted expected cost of the unit years of shortage incurred between τ and $\tau + t$ is, when averaged over $t < \tau$

$$\hat{\pi} \int_0^{\tau} \int_{\tau}^{\tau+t} \sum_{x=\xi}^{\infty} (x - \xi)e^{-i\zeta} \left[\sum_{j=1}^{x} d(j|t) V_{x-j}(\zeta - t) \right] g(t)\, d\zeta\, dt \tag{8-24}$$

It is actually more difficult to compute the expected fixed backorder cost incurred between τ and $\tau + t$ because of the continuous discounting. We cannot simply compute the expected number incurred between τ and $\tau + t$, then multiply by π and a discount factor. The backorders must be costed and discounted at the point of time when they occur. To do this we define $W_k(n + k; t)\, dt$ to be the probability that in a time interval of length t

following a demand n units are demanded, and between t and $t + dt$ a demand for k units occurs. It is then easy to give an expression for the discounted expected fixed cost of backorders incurred between τ and $\tau + t$. When averaged over $t < \tau$, it is

$$\pi \int_0^\tau \int_\tau^{\tau+t} e^{-i\zeta} \sum_{k=1}^\infty \sum_{x=\xi}^\infty \sum_{j=1}^x k W_k(x - j + k; \zeta - t) \, d(j|t) \, g(t) d\zeta \, dt \, +$$

$$\pi \int_0^\tau \int_\tau^{\tau+t} e^{-i\zeta} \sum_{x=1}^{\xi-1} \sum_{k=\xi-x}^\infty \sum_{j=1}^x (k + x - \xi) W_k(x - j + k; \zeta - t) \, d(j|t) g(t) d\zeta \, dt$$

$$(8\text{-}25)$$

The second term in (8-25) arises because x may be less than ξ while $x + k$ is greater than ξ.

The $W_k(n + k; t)$ can be computed recursively just as the $V_n(t)$. It is clear that

$$W_k(n + k; t) = \int_0^t \sum_{m=1}^n d(k|t - \zeta) g(t - \zeta) W_m(n; \zeta) \, d\zeta, \quad n \geq 1 \quad (8\text{-}26)$$

and

$$W_k(k; t) = d(k|t) g(t) \quad (8\text{-}27)$$

The expected discounted cost of carrying inventory from τ to $\tau + t$ is, when averaged over $t < \tau$

$$IC \int_0^\tau \int_\tau^{\tau+t} \sum_{x=1}^\xi (\xi - x) e^{-i\zeta} \left[\sum_{j=1}^x d(j|t) V_{x-j}(\zeta - t) \right] g(t) \, d\zeta \, dt \quad (8\text{-}28)$$

We must compute now the costs corresponding to those above for the case where $t \geq \tau$. From τ to t the on hand inventory is ξ (and no backorders exist for this time interval since by assumption $\xi \geq 0$). However, from t to $\tau + t$, the computation must be made as above. The discounted expected cost of the unit years of shortage incurred from t to $\tau + t$ averaged over $t \geq \tau$ is

$$\hat{\pi} \int_\tau^\infty \int_t^{\tau+t} \sum_{x=\xi}^\infty (x - \xi) e^{-i\zeta} \left[\sum_{j=1}^x d(j|t) V_{x-j}(\zeta - t) \right] g(t) \, d\zeta \, dt \quad (8\text{-}29)$$

Similarly, the discounted expected fixed cost of backorders incurred from t to $\tau + t$ averaged over $t \geq \tau$ is

$$\pi \int_\tau^\infty \sum_{j=\xi}^\infty (j - \xi) e^{-it} \, d(j|t) g(t) \, dt$$

$$+ \pi \int_\tau^\infty \int_t^{\tau+t} e^{-i\zeta} \sum_{k=1}^\infty \sum_{x=\xi}^\infty \sum_{j=1}^x k W_k(x - j + k; \zeta - t) \, d(j|t) g(t) \, d\zeta \, dt$$

$$+ \pi \int_\tau^\infty \int_t^{\tau+t} e^{-i\zeta} \sum_{x=1}^{\xi-1} \sum_{k=\xi-x}^\infty \sum_{j=1}^x (k + x - \xi) W_k(x - j + k; \zeta - t)$$

$$d(j|t)g(t) \, d\zeta \, dt \qquad (8\text{-}30)$$

The first term arises because of the possibility of incurring fixed backorder costs when the demand occurs at time t.

The expected carrying cost from time τ to $\tau + t$ averaged over $t \geq \tau$ is

$$IC \int_\tau^\infty \int_\tau^t e^{-i\zeta} \zeta g(t) \, d\zeta \, dt + IC \int_\tau^\infty \int_t^{\tau+t} \sum_{x=1}^\xi (\xi - x)e^{-i\zeta}$$

$$\left[\sum_{j=1}^x d(j|t) V_{x-j}(\zeta - t) \right] g(t) \, d\zeta \, dt \qquad (8\text{-}31)$$

The discounted expected cost of carrying inventory and of backorders from τ to $\tau + t$ averaged over all t can then be written

$$f(\xi) = ICD(\xi) + \pi E(\xi) + \hat{\pi} B(\xi) \qquad (8\text{-}32)$$

where

$$D(\xi) = \sum_{x=0}^\xi (\xi - x)\eta(x) \qquad (8\text{-}33)$$

$$B(\xi) = \sum_{x=\xi}^\infty (x - \xi)\eta(x) \qquad (8\text{-}34)$$

$$E(\xi) = \sum_{x=0}^{\xi-1} \sum_{k=\xi-x}^\infty (x + k - \xi)\theta(k, x) + \sum_{x=\xi}^\infty \sum_{k=1}^\infty k\theta(k, x)$$

$$+ \sum_{x=\xi}^\infty (x - \xi)\theta(0, x) \qquad (8\text{-}35)$$

and

$$\eta(x) = \int_0^\tau \int_\tau^{\tau+t} e^{-i\zeta} \left[\sum_{j=1}^x d(j|t) V_{x-j}(\zeta - t) \right] g(t) \, d\zeta \, dt$$

$$+ \int_\tau^\infty \int_t^{\tau+t} e^{-i\zeta} \left[\sum_{j=1}^x d(j|t) V_{x-j}(\zeta - t) \right] g(t) \, d\zeta \, dt, \qquad x = 1, 2, 3 \ldots$$

$$(8\text{-}36)$$

$$\eta(0) = -\frac{1}{i} \int_\tau \left[e^{-it} - e^{-i\tau} \right] g(t) \, dt \qquad (8\text{-}37)$$

and

$$\theta(k, x) = \int_0^\tau \int_\tau^{\tau+t} e^{-i\zeta} \left[\sum_{j=1}^x W_k(x - j + k; \zeta - t) \, d(j|t) \right] g(t) \, d\zeta \, dt$$

$$+ \int_\tau^\infty \int_t^{\tau+t} e^{-i\zeta} \left[\sum_{j=1}^x W_k(x - j + k; \zeta - t) \, d(j|t) \right] g(t) \, d\zeta \, dt,$$

$$k = 1, 2, \ldots$$

$$x = 1, 2, \ldots \qquad (8\text{-}38)$$

$$\theta(0, x) = \int_\tau^\infty e^{-it} \, d(x|t) g(t) \, dt, \quad x = 1, 2, \ldots \qquad (8\text{-}39)$$

Having computed the expected discounted costs $f(\xi)$ of carrying inventory and of backorders incurred from τ to $\tau + t$ and averaged over t, we can then immediately write down the functional equation for $Z(\xi)$. It is

$$Z(\xi) = f(\xi) + \int_0^\infty \sum_{j=1}^\infty e^{-it} \, d(j|t) g(t) \{\min_{y \geq 0}[A\delta + Cy + Z(\xi + y - j)]\} \, dt$$

Thus, since $Z(\xi + y - j)$ is independent of t

$$Z(\xi) = f(\xi) + a \sum_{j=1}^\infty p(j) \{\min_{y \geq 0}[A\delta + Cy + Z(\xi + y - j)]\} \qquad (8\text{-}40)$$

where

$$\int_0^\infty e^{-it} \, d(j|t) g(t) \, dt = ap(j) \qquad (8\text{-}41)$$

and

$$a = \int_0^\infty g(t) e^{-it} \, dt \qquad (8\text{-}42)$$

Hence

$$\sum_{j=1}^\infty p(j) = 1$$

and the $p(j)$ can be thought of as probabilities. Note that a is simply the expected value of the discount factor over the time until the next demand occurs.

The functional equation (8-40) differs from other dynamic programming problems that we have studied in that the minimization over y must be carried out before summing over j, i.e., y^* is a function of $\xi - j$, not of ξ. The intuitive reason for this is clear. The optimal quantity to procure will depend on the number of units demanded when the next demand occurs.

The solution to the functional equation will yield $Z(\xi)$ and $y^*(\xi - j)$. The function $y^*(\xi - j)$ provides the optimal operating doctrine which we are seeking.

8-7 Optimality of Rr Policies for Transactions Reporting Systems

Intuitively, one would expect that an Rr policy would be optimal for transactions reporting systems of the type discussed in the previous section. We here wish to show that, normally, an Rr policy will be optimal. From the results of Sec. 8-4 we know that an Rr policy will be optimal if $f(\xi)$ is convex when the variable ξ is treated as continuous and the unit cost is constant (proof?). To see that $f(\xi)$ will normally be convex, note that $ICD(\xi) + \hat{\pi}B(\xi)$ can be written

$$\sum_{x=0}^{\infty} l(\xi - x)\eta(x) \tag{8-43}$$

where

$$l(\xi - x) = \begin{cases} IC(\xi - x), & \xi - x \geq 0 \\ \hat{\pi}(x - \xi), & \xi - x < 0 \end{cases} \tag{8-44}$$

Thus $l(\xi - x)$ is a convex function of ξ for a given x (plot $l(\xi - x)$ as a function of ξ). Now since $\eta(x) \geq 0$, it follows that $ICD(\xi) + \hat{\pi}B(\xi)$ is a convex function of ξ. This is to be proved in Problem 8-7. The term $\pi E(\xi)$ will not necessarily be convex for all ξ. In Problem 8-7, we ask the reader to explain why this is the case. However, $\pi E(\xi)$ will usually be convex for ξ in the range of interest. Therefore, we normally expect $f(\xi)$ to be convex, and hence an Rr policy will be optimal, provided that the unit cost is constant.

In the event that units are demanded one at a time and transactions reporting is used, it is possible to show that an Rr policy is optimal under much more general conditions than those discussed above. For this case, an Rr policy will be optimal provided only that the expected carrying and backorder costs incurred between τ and $\tau + t$ depend on ξ alone and hence can be written $f(\xi)$. This will be true independently of the shape of $f(\xi)$. Here, it need not be assumed that the unit cost of the item is constant. An Rr policy will be optimal even if quantity discounts are available. The proof of these facts is left for Problem 8-20.

It is possible to evaluate numerically $Z(\xi)$ and $y^*(\xi - j)$, and hence R^*, r^*, using the same sort of procedure suggested in Sec. 8-5 for a periodic review system. We approximate the infinite stage process by n stages, so that (8-40) is replaced by

$$Z_n(\xi) = f(\xi) + a \sum_{j=1}^{\infty} p(j) \{\min_{y \geq 0}[A\delta + Cy + Z_{n-1}(\xi + y - j)]\} \quad (8\text{-}45)$$

$$Z_1(\xi) = f(\xi) \quad (8\text{-}46)$$

Then $y_n^*(\xi - j)$ is taken to be $y^*(\xi - j)$. Since for the transactions reporting system being studied, a stage refers to the time between two successive demands, n will in general need to be quite large before $y_n^*(\xi) = y^*(\xi)$. Here, the value of n required can vary widely depending on the mean rate of demand. An n of several thousand may be required, or, for very low mean rates of demand, an n of less than one hundred may be satisfactory. For medium or high mean rates of demand, many more stages will be required than for a periodic review system with the same mean rate of demand. On the other hand, it is not necessary here to run the problem many times to find the optimal T, as required in the periodic review case. The task of computing the optimal operating doctrine for a transactions reporting system in this way could be quite time consuming even for a large digital computer; however, it can be accomplished. Later we shall introduce a somewhat simpler procedure for determining R^* and r^* which makes use of the average annual cost expression. This simpler procedure still requires the use of a large scale computer, however.

8-8 Explicit Solution of the Functional Equation when a Poisson Process Generates Demands and Units are Demanded One at a Time

It is an interesting fact that the functional equation (8-40) can be solved explicitly for $Z(\xi)$. We shall illustrate here how this can be done in the case where a Poisson process generates demands and units are demanded one at a time. In the next section, the more general case will be considered. The explicit solution of the functional equation makes it possible to also obtain an explicit expression for the average annual cost, thus establishing a link between the functional equation approach and that used in Chapter 4. For the case of a Poisson process generating demands with units being demanded one at a time, we shall obtain the average annual cost in this way and show that it is precisely the same as that obtained in Chapter 4.

When units are demanded one at a time, the functional equation (8-40) can be written

$$Z(\xi) = f(\xi) - aC\xi + \min_{y \geq 0} \{aA\delta + a(\xi + y)C + aZ(\xi + y - 1)\} \quad (8\text{-}47)$$

Now an Rr policy must be optimal in this case. We can write $R^* = r^* + Q^*$. The quantity procured will always be Q^*. Let $r^* + 1$ be the largest value of ξ such that in (8-47), $y^* > 0$. Also, write

$$F(x) = Cx + Z(x - 1) \quad (8\text{-}48)$$

and let $\min_x F(x)$ be taken on at $x = R^* + 1$. Then

$$Z(r^* + 1) = f(r^* + 1) + aCQ^* + aA + aZ(R^*) \qquad (8\text{-}49)$$

For $\xi > r^* + 1$, no order will be placed when the next demand occurs. Thus

$$Z(r^* + 2) = f(r^* + 2) + aZ(r^* + 1) \qquad (8\text{-}50)$$

$$Z(r^* + 3) = f(r^* + 3) + aZ(r^* + 2) \qquad (8\text{-}51)$$

$$\vdots$$

$$Z(R^*) \quad = f(R^*) + aZ(R^* - 1) \qquad (8\text{-}52)$$

When the system is operated optimally, the inventory position will never get above R^*, since one never orders above R^*. Now substitute (8-49) into (8-50), the resulting equation into (8-51), etc. This yields

$$Z(r^* + k) = \sum_{j=1}^{k} a^{k-j} f(r^* + j) + a^k[A + CQ^* + Z(R^*)],$$

$$k = 1, \ldots, Q^* \qquad (8\text{-}53)$$

In particular

$$Z(R^*) = \sum_{j=1}^{Q^*} a^{Q^*-j} f(r^* + j) + a^{Q^*}[A + CQ^* + Z(R^*)]$$

or

$$Z(R^*) = \frac{1}{1 - a^{Q^*}} \left[\sum_{j=1}^{Q^*} a^{Q^*-j} f(r^* + j) + a^{Q^*}(A + CQ^*) \right] \qquad (8\text{-}54)$$

Here we have obtained an explicit expression for $Z(R^*)$. Substitution of (8-54) into (8-53) yields explicit expressions for each $Z(r^* + k)$, i.e.,

$$Z(r^* + k) =$$

$$\sum_{j=1}^{k} a^{k-j} f(r^* + j) + \frac{a^k}{1 - a^{Q^*}} \left[A + CQ^* + \sum_{j=1}^{Q^*} a^{Q^*-j} f(r^* + j) \right]$$

$$= \frac{a^k}{1 - a^{Q^*}} \left[A + CQ^* + \sum_{j=1}^{k} a^{-j} f(r^* + j) + a^{Q^*} \sum_{j=k+1}^{Q^*} a^{-j} f(r^* + j) \right],$$

$$k = 1, \ldots, Q^* \qquad (8\text{-}55)$$

Recall that $Z(\xi)$ can be interpreted as the discounted value of all future costs (with the convention that no carrying or backorder costs are incurred until a lead time has elapsed) when the inventory position is ξ immediately after a demand, and an optimal policy is followed for all future times. We have noted previously that an Rr policy is optimal, and hence, when the system is operated optimally, ξ will only have one of the values $r^* + 1, \ldots, r^* + Q^* = R^*$. For each of these ξ values, we have in (8-55) an explicit expression for $Z(\xi)$.

We shall now define a new function $\mathfrak{z}(\xi; R, r)$ as follows: $\mathfrak{z}(\xi; R, r)$ is the discounted expected value of all future costs evaluated immediately after the occurrence of a demand (time 0) when an Rr policy is used to operate the system with the reorder point being r, and $Q = R - r$ the order quantity (note that R and r need not be the optimal values of these quantities), and ξ is the inventory position at time 0 after an order has been placed if it is called for. As usual, it is assumed that no carrying or backorder costs incurred until a lead time has elapsed are included, i.e., until time τ. The function $\mathfrak{z}(\xi; R, r)$ then satisfies the functional equation

$$\mathfrak{z}(\xi; R, r) = f(\xi) + a\mathfrak{z}(\xi - 1; R, r), \quad \xi = r + 2, \ldots, R$$

$$\mathfrak{z}(r + 1; R, r) = aA + aCQ + f(r + 1) + a\mathfrak{z}(R; R, r)$$

(8-56)

since, when this Rr doctrine is used, the only possible values of ξ are $r + 1, \ldots, R$. Thus equations (8-49) through (8-52) are satisfied if Z is replaced by $\mathfrak{z}$ and the asterisks on r, R, and Q are omitted. Hence an explicit solution for $\mathfrak{z}(\xi; R, r)$ if given by (8-55), if Z is replaced by $\mathfrak{z}$ and the asterisks are omitted on r and Q. Note that

$$Z(r^* + k) = \mathfrak{z}(r^* + k; R^*, r^*), \quad k = 1, \ldots, Q^*$$

It will now be shown how to relate $\mathfrak{z}(\xi; R, r)$ to the average annual cost $\mathcal{K}(Q, r)$. To do this, consider an ensemble of identical systems in statistical equilibrium. If over any given interval of time of length Δt, we determine the ensemble average of the costs incurred over this time interval and then divide by Δt, the result obtained, when expressed in the dimensions of dollars per year, will be simply the average annual cost $\mathcal{K}(Q, r)$, for any $\Delta t > 0$, however small. Furthermore, the rate of incurring costs $\mathcal{K}$ which is obtained will be independent of time. Now consider the quantity $\mathcal{L}$ defined by

$$\mathcal{L} = \int_0^\infty e^{-it}\mathcal{K} \, dt = \mathcal{K} \int_0^\infty e^{-it} \, dt = \mathcal{K}/i$$

Thus

$$\mathcal{K} = i\mathcal{L}$$

(8-57)

$\mathcal{L}$ has the following interpretation. If we begin observation of the ensemble of systems at a given point in time, and for each system in the ensemble, we continuously determine the total costs, discounted to time t, incurred since we began observation, then $\mathcal{L}$ would be the limit of the ensemble average of these costs as the time over which observations are made becomes infinite. Equation (8-57) is the familiar expression relating the present worth to average annual cost.

We must now relate $\mathcal{L}$ to the $\mathfrak{z}(\xi; R, r)$. Recall that $\mathfrak{z}$ is the discounted expected cost for a single system, given that we begin observation immediately after a demand occurs, and the inventory position is ξ at the time observation is begun, with the further restriction that no carrying or backorder costs are included until a lead time has elapsed. From this definition, the reader might feel that

$$\mathcal{L} = \frac{1}{Q} \sum_{k=1}^{Q} \mathfrak{z}(r + k; R, r)$$

since as shown in Chapter 4, the probability that the inventory position will be $r + k$ at an arbitrary point in time is $1/Q$, so that the fraction of the systems in the ensemble which have the inventory position $r + k$ when we began observation should be $1/Q$. This is not quite correct, however, because of the way in which $\mathfrak{z}(r + k; R, r)$ was defined. Recall that in the definition of $\mathfrak{z}(r + k; R, r)$ no carrying or backorder costs incurred between times 0 and τ were included. On the other hand, $\mathcal{L}$ includes these costs. Furthermore, $\mathfrak{z}(r + k; R, r)$ is defined only at points in time immediately after the occurrence of a demand and not at an arbitrary point in time. However, as the interest rate becomes smaller and smaller, both of these differences disappear, since then the carrying and backorder costs incurred from 0 to τ, and the correction to the cost arising from starting at an arbitrary point in time rather than immediately after a demand becomes a negligible fraction of the total discounted cost. This discussion then shows that $\mathcal{K}$ should be given by

$$\mathcal{K} = \lim_{i \to 0} \frac{i}{Q} \sum_{k=1}^{Q} \mathfrak{z}(r + k; R, r) \tag{8-58}$$

When we compute

$$\lim_{i \to 0} i\mathfrak{z}(r + k; R, r)$$

it turns out that the same result is obtained for each $k = 1, \ldots, Q$. We ask the reader to prove this in Problem 8-11. The intuitive reason for this is that as $i \to 0$, the contribution of the costs which depend on the starting inventory position become a negligible part of the total discounted cost. Because of this we have the simpler result

$$\mathcal{K} = \lim_{i \to 0} i\mathfrak{z}(r + k; R, r), \quad k = 1, \ldots, Q \tag{8-59}$$

or in particular

$$\mathcal{K} = \lim_{i \to 0} i\mathfrak{z}(R; R, r) \tag{8-60}$$

Using (8-60), we shall now compute $\mathcal{K}$ when a Poisson process generates demands, and show that precisely the same result is obtained as was obtained in Chapter 4. When a Poisson process generates demands, $g(t) = \lambda e^{-\lambda t}$ and from (8-42)

$$a = \lambda \int_0^\infty e^{-(\lambda+i)t}\, dt = \frac{\lambda}{\lambda + i} \qquad (8\text{-}61)$$

Thus

$$\lim_{i \to 0} a^{Q-i} = 1, \quad j = 0, \ldots, Q \qquad (8\text{-}62)$$

and

$$\lim_{i \to 0} \frac{i}{1 - a^Q} = \lim_{i \to 0} \frac{i}{1 - 1 + \dfrac{Q}{\lambda} i - \dfrac{Q(Q+1)}{2\lambda^2} i^2 + \cdots} = \frac{\lambda}{Q} \qquad (8\text{-}63)$$

where in the denominator, we have expanded a^Q by the binomial theorem. Hence from (8-54)

$$\mathcal{K} = \lim_{i \to 0} i\mathfrak{s}(R; R, r) = \frac{\lambda}{Q} A + \lambda C + \frac{\lambda}{Q} \sum_{k=1}^Q f(r + k) \qquad (8\text{-}64)$$

where in $f(r + j)$, we set $i = 0$.

It remains to evaluate $f(r + j)$. To do this we must first compute $\eta(x)$ and $\theta(k, x)$. When units are demanded one at a time and a Poisson process generates demands, $d(1|t) = 1$, $d(j|t) = 0$, $j \neq 1$, $V_x(t) = p(x; \lambda t)$, $W_k(n + k; t) = 0$, $k \neq 1$, and $W_1(n + 1; t) = \lambda p(n; \lambda t)$, since $W_1(n + 1; t)\, dt$ is the probability that n demands occur in a time t following a demand and a demand occurs between t and $t + dt$.

From (8-36), we see on making the substitution of variable $T = \zeta - t$, for fixed t, that when $i = 0$

$$\eta(x) = \lambda \int_0^\tau \int_{\tau-t}^\tau p(x - 1; \lambda T)e^{-\lambda t}\, dT\, dt + \lambda \int_\tau^\infty \int_0^\tau p(x - 1; \lambda T)e^{-\lambda t}\, dT\, dt,$$
$$x = 1, 2, \ldots \qquad (8\text{-}65)$$

We now change the order of integration of the first term by use of the familiar geometrical analysis employed in Chapter 3. This yields for the first term

$$\lambda \int_0^\tau \int_{\tau-T}^\tau p(x - 1; \lambda T)e^{-\lambda t}\, dt\, dT$$

which when combined with the second term yields

$$\eta(x) = \lambda \int_0^\tau \int_{\tau-T}^\infty p(x - 1; \lambda T)e^{-\lambda t}\, dt\, dT$$

We can now readily evaluate this integral explicitly. It is

$$\eta(x) = e^{-\lambda\tau} \int_0^\tau \frac{(\lambda T)^{x-1}}{(x-1)!} \, dT = \frac{1}{\lambda} p(x; \lambda\tau), \quad x = 1, 2, \ldots \quad (8\text{-}66)$$

From (8-37) we see that

$$\eta(0) = \lim_{i \to 0} -\frac{\lambda}{i}\left[\frac{1}{i+\lambda} - \frac{1}{\lambda}\right] e^{-(i+\lambda)\tau} = \frac{1}{\lambda} e^{-\lambda\tau} = \frac{1}{\lambda} p(0; \lambda\tau) \quad (8\text{-}67)$$

Since $W_1(x+1; t) = \lambda V_x(t) = \lambda p(x; \lambda t)$, we see on comparison of (8-36) and (8-38) that

$$\theta(1, x) = p(x; \lambda\tau) \quad (8\text{-}68)$$

From (8-32) it immediately follows that

$$
\begin{aligned}
f(r+k) &= \frac{IC}{\lambda} \sum_{x=0}^{r+k} (r+k-x)p(x; \lambda\tau) + \pi \sum_{x=r+k}^{\infty} p(x; \lambda\tau) \\
&\quad + \frac{\hat{\pi}}{\lambda} \sum_{x=r+k}^{\infty} (x-r-k)p(x; \lambda\tau) \\
&= \frac{IC}{\lambda}(r+k-\mu) + \pi \sum_{x=r+k}^{\infty} p(x; \lambda\tau) \\
&\quad + \frac{1}{\lambda}(\hat{\pi}+IC) \sum_{x=r+k}^{\infty} (x-r-k)p(x; \lambda\tau)
\end{aligned}
\quad (8\text{-}69)
$$

Hence, according to (8-64), $\mathcal{K}$ should be

$$
\begin{aligned}
\mathcal{K} &= \frac{\lambda}{Q} A + \lambda C + \frac{IC}{Q} \sum_{k=1}^{Q} (r+k-\mu) + \frac{\pi\lambda}{Q} \sum_{k=1}^{Q} P(r+k; \lambda\tau) \\
&\quad + \frac{\hat{\pi}+IC}{Q} \sum_{k=1}^{Q} \sum_{x=r+k}^{\infty} (x-r-k)p(x; \lambda\tau) \\
&= \frac{\lambda}{Q} A + \lambda C + IC\left[\frac{Q}{2} + \frac{1}{2} + r - \mu\right] + \frac{\pi\lambda}{Q} \sum_{u=r+1}^{r+Q} P(u; \lambda\tau) \\
&\quad + \frac{\hat{\pi}+IC}{Q} \sum_{y=r+1}^{r+Q} \sum_{x=y}^{\infty} (x-y)p(x; \lambda\tau)
\end{aligned}
\quad (8\text{-}70)
$$

However

$$\sum_{y=v}^{\infty} \sum_{x=y}^{\infty} (x-y)p(x; \lambda\tau) = \sum_{j=0}^{\infty} \sum_{w=v}^{\infty} (w-v)p(w+j; \lambda\tau)$$

$$= \sum_{w=v}^{\infty} (w-v)P(w; \lambda\tau)$$

on making the change of variables $y = v + j$, $w = x - j$. Thus we see that $\mathcal{K}$ is indeed equivalent to the average annual cost expression obtained in Chapter 4. Of course, here $\mathcal{K}$ includes the average annual cost of the units λC.

8-9 Explicit Solution of the Functional Equation in the General Case

It is possible to solve (8-40) explicitly for $Z(\xi)$ in the general case, but the task is somewhat more difficult than when units are demanded one at a time. Assume that an Rr policy is optimal. Then let r^* be the value of the inventory position such that if $\xi \leq r^*$ after a demand occurs an order will be placed. Assume that when an order is placed the inventory position is brought up to a level R^*. If the inventory position is $r^* + 1$ immediately after a demand occurs, it is certain that an order will be placed after the next demand occurs. Similarly, if the inventory position is $r^* + 2$ immediately after a demand, it will be $r^* + 1$ after the next demand if only a single unit is demanded and will be R^* if two or more units are demanded, since in this case an order will be placed. Thus

$$Z(r^* + 1) = f(r^* + 1) + a[A + Z(R^*)]$$

$$+ aC \sum_{j=1}^{\infty} (R^* - r^* + j - 1)p(j) \tag{8-71}$$

$$Z(r^* + 2) = f(r^* + 2) + aP(2)[A + Z(R^*)] + ap(1)Z(r^* + 1)$$

$$+ aC \sum_{j=2}^{\infty} (R^* - r^* + j - 2)p(j) \tag{8-72}$$

$$Z(r^* + 3) = f(r^* + 3) + aP(3)[A + Z(R^*)] + ap(1)Z(r^* + 2)$$

$$+ ap(2)Z(r^* + 1) + aC \sum_{j=3}^{\infty} (R^* - r^* + j - 3)p(j)$$

$$\tag{8-73}$$

$$\vdots$$

$$Z(R^* - 1) = f(R^* - 1) + aP(R^* - r^* - 1)[A + Z(R^*)]$$

$$+ ap(1)Z(R^* - 2) + ap(2)Z(R^* - 3)$$

$$+ \ldots + ap(R^* - r^* - 2)Z(r^* + 1)$$

$$+ aC \sum_{j=R^*-r^*-1}^{\infty} (j + 1)p(j) \tag{8-74}$$

$$Z(R^*) = f(R^*) + aP(R^* - r^*)[A + Z(R^*)]$$
$$+ ap(1)Z(R^* - 1) + ap(2)Z(R^* - 2)$$
$$+ \ldots + ap(R^* - r^* - 1)Z(r^* + 1) + aC \sum_{j=R^*-r^*}^{\infty} jp(j)$$

$$(8\text{-}75)$$

where $P(j)$ is the complementary cumulative of $p(j)$.

Let us now solve explicitly for $Z(R^*)$ by substituting (8-74) into (8-75), then $Z(R - 2)$ into the resulting expression, etc. On substitution of (8-74) into (8-75) we obtain

$$Z(R^*) = f(R^*) + ap(1)f(R^* - 1) + a[P(R^* - r^*)$$
$$+ ap(1)P(R^* - r^* - 1)][A + Z(R^*)] + [a^2p^2(1)$$
$$+ ap(2)]Z(R^* - 2) + [a^2p(1)p(2) + ap(3)]Z(R^* - 3)$$
$$+ \ldots + [a^2p(1)p(R^* - r^* - 2)$$
$$+ ap(R^* - r^* - 1)]Z(r^* + 1)$$

$$+ aC \left[\sum_{j=R^*-r^*}^{\infty} jp(j) + ap(1) \sum_{j=R^*-r^*-1}^{\infty} (j+1)\,p(j) \right] \quad (8\text{-}76)$$

On continuing the substitution, one quickly determines that the coefficient of $f(R^* - h)$ will be the probability of having h units demanded in 1 or 2 or, . . . , or h demands, and with a discount factor included for each of the demands. Thus, if $X(h)$ is the coefficient of $f(R^* - h)$

$$X(1) = ap(1), \quad X(2) = a^2p^2(1) + ap(2),$$
$$X(3) = a^3p^3(1) + 2a^2p(1)p(2) + ap(3)$$

or in general

$$X(h) = \sum_{u_1,\ldots,u_h} \frac{\left(\sum\limits_{j=1}^{h} u_j \right)!}{u_1!\, u_2! \ldots u_h!} \prod_{j=1}^{h} [ap(j)]^{u_j} \quad (8\text{-}77)$$

where the u_j are non-negative integers satisfying

$$\sum_{j=1}^{h} ju_j = h$$

It is also possible to generate the $X(h)$ in a different way. Define the quantities $X_n(k)$ recursively as follows

$$X_n(k) = \sum_{j=1}^{k} ap(j)X_{n-1}(k - j), \quad n = 2, 3, \ldots; \quad k = 1, 2, \ldots \quad (8\text{-}78)$$

and

$$X_1(k) = ap(k), \quad k = 1, 2, \ldots$$

and

$$X_n(0) = 1, \quad n = 1, 2, \ldots$$

The quantity $X_n(k)$ is almost the n-fold convolution of $ap(k)$ as defined in Sec. 3-9. It differs, however, in that we sum from $j = 1$ in (8-78) rather than from $j = 0$, and that we use the artificial convention $X_n(0) = 1$, whereas in reality, $ap(0) = 0$, because when a demand occurs at least one unit must be demanded. Intuitively, $X_n(k)$ is the probability, suitably discounted, that k units are demanded in 1 or 2 or . . . or n demands. Thus

$$X(h) = X_h(h) \tag{8-79}$$

The final coefficient of $[A + Z(R^*)]$ will be

$$a \sum_{h=0}^{R^*-r^*-1} X(h)P(R^* - r^* - h)$$

where $X(0) = 1$. This is the probability, suitably discounted, that 1 or 2 or, . . . , or $R^* - r^*$ demands are required before the inventory position moves from R^* and crosses (or reaches) the value r^*. The coefficient of C will be

$$\bar{Q}(a) = a \sum_{h=0}^{R^*-r^*-1} X(h) \left[\sum_{j=R^*-r^*-h}^{\infty} (j + h)p(j) \right] \tag{8-80}$$

and is simply the expected size of the order suitably discounted.

With the above information, we can then write

$$Z(R^*) = \sum_{h=0}^{R^*-r^*-1} X(h)f(R^* - h) + C\bar{Q}(a)$$

$$+ a \left[\sum_{h=0}^{R^*-r^*-1} X(h)P(R^* - r^* - h) \right] [A + Z(R^*)] \tag{8-81}$$

or

$$Z(R^*) =$$

$$\frac{aA \displaystyle\sum_{h=0}^{R^*-r^*-1} X(h)P(R^* - r^* - h) + C\bar{Q}(a) + \displaystyle\sum_{h=0}^{R^*-r^*-1} X(h)f(R^* - h)}{1 - a \displaystyle\sum_{h=0}^{R^*-r^*-1} X(h)P(R^* - r^* - h)}$$

$$\tag{8-82}$$

We leave for Problem 8-12 the details of obtaining explicit expressions for the other $Z(r^* + k)$. Problem 8-12 also asks the reader to show that $\lim_{i \to 0} [iZ(r^* + k)]$ is the same for each k, $k = 1, \ldots, Q$, as would be expected.

To relate what we have obtained here to the average annual cost $\mathcal{K}(R, r)$ we introduce the function $\mathfrak{z}(\xi; R, r)$ defined in the previous section. We note that equations (8-71) through (8-75) still hold if we remove the asterisks on R and r and replace $Z(r^* + k)$ by $\mathfrak{z}(r + k; R, r)$. Thus an explicit solution for $\mathfrak{z}(R; R, r)$ is given by (8-82) when the asterisks on R and r are deleted. Furthermore, $\lim_{i \to 0} [i\mathfrak{z}(r + k; R, r)]$ is the same for each k, $k = 1, \ldots, Q$. Therefore, from the discussion of the previous section, it should be true that

$$\mathcal{K}(R, r) = \lim_{i \to 0} i\mathfrak{z}(R; R, r) \tag{8-83}$$

Here we have a means for obtaining an explicit expression for the average annual cost which could be used to determine the optimal values of R and r. For any particular process generating demands, such as a stuttering Poisson process, it is rather cumbersome to evaluate $\mathcal{K}(R, r)$ directly, although it can be done. In Problem 8-21 we ask the reader to derive $\mathcal{K}(R, r)$ from (8-83) in the case where the number of units demanded in any time interval has a stuttering Poisson distribution. Problem 8-22 then requires that $\mathcal{K}(R, r)$ in this case also be derived by computing the expected cost per cycle and multiplying by the average number of cycles per year, and shown to be the same as the expression obtained from (8-83). It would not be easy to compute manually numerical values of R^* and r^* using $\mathcal{K}(R, r)$. However, the computation can be carried out quite easily on a digital computer. The determination of R^* and r^* on a digital computer using $\mathcal{K}(R, r)$ would normally require considerably less time than the solution of the n stage dynamic programming problem suggested in Sec. 8-7.

8-10 Explicit Solution of the Functional Equation for the Steady State Periodic Review Model

The material developed in the last few sections suggests that it should also be possible to solve explicitly the functional equation for a periodic review system. We shall show that this can indeed be done. This in turn will provide another means for computing the average annual cost of an $\langle R, r, T \rangle$ model. It will, of course, be the same expression that was obtained in Chapter 5. In order to solve explicitly the functional equation, it must be formulated so that the ξ in $Z(\xi; T)$ is the inventory position at a review time after any order has been placed, not before the placing of an order.

Let us then define $Z(\xi; T)$ to be the discounted expected costs over all future time when an optimal policy is followed for all future times, and we begin at a review time with the inventory position being ξ, after any order has been placed. As usual, we do not include any carrying or backorder costs incurred until a lead time has elapsed. Then it is clear that the functional equation becomes

$$Z(\xi; T) = f(\xi; T)$$
$$+ a \sum_{x=0}^{\infty} p(x; T)\{\min_{y \geq 0} [A\delta + Cy + Z(\xi + y - x; T)]\} \quad (8\text{-}84)$$

which has precisely the same form as (8-40). We have omitted the J which appears in (8-4), since it has no influence on the computations for a given T. Now, of course, $p(x; T)$ is the probability that x units are demanded in a period, and $f(\xi; T)$ is the expected cost of carrying inventory and of backorders in the period from τ to $\tau + T$, discounted to time 0, if the inventory position is ξ at time 0 (the review time) after the placing of any order.

Assume that an Rr policy is optimal. Then if the inventory system is operated optimally, the inventory position at a review time after any order has been placed will only have the values $r^* + 1, r^* + 2, \ldots, R^*$. Thus, for these values, (8-84) becomes

$$Z(r^* + 1; T) = f(r^* + 1; T) + ap(0; T)Z(r^* + 1; T)$$
$$+ aP(1; T)[A + Z(R^*; T)]$$
$$+ aC \sum_{x=1}^{\infty} (R^* - r^* + x - 1)p(x; T) \quad (8\text{-}85)$$

$$Z(r^* + 2; T) = f(r^* + 2; T) + ap(0; T)Z(r^* + 2; T)$$
$$+ ap(1; T)Z(r^* + 1; T) + aP(2; T)[A + Z(R^*; T)]$$
$$+ aC \sum_{x=2}^{\infty} (R^* - r^* + x - 2)p(x; T) \quad (8\text{-}86)$$

$$\vdots$$

$$Z(R^* - 1; T) = f(R^* - 1; T) + ap(0; T)Z(R^* - 1; T)$$
$$+ ap(1; T)Z(R^* - 2; T)$$
$$+ \ldots + ap(R^* - r^* - 2; T)Z(r^* + 1; T)$$
$$+ aP(R^* - r^* - 1; T)[A + Z(R^*; T)]$$
$$+ aC \sum_{x=R^*-r^*-1}^{\infty} (x + 1)p(x; T) \quad (8\text{-}87)$$

$$Z(R^*; T) = f(R^*; T) + ap(0; T)Z(R^*; T) + ap(1; T)Z(R^* - 1; T)$$

$$+ ap(2; T)Z(R^* - 2; T)$$

$$+ \ldots + ap(R^* - r^* - 1; T)Z(r^* + 1; T)$$

$$+ aP(R^* - r^*; T)[A + Z(R^*; T)] + aC \sum_{x=R^*-r^*}^{\infty} xp(x; T) \quad (8\text{-}88)$$

where $P(x; T)$ is the complementary cumulative of $p(x; T)$. These equations differ from (8-71) through (8-75), because in the periodic review case, it is possible to have no demands occur in a period, and hence $p(0; T)$ appears. Equations (8-85) through (8-88) can be used to solve explicitly for $Z(R; T)$. The solution, which the reader is asked to obtain in Problem 8-13, is

$$Z(R^*; T) = \frac{aA \sum_{n=0}^{\infty} \sum_{h=0}^{R^*-r^*-1} a^n p^{(n)}(h; T) P(R^* - r^* - h; T)}{1 - a \sum_{n=0}^{\infty} \sum_{h=0}^{R^*-r^*-1} a^n p^{(n)}(h; T) P(R^* - r^* - h; T)}$$

$$+ \frac{C\overline{Q} + \sum_{n=0}^{\infty} \sum_{h=0}^{R^*-r^*-1} a^n p^{(n)}(h; T) f(R^* - h; T)}{1 - a \sum_{n=0}^{\infty} \sum_{h=0}^{R^*-r^*-1} a^n p^{(n)}(h; T) P(R^* - r^* - h; T)} \quad (8\text{-}89)$$

where $p^{(n)}(h; T)$ is the n-fold convolution of $p(x; T)$, and by definition

$$p^{(0)}(0; T) = 1; \quad p^{(0)}(h; T) = 0, \quad h = 1, 2, \ldots$$

We leave for Problem 8-14 the evaluation of the other $Z(r^* + k; T)$, $k = 1, \ldots, R^* - r^* - 1$. In Problem 8-15 we ask the reader to show that

$$\lim_{i \to 0} iZ(r^* + k; T), \quad k = 1, \ldots, R^* - r^*$$

is the same for each k, and hence the average annual cost is this common limit.

The above results can be used to obtain an explicit expression for the expected annual cost. To do this we as usual define a function $\mathfrak{z}(\xi; R, r, T)$ to be the discounted expected cost at a review time if an Rr policy is used with the critical numbers R and r (note that R and r can be different than R^* and r^*), and if the inventory position is ξ after taking whatever action is appropriate. It then follows that equations (8-85) through (8-88) still hold if $Z(\xi; T)$ is replaced by $\mathfrak{z}(\xi; R, r, T)$ and the asterisks are removed from R and r. Thus an explicit solution for $\mathfrak{z}(R; R, r, T)$ is given by

(8-89) on removing the asterisks from R and r. It also follows that $\lim_{i \to 0} i\partial(\xi; R, r, T)$ is the same for each $\xi, \xi = r + 1, \ldots, R$. Consequently, the average annual cost, exclusive of review costs, is

$$\mathcal{K}_T(R, r) = \lim_{i \to 0} i\partial(R; R, r, T) \qquad (8\text{-}90)$$

The average annual cost including the review costs is

$$\mathcal{K}(R, r, T) = \frac{J}{T} + \mathcal{K}_T(R, r) \qquad (8\text{-}91)$$

In this way one can obtain an explicit expression for the expected annual cost of a periodic review system using an Rr policy. Problem 8-16 requires the proof that the result obtained here is the same as that obtained in Chapter 5.

8-11 The Lost Sales Case

The functional equation approach of dynamic programming is of little assistance in studying steady state models for the lost sales case. To illustrate the problems encountered, we shall study a periodic review system in which the procurement lead time is constant, and precisely $m \geq 1$ orders are outstanding at any given review time before any order is placed. In this case the Z function cannot be made to involve just a single argument. Suppose that ζ is a review time, and that quantities $w_1, \ldots, w_m$ were ordered at times $\zeta - T, \zeta - 2T, \ldots, \zeta - mT$ respectively. Also assume that ξ is the *on hand* inventory at time ζ. Z will now depend on $\xi, w_1, \ldots, w_m$.

Let $Z(\xi, w_1, \ldots, w_m)$ be the discounted expected cost over all future times when an optimal decision is made at time ζ and at all future times, and the time between reviews is T. Here we shall begin computing carrying costs and the cost of lost sales at time ζ, and the delay of a lead time will not be introduced. The task of setting up the functional equation for Z is not quite so straightforward as in the backorders case. Note first that when lead times are constant, only the order placed at time $\zeta - mT$ will arrive between ζ and $\zeta + T$. Suppose that this order for a quantity $w_m \geq 0$ arrives at time $\zeta + \hat{\imath}$. Let $p_1(x_1)$ be the probability that x_1 units are demanded from ζ to $\zeta + \hat{\imath}$ and $p_2(x_2)$ be the probability that x_2 units are demanded in the interval $\zeta + \hat{\imath}$ to $\zeta + T$. If $x_1 < \xi$ and $x_2 \leq w_m + \xi - x_1$, the on hand inventory at time $\zeta + T$ is $\xi + w_m - x_1 - x_2$. If $x_1 > \xi$ and $x_2 \leq w_m$, the on hand inventory at time $\zeta + T$ is $w_m - x_2$. Finally, the on hand inventory at time $\zeta + T$ will be zero if $x_1 < \xi$ and $x_2 > w_m + \xi - x_1$ or if $x_1 \geq \xi$ and $x_2 > w_m$.

Thus, if x_1, x_2 are independent random variables

$$Z(\xi, w_1, \ldots, w_m) = J + f(\xi, w_m) + \min_Q \{A\delta + CQ$$

$$+ a \sum_{x_2=0}^{w_m+\xi-x_1} \sum_{x_1=0}^{\xi-1} p_1(x_1)p_2(x_2)Z(\xi + w_m - x_1 - x_2, Q, w_1, \ldots, w_{m-1}) \quad (8\text{-}92)$$

$$+ a \sum_{x_2=0}^{w_m} \sum_{x_1=\xi}^{\infty} p_1(x_1)p_2(x_2)Z(w_m - x_2, Q, w_1, \ldots, w_{m-1})$$

$$+ a \left[\sum_{x_2=w_m+\xi-x_1+1}^{\infty} \sum_{x_1=0}^{\xi-1} p_1(x_1)p_2(x_2) \right.$$

$$\left. + \sum_{x_2=w_m+1}^{\infty} \sum_{x_1=\xi}^{\infty} p_1(x_1)p_2(x_2) \right] Z(0, Q, w_1, \ldots, w_{m-1})$$

where $f(\xi, w_m)$ is the expected cost of carrying inventory and of lost sales incurred from ζ to $\zeta + T$ (not $\zeta + \tau$ to $\zeta + \tau + T$). We ask the reader in Problem 8-17 to write out $f(\xi, w_m)$ explicitly.

Z is now a function of $m + 1$ variables rather than just a single variable as in the backorders case. None of the methods used previously can be applied to the functional equation (8-92). Indeed, it does not seem easy to use it either in discussing the optimality of an Rr policy or as an aid in obtaining the average annual cost. We shall not attempt to carry any farther the analysis of the lost sales case. In Problem 8-18 we ask the reader to obtain the functional equation in the case where no orders are outstanding at a review time.

REFERENCES

1. Arrow, K. J., T. Harris, and J. Marschak, "Optimal Inventory Policy," *Econometrica*, **XIX**, 1951, pp. 250–272.

2. Arrow, K. J., S. Karlin, and H. Scarf, *Studies in the Mathematical Theory of Inventory and Production.* Stanford, California: Stanford University Press, 1958.

3. Beckmann, M., and R. Muth, "An Inventory Policy for a Case of Lagged Delivery," *Management Science*, Vol. 2, No. 2, Jan. 1956, pp. 145–155.

4. Beckmann, M., "An Inventory Model for Arbitrary Interval and Quantity Distributions of Demand," *Management Science*, Vol. 8, No. 1, Oct. 1961, pp. 35–37.

5. Bellman, R., I. Glicksberg, and O. Gross, "On the Optimal Inventory Equation," *Management Science*, Vol. 2, No. 1, Oct. 1955, pp. 83–104.

6. Dvoretzky, A., J. Kiefer, and J. Wolfowitz, "The Inventory Problem: I, Case of Known Distributions of Demand; II, Case of Unknown Distributions of Demand," *Econometrica*, **XX**, Nos. 2–3, 1952, pp. 187–222 and 450–466.

7. Dvoretzky, A., J. Kiefer, and J. Wolfowitz, "On the Optimal Character of the (s, S) Policy in Inventory Theory," *Econometrica*, **XXI**, 1953, pp. 586–596.

8. Massé, P. B. D., *Les Réserves et la régulation de l'avenir dans la vie économique.* Paris: Hermann and Cie, 1946.

9. Scarf, H., "The Optimality of (S, s) Policies in the Dynamic Inventory Problem," in *Mathematical Methods in the Social Sciences*, (K. J. Arrow, S. Karlin, and P. Suppes, editors). Stanford, California: Stanford University Press, 1960, pp. 196–202.

PROBLEMS

8-1. Write out explicitly $E_T(\xi + Q; T)$, $B_T(\xi + Q; T)$ defined in Eq. (8-1) for the case where the number of units demanded in any time interval is Poisson distributed.

8-2. For the model discussed in Sec. 8-2, prove that if $A = 0$, then $Z_n(\xi; T)$ and $Z(\xi; T)$ are convex, thus implying that an order up to R policy is optimal. Carry out the proof directly, and do not simply specialize the A-convex arguments to this case.

8-3. When $f(y)$ is differentiable everywhere, show the equivalence between the definition of a convex function given in Problem 2-6 and that represented by Eq. (8-15).

8-4. Prove the four properties of A-convex functions listed in Sec. 8-4.

8-5. Prove that when $f(y; T)$ is a convex function which is everywhere differentiable, then $F_n(y; T)$ defined by Eq. (8-11) is continuous and differentiable everywhere. To do this, first show that $F_1(y; T)$ is continuous and differentiable everywhere. Then show that $Z_1(\xi; T)$ is continuous everywhere. Thus show that $F_2(y; T)$ is continuous and differentiable everywhere, etc.

8-6. Consider the definition of $\eta(x)$ for $x > 0$ given by Eq. (8-36). Show that if units are demanded one at a time

$$\eta(x) = \int_0^\tau V_{x-1}(\tau - t)e^{-it} \int_t^\infty g(\zeta)e^{-i\zeta}\, d\zeta\, dt$$

Can you make a similar transformation for $\theta(1, x)$?

8-7. In Sec. 8-7, prove that $ICD(\xi) + \hat{\pi}B(\xi)$ is a convex function of ξ. Explain why $E(\xi)$ need not be convex. *Hint:* Consider what can happen for small ξ.

8-8. Modify Eqs. (8-29), (8-30) and (8-31) for the case where ξ is allowed to be negative. What influence does this have on the functional equation for $Z(\xi)$?

8-9. In Sec. 8-6, show how to simplify the computation of the expected number of backorders incurred between τ and $\tau + t$ when the interest rate $i = 0$.

8-10. Derive in detail Eq. (8-55).

8-11. Compute

$$\lim_{i \to 0} iZ(r^* + k), \quad k = 1, \ldots, Q^*$$

where $Z(r^* + k)$ is given by Eq. (8-55), and demonstrate that the same answer is obtained for each value of k.

8-12. By use of Eq. (8-82) obtain an explicit expression for the other $Z(r^* + k)$, $k = 1, \ldots, Q^* - 1$. Show that $\lim_{i \to 0} [iZ(r^* + k)]$ is the same for each k.

8-13. Obtain Eq. (8-89) from Eqs. (8-85) through (8-88). *Hint:* There are many ways in which one can manipulate the equations in attempting to solve explicitly for $Z(R; T)$. Difficulty can be encountered unless the substitutions are carried out in a particular way. Begin with Eq. (8-88). Replace the $Z(R^*; T)$ whose coefficient is $ap(0; T)$ by the right hand side of Eq. (8-88); replace $Z(R^* - 1; T)$ by the right hand side of Eq. (8-87), etc. This yields

$$Z(R^*; T) = f(R^*; T) + ap(0; T)f(R^*; T)$$

$$+ ap(1; T)f(R^* - 1; T) + ap(2; T)f(R^* - 2; T)$$

$$+ \ldots + ap(R^* - r^* - 1; T)f(r^* + 1; T)$$

$$+ a^2 p^{(2)}(0; T)Z(R^*; T) + a^2 p^{(2)}(1; T)Z(R^* - 1; T)$$

$$+ \ldots + a^2 p^{(2)}(R^* - r^* - 1; T)Z(r^* + 1; T)$$

$$+ a\{[1 + ap(0; T)]P(R^* - r^*; T) + ap(1; T)P(R^* - r^*$$

$$- 1; T) + \ldots + ap(R^* - r^* - 1; T)P(1; T)\}[A$$

$$+ Z(R^*; T)] + aC[1 + ap(0; T)] \sum_{x = R^* - r^*}^{\infty} xp(x; T)$$

$$+ a^2 Cp(1; T) \sum_{x = R^* - r^* - 1}^{\infty} (x + 1) p(x; T)$$

$$+ a^2 Cp(2; T) \sum_{x = R^* - r^* - 2}^{\infty} (x + 2) p(x; T) + \cdots$$

$$+ a^2 Cp(R^* - r^* - 1; T) \sum_{x = 1}^{\infty} (R^* - r^* + x - 1) p(x; T)$$

Now repeat the substitution process with the above.

8-14. Evaluate explicitly, using Eq. (8-89), the other $Z(r^* + k; T)$ for a periodic review system.

8-15. By use of the results obtained in Problem 8-14 show that

$$\lim_{i \to 0} i Z(r^* + k; T), \quad k = 1, \ldots, R^* - r^*$$

is the same for each value of k.

8-16. Compute explicitly $\mathcal{K}_T(R, r)$ defined by Eq. (8-90) making use of Eq. (8-89), and show that Eq. (8-91) is precisely what was obtained in Chapter 5.

8-17. Write out explicitly $f(\xi, w_m)$ defined in Sec. 8-11.

8-18. Derive the equivalent of Eq. (8-92) for the case where no orders are outstanding at a review time.

8-19. Prove that for the simple deterministic system discussed in Chapter 2 where no stockouts are allowed that an Rr operating doctrine is optimal. Show that an Rr doctrine remains optimal when backorders are allowed.

8-20. Prove that for transactions reporting systems in which units are demanded one at a time, an Rr operating doctrine is optimal provided only that the expected carrying and backorder costs incurred in the time period τ to $\tau + t$ following a demand (τ being the constant lead time and t the time until the next unit is demanded) depends only on ξ, the inventory position of the system immediately following the demand after whatever action is appropriate has been taken. Show that this is true even if the unit cost of the item is not constant. Show that this is true even if the unit cost of the item is not constant. *Hint:* Consider first the case where the unit cost is constant. Let $F(y)$ be defined as in Sec. 8-8. Suppose that the absolute minimum of $F(y)$ is taken on at $y = R$. Then show both for the case where the demand variable is treated as discrete and where it is treated as continuous, that when the system is operated optimally, an Rr policy is optimal regardless of what the shape of $F(y)$ may be. Show that this is true even if R is not unique. How is r determined? Is it necessarily true that r is the largest value if $y < R$ such that $F(r) \geq A + F(R)$? Next consider the case where the unit cost is not constant.

8-21. Compute $\mathcal{K}(R, r)$ using Eq. (8-83) for the case where the number of units demanded in any time interval has a stuttering Poisson distribution.

8-22. Compute $\mathcal{K}(R, r)$ for the case where the number of units demanded in any time interval has a stuttering Poisson distribution by computing the expected cost per cycle and then multiplying by the average number of cycles per year. Show that result is the same as that obtained in Problem 8-21. *Hint*: A cycle may require 1, 2, . . . , $R - r$ demands. What then is the expected length of a cycle? Let $f(r + k)$ be the expected cost incurred from time $\zeta + \tau$ to $\zeta + \tau + t$ when the inventory position is $r + k$ immediately after a demand at time ζ, and t is the time until the next demand. At the beginning of a cycle the inventory position is R. What is the probability that it will be $r + k$ at some time during the cycle? Hence, what is the expected cost per cycle?

8-23. Read Problem 2-69. Show that when demand is treated as a stochastic variable, it still remains true that when minimizing the present worth of all future costs, rather than the average annual cost, one should not include the rate of return in the inventory carrying charge. Show, however, that if this is done, then after performing the limiting processes discussed in this chapter to obtain the average annual cost, it is necessary in the resulting expression to add back into the carrying charge the rate of return.

8-24. In Sec. 8-4 we proved that if $f(y; T)$ is convex then $F(y; T)$ cannot have a relative maximum at a point y for which $F(y; T) > A + F(R^*; T)$. Show that it is allowable for $F(y; T)$ to have a relative maximum at a point y such that $F(y; T) = A + F(R^*; T)$, without destroying the optimality of an Rr policy. Illustrate this geometrically.

8-25. Use Eq. (8-2) to provide a rigorous proof of Eq. (8-3).

8-26. Under what conditions is an Rr policy optimal for the dynamic model of Sec. 7-6 (possibly with different values of R and r for each period)?

PROBLEMS

OF PRACTICAL APPLICATION

"How chances mock,

And changes fill the cup of alteration

with divers liquors!"

Shakespeare, Henry IV, Part II

9-1 Introduction

The old adage that there can be many a slip from the cup to the lip seems to be especially descriptive of the problems encountered in any attempt to implement an operating doctrine obtained by analysis of a mathematical model in a real world inventory system. In this chapter we wish to turn our attention from the main theme of this work, which has been the construction and analysis of mathematical models of inventory systems, to problems of implementation, i.e., of practical application. We do not intend this to be a set of instructions on how a model should be implemented, since it is not clear that such a set of rules could be devised to cover all situations, and even if it could, more than a single volume would be required to discuss these rules. Rather, we would like to point up the sorts of problems that can arise, and insofar as possible, suggest ways to avoid them or solve them. Unfortunately, however, there are no easy solutions to most of these problems, and in a fairly large number of cases, no satisfactory solutions at all have been devised. We shall find it convenient to discuss the various problems under the headings of: the relevance of the model, data problems, multi-item problems, personnel problems and procedural problems, and problems of evaluation. If nothing else, this chapter should make the reader aware that a successful application will require more than the formulation of an appropriate mathematical model.

9-2 Relevance of the Model

It has been noted previously that some simplifications and approximations will always be needed when constructing a mathematical model of any real world system. However, one must be extremely careful in developing a model to be sure that it represents with sufficient accuracy the essential characteristics of the system which are important determinants of what the operating doctrine should be. If this is not done, the results obtained by use of the model can easily lead to operating rules which are worse than those currently in use, or worse than those which could be derived from simple heuristic intuitive considerations. It would hardly seem necessary

401

to emphasize this point, and yet, the authors have encountered many instances in practice where attempts have been made to use models in situations where they were completely inapplicable, simply because the model was available for use. One rather obvious misuse of a model which the authors have encountered was in a military supply system where an attempt was made to apply a steady state model of the type discussed in Chapter 4 to spare parts for a military aircraft which would be phased in and out in a relatively few years. The model was completely inapplicable since the mean rate of demand was continually changing with time, and since explicit account should have been taken of the fact that the parts would be obsolete when the aircraft was phased out. A more appropriate model would have been some form of dynamic model such as those discussed in Chapter 7.

The inadequacy of a model for some particular application is not always so obvious as that referred to above, but nonetheless can lead to equally disastrous results if applied. A good example of this concerns an application made in that part of a military supply system concerned with stockage of electronic components. A large number of different electronic components were carried in stock. The basic idea was to use a steady state model such as the one described in Chapter 4, to set order levels and reorder points for each of the items. Previously, the system had been operating using periodic review. This in itself was reasonable enough, since the mean rate of demand for many of the items was essentially constant over a fair period of time, and since the system had installed a digital computer which made it possible to use what was, for practical purposes, a transactions reporting system.

However, it was recognized that the order quantities could not necessarily be used directly, since each year only a certain sum of money determined by the budget could be spent on procurements. Hence it was necessary to take into account, in one way or another, the budget constraint on procurement expenditures. At this point, the following procedures were attempted. It was decided to choose the order quantities Q_j and reorder points r_j, for each of the n items, by minimizing the average annual cost $\mathcal{K}$ for all n items, in such a way that the expected procurement costs would not exceed the budgetary limitation. To do this, the cost of a backorder for unit j was assumed to have the form $\theta t \sqrt{C_j}$, where C_j is the unit cost of the item, t is the length of time for which the backorder exists, and θ is a parameter independent of j, to be determined in such a way that the budget constraint was to be satisfied. Note that in this model there is no fixed cost of a backorder. (The reasoning which led to the choice of $\hat{\pi}_j = \theta \sqrt{C_j}$ is somewhat obscure, but is probably irrelevant, since the same problems would have in all likelihood been encountered if $\hat{\pi}_j$ was taken equal to θf_j for any arbitrarily selected number f_j.) Then the function to be minimized was

$$\mathcal{K} = \sum_{j=1}^{n} \left\{ \frac{\lambda_j}{Q_j} A_j + IC_j \left[\frac{Q_j}{2} + \frac{1}{2} + r_j - \mu_j \right] + (\theta\sqrt{C_j} + IC_j)B_j(Q_j, r_j) \right\}$$

where all quantities not defined above have their usual meaning. The minimization was carried out for various values of θ yielding $\mathcal{K}^*(\theta)$, $Q_j^*(\theta)$, $r_j^*(\theta)$, $j = 1, \ldots, n$. Then θ was chosen so that the expected procurement expenditures were equal to the sum available in the budget.

It happened that, in the particular year in which the model was introduced, the budget was extremely tight. Because of this, θ turned out to be a very small number, so that the cost of a unit year of shortage was small. For example, on some tubes, the cost of a unit year of shortage came to the absurdly small value of \$0.75. The reorder points determined in this way were quite low. In many cases, they were so low that the safety stock was negative (i.e., r_j was less than μ_j). The r_j were in general considerably lower than the on hand inventory at the beginning of the year. On the other hand, the Q_j was not especially small, since in the model, the contribution of the $r_j + Q_j$ terms to the backorder cost were ignored, and thus Q_j could not be less than the Wilson Q.

The Q_j and r_j values obtained from the above model were used in the real world system. What happened was as follows: The system began using up the on hand inventory for all items, and when (the very low) reorder points were reached, orders for the rather large quantities Q_j were placed as needed. Before the end of the year, the entire budgeted sum had been spent, and the system was about to run out of stock on many items—on some because an order had been placed but the safety stock was negative, and on others because the reorder points had to be passed because no funds were available. At this point a crisis was reached which required special legislation to obtain emergency funds for restocking through the sending of expedited procurement orders to suppliers.

The application just discussed provides an excellent example of a case where the results obtained using a mathematical model were much worse than would have been obtained using the standard procedures that were already in existence. It was entirely inappropriate, of course, to attempt to apply a steady state model to a situation where there was a fixed annual procurement budget, and even worse to do it on the basis of introducing a constraint on expected expenditures where the backorder cost was varied to bring expected expenditures in line with the budget (since varying the backorder cost did not have a great influence on the Q_j). The proper procedure for operating a system in the face of a tight budget is very complex. One must in general use hand to mouth buying (i.e., buy in very small quantities), and insofar as possible attempt to postpone as many procurements as possible until right after the beginning of the next budgetary year when more funds will be available. None of the models developed in this text are capable of handling such a problem and, indeed, no such models have been developed. It is clear that on the average, the budget must be sufficient to procure the average annual demand, or the system cannot continue to operate. However, by clever manipulation, it can survive particular years with tight budgets.

There exist many other ways in which a model can be improperly applied. We shall now briefly mention several of these. For example, consider a situation in which the mean rate of demand is fairly low while the number of units demanded per demand varies widely. Here it would be very dangerous to use the steady state model developed in Chapter 4 for Poisson demands, even if the mean rate of demand remained constant over time, since the variance in the order size could cause the safety stock determined from the model to be much too small. Other misapplications have involved attempts to apply a steady state model to a department store item, 50 percent of which was sold during the Christmas season, or the attempt to use results computed from a transactions reporting model in a periodic review system.

The above have illustrated actual cases where models have been misapplied. The reader should not infer from the above that a model will never be satisfactory unless it replicates very closely the behavior of the real world. For example, it may be perfectly satisfactory to apply a steady state model to a situation in which there is a moderate amount of seasonality in demand, i.e., the additional savings which could be obtained by using an operating doctrine based on a dynamic model over the costs incurred by using a $\langle Q, r \rangle$ model with a fixed Q and r (computed using the average demand rate) may not justify its use, perhaps because it is too difficult to get the clerical people to use a changing Q and r. It is quite easy to obtain a rough estimate of the differences in ordering and holding costs obtained by using a fixed Q and one that varies with the season. All one needs to do is compare the results of the simple deterministic lot size model of Chapter 2 with the deterministic dynamic lot size model of Chapter 7. Sample calculations quickly reveal that even with sizable seasonal patterns, the cost differences can be very small. Thus in many instances the use of a constant Q could be easily justified. It is somewhat more difficult to determine whether or not it is reasonable to keep r constant at the value determined from the steady state model also (i.e., have a constant safety stock). This depends in part on the relative magnitude of the stockout costs and carrying costs. A natural way to investigate whether or not the use of a constant r value determined from the $\langle Q, r \rangle$ model would be satisfactory would be to use simulation.

Simulation is a very useful tool for studying how any operating doctrine can be expected to behave in the real world system. In particular, simulation is helpful in studying what sort of behavior can be expected when using an operating doctrine obtained from a mathematical model under conditions different from those assumed in deriving the operating doctrine. The procedure is to simulate in time the behavior of the system when using a specified operating doctrine. This is done by generating random numbers giving the times between the occurrence of demands and the number of units demanded. These random numbers are generated in such a way that they have the statistical properties which characterize the stochastic processes generating demands and the order sizes for the actual system. Given the time pattern of demands, one can then determine the inventory level as a function of time, the points at which orders should be placed (if lead times must be represented as stochastic variables, random numbers will be generated giving the length of the lead time), the backorders as a function of time, etc. By use of this information, one can compute annual costs, the fraction of time out of stock, etc. Hence one can compare an operating doctrine obtained from a mathematical model with the operating doctrine actually in use, to see how much improvement can be expected; or an operating doctrine obtained from a simplified model with that obtained from a more exact model, to see if the cost differences are significant enough to warrant using the more complicated doctrine; or one can study some heuristic modifications of an operating doctrine obtained from a simplified model to see if an even better operating doctrine can be obtained.

The simplest simulations can be carried out by hand. Usually, however, a digital computer will be needed, since the simulation must be carried out for a sufficient length of time, or repeated a sufficient number of times, so that the various measures of effectiveness which one wants to compute will be representative of their expected values. This may require the generation of 100,000 or more random numbers. The arithmetic associated with the bookkeeping for all this becomes impossibly laborious, and hence a computer is needed. In practice, simulation has not been used extensively to analyze operating doctrines for a system. The reason is that it is too expensive and too time consuming. In the future, however, as computers become faster, and cheaper to use, one might expect to see simulation used much more than it is at present.

9-3 Data Problems

Once a satisfactory mathematical model of some real world situation has been developed, there remains the problem of determining empirically the values of the various parameters, and perhaps also the nature of certain functions which appear in the model, before it is possible to use it to obtain an explicit operating doctrine. In order to obtain these parameters and functions, it is necessary to use data obtained from the actual system.

Unfortunately, for a variety of reasons which will be examined in more detail below, it is often quite difficult to obtain the data needed. Even when some data are available, it is frequently exceptionally difficult to compute the parameters and functions needed in the model with great accuracy. Fortunately, the optimal profit or cost often does not change radically with small changes in the parameters, and hence good results can be obtained without knowing many of the parameters with great accuracy. It is very helpful, however, to determine which parameters, when changed, have the greatest influence in changing the optimal profit or cost, since the greatest effort should then be concentrated on obtaining accurate values of these parameters. In order to determine the critical parameters, it is necessary to perform a sensitivity analysis, simply by determining what happens when a parameter is changed. Some examples of this have been given in previous chapters.

In the next several sections we wish to discuss in more detail the problems involved in determining the parameters and functions needed in the mathematical model. It will be convenient to subdivide the discussion of these data problems into the following categories: (a) the demand distribution, (b) the lead time distribution, and (c) the costs.

9-4 The Demand Distribution

All inventory models require some information concerning the demand for the item under consideration. In the simplest deterministic model only a single parameter, the demand rate is needed. For other models it may be necessary to determine the nature of the process generating demands, and the nature of the distribution of the quantity demanded per demand. It may even be necessary to predict how these will change over some future time period. In order to make even the simplest estimate of the demand rate, historical data are needed. It is surprising how often one finds that no demand data whatever are available in usable form, and hence, before any attempt can be made to apply the operating doctrine obtained from the mathematical model, it is necessary to collect such data. In essentially all cases, the data available will be sales data, and these will be equivalent to demand data only if no sales are lost. When lost sales are possible, then sales data will not yield precisely demand data. Even in the case where all demands are backordered, sales data can distort the picture if they are based on the time of filling an order, because, when some demands must be backordered, the time pattern of filling orders will be different from the time pattern of the original demands. One normally has no alternative but to use the sales data as demand data. In the lost sales case, one could, if the average fraction of the time out of stock was known, correct the mean rate of demand obtained from sales data by dividing by the average fraction of time for which the system has stock on hand. Generally, however, the fraction of the time out of stock is not available and is difficult to measure. Fortunately, it is often small and hence not too much of a problem.

Let us now assume that some sort of demand (i.e., sales) data are available, and let us then see what problems arise in attempting to use these to obtain the parameters of the demand distribution needed in the model. First, we shall study the case where the model being used assumes that the stochastic process generating demands does not change with time. Before any attempt at parameter estimation is made, one should examine the situation to determine whether or not the assumption of a constant mean rate of demand is reasonable. Usually, in the real world, the mean rate of demand will not be strictly constant, and what one really wants to decide is whether over a suitable time interval (perhaps a year or so) the mean rate of demand is essentially constant. It is very difficult to make this decision on a quantitative basis since this would require comparing the cost using an operating doctrine obtained from a model which assumes a constant demand rate and those using an operating doctrine obtained from a dynamic model. To make such comparisons could require a great deal of work, and might even require the use of a large computer to make a detailed simulation. To do all this is usually much too time consuming and expensive (and even if it was done the results might be misleading because of the difficulties in predicting how the mean rate of demand would change with time for use in the dynamic model). Instead one makes the decision on a very qualitative basis, often without a detailed study of the data. Frequently, it is sufficient to know what sort of item is being dealt with. If it is a staple item, which does not have an extreme seasonal pattern, and for which obsolescence is not an immediate problem, one will usually use a model which assumes that the mean rate of demand is constant, simply because the probable savings that could accrue from using a more complicated dynamic model do not justify the relatively high costs of its use. If the mean rate of demand is changing somewhat with time, one can simply recompute the operating doctrine at some regular interval, such as once a year. On the other hand, if the item is a high fashion item, which is only sold during one period of the year, or is an item which is to be phased in and out over a relatively short period, it will frequently be ill advised to use a model that assumes the mean rate of demand to be constant.

If one wants to determine the behavior of the mean rate of demand over time in more detail, it is convenient to use a control chart type of analysis in doing so. As a measure of the demand rate one will use the demand per time period, i.e., the daily, weekly, or monthly demand. This will be plotted on a graph as a function of time. Using the demand per time period data, one will then compute from the data available the average demand per period $\bar{d}$ and the standard deviation of the average demand per period S_d. On the graph where the demand data are plotted, lines for $\bar{d}$, $\bar{d} + 3S_d$ and $\bar{d} - 3S_d$ are also plotted. This may yield results such as those shown in Figs. 9-1 and 9-2. The chances that a point will lie outside the control limits $\bar{d} + 3S_d$ or $\bar{d} - 3S_d$ are very small if the mean rate of demand is indeed constant.

If the data behave like those shown in Fig. 9-1, then statistically there is no reason to believe that the data were not generated by a stochastic process in which the mean rate of demand is constant. On the other hand, if the data behaved like those in Fig. 9-2, it seems clear that the mean rate of demand is increasing with time. In both cases, however, one might use

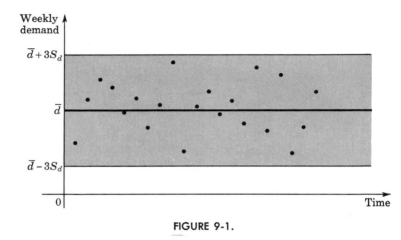

FIGURE 9-1.

an operating doctrine obtained from a model which assumed that the mean rate of demand was constant. Indeed one could use graphs such as Figs. 9-1, and 9-2 to indicate when it was desirable to change the parameters in the model and recompute the operating doctrine. The recomputation (or at least an investigation of whether or not a recomputation should be made) would be triggered by having a point fall outside the control limits. For such purposes, however, it would not necessarily be desirable to have the control limits lie at $\bar{d} + 3S_d$ and $\bar{d} - 3S_d$. It might be noted that the sort of results one obtains on graphs like Fig. 9-1 can be strongly dependent on the time period chosen, i.e., whether one uses the daily, weekly, or monthly demand. For example, the daily demand on Mondays may always be very low while it is always very high on Fridays. Hence for this unit of measure, a control chart would indicate that the mean rate of demand was not constant. On the other hand, the mean rate of demand on a weekly basis might be quite constant. The interval should be chosen to be as large as possible consistent with the data available, and any other requirements such as those that will be discussed later. It should not, however, be larger than either the lead time or the average time between the placement of orders.

We shall now turn to the details of estimating the demand parameters or the demand distribution needed in the model. If the model is a deterministic one which requires only the mean rate of demand, we would divide the total demand, over the longest possible time period for which it is believed that the demand rate is representative of the current demand rate,

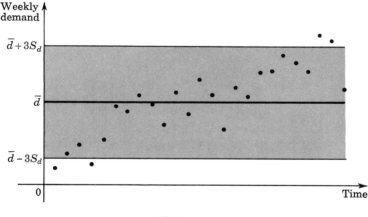

FIGURE 9-2.

by the length of the period in years to obtain λ. When demand is treated as a stochastic variable, the model may use some theoretical distribution, for which it is only necessary to estimate the parameters in the distribution, or it may be possible to use an empirically determined distribution, so that in such a case, it is necessary to determine the entire distribution.

Let us first examine the case where the model allows the use of an empirically determined distribution, and it is desired to use such a distribution. To be specific, let us imagine that we are using one of the simple $\langle Q, r \rangle$ models developed in Secs. 4-2 and 4-3. Assume also that the lead time can be imagined to be a constant τ. We shall defer a discussion of the additional complications introduced by stochastic lead times to the next section. To determine the density $p(x; \tau)$ that x units are demanded in the lead time, we might proceed by dividing the total time period over which we have useful data into intervals of length τ. For each such time interval we determine how many demands occurred. Then we construct a histogram by finding the fraction of the time intervals which have demands lying in each of some suitably chosen demand intervals of length Δx. When plotted graphically one might get a result such as that shown in Fig. 9-3.

Unfortunately, the procedure just suggested often cannot be used. The reason for this is that if τ is fairly long, only a very small number of time intervals of length τ will be available in the time period over which useful data are available. In order to use the above technique, one should have something like at least 50 intervals of length τ in the demand history, if one is to obtain a histogram which contains any detail. Often this cannot be done.

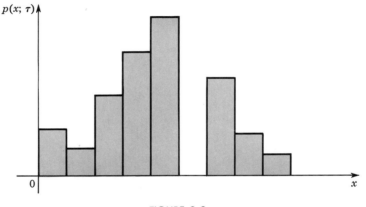

FIGURE 9-3.

Thus we must use a different procedure to obtain $p(x; \tau)$ empirically. An alternative procedure is to proceed as follows. The demand data are used to obtain a histogram for the demand over a shorter time period of length t, say one day or one week; t can be chosen so that $\tau = nt$ where n is an integer. Then, if we assume that demands in different periods of length t are independent, $p(x; \tau) = p^{(n)}(x; t)$, i.e., by taking the n-fold convolution of $p(x; t)$, one obtains $p(x; \tau)$. However, it is very tedious to attempt to compute by hand the n-fold convolution of an empirical density function, especially if n is fairly large and x can take on a considerable range of values. The computation can be made either directly from the definition or through use of the generating function. The computation could be carried out quite readily on a computer, however. The results of the computation, when plotted, would yield a histogram such as Fig. 9-3.

Once $p(x; \tau)$ is obtained then it is a simple matter to obtain $P(x; \tau)$, the complementary cumulative of $p(x; \tau)$. When plotted graphically, it would look something like that shown in Fig. 9-4. In principle, then one can proceed to use the model. In addition to $P(r; \tau)$, one needs $\bar{\eta}(r) = \sum_{x=r}^{\infty} (x - r)p(x; \tau)$, which can be easily computed numerically (at least on a computer it would be easy). Frequently, another trouble arises in using $P(x; \tau)$. When stockout costs are high, $P(r^*; \tau)$ will be very small, i.e., the only part of the distribution which is important is that far out on the right hand tail of $p(x; \tau)$. However, events lying far out on the right hand tail of $p(x; \tau)$ are quite rare, and for this reason an extremely long

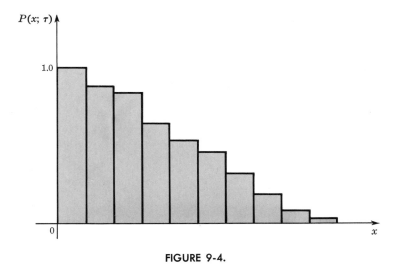

FIGURE 9-4.

history of demand would be needed to obtain an accurate representation of the tail of the distribution. Only under special circumstances can one get an accurate representation of the tail of the distribution, which is really the only important part for inventory problems. When the tail of the distribution is poorly represented, then serious errors can be made in computing the reorder level and safety stock.

In periodic review models, any attempt to use an empirical distribution involves all the difficulties mentioned above plus an additional difficulty. For example, for the simplest order up to R model, recall that R depends on the demand in the time $\tau + T$. Hence, if one desires to optimize with respect to T, it is necessary to generate a new empirical distribution for each different T value used. This is impossibly laborious to carry out by hand, although it could be done quite readily on a computer.

The above discussion has pointed out that, in many instances, severe difficulties may be encountered in any attempt to use an empirical demand distribution—even in the simplest of inventory models. It should be clear that the difficulty would be compounded if a model with $\hat{r} \neq 0$ was being used, since then the distribution would need to be known as a function of time. Perhaps the most serious deficiency in attempting to use an empirical distribution is the fact that often only the tail of the distribution is important, and not enough data are available to represent it accurately. Thus, although there do arise situations in which one can and will find it desirable to use an empirical distribution, there are equally well many situations where it is exceptionally difficult to use an empirical distribution, and, in such cases, one is essentially forced to use a theoretical distribution.

There is one type of inventory model where one can frequently use an empirical distribution with relative ease. This is the single period model. There are two reasons why an empirical distribution can often be used here. First, one can obtain the histogram for the period's demand directly, and without performing a convolution. Secondly, there may be no stockout cost or a relatively low stockout cost, so that one does not need to move so far out on the tail of the distribution to determine the order quantity. Thus it is not so important that the extreme tail of the distribution be so accurately known.

Let us next consider the case where the model makes use of a theoretical distribution, and it is only necessary to estimate the parameters of this distribution. When the lead time demand is relatively low, the theoretical distribution usually used will be the Poisson. The only parameter needed is the mean rate of demand λ, and it can be determined simply by dividing the total number of units demanded over the relevant historical period by the length of the interval in years. In addition to doing this, it is helpful, if possible, to check to see how well the Poisson assumption seems to apply. In the real world, it will normally be true that the number of units demanded in any time period will not be strictly Poisson distributed, if for no other reason, simply because the order size is not always unity. Often it is very difficult to obtain information on the distribution of the order sizes. It is desirable to learn as much as possible about this, however. One crude but simple way of checking on the goodness of the Poisson assumption is to obtain a histogram for the demand in some period such as a day or week, and compute the mean and variance of the histogram. If the variance is quite different from the mean, this suggests that the assumption that the number of units demanded in any time period is Poisson is not too good. In cases where the lead time demand is so low that the normal approximation cannot be applied and the data indicate that the Poisson assumption is far removed from reality, then one may be forced to go to some other theoretical distribution of demand such as the stuttering Poisson. One would do this only if the item was very important since a considerable amount of extra effort would be needed to program a computer to make the computations which determine the optimal operating doctrine.

When the normal distribution is the theoretical distribution used in the model, λ is determined as above. Now, however, one also needs D, where by definition $\sigma^2 = Dt$ for any time interval t. To compute D one would, as usual, select a time period t such as a day or a week and compute the variance S^2 of the demand over this period; D would then be obtained from $D = S^2/t$.

It remains to discuss cases where the mean rate of demand changes with such rapidity that a dynamic model must be used. The dynamic models developed in this text assume that for each future time period, the system knows precisely what the distribution of demand will be. In the real world, of course, considerable difficulties are encountered merely in attempting to predict what the mean demand will be for each future period, not to mention the precise nature of the distribution. Indeed, it is impossible to predict even the mean demand for any future period with complete accuracy. We shall now consider briefly some of the problems involved in making demand predictions, and we shall also consider some of the techniques which can be used for this purpose.

9-5 Demand Prediction

Central to any attempt to use a dynamic model is the procedure used for making predictions or forecasts. The nature of the predicting technique used can vary widely. It may, for example, involve only the use of historical data on the item itself, it may involve predictions on the general state of the economy, or it may be based on future planned requirements (in the case of spare parts, etc.).

We shall not discuss prediction techniques in detail, since different circumstances require widely varying approaches. We shall, however, briefly examine several of the more simple ones. Consider first the problem of predicting the demand for things like spare parts, which depend on the usage of some other piece of equipment. This is an important problem in any military supply system. To be specific, imagine that we are attempting to predict demand for a spare part for a certain aircraft over a given future period of time. The typical procedure which has been used in the military to do this is to establish, on the basis of historical data, a usage rate, given as the average number of spares needed per flying hour. Then the total number of expected flying hours for all the aircraft of the type under consideration during the interval of interest is estimated from current plans. Multiplication of the usage rate by the expected number of flying hours gives the expected demand for the spare part over the interval under consideration. The accuracy of the forecast depends on both the accuracy of the usage rate and the accuracy of the prediction of the number of flying hours. In practice predictions are often considerably in error, both because it is difficult to obtain an accurate estimate of the usage rate, and because it can be exceptionally difficult to predict what the flying hours will be. It is especially difficult to obtain accurate values for the usage rate for very low demand spare parts (this includes a majority of the spare parts), since the aircraft is obsolete before a sufficient demand history is obtained to yield an accurate value. A great deal of effort has gone into trying to find ways to accurately predict usage rates, but, as yet, none of these has been very successful.

It should be noted that in the above technique for predicting spare parts demand, no attempt was made to introduce probabilistic considerations. Clearly, in a situation like this it is very difficult to attempt to describe what the probability density for the demand for the spare part will be in some future period. There would be randomness in the demand for spares even if the flying hours could be predicted with accuracy. In cases like this, when working with a dynamic model which requires the specification of a demand distribution, one is essentially forced to use a theoretical distribution such as the Poisson. If the distribution also requires the specification of a variance, about the best one can do is to make a crude guess as to what its value may be.

It might be of interest to point out the sort of operating doctrine that has actually been used by the military for some years for spare parts. A periodic review system is used, with the review period being normally three months, six months, or one year. Let T be the time between reviews in months. The operating procedure is to attempt to always keep a safety stock of k months demand on hand (k may vary from 1.5 to 12 months). At a review time supply officers send in their estimates of what demand will be for the period of length $\tau + T + k$, where τ is the lead time in months. These estimates are aggregated over all air bases and repair facilities to yield the expected demand d over this period. Suppose that at the review time the inventory position of the system is R. Then the quantity ordered is $d - R$ if $d - R > 0$, and nothing otherwise. This operating doctrine does not take into account costs or probabilistic considerations. The value of k is usually set arbitrarily, and is the same for broad categories of items. At the present time the military is attempting to improve its procedures for controlling inventories of spare parts. It is not a simple matter to obtain really useful mathematical models, however, because of the prediction problems referred to above.

Let us now turn our attention to situations in which predictions are made using historical data and nothing else. We shall assume that a dynamic periodic review model of the type discussed in Chapter 7 is being used, and that at each review time a new prediction is made. We shall first examine techniques that are useful when there is no strong seasonal pattern. The two procedures which have gained widest acceptance are (1) to fit a least squares line to the historical data, and (2) to use exponential smoothing.

The least squares technique assumes that the demand d_j in period j can be predicted using $d'_j = aj + b$, where a, b are determined from historical data by minimizing

$$F = \sum_j (d_j - d'_j)^2 = \sum_j (d_j - aj - b)^2 \tag{9-1}$$

In the above, d'_j is the predicted demand for period j and d_j is the actual demand for period j. Assume that a, b are to be determined by using the demands in the previous N periods. We shall imagine that the current time t is a review time, and that the time period from t to $t - T$, T being the time between reviews, will be referred to as period 0, the period from $t - T$ to $t - 2T$ as period -1, etc. Thus the numbers of the N periods to be used in determining a and b will be $0, -1, \ldots, -(N - 1)$. To determine a and b, we set $\partial F/\partial a = \partial F/\partial b = 0$ and solve the resulting equations for a and b. Then from (9-1)

$$\frac{\partial F}{\partial a} = -2 \sum_{j=0}^{-(N-1)} j(d_j - aj - b) = 0,$$

$$\frac{\partial F}{\partial b} = -2 \sum_{j=0}^{-(N-1)} (d_j - aj - b) = 0 \tag{9-2}$$

Now

$$\sum_{j=0}^{-(N-1)} j = \frac{-N(N-1)}{2}; \quad \sum_{j=0}^{-(N-1)} j^2 = \frac{1}{6} N(N-1)(2N-1)$$

Also, let

$$U = \sum_{j=0}^{-(N-1)} d_j; \quad V = \sum_{j=0}^{-(N-1)} jd_j \tag{9-3}$$

Then the solution to the equations (9-2) is

$$a = \frac{12}{N(N-1)(N+1)} \left[V + \frac{N-1}{2} U \right]; \quad b = \frac{U}{N} + a\left(\frac{N-1}{2}\right)$$

so that

$$d'_j = \frac{U}{N} + a\left[j + \frac{N-1}{2}\right]$$

$$= \frac{U}{N} + 12\left[\frac{V + \frac{N-1}{2}U}{N(N-1)(N+1)}\right]\left[j + \frac{N-1}{2}\right], \quad j = 1, 2, 3, \ldots \quad (9\text{-}4)$$

Equation (9-4) tells how to compute the predicted demand for period j, $j = 1, 2, \ldots$, using data for the demands in periods $0, -1, \ldots, -(N-1)$. Note that period 1 occurs between t and $t + T$, period 2 between $t + T$ and $t + 2T$, etc. Observe also, that U/N is simply the average demand in periods $0, -1, \ldots, -(N-1)$, so that (9-4) indicates that the predicted demand is the average over the past N periods plus a trend correction.

In (9-4) only U and V depend on historical data. It is unnecessary to recompute U and V from their definitions each time a new prediction is made. Instead, it is easier to compute the new values of U and V from the previous values. Let $\hat{U}$ and $\hat{V}$ refer to the values of these variables computed at time $t + T$, i.e., using $d_1, d_0, \ldots, d_{-(N-2)}$, and U and V the values computed at time t, i.e., using $d_0, d_{-1}, \ldots, d_{-(N-1)}$. Then it is easy to see that

$$\hat{U} = d_1 + U - d_{-(N-1)}; \quad \hat{V} = V - U + Nd_{-(N-1)} \quad (9\text{-}5)$$

It is much easier to compute $\hat{U}$ and $\hat{V}$ from (9-5) rather than directly from their definitions.

By use of (9-4) and (9-5), it is quite simple, either manually or on a computer, to predict the demand in each of the future periods needed and also to predict (at least approximately) the lead time demands needed.

The uncertainty in the predicted demand will increase with j, i.e., the farther one moves into the future. It is desirable when possible to get some estimate of this uncertainty as a function of j (the number of periods in the future for which prediction is made). If sufficient historical data are available, this can be done by computing a histogram for the distribution of forecast errors. This is accomplished by using (9-4) to predict the demand j periods in the future and then comparing it with the actual demand. The difference between the actual demand and the forecast demand is called the forecast error. By doing this for as many historical points as possible, one can obtain a histogram of forecast errors for each value of j. Let S_j^2 be the variance of the distribution of forecast errors when predicting j periods into the future. If the dynamic model uses a theoretical distribution such as the normal, then for period j one can use S_j^2 for the variance of the period's demand. Similarly, be adding the appropriate variances, one can at least roughly estimate the variance of the lead time demands.

We gave no indication above as to how to choose N, the number of past periods demand that are used in making the predictions. One way to select N is to pick the N which minimizes the variance of the distribution of forecast errors for a given j, or minimizes some combination of the variances over all j. This could be a tedious computation to make manually, but it could easily be carried out on a computer.

One difficulty with using a least squares line for prediction is that it is always necessary to have available the demand N periods back. This can take up an unnecessarily large amout of storage in a computer when many items are being handled. The exponential smoothing method of predicting eliminates this problem. Given any time sequence of data with f_j being the value of the variable for period j, then the smoothed value of the variable for period j, denoted by $\bar{f}_j$, is

$$\bar{f}_j = \alpha f_j + (1 - \alpha)\bar{f}_{j-1}, \quad 0 < \alpha < 1 \tag{9-6}$$

i.e., the smoothed value for period j is α times the value of the variable for period j plus $(1 - \alpha)$ times the smoothed value for period $j - 1$, where α is a positive number less than unity. Since $\bar{f}_j$ involves $\bar{f}_{j-1}$, it is clear that all previous data are included in obtaining $\bar{f}_j$, i.e., from repeated substitution

$$\bar{f}_j = \alpha f_j + \alpha(1 - \alpha)f_{j-1} + (1 - \alpha)^2\bar{f}_{j-2}$$

$$= \alpha f_j + \alpha(1 - \alpha)f_{j-1} + \alpha(1 - \alpha)^2 f_{j-2} + \ldots \tag{9-7}$$

Let us now see how exponential smoothing can be used in demand prediction. The same terminology will be used as in the least squares case. The present time is t and we wish to predict the demand in period j, $j = 1$, $2, \ldots$, i.e., in the time interval $t + (j - 1)T$ to $t + jT$. The demand in the interval $t - T$ to T will be denoted by d_0, in the interval $t - 2T$ to $t - T$ by d_{-1}, etc. We might, using the exponential smoothing formula, compute d'_j, the predicted value of d_j, from

$$d'_j = \bar{d}_0 = \alpha d_0 + (1 - \alpha)\bar{d}_{-1} \tag{9-8}$$

This would be equivalent to using $d'_j = U/N$ in the least squares case. It will always introduce a lag when there is a trend in the data.

Suppose that demand has been increasing linearly, i.e., at a constant rate. We shall now determine the trend correction needed in (9-8). Assume that the demand can be written $\delta + \rho j$ where ρ is the increase in demand per period. Then

$$\bar{d}_0 = \alpha\delta + \alpha(1 - \alpha)[\delta - \rho] + \alpha(1 - \alpha)^2[\delta - 2\rho]$$

$$+ \alpha(1 - \alpha)^3[\delta - 3\rho] + \ldots$$

$$= \delta - \alpha(1 - \alpha)\rho[1 + 2(1 - \alpha) + 3(1 - \alpha)^2 + \ldots]$$

$$= \delta - \frac{1 - \alpha}{\alpha}\rho \tag{9-9}$$

In reality, $d_j = \delta + \rho j$. Thus $\overline{d}_0$ must be increased by

$$\left[j + \frac{1 - \alpha}{\alpha} \right] \rho$$

to obtain the correct result.

In the real world we must estimate ρ also. We can do this using exponential smoothing. Let

$$\rho_j = \overline{d}_j - \overline{d}_{j-1} \tag{9-10}$$

Then the smoothed value of ρ will be computed using

$$\overline{\rho}_0 = \alpha \rho_0 + (1 - \alpha)\overline{\rho}_{-1} \tag{9-11}$$

The formula for d'_j will then be

$$d'_j = \overline{d}_0 + \left[j + \frac{1 - \alpha}{\alpha} \right] \overline{\rho}_0 \tag{9-12}$$

Equation (9-12) is the equivalent for exponential smoothing of (9-4) for least squares prediction. Again one can determine a histogram for the distribution of forecast errors for each j, and also determine the variance S_j^2. The value of α can be chosen so as to minimize the variance of the distribution of forecast errors for a given j.

To see why (9-6) is referred to as exponential smoothing write $\alpha = \gamma \Delta t$ and take the limit as $\Delta t \rightarrow 0$ while holding γ constant. This yields the following differential equation for continuous exponential smoothing

$$\frac{1}{\gamma} \frac{d\overline{f}}{dt} + \overline{f} = f(t) \tag{9-13}$$

The solution to this equation is

$$\overline{f} = \gamma \int_{-\infty}^{t} e^{-\gamma(t-\zeta)} f(\zeta) \, d\zeta \tag{9-14}$$

if $\overline{f}(-\infty) = 0$, and $\overline{f}$ is an exponentially weighted average of all past values of f.

In situations where a seasonal pattern is the most important aspect of the demand pattern, it is common to predict that sales this season will be equal to sales last season at the same point in the season plus a percentage correction appropriate to the general state of business, or any other relevant figures. Being at the same point in the season as last year does not necessarily mean the same date, since the season may be determined by the date of occurrence of some special event such as Easter, and hence the seasonal dates can fluctuate from year to year. It is an interesting fact that for many seasonal items, the percentages of the total season's sales which are sold in given periods of time measured from the start of the season remain remarkably constant from one season to the next. In this way, the total sales for the season can be predicted with some accuracy after only the first few weeks. At least one very large retail chain makes use of these seasonal percentages to make early estimates of the total season's sales for purposes of placing additional orders, or for markdowns.

9-6 The Lead Time Distribution

It was pointed out in the previous section that it is often true that demand data needed in the application of an inventory model are not available. This is even more true with lead time data, especially if lead times are fairly long and orders are not placed too frequently. It is rare indeed when sufficient data are available to yield a detailed histogram for the lead time distribution. Sometimes, about the best one can do is to obtain crude estimates of what the maximum and minimum lead times are. In such a case, about all that can be done is to average them to yield the mean lead time, and to estimate the standard deviation to be the range divided by six (since often six standard deviations, three on either side of the mean, will include essentially all of a density function).

In practice many other problems may arise with lead times besides those of trying to estimate the lead time distribution. There may not, in fact, be any stationary lead time distribution, since lead times may be continually changing with time. Furthermore, it may turn out on occasions that orders are split and the entire order is not shipped at one time. In addition, there may exist the possibility of expediting orders if an out of stock condition appears imminent. Although some of these additional complications can be included in the mathematical model, it usually turns out that the model becomes so much more difficult to work with and requires so much additional data which are hard to obtain, that it is not worthwhile to attempt to include them rigorously.

We have noted in the previous section the difficulties involved in attempting to use an empirically determined demand distribution in a mathematical model. The difficulties are compounded, of course, if one attempts to use both empirically determined lead time and demand distributions, since then one must generate numerically the marginal distribution of lead time demand. This in turn requires that the demand distribution for each possible lead time must be found. It is only in very special cases that this marginal distribution can be determined with sufficient accuracy to warrant the effort required to obtain it. One can, however, use an empirically determined lead time distribution with a theoretical, discrete, demand distribution such as the Poisson, for if it is assumed that the lead time τ can only assume one of a finite number of values t_i with probability $l(t_i)$, then the marginal distribution of lead time demand is given by (3-66). The use of such a marginal distribution can complicate hand computations, but would not be hard for a computer to work with. Of course, one can also use some theoretical distribution, such as a gamma distribution, for a lead time density, determining its mean and variance from the empirical data. Then the marginal distribution of lead time demand can be determined analytically, when a theoretical distribution is also used to represent the number of units demanded over any interval. If the demand variable is treated as continuous, or is represented by the normal density, one will usually assume that the marginal distribution of lead time demand is also normal with its mean and variance given by the results of Problem 3-12, where the mean and variance of the lead time are estimated from the empirical data, as are λ and D for the demand variable.

When the lead time variance is significant, it can be dangerous to use a model which assumes a constant lead time, if one uses the mean lead time in the model, since this can lead to seriously underestimating the average fraction of the time that the system is out of stock. Consequently, the safety stock determined from the model may be too low. However, one can often get by quite well using a model which assumes that the lead time is constant, if instead of using the mean lead time in the model one uses something like the maximum lead time or the mean lead time plus one standard deviation. In situations where the lead time data are so meager that it is essentially impossible to say much about the lead time distribution, one has little choice but to do something like the above.

9-7 Determination of Costs

The types of costs which are relevant in working with inventory models have been discussed in Chapter 1. These costs include the costs of the units, the fixed ordering costs, carrying costs, stockout costs, and the cost of operating the information processing system. All these costs can be difficult to determine in certain cases, and some are almost always difficult to determine. Regarding this determination, there is not a great deal that can be said to be really useful in a wide variety of situations; so we shall only make a few brief remarks.

Stockout costs are often the most difficult to determine. They cannot normally be measured directly, since they usually include such intangibles as good will losses. Consequently, the usual procedure, if stockout costs are specified at all, is for someone to make a guess as to what they are. Fortunately, as we have illustrated previously by example, the optimal policy tends not to be very sensitive to these costs, and hence an estimate that is of the right order of magnitude will often suffice. In the text it was shown how to obtain operating doctrines by specifying the maximum allowable average fraction of time out of stock (and/or the expected number of backorders at any point in time). If such a technique is used, one should, after computing the operating doctrine, examine the imputed stockout cost to see whether or not it is reasonable. If it is not, the basis for specifying the average fraction of time out of stock should be re-examined.

Recall from Chapter 1 that except for costs such as warehouse rental, which depend on the maximum inventory level, the rate of incurring carrying costs is assumed to be proportional to the investment in inventory, and that the factor of proportionality is the carrying charge I, which has the dimensions of dollars per year per dollar invested in inventory. Furthermore, I can be written $I_1 + I_2 + \ldots$, since I is the sum of several contributions to the carrying cost. As has been noted in Chapter 1, the most important component of the carrying cost is often an opportunity cost—the rate of return. It is exceptionally difficult in any specific case to determine precisely what maximum rate of return an organization could obtain by investing funds elsewhere. Instead, a firm will frequently specify the rate of return it desires on invested capital, and this can be used for the rate of return in the carrying charge. Usually, this value will be at least 10 percent so that I_1, the contribution to I from the rate of return factor, will be 0.10 or greater. For nonprofit organizations, such as military supply systems, the rate of return in the usual sense is not so relevant because it would not be possible to invest funds for profit (except perhaps by earning interest in a bank). However, there is very definitely an opportunity cost in this case too, since if funds were not invested in inventory, they could be used to buy more new planes or missiles which would have provided additional security, etc. It is harder to obtain a measure of the opportunity cost in this case, but it seems that here the rate should also be reasonably high, probably 10 percent or even more.

The other contributions to the carrying charge may include such things as insurance, breakage and pilferage, and taxes. Recall that taxes should be included in the carrying charge only when no special efforts are made to reduce inventories at certain times to avoid taxes. When no such efforts are made, then, on the average, the annual tax costs will be proportional to the average investment in inventory, so that I_2, the contribution to I from taxes, will be the tax rate in dollars per year per dollar invested in inventory. This tax rate will usually not be linear over wide ranges, and that range should be used which one expects will include the optimal average inventory. Often, management will attempt to make insurance cover the expected average inventory for the period of coverage, and in this case I_3, the contribution to I from insurance costs, will simply be the insurance cost in dollars per year per dollar investment in inventory, at the rate appropriate to the expected average inventory level. Other contributions to I can be evaluated in the same way. For example, to compute I_4, the contribution to I of the costs of breakage and pilferage, we can add up the total costs from this source over the length of time for which relevant historical data are available, and divide by the integral of the investment in inventory over that time, i.e., divide by the dollar-years of storage incurred. The final value of I is determined by adding up all its components I_1, I_2, etc. Typically, the final value of I will be at least 0.20. Reasonable real world values for I range from something like 0.15 to 0.35. Firms often make a mistake of using a value of I which is much too low in computing inventory carrying charges. For example, the military long used a value of $I = 0.03$, and has changed this only recently.

In principle, the task of determining A, the fixed cost of placing an order is straightforward. One traces through in detail the process of placing and receiving an order. Then the costs of forms, telephone calls, computer time, etc., are determined. In addition, the amount of time that each individual spends in processing the order is determined. These times are multiplied by the appropriate wage rate (including benefits) to yield the labor costs. All these are totaled to yield A. If a factory is part of the system, and the item is produced in lots, then the setup cost for a production run will also be included in A.

Various sorts of difficulties can arise in the determination of A. For example, if the system is quite small and there are only a few people on the payroll, the steplike behavior shown in Fig. 1-4. This sort of behavior can be accounted for with the models developed as follows: Assume that n people are to be employed, and let h_n be the maximum number of orders which they can process on the average per year. Then, using the Lagrange multiplier technique, determine the minimum average annual cost $\mathcal{K}_n^*$ when h_n is the upper limit on the average number of orders placed per year. Now add the annual wage costs of the n employees to $\mathcal{K}_n^*$. Repeat the process for $n + 1$ employees. In this way, the optimal number of employees can be determined. In military systems that use military personnel to process orders, it may not be the wage rates of the personnel which are relevant in determining A; they might be in the service regardless of whether or not any orders are placed. Instead, it is an opportunity cost that is of interest in this case, i.e., what could they be doing if they were not processing orders? Clearly, this opportunity cost may be somewhat difficult to determine.

The cost of the units themselves is usually the easiest of the costs to determine. Recall, however, that because of the way the models were set up in this text, the cost of the units includes transportation costs and any other costs of placing an order which vary with the order size. In the text we investigated incremental and "all units" quantity discounts, and noted that the computational effort required to determine Q^* and r^* may be increased considerably in this case. There are occasions in the real world where discounts of this sort are important and must be taken into account. Fortunately, however, there is another type of quantity discount which seems to be more popular, and which is also easier to handle. This discount is based on the total quantity purchased per year—not on the size of any individual order. For situations where the mean rate of demand is fairly constant, the average amount procured per year will be fixed independently of the operating doctrine (at least for the backorders case, and also for the lost sales case if the system is seldom out of stock) so that the average discount is predetermined. In this case one can treat the unit cost as a constant, independent of the operating doctrine. The unit cost should, however, be modified to reflect the discount.

Finally, let us consider the costs involved in operating the information processing system. In general, these costs will include all the costs associated with maintaining inventory records, including wage costs, computer costs, material costs, etc. Also included will be the costs of making physical inventory counts and the cost of making demand forecasts. In the text, it was assumed that the cost of a review for periodic review systems and the cost of operating a transactions reporting system were independent of the operating doctrine. This need not be true when the parameters of the operating doctrine are varied over a wide range. If one could determine precisely how these costs varied with the parameters of the operating doctrine, these appropriate functions could be included in the cost expression. Generally, however, it is adequate to assume that they are independent of the operating doctrine.

9-8 Multi-Item Problems

Most inventory systems stock a rather large number of items. It is not at all uncommon to find that 10,000 or more items are stocked, and even 100,000 or more will be stocked by a large department store. The control of such a large number of items presents many problems that do not arise in considering just a single item. It is one thing to try to develop an optimal operating doctrine for just a single item, but it is something quite different to attempt to develop optimal operating doctrines for 10,000 or 100,000 items.

It has often been typical of both industry, the retail trade, and the military to treat broad categories of items in the same way. For example, every six months a military installation might review many items, and then order an amount that would bring the inventory position up to a six months supply, plus average lead time demand, plus k months demand for safety stock. The same value of k would be used for each item. This is in general a very poor policy to follow. If nothing else, the models developed in this text have clearly indicated that different items should be treated differently, depending on the nature of the costs and stochastic processes involved. However, it can become impossibly expensive if one attempts to develop and use sophisticated operating doctrines on each of 100,000 items. For example, if 10,000 items were being controlled, one might need a very large computer. If 100,000 items were being managed, several of the largest computers available might be needed. Just the operation of several computers could easily amount to an expense of two or three million dollars per year. The answer to this problem lies in dividing the items up into a number of groups, with items in the different groups being treated differently.

Recent studies in both the military, retail stores, and industry have all reached the same interesting conclusion that, in general, a very small fraction of the total number of items stocked account for a very large fraction of the dollar volume of business involved. Frequently this will be something like ten percent of the items, accounting for eighty to ninety percent of the dollar volume. These studies have led many large inventory systems to change the way in which they control the items they stock. Now, the items are broken down into several categories, usually three, and items in different categories are treated differently. The items in the three different categories might be referred to as high, medium, and low value items. In the military, for example, the high value items would be controlled very closely, using the best means available. For items with a relatively constant demand rate, transactions reporting might be used along with a $\langle Q, r \rangle$ model. For items with strongly time dependent demands, the best available dynamic model might be used. In the case of medium value items, somewhat less costly control procedures would be used. For example, periodic review might be used for all items, with only two or three possible review intervals allowed. Here also, an effort would be made to account for the nature of the demand distribution and the costs in determining the safety stocks to be kept. In the case of low value items, no attempt would be made to use a sophisticated operating doctrine. All items might be reviewed once per year. The safety stock for all these items would be more or less arbitrarily set at k months of supply. By use of a control system of this sort, one keeps down the cost of control while still doing a good job of controlling the most important items. A similar sort of procedure might be used in a department store. In this case, however, periodic review would probably be used for all items, with shorter review periods for the high value items. The review periods might range from one day to two weeks for high value items, one week to one month for medium value items, and two weeks to six months for low value items.

We have previously suggested that there will often be interactions between items carried by the inventory system. Almost any interactions involving a large number of items are difficult to account for in practice. We studied in previous chapters how to handle constraints on floor space, the number of orders which can be placed, or the allowable investment in inventory. With 10,000 or 100,000 items it would be very difficult to attempt to compute optimal operating doctrines in the presence of such constraints. We also noted that it is difficult to give a satisfactory treatment of such constraints in the presence of uncertainty. Fortunately, in the real world, constraints of this sort are usually not sufficiently stringent that they need to be introduced explicitly. Perhaps the most important real world constraints are budgetary restrictions on the amount that can be spent on procurements. These are more important in the military than in private industry, where there can be a greater degree of flexibility. However, as we noted previously, there is no simple way of including such budgetary constraints in a model.

9-9 Personnel and Procedural Problems

The development of an appropriate mathematical model and the gathering of the data necessary for the formulation of an operating doctrine that controls an item or items in an inventory system are only part of the job required to achieve a successful application. One must, in addition, take steps to make sure that the operating doctrine will be used properly in practice. This means that one must make every effort to ensure that the people who operate the system perform their tasks correctly. In order to do so, they must receive the proper training. This is not sufficient, however. It is also necessary that the system of incentives which is operative in the system actually encourages the proper performance of the duties. Often, for one reason or another, there will be antagonism on the part of certain individuals toward the introduction of a new system. Every effort must be made to overcome this antagonism, or if this is impossible, to introduce checking procedures to make certain that these individuals do not completely destroy the advantages of the new system by intentionally doing the wrong thing.

In order to be sure that all personnel perform their tasks properly, it will normally be necessary to prepare detailed, step by step instructions to cover every possible contingency which may arise. Generally, it is a difficult task to make these instructions clear and understandable. Often, because there are so many different cases to consider, the instructions become so complicated that not even a lawyer can interpret them. By devising suitable forms for keeping records and making reports, it is possible to increase considerably the efficiency with which the system can be operated. As with instructions, these forms must be such that those using them can understand them. Frequently, one will have to break down the details for using them to the point where even the color of pencil to be used in making certain notations is indicated.

Some examples, taken from actual real world situations, may help to emphasize some of the above points. One large department store instituted a lot size-reorder point operating doctrine for a great many items in the housewares department where the mean rate of demand is reasonably constant over time, with the exception of the Christmas season. Initially, the buyers were strongly opposed to the introduction of such a system. Usually, the buyer in a department store has a great deal of freedom in determining what to buy, when to buy, how much inventory to carry, when to take markdowns, etc. The buyer himself makes all these decisions for the items under his jurisdiction. With the new system, the buyer had no control over how much to stock or when to place orders. In fact, all the ordering decisions which were previously made by the buyer were, under the new system, made by clerks in the accounting office which previously had nothing to do with these decisions. The buyers no doubt opposed the introduction of the new system partly because they were afraid that their jobs were being downgraded. Probably another reason that they opposed it was because they were afraid of what would be discovered. On making checks prior to introducing the system, all sorts of shocking things came to light, such as the appearance of a fifteen years' supply of some items on hand, the stocking of a huge number of different brands of a particular item such as coffee pots (in different parts of the store, without one buyer knowing what the other was doing), items that could no longer be sold because they were obsolete and the buyer had not taken a markdown at the proper time, etc.

Initially, things did not go at all smoothly on introducing the new system. The greatest difficulty was in getting people to do the right things. The clerks would mix up stock numbers and count the wrong items, or they would not make the counts correctly. In the accounting department, orders would not be placed when the reorder points were reached, the wrong item would be ordered, or the wrong quantity would be ordered. In time, these difficulties were corrected to a considerable extent. Furthermore, most of the buyers did become more enthusiastic about the system since it relieved them of a considerable amount of work and, in addition, made it possible for them to blame someone else if things went wrong.

The operation of some military supply systems provides an excellent example of situations where the system of rewards and punishments for the operating personnel tends to make them behave in a way completely contrary to the behavior desired. Just like the buyer in a department store, the base supply officer at a military installation has considerable freedom in deciding how much of various items to stock despite rules and regulations which, theoretically, determine what the inventory levels should be. The supply officer's commanding officer is the line officer in command of the base. The main concern of the base commander is that all planes should be in flying condition, or that all ships be seaworthy and with all systems operational. Consequently, if a plane is grounded because there is a stock-out of some spare part, the base supply officer will be heavily penalized and may receive a black mark on his record. On the other hand, there are no equivalent demerits for keeping too much inventory. Thus, the logical thing for the supply officer to do is to keep as much of everything on hand as possible. This is precisely what he does do, and this leads to much higher stocks at bases than are really needed.

Another example of this same sort of phenomenon occurs when some part is in short supply throughout the entire military supply system. Then the item is placed on what is called a critical list, and all base supply officers are supposed to report how much they have of this item, so that if someone needs it desperately, the item can be shipped from one base to another. What actually happens when an item is placed on the critical list is that all base supply officers attempt to hoard the item, and will not part with any of it under any circumstances. Thus the situation is really made worse rather than better.

To get some feeling as to the problems that can be involved in attempting to write down a precise set of instructions as to how a system should be operated, one only need look at a set of military supply manuals. These consist of a set of thirty or more volumes that presumably state in detail precisely how the system should be operated. However, on attempting to determine what should be done by reading these manuals, one soon becomes hopelessly confused. It is essentially impossible to discover from them how the system should be operated. This is in part due to the complexity of the whole system, and in part due to the way in which the manuals are written. No one person knows enough about the whole system to say how it should be operated. Different people write different volumes in the set, and, consequently, this makes it difficult even to have them consistent, let alone coherent.

9-10 The Evaluation Problem

Frequently, the most neglected part of any application of an inventory model to a real world situation is an objective evaluation of how well it worked. Even under ideal conditions, it can often be difficult to quantify in monetary terms precisely how much improvement there has been. In some cases, the improvement is so startling that even though one cannot say precisely what the average annual reductions in cost are, it is clear that they are substantial; a more detailed evaluation is unnecessary. However, in such situations, it is usually also true that almost any rational procedure for operating the system would have yielded a remarkable improvement, and hence the improvement cannot be attributed to the use of any particular mathematical model. In cases where the use of a mathematical model leads to a reduction in average on hand inventory, a reduction in the average fraction of time out of stock, and a reduction in the average annual rate of placing orders, then, provided that it was not necessary to hire extra people to help operate the new system, it is clear that there has been an improvement. However, there still remains the question as to whether the new system will effect sufficient cost reductions to pay for the cost of installing it. The cost of installing a new system based on the use of mathematical models is often fairly high. In very large inventory systems where a very small percentage improvement could mean several hundred thousand to a million dollars per year reduction in carrying costs alone, it is very easy to justify spending rather large sums in an attempt to make improvements. As the system becomes smaller and smaller, however, it becomes increasingly difficult to justify large expenditures for the introduction of a sophisticated control system.

The department store referred to in the previous section provides a good illustration of the sort of problem that one encounters in attempting an evaluation of any application. The management had no idea at all as to whether costs were reduced or profits increased as a result of the change. Furthermore they knew of no way to determine this. They did feel that a great deal was gained by having better control over inventories and by having a clearer picture of what was going on. Furthermore, they knew that something was gained by relieving the buyers of the task of controlling the inventories of all the items, but they did not know how to balance this against the additional costs incurred in accounting. The authors have investigated applications in several department stores throughout the country and in every case the situation was the same. The management really had no idea as to how much better the new system was than the old one, or whether it was really any better at all. The same sorts of difficulties encountered by the management in the department stores is also encountered in industrial applications. The situation is even more difficult in military installations, where it is almost impossible to make an evaluation on a cost basis alone, since so many of the costs are not directly measureable (viz., the cost of having an ICBM inoperable because of the lack of some spare part).

There is another reason why evaluations are often difficult to make. This reason is especially applicable when an outside organization is called upon to make the application. The management personnel who were responsible for an application will do everything possible to make it seem a success, and they will make every effort possible to cover up any defects in the system. On the other hand, if it really is a spectacular success, then in some industries the management will also attempt to keep the entire operation a secret from the outside world and their competitors.

9-11 Summary

In this chapter we have attempted to point out some of the difficulties which can be encountered in making practical applications. We have not discussed how one can treat complex multi-echelon systems which is the form taken on by many military supply systems, where a single organization operates the entire system. Here one has all the problems dealt with in this chapter, plus the difficult task of attempting to make all parts of the system mesh properly. As has been noted in Chapter 1, no general models have been developed that show how the various parts should mesh together. Hence, here, one has to face unsolved theoretical problems as well as problems of practical application. Even within the range of systems considered in this chapter, however, it was seen that many formidable practical problems must be overcome before one can achieve a successful practical application.

It is not true, of course, that in every application all the problems discussed in this chapter will be major obstacles to be overcome. Some applications are relatively easy and some are difficult. The problems which can arise were considered, not to discourage the reader from attempting practical applications, but, rather, to prepare him for the sorts of difficulties which may be encountered, in order that he may be better prepared to cope with them.

REFERENCES

1. Brown, R. G., *Statistical Forecasting for Inventory Control.* New York: McGraw-Hill Book Co., 1959.

   A number of different techniques for forecasting demand using only historical data are examined. Included are discussions of exponential smoothing and the use of a least squares line. Usually, no derivations are given, however.

2. Fetter, R. B., and W. C. Dalleck, *Decision Models for Inventory Management.* Homewood, Illinois: Richard D. Irwin, Inc., 1961.

3. Magee, J. F., *Production Planning and Inventory Control.* New York: McGraw-Hill Book Co., 1958.

4. Whitin, T. M., *The Theory of Inventory Management, Rev. ed.*, Princeton, N.J.: Princeton University Press, 1957.

PROBLEMS

9-1. The daily sales of a certain item in a department store have been observed for 60 days. It has been found that never more than three units are demanded and the frequencies with which 0, 1, 2, 3 units were demanded are 15, 10, 20, 10, 5 respectively. The procurement lead time is always four days. Determine from the empirical data the marginal distribution of lead time demand.

9-2. Suppose that in Problem 9-1, one additional day is observed, and the demand is for 6 units. How does this change the marginal distribution of lead time demand?

9-3. Consider the demand data given in Problem 9-1. Assume that the lead time is always either 2 days or 3 days, with the probability of two days being 0.3. Determine the marginal distribution of lead time demand.

9-4. The weekly demand for an item has had in the recent past the following values on successive weeks: 25, 10, 15, 16, 9, 30, 17, 18, 8, 25, 26, 14, 12, 9, 15, 18, 7, 11, 19, 15, 28, 17. By use of a moving average having $N = 3$ and without a trend correction, estimate the demand two periods in advance for each week, beginning with the third in the demand history, and compare with the actual demand. Repeat the procedure using Eq. (9-4), which includes the trend correction, to make the prediction. Plot the results obtained, showing the predicted values and actual demand as a function of time. Compute a histogram of forecast errors for the case where the trend correction was included in making the prediction.

9-5. Repeat Problem 9-4 using exponential smoothing with $\alpha = 0.15$.

9-6. Assume that for all past time the demand per period has been 10 units. Then beginning at time 0, the demand per period begins to increase at the rate of 2 units per period, so that $d_j = 10 + 2j$. Plot d_j and $d'_j = U/N$ when $N = 4$. Also plot d_j and $d'_j = \overline{d}_j = \alpha d_j + (1 - \alpha)\overline{d}_{j-1}$, $\alpha = 0.20$. Does the lag $d_j - d'_j$ behave in the way one would expect it to?

9-7. Assume that for all past time, the demand per period has been 10 units. Suddenly at $t = 0$, the demand per period jumps to 20 units and remains constant at that value. Plot d_j and d'_j, where d'_j is computed from Eq. (9-4) for $N = 4$, and the prediction being made for the next period.

9-8. Repeat Problem 9-7 using Eq. (9-12) with $\alpha = 0.2$, and again making the prediction for the next period.

9-9. Solve Eq. (9-13) when

$$f(t) = \begin{cases} 0, & t < 0 \\ 6t, & t \geq 0 \end{cases}$$

Plot $\bar{f}(t)$ and $f(t)$ on the same graph.

9-10. Solve Eq. (9-13) when

$$f(t) = \begin{cases} 0, & t < 0 \\ 20, & t \geq 0 \end{cases}$$

Plot $\bar{f}(t)$ and $f(t)$ on the same graph.

9-11. Discuss the way one could introduce an expedited procurement into a $\langle Q, r \rangle$ model of the type discussed in Chapter 4. Assume that an order is expedited if the on hand inventory falls to a given value, and that an expedited order takes a time $\hat{\tau} < \tau$ to arrive. If the time until the arrival of the next order is less than $\hat{\tau}$, no expedite order is placed. The cost of expediting is π^*. What sorts of complications develop? Would it be easy to work out Q^* and r^* for this model?

9-12. Discuss in detail the way in which a generating function could be used to obtain the n-fold convolution of an empirical demand distribution.

9-13. Discuss how one might compute the n-fold convolution of an empirical demand distribution on a computer, directly from its definition, and without the use of generating functions.

APPENDICES

APPENDIX 1

A1-1 Constraints and Lagrange Multipliers

Consider the problem of minimizing the continuous and differentiable function $z = f(x_1, \ldots, x_n)$ subject to the constraint $g(x_1, \ldots, x_n) = \alpha$, where $g(x_1, \ldots, x_n)$ is also continuous and differentiable. Since the variables are not independent, it is no longer true that the optimal set of x_j values must satisfy $\partial f/\partial x_j = 0, j = 1, \ldots, n$. However, a procedure for solving this problem would be to use the constraint to solve for one of the variables, say x_n, to yield $x_n = h(x_1, \ldots, x_{n-1})$. This expression for x_n is then substituted into f to yield a function $\hat{f}$ of $n - 1$ variables. In this form the methods for finding unconstrained minima can then be applied, i.e., we solve $\partial \hat{f}/\partial x_j = 0, j = 1, \ldots, n - 1$ where, since

$$\hat{f}(x_1, \ldots, x_{n-1}) = f[x_1, \ldots, x_{n-1}, h(x_1, \ldots, x_{n-1})]$$

$$\frac{\partial \hat{f}}{\partial x_j} = \frac{\partial f}{\partial x_j} + \frac{\partial f}{\partial x_n}\frac{\partial h}{\partial x_j}, \quad j = 1, \ldots, n - 1 \tag{A1-1}$$

However, from $g(x_1, \ldots, x_n) = \alpha$, we see that

$$\frac{\partial g}{\partial x_j} + \frac{\partial g}{\partial x_n}\frac{\partial h}{\partial x_j} = 0 \quad \text{or} \quad \frac{\partial h}{\partial x_j} = -\frac{\partial g/\partial x_j}{\partial g/\partial x_n}; \quad \partial g/\partial x_n \neq 0$$

so

$$\frac{\partial \hat{f}}{\partial x_j} = \frac{\partial f}{\partial x_j} - \frac{\dfrac{\partial f}{\partial x_n}}{\dfrac{\partial g}{\partial x_n}}\frac{\partial g}{\partial x_j} = 0, \quad j = 1, \ldots, n - 1 \tag{A1-2}$$

Now if $x_1^*, \ldots, x_n^*$ are the minimizing values, write $\eta = -\partial f/\partial x_n/\partial g/\partial x_n$ where $\partial f/\partial x_n$ and $\partial g/\partial x_n$ are evaluated at $x_1^*, \ldots, x_n^*$. Therefore the optimal x_j values must satisfy the $n + 1$ equations

$$\frac{\partial f}{\partial x_j} + \eta\frac{\partial g}{\partial x_j} = 0, \quad j = 1, \ldots, n; \quad g(x_1, \ldots, x_n) = \alpha \tag{A1-3}$$

Here we have $n + 1$ equations to be solved for $x_1^*, \ldots, x_n^*$ and η. The form (A1-3) is very convenient to use, since all the variables are treated symmetrically, and it is equivalent to (A1-2) if $\partial g/\partial x_n \neq 0$ at $x_1^*, \ldots, x_n^*$. In fact, we can use the equations (A1-3) to determine $x_1^*, \ldots, x_n^*$ provided that not all derivatives $\partial g/\partial x_j$ vanish at $x_1^*, \ldots, x_n^*$. It seldom happens that these derivatives do all vanish at $x_1^*, \ldots, x_n^*$. Hence the above procedure will work normally.

The necessary conditions (A1-3) which the x_j^* must satisfy can be obtained simply as follows. Form the function

$$F(x_1, \ldots, x_n, \eta) = f(x_1, \ldots, x_n) + \eta[g(x_1, \ldots, x_n) - \alpha] \qquad \text{(A1-4)}$$

Then

$$\frac{\partial F}{\partial x_j} = \frac{\partial f}{\partial x_j} + \eta\, \frac{\partial g}{\partial x_j}, \quad j = 1, \ldots, n; \quad \frac{\partial F}{\partial \eta} = g - \alpha \qquad \text{(A1-5)}$$

Hence, on setting $\partial F/\partial x_j = 0$, and $\partial F/\partial \eta = 0$, we obtain (A1-3). The parameter η which we introduced above is referred to as a Lagrange multiplier. The procedure of determining the conditions satisfied by the x_j, $j = 1, \ldots, n$, that minimize z subject to the constraint $g = \alpha$, by forming the function F and setting the partial derivatives of F with respect to the x_j and η equal to zero, is referred to as the method of Lagrange multipliers.

The Lagrange multiplier technique can also be used when there are two or more constraints. Suppose that we wish to minimize $z = f(x_1, \ldots, x_n)$ subject to $g_1(x_1, \ldots, x_n) = \alpha_1$, $g_2(x_1, \ldots, x_n) = \alpha_2$. We introduce two Lagrange multipliers η, θ and form the function

$$F(x_1, \ldots, x_n, \eta, \theta) = f(x_1, \ldots, x_n) + \eta[g_1(x_1, \ldots, x_n) - \alpha_1]$$
$$+ \theta[g_2(x_1, \ldots, x_n) - \alpha_2] \qquad \text{(A1-6)}$$

The necessary conditions which the x_j that minimize z subject to the two constraints must satisfy are

$$\frac{\partial F}{\partial x_j} = 0 = \frac{\partial f}{\partial x_j} + \eta\, \frac{\partial g_1}{\partial x_j} + \theta\, \frac{\partial g_2}{\partial x_j}$$

$$\frac{\partial F}{\partial \eta} = g_1 - \alpha = 0; \quad \frac{\partial F}{\partial \theta} = g_2 - \alpha = 0$$

$$\text{(A1-7)}$$

Here we have $n + 2$ equations to solve for the $n + 2$ variables x_j, $j = 1, \ldots, n$, η, and θ. This procedure will work provided that the rank of the $(2 \times n)$ matrix $\|\partial g_i/\partial x_j\|$, $i = 1, 2; j = 1, \ldots, n$, is 2 at the minimizing point. The proof that this procedure works is the same as for the one variable case, except that now one must use the two constraints to solve explicitly for two of the variables.

Often when solving constrained optimization problems of the type discussed above, there are the additional restrictions that $x_j \geq 0$ for some or all of the variables. In this case, the set of optimal x_j need not satisfy

(A1-3) or (A1-7), since one or more x_j^* may be 0, i.e., be on the boundaries of the region defined by $x_j \geq 0$, $j = 1, \ldots, n$ (this is called the non-negative orthant). If there exists the possibility that the optimum has one or more $x_j = 0$, then one must also find all the relative minima lying on those boundaries of the non-negative orthant which correspond to the variables which are required to be non-negative. To do this, one goes through the same procedure outlined above first holding one of the variables required to be non-negative at a zero level. This is done for each variable required to be non-negative. Then the problem is solved for two of the variables set equal to zero. This is done for all possible combinations of two of the variables required to be non-negative set equal to zero. Then three variables are set equal to zero, etc. The absolute minimum will be the smallest of all the relative minima obtained with 0, 1, 2, ... variables set to zero. It can be a very arduous task to check all the boundary minima. Fortunately, for the problems of interest in this text, these boundary minima do not usually occur.

A1-2 Interpretation of Lagrange Multipliers

Let us return to the study of the problem which seeks to find non-negative values of $x_1, \ldots, x_n$ which minimize $z = f(x_1, \ldots, x_n)$ subject to the constraint $g(x_1, \ldots, x_n) = \alpha$. If z^* is the minimum value of z subject to the constraint, then z^* will in general depend on the value of α, i.e., z^* is a function of α. Similarly, the Lagrange multiplier η will also depend on α, i.e., η is a function of α. We would now like to show that $\partial z^*/\partial \alpha = -\eta$ where both sides of the equation are evaluated at the same value of α.

To prove that $\partial z^*/\partial \alpha = -\eta$, let $x_1^*, \ldots, x_n^*$ be a set of x_j values which yield z^*. These x_j^* values will also be functions of α. Thus

$$\frac{\partial z^*}{\partial \alpha} = \sum_{j=1}^{n} \frac{\partial f}{\partial x_j^*} \frac{dx_j^*}{d\alpha}$$

However, because of (A1-3)

$$\frac{\partial f}{\partial x_j^*} = -\eta \frac{\partial g}{\partial x_j^*}$$

so

$$\frac{\partial z^*}{\partial \alpha} = -\eta \sum_{j=1}^{n} \frac{\partial g}{\partial x_j^*} \frac{dx_j^*}{d\alpha} \tag{A1-8}$$

Next we note that the constraint $g(x_1, \ldots, x_n) = \alpha$ must always be satisfied (i.e., it must be an identity in α). Hence, differentiating the constraint with respect to α we obtain

$$\sum_{j=1}^{n} \frac{\partial g}{\partial x_j^*} \frac{dx_j^*}{d\alpha} = 1 \qquad\qquad (\text{A1-9})$$

or on substitution of (A1-9) into (A1-8), $\partial z^*/\partial \alpha = -\eta$ which is what we wanted to prove. The same procedure can be used to show that if there are $m < n$ constraints, then $\partial z^*/\partial \alpha = -\eta_j$, $i = 1, \ldots, m$. The proof is more difficult for this case, however, and will not be presented here.

The above result can be given an interesting economic interpretation. In this book z usually represents the average annual cost, and the constraints will represent limitations on the physical resources such as capital or floor space. Then, by its dimensions, η_i must be a value or cost per unit of resource i. Intuitively, we see from $\partial z^*/\partial \alpha_i = -\eta_i$ that η_i is the amount by which the minimum cost can be reduced by adding one additional unit of resource i. The Lagrange multipliers can thus be considered to be the imputed values or shadow prices of the resources.

A1-3 Inequality Constraints

The constraints on a problem which are of interest to us in this work usually take the form $g_i(x_1, \ldots, x_n) \leq \alpha_i$ rather than $g_i(x_1, \ldots, x_n) = \alpha_i$. Intuitively, the constraint requires that no more than a given amount of a resource can be used; it is permissible to use less than the maximum amount, however. We now wish to show that the Lagrange multiplier technique can be generalized to handle inequality constraints.

To begin the discussion imagine that we wish to determine non-negative variables $x_1, \ldots, x_n$ which minimize $z = f(x_1, \ldots, x_n)$ subject to $g(x_1, \ldots, x_n) \leq \alpha$. Let $x_1^*, \ldots, x_n^*$ be the set of non-negative x_j values which minimize z subject to the constraint. Then either: (1) $g(x_1^*, \ldots, x_n^*) = \alpha$ or (2) $g(x_1^*, \ldots, x_n^*) < \alpha$. If (1) holds the constraints it is said to be active; a constraint is active if it holds as a strict equality at the minimizing point. A constraint is called inactive if it holds as a strict inequality at the minimizing point. A constraint must be either active or inactive. The important thing to observe is that if the constraint is inactive then the minimizing point is the same whether or not we consider the constraint when solving the problem. If the constraint is active, then the minimizing point is the same as would be obtained if we solved the problem assuming that the constraint always held as a strict equality.

After one final observation, we shall be able to present a method for solving the problem of interest. Let z_u^* be the minimum value of z for non-negative x_j in the absence of the constraint, and let z_1^* be the minimum value of z for non-negative x_j subject to the constraint $g(x_1, \ldots, x_n) = \alpha$. Then it is true that $z_u^* \leq z_1^*$, since the point which yields z_1^* is also an allowable solution to the unconstrained problem. More generally, if z_m^* is the minimum value of z for non-negative x_j subject to the m constraints $g_i(x_1, \ldots, x_n) = \alpha_i$, and z_{m+1}^* is the minimum of z for non-negative x_i subject to $m + 1$ constraints (m of the constraints being the same as those referred to above) of the form $g_i(x_1, \ldots, x_n) = \alpha_i$ then $z_{m+1}^* \geq z_m^*$, since the point which yields z_{m+1}^* is an allowable solution to the problem with m constraints.

It is now clear how to solve the problem of finding non-negative x_j which minimize $z = f(x_1, \ldots, x_n)$ subject to the inequality constraint $g(x_1, \ldots, x_n) \leq \alpha$. We first find the point which minimizes z for non-negative x_j ignoring the constraint, i.e., we first solve the unconstrained problem. If the solution so obtained satisfies the constraint, it follows from the previous paragraph that it is the optimal solution. If the point so obtained does not satisfy the constraint, then the constraint will be active, and we solve the problem of finding non-negative x_j which minimizes z subject to the equality constraint $g(x_1, \ldots, x_n) = \alpha$. This problem can be solved by introducing a Lagrange multiplier as discussed in Sec. A1-1. The minimizing point so obtained will also be the optimal solution to the given problem. When the constraint is an inequality, more effort may be required to solve the problem than for the case where the constraint is a strict equality, since it is also necessary to solve the unconstrained problem.

Consider now the case where we wish to find non-negative variables which minimize $z = f(x_1, \ldots, x_n)$ subject to the two inequality constraints $g_1(x_1, \ldots, x_n) \leq \alpha_1$, $g_2(x_1, \ldots, x_n) \leq \alpha_2$. The procedure is to first solve the problem ignoring both constraints. If the minimizing point so obtained satisfies both constraints it is the optimal solution to the given problem. If it does not satisfy both constraints, then at least one of the constraints will be active. In such a situation, the next step is to solve the problem of finding non-negative x_j which minimize z subject to the constraint $g_1(x_1, \ldots, x_n) = \alpha_1$ (ignoring the other constraint). If the solution so obtained satisfies the other constraint, it is optimal. If it does not, we next find the set of non-negative x_j which minimize z subject to $g_2(x_1, \ldots, x_n) = \alpha_2$, (ignoring the constraint $g_1(x_1, \ldots, x_n) \leq \alpha_1$). If the solution so obtained satisfies $g_1(x_1, \ldots, x_n) \leq \alpha_1$ it is optimal. When it does not, we are sure that both constraints will be active, and we determine the set of non-negative x_j which minimize z subject to the two constraints $g_1(x_1, \ldots, x_n) = \alpha_1$, $g_2(x_1, \ldots, x_n) = \alpha_2$. The resulting set of x_j will be the optimal solution to the given problem.

The same procedures can be used to solve problems involving three or more inequality constraints. However, the effort required to solve the problem increases rapidly with the number of constraints.

APPENDIX 2

A2-1 Introduction

To determine optimal values of the parameters associated with an operating doctrine, it is often necessary to solve numerically an equation such as $f(x) = 0$ or a set of equations such as $f_1(x, y) = 0$, $f_2(x, y) = 0$. We shall discuss a useful technique for solving numerically equations such as the above. It is known as Newton's method. We shall also discuss a technique called the method of "steepest descents" for minimizing the cost expression directly, rather than solving a set of equations obtained by setting the derivatives of the cost equal to zero.

A2-2 Newton's Method

Consider the problem of solving the equation $f(x) = 0$. Suppose that x_0 is an approximate solution, i.e., $f(x_0)$ is close to 0. Then using the first two terms of the Taylor expansion we have

$$f(x) \approx f(x_0) + \frac{df(x_0)}{dx} (x - x_0) \tag{A2-1}$$

when x is close to x_0. In (A2-1) $df(x_0)/dx$ is the derivative of f with respect to x evaluated at x_0. We wish to determine x such that $f(x) = 0$. Setting $f(x) = 0$ in (A2-1), we obtain

$$x - x_0 = \Delta x = -f(x_0)/(df(x_0)/dx) \tag{A2-2}$$

We can then try $x_1 = x_0 + \Delta x$ as the new estimate of the solution to $f(x) = 0$. This process is repeated and at the $(n + 1)$st stage

$$\Delta x_n = -f(x_n)/(df(x_n)/dx) \tag{A2-3}$$

and $x_{n+1} = x_n + \Delta x_n$. The procedure just outlined is an iterative procedure for finding the solution to $f(x) = 0$, and is referred to as Newton's method. It is not necessarily true, however, that the procedure will converge to the solution to $f(x) = 0$. The method will converge if df/dx and d^2f/dx^2 do not change signs in the interval between x_0 and the root of $f(x) = 0$.

The same procedure can be used to solve $f_1(x, y) = 0$, $f_2(x, y) = 0$. Assume that at the $(n + 1)$st stage the approximate roots are x_n, y_n. Then write

$$0 = f_1(x_n, y_n) + \frac{\partial f_1(x_n, y_n)}{\partial x} (x_{n+1} - x_n)$$

$$+ \frac{\partial f_1(x_n, y_n)}{\partial y} (y_{n+1} - y_n) \approx f_1(x_{n+1}, y_{n+1})$$

$$0 = f_2(x_n, y_n) + \frac{\partial f_2(x_n, y_n)}{\partial x} (x_{n+1} - x_n)$$

$$+ \frac{\partial f_2(x_n, y_n)}{\partial y} (y_{n+1} - y_n) \approx f_2(x_{n+1}, y_{n+1})$$

so that

$$\Delta x_n = x_{n+1} - x_n = \frac{1}{J} \begin{vmatrix} -f_1 & \partial f_1/\partial y \\ -f_2 & \partial f_2/\partial y \end{vmatrix}$$

$$= \frac{1}{J} \left[f_2(x_n, y_n) \frac{\partial f_1(x_n, y_n)}{\partial y} - f_1(x_n, y_n) \frac{\partial f_2(x_n, y_n)}{\partial y} \right] \quad (A2\text{-}4)$$

$$\Delta y_n = y_{n+1} - y_n = \frac{1}{J} \begin{vmatrix} \partial f_1/\partial x & -f_1 \\ \partial f_2/\partial x & -f_2 \end{vmatrix}$$

$$= \frac{1}{J} \left[f_1(x_n, y_n) \frac{\partial f_2(x_n, y_n)}{\partial x} - f_2(x_n, y_n) \frac{\partial f_1(x_n, y_n)}{\partial x} \right] \quad (A2\text{-}5)$$

where

$$J = \frac{\partial f_1(x_n, y_n)}{\partial x} \frac{\partial f_2(x_n, y_n)}{\partial y} - \frac{\partial f_1(x_n, y_n)}{\partial y} \frac{\partial f_2(x_n, y_n)}{\partial x} \quad (A2\text{-}6)$$

Then $x_{n+1} = x_n + \Delta x_n$, $y_{n+1} = y_n + \Delta y_n$. Again it is not necessarily true that this iterative scheme will converge. The conditions for convergence are not so simple as in the one variable case, and we shall not consider them.

Of course, if the roots of $f(x) = 0$ or $f_1(x, y) = 0$, $f_2(x, y) = 0$ are not unique, Newton's method does not provide a way for finding all roots. There does not seem to be any simple way to do this in general.

A2-3 The Method of Steepest Descents

For most of the models formulated in this text, the optimal operating doctrine was determined by minimizing some cost expression such as the average annual cost $\mathcal{K}$. Newton's method provided a way of solving equations such as $\partial \mathcal{K}/\partial Q = \partial \mathcal{K}/\partial r = 0$, which are necessary conditions that Q and r must satisfy if they minimize $\mathcal{K}$. The method of steepest descents works with $\mathcal{K}$ directly, and proceeds to minimize $\mathcal{K}$ rather than to solve equations such as $\partial \mathcal{K}/\partial Q = \partial \mathcal{K}/\partial r = 0$. Assume that $\mathcal{K}$ is a function of two variables Q and r, and that it is desired to determine the absolute minimum of $\mathcal{K}$.

Suppose that we begin with any values Q_0, r_0, and compute $\mathcal{K}(Q_0, r_0)$. We wish to determine values Q_1, r_1 such that $\mathcal{K}(Q_1, r_1) < \mathcal{K}(Q_0, r_0)$. Now $\partial \mathcal{K}/\partial Q$, $\partial \mathcal{K}/\partial r$ tell us how $\mathcal{K}$ is changing with respect to Q and r at any given point, i.e., they indicate how Q and r should be changed so as to decrease $\mathcal{K}$. Consider

$$Q_1 = Q_0 - \theta \frac{\partial \mathcal{K}(Q_0, r_0)}{\partial Q}; \quad r_1 = r_0 - \theta \frac{\partial \mathcal{K}(Q_0, r_0)}{\partial r}, \quad \theta > 0 \quad (A2\text{-}7)$$

Then if θ is sufficiently small, $\mathcal{K}(Q_1, r_1) < \mathcal{K}(Q_0, r_0)$ unless $\partial \mathcal{K}/\partial Q = \partial \mathcal{K}/\partial r = 0$ at Q_0, r_0. When θ is the same in both expressions in (A2-7), we say that we are using the method of steepest descents, since it can be shown that we move in the direction of the greatest rate of decrease in $\mathcal{K}$.

The procedure then is to compute a Q_1 and r_1 using (A2-7). The value of θ is selected arbitrarily. The proper values to use will automatically suggest themselves as the problem is solved, since if θ is too large, the minimum will be overshot, and if θ is too small, it will take a long time to reach the minimum. Then $\mathcal{K}(Q_1, r_1)$ is computed. If $\mathcal{K}(Q_1, r_1) < \mathcal{K}(Q_0, r_0)$, then $\partial \mathcal{K}/\partial Q$, $\partial \mathcal{K}/\partial r$ are recomputed at Q_1, r_1 and new values of Q, r are found from (A2-7), where now Q_1, r_1 become Q_0, r_0. When $\mathcal{K}(Q_1, r_1) \geq \mathcal{K}(Q_0, r_0)$ select a smaller θ and repeat the process. Just as with Newton's method troubles with convergence may be encountered with the method of steepest descents. The value of θ may be changed at each iteration, if desired.

To use Newton's method, the first derivatives of f_1, f_2 are needed. These are the second derivatives of $\mathcal{K}$. The method of steepest descents uses only the first derivatives of $\mathcal{K}$. If the derivatives are difficult to evaluate numerically, the method of steepest descents requires less computation per iteration. On the other hand, it may require more iterations unless θ is wisely chosen each time.

APPENDIX 3

In the following properties, $p(r; \mu)$, $P(r; \mu)$, $\gamma(t; \alpha, \beta)$, $b_N(j; n, \rho)$ are defined by

$$p(r; \mu) = \frac{\mu^r}{r!} e^{-\mu}; \quad P(r; \mu) = \sum_{j=r}^{\infty} p(j; \mu), \quad r = 0, 1, 2, \ldots$$

$$\gamma(t; \alpha, \beta) = \frac{\beta(\beta t)^{\alpha} e^{-\beta t}}{\Gamma(\alpha + 1)}, \quad \alpha > -1, \beta > 0$$

$$b_N(j; n, \rho) = \frac{\Gamma(j + n)}{j! \Gamma(n)} \rho^n (1 - \rho)^j, \quad j = 0, 1, 2, \ldots$$

The properties hold for all $\mu > 0$ and all non-negative integers r^*. The differencing operator $\Delta\{f(r)\}$ is defined by $\Delta\{f(r)\} = f(r) - f(r - 1)$. $\Gamma(x)$ is the gamma function of argument x.

1. $rp(r; \mu) = \mu p(r - 1; \mu)$

2. Let $\mu_m(r) = \sum_{j=r}^{\infty} j^m p(j; \mu)$, $m = 0, 1, 2, \ldots$

Then,

$$\mu_m(r) = \mu \sum_{x=0}^{m-1} \binom{m - 1}{x} \mu_x(r - 1), \quad m = 1, 2, \ldots$$

3. $\sum_{j=r}^{\infty} jp(j; \mu) = \mu P(r - 1; \mu)$

4. $\sum_{j=r}^{\infty} j^2 p(j; \mu) = \mu P(r - 1; \mu) + \mu^2 P(r - 2; \mu)$

5. $\sum_{j=r}^{\infty} j^3 p(j; \mu) = \mu^3 P(r - 3; \mu) + 3\mu^2 P(r - 2; \mu) + \mu P(r - 1; \mu)$

---

* Although r is to be non-negative, it is possible in some of the properties to have a negative argument for p or P when $r < 3$. These properties will be correct for such r if the convention is used that $p(j; \mu) = 0$, $P(j; \mu) = 1$ for j a negative integer.

6. $\displaystyle\sum_{j=r}^{\infty} P(j;\mu) = \mu P(r-1;\mu) + (1-r)P(r;\mu)$

7. Let $\Omega_m(r) = \displaystyle\sum_{j=r}^{\infty} j^m P(j;\mu), \ m = 0, 1, 2, \ldots$

Then,

$$\Omega_m(r) = \frac{1}{m+1}\left\{ \sum_{x=0}^{m-1} (-1)^{m+1-x}\binom{m+1}{x}\Omega_x(r) + \mu_{m+1}(r) \right.$$

$$\left. - (r-1)^{m+1}P(r;\mu) \right\}, \quad m = 1, 2, \ldots$$

8. $\displaystyle\sum_{j=r}^{\infty} jP(j;\mu) = \frac{\mu^2}{2} P(r-2;\mu) + \mu P(r-1;\mu) - \frac{r(r-1)}{2} P(r;\mu)$

9. $\displaystyle\sum_{j=r}^{\infty} j^2 P(j;\mu) = \left[-\frac{r^3}{3} + \frac{r^2}{2} - \frac{r}{6} \right] P(r;\mu) + \mu P(r-1;\mu)$

$$+ \frac{3\mu^2}{2} P(r-2;\mu) + \frac{\mu^3}{3} P(r-3;\mu)$$

10. $\displaystyle\sum_{j=r}^{\infty} (j-r)p(j;\mu) = \sum_{j=0}^{\infty} jp(r+j;\mu) = \sum_{j=r+1}^{\infty} P(j;\mu)$

$$= \mu P(r-1;\mu) - rP(r;\mu)$$

$$= \mu p(r;\mu) + (\mu - r)P(r+1;\mu)$$

11. $\displaystyle\sum_{j=0}^{r} (r-j)p(j;\mu) = r - \mu + \mu P(r;\mu) - rP(r+1;\mu)$

12. $rP(r+1;\mu) = rP(r;\mu) - \mu p(r-1;\mu)$

13. $\mu P(r;\mu) - rP(r+1;\mu) = \mu P(r-1;\mu) - rP(r;\mu)$

14. $\dfrac{dp(r;\mu)}{d\mu} = p(r-1;\mu) - p(r;\mu)$

15. $\dfrac{dP(r;\mu)}{d\mu} = p(r-1;\mu)$

16. $\displaystyle\int_0^T p(r;\lambda t)\, dt = \frac{1}{\lambda} P(r+1;\lambda T)$

17. $\displaystyle\int_0^T t^n p(r;\lambda t)\, dt = \frac{1}{\lambda^{n+1}} \frac{(n+r)!}{r!} P(n+r+1;\lambda T), n = 0, 1, 2, \ldots$

18. $\displaystyle\int_0^T P(r;\lambda t)\, dt = \frac{1}{\lambda} \sum_{j=r+1}^{\infty} P(j;\lambda T) = TP(r;\lambda T) - \frac{r}{\lambda} P(r+1;\lambda T)$

19. $\displaystyle\int_0^T t^n P(r;\lambda t)\,dt = \frac{1}{\lambda^{n+1}}\sum_{j=r}^\infty \frac{(n+j)!}{j!}\,P(n+j+1;\lambda T) = \frac{T^{n+1}}{n+1}\,P(r;\lambda T)$

$$-\frac{1}{\lambda^{n+1}}\left(\frac{1}{n+1}\right)\frac{(n+r)!}{(r-1)!}\,P(n+r+1;\lambda T),$$

$$n = 0, 1, 2, \ldots$$

20. $\displaystyle\int_0^T (T-t)^n p(r;\lambda t)\,dt = \sum_{x=0}^n (-1)^x\binom{n}{x}\frac{T^{n-x}}{\lambda^{x+1}}\frac{(x+r)!}{r!}\,P(x+r+1;\lambda T)$

21. $\displaystyle\int_0^T (T-t)^n P(r;\lambda t)\,dt = \sum_{x=0}^n (-1)^x\binom{n}{x}\frac{T^{n-x}}{\lambda^{x+1}}\left(\frac{1}{x+1}\right)[(\lambda T)^{x+1}P(r;\lambda T)$

$$-\frac{(x+r)!}{(r-1)!}\,P(x+r+1;\lambda T)]$$

22. $\displaystyle\int_0^\infty \gamma(t;\alpha,\beta)p(r;\lambda t)\,dt = b_N\left(r;\alpha+1,\frac{\beta}{\lambda+\beta}\right)$

23. $\displaystyle\int_0^\infty \gamma(t;\alpha,\beta)p[r;\lambda(t+T)]\,dt = \sum_{j=0}^r p(r-j;\lambda T)b_N\left(j;\alpha+1,\frac{\beta}{\lambda+\beta}\right)$

24. $\displaystyle\int_0^\infty \int_0^t \gamma(t;\alpha,\beta)p(r;\lambda\tau)\,d\tau\,dt = \frac{1}{\lambda}\left[1 - \sum_{j=0}^r b_N\left(j;\alpha+1,\frac{\beta}{\lambda+\beta}\right)\right]$

25. $\displaystyle\int_0^\infty \int_0^{t+T} \gamma(t;\alpha,\beta)p(r;\lambda\tau)\,d\tau\,dt$

$$= \frac{1}{\lambda}\left[1 - \sum_{j=0}^r \sum_{i=0}^j p(j-i;\lambda T)b_N\left(i;\alpha+1,\frac{\beta}{\lambda+\beta}\right)\right]$$

26. $\Delta\{\mu_1(r)\} = -(r-1)p(r-1;\mu) = -\mu p(r-2;\mu)$

27. $\Delta\{1-\mu_1(r+1)\} = \Delta\left\{\sum_{j=0}^r jp(j;\mu)\right\} = rp(r;\mu) = \mu p(r-1;\mu)$

28. $\Delta\left\{\sum_{j=r}^\infty (j-r)p(j;\mu)\right\} = -P(r;\mu)$

APPENDIX 4

In the following properties, $\phi(r)$, $\Phi(r)$ are defined as follows:

$$\phi(r) = \frac{1}{\sqrt{2\pi}} e^{-r^2/2}; \quad \Phi(r) = \int_r^\infty \phi(x) \, dx$$

where r can be positive, negative, or zero.

1. $\displaystyle\int_r^\infty x\phi(x) \, dx = \phi(r)$

2. $\displaystyle\int_r^\infty x^n\phi(x) \, dx = r^{n-1}\phi(r) + (n-1)\int_r^\infty x^{n-2}\phi(x) \, dx, \; n = 2, 3, \ldots$

3. $\displaystyle\int_r^\infty x^2\phi(x) \, dx = \Phi(r) + r\phi(r)$

4. $\displaystyle\int_r^\infty x^3\phi(x) \, dx = (r^2 + 2)\phi(r)$

5. $\displaystyle\int_r^\infty x^n\Phi(x) \, dx = -\frac{1}{n+1} r^{n+1}\Phi(r) + \frac{1}{n+1}\int_r^\infty x^{n+1}\phi(x) \, dx,$
$$n = 0, 1, 2, \ldots$$

6. $\displaystyle\int_r^\infty \Phi(x) \, dx = \phi(r) - r\Phi(r)$

7. $\displaystyle\int_r^\infty x\Phi(x) \, dx = \tfrac{1}{2}[(1 - r^2)\Phi(r) + r\phi(r)]$

8. $\displaystyle\int_r^\infty x^2\Phi(x) \, dx = \tfrac{1}{3}[(r^2 + 2)\phi(r) - r^3\Phi(r)]$

9. $\displaystyle\int_{T_1}^{T_2} \frac{1}{(Dt)^{1/2}} \phi\left[\frac{x - \lambda t}{(Dt)^{1/2}}\right] dt = W_0(x, T_2) - W_0(x, T_1), \; T_1, T_2 > 0$

$$W_0(x, T) = \frac{1}{\lambda} \Phi\left[\frac{x - \lambda T}{(DT)^{1/2}}\right] - \frac{1}{\lambda} e^{2\lambda x/D} \Phi\left[\frac{x + \lambda T}{(DT)^{1/2}}\right]$$

10. $\int_{T_1}^{T_2} \left(\dfrac{t}{D}\right)^{1/2} \phi\left[\dfrac{x - \lambda t}{(Dt)^{1/2}}\right] dt = W_1(x, T_2) - W_1(x, T_1), \quad T_1, T_2 > 0$

$$W_1(x, T) = \dfrac{D}{\lambda^3}\left(1 + \dfrac{\lambda x}{D}\right)\Phi\left[\dfrac{x - \lambda T}{(DT)^{1/2}}\right] - \dfrac{2(DT)^{1/2}}{\lambda^2}\phi\left[\dfrac{x - \lambda T}{(DT)^{1/2}}\right]$$
$$+ \dfrac{1}{\lambda^2}\left(x - \dfrac{D}{\lambda}\right)e^{2\lambda x/D}\Phi\left[\dfrac{x + \lambda T}{(DT)^{1/2}}\right]$$

11. Let

$$J_n(x, T_1, T_2) = \int_{T_1}^{T_2} \dfrac{t^n}{(Dt)^{1/2}} \phi\left[\dfrac{x - \lambda t}{(Dt)^{1/2}}\right] dt, \quad n = 0, 1, 2, \ldots; T_1, T_2 > 0$$

Then

$$J_{n+1}(x, T_1, T_2) = \dfrac{2(DT_1)^{1/2}T_1^n}{\lambda^2}\phi\left[\dfrac{x - \lambda T_1}{(DT_1)^{1/2}}\right] - \dfrac{2(DT_2)^{1/2}T_2^n}{\lambda^2}\phi\left[\dfrac{x - \lambda T_2}{(DT_2)^{1/2}}\right]$$
$$+ \dfrac{(2n + 1)D}{\lambda^2}J_n(x, T_1, T_2) + \dfrac{x^2}{\lambda^2}J_{n-1}(x, T_1, T_2),$$
$$n = 0, 1, 2, \ldots$$

12. $\int_{T_1}^{T_2} \dfrac{t^{3/2}}{D^{1/2}} \phi\left[\dfrac{x - \lambda t}{(Dt)^{1/2}}\right] dt = W_2(x, T_2) - W_2(x, T_1), \quad T_1, T_2 > 0$

$$W_2(x, T) = \dfrac{1}{\lambda^3}\left[x^2 + \dfrac{3Dx}{\lambda} + \dfrac{3D^2}{\lambda^2}\right]\Phi\left[\dfrac{x - \lambda T}{(DT)^{1/2}}\right]$$
$$- \dfrac{2(DT)^{1/2}}{\lambda^2}\left[T + \dfrac{3D}{\lambda^2}\right]\phi\left[\dfrac{x - \lambda T}{(DT)^{1/2}}\right]$$
$$+ \left[\dfrac{3D}{\lambda^4}\left(x - \dfrac{D}{\lambda}\right) - \dfrac{x^2}{\lambda^3}\right]e^{2\lambda x/D}\Phi\left[\dfrac{x + \lambda T}{(DT)^{1/2}}\right]$$

13. $\int_{T_1}^{T_2} \dfrac{t^{5/2}}{D^{1/2}} \phi\left[\dfrac{x - \lambda t}{(Dt)^{1/2}}\right] dt = W_3(x, T_2) - W_3(x, T_1), \quad T_1, T_2 > 0$

$$W_3(x, T) = \dfrac{1}{\lambda^4}\left[x^3 + \dfrac{6x^2 D}{\lambda} + \dfrac{15xD^2}{\lambda^2} + \dfrac{15D^3}{\lambda^3}\right]\Phi\left[\dfrac{x - \lambda T}{(DT)^{1/2}}\right]$$
$$- \dfrac{2(DT)^{1/2}}{\lambda^2}\left[T^2 + \dfrac{5D}{\lambda^2}\left(T + \dfrac{3D}{\lambda^2}\right) + \dfrac{x^2}{\lambda^2}\right]\phi\left[\dfrac{x - \lambda T}{(DT)^{1/2}}\right]$$
$$+ \left[\dfrac{15D^2}{\lambda^6}\left(x - \dfrac{D}{\lambda}\right) - \dfrac{6Dx^2}{\lambda^5} + \dfrac{x^3}{\lambda^4}\right]e^{2\lambda x/D}\Phi\left[\dfrac{x + \lambda T}{(DT)^{1/2}}\right]$$

14. Let

$$R_n(x, T_1, T_2) = \int_{T_1}^{T_2} t^n \Phi\left[\dfrac{x - \lambda t}{(Dt)^{1/2}}\right] dt, \quad n = 0, 1, 2, \ldots; T_1, T_2 > 0$$

Then

$$R_n(x, T_1, T_2) = \dfrac{1}{n + 1}T_2^{n+1}\Phi\left[\dfrac{x - \lambda T_2}{(DT_2)^{1/2}}\right] - \dfrac{1}{n + 1}T_1^{n+1}\Phi\left[\dfrac{x - \lambda T_1}{(DT_1)^{1/2}}\right]$$
$$- \dfrac{\lambda}{2(n + 1)}J_{n+1}(x, T_1, T_2) - \dfrac{x}{2(n + 1)}J_n(x, T_1, T_2)$$

15. $\dfrac{\partial}{\partial x} R_n(x, T_1, T_2) = -J_n(x, T_1, T_2)$

and

$$R_n(x, T_1, T_2) = -\int_x^{\infty} J_n(\xi, T_1, T_2)\, d\xi$$

16. $\displaystyle\int_{T_1}^{T_2} \Phi\left[\dfrac{x - \lambda t}{(Dt)^{1/2}}\right] dt = V_0(x, T_2) - V_0(x, T_1)\ ,\ T_1, T_2 > 0$

$$V_0(x, T) = \left[T - \dfrac{x}{\lambda} - \dfrac{D}{2\lambda^2}\right] \Phi\left[\dfrac{x - \lambda T}{(DT)^{1/2}}\right] + \dfrac{(DT)^{1/2}}{\lambda} \phi\left[\dfrac{x - \lambda T}{(DT)^{1/2}}\right]$$

$$+ \dfrac{D}{2\lambda^2} e^{2\lambda x/D} \Phi\left[\dfrac{x + \lambda T}{(DT)^{1/2}}\right]$$

17. $\displaystyle\int_{T_1}^{T_2} t\, \Phi\left[\dfrac{x - \lambda t}{(Dt)^{1/2}}\right] dt = V_1(x, T_2) - V_1(x, T_1),\quad T_1, T_2 > 0$

$$V_1(x, T) = \dfrac{1}{2}\left[T^2 - \dfrac{x^2}{\lambda^2} - \dfrac{2Dx}{\lambda^3} - \dfrac{3D^2}{2\lambda^4}\right] \Phi\left[\dfrac{x - \lambda T}{(DT)^{1/2}}\right]$$

$$+ \dfrac{(DT)^{1/2}}{2\lambda^2}\left[\lambda T + \dfrac{3D}{\lambda} + x\right] \phi\left[\dfrac{x - \lambda T}{(DT)^{1/2}}\right]$$

$$- \dfrac{D}{2\lambda^3}\left[x - \dfrac{3D}{2\lambda}\right] e^{2\lambda x/D} \Phi\left[\dfrac{x + \lambda T}{(DT)^{1/2}}\right]$$

18. $e^{2\lambda x/D} \phi\left[\dfrac{x + \lambda t}{(Dt)^{1/2}}\right] = \phi\left[\dfrac{x - \lambda t}{(Dt)^{1/2}}\right]$

19. $\dfrac{d\Phi(r)}{dr} = -\phi(r)$

20. $\dfrac{\partial}{\partial x} \Phi\left[\dfrac{x - \lambda t}{(Dt)^{1/2}}\right] = -\dfrac{1}{(Dt)^{1/2}} \phi\left[\dfrac{x - \lambda t}{(Dt)^{1/2}}\right]$

21. $\dfrac{\partial}{\partial t} \Phi\left[\dfrac{x - \lambda t}{(Dt)^{1/2}}\right] = \dfrac{1}{2}\left[\dfrac{\lambda}{(Dt)^{1/2}} + \dfrac{x}{D^{1/2}t^{3/2}}\right] \phi\left[\dfrac{x - \lambda t}{(Dt)^{1/2}}\right]$

22. $\dfrac{\partial}{\partial x} \phi\left[\dfrac{x - \lambda t}{(Dt)^{1/2}}\right] = -\left[\dfrac{x - \lambda t}{Dt}\right] \phi\left[\dfrac{x - \lambda t}{(Dt)^{1/2}}\right]$

23. $\dfrac{\partial}{\partial t} \phi\left[\dfrac{x - \lambda t}{(Dt)^{1/2}}\right] = \dfrac{1}{2Dt}\left[\dfrac{x^2}{t} - \lambda^2 t\right] \phi\left[\dfrac{x - \lambda t}{(Dt)^{1/2}}\right]$

24. $\displaystyle\int_r^{\infty} x\phi\left(\dfrac{x - \mu}{\sigma}\right) dx = \sigma^2\phi\left(\dfrac{r - \mu}{\sigma}\right) + \mu\sigma\Phi\left(\dfrac{r - \mu}{\sigma}\right)$

25. $\dfrac{1}{\sigma}\displaystyle\int_r^{\infty} (x - r)\phi\left(\dfrac{x - \mu}{\sigma}\right) dx = \int_r^{\infty} \Phi\left(\dfrac{x - \mu}{\sigma}\right) dx$

$$= \sigma\phi\left(\dfrac{r - \mu}{\sigma}\right) - (r - \mu)\Phi\left(\dfrac{r - \mu}{\sigma}\right)$$

26. $\displaystyle\int_r^\infty x\Phi\left(\frac{x-\mu}{\sigma}\right)dx$

$$= \frac{1}{2}\left\{(\sigma^2+\mu^2-r^2)\Phi\left(\frac{r-\mu}{\sigma}\right) + \sigma(r+\mu)\phi\left(\frac{r-\mu}{\sigma}\right)\right\}$$

27. $\displaystyle\int_r^\infty x^2\Phi\left(\frac{x-\mu}{\sigma}\right)dx = \frac{1}{3}\left(\mu^3+3\mu\sigma^2-r^3\right)\Phi\left(\frac{r-\mu}{\sigma}\right)$

$$+ \frac{\sigma}{3}\left(r^2+\mu r+\mu^2+2\sigma^2\right)\phi\left(\frac{r-\mu}{\sigma}\right)$$

28. $\displaystyle\int_r^\infty e^{2\lambda x/D}\Phi\left(\frac{x+\mu}{\sigma}\right)dx = \frac{D}{2\lambda}\left\{\Phi\left(\frac{r-\mu}{\sigma}\right) - e^{2\lambda r/D}\Phi\left(\frac{r+\mu}{\sigma}\right)\right\}$

INDEX

DATE DUE